TECHNOLOGICAL INNOVATION AND ECONOMIC PERFORMANCE

TECHNOLOGICAL INNOVATION AND ECONOMIC PERFORMANCE

Edited by

Benn Steil

David G. Victor

Richard R. Nelson

A Council on Foreign Relations Book

PRINCETON UNIVERSITY PRESS   PRINCETON AND OXFORD

Founded in 1921, the Council on Foreign Relations is a
nonpartisan membership organization, research center, and
publisher. It is dedicated to increasing America's understanding
of the world and contributing ideas to U.S. foreign policy. The
Council accomplishes this mainly by promoting constructive
discussions and by publishing *Foreign Affairs*, the leading journal
on global issues. The Council is host to the widest possible range
of views, but an advocate of none, though its research fellows
and Independent Task Forces do take policy stands.

From time to time books and reports written by members of the
Council's research staff or other are published as "A Council on
Foreign Relations Book."

THE COUNCIL TAKES NO INSTITUTIONAL POSITION ON
POLICY ISSUES AND HAS NO AFFILIATION WITH THE U.S.
GOVERNMENT. ALL STATEMENTS OF FACT AND
EXPRESSIONS OF OPINION CONTAINED IN ALL ITS
PUBLICATIONS ARE THE SOLE RESPONSIBILITY OF THE
AUTHORS.

ISBN: 0-691-08874-8 (cloth), 0-691-09091-2 (paper)

This book has been composed in New Baskerville
Printed on acid-free paper ∞
www.pup.princeton.edu
Printed in the United States of America
10 9 8 7 6 5 4 3 2 1
10 9 8 7 6 5 4 3 2 1
(Pbk.)

Contents

Contributors

Charles W. Calomiris, Columbia Business School
Ian Domowitz, Pennsylvania State University
Robert E. Evenson, Yale University
Charles H. Fine, Massachusetts Institute of Technology
Robert J. Gordon, Northwestern University
Richard N. Langlois, University of Connecticut
Josh Lerner, Harvard Business School
Markku Malkamäki, Evli, Ltd.
Patrick A. Messerlin, Institut d'Etudes Politiques de Paris
Joel Mokyr, Northwestern University
David C. Mowery, Haas School of Business, University of California, Berkeley
Richard R. Nelson, Columbia University
Stephen Nickell, London School of Economics
Gary P. Pisano, Harvard Business School
Adam S. Posen, Institute for International Economics
Daniel M.G. Raff, The Wharton School, University of Pennsylvania
Horst Siebert, The Kiel Institute of World Economics
Timothy Simcoe, Haas School of Business, University of California, Berkeley
Benn Steil, Council on Foreign Relations
Michael Stolpe, The Kiel Institute of World Economics
John Van Reenen, University College, London
David G. Victor, Council on Foreign Relations
Matti Virén, University of Turku

Since the end of the cold war period, it has become increasingly apparent that the traditional political and military focus of diplomacy needs to be augmented by economic diplomacy. American economic hegemony has never been clearer. Since the end of the 1970s, the United States has generated a disproportionate share of the world's wealth and with it, political power. It appears that the United States has developed a very robust economic system, in part based on this country's success in aggressively pursuing technological change. If these apparent advantages continue to yield superior economic results, American hegemony will increase, perhaps to unhealthy levels.

Given the current situation, it is more important than ever that policymakers clearly understand the determinants of economic success based on technological change. These relationships are nevertheless still quite murky; characterized more by Rudyard Kiplingesque "just so" stories of economic success based on technological change, than by well documented cross-national, cross-industry studies. We need to put more facts together to reveal the true nature of these most important relationships.

This volume is a step in that direction. Benn Steil, David Victor, Richard Nelson, and the chapter authors, many of whom are not American nor living in the United States, have taken an important step forward in this careful historical study of the complex relationships between technological change and economic success. Collectively, this group of scholars has reached three conclusions:

- First, the flexibility of market-oriented, capitalist modes of production is most conducive to fostering economic success based on technological innovation. Alternative modes of market organization can produce spurts of growth when the stars align and technological bets happen to pay off, but sustained performance requires the discipline of the market.

- Second, technological progress has to be seen in a wider context than research and development or patents. Rather, technological progress is often embodied in new corporations which have relatively little formal R&D, but which are able to capitalize very effectively on the efforts of others.

- Third, the studies suggest that when the economic history of the past 100 years is viewed as a whole, technological innovation is increasingly becoming the central organizing principle for managers and policymakers. As Schumpeter pointed out more than 70 years ago, "The problem that is usually being visualized is how capitalism administers existing structures, whereas the relevant problem is how it creates and destroys them."

This volume is important because it documents those conclusions thoroughly with specific case studies drawn from nine countries and nine industries. This study focuses the terms of the debate very clearly, and the cases point the way towards pragmatic discussions of policy options. We hope that this volume will stimulate those discussions.

While this study has focused on the developed world, it may find interested readers in the developing world as well. I am reminded of a meeting in 1995 of several U.S. representatives with former South Korean Prime Minister H.K. Lee.[1] The former Prime Minister made the point that, in his view, the number one challenge facing South Korea in the mid-1990s was increasing South Korea's innovativeness as a source of economic competitiveness. He pointed out that the Korean "miracle" had been based on copying the Japanese industrialization strategy. That strategy had reached its limits, and he felt the dam was bound to burst at some point. Since that time, the dam has burst,

---

[1] Adapted from Foster, R.N. and S. Kaplan. 2001. *Creative Destruction*, Currency Books.

and many Korean companies have had to seek bankruptcy protection. The failure to provide for indigenous capacity to refresh Korean industry undermined the Korean miracle.

Lee recalled being present when the economic policy of the country was being shaped in the early days after the Korean War. He said, "We felt that if we only achieved world scale operations we would have a seat at the table. We would be respected members of the international economic community, and that was our goal. We were successful in reaching our goal." "However", he went on, "while our strategy of industrial organization gave us the scale we sought, we still found we had no seat at the table. We were not welcome because we had copied what others had done. We had not built the capability to contribute to further advances because we did not know how to innovate. Now we must learn." We all need to learn, and this volume is a solid step forward in that process.

Of course, this study will not be the last of its kind. Indeed a measure of its effectiveness will be the extent to which it triggers other studies in other countries to examine and test the conclusions presented here. Hopefully, through the offices of the Council on Foreign Relations and other organizations, the pace and breadth of the debate will increase.

Richard N. Foster
New York
July, 2001

Acknowledgments

On behalf of the Council on Foreign Relations, we would like to express our sincere thanks to McKinsey and Company, Xerox Corporation, Instinet Corporation, and Peter J. Solomon for funding this massive research project. We are also grateful to the Linda J. Wachner Senior Fellowship in U.S. Foreign Economic Policy, the Robert Wood Johnson 1962 Charitable Trust, and the John D. and Catherine T. MacArthur Foundation for additional support of our tenure at the Council. We would also like to offer our personal thanks to the Council President, Les Gelb, and Director of Studies, Larry Korb, for their support and encouragement.

We are particularly grateful to Dick Foster, who was a constant source of encouragement and sage advice. He first urged the Council to undertake this study, and then expertly chaired the meetings at which the authors and many Council members reviewed drafts of the studies which we now proudly present in this volume.

Benn Steil
David Victor
Project Co-Directors

Part I

INTRODUCTION

Introduction and Overview

Benn Steil, David G. Victor, and Richard R. Nelson

The exceptional performance of the U.S. economy during the late 1990s has, once again, put a spotlight on technological innovation. Some speculate that the acceleration of American economic growth beginning in the mid-1990s was a passing phase that will be erased with the next swing in the business cycle. Others claim that it foretells the coming of an extended wave of economic growth worldwide—bankable evidence, finally, of a new "industrial revolution" centered on information technology, the Internet and biotechnology. Which side claims victory in this effort to untangle the sources of innovation and economic performance is more than an academic matter. The contrasting performance of the United States with Japan and the other leading industrial economies, along with the rising imperative for firms to compete in a "globalizing" world economy, has focused the attention of policy makers as never before on creating the conditions that foster innovation and the means of translating it into growth.

The chapters that follow put the issues into historical perspective—starting with the first industrial revolution—and then probe two central questions through fifteen case studies. First, what are the drivers of technological innovation? Second, what factors determine the ability of firms and governments to translate innovation into economic wealth?

The studies in Part I cover nine advanced industrialized nations that account for nearly half of the world's economic output and largely define the "efficient frontier" of technological innovation in the global economy—

the United States, Japan, Germany, France, the United Kingdom, and four Nordic countries (Denmark, Finland, Norway, and Sweden). Gross domestic product (GDP) and population data are provided in Tables 1.1 and 1.2, and per-capita income is shown in Figure 1.1.

The nine studies in Part II focus on industries where radical innovation has been readily apparent, pervasive and critical (e.g., semiconductors, the Internet, and pharmaceutical biotechnology) as well as a selection of major "old economy" industries where innovation in recent decades generally has been more incremental (e.g., automobiles and electric power). Some of these industries have long histories of innovation (e.g., agriculture) while others are fundamentally based on recent technological opportunities (e.g., electronic trading of securities).

The studies employ the concept of an "innovation system"—the cluster of institutions, policies, and practices that determine an industry or nation's capacity to generate and apply innovations. With our focus on innovation systems, this book follows in the tradition of the country studies compiled by Nelson (1993), which introduced the concept of a "national innovation system," and the industry studies assembled by Mowery and Nelson (1999).

For decades, scholars and policy makers have sought to identify the technological headwaters of economic growth. In the 1980s, the exceptional performance of the Japanese economy led many to admire and fear the "Japanese model." Historians, probing for the cycles of history, portrayed Japan's rise and America's relative decline as inevitable developments—most famously, Paul Kennedy (1987), but also foreshadowed by Robert Gilpin (1981) and others who sought to link shifts in economic

We are particularly grateful to Robert Gordon and Richard Foster for detailed critiques of earlier drafts of this chapter.

TABLE 1.1
Total Income (GDP, billion U.S.$ converted with purchasing power parity, constant 1995 U.S.$)

	1970	1980	1990	1999
Denmark	62	79	100	134
Finland	46	66	93	110
France	629	883	1136	1248
Germany	na	na	1536[a]	1835
Japan	1016	1615	2499	2937
Norway	39	64	84	118
Sweden	108	134	178	189
United Kingdom	609	761	1048	1277
United States	3497	4767	6525	8582
Percent of World	na	na	44%	41%

Sources: GDP from World Bank (2001); PPP conversions from OECD *Purchasing Power Parities of OECD Countries* as World Bank PPP statistics are highly incomplete prior to 1990 and nonexistent prior to 1975; GDP deflator from World Bank (2001). Fraction of world economy estimated with PPP statistics from World Bank (2001).

[a] Data for 1991, first year of unified German statistics.

TABLE 1.2
Total Population (millions)

	1970	1980	1990	1999
Denmark	4.9	5.1	5.1	5.3
Finland	4.6	4.8	5.0	5.2
France	51	54	57	59
Germany	78	78	79	82
Japan	104	117	124	126
Norway	3.9	4.1	4.2	4.4
Sweden	8.0	8.3	8.6	8.9
United Kingdom	56	56	58	59
United States	205	227	249	278

Source: World Bank (2001).

power to the wars that often occur during changes in the international pecking order.

Confronted with an ascendant Japan, political economists wondered whether the apparent efficiency of the Japanese semi-command economy would trounce the more open markets and weaker central governments that were the hallmarks of Western, liberal democratic societies.

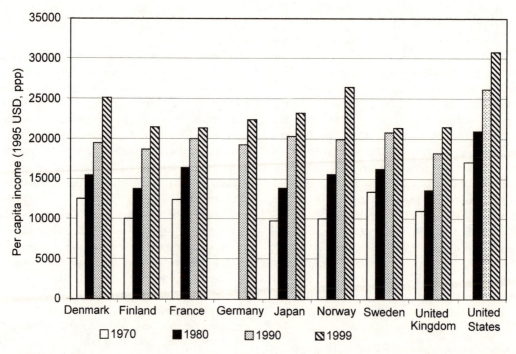

Figure 1.1 Per Capita Income (constant 1995 U.S.$ per person). *Source:* income as in Table 1.1; population from World Bank (2001). The first German data point is 1991.

The theories were reminiscent of the 1940s, when Western commentators such as George Orwell worried that decentralized liberal societies would not be able to stand against the supposedly efficient military-industrial phalanx of the Soviet Bloc. Today, scholars and pundits are reviving Joseph Schumpeter for his visions of "creative destruction"—spurts of innovation that destroy technological paradigms and pulse the economy to greater wealth. Yet in the late 1940s, Schumpeter was best known for his gloomy prognosis for capitalism and democracy at the hands of central planning (Schumpeter, 1942).

In the past five years, these theories on planning and markets have crashed—and in a way that, again, has put the spotlight on innovation. The Japanese economy has been dormant since the stock market and real estate bubbles burst nearly a decade ago, and severe fragility in the banking sector continues to stalk the economic landscape. By the year 2000—with the longest economic expansion on record, five years of exceptional growth in productivity, low unemployment, and low inflation—the "miracle" of the U.S. economy had rekindled debate over the best model for generating sustained high economic growth. Reflecting the times, today's consensus extols decentralized private investment as the prime source of innovation and market flexibility as the best conduit for translating innovation into economic performance. Rather than celebrating the rise of powerful central states and stewards of semi-command economies, many political economists now see liberal democratic societies based on open markets not only as efficient, but as the endpoint of political evolution—the "end of history," to cite Hegel's promoter of the 1990s, Francis Fukuyama (1992). The actual practice of economic policy in the advanced economies has never had more of a singular focus on encouraging innovation than it does today. Governments now routinely craft a wide array of policies—in the areas of labor markets, immigration, education, antitrust, and public investment—principally by the desire to make their nations more innovative and more receptive to the deployment of new technologies, products and processes.

In the next section, we briefly review how economists have traditionally measured innovation and attributed its sources and impact. We also examine two sets of general conclusions from the studies—on the macroeconomic and microeconomic sources and impacts of innovation.

1.1. Measures and Sources of Innovation

In the early part of the twentieth century, Joseph Schumpeter (1912/1934, 1942) argued that ongoing industrial innovation was the most important feature and fruit of capitalist economic systems. Schumpter argued that the focus of most economists in his day on conditions of static economic efficiency was misplaced. In stressing the centrality of technological advance and innovation, Schumpeter resurrected an earlier, long tradition of distinguished economists. A significant portion of Adam Smith's *The Wealth of Nations* (1776), for example, is about the process of innovation—think of his famous pinmaking example, which involves an elaborate discussion of the invention of new machinery that increased labor productivity associated with (as both cause and effect) the progressive division of labor—and about the sources of major cross-country differences in the ability to generate wealth. Schumpeter has been an inspiration for a considerable body of research by economists on the factors that lead to industrial innovation and wealth creation. Recent books by Vernon Ruttan (2001) and by Freeman and Louca (2001) provide accessible overviews of writings by economists on technological innovation.

At the time that Schumpeter first wrote about innovation, economists did not have access to the concepts and measures of "gross national product," which would later permit them actually to measure economic growth and to analyze its sources. After World War II these new statistics gradually became available, and economists working with them were able to provide the first quantitative estimates of the importance of technological advance to the rising living standards that had been achieved in the United States and other advanced industrial nations.

TABLE 1.3
Labor Productivity (value added, 1990 U.S.$, per work hour)

	1980	1990	1995	1997
Denmark	17.50	20.93	23.88	24.55
Finland	14.50	20.30	23.40	24.00
France	22.16	28.94	31.10	32.18
Germany	20.28	25.84	28.86	na
Japan	13.83	18.75	20.53	21.19
Norway	na	na	na	na
Sweden	20.19	22.60	24.63	25.73
United Kingdom	18.32	22.77	25.54	26.40
United States	25.49	28.47	30.00	30.66

Source: International Labor Organization, *Key Indicators of the Labor Market 1999.*

Of these, a seminal paper by Solow (1957), along with studies by Abramowitz (1956) and Denison (1962), had particular impact on the thinking of economists. These studies offered a method of accounting for the sources of growth, known today as "growth accounting." The studies by Solow and Abramowitz, and many since, suggested that technological change accounted for far more than half of the observed rise in labor productivity and national income. The primary importance of technological change has resurfaced in the "new" or "endogenous" growth theory in economics (see Lucas, 1988; Romer, 1990).

Most current growth accounting studies aim to explain changes in labor productivity—the value added in the economy per hour worked, as shown in Table 1.3. By simple identity, the total size of the economy is the product of labor productivity and the total number of hours worked. In turn, total hours worked is a function of the total population (Table 1.2), the fraction of the population at work (Table 1.4), and hours per worker (Figure 1.2). Before looking to technological change as a source of economic growth, one must first account for these elements of the labor force, which vary substantially across the countries.[1] But for

[1] For a recent study that accounts for the diverse factors that explain the differences in economic growth in the OECD nations, see Scarpetta et al. (2000).

Denmark and Norway, a higher fraction of the U.S. population is at work than in any other of these nine countries. Working hours are up to one-third longer in the United States and Japan than in the others. Over the long term, working hours tend to decline as economies grow and workers substitute leisure for their labor; only a small fraction of today's workforce puts in the hours that were the norm for most of the industrial and agricultural workforce in the nineteenth century (Ausubel and Grübler, 1995), although working time often increases during periods of economic boom, as in the past decade in the United States.

The growth accounting method is typically used to parse labor productivity into the sum of two effects. One is "capital deepening"—the increase in capital services available per worker. If firms make capital investments—two robots on an assembly line where only one used to assist human laborers—then labor productivity can rise even though workers do not change their habits, and the tradeoffs between investment in labor and capital do not change. As Robert Gordon (chapter 3) argues, a significant portion of the growth in the U.S. economy in the late 1990s can be ascribed to capital deepening—in particular, massive investment in computers. How to measure the capital deepening effect is, however, hotly disputed, in part because it is hard to know how to compare and depreciate investments in technologies like computers, for which performance and prices are changing rapidly.

TABLE 1.4
Fraction of the Population Employed

	1973	1979	1990	1995	1999
Denmark	75.2	75.1	75.4	73.9	76.5
Finland	70.0	71.1	74.7	61.9	66.0
France	65.9	64.4	59.9	59.0	59.8
Germany	68.7	66.2	66.4	64.7	64.9
Japan	70.8	70.3	68.6	69.2	68.9
Norway	67.7	74.2	73.1	73.5	78.0
Sweden	73.6	78.8	83.1	72.2	72.9
United Kingdom	71.4	70.8	72.4	69.3	71.9
United States	65.1	68.0	72.2	72.5	73.9

Source: OECD *Employment Outlook* (1995, 2000).

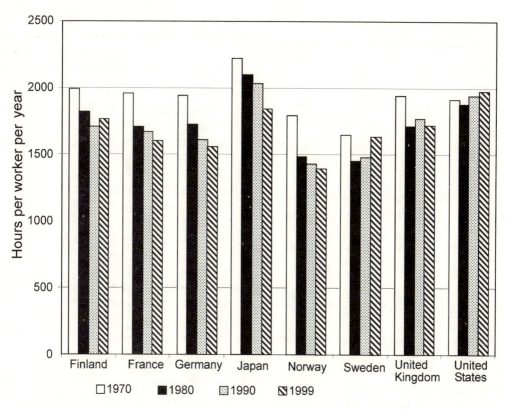

Figure 1.2 Hours per worker (annual). German statistics for West Germany; first Japanese data point is 1972 (earlier data not reported); Danish data not reported. *Source:* OECD *Employment Outlook* (Paris: OECD), various years.

After subtracting the measure of capital deepening, what is left over is the "Solow residual;" now termed "total factor productivity (TFP)" (or sometimes called "multi-factor productivity (MFP)"). This residual factor includes effects from changing technology: for example, if plant managers find a way to lift worker productivity by improving robots on an assembly line, rather than simply buying more robots, the effects are captured in TFP. Table 1.5 shows estimates for the two constituents that contribute to changes in labor productivity— capital deepening and the residual TFP—for all the countries examined in this book.

Growth accounting has come in for some serious criticism, and thus we use it only to set the scene—to provide a broad brush painting of the patterns and puzzles that must be explained by looking at the more micro forces at work inside national economies and specific industries. Generally, the critiques have focused on two lines of argument.

First, the methods and measures that comprise growth accounting are hotly contested. As noted, estimates for "capital deepening" can be flawed, which in turn affect the residual TFP. Moreover, treating TFP as a catch-all residual attributes to "technological change" factors that may not be technological, such as changes in labor quality (e.g., the education level of the work force). Some studies, such as by Oliner and Sichel (2000), have explicitly sought to disaggregate labor quality from TFP, but studies employing comparable methods are not available across all the countries.[2] Thus, in Table 1.5 we show estimates for TFP that include labor quality as well as the dog's breakfast of other factors that end up in the residual. The methods of growth accounting are also vulnerable to criticism because most of the

[2] But see the effort to account for differences in labor quality ("human capital") across nations through the use of international test scores, reported in Barro (2001).

TABLE 1.5
Labor Productivity and its Components

	1981–9	1990–5	1996–9
Denmark			
Labor Productivity	2.53	3.69	0.86
of which capital deepening	na	1.27	0.56
of which TFP	na	2.37	0.31
Finland			
Labor Productivity	3.85	3.91	3.10
of which capital deepening	na	na	−0.53
of which TFP	na	na	3.70
France			
Labor Productivity	3.41	2.26	1.61
of which capital deepening	1.10	1.35	0.50
of which TFP	2.26	0.89	1.12
Germany			
Labor Productivity	na	2.26	2.14
of which capital deepening	na	1.22	1.06
of which TFP	na	1.02	1.07
Japan			
Labor Productivity	3.12	2.89	2.07
of which capital deepening	1.15	1.56	1.23
of which TFP	2.00	1.31	0.85

TABLE 1.5 (*continued*)

	1981–9	1990–5	1996–9
Norway			
Labor Productivity	1.44	3.18	1.39
of which capital deepening	0.92	0.66	0.29
of which TFP	0.50	2.48	1.13
Sweden			
Labor Productivity	1.52	2.11	1.73
of which capital deepening	0.61	0.89	na
of which TFP	0.92	1.19	na
United Kingdom			
Labor Productivity	3.37	1.78	1.47
of which capital deepening	0.42	0.57	0.54
of which TFP	2.90	1.21	0.95
United States			
Labor Productivity	1.59	1.47	2.57
of which capital deepening	0.73	0.68	1.11
of which TFP	0.86	0.79	1.47

Source: Gust and Marquez (2000). U.S. data based on BLS statistics; all others based on OECD.

components of labor productivity vary with the business cycle. For example, in normal business cycles, capital deepening is intense in the early stages of the cycle because the increase in capital investment exceeds the rise in employment; labor quality usually declines during the cycle as less skilled workers enter the workforce. Yet there is no single method for removing cyclical effects to uncover the magnitude of any fundamental long-term shift, such as whether the jump in the growth of productivity in the late 1990s in the United States is a permanent trace of the "New Economy" or merely transient.

The other line of criticism is more fundamental. The logic of growth accounting only holds up for small, relatively isolated changes in technology and other factors of production. When the changes are large and dispersed over long periods of time, interaction effects are large relative to the direct effects, and it makes no sense to "divide up the credit" among separate factors. Over time, changes in worker skills, the available physical capital per worker, and advances in technology have been very strong complements, and it is impossible to isolate the impact of one of these changes from the other (e.g., Nelson, 1998). Moreover, technological changes often cause profound changes in the institutions that govern the economy, and it is difficult to take the pulse of that process applying the blunt, broad categories of growth accounting. For example, the advent of electric power had little impact on productivity until factory floors and production processes had been fundamentally reorganized to take advantage of it: that slow process has been revealed only through detailed firm-level historical studies (e.g., Devine, 1983; David, 1990). Similarly, the economic benefits of computers and the Internet are only becoming apparent as firms reorganize their internal processes and external relations (e.g., see Brynjolfsson and Hitt, 2000), and these impacts are only indirectly revealed in growth accounts.[3]

1.2. Sources of Innovation

Below we survey some of key features of industrial innovation that scholars have identified, citing some of the major studies and providing illustrations from our own case studies.[4] We first look at the attributes of technologies themselves, and how they may affect the pace and impact of innovation. We then examine the actors, institutions, and policies that affect innovation.

1.2.1. Technological Opportunity and Uncertainty

Differences in technological opportunities across fields, and across eras, have been a driving force determining the path of technological progress (see Klevorick et al., 1995). Advances in chemical technologies—from dyestuffs to synthetic materials to pharmaceuticals—along with electrical and electronic technologies—from electric lighting and telephones to street cars and electric motors—were engines of economic growth during the first half of the twentieth century. Abundant opportunities for technological change in these areas, driven by scientific breakthroughs in specific areas, led to abundant economic change. As opportunities to advance particular technologies become exhausted, the pace of change naturally slows. Thus, Boeing 747s are still a backbone of

commercial aviation today, 32 years after their first flight—whereas prior to 1969, each generation of aircraft was obsolete within a decade. Similarly, the maximum size of steam electric generators today is no greater than in the late 1960s, after having risen steadily for decades (Victor, chapter 16).

According to this "supply push" view of technological change, the opportunities for technological change are not only a function of the technologies themselves but also the state of the underlying "science"—general knowledge about physical properties and laws. For example, advances in the basic sciences of chemistry and physics helped to drive the chemical and electric revolutions of the twentieth century. Today, basic knowledge about biological sciences, such as the techniques of recombinant DNA invented in 1973, has made possible the creation of transgenic crops and novel pharmaceuticals (Evenson, chapter 15; Pisano, chapter 14). But science has not always been a driver of new technology. Mokyr (chapter 2) shows that science played essentially no role in the emergence of steam power and the technological revolution that it caused in the late eighteenth century; nor did basic science play much role in the emergence of industrial steelmaking in the nineteenth century and the industrial revolution that it gave rise to in areas such as railroad transport. Rather, science and technology often ran in the opposite direction—the invention of the steam engine, for example, helped to create the field of modern thermodynamics. Today, even though organized science is playing a central role in biotechnology, medicine, chemicals, and semiconductors, a good deal of technological change in these fields is the byproduct of incremental tinkering and engineering rather than changes in fundamental knowledge.

Although technological opportunities define a frontier for possible technological change, the process of searching for that frontier is marked by pervasive uncertainty (see, e.g., Rosenberg, 1996). While certain broad trends may be predictable—for example, Moore's Law about the progressive miniaturization of the components of integrated circuits has held up for decades—the precise pathways to particular

---

[3] Nonetheless, there are several good studies that have sought to isolate the effects of IT on the economy and productivity by using the techniques of growth accounting (Jorgenson and Stiroh, 2000; Oliner and Sichel, 2000; Whelan, 2000; Litan and Rivlin, 2001).

[4] See Freeman and Soete (1997) for a more detailed survey.

advances are extraordinarily difficult to predict in advance, and knowledgeable experts tend to differ regarding where they would lay their own bets. For example, very few scientists and pharmaceutical companies foresaw the impact of new understandings and techniques in biotechnology before these were literally upon them, and the early beliefs about how biotechnology would prove most fruitful in pharmaceutical development turned out to be incorrect (see, e.g., Henderson et al., 1999; Pisano, chapter 14). Similarly, in the late 1970s, at the dawn of the personal computer market, few predicted the widespread market that would arise or that assemblages of small computers would begin to replace mainframes, the dominant technology of the day (Bresnahan and Malerba, 1999; Langlois, chapter 10). While at present there are many strong opinions regarding the future of the Internet, it is a safe conjecture that most of these will turn out to be incorrect.

That technological change is both central to the process of wealth creation and difficult to predict helps to explain why a long historical perspective reveals a high rate of turnover among leading firms—managers often bet inaccurately on the future of technology, and even when they understand the technological potential, they are often unable to reorganize their firms to seize them (see, e.g., Foster, 1986; Christensen, 1997; Foster and Kaplan, 2001). As Schumpeter pointed out long ago, competition under capitalism is to a considerable extent competition through innovation and then trial by actual experience. It is the uncertainties associated with technological advance and industrial innovation that explain why capitalist economic systems have performed so much better than more centrally planned ones (Nelson, 1990).

1.2.2. Actors, Institutions, and Policies

Scholars of technological innovation have long struggled to understand why it is that innovative effort tends to be allocated so unevenly across sectors and tasks. Thus, by all measures, such as spending on research and development (R&D) or patents, innovative effort today is very high in many areas of electronics and pharmaceuticals, but there is comparatively little innovative effort going on related to furniture or shoes. Moreover, technological change in the marketplace seems to track with innovative effort. Where innovative effort is intense, such as in computers, the actual application of new technologies in the marketplace is relatively rapid. What accounts for these patterns?

Part of the answer lies in the distribution of technological opportunities, just discussed, and part is to be found in the institutions and public policies that affect how innovators behave and how new technologies are applied. Broadly, economists have looked at four areas of the marketplace that affect innovation:

- the size of the market
- the appropriability of new ideas
- the structure of the industry and
- investment in public knowledge and institutions

1.2.2.1. The Size of the Market

While it long has been a shibboleth that "necessity is the mother of intention," Jacob Schmookler (1966) was the first to provide convincing statistical evidence that inventive effort, as measured by patents in the field, tended to be greater the greater the sales of the products to which the patents were related. Also, changes in the allocation of patenting tended to follow changes in the allocation of sales across different industries and product groups. Large markets attracted efforts at innovation. In a way, this is not surprising. A large market for a particular product means that an invention that makes that product better, or enables it to be produced more efficiently, itself has the opportunity of delivering large profits to the innovator. Moreover, in large markets there are also typically large numbers of people who have experience with and knowledge about the product and underlying process technologies who can make further improvements and complementary innovations.

Market size is not a fixed quantity; nor is it easy to estimate market size accurately, especially for radical innovations that cause transformations in markets rather than incremental changes. It is very difficult to forecast how much demand there would be for a radically improved (or very different version of a) product than is presently marketed (Rosenberg, 1996, presents a number of fascinating examples). It is even more difficult to foresee the market for a product that enables needs to be met that no current product is capable of meeting. Through the 1970s, before widespread use of integrated circuits, analysts vastly underestimated the future market for integrated circuits (Langlois, chapter 10).

Market size is not only a function of geography and technology, but also of policy decisions relating to such factors as technical standards and trade barriers. Governments and industry associations set standards that affect the size of the market for novel products and services. For example, the study of agriculture by Evenson (chapter 15) documents the efforts by opponents of engineered food products to use food safety standards as a means to bar this new technology from the market, as well as labeling regulations to empower wary consumers to shun the products. More broadly, policies to lower tariffs and other trade barriers offer access to larger markets—which is of particular importance to countries with small home markets. Thus, small countries with open borders, such as the Netherlands and Singapore, have been among the fastest growing national economies over the past century—able to access large markets for new products even when the home market is small. Other factors that affect the size of the market include language. For example, English language software houses have been able to dominate the software industry worldwide because English is the second language of educated people in much of the world.

1.2.2.2. Appropriability

The lion's share of industrial research, and of individual efforts at inventing, is done in the hope that the results will prove profitable. Profitability is a function of many factors, such as financing strategies, competition, potential for cost reduction, and firm management. The literature on innovation, however, gives particular attention to how innovators can appropriate a portion of the returns from their successful work.

When most people think about how innovators appropriate returns, they think about patents, or intellectual property rights. However, results from a large number of studies now demonstrate that patent protection is the central vehicle for investors to reap returns in only a few industries; prominent among them, pharmaceuticals, fine chemical products, and agricultural chemicals (see, e.g., Levin et al., 1987; Cohen et al., 2000). In a wide range of other industries, including many where technological advance has been rapid and firms invest significant resources in R&D, patents are not particularly effective. For many years firms invested heavily in R&D in the semiconductor and computer industries, and profited from their successes, despite the fact that patent protection was weak in these areas. Patent protection remains weak in many areas of telecommunications technology. Moreover, in some areas firms shun patents - preferring secrecy as a protector of novel ideas—because the patenting process, by design, requires the release of design information. Apart from commercial considerations, there are conflicting ideas about the appropriate rules for ownership of fundamental discoveries. As Gary Pisano (chapter 14) recounts, the university researchers who made one of the key discoveries in the development of the modern pharmaceuticals industry, the monoclonal antibody technique, did not patent their innovation specifically because they wanted the ideas to remain in the public domain and available to all. That was in the early 1970s; today, such a unilateral expression of what is "right" would be harder for researchers to adopt. All major research universities in the United States, and some universities overseas, have technology transfer offices that typically require researchers to patent and license the results of university research. In practice, most universities have not found license fees to be a large source of revenue, and many scholars increasingly question the desirability of these new policies of universities to patent what earlier they simply put into the public domain (Mowery et al., 2001).

The different strategies for protecting and appropriating new ideas pose special problems

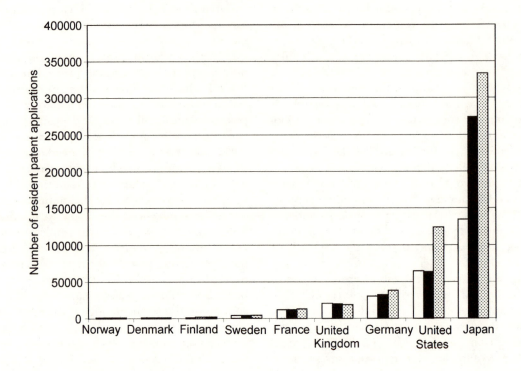

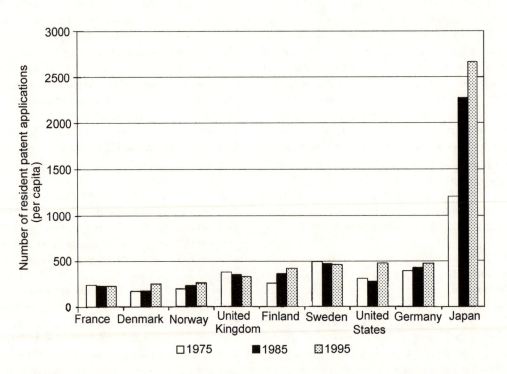

Figure 1.3 Patent applications by national residents in their home patent office, absolute quantity (top) and per capita (bottom). *Source:* OECD *Basic Science and Technology Statistics* (1993, 1998).

for economists who want to measure patterns of innovation. A common approach is to measure patents, as shown in Figure 1.3 for the nine countries examined in this book. But such data are hard to put into practical use. Not only are patents poor indicators of innovation in many fields, but there are also considerable cross-jurisdiction variations in rules that make it difficult to compare patent statistics across countries. For example, patent offices in the United States and Europe have ruled on the patentability of novel life forms differently, with the result that patent registers in these jurisdictions will differ even if the output of life science innovations were the same. Transaction costs and disclosure rules also vary and affect patent measures of innovation. Relative to the United States, filing fees (including translation costs) at the European Patent Office are significantly higher, which partially explains why total patenting activity in European countries is lower than in the United States and skews patenting towards large, well-organized firms that can pay these costs, as well as less speculative filings. Because there is no single international patent office, but patent protection is needed in many jurisdictions, international patent filings have swelled in the last decades. About half the patent applications to the U.S. patent office are filed by residents in countries other than the United States.

Other measures of innovative output include scientific papers and citations to scientific papers. But those measures are also unsatisfying for the same reasons that patent statistics can be misleading—sheer numbers do not distinguish the revolutionary from the mundane, and some genuine innovations are never published in the professional peer reviewed literature. Analysis of the citation rates can help identify important papers, but it does not distinguish commercially important ideas from scientific curiosities.

Royalties and license fees offer another measure of innovative output, and one that is a direct measure of market value. Figure 1.4 shows the flow of royalties and license fees between the United States and other countries in this study. The figure reveals the concentration of commercially valuable innovation in the United States and contrasts sharply with the impression

from patent statistics (Figure 1.3), which suggest that Japan is the world's leading innovator.

1.2.2.3. Firms and the Structure of Industry

Since the time of Schumpeter, there has been continuing dispute in economics regarding the kinds of firm and the structure of industry that are most conducive to innovation and technological change. Much of that dispute has been about whether the resources and technological and marketing experience that large established firms can bring to industrial innovation is more important than the fresh approaches and flexibility that new firms can bring. Scholars who have studied this question in detail have generally concluded that the answer depends very much on the specific industry and the technology (Cohen and Levin, 1989).

In industries where progress rests on a relatively stable set of technologies and sciences, and the nature of product innovation does not open up radically new markets, there are strong tendencies for a relatively concentrated industrial structure to evolve, with only limited entry. One has seen this in the case of industries like automobiles, large electrical equipment, aircraft, and chemicals (see, e.g., Utterback and Suarez, 1993). The study on automobile production by Fine and Raff in this volume (chapter 17) shows that General Motors has been able to hold on to a large share of the U.S. market despite a relatively poor record of innovation and management over recent decades, although the rate of market change appears to be increasing with the continued opening of markets to foreign competition. On the other hand, when the technologies that underlie products and processes are prone to change radically, which often opens up large new markets, established firms may have no particular advantage. Indeed, they may be highly disadvantaged relative to newcomers who are not weighed down by obsolescent processes and production technologies. An established firm, selling to a particular collection of users, is often blind to potential new markets involving users with very different needs (Foster, 1986; Christensen, 1997).

When the underlying technological and scientific basis is shifting rapidly, the success of

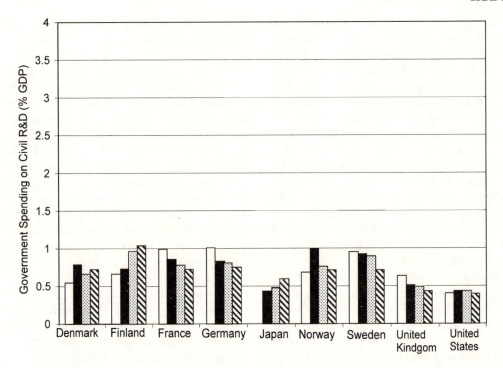

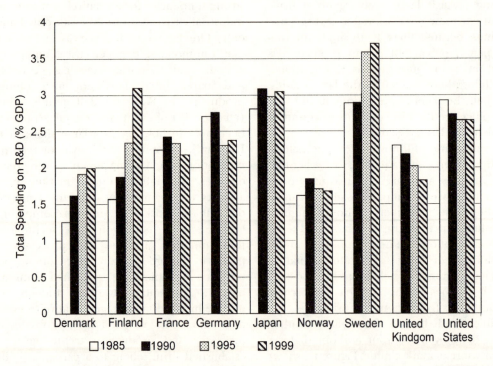

Figure 1.4 Expenditure on R&D as a percentage of GDP. Top panel shows spending by government on civil R&D, which is an indicator of government investment in the "public good" of new knowledge outside the military sector. Bottom panel shows total public and private spending on R&D, which is the broadest measure of social investment in new technology. 1990 and earlier civil R&D statistics for Japan unavailable (1991 shown). 1999 civil R&D statistics unavailable for France (1998 shown). For total R&D spending, final data points are 1998 for France, Japan, and United Kingdom; 1997 for Sweden. *Source:* OECD, *Main Science and Technology Indicators* (Paris: OECD), various years.

a national economy may depend to a considerable extent on the pace of firm turnover. Countries which maintain policies that facilitate turnover—for example, where liquid capital markets ease the financing of new entrants, and bankruptcy law lubricates the exit of failing firms—will tend to perform better than those that attempt to protect incumbent market shares, such as through public funding of ailing "national champions." Indeed, the strength of U.S. industry in IT and biotechnology rests in part on the striking openness of the American economy to turnover of firms.

1.2.2.4. Public Knowledge and Institutions

Although much of the writings by economists regarding innovation and technological advance focuses on business firms in competition, scholars have long understood that there is another important side to the process—knowledge and skills that are public goods, available to all. Some of these public goods are the result of discoveries made and training provided in private firms that "leak out" into the wider economy. But in many fields, a large portion is the result of the research and dissemination efforts of universities and other public research institutions funded mainly by governments. Much of this publicly funded research takes the form of "basic research" and is funded by

TABLE 1.6

Gross Expenditure on Research and Development (millions of current U.S.$, PPP)

	1985	1990	1995	1999
Denmark	785	1384	2194	2720
Finland	879	1542	2197	3652
France	14571	23762	27595	27880[b]
Germany	19984	31935	39366	46218
Japan	40064	66965	85256	92663[b]
Norway	940	1315[a]	1733	21456
Sweden	3068	4180[a]	6069	6845[b]
United Kingdom	14444	19955	21604	23445[b]
United States	116026	149225	183694	243548

Source: OECD *Main Science & Technology Indicators* (1991, 1993, 1995, 1999, 2000).

[a] 1990 data for Norway and Sweden from 1991.

[b] 1999 data for France, Japan, and United Kingdom from 1998; for Sweden from 1997.

governments according to the traditional justification for spending on public goods: such research yields fundamental knowledge that is beneficial to society as a whole, and private firms would not invest adequately in basic science because the benefits are difficult to appropriate.

Comparable data on investment in "basic research" are not available for all the countries in this study. To illustrate the level of investment, therefore, Figure 1.4 (top panel) shows data that are more readily available and easier to compare across countries—public spending on civilian R&D. The reader should be mindful that this method of measuring basic research investment, although the best available, is flawed. Data on public civilian R&D spending overstate the true investment in basic research insofar as government R&D budgets include costly development projects in addition to pure basic research. On the other hand, data such as shown in Figure 1.4 (top panel) understate the true level of social investment into basic research because governments are not the sole source of basic research funding. In some fields, such as biology, private firms and foundations spend heavily on basic research—pharmaceutical companies, for example, invest in basic research in part to discover new drugs and in part to build an in-house capacity to understand new results at the frontiers of science (Cockburn and Henderson, 1998; Pisano, chapter 14). Such data also understate the true investment in basic research in countries that have large military (i.e., noncivilian) R&D programs, as in the United States. Most military R&D spending is applied to particular purposes, but some is devoted to "basic research" that spills over into general public knowledge; however, it is extremely difficult to separate applied from basic research, not least because military R&D objectives are often shrouded in secrecy. For comparison, the bottom panel of Figure 1.4 shows total spending on R&D—private and public, civilian and military—as a fraction of economic output. Table 1.6 shows the absolute quantities.

Among the patterns evident in Figure 1.4 is the increased spending on R&D by the Finnish government and private sector starting in the

early 1990s and inspired by the effort to make
Finland a globally competitive high-tech economy (see Virén and Malkamäki, chapter 8). It is
also interesting to note that despite the widespread belief that basic science underpins technological progress, in all five of the largest
industrialized countries examined in this
study, total spending on R&D as a fraction of
economic output has actually declined. In
most of those countries, public civilian spending on R&D as a fraction of economic output
has also shrunk.

Popular perception sites the locus of basic
research activities at universities in areas such
as astronomy, solid-state physics, and molecular
biology—and indeed the latter two of these
fields have provided the basic conceptual
underpinnings for the development of microelectronics and biotechnology. However, a very
significant portion of the major research done
in universities and public institutions is in more
applied fields such as material science, computer science, pathology, oncology, and the engineering disciplines (see Klevorick et al., 1995).
Academic medical centers are important
sources of medical innovation. Engineering
schools often develop the early versions of
important new process and product technologies that are later picked up by industry. Publicly
funded agricultural research stations have
played critical roles in many countries by lifting
crop yields through programs to apply new seed
technologies and educate farmers in new farming techniques (Hayami and Ruttan, 1971). In
all these fields, the lines between public and
private research—and between basic and
applied research—are extremely difficult to
draw. Governments and private companies
often build public-private partnerships to invest
in new technologies; the private sector is a
major investor in basic research, especially in
biology; and policies such as the "Bayh-Dole
Act" in the United States are explicitly designed
to ease the transfer of results from publicly
funded research programs into privately held
companies.

In addition to funding of R&D, public institutions play at least two other critical roles in the
innovation process. First, public institutions are
central to training that affects the quality of the
labor force and innovative potential. Much
attention has focused on the role of universities
and public research laboratories as the sites for
exchanges between public and private research
activities as well as advanced (doctoral) training. Public institutions also play critical roles
earlier in the educational process, laying the
foundation of basic skills. Because the educational process typically delivers benefits to the
economy only slowly—literally, the timescales
are generational—the quality of the workforce
also depends on immigration policies that can
augment (or drain) a skilled workforce more
quickly. Second, public institutions are themselves often large markets for innovative
products—they can spur innovation through
their own buying habits. Militaries, in particular,
make large procurements of novel products
and have played critical roles in the development of infant technologies in the Internet
(Mowery and Simcoe, chapter 9) and semiconductors (Langlois, chapter 10).

1.3. Country Performance

In the absence of a single unifying "theory of
innovation," scholars have focused their analytical lenses on a wide array of putative drivers of
innovation and mechanisms which might link
innovation and economic performance. In the
country study chapters that follow, we asked
each of the authors to examine a common list
of specific factors—such as capital markets,
labor markets, education systems, R&D policies
and spending, industry structures, intellectual
property protection, and trade policies—and
to focus on those that appear best to answer
the two central questions of this book: what
drives innovation, and what explains the translation of innovation into measures of economic
performance? Each chapter provides a survey of
the economic performance in the selected
country, or countries, since 1970, and then
probes the operation of the "national innovation system" and its impact on that performance. We asked the authors to examine
significant scientific and commercial advances
in the country over the last thirty years, conspicuous contributions to technological innovation,

and conspicuous failures. Many of the chapters include vignettes that explore particular examples—such as the "Minitel" rival to the Internet in France, or the radical transformation of Nokia in Finland—and put them into the context of the larger national story. We hope the reader will conclude that we struck roughly the right balance between a "cookie cutter" approach, which facilitates comparison across the country studies, and flexibility to allow for a more qualitative approach to studying idiosyncratic national institutions and practices. Our advance on the first comparative study using this method (Nelson, 1993) is to probe those national institutions and practices in much greater depth and with richer comparisons.

We focus here on three broad observations from the country studies.

First, innovation scholarship has generally given inordinate attention to R&D spending. R&D conforms with the "pipeline" concept of technological change—new ideas emerge from laboratory research, are "developed" in semi-commercial settings, and then applied. Few believe that this model is more than a crude caricature, but it is a simpler analytical device than any of the alternatives. R&D is the only major input to the innovation process that can be measured easily and systematically, and comparative studies of innovation tend to focus, not surprisingly, where comparative measures are most readily available. Yet the country studies show that relatively little of the innovation story in each country is a function of R&D. Even stories that appear to illustrate the centrality of R&D policy, in fact, show a diverse range of factors at work. The dominance of the U.S. pharmaceutical industry, for example, is not only a byproduct of liberal spending by the U.S. government on basic research in the health sciences, but also of policies such as the Bayh-Dole Act that allow private institutions to claim (and develop) the intellectual property from government-funded research.

Second, the case studies suggest that there has been some convergence in innovation systems and economic policies across all nine countries. In 1970, economic policies in many of these countries involved very considerable government intervention—particularly in the areas of capital markets, industrial policy, and labor markets. Yet over the past fifteen years, all of these countries have sought to pare down the role of government and to allow markets a greater role in allocating resources. That process has led not only to substantial policy changes within countries, but also to convergence across countries. In some countries, these changes were relatively dramatic and sudden—such as occurred during the Thatcher program of privatization and deregulation in the United Kingdom during the 1980s, or the radical economic restructuring in Finland which followed the collapse of its largest trading partner, the Soviet Union. Economic liberalization is hardly complete, nor is the trend inexorable, however. The chapter on Germany, for example, focuses on persistent barriers to innovation and innovation diffusion deriving from capital market structure, labor market regulation, and a relatively rigid system of higher education.

The critical importance of capital markets in the innovation process was powerfully illustrated in the United States in the 1990s, as equity capital poured into "New Economy" enterprises, rapidly transforming the composition of the major stock market indexes. Whereas "irrational exuberance" may have infused the Nasdaq market in the late 1990s, it would seem equally clear that the astounding growth of the U.S. IT sector could never have occurred without the presence of highly liquid capital markets (and the venture capital growth which such markets enabled). The prominence of the Lamfalussy "Wise Men" Committee in the European Union, which focused on the need to accelerate significantly the process of securities market integration in Europe, owed much to the example set by the United States over the previous decade.

The chapters also illustrate that governments have not solved some of the fundamental problems that come with a shift to markets, such as the under-provision of public goods. In many countries there is evidence of under-investment in public goods such as basic research. In some countries that have privatized and deregulated electric power generation, for example, investment in basic research related to energy, such as metallurgy and certain branches of physics, has plummeted. Several of the country studies also highlight problems relating to the level and targeting of education spending in an era of contractionary fiscal policy.

Third, looking across the nine country studies, the strongest common thread is most clearly discerned at its two extreme points: the United States and Japan. If we want to understand the relation between innovation and economic performance, innovation turns out to be both essential and inconsequential—dependent entirely on what sectors and what time frame one chooses to focus on.

As Robert Gordon's (chapter 3) seminal work on the U.S. economy has indicated, innovation in the computer industry has dramatically increased productivity in that sector, but the nature and extent of the spillover has been misunderstood. Since 1995, there has been a significant increase in productivity in the computer and computer peripherals industry—an industry which accounts for a relatively small but growing proportion of the U.S. economy (currently about 4 percent). Furthermore, there has been a clear productivity spillover effect from investment in computers in the noncomputer economy. However, for the 88 percent of the economy outside of durable manufacturing, there has been no acceleration of TFP growth. Computer capital did contribute to "capital deepening" across the economy, in the form of faster growth of capital relative to labor, but did not contribute a higher rate of return than other types of capital—meaning that there was no measurable transformative effect on business practices and productivity in the noncomputer economy over the period studied. Over a much longer observation period, we may indeed come to witness such a transformative effect. Yet if the growth of computer investment should slow in the next five years to a rate more similar to that which prevailed prior to 1995, then over half the productivity growth revival we have witnessed since 1995 may also disappear. In short, computers are indeed a major technological innovation, one whose impact has been significant across a range of industries in durable manufac-

turing, but one whose status as the driver of a putative "New Economy" is still an open issue.

Given the current popular focus on innovation, it is not surprising that many have sought to attribute the near decade-long Japanese economic malaise to Japan's inability to innovate sufficiently. As Posen (chapter 4) concludes, "Accepting an imperfect, or at least very long-term connection between [innovation and economic performance] is to be preferred to making a circular argument, as some do, that the reason Japanese economic performance is poor is because the entire national innovation system that once worked for Japan is 'inappropriate' for today's world and technology, and the reason that we know the innovation system is inappropriate is that performance is poor." Posen demonstrates very persuasively that, along numerous dimensions, Japan is simply no less "innovative" today than it was in the 1980s. To be sure, there are conspicuous long-standing deficiencies in the Japanese national innovation system, deficiencies which help to explain why "There has been little or no diffusion of technological progress or productivity enhancing practices from the 10 percent of the Japanese economy that is export competitive to the 90 percent of the Japanese economy that is not." Yet the focus on finding sources of Japanese innovation failure, a mirror image of innovation exuberance in the United States, has resulted in far too little attention being paid to deep-seated structural and macroeconomic failures. For example, liberalization of the Japanese financial, retail, and telecommunications sectors would result in twice the national productivity growth that the United States experienced over the course of the 1990s (OECD, 1998b). If the United States had suffered from comparable structural problems or deflationary pressures, there would undoubtedly be no discernable "New Economy." Whether or not the United States has in fact developed a "New Economy," it is clear that the United States is now reaping the benefits of a successful but extended battle to control inflation and inflation expectations, liberalization of the telecommunications sector, and reform of banking regulation. As investment in innovation depends fundamentally on monetary stability, fiscal incentives, and effective regulation and competition policy, it is not possible to assess properly the role of innovation or innovation policies in the United States or Japan without taking explicit account of the wider economic environment in which they are embedded.

1.4. Government and Industry in a "New Economy"

In the industry studies, we asked the authors to focus on those national markets that appear to define the "efficient frontier" of innovation, or the yardstick against which performance in the industry worldwide is generally measured. Relevant indicators of performance obviously vary considerably across industries. The securities trading chapter, for example, focused on the impact of technological innovation in trading systems on the cost of capital to those companies whose securities are traded on such systems. Here, we focus on some of the key policy issues emerging from the research across the selected industries.

Thinking regarding the role of government in the marketplace has undergone enormous change over the past twenty years, particularly in Europe. The term "industrial policy" is very rarely used these days even among those highly sympathetic to government intervention. But the rise in interest in the economic role of innovation has been accompanied by a corresponding rise in interest in the role of government as a catalyst for innovation and diffusion of innovations across the economy.

Recent technological innovations have tended to be concentrated in industries with very particular economic characteristics. Many of these industries, particularly those analyzed in this volume, are marked by some combination of:

- significant economies of scale
- network externalities
- complementarity and standardization
- switching costs
- intellectual property as a principal output

Virtually every part of the computer industry—whether focused on hardware, software, or communications—exhibits these characteristics to a greater or lesser degree. The defining feature of this and other network industries, where users of a product benefit from the addition of new users, is that competitive equilibria do not exist. Market failures may therefore occur. Dominant firms facing ineffective competition may generate resource misallocation. Externalities may result in standardization around products which are inferior, but happen to come on the market earlier. Inability to appropriate the full commercial benefits of research may result in socially suboptimal levels of R&D investment.

It is not surprising, therefore, that the major agenda items dominating the debate over the interaction between government and industry in the innovation process are competition, government financial support, and intellectual property rights (IPR). Whereas the industries we have examined in this project occupy markets with quite varied economic characteristics and historical relationships with government, we believe some important policy lessons may be drawn.

1.4.1. Competition Policy

Network industries complicate competition policy. This can be illustrated by reference to the two conceptual components of economic efficiency: allocative and productive efficiency. Allocative efficiency concerns the relation between price and marginal cost, and is a function of market power. More competition, or potential competition, reduces market power and increases allocative efficiency. Productive efficiency concerns the unit costs associated with the production of goods and services, and is a function of factors such as economies of scale and network externalities. Mergers may reduce the long-run average cost of firms, and thereby increase productive efficiency. They may also increase market power, and thereby reduce allocative efficiency. It is the task of antitrust analysis to determine which effect is predominant in any given case.

New industries, and new manifestations of old ones, seem particularly apt to exhibit a sharp contrast between the two types of effi-

ciency, and thereby pose difficult analytical challenges for antitrust authorities. Computer-
based products such as operating systems and
trading architectures exhibit enormous
network externalities, such that the more
users that coalesce around a given product,
the more benefit is conferred on each user.
The potential customer reach of such products
is frequently global, even when the owner does
not intend it to be: Internet-based applications
are the clearest example. Defining the relevant
market for both geographic and product identification purposes (what exactly is an "operating system"?) can frequently be very difficult.
Different national competition authorities
applying identical principles in identical cases
are apt to reach different conclusions or specify
different remedies. Where nonefficiency
concerns, such as income distribution effects,
are allowed to come into play, the potential
for cross-border antitrust conflict can only
increase as the "New Economy" expands. And
as Posner (1999: 51) has highlighted, it is large
firms rather than monopolists as such to which
political concern is generally directed. Many of
the New Economy enterprises will boast enormous market capitalizations without clearly
exhibiting market power, yet are likely to
receive antitrust attention, particularly outside
their legal home base, merely because of the
size of their equity base (see Evenett et al.,
2000).

The evidence suggests that governments
need to distinguish clearly between dominant
firms which have emerged through government
ownership or protection, and those which have
emerged through the competitive process in
the private sector. French government policy
to develop Minitel usage among the populace,
for example, suffered considerably from failure
to introduce competition into the telecommunications market—controlled by state-owned
France Telecom (see Messerlin, chapter 6). In
the United States, Securities and Exchange
Commission (SEC) policy designed to shackle
emerging for-profit electronic trading system
operators to the rules and institutions of the
incumbent monopoly Nasdaq market, owned
by the quasi-governmental National Association
of Securities Dealers, led to increased fragmen-

tation of trading, contrary to the SEC's aims,
and calcification of Nasdaq's outdated dealer
market structure. Privatizing and demutualizing
Nasdaq would have been a more effective
response to the emergence of competitive electronic trading systems—a conclusion supported
by the European experience with freer competition among exchanges (see Domowitz and
Steil, chapter 12). Many industries which have
traditionally been held to exhibit "natural
monopoly" characteristics have been revealed,
largely through technological innovation, to
have sustained monopolies only because of
the persistence of government control, patent
protection, and other forms of state intervention (Shy, 2001). Activist competition policy is
necessary to allow competition and innovation
to emerge. However, the competition-driven
emergence of dominant firms in network industries, such as Microsoft in computer operating
systems, presents a much less clear-cut case for
radical government intervention—such as
Judge Penfield Jackson's break-up order (over-
turned in June 2001). Consumer harm from
losses in allocative efficiency may be swamped
by gains in productive efficiency, and the
dismantling of such firms may result in higher
prices for complementary products, which typically cross-subsidize each other.

1.4.2. Financial Support

The story of the U.S. government's role in the
creation of the Internet is legendary, but, as
with all legends, one must be careful to draw
the right message. The U.S. government never
set out to build an "Internet" as such—rather,
the Internet is the ever-evolving outcome of
numerous distinct projects funded by different
government agencies, often with conflicting
aims (see Mowery and Simcoe, chapter 9). As
such, U.S. government support for the Internet
bears a far better relation to funding for basic
noncommercial science than, say, French
government support for the Minitel. In the
latter case, the clear intention was to establish
a closed national telephone-based network,
built on a single set of standards by designated
monopoly suppliers. French officials displayed
exceptional foresight in the development of

the network, but only perfect foresight would have prevented its undoing. Without the benefit of competitive forces to encourage experimentation, diversify sources, lower prices, expand services, and enable foreign access, the Minitel became merely a useful, but costly, short-lived product which significantly inhibited French adoption of the Internet. Government support for innovation is most likely to be effective where it is distinctly lacking in such "intentionality"—that is, where it is aimed at stimulating research with no immediate route to commercialization. The private sector is best placed to evaluate the risks and rewards of commercial R&D. Government funding should focus on basic science which would not otherwise be funded, owing to the extreme uncertainty as to future commercial applications and value.

More fundamentally, the studies in this volume suggest strongly that the traditional association of innovation with corporate R&D is increasingly misplaced in the context of the rapidly evolving financial marketplace. In particular, venture capital is playing an increasingly important role in funding technological innovation. Lerner (chapter 13) documents the striking finding that one dollar of venture capital funding results in a patenting level typically associated with three to four dollars of traditional corporate R&D. Of course, venture capital and intrafirm R&D may fund different activities, so that this observation does not speak to the relative efficiency of the two sources of investment. Yet it does suggest that government efforts to stimulate commercial innovation should not focus on large incumbent firms when the elimination of tax and regulatory impediments to private venture capital funding may achieve far more with lower cost and less distortion to competition.

1.4.3. Intellectual Property

Intellectual property is the primary product of the "New Economy." As such, it is hardly surprising that the pressure on developed country governments to grant and enforce legal protection to intellectual property has grown dramatically over the past decade. As intellectual property is typically characterized by a very high ratio of fixed to marginal production costs, innovators have a strong prima facie case for protection against free riding. Critically, however, protection for intellectual property beyond that required to stimulate its production will have an even more stultifying effect on the diffusion of economic benefits than would be the case for more familiar products with a lower ratio of fixed to marginal cost. Policies which increase rewards to innovators are likely to increase the cost of diffusing innovations through new and better products and services. The economic benefits of technology commercialization can be too easily overlooked in creating protection for all forms of innovation.

Furthermore, whereas the standard economic models tend to see the costs of strong patent protection simply in terms of diminished use and diffusion of a given invention, in some industries and technologies excessive patent protection can actually slow down technical progress. Such problems arise in at least two different types of situations. The first is in industries where products involve a large number of different components, and where the holding of component patents by different parties can make it very difficult for an inventor or company to advance the system as a whole, without infringing somebody's patent (Hall and Ziedonis, 2001). The second is when patents are given on scientific discoveries that are far "upstream" from practical application, and thus restrict the range of inventors who are free to use that scientific finding as a basis for new practical products and processes. This issue is currently very prominent in biotechnology.

The proper scope of intellectual property rights is a matter of public policy concern and is currently the subject of intense debate. In the United States, dramatic changes on a variety of technological fronts, and in the patent system itself, have combined to create a great deal of uncertainty and also a surge in patenting activity. Hall and Ziedonis (2001) found that the strengthening of U.S. patent rights in the 1980s spawned "patent portfolio races" among capital-intensive semiconductor firms; firms which do not rely heavily on patents to appropriate returns to R&D. These races appeared to be fuelled by "concerns about being held up by external patent owners, and at negotiating access to external technologies on more favorable terms" (Hall and Ziedonis, 2001: 104). A 1998 court decision upholding a patent on software that uses a method for computing mutual fund closing prices that had been in use for many years appears to extend fairly strong property rights to the software domain. There are concerns that the courts will take a similar stance with respect to the issue of so-called "business method" patents (see Mowery and Simcoe, chapter 9). In the wake of the decision, business method patenting and patent litigation has expanded dramatically, raising the specter of an explosion of litigation focused on technical methods long in use, but patented only recently (by a later adopter).

As such property conflicts sweep across the terrain of Internet commerce, encompassing such general techniques as "one click" ordering and "reverse auctions," the effects on the evolution the Internet—and, indeed, the wider economy—may be very considerable. As Mowery and Simcoe emphasize, "national IPR systems and national economies ... 'co-evolve' in a complex, path-dependent, and interactive fashion." Given the explosive rise of the Internet as a fundamental tool of mass communication, information diffusion, and commerce, we fear that the wholesale intrusion of state protection for dubious forms of intellectual property may have a chilling effect on competition and innovation diffusion.

If a silver lining can be discerned, it is beyond the borders of the United States, where e-commerce is likely to expand rapidly and where U.S. business method patents are likely to be ineffective. The growing internationalization of the Internet suggests that it will, in the long run, prove impossible for any one state authority to enforce rights or standards. Expect e-commerce therefore to represent an increasingly important component of a complex and expanding agenda for U.S.–E.U. negotiations on cross-border competition policy.

2

Innovation in an Historical Perspective: Tales of Technology and Evolution

Joel Mokyr

2.1. Introduction

Are we living in the middle of an Industrial Revolution? The easy answer is, of course, that it is too soon to tell (Mokyr, 1997). Before a more specific argument can be made, it is essential to show what precisely was revolutionary about previous Industrial Revolutions and what elements made them so. Contemporaries of events that were at the start of what later turned out to be truly historical watersheds were not always cognizant of what was happening around them. The people alive during the first Industrial Revolution in the late eighteenth century were not fully aware of living in the middle of a period of dramatic and irreversible change. Most of the promises and future benefits of the technological changes were still unsuspected. Adam Smith clearly could not have much sense of the impact of the innovations taking place around him in 1776. Napoleon famously referred to Britain as a nation of shopkeepers, not of "cotton-spinners" or "steam-engine operators." By the time of the battle of Waterloo, however, this had already changed.[1] By the mid-nineteenth century, a growing awareness of the importance of technology in changing the world can be seen everywhere. Horace Greeley, the editor of the *New York Tribune*, pronounced in 1853 that "we have universalized all the beautiful and glorious results of industry and skill ... we have democratized the means and appliances of a higher life." These were to some extent prophetic

words, since only the second Industrial Revolution brought technological progress to the advantage of the consumer. By the end of the nineteenth century, James P. Boyd, the author of *Triumphs and Wonders of the 19th Century, The True Mirror of a Phenomenal Era*, concluded that the invention and progress which have most affected the life and civilizations of the world, "the nineteenth century has achieved triumphs ... equal, if not superior to all centuries combined" (Smith, 1994: 5–7).

Terms like "revolution" tend to be overused and abused by historians. They draw attention. They sell books. But do they have historical content? In economic history, especially, melodramatic terms have a bad name, because the field tends to be relatively *un*dramatic. Most of the things that play a role in modern economic growth are gradual, slow, and almost imperceptible: the dissemination of technological ideas, the accumulation of capital, even in most cases the changes in economic institutions were rarely very spectacular. In those cases in which a genu-

I am indebted to Robert J. Gordon, Richard R. Nelson and the editors for helpful comments. This chapter is based on material taken from my forthcoming book, *The Gifts of Athena: Historical Origins of the Knowledge Economy*, to be published by Princeton University Press.

[1] The Scottish merchant and statistician Patrick Colquhoun, only twenty-five-years Smith's junior, wrote in 1814 in a celebrated paragraph that "It is impossible to contemplate the progress of manufactures in Great Britain within the last thirty years without wonder and astonishment. Its rapidity, particularly since the French Revolutionary Wars, exceeds all credibility." At about the same time, the great manufacturer Robert Owen noted that "The manufacturing system has already so far extended its influence over the British Empire, as to effect an essential change in the general character of the mass of the people. This alteration is still in rapid progress ... This change has been owing chiefly to the mechanical inventions which introduced the cotton trade into this country ... the immediate effects of this manufacturing phenomenon were a rapid increase in the wealth, industry, population, and political influence of the British Empire." For details, see Mokyr (1998a: 3–5).

inely dramatic invention occurred, its immediate impact on productivity was often negligible and if it occurred at all, took many years to be felt through the economy. The first Industrial Revolution used to be regarded as the most dramatic watershed event of the economic history of mankind since the invention of agriculture and has often been mentioned in one breath with the drama-laden contemporaneous French Revolution. It has now been shown to have had only minor effects on economic growth before 1815 and practically none on real wages and living standards before 1840, more than a century after the appearance of the first steam engine. The second Industrial Revolution, similarly, was slow in manifesting its full impact on the economies in question and it took much of the twentieth century to work out its effects fully. The paragon of the putative third Industrial Revolution, the computer, has still apparently not wholly lived up to the hopes and expectations regarding productivity and output.

It is ahistorical to think about Industrial Revolutions of any kind as a set of events which abruptly raise the rate of sustained economic growth by a considerable amount. Most of the effects on income per capita or economic welfare are slow in the coming, and spread out over long periods. Instead, we should recognize that even though the dynamic relation between technological progress and per capita growth is hard to pin down and measure, it is the central feature of modern economic history. We do not know for sure how to identify the technology-driven component of growth, but we can be reasonably sure that the unprecedented (and to a large extent undermeasured) growth in income in the twentieth century would not have taken place without technological changes. It seems therefore more useful to measure "industrial revolutions" in terms of the technological capabilities of a society based on the knowledge it possesses and the institutional rules by which its economy operates. These technological capabilities include the potential to produce more goods and services which enter gross domestic product (GDP) and productivity calculations, but they could equally affect aspects that are poorly measured by our standard measures of economic performance, such as

the ability to prevent disease, to educate the young, to preserve and repair the environment, to move and process information, to coordinate production in large units, and so on. By those standards, it is hard to deny that the 1990s have witnessed an Industrial Revolution, but we need to assess it in terms of those capabilities, with the macroeconomic consequences, eventual but much delayed.

2.2. Knowledge and Economic Growth

Dramatic or not, technological progress has been the central driving force in modern economic growth. Historically this has not always been the case. Economic growth in pre-1750 was by no means always negligible, but it tended to be more heavily fueled by institutional change and the effects it had on trade creation and the allocation of resources. Processes such as improved property rights and better organized markets can create considerable wealth, and did so in various stages in Northern Italy, in England, and in the Low Countries. Technology had some striking achievements in the centuries before the Industrial Revolution, but all things considered, it probably accounted for limited growth.[2] The British Industrial Revolution (1760–1830) marks the first event in which changes in technology indisputably occupy the center of the stage due to an acceleration in the rate of innovation. Two other such accelerations can be tentatively identified: the "second" Industrial Revolution which started after 1860, and the closing decades of the twentieth century.

Whether such accelerations qualify these epochs for a "revolutionary" label remains a matter of semantics. The argument in this chapter is that these accelerations are neither complete accidents nor were entirely generated internally by inexorable factors such as market conditions or the institutional environment. Instead, we return to an argument made by

[2] The assessment of its role is complicated by the impact that technology had on the creation of markets and international trade through improvements in shipping and navigation.

Simon Kuznets (1965: 84–87). Kuznets wrote flat-out that modern economic growth was based on the growth of the stock of useful or "tested knowledge." He argued that "one might define modern economic growth as the spread of a system of production ... based on the increased application of science." This seemed obvious to Kuznets because after all, "science is controlled observation of the world around us [whereas] economic production is manipulation of observable reality for the special purpose of providing commodities and services desired by human beings."

Few scholars would take issue with Kuznets's dictum that useful knowledge lies at the core of modern economic growth. In the past centuries too, additional factors were at work: capital accumulation, gains from trade, and improved factor allocations. Yet it is generally felt that without modern technology, Europe and the West might have ended up like China after 1800, when the gains from internal trade ran into diminishing returns and supporting institutions such as internal law and order were weakened by political instability. The exact definition of "useful knowledge" and how we approach its unusual dynamics in the past quarter millennium have barely been touched upon by economic historians.

Kuznets's definition, however, creates a dilemma for economic historians. It is agreed by historians of science and economics historians that the component of "science" properly speaking in the classical Industrial Revolution was quite modest, and that the tight interaction of scientific knowledge and engineering, applied chemistry, agriculture and so on postdate the middle of the nineteenth century. Even then, as discussed later, this connection remained quite tenuous in many fields. It is therefore obvious that Kuznets's transition from "useful knowledge" to "science" is not entirely satisfactory. Science was and is only a small part of what can be called "useful" knowledge. Useful knowledge includes *all natural phenomena and regularities* and, as such, it contains what we call science as a subset. It is true, perhaps, that by now most such regularities and phenomena that can be readily observed are known, so that any increments in the set of useful knowledge are likely to come from trained experts, but this is clearly a relatively recent development.

"Knowledge," as a historical factor, however, is a difficult concept. Epistemologists have for millennia argued about how we "know" things and what it means for something to be "known." Despite the central role that technology and human knowledge play in modern economic growth, economists have rarely spent much time worrying about the more subtle aspects of epistemology and probably rightly so. In technology, after all, we are not interested in whether something is "true" but whether it works. An invention based on a mistaken insight can at times enhance productivity and in that case the unsound foundation may seem immaterial. It would be impossible to understand the development of technology without realizing the knowledge and assumptions on which techniques rest. As an economic concept, knowledge is also slippery. It is a nonrival public good (sharing it does not reduce the amount available to the original owner), yet it is often excludable (it can be kept secret). Acquiring it can be costly to the individual, yet there is not much correlation between the costs of its acquisition and its marginal product. Knowledge does not follow simple rules of arithmetic and additivity, and it is highly self-referential (there is a lot of knowledge about knowledge). *New* knowledge's characteristics as a commodity have always been difficult to incorporate in a price-theoretic framework, and while certain kinds of patentable knowledge have come close, the patent system, even when it existed, has been notoriously uneven in its ability to protect and encourage new knowledge.

In recent decades, a growing number of scholars have argued that it is more enlightening to take an evolutionary approach to technological knowledge. This approach combines the evolutionary epistemology pioneered by Campbell and his colleagues with notions of "cultural evolution" and treats knowledge as produced by the system through a stock of information that is transmitted through time by "agents" who select and then "retain" (carry) it. The literature on this topic is quite large and growing rapidly. Surveys on the topic are readily available (Dosi and Nelson, 1994; Nelson, 1995b; Saviotti, 1996).

Can such an approach be used to shed light on the economic history of technological change? One way of applying this framework to economic history is to differentiate between *propositional* knowledge serving as background knowledge ("knowledge what") and *prescriptive* knowledge, which consists of "instructions" that constitute techniques or "routines" ("knowledge how to"). This distinction is neither original nor uncontroversial.[3] What is important is not so much to create taxonomies, as to realize that the relationship between these different kinds of knowledge was critical to the historical outcomes. Fundamentally, new techniques are created when in one form or another, useful knowledge is "mapped" onto a set of instructions which constitute a technique.[4] Much of this underlying knowledge maybe tacit and very poorly understood, but something has to be there for a technique to emerge. It is important to realize that this mapping involves a variety of agents, since the people who build artifacts and design techniques, much less those who carry them out, are not necessarily the ones who possess the knowledge. This means that *access* to propositional knowledge is as important as the amount known.

This setup leads directly to the concept of the *epistemic base* of a technique as that part of "propositional knowledge" of natural regularities and phenomena on which techniques in use are based (Mokyr, 2000). There is some minimum epistemic base without which techniques cannot be conceived, but for many techniques in use in 1750, this minimum may have been quite small.[5] The epistemic base *can* be much wider than the minimum: modern science knows a great deal more about the statistical mechanics of boiling water than is necessary to make a cup of tea. A narrow epistemic base of a technology that is in use means that people were able to figure out *what* worked, but did not understand *how* and *why* things worked. Further improvements, adaptations to changing circumstances, and new applications and extensions would be more difficult if the epistemic base was narrow. Further "research" would be encumbered by not knowing what does *not* work.[6]

The epistemic basis of a technique constitutes a "fixed factor" in the sense that continuous improvements in techniques in use without a growth in the underlying knowledge ran into something akin to diminishing returns. While it may not be *invariably* true that a deeper understanding of the physical processes at work is a sufficient condition for technological change to be self-sustaining, societies with little understanding of the processes they exploit would be limited in their progress.[7] There can

---

[3] The distinction between the two types of knowledge parallels the distinction made famous half a century ago by Gilbert Ryle (1949), who distinguished between knowledge "how" and knowledge "what." Ryle rejected the notion that one can meaningfully distinguish *within a single individual* knowledge of a set of parameters about a problem and an environment from a set of instructions derived from this knowledge that directs an individual to take a certain action. Michael Polanyi (1962: 175) points out that the difference boils down to observing that knowledge "what" can be "right or wrong" whereas "action can only be successful or unsuccessful." He also notes that the distinction is recognized by patent law, which patents inventions but not discoveries. The application of this dichotomy to the analysis of technological change was pioneered by Arora and Gambardella (1994) whose term for "useful knowledge" is "abstract and general knowledge" – although there is no particular reason why useful knowledge could not be both concrete and specific.

[4] There is a somewhat forced analogy between the dichotomy between the two types of knowledge and the distinction made between genotype and phenotype in biology. For a discussion of the merits and pitfalls of such isomorphisms, see Mokyr (1998b, 2000c).

[5] Some rather simple techniques might have an almost completely degenerate epistemic base, which means that the only knowledge on which they rest is that "this technique works." Such singleton techniques are discovered by accident or through exhaustive experimentation, and usually constitute dead ends in technological development.

[6] One thinks somewhat wistfully about the alchemical work of Newton (who wrote almost a million words on alchemy) and many other brilliant scientists such as Robert Boyle. Modern scholarship has shown that Newton, rather than being superstitious, was consistent with the best practice theories of his time (Brock, 1992: 30–32).

[7] When the natural processes at work are complex or misunderstood, progress can take place through a purely experimental approach, or by establishing exploitable empirical regularities through statistical techniques. Yet even such inductive-empirical methodologies of inquiry require epistemic bases such as statistical inference techniques.

be little doubt that the widening of the epistemic base in modern times was a critical element in sustaining technological progress. Nelson (2000: 74) has even maintained that "nowadays, of course, most technologies are understood, in part at least, 'scientifically'". *Understanding* a technique is, however, a relative concept: we may understand more about why certain techniques work than earlier generations, but we do not *really* know why physics and chemistry work the way they do either and we cannot be ontologically certain that our way of thinking about nature is the "right" or the only one (Cohen and Stewart, 1994). Such relativism, however, has its limits: for each technique there is some minimum epistemic base without which it cannot exist. This basis may not be *unique*, but it can grow and change, and as it does, it holds one key to the economic history of technological change.

One distinction used here is that between macroinventions and microinventions first introduced in Mokyr (1990b). The distinction between the two is largely based on the epistemic distance between them and the prescriptive knowledge previously available. A macroinvention is one that cannot be considered an improvement or an elaboration of existing techniques even though it, too, must rely on an existing epistemic base. The main characteristics of a macroinvention are an observable epistemological discontinuity from what was possible before. Over the years, biologists have changed their minds on the likelihood of such "saltations." The geneticist Richard Goldschmidt referred to them in a memorable term as "hopeful monstrosities" but it seems that even the believers in "punctuated equilibrium" no longer believe that biology can be *that* abrupt. In nature, "hopeful monstrosities" do not suddenly create new species.[8] There are points in the history of technology that we can identify as such hopeful monstrosities. One thinks instinctively of Newcomen's famous Dudley Castle 1712 steam pump, the "Silent Otto" (a monstrously noisy—its name notwithstanding—early version of the internal combustion engine), the first hot-air balloon, Babbage's difference engine, or even the ENIAC computer. We are interested in these cases precisely because we know what

came before and after, and the huge leap represented by these machines and how they subsequently changed history.

One useful way to think about the economic history of technological progress is to think of it in terms of evolutionary trajectories that begin through a sudden novelty or macroinvention, which then are continuously improved and refined through a multitude of microinventions. Those myriad of small, incremental, mostly anonymous improvements and refinements that debug and modify the new idea so as to turn it into something workable and efficient, basically draw from the same or very close parts of the epistemic base. When this useful knowledge is exhausted, stasis is likely to set in until "punctuated" by a new macroinvention. It could be said that microinventions occur within an existing technological paradigm and are part of "normal technological change" whereas macroinventions require stepping outside accepted practice and design, an act of technological rebellion and heresy. Their success is in opening new doors, while microinventions fill gaps. In terms of their contribution to such economic variables as GDP growth and productivity increase, macroinventions are dwarfed by the effects of technological drift. But without great daring insights that represent a radical break of some sort with the past, such increments would inevitably grind to a halt.

2.3. The First Industrial Revolution

A renewed emphasis of "knowledge" in the first Industrial Revolution of 1760–1830 has been proposed recently in Mokyr (2000a). The

---

[8] See, for instance, Charlesworth and Templeton (1982). Yet none of that would contradict the commonplace observation that there are periods in which evolutionary innovation was very rapid and feverish, and others in which it proceeded, if at all, at a glacial rate. Perhaps, then, biological evolution did not have its steam engine or its mechanical clock, but it did have periods much like the Industrial Revolution in which change was unusually rapid, even on a different time scale. Such periods of "adaptive radiation" during which innovation was fast and radical have been documented at the beginning of the cenozoic with the spectacular proliferation of mammals (Stanley, 1981: 91–3.)

economic significance of the Industrial Revolution is not so much in the great gadgets that were invented in the "years of miracles" between 1760 and 1790, but rather that the process of innovation did not run into diminishing returns and peter out after 1800 or 1820. This is what had always happened in the past when Europe (or non-European societies) had experienced a cluster of macroinventions. The point is, above all, to explain why.

There are at least two reasons for the failure of technological progress in the pre-1750 environment to generate *sustained* economic growth. One of them was institutional negative feedback. When economic progress took place, it almost always generated a variety of social and political forces that, in almost dialectical fashion, ended up terminating it. Prosperity and success led to the emergence of rent-seekers and parasites in a variety of forms and guises who eventually slaughtered the geese that laid the golden eggs. Tax collectors, foreign invaders, and distributional coalitions such as guilds and monopolies in the end extinguished much of the growth of Northern Italy, Southern Germany and the Low Countries.

The other reason is that before 1750, most techniques in use or known to be feasible rested on very narrow epistemic bases.[9] The famed inventions that formed the basis of the Industrial Revolution were accompanied by a deepening as well as a widening of the epistemic base of the techniques in use. Perhaps, by our standards, the direct technological achievements of the scientific revolution appear to be modest, and there is clearly much to recommend A. Rupert Hall's view that the early inventions of the Industrial Revolution lacked support in science proper (Hall, 1974). Yet, as I argued above, this is an overly restricted definition of the knowledge base of technology. Propositional knowledge included a great deal

more knowledge that we would call "useful" but which was more artisanal knowledge than "science": examples are the lubricating qualities of oils, the hardness and durability of different kinds of woods, the location of minerals, the direction of the trade winds, and the strength and dietary needs of domestic animals. On the eve of the Industrial Revolution, with "science" in the modern sense in its infancy, this was most of what there was of the set of propositional knowledge.[10]

In the decades around 1800, advances in chemistry, mechanics, energy, material science, and medicine continuously expanded the informal and formal parts of useful knowledge, including—but not limited to—the well-known scientific advances of Lavoisier, Cavendish, Dalton, and their colleagues. This development was fueled by the self-propelled internal growth of propositional knowledge as well as by the feedback of technological breakthroughs into science and engineering. Before 1850, the contribution of *formal* science to technology was probably modest. Much of the technological progress in the first half of the nineteenth century came from the semi-formal and pragmatic useful knowledge generated by the great engineers of the Industrial Revolution: Maudslay, the Brunels, the Stephensons, Roberts, Neilson, and their colleagues. This does not really invalidate the argument that the interaction between propositional knowledge and prescriptive knowledge was the driving force behind technological expansion, only that we are missing most of the action if we concentrate our efforts on formal science. Two stereotypic cartoons, the one of an ignorant amateur "tinkerer" who stumbled into great inventions through a combination of inspired intuition and sheer luck, and that of the methodical, well-informed scientist whose rigorous papers inform applied scientists and engineers of the natural exploitable regularities are mostly

---

[9] In some areas, the epistemic base was reasonably broad but, by our standards, misconceived. Thus, eighteenth century metallurgy relied on phlogiston theory which, despite some useful implications, was shown to be false by Lavoisier. Much of medicine around 1750 still relied on the humoral theory of disease.

[10] Many of the great discoveries of the Scientific Revolution were in areas that had little direct applicability such as cosmology and optics. This gradually began to change in the eighteenth century with the application of calculus to problems in hydraulic engineering and construction.

ahistorical. In between, there was a semi-directed, groping, bumbling process of trial and error with occasional successes, squeezing a messy, poorly defined blob of useful knowledge, some of it formal and codified, some of it simply passed on orally in terms of "this works and this does not" mapping into "here is how you do this."

What made the difference between the innovations of the 1760s and 1770s, and those of the fifteenth century? As argued in detail in Mokyr (2000a), the scientific revolution and the enlightenment helped expand the epistemic base of techniques in use and thus create the conditions for more sustainable technological progress. Not only that, they expanded the set of propositional knowledge in a variety of ways; they also deepened it by making access to the knowledge easier and cheaper. This was in part a consequence of *social* access: the seventeenth century developed the notion of open science, published upon discovery. The social prestige of science and "useful arts" gradually increased over the eighteenth century in Britain, creating a closer connection between entrepreneurs and people with technical knowledge.[11] The eighteenth century also produced more efficient storage devices (textbooks, encyclopedias), search engines (indices, experts), and even improved and streamlined the language of technical communication. For an Industrial Revolution to produce sustainable technological progress, then, it requires not just new knowledge but the ability of society to access this knowledge, use it, improve it, and find

new applications and combinations for it. As Headrick (2000) has stressed, the age of the Industrial Revolution through a variety of technological and institutional innovations did exactly that.

Besides the widening of the epistemic basis of technology, technology in the first Industrial Revolution co-evolved with the new institutions of industrial capitalism. Institutional evolution in many ways followed its own dynamic. For instance, the repeal of the Bubble Act in 1825, as has been shown by Harris (2000) was in large part the result of a power struggle between parties that believed they stood to gain from it. The creation of modern management ran into endless difficulties as documented in the late Sidney Pollard's still unsurpassed classic (Pollard, 1965). Yet ultimately the feedback from technology to institutions was positive. Rent-seeking and unproductive behavior never disappeared in any human society, but in the years after 1815 in the West they were more and more subjugated by a free market liberal ideology which provided incentives for entrepreneurial behavior that on a wide front enhanced efficiency and productivity. Had institutional feedback been negative, as it had been before 1750, technological progress would have been on the whole short-lived.

How revolutionary was the Industrial Revolution? Modern economic historians have emphasized the continuities as much as the transformations. Steam engines looked and were spectacular, but water power continued to play an important role everywhere. Cotton was equally revolutionary, but the other textiles (wool, linen and silk) were much slower to change—although eventually they all did. Apparel making and millinery remained manual, domestic industries until well into the nineteenth century. The Cort process revolutionized wrought iron, but the making of cheap steel for industrial purposes remained out of reach until the 1850s. The great changes in industrial engineering—interchangeable parts, continuous flow processes, mass production of cookie-cutter standardized products— were all in the air at the time, but were not realized at an economically significant scale until the second half of the nineteenth

[11] William Eamon (1990), and more recently Paul David (1997) have pointed to the Scientific Revolution of the seventeenth century as the period in which "open science" emerged, when knowledge about the natural world became increasingly nonproprietary and scientific advances and discoveries were freely shared with the public at large. Thus, scientific knowledge became a public good, communicated freely rather than confined to a secretive exclusive few as had been the custom in medieval Europe. Margaret Jacob (1997: 115) has argued that by 1750, British engineers and entrepreneurs had a "shared technical vocabulary" that could "objectify the physical world" and that this communication changed the Western world forever. These shared languages and vocabularies are precisely the stuff of which reduced access costs are made of.

century.[12] Much of the British economy was affected very little until the middle of the nineteenth century; productivity growth was minimal and income per capita edged upward very slowly before 1830; real wages hardly rose until the mid-1840s.

The technological changes that occurred in Western Europe between 1760 and 1800 heralded a new age in the way that new instructional knowledge was generated. It was slowly becoming less random and serendipitous. This was the result of the widening of the epistemic base of technological knowledge, and improved access to propositional knowledge by engineers and entrepreneurs. As a result, the 1820s witnessed another "wave" of inventions which, while perhaps not quite as pathbreaking as the classic inventions of the "annus mirabilis" of 1769, created a second wind which prevented the process from slowing down. In the iron industry, for example, Neilson's hot blast (1828) sharply reduced fuel costs in blast furnaces, and the self-actor was perfected by Richard Roberts in the late 1820s. In energy production, the continuous improvement in engine design and transmission in the 1820s by a large team of engineers led to Stephenson's locomotive in 1828. Many of the important inventions of this period were anything but "serendipitous" but the result of more or less directed searches and concentrated efforts of informed engineers. Some of the ideas generated in this period, however, were not realized until after 1860, which is widely agreed to merit the title the second Industrial Revolution.

2.4. The Second Industrial Revolution

It is part of accepted wisdom that the techniques that came into being after 1860 were the result of applied science which had made enormous advances in the first two-thirds of the nineteenth century. In some industries this is surely true: one can hardly imagine the advances in the chemical industry after 1860 without the advances in organic chemistry that followed Von Liebig and Wöhler's work in the 1820s and 1830s.[13] Yet, as always, there was more continuity than is often allowed for. Invention by trial and error, luck, and instinct were not replaced entirely by a complete and full understanding of the natural processes at work. The two types of knowledge continuously kept reinforcing each other.

A full survey of the technological advances during the second Industrial Revolution is not possible here, but a few illustrative examples may help us understand the subtle interplay between epistemic base and technique in this period.[14] Perhaps the paradigmatic industry of this period is steel; the breakthrough invention here, the Bessemer process of 1856, was made by a man who, by his own admission, had "very limited knowledge of iron metallurgy" (Carr and Taplin, 1962: 19).[15] His knowledge was limited to the point where the typical Bessemer blast, in his own words was "a revelation to me, as I had in no way anticipated such results." Yet the epistemic base was by no means degenerate: Bessemer knew enough chemistry to

[12] The famous Portsmouth block-making machines, devised by Maudslay together with Marc Brunel around 1801 to produce wooden gears and pulleys for the British Navy, were automatic and in their close coordination and fine division of labor, resembled a modern mass-production process in which a labor force of ten workers produced a larger and far more homogeneous output than the traditional technique that had employed more than ten times as many (Cooper, 1984). For an early application of the idea of interchangeability in France's musket making industry, see Alder (1997). The continuous flow process of the early mechanical spinning mills is emphasized by Chapman (1974).

[13] In organic chemistry, the pivotal breakthrough in the useful knowledge set was probably the understanding of the structure of the benzene molecule by the German chemist August von Kekulé in 1865, after which the search for synthetic dyes became simpler and faster. Benzene had been known for a few decades, and the first artificial dye had been synthesized a decade earlier by Perkin, so the discovery of the chemical structure counts as a classical broadening of the epistemic base.

[14] A more detailed survey can be found in Mokyr (1999), available in English on http://www.faculty.econ.northwestern.edu/faculty/mokyr/

[15] This example is also used by Arora and Gambardella (1994).

recognize that the reason why his process succeeded and similar experiments by others had failed was that the pig iron he had used was, by accident, singularly free of phosphorus and that by adding carbon at the right time, he would get the correct mixture of carbon and iron, that is, steel. He did not know enough, however, to come up with a technique that would rid iron of the phosphorus; this took another twenty years, when the basic process was discovered. Moreover, the epistemic base at the time was much larger than Bessemer's knowledge. This is demonstrated by the recognition, by an experienced metallurgist named Robert Mushet, that Bessemer steel suffered from excess oxygen, which could be remedied by the addition of a decarburizer consisting of a mixture of manganese, carbon, and iron. The Bessemer and related microinventions led, in the words of Donald Cardwell (1994: 292) to "the establishment of metallurgy as a study on the border of science and technology."

Energy utilization followed a comparable pattern. Engines in the sense we would recognize them today, that is, devices that convert heat to work in a controlled way, had existed since the first Newcomen machines, but the physics underlying their operation and governing their efficiency was not properly understood. A good intuition coupled with a sound experimental method were, up to a point, good substitutes for formal science and helped James Watt to transform a crude and clumsy contraption into a universal source of industrial power. Richard Trevithick, Arthur Woolf and their followers created, in the first decades of the nineteenth century, the more compact high pressure engine. But the science that established the efficiency of such engines did not exist. Perhaps typical of the division of labor between Britain and France, the first enunciation of the principles at work here—efficiency was a function of the differences in temperature—were laid out by a French engineer, Sadi Carnot, in 1824 after observing the differences in efficiency between a high pressure Woolf engine and an older model.[16] The next big step was made by an Englishman, James P. Joule who showed the conversion rates from

work to heat and back. Joule's work and that of Carnot were then reconciled by a German, R.J.E. Clausius (the discoverer of entropy), and by 1850 a new branch of science dubbed by William Thomson (later Lord Kelvin) "thermodynamics" had emerged (Cardwell, 1971, 1994).[17] Yet this expansion of the epistemic base on which engines rested would have been irrelevant had it not led to applications in engineering which made old engines better as well as creating new ones. William Rankine, the author of *Manual of the Steam Engine* (1859) made thermodynamics accessible to engineers and Scottish steam engines made good use of the Carnot principle that the efficiency of a steam engine depended on the temperature range over which the engine worked.[18] One of Rankine's disciples, John Elder, developed the two-cylinder compound marine engine in the 1850s, which eventually sealed the victory of steam over sailing ships. An odd curiosum in this context is the somewhat obscure pamphlet published in 1862 by Alphonse Beau de Rochas which theoretically proved that the Carnot principles applied to all heat engines, and that the most efficient system would be a four-stroke cycle. Not long after, N.A. Otto started to work on an internal combustion gas engine, and in 1876 filed a patent based on the same four-

[16] Sadi Carnot, *Reflexions sur la Puissance Motrice du Feu* [1824], 1986. In his introduction, Fox points out that French technology was widely regarded to be behind British in all matters of power engineering, yet French engineering was distinctly more theoretical than British and there was a flurry of interest in the theory of heat engines. Carnot's work was incomplete and initially had little in it to be of help to engineers, but it was rediscovered by Thomson in the 1840s.

[17] Continuous work combining experiment and theory in thermodynamics continued for many decades after that, especially in Scotland and in Mulhouse, France, where Gustave Adolphe Hirn led a large group of scientists.

[18] Rankine did more than anyone in his time to bridge the gap between science and engineering by writing four textbooks that made the findings of the new science available to engineers. His *Manual of Applied Mechanics* went through 21 editions to 1921, and the *Manual of the Steam Engine* through 17 editions to 1908 (Cardwell, 1994: 335, 529).

stroke principle. Yet apparently the two were independent events.[19]

A third example of the widening of the epistemic base of technology leading to the emergence and then continuous improvement of techniques is the emergence of the telegraph. Many eighteenth century scientists, such as the great French physicist Coulomb, believed that magnetism and electricity were unrelated. But in 1819 a Danish physicist, Hans Oersted, brought a compass needle near a wire through which a current was passing. It forced the needle to point at a right angle to the current. It turned out that electricity and magnetism were related after all. Electro-magnetism, once discovered, was turned into a legitimate field of inquiry by the work of William Sturgeon, Michael Faraday and above all Joseph Henry who advised both the Englishman Wheatstone and the American Morse. The telegraph was associated with a string of inventors, the most important of whom were: S.T. von Soemmering, a German, who was the first to demonstrate its capabilities in 1810; William Cooke, an Englishman who patented a five-needle system to transmit messages (1837); and Samuel Morse, an American, who invented the code named after him that made the single-needle system feasible. The first successful submarine cable was laid by Thomas Crampton's Company between Dover and Calais in 1851, and became a technological triumph that lasted thirty-seven years. The idea of utilizing electrical current to affect a magnetized needle to transmit information at a speed much faster than anything previously possible was a classic macroinvention. Long-distance telegraph, however, required many subsequent microinventions. Submarine cables were found to be a difficult technology to master. Signals were often weak and slow, and the messages distorted. Worse, cables were

subject at first to intolerable wear and tear.[20] The techniques of insulating and armoring the cables properly had to be perfected, and the problem of capacitance (increasing distortion on long-distance cables) had to be overcome. Before the telegraph could become truly functional, the physics of transmission of electric impulses had to be understood. Physicists, and above all Lord Kelvin, made fundamental contributions to the technology. Kelvin invented a special galvanometer, and a technique of sending short reverse pulses immediately following the main pulse, to sharpen the signal (Headrick, 1989: 215–218). In this close collaboration between science and technology, telegraphy was clearly a second generation technology.

Yet it would be a mistake to suppose that all new technology during the second Industrial Revolution required broad bases in useful knowledge. The complex relationship between propositional and prescriptive knowledge is illustrated by the profound difference between two pathbreaking inventions of the second Industrial Revolution: aspirin (discovered in 1897) and electric generators (perfected between 1865 and 1880). Aspirin had a very narrow epistemic base. In 1763 a British clergyman, the Rev. Edmund Stone drew attention to willow bark which, he thought, would serve as a remedy against ague (malaria) because willows grew in damp places and God planted cures where diseases originated (Porter, 1997: 270). Not much was done with this "insight" until the 1820s, when chemists became interested in it once again. It was recognized that the active ingredient was salicin, and later the German Löwig obtained salicylic acid. While the chemical structure of these substances was known, they had little medical value because of severe side effects. These were eliminated when Felix Hoffman stumbled on the acetyl compound of salicylic acid, later known as aspirin. It was a true wonder-drug: effective, without serious negative side effects, and cheap to produce. His employer, Bayer, hit the jackpot. Yet no one knew how and why aspirin did what it did. It was not until the 1970s that aspirin's physiological modus operandi became more evident. With this extension of the epistemic base of

---

[19] Otto vehemently denied having any knowledge of Beau de Rochas's work, and given its limited diffusion, most scholars find that claim plausible (Bryant, 1967: 656).

[20] Of the 17,700 kilometers of cable laid before 1861, only 4800 kilometers were operational in that year – the rest was lost. The transatlantic cable, through which Queen Victoria and President Buchanan exchanged their famous messages in August 1858, ceased to work three months later.

an existing technique, further adaptations were possible.[21]

The refinement of electricity generation, on the other hand, could not make much commercial progress before some of the principles had been worked out. Faraday's narrow-based discovery of the dynamo demonstrated the possibility of generating electricity by mechanical means in 1831.[22] The technical problem with which engineers struggled for decades was the generation of electricity in quantities and at prices that would make it economically viable. The pioneers of the telegraph, Cooke and Wheatstone, patented the magneto in 1845. Joule had shown a few years earlier that the magneto converts mechanical energy into electricity (and not, as was believed until then, magnetism into electricity). The important implication of this insight was that the huge amount of mechanical power that the steam engines in the middle of the nineteenth century could create was convertible into electrical energy.[23] Although not all the physics underlying that had been worked out by 1865, Joule's work suggested how it could be done. A full generation after Faraday, the discovery of the principle of self-excitation in 1866–7 led to the construction of large generators in the early 1870s and eventually to the electrical revolution.[24] Yet the *exact* physical processes that underlie the generation of electrical power were not really understood until much later.

In short, after 1850, engineers in many areas increasingly engaged in "Research and Development" (the term is slightly anachronistic for the nineteenth century) that was less experimental and more directed. Many advances were made simply because the limitations of the narrow epistemic bases of old technologies were shed. This does not mean that there were no techniques in use that still rested on very narrow epistemic bases. But in industry after industry, the knowledge base expanded. The driving force behind progress was not just that more was known, but also that institutions and culture collaborated to create better, cheaper, access to the knowledge base.[25]

The economies that were most successful in the second Industrial Revolution were those in which these connections were the most efficient. The institutions that created these bridges are well understood: universities, polytechnic schools, publicly funded research institutes, museums, agricultural research stations, and research departments in large financial institutions. Improved access to useful knowledge took many forms: cheap and widely diffused publications disseminated useful knowledge. Technical subjects penetrated

---

[21] The pathbreaking work was carried out by John Vane, who showed how aspirin inhibited the formation of prostaglandins. Following this insight, other anti-inflammatory drugs such as ibuprofen were developed. See Landau, Achilladelis and Scriabine (1999: 246–51).

[22] The first working dynamo was constructed a year later by Hippolyte Pixii in Paris. Faraday himself oddly lost interest in the mechanical production of electricity soon after.

[23] Oddly, few physicists understood what Joule argued or took the trouble to try, given that he was a professional brewer and an amateur scientist. Fortunately, young William Thomson was one of the few who realized its importance and collaborated with Joule for many years.

[24] The self-excited electric generator was a classic case of simultaneous, independent invention by Werner von Siemens, Charles Wheatstone, C.F. Varley and others. The first working generators were constructed in the early 1870s by Z.W. Gramme.

[25] In the words of Charles Parsons (1911), the co-inventor of the steam turbine (1884), which revolutionized both marine propulsion and electricity generation, "In modern times the progress of science has been phenomenally rapid. The old methods of research have given place to new. The almost infinite complexity of things has been recognized and methods, based on a co-ordination of data derived from accurate observation and tabulation of facts, have proved most successful in unravelling the secrets of Nature … In the practical sphere of engineering the same systematic research is now followed, and the old rule of thumb methods have been discarded. The discoveries and data made and tabulated by physicists, chemists, and metallurgists, are eagerly sought by the engineer, and as far as possible utilized by him in his designs. the staff. In many of the best equipped works, also, a large amount of experimental research, directly bearing on the business, is carried on by the staff … it may be interesting to mention that the work [on the steam turbine] was initially commenced because calculation showed that, from the known data, a successful steam turbine ought to be capable of construction. The practical development of this engine was thus commenced chiefly on the basis of the data of physicists …"

school curricula in every country in the West, although interestingly enough Britain, the leader in the first Industrial Revolution was the laggard here. Textbooks, professional journals, technical encyclopedias, and engineering manuals appeared in every field, providing easier access to information. The professionalization of experts meant that anyone who needed some piece of useful knowledge could always find someone who knew how or where to find it.

As in the earlier period, the growing interaction between propositional and prescriptive knowledge took two basic forms. One was technical and concerned mostly the nature of knowledge itself. What is called here "useful" knowledge increasingly mapped into new techniques, but the positive feedback between the two types of knowledge led to continuous mutual reinforcement. This positive feedback took a variety of forms. One was that technology simply posed well-defined problems to the scientists and focused their attention on some areas that were well defined and turned out to be solvable. As noted above, thermodynamics emerged in part as an endogenous response to theoretical problems posed by the operation of the steam engine.[26] The other channel through which the feedback from techniques

to useful knowledge worked was through improved instruments and laboratory equipment and methods.[27] Our senses limit us to a fairly narrow slice of the universe which has been called a "mesocosm": we cannot see things that are too far away, too small, or not in the visible light spectrum (Wuketits, 1990: 92, 105). The same is true for any of our senses and the computational ability of our brains. Technology consists in part of helping us to learn about natural phenomena we were not meant to see or hear by human evolution. Once these phenomena are known, they can provide us with ever more powerful tools to observe ever more remote phenomena; we can proceed to manipulate these further and so on.[28]

The nature of what *kind* of knowledge was admissible as the basis for techniques also changed after 1830. An important element of the second Industrial Revolution was the growing recognition and admissibility of statistical evidence to establish natural regularities. The use of statistics has eighteenth century origins, but the widespread use of statistical data as a legitimate source of knowledge can be pinpointed to the work of Quetelet, Chadwick,

---

[26] Less well known, but pointing very much in the same direction, is the interaction between the techniques of food canning and the evolution of bacteriology. The canning of food was invented in 1795, right in the middle of the Industrial Revolution, by a French confectioner named Nicolas Appert. He discovered that when he placed food in champagne bottles, corked them loosely, immersed them in boiling water, and then hammered the corks tight, the food was preserved for extended periods. Neither Appert nor his English emulators who perfected the preservation of food in tin-plated canisters in 1810 knew precisely why and how this technique worked, since the definitive demonstration of the notion that microorganisms were responsible for putrefaction of food was still in the future. The canning of food led to a prolonged scientific debate as to what caused food to spoil, a debate that was not finally put to rest until Pasteur's work in the early 1860s. Pasteur knew of course of Appert's work, and his work clearly settled the question of why the technique worked. In the terminology proposed earlier, the epistemic base of food canning became wider, and the optimal temperatures for the preservation of various foods with minimal damage to flavor and texture could be worked out.

[27] This is emphasized by Dyson (1997: 49–50). The invention of the modern microscope by Joseph J. Lister (father of the famous surgeon) in 1830 serves as a good example. Lister was an amateur optician, whose revolutionary method of grinding lenses greatly improved image resolution by eliminating chromatic and spherical aberrations. The invention was used to construct a theoretical basis for combining lenses and reduced average image distortion by a huge proportion, from 19 to 3 percent. Lister was the first human being ever to see a red blood cell. This invention changed microscopy from an amusing diversion to a serious scientific endeavor and eventually allowed Pasteur, Koch and their disciples to refute spontaneous generation and to establish the germ theory. The germ theory was one of the most revolutionary changes in useful knowledge in human history and mapped into a large number of new techniques in medicine, both preventive and clinical. Today's work in experimental biology would be impossible without X-ray crystallography and magnetic resonance imaging, to say nothing of powerful computers.

[28] As evolutionary theorists such as Vermeij (1993) and system analysts such as Kauffman (1995) have pointed out, dual systems that interact in such a way can reach a critical point, at which they become dynamically unstable and start to diverge from an equilibrium.

Farr, Villermé, and their colleagues in the 1820s and 1830s.[29] This work led to an enormous expansion of the epistemic base of medical techniques and to the identification of the causes of disease and their channels of transmission (Mokyr, 1996) and from there to techniques that prevented diseases from breaking out and reduced mortality long before effective cures had been found. By the beginning of the twentieth century, the theory of evolution had become widely accepted and genetics was rediscovered, and statistics found a variety of new applications, especially in the work of Francis Galton and Karl Pearson.

Without a widening epistemic base, the continuous development of techniques will eventually run into diminishing returns simply because the natural phenomena can be understood only partially, and arguably only superficially. It is, of course, unclear where precisely the point of diminishing returns occurs. What complicates matters is that even when a large number of new techniques rest on a fixed epistemic basis, these techniques could recombine into compound techniques and thus technological creativity could continue expanding even when the epistemic base was fixed. Ultimately, however, if the epistemic base does not expand, technological progress will slow down.

The concept of growing access to a common knowledge base as a catalyst in technological progress in the second Industrial Revolution cannot be proven rigorously, but a fair amount of historical evidence can be amassed to support it. An example is the simultaneity of many major inventions. The more a new technique depends on an epistemic base that is in the common domain and accessible to many inventors at low cost, the more likely it is that more than one inventor will hit upon it at about the same time. As such useful knowledge became increasingly accessible and universal, it is hardly surprising that many of the inventions of the period were made independently by multiple inventors who beat one another to the patent office door by a matter of days.[30]

Beyond that, again, was the further level of interaction and feedback between human knowledge and the environment in which it operates. The significance of the co-evolution of technological knowledge and institutions during the second Industrial Revolution has been noticed before. Nelson (1994) has pointed to a classic example of such co-evolution, namely the growth of the large American business corporation in the closing decades of the nineteenth century which evolved jointly with the high throughput technology of mass production and continuous flow. Many other examples can be cited, such as the miraculous expansion of the British capital market which emerged jointly with the capital-hungry early railroads and the emergence of universities and technical colleges combining research and teaching.[31] The feedback between institutions and technology, as argued above, is not necessarily always positive. Technological success often creates vested interests that protect assets from being jeopardized by further invention. In the highly competitive and open economies of the second Industrial Revolution, however, such negative feedbacks were swamped by positive ones, and on the whole the institutions of mature industrial capitalism reinforced the growth of useful knowledge and vice versa. The complexity of two overlapping systems of positive feedback is immense, but it clearly is capable of producing continuous expansion.

[30] The phenomenon of independent simultaneous invention has often been interpreted as supporting the effect of demand conditions on the search for innovation, but obvious the ability of inventors to draw on similar bases in useful knowledge provides a complementary explanation. See Merton (1961) for a survey of the literature.

[31] An especially good and persuasive example is provided by Murmann (1998) who describes the co-evolution of technology and institutions in the chemical industry in Imperial Germany, where the new technology of dyes, explosives, and fertilizers emerged in constant interaction with the growth of research and development facilities, institutes of higher education, and large industrial corporations interested in industrial research.

[29] For some insights in the emergence of the statistical method in post-1830 Europe, see especially Porter (1986) and Cullen (1975).

2.5. A Third Industrial Revolution?

The thirty years or so that followed the beginning of World War I were odd in at least three respects. First, it was a period of major political and economic upheavals which affected the growth and productivity in many of the leading industrial countries, although in different ways. Second, as DeLong (2000) has recently reminded us, not withstanding these disruptions, the twentieth century was a period of unprecedented growth. Third, much of this growth was technological in nature, yet relative to what we may perhaps expect, there is a surprising scarcity of true macroinventions in the period between 1914 and 1973 compared to the preceding decades. While science and useful knowledge in general kept expanding at an exponential pace, it actually produced few radical new departures, and the ones that took place had a comparatively modest impact on the economy. Instead, a continuous flow of *micro*inventions was the driving force behind much of the economic growth, such as it was, in the period 1914–50. In automobiles, chemicals, energy supply, industrial engineering, food processing, telephony and wireless communications, and synthetic materials, the developments after 1914 fit this pattern. Micro-inventions tend to be the result of directed and well-organized searches for new knowledge, what the twentieth century has increasingly termed R&D. The striking phenomenon here is that it took a very long time until these microinventions started running into diminishing returns and their effects on the standard of living were pervasive and ubiquitous. The main cause for this persistence and sustainability of technological progress was the widening of the epistemic base of techniques *already in existence* (some of them, admittedly, barely) in 1914, creating continuous opportunities for economic expansion and productivity growth.[32] When that base was narrow, as was the case in pharmaceutics and synthetic materials, progress was slow and depended on serendipity. When that base was wider, as was the case in engineering and metallurgy, progress was relentless and continuous. Yet by the definitions employed above, this progress does not qualify as an "Industrial Revolution."

As noted, then, the number of epochal *macro*-inventions in the 1914–50 period was comparatively small. Nuclear power, of course, would rank at the top of those. It demonstrates that the minimum epistemic base for some technologies had become very extensive. Quantum mechanics and nuclear physics were without doubt a major expansion of the set of useful knowledge, and the use of nuclear power was a true discontinuity: apart from occasional and fairly rare uses of tidal mills and geothermal heat, *all* energy had come from the sun. Nuclear power, however, did not lead to the usual pattern of diffusion and microinventions. While gradual improvements in the technique continued from the 1950s on, the costs of nuclear fission reactors in thermal or fast breeder versions never quite became sufficiently low to drive out fossil fuels and the safety and disposal problems have remained hard to solve (Victor, 2001). More than any technology since the Industrial Revolution, it has become a target of political opposition. Nuclear fusion, which had the potential to produce limitless energy at low prices, so far has failed to become a reality outside hydrogen weapons. One might say that the minimum epistemic base of handling materials at exceedingly high temperatures has not been attained.

The other major macroinvention in the first half of the twentieth century was antibiotics (Kingston, 2000). It too followed a rather unusual path, but for quite different reasons. The minimum epistemic base for antibiotics to work was the knowledge that specific germs existed and that they caused diseases. Yet Alexander Fleming's discovery that certain molds were bactericidal and could be deployed in

[32] Consider the following quote from a recent newspaper essay on the "New Economy": "The computer, of course, is at its heart—but not as a miracle machine spinning a golden future comparable to the industrial leap forward that came in the late 19th and early 20th centuries. Then, the electric motor, the light bulb, the internal combustion engine, petroleum, natural gas and numerous new chemicals all came on the scene—rearranging the economy and making it vastly more productive. The electric motor alone made possible the factory assembly line and mass production." Note that no such "industrial leap" is identified for the post-1914 period. See Uchitelle (2000b).

combating infectious disease was famously accidental. How and why they did so was unknown at the time. While fortune once again favored the prepared minds of Howard Florey and Ernst Chain, the modus operandi of antibiotics and much of the rest of our materia medica in existence was not understood when first employed and thus, in the terminology developed above, operated on a narrow epistemic base. The difference from other technologies was that antibiotics, much like insecticides, are subject to a negative feedback mechanism (due to the mutation of living species to make them immune to harmful substances), which after a while weakens their effectiveness and requires constant innovation just to keep the benefits from vanishing.

Between about 1950 and 1985, the pharmaceutical industry went through an unprecedented process of expansion. Yet much of this progress was attained on a narrow epistemic base. The industry developed a methodology known as "random screening" which is essentially a systematic application of the archaic "try every bottle on the shelf" principle. This method worked quite well, but it would eventually have run into diminishing returns had it not received a positive feedback shock from the growth in molecular biology from the mid-1970s on. As the cellular and molecular mechanisms of the operation of drugs became clearer, the screening method became more sophisticated and efficient. The expansion was further based, as Henderson et al. (1999) point out, on the sheer massive magnitude of unmet needs and research opportunities. Until 1950 medical science could cure few, if any diseases; the advances after that permitted cures as well as the alleviation of many symptoms.

Much as nineteenth century thermodynamics and chemistry provided the expansion of the epistemic base of the inventions of the Industrial Revolution and prevented it from fizzling out, the DNA revolution augmented the base of the pharmaceutical techniques developed in the 1950s and 1960s. It is this event, then, that is truly revolutionary in that it provided a means for technological change to avoid the trap of diminishing returns.[33] Pisano (2001) points out that this involved a change in the *methods* of R&D and refers to the phenomenon as the Molecular Biology *Revolution*. Genetic engineering took two rather distinct paths: the use of the new knowledge to improve the manufacture of substances whose modus operandi was already understood, and the use of advanced genetics in the discovery of new drugs moving from a process of more or less random discovery to one of "guided discovery."[34] Increasingly, we have the ability to *design* new drugs rather than *discover* them through recombinant DNA and monoclonal antibody techniques. As Evenson (2001) amply illustrates, the importance of this knowledge to agriculture is at least as important as in medicine. The importance of biological innovation in agriculture is not new (Olmstead and Rhode, 2000) but the developments in molecular biology promise solutions in pesticides and the use of marginal soils far beyond anything possible before 1970.[35] The truly revolutionary aspect, again, was not in the innovations themselves but in the creation of a useful knowledge base that made *sustained* innovation possible. In that regard, the revolution in cellular and molecular biology differed from that in nuclear physics. Yet they share the deepest common denominator of progress in the post Industrial Revolution technological era, namely a wide and widening epistemic base. Rather than the stochastic trial-

---

[33] For an excellent discussion, see Ruttan (2000). As he points out, the fundamental notion is not just that the DNA molecule contains critical information about life, but that microbes can exchange this genetic information. The breakthroughs in the applications of these insights occurred in the mid-1970s with the development of recombinant DNA by Cohen and Boyer and the fusion techniques developed by Milstein and Köehler.

[34] Henderson et al. (1999: 282ff). The authors point out that the two paths initially required quite different forms of industrial organization but have recently converged.

[35] Olmstead and Rhode demonstrate the possibilities of land-augmenting technological progress on a narrow epistemic base in the nineteenth century: through trial and error, it was discovered which varieties of vines were resistant to phylloxera, which parasites could be used to fight harmful pests, and how different varieties of wheat permitted the fine calibration of the growing season.

and-error method that characterized invention before 1800, progress is achieved increasingly by relying on a deeper understanding of the natural regularities at work.

There were, of course, other major break-throughs in the post-1914 decades: for example, the jet engine, catalytic cracking, and the emergence of man-made fibers and substances. Many of these were, however, improvements upon *existing* techniques rather than totally new techniques.[36] Perhaps the most discontinuous breakthroughs in the 1920s were in physiology: the discovery of insulin in 1922 and its extraction from animal pancreas which made the treatment of diabetes patients possible, and the growing realization that trace elements (termed vitamins in 1920) played a major role in preventing a series of diseases. The useful knowledge about nutrition mapped directly into a series of techniques employed by households in preparing food for their families, as well as the food industry which fortified products such as margarine with these trace elements to ensure adequate intake.

Much of the progress in the twentieth century consisted of what we might call "hybrid" inventions, which combined components that had been worked out before 1914 in novel ways. The principles of the use of electrical power to run engines, activate vacuum tubes and heat objects could be combined into radios, dishwashers, vacuum cleaners, fans, and virtually every other household appliance. Other pre-1914 inventions formed the basis of much industrial development until 1950 and beyond. The internal combustion engine and its cousin, the Diesel engine—both up and running by 1914—eventually replaced steam as the main source of power.

The story of the chemical industry is a bit more complex (Arora, Landau, and Rosen-

berg, 1998). Much of the chemical science underlying the synthetic materials industry was simply not around in 1914. A few synthetics such as celluloid and bakelite were developed on a very narrow epistemic base.[37] Even so, some true macroinventions predate 1914.[38] The chemical science underlying the technology co-evolved in classic fashion with the techniques. The same is true for aerodynamics where the epistemic base kept expanding as a response to technical successes, but which served as a further input into their design. The Wright brothers flew in 1903, a year before Ludwig Prandtl, the great theorist of aerodynamics, moved to Göttingen.[39] Only in 1918 did he publish his magisterial work on how wings could be scientifically rather than empirically designed and the lift and drag precisely calculated (Constant, 1980: 105; Vincenti,

---

[37] Bakelite was patented in 1909 and manufactured on a commercial scale from 1910, but its chemical formula was not even established until 20 years later. Rosenberg (1998: 212) also points out that pilot plants were necessary simply because no body of scientific knowledge could answer the necessary questions.

[38] Of those, the technique to fix ammonia from the atmosphere perfected by Fritz Haber and his associates around 1910 must count as one of most momentous in modern history. Nitrates were the critical ingredient in both the fertilizer and the explosives industries and its fixation from the atmosphere had far-reaching consequences including the prolongation of World War I. Thermal cracking, which separates the long-chain hydrocarbons of petroleum into smaller but more important ones such as gasoline was first employed commercially in 1913 by Standard Oil researcher, William Burton. Catalytic cracking was developed by Eugène Houdry in the 1920s and speeded up the process considerably.

[39] Much of the knowledge in aeronautics in the early days was experimental rather than theoretical such as attempts to tabulate coefficients of lift and drag for each wing shape at each angle. The Wright brothers relied on published work (especially by Otto Lilienthal) available at the time to work out their own formulas, but they also ended up working closely with the leading aeronautical engineer of the time, Octave Chanute, who supplied them with advice right up to Kitty Hawk (Crouch, 1989). It is clear that the Wright brothers were avid consumers of engineering science and that their greatness lay in the mapping function; however, before and even after their success, best-practice knowledge was limited.

---

[36] The definition of a macroinvention does not exclude the possibility that the ultimate form the technique takes is the result of a number of discontinuous complementary breakthroughs. The best example is the steam engine, which arguably was not complete until the reciprocal (double-acting) cylinder and the separate condenser were added by Watt. It seems a matter of taste whether we would think of the jet engine and plastics in the same terms.

1990: 120–5). Not all advances in airplane design were that neatly based on expansions of their epistemic base, and the ancient methodology of trial and error was still widely used in the search for the best use of flush riveting in holding together the body of the plane (Vincenti, 1990: 170–99) or the best way to design landing gear (Vincenti, 2000).[40]

Much of the productivity increase in the twentieth century, then, was the result of the perfection of production techniques and process innovation. Again, there was little truly new about the growth of these ideas beyond what had been around in 1914, but the scale of organization and accuracy of detail continued to grow. These led to a continuous transformation in organizational methods, most obviously in mass production in manufacturing techniques but eventually in services and agriculture as well. For better or for worse, these changes have become known as "the American system of manufacturing" (actually their historical roots were complex), and they were disseminated to the rest of the industrialized world. It is perhaps a matter of semantics whether we think of these changes as "technological" or "organizational." What matters is that they co-evolved with the ability of the capital goods industry to produce the tools and machinery that made their deployment practical, relying on an ever growing epistemic based of materials and mechanical engineering.

The modernization of techniques can be broken down into a number of elements. The first is *routinization* which made production processes interchangeable. Thus, assembly, welding, painting, and packing all became increasingly similar across different products, with obvious implications for the specificity of human capital and skills. Another component was *modularization* meaning that identical parts were fully interchangeable. The advantages of

modularization had been realized since Christopher Polhem in the early eighteenth century, but the precision engineering that made it possible on an almost universal scale required machine tools that became available only in the twentieth century.[41] Modularization was closely related to *standardization* meaning that all products of a particular type were identical. Standardization, much like modularization, helped not just during the production stage of output but also in the maintenance of durable equipment. Whoever could repair one model T could repair *any* model T. It was also essential to mass-marketing through catalogs and price lists. Mass production also entailed *acceleration* through continuous flow production. Continuous flow could be assembly or *dis*assembly (as in the stockyards), as well as in continuous physical and chemical processes (grain milling, refining).[42] Finally, in some applications there was a trend toward *miniaturization* (space saving) such as in the design of smaller motors and less clumsy microelectronics resulting in modern nanoelectronics.

In parallel with changes in the organization of production was the growing specialization of labor. Trends in specialization are actually complex: the routinization of production, as Marx already pointed out, was fundamentally de-skilling, and production employed undifferentiated homogeneous labor, performing simple tasks on machines that were increasingly user friendly at least in the sense that their operation was simple enough. Yet the division of labor became more and more refined in the twentieth century and led to a myriad of highly specialized occupations and tasks. The advantages of the division of labor and specialization

---

[40] The hardening-process of aluminum in which the metal hardens slowly over the week following heating and quenching was discovered accidentally by Alfred Wilm in 1909 and eventually led to the use of aluminum in all aircraft construction. Metallurgists had a difficult time explaining the phenomenon of age hardening, but it took years until even a partial epistemic base had been uncovered (Alexander, 1978: 439).

[41] Hounshell (1984: 232–33) notes that by 1913, when Ford initiated his line assembly techniques, the machine industry was capable – perhaps for the first time – of manufacturing machines that could turn out large amounts of consistently accurate work.

[42] Von Tunzelmann (1995) who stresses the importance of time-saving technological changes, has identified at least four components of the speed of production: higher speed of operation, less down-time due to more reliable and easy-to-repair equipment, faster inter-process coordination, and faster intra-process coordination.

have been commented upon ever since Adam Smith wrote his famous first chapter. His idea of the advantages of the division of labor were the growing familiarity of a worker with the process he is assigned to; his ability to produce improvements on it once he is thoroughly familiar with it; and the savings of time involved in moving from one task to another. The idea of the division of labor proposed by Smith was further picked up by Charles Babbage (1835: 175–6) who noted that specialization was not only useful for the reasons laid out by Smith, but also because workers had different inherent skill and strength endowments and it would be wasteful for employees to carry out tasks for which they were overqualified. An optimal matching of tasks to (exogenous) ability was a key to efficiency (Rosenberg, 1994: 28–9). A third argument for the division of labor is that with the growth of the knowledge base that each firm or plant needs to possess (its "core competence"), specialization is inevitable simply because the amount of knowledge is larger than one individual can possess.[43] This point was formalized and elaborated upon in a seminal paper by Becker and Murphy (1992), which suggested a new interpretation of the role of the firm. Given the limitations on what each worker can know, they maintain, the total knowledge that the firm has to possess is chopped up into manageable bites, divided amongst the workers, and their actions are then coordinated by management.[44] In addition to Smith's dictum about the division of labor being limited by the size of the market, the division of labor is limited from below by the size of the knowledge set that is necessary to employ best-practice techniques. The point is not just that each worker knows what he/she needs to know to carry out his/her task, but that he/she becomes in charge of a subset of the total knowledge required so that others can ask him/her when

needed. This model predicts that when the amount of knowledge is small, plants can be small and coincide with households; when it expands it will require either a sophisticated and efficient network for the distribution of knowledge or a different setup of the unit of production (or a combination of the two). Modern manufacturing as it emerged in the twentieth century depended largely on the presence of in-house experts, not just in engineering, chemistry, and mechanics, but also in accounting, marketing, labor management, finance, and so on. Yet this setup is a function of the technology of the transmission of and access to knowledge.

The co-evolution of institutions and technology assumed new forms in the twentieth century.[45] Perhaps the most important development of the twentieth century is the change in the nature of the process of invention with the emergence of corporate, university, and government-sponsored R&D, what Mowery and Rosenberg (1998) have called the "institutionalization of innovation."[46] A long and inconclusive debate emerged whether individual independent inventors would eventually be made redundant by this development (Jewkes, Sawers, and Stillerman, 1969). After 1945

---

[43] The "core competence" of a firm is different from the term "epistemic base" used here. An epistemic base is knowledge that has to be possessed by *someone* in an economy for a set of instructions to be written down. Actually carrying out such instructions involve quite different knowledge, just as inventing a bicycle, manufacturing one, and riding one all involve different kinds of skills and knowledge.

[44] A similar point is made by Pavitt and Steinmueller (1999: 15–16) in the context of the knowledge *generating* activities in the firm (that is, R&D). They point out that uncertainty and much tacit knowledge require "physical and organizational proximity" that guarantees efficient coordination of the knowledge-generating and the production and marketing functions of the firm. The skills involved in this coordination are themselves tacit and hence some meetings and personal contact remain important in industries that rely on a high degree of innovation; yet this does not mean that outsourcing to individuals working normally from other locations would be effective.

[45] For a similar use of the term in the context of the computer hardware industry, see Bresnahan and Malerba (1999).

[46] Here, too, there were clear-cut nineteenth century roots. The great German dye manufacturers and large US corporations such as GE and Alcoa established the corporate research laboratory and the university as the prime loci where the technological frontier was pushed out, but the spread of this idea to the rest of the economy was slow and gradual.

circumstances favored a shift toward in-house research, particularly in industries such as chemicals and electrical equipment (Mowery, 1995). In-house research and inter-firm transfers of technology were to a large extent complementary but their shifting weight demonstrates the kind of institutional agility necessary for a successful co-evolution. Of particular importance, as emphasized above, is the connection between the people who know the science and those who map it into new techniques.[47]

The twentieth century was the one century in which both the nature and the speed of technological progress were actively determined by politics. Governments invested in and encouraged research for strategic reasons.[48] Defense accounted for the lion's share of federal R&D spending in the United States, and the Federal government financed a substantial proportion of R&D. In other countries, governments and other coordinating agencies played an equally important role in large part out of recognition of the likely failure of private research to provide the optimal mix and quantity of new useful knowledge, and in part for purely nationalist reasons. Much of the history of technology in the twentieth century can be described as a continuous search for the right "mix" of private and public efforts in R&D.[49] The fundamental

dilemma is well known to any economist: the private sector systematically underinvests in R&D because of the appropriability problems in the market for useful knowledge and their failure to take into account the externalities involved. Government agencies, however, in both market and command economies have systematically done a poor job in picking winners and have only haphazardly contributed to civilian techniques.

Capital markets provided another source of institutional agility. In the United States, venture capital markets emerged in the 1980s and 1990s and played a major role in the emergence of biotechnology, semiconductors, and software, among others (Mowery and Nelson, 1999: 363). Such institutions were almost unique to the United States, and explain its continued industrial leadership. The dynamic of modern technology, however, is that because of the openness and continued international transfer of technology, advances made in the United States due to better capital markets, patent protection, or another type of institution, were soon accessible to other nations.

The 1940s witnessed the emergence of three spectacular macroinventions: nuclear power, antibiotics and the semiconductor.[50] While all emerged in the 1940s, electronics is the only area in which the continuous feedback between propositional and prescriptive knowledge, as well as recombination with other inventions led to a sustained and continuous growth that to date shows no evidence of slowing down and is believed by many to herald a "new economy." Helpman and Trajtenberg (1998) have pointed to the semiconductor's unusual properties as an innovation: its ability to recombine with other techniques and its complementarity with downstream innovations, and its consequent pervasiveness in many applications, meriting the term General Purpose Technology (GPT). There have been few comparable macroinventions since the emergence of electricity in the

---

[47] It is telling that Henderson et al. (1999: 298) point to the institution most responsible for the success of American biotechnology as the "academic norms that permitted the rapid translation of academic results into competitive enterprises." Successful academics in biotechnology and computer science, among others, moved easily between the academe and the start-up, whereas elsewhere the ivory towers remained largely aloof from the technological revolution around them.

[48] Mowery and Rosenberg (1998: 28) note the irony in the post-1945 view that the great research projects of World War II (Manhattan Project, antibiotics, and synthetic rubber) demonstrated the capabilities of "Big R&D" to enhance social welfare.

[49] As Langlois (2001) points out, the modern computer combines the outcome of research initiated and financed by the government for computing machines with the private research efforts that led to the development of semiconductor technology.

[50] There are many excellent histories of the computer despite their obvious built-in obsolescence. See for instance Campbell-Kelly and Aspray (1996).

late nineteenth century.[51] What has happened is the emergence of a large cluster of separate inventions with an unusual propensity to recombine with one another and to create synergistic innovations which vastly exceeded the capabilities of the individual components. Around 1955, vacuum tubes were replaced by the junction transistors invented by Robert Shockley a few years earlier. In the 1980s and 1990s, high-speed microprocessors combined with lasers, fiber optics, satellites, software technology and new breakthroughs in material science and electronics made high density ROM storage possible. The so-called Information and Communication Technology (ICT) revolution is not identical to the computer, and many of the debates on the impact of "the computer" on productivity in the 1990s miss the point for that reason. Mainframe computers in the 1950s and 1960s and even the early personal computer (at first little more than a glorified typewriter and calculator) were not really a revolutionary GPT, their many uses notwithstanding. The 1990s witnessed the integration of microprocessors with scores of old technologies (such as household appliances) and new ones (cell phones, medical equipment). The ultimate impact of ICT, however, goes far beyond its ability to combine with other techniques.

It always seems rash and imprudent for historians to analyze contemporary events as if they occurred sufficiently in the past to be analyzed

with some perspective. But the arguments made above suggest that the cluster of innovations around semiconductors and their applications will be viewed by future historians not only as a macroinvention, but also as the kind of discontinuity that separates one era from another, much like the two previous Industrial Revolutions. For such a statement to be true, there has to be more than a GPT such as steam power or electricity or chemical engineering (Rosenberg, 1998). There has to be a profound change in the generation and deployment of knowledge. The significance of the information revolution is not that we can read on a screen things that we previously read in the newspaper or looked up in the library, but in the decline of marginal access costs to codified knowledge *of any kind*. The hugely improved communications and the decline in storage and access costs to knowledge may turn out to be the pivotal event of the two closing decades of the twentieth century.

The significance of ICT, then, is not just in its direct impact on productivity but that it is a *knowledge technology* and thus affects every other technique in use. Given the huge dimensions that the set of useful knowledge has attained in the twentieth century (and its continuing exponential growth), ever-increasing specialization and narrow-based expertise is inevitable. Access in the form of search engines that allow an individual to find some known piece of useful knowledge at low cost becomes critical. Indeed, it must be true that had useful knowledge grown at the rate it did without changes in the technology of access, diminishing returns must have set in just due to the difficulties in information management on a gigantic scale. The segment of knowledge that each individual possesses is declining proportionally (even if it increases in total terms). An increasingly fine division of knowledge requires ever improving access relations between individuals, and between individuals and storage devices. It may be that Internet 2 will be the culmination of this process, but in fact access has been improving for decades now in the form of computer-based information databases such as computerized library catalogs, databases, and online access channels

---

[51] The transistor is a good example of the concepts of knowledge employed in this chapter, as already noted in a classic paper by Nelson (1996). The epistemic base consisted of the natural regularity of the behavior of silicons as semiconducting materials, and the work of A.H. Wilson had explained this in terms of quantum mechanics in 1931. Much of the theory, however, was not fully understood until Shockley (1949) wrote his book in which he showed how and why the junction transistor would work. As Nelson remarks, "the theory was the invention" (Nelson, 1996: 170). Yet the continuous progress in computer technology could not have taken place without a wide epistemic base. Jean Hoerni's invention of the planar process, widely acknowledged to be the breakthrough that made progress in integrated circuits possible, could not have taken place without a thorough knowledge of the chemical and physical qualities of silicone (Langlois, 2001; Ceruzzi, 1998: 186).

such as Medline. As people who carry out technological instructions—let alone those who write new ones—have to access more and more useful knowledge, the means by which they can access, sort, evaluate, and filter this knowledge is crucial.

Above all, it is that aspect of information technology that holds the key to the future of technological creativity in our time. The uniqueness of the late twentieth century is that the body of useful knowledge has become vast, and that it has come to depend on access-cost-reducing technology without which it would never have advanced as fast as it has. If the Industrial Revolution witnessed an expansion of useful knowledge to the point where no *single individual* could possess it all and therefore growing intra-firm specialization was necessary, the closing decades of the twentieth century required far more than that. The internet and its "search engines" are one element in this. Equally important is the institutional element of the establishment of social conventions of rhetoric and acceptability, coupled with growing professionalization and the formalization of expertise.

Declining access costs are instrumental in the rapid diffusion of new useful knowledge, not just because techniques cannot be employed before the minimum epistemic base is available, but also because in many cases each user has idiosyncratic needs and uses, and has to adapt the technique to his or her specific conditions. This is surely true for agriculture, but holds with equal force in the service industries and manufacturing. Hence, what a new user needs is a way of answering specific questions he or she has while actually implementing a technique, and it is these questions that can often be answered by rapid and cheap communications. The most effective and cheapest way to communicate is still to speak with someone in the same room, and the resurgence of the silicon valley industrial district is no accident. But ICT may in the end destroy its own parents: with the virtual reality implied in the high speed processing and huge bandwidth of Internet 2, many of the externalities in the generation of knowledge may soon become distance-independent, and concepts like the virtual industrial district are almost upon us.

Furthermore, falling access costs have stimulated technological progress through another phenomenon, technological hybrids and recombinations (what one might call technological compounds). If we consider each technique to be a "unit" of analysis, much like in evolution these units can interact with other units to produce entirely new entities. Most modern devices represent such compounds, often scores or even hundreds of them.[52] The notion that existing techniques could recombine into new ones is not a novel one (Weitzman, 1993), but in our framework it has deeper significance. It means that techniques can not only incorporate other techniques whole (which we might call "hybrids") but also import subsets of their instructions and their epistemic bases and combine these with their own (which would more properly be thought of as a recombination).[53] Hybrids and recombinations are not the same: there is a conceptual difference between the combination of an internal combustion engine, a propeller, and a glider joining them together to make an airplane, and the application of mechanical knowledge underlying bicycle repairs in solving the specific problems that occur in airplane construction.[54] Either way, however, better access to knowledge will not only make it more likely that best-prac-

---

[52] The degree to which technology is "recombinant" can be approximated, however imperfectly, by the degree of citations to other patents and scientific literature in patent applications. Considerable research has gone into the topic of patent citations, and recent work shows that a fair number of citations take place to other patents that are reasonably unrelated. Unfortunately this information had to be attained from an ex post survey of the patentees and thus the inference is from a small sample and for 1993 only. It is striking, however, that, on a rank from 1 (unrelated) to 5 (closely related), 44 percent of the citations did not rank above 2. The data pertain to 1993 patents and therefore predate the Internet. See Jaffe, Trajtenberg, and Fogarty (2000).

[53] Just as we can define "general purpose technology" as techniques that can readily hybridize with others (electrical power being an obvious example), we can think of "general purpose knowledge" which maps into a large number of techniques and allows them to recombine. I am indebted for this point to Richard G. Lipsey.

tice techniques are widely employed, but will generate the emergence of these compound innovations.

But what, exactly, do we mean by "better access"? Even scientific knowledge in the public domain needs to be found, interpreted by specialists, and reprocessed for use. The most widely discussed issue is that of tacit versus codified knowledge (Cowan and Foray, 1997). It may or may not be the case that modern technology is more codified and thus is more accessible by normal channels. What is clear is that there is still a great deal of tacit knowledge, which cannot be readily acquired from storage devices and can only be accessed by hiring the people who possess it. However, modern ICT makes it easier to find the people who possess that tacit knowledge, and hire them, if possible, on an ad hoc basis. Technical consultants and "just in time expertise" to whom specific tasks can be subcontracted out have become far more pervasive. One reason may be that modern ICT makes it easier to track down where this knowledge can be found (or, one step removed, who knows where this knowledge can be found, and so on). The problem, however, is not just access to knowledge but also its reliability. Knowledge supplied to us by strangers in a nonrepeated context could have serious verifiability problems. What needs to be explored is the impact of better ICT on the reputation mechanisms that protect users from false and misleading information, and to

what extent the access technology will co-evolve with institutions that in one form or another permit users to assess its veracity.

2.6. Conclusions

If we are living in the middle of something we suspect future historians will regard as another Industrial Revolution, we need to define with some care what is meant by that. The productivity and growth implications of revolutions in knowledge are at the core of much of the literature in the economics of technological change and productivity measurement. Oddly enough, however, economists (with a few notable exceptions such as F.M. Scherer, Richard Nelson and Nathan Rosenberg) have not gotten much into the "black box" of knowledge evolution in the past. Models of endogenous growth have attempted to open these black boxes, but have just found another black box inside. Endogenous growth models analyze the production of new knowledge in terms of R&D and investment in human and physical capital, but they do not really bother with the epistemological issues of how knowledge is generated and communicated. Decomposing useful knowledge into its componenets as defined here and examining their interaction, as well as in Mokyr (2000a,b), takes a small step in the understanding of what is inside this black box. As has been argued by many analysts in the evolutionary epistemology school (e.g., Plotkin, 1993; Wuketits, 1990), human knowledge can be and needs to be analyzed as part of a larger evolutionary paradigm. This effort was started in economics by Nelson and Winter in 1982, but thus far has been little applied to economic history, where its marginal product seems particularly high. What is argued here is that the interaction between knowledge "what" and knowledge "how" created, under the right circumstances, an explosive dynamic that led to sudden surges in technology that we may call Industrial Revolutions. In the very long run, such surges have profound effects on economic growth and productivity, but the phenomenon itself should be analyzed distinct from its consequences.

---

[54] Many techniques can be identified as being particularly amenable to recombination. Historically in the West, watch making is probably the best example as a set of techniques with considerable spillovers of this kind. Watch-making knowledge was used in the making of instruments and fine machinery of all kinds and some watch makers made important inventions. The best-known inventors trained as clock makers were Benjamin Huntsman, the originator of the crucible steel technique, and John Kay (not to be confused with the inventor of the flying shuttle of the same name), who helped Arkwright in developing the water frame. Gunmaking played a somewhat similar role at some junctures, especially in the case of John Wilkinson whose boring machines helped Watt build his cylinders. In a modern context, Nelson (1996: 171) has pointed to the theory on which semiconductors were based as the source of better thermoelectric devices and the Bell solar battery.

This approach may also help in clarifying the role of institutions in the growth of technology in the past two centuries. Institutions play a central role in two different processes. One is the growth of useful knowledge itself, much of it motivated by purely epistemic considerations (i.e., curiosity about nature). The existence of organizations in which such knowledge is expanded, preserved, and diffused (such as academies, universities, research institutes, R&D departments) and the rules by which they play (such as open science, credit by priority, reproducibility of experiment, rhetorical rules, acceptance of expertise and authority), together with the perceived needs and priorities of the social environment in which they operate, help determine its historical path. The other is the mapping of this knowledge onto techniques. The institutions that play a role here are of course the usual ones that determine economic performance: incentives, property rights, relative prices. It should be stressed that through much of human past, the people who studied nature (natural philosophers and scientists) and those who were active in economic production (craftsmen, engineers, entrepreneurs) were often disjoint historical groups. Those who carried out the mapping needed to access the useful knowledge, and large social gaps between the *savans* and the *fabricans* were detrimental to technological progress.

Some nations were more attracted to the formal study of nature, while others were more inclined to look for applications. In the industrialized West as it emerged in the nineteenth century, a rough division of labor on the matter emerged.[55] Yet the free flow of information across national boundaries meant that American engineers could and did access French physics when they needed it and British manufacturers could rely on German and Belgian chemistry. This openness was enhanced both by institutions and technology. It created a

positive feedback mechanism that had never existed before, not among the scientists of the Hellenistic world, not among the engineers of Song China, and not even in seventeenth century Europe. In that sense, Kuznets's insight is fully vindicated.

The historical experience of economic growth also suggests to modern economists that an emphasis on aggregate output figures and their analysis in terms of productivity growth may be of limited use if we are interested in its full impact on economic welfare and the quality of material life. The full *economic* impact of some of the most significant inventions in the last two centuries would be largely missed in that way. One reason for that was recently restated by DeLong (2000). Income and productivity measurement cannot deal very well with the appearance of entirely new products. The Laspeyre index of income measures a basket from some year in the past and asks how much it would have cost today; that is, comparing the standard of living at some point in the past asks essentially how much *our* income would have bought in terms of the goods available in the past. But the whole point of technological progress is not just that these goods can be made cheaper. New consumer goods not even dreamed of in an earlier age make such welfare comparisons useless. In that regard we see a progression from the first to the second Industrial Revolution and even more into the twentieth century. The first Industrial Revolution in the late eighteenth and early nineteenth centuries created few new consumer goods, and consumption baskets in 1830 were not radically different than in 1760. This was no longer the case in 1914, and by the end of the century new goods that satisfied needs unsuspected a century earlier (walkman radios, multivitamin pills, internet service providers) or needs that previously simply could not be satisfied (e.g., hip replacement surgery or telecommunication satellites) keep emerging at an accelerating pace. What that means is that not only do traditional measures underestimate the rate of progress, but they do so at a rate that grows over time.

Moreover, goods become different, and improve in ways that are difficult to

---

[55] In the 1830s, De Tocqueville observed that Americans were not much interested in theory and the abstract parts of human knowledge. Rosenberg (1998b: 196) observed that this attitude was to characterize American culture for many decades to come.

measure.[56] Some of these aspects are almost impossible to quantify: reduced wear and tear, ease of repair and maintenance, and improved user friendliness come to mind.[57] It has also been pointed out repeatedly that increased diversity and choice by themselves represent welfare improvements, and that modern technology allows customers to "design" their own final product from modular components thus creating mass customization (Cox and Alm, 1998).

But more is involved than that.[58] Improved access to useful knowledge through electronic means implies that, insofar as the function of the firm (or, to be precise, the plant) is to facilitate communication between workers of different specialization, the ICT revolution means that geographical proximity is less and less required for such contact. We do not know to what extent the modern workplace as a separate entity from the household owes its existence to the need to exchange and access knowledge, but the sharp increase in telecommuting and telecottaging in recent years suggests a possible trend in that direction. If so, the welfare implications could be even more dramatic than DeLong suggests, since the social costs of commuting are a deadweight burden on society (much like any other transaction or trading cost), and because an enormous amount of capital in dwellings and buildings is inefficiently utilized by partial occupation, to say nothing of other social costs. It would be wildly optimistic to predict that within a short time ICT will reverse the effects of two centuries of economic change, but at the very least we could recognize that, aside from productivity, other dimensions of the nature of work are strongly affected by technological change and they affect economic welfare and performance in many unexpected ways.

---

[56] DeLong (2000: 7) chooses a particularly felicitous example. In 1895, a copy of the *Encyclopedia Britannica* cost US$35, whereas today a print version cost US$1250, about one-quarter in terms of labor cost. But a different good, the *Encyclopedia Britannica on CD ROM* today costs only US$50.00. How are we to compare the two? Assuming that in both cases, the content reflects an equally exhausting and reliable picture of the world, the CD ROM has some major advantages besides cost: it is easier to store, and access to information is faster and more convenient. It also includes more powerful imagery (through video clips) and audio. In short, readers in 1895 with a fast computer would have in all likelihood preferred the CD ROM version.

[57] This point is ignored in William Nordhaus's (1997) otherwise pathbreaking paper on the real cost of lighting. The true consumer gain from switching from candles or oil lamps to electric light was not just in that electric light was cheaper, lumens per lumens. It is also that electric light was easier to switch on and off, reduced fire hazard, reduced flickering, did not create an offensive smell and smoke, and was easier to direct.

[58] The following paragraph draws on Mokyr (2000b).

Part II

COUNTRY STUDIES

3

The United States

Robert J. Gordon

This chapter examines the sources of the U.S. macroeconomic miracle of 1995–2000 and attempts to distinguish between permanent sources of U.S. leadership in high-technology industries, in contrast with the particular post-1995 episode of technological acceleration, and with other independent sources of the economic miracle unrelated to technology. The core of the U.S. achievement was the maintenance of low inflation in the presence of a decline in the unemployment rate to the lowest level reached in three decades. The post-1995 technological acceleration, particularly in information technology (IT) and accompanying revival of productivity growth, directly contributed both to faster output growth and to holding down the inflation rate, but inflation was also held down by a substantial decline in real nonoil import prices, by low energy prices through early 1999, and by a temporary cessation in 1996–8 of inflation in real medical care prices. In turn, low inflation allowed the Fed to maintain an easy monetary policy that fueled rapid growth in real demand, profits, and stock prices, which fed back into growth of consumption in excess of growth in income.

The technological acceleration was made possible in part by permanent sources of U.S. advantage over Europe and Japan, most notably the mixed system of government and privately funded research universities, the large role of US government agencies providing research funding based on peer review, the strong tradition of patent and securities regulation, the leading worldwide position of US business schools and US-owned investment banking, accounting, and management consulting firms, and the particular importance of the capital market for high-tech financing led by a uniquely dynamic venture capital industry. While these advantages help to explain why the IT boom happened in the United States, they did not prevent the United States from experiencing a dismal period of slow productivity growth between 1972 and 1995 nor from falling behind in numerous industries outside the IT sector.

The 1995–2000 productivity growth revival was fragile, both because a portion rested on unsustainably rapid output growth in 1999–2000, and because much of the rest was the result of a doubling in the growth rate of computer investment after 1995 that could not continue forever. The web could only be invented once, Y2K artificially compressed the computer replacement cycle, and some IT purchases were made by dot-coms that by early 2001 were bankrupt. As an invention, the web provided abundant consumer surplus but no recipe for most dot-coms to make a profit from providing free services. High-tech also included a boom in biotech and medical technology, which also provided consumer surplus without necessarily creating higher productivity, at least within the feasible scope of output measurement.

3.1. Introduction

The miracle of U.S. economic performance between 1995 and mid-2000 was a source of pride at home, of envy abroad, and of puzzle-

I am grateful to Richard Nelson, Benn Steil, and David Victor for helpful comments and to Stuart Gurrea for preparing the figures.

ment among economists and policy makers.[1] The Federal Reserve presided over quarter after quarter of output growth so rapid as to break any speed limit previously believed to be feasible. As the unemployment rate inched ever lower, reaching 3.9 percent in several months between April and October, 2000, the Fed reacted with a degree of neglect so benign that late in the year 2000 short-term interest rates were barely higher than they had been five years earlier and long-term interest rates were considerably lower.[2]

The miracle began to unravel in the U.S. stock market, when the tech-influenced Nasdaq stock market index fell by half between March and December, 2000. Soon the unraveling reached the real economy, with a steady decline in the *growth rate* of computer investment after the beginning of 2000 and a decline in the *level* of industrial production after September. As this chapter went to press, it was not yet clear whether the evident slowdown in U.S. economic activity in 2000–1 would be of short or long duration, and to what extent the pillars of the 1995–2000 miracle would crumble or just shed a bit of dust.

Whatever the ultimate dimensions of the post-2000 economic slowdown and its aftermath, much of the 1995–2000 achievement was sure to remain, including the fruits of the post-1995 productivity growth revival, the investment goods and consumer durables that were produced during the investment boom, and acknowledged U.S. leadership in the IT industries that had sparked the boom. This chapter is primarily concerned with the conjunction of events that help us to understand the miracle, including those transitory components of the 1995–2000 economic environment which ultimately disappeared and help us understand why the period of rapid growth eventually came to an end.

The essence of the miracle was the conjunction of low unemployment and low inflation. Fed policy avoided any sharp upward spike in short-term interest rates such as had happened during the previous expansion in 1988–9 because of the perception that accelerating inflation was not a problem, despite a much lower unemployment rate than the minimum achieved in the earlier expansion. Policy reactions were less aggressive in the late 1990s than in the late 1980s, because the economy appeared to have experienced a sharp change in behavior along at least two dimensions. Unemployment could be allowed to decline because inflation remained low. The second change of behavior was in the growth of productivity. After resigned acceptance of the so-called "productivity slowdown," more than two decades following 1973 when output per hour grew at barely 1 percent per annum (well under half of the rate experienced before 1973), analysts were astonished to observe productivity growth at a rate of nearly 3 percent as the average annual rate for 1996–2000 and an unbelievable 5.3 percent in the four quarters ending in mid-2000.[3]

Falling unemployment, low inflation, and accelerating productivity growth brought many other good things in their wake. In February, 2000, the U.S. economy set a record for the longest business expansion since records began in 1850. Profits surged and, at least until early in the year 2000, stock market prices grew even faster than profits, showering households with unheard-of increases in wealth that in turned fueled a boom in consumption and an evaporation of household saving (at least as conventionally measured, excluding capital gains). The Federal government participated in the good times, enjoying a 64 percent increase in personal income tax revenues between 1994 and 1999, fueled by strong income growth and the capital gains resulting from a tripling of stock

---

[1] Lawrence Summers spoke for many economists and policy makers recently when he characterized this widespread puzzlement as "paradigm uncertainty." See *Business Week*, "The Economy: A Higher Safe Speed Limit," April 10, 2000: 242.

[2] The Treasury bill rate in September, 2000 at 6.00 percent was barely higher than the 5.64 percent registered in December, 1994, while the 30-year government bond rate over the same period fell from 7.87 percent to 5.83 percent.

[3] Part of this change in perception was an illusion based on a change in the measuring rod. The annual growth rate of output per hour for 1972–95 was 1.1 percent per year based on data available prior to 1999 but jumped to 1.5 percent per year as a result of data revisions announced in late 1999.

market prices over the same interval.[4] And the gains from the boom were not limited to the top 5 or 10 percent of the income distribution. For the first time since the early 1970s, gains in real income were enjoyed by households in the bottom half of the income distribution, and in April, 2000, the unemployment rates for blacks and Hispanics reached the lowest levels ever recorded.[5]

Perhaps the greatest contrast of all was between the glowing optimism in early 2000 that all was right with the U.S. economy, especially in contrast to most of the other developed nations, whereas a decade earlier nothing seemed to be going right. In 1990 Japan had been king of the mountain, and the United States then appeared to be clearly inferior to Japan along almost every dimension, including inflation, unemployment, productivity growth, technical dynamism, and income inequality. The emerging economic slowdown in late 2000 and early 2001 suggested that the U.S. switch from an inferiority to a superiority complex had been too abrupt, and that the miracle of the late 1990s had perhaps been less permanent and complete than economic pundits had proclaimed only a year earlier.

If there was a consensus about anything as the boom years of the miracle were followed by a slowdown and perhaps a subsequent recession, it was that the core of the miracle was an acceleration in technological progress centered around the "New Economy" of computers, IT more generally, and the Internet, and that the clearest manifestation of the miracle in the economic data—the post-1995 productivity growth revival—could be traced directly to the IT revolution. One way of describing the changing relationship between technology and economic performance is through Robert M. Solow's famous 1987 saying that "we can see

the computer age everywhere but in the productivity statistics." For a decade economists took "Solow's paradox" as a truism, noting the continuing co-existence of explosive growth in computer use and dismal growth in labor productivity, and they differed only in their explanations.[6] But by 1999–2000 a consensus emerged that the technological revolution represented by the New Economy was responsible directly or indirectly not just for the productivity growth acceleration, but also the other manifestations of the miracle, including the stock market and wealth boom and spreading of benefits to the lower half of the income distribution. In short, Solow's paradox is now obsolete and its inventor has admitted as much.[7]

This chapter explores the interrelations between the ebb and flow of U.S. economic performance and the role of technology. We quantify the role of technology in general and IT in particular in achieving the U.S. productivity acceleration of the late 1990s and provide an analysis that suggests that some of the acceleration may be temporary and may not persist. In determining the role of alternative sources of the technological acceleration and U.S. domination of IT manufacturing and software production, we explore the role of mechanisms and incentives in the private sector, foreign competition, and government policy. The role in the U.S. success of its heterogeneous system of public and private universities, peer-reviewed government research grants, and strong tradition of patent and securities regulation are also emphasized. The chapter concludes with observations on the role of immigration as a source of recent U.S. success and an area where policy has an important role to play. Throughout the analysis, the U.S. success story is qualified not just by the emergence of an economic downturn in 2000–2001, but also by the remaining less favorable elements of U.S. exceptionalism

---

[4] The S&P 500 stock market index increased from an average of 455 in December, 1994, to 1505 in the week ending April 1, 2000 and was still above 1400 in early November, 2000.

[5] Data on real family incomes show a pattern of equal growth rates by income quintile for 1947–79 but sharp divergence between decreases at the bottom and increases at the top during 1979–97 (see Mishel et al., 1999: 52, Figure 1E).

[6] The explanations included "the computers are not everywhere," or "there must be something wrong with the productivity statistics," or "there must be something wrong with the computers." The best compendium and assessments of these and other alternative explanations is provided by Triplett (1999).

[7] Solow is quoted as such in Uchitelle (2000).

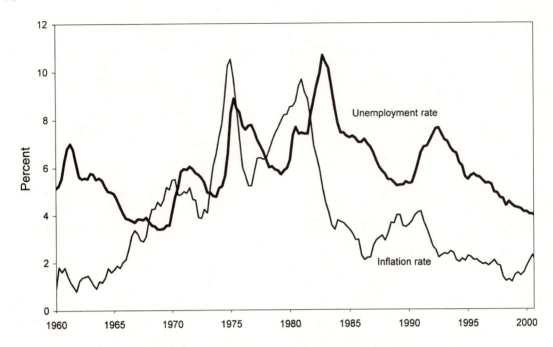

Figure 3.1 Unemployment rate vs. inflation rate, 1960–2000.

when viewed from abroad, especially rising economic inequality that limited the spread of the "miracle" across the income distribution.

3.2. Dimensions of Macroeconomic Performance

We begin by examining several indicators of economic performance and discuss several hypotheses that have been suggested to explain the multidimensional improvement of performance in the late 1990s.

3.2.1. Inflation and Unemployment

Figure 3.1 plots the unemployment rate on the same scale as the inflation rate for the Personal Consumption deflator.[8] The unemployment rate in 1999–2000 fell to 4 percent, the lowest rate since the 1966–70 period during which

[8] The deflator for Personal Consumption Expenditures, part of the National Income and Product Accounts, is preferable to the Consumer Price Index (CPI) because it has been revised retrospectively to use a consistent set of measurement methods, whereas the CPI is never revised.

inflation accelerated steadily. Yet in 1998 and early 1999, prior to the 1999–2000 upsurge in oil prices, inflation not only failed to accelerate but rather decelerated.

Taking a general view of the unemployment–inflation relationship, it appears superficially that the only support for a negative Phillips curve unemployment–inflation tradeoff is based on the 1960s Viet Nam-era experience, with a bit of further support from the economic expansion of 1987–90. In other periods, especially during 1972–85 and 1995–9, the unemployment and inflation rates appear to be positively correlated, with the unemployment rate behaving as a lagging indicator, moving a year or two later than inflation. While this appearance of a positive tradeoff led some economists, notably Robert E. Lucas, Jr. and Thomas Sargent back in the 1970s to declare the Phillips curve to be "lying in wreckage," at the same time a more general model of inflation determination was developed that combined an influence of demand (i.e., a negative short-run relation between inflation and unemployment), supply (in the form of "supply shocks" like changing real oil prices), slow inertial adjustment, and long-run independence of inflation and the unemployment rate.[9] During the 1980s and the first half of the 1990s this more general model was adopted as the main-stream approach to inflation determination by textbook authors and policy makers alike, but in the late 1990s it was challenged again by the simultaneous decline in unemployment and deceleration of inflation evident in Figure 3.1.

At the end of the decade no consensus had yet emerged to explain the positive correlation of inflation and unemployment in the late 1990s. I have attempted to use a common framework to explain why the performance of the 1970s was so bad and that of the 1990s was so good, pointing to the role of adverse supply shocks in the earlier episode and beneficial supply shocks more recently. In my interpreta-tion (1998) inflation in 1997–8 was held down by two "old" supply shocks, falling real prices of imports and energy, and by two "new" supply shocks, the accelerating decline in computer prices (see Figure 3.9) and a sharp decline in the prices of medical care services made possi-ble by the managed care revolution. In retro-spect, my analysis, while still valid regarding the role of the supply shocks, did not place suffi-cient emphasis on the productivity growth revi-val as an independent source of low inflation. Between 1995 and late 2000, wage growth accel-erated substantially from 2.1 to above 6 percent at an annual rate, thus appearing to validate the Phillips curve hypothesis of a negative tradeoff between unemployment and wage growth.[10] However, soaring productivity growth during the same period prevented faster wage growth from translating into growth in unit labor costs (defined as wage growth minus productivity growth). If productivity growth were to decele-rate, then it added one more element to the list of transitory elements that had held down infla-tion in the late 1990s. Any of the items on the list—falling relative import and energy prices, a faster rate of decline in computer prices,

moderate medical care inflation, and the productivity growth revival itself—could turn around and put upward rather than downward pressure on the inflation rate. This had already begun to happen as a result of higher energy prices, as the growth rate of the price index for personal consumption expenditures had already more than doubled from 1.1 percent in 1998 to 2.4 percent in 2000.

Figure 3.2 compares (with annual rather than quarterly data) the actual unemployment rate with the natural unemployment rate (or NAIRU). The concept of the natural unemploy-ment rate used here attempts to measure the unemployment rate consistent with a constant rate of inflation in the absence of the "old" supply shocks, changes in the relative prices of imports and energy.[11] The acceleration of infla-tion during 1987–90 and the deceleration of inflation during 1991–5 are explained by move-ments of the actual unemployment rate below and then above the natural rate. It is the dip of the actual unemployment rate below the natural unemployment rate in 1997–2000 which raises questions about the behavior of inflation.[12] Perhaps the natural rate has declined more than is depicted here.[13,14]

[11] Allowance is also made for the role of the imposition and removal of the Nixon era price controls during 1971–4.

[12] In Figure 3.1 the decline of inflation in 1997–8 and its resurgence in 1999–2000 can be explained entirely by the "old" supply shocks, the behavior of the real prices of imports and energy.

[13] Subsequent to my research on the NAIRU (Gordon, 1998), Eller (2000) has updated my research and made numerous improvements in my specification. However, Eller is unable to find any technique which yields a NAIRU below 5.0 percent in late 1999.

[14] In addition to the role of computer prices and medical care prices in holding down inflation relative to that which would be predicted by the unemployment gap in Figure 3.2, several other changes in labor markets are considered by Katz and Krueger (1999). These include a declining share of youth in the working-age population, the imprisonment of some young adult males who would otherwise be unem-ployed, and the increased role in matching jobs and the unemployed played by temporary help agencies. The bene-fit of legal and illegal immigration in providing an addi-tional supply of workers needed by tight labor markets can be added to this list (see section 3.4.2.6).

[9] The more general approach was developed by Gordon (1977, 1982). The evolution of this approach is described by Gordon (1997).

[10] These figures refer to the growth in nonfarm private compensation per hour.

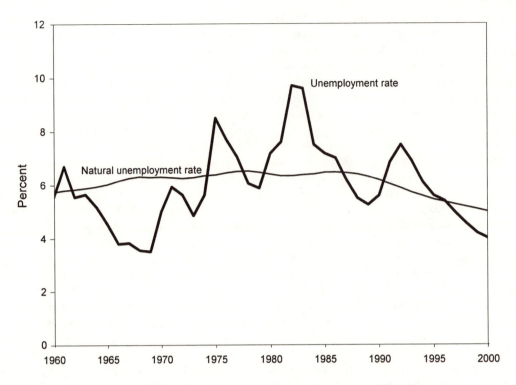

Figure 3.2 Unemployment rate vs. natural unemployment rate, 1960–2000.

3.2.2. Monetary Policy, the "Twin Deficits," Saving, and Investment

The response of the Fed's monetary policy is summarized in Figure 3.3, which displays annual values of the Federal funds rate, which is controlled directly by the Fed, and the corporate bond rate. The Federal funds rate barely changed on an annual basis in the five years 1995–9 and during that period was much lower than reached in previous tight money episodes in 1969, 1974, 1981, and 1989, each of which can be interpreted as the Fed's response to an inflation acceleration that did not occur in 1995–9. Throughout the 1990s the corporate bond rate declined, reflecting both the behavior of short-term interest rates and also the perception that corporate bonds had become less risky as memories of the most recent 1990–1 recession receded into the past. The level of the corporate bond rate in 1999 was lower than in any year since 1969, helping to explain the longevity of the economic

expansion and the ongoing boom in investment.

Until the late 1990s the U.S. economy appeared to be plagued by the "twin deficits," namely the government budget deficit and current account deficit.[15] In the casual discussion of causation that became typical during the 1980s and early 1990s, U.S. domestic saving was barely sufficient to finance domestic investment, requiring that any government deficit be financed by foreign borrowing. When both the government budget surplus and current account surplus are plotted as a share of gross domestic product (GDP), as in Figure 3.4, we see that a tight relation between the "twin surpluses" or "twin deficits" is more the exception than the rule and occurred most notably

---

[15] All references to the government budget deficit in this chapter refer to the combined current surplus or deficit of all levels of government–federal, state, and local. See *Economic Report of the President,* January 2001: 371, Table B-82, third column.

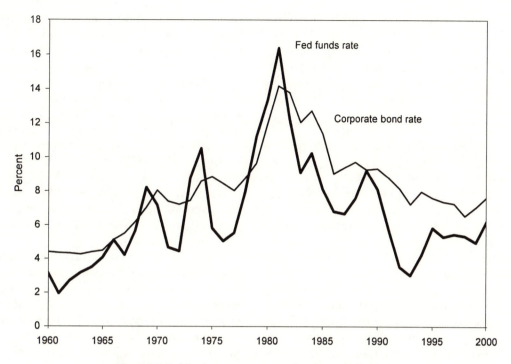

Figure 3.3 Fed funds rate vs. corporate bond rate, 1960–2000.

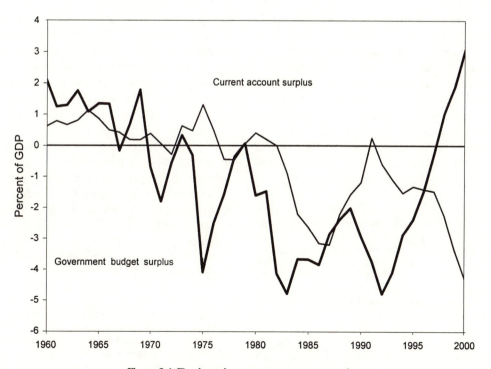

Figure 3.4 Fiscal surplus vs. current account surplus.

during the intervals 1960–70 and 1985–90.[16] In the 1990s the two deficits have moved in opposite directions to an unprecedented degree— the arithmetic difference between the government surplus and current account surplus changed from −4.2 percent of GDP in 1992 to +7.3 percent of GDP in 2000, a swing of 11.5 percent of GDP, or more than U.S.\$1 trillion.

This dramatic swing is easy to explain qualitatively if not quantitatively. A booming economy boosts the government budget surplus as revenue rises more rapidly than expenditures but also turns the current account toward deficit as imports grow more rapidly than exports. The magnitude of the current account deterioration seems roughly consistent with the excess of economic growth in the United States compared to its trading partners (the ability of which to purchase U.S. exports during 1998–9 was impaired by the financial crises in Asia, Brazil, and Russia, and continuing stagnation in Japan). But the magnitude of the government budget improvement appears to defy explanation, as each successive forecast by the Congressional Budget Office has become waste paper almost as fast as it has been published. Landmarks in the budget turnaround were the tax reform legislation of 1993 and 1996 and the huge surge of taxable capital gains generated by the stock market boom.

During the long period during which the government ran a budget deficit, a consensus emerged that the main harm done by the deficit was the erosion of "national saving," the sum of private saving and the government surplus.[17] Since private investment could exceed national saving only through foreign borrowing, a low rate of national saving inevitably implied a squeeze on domestic investment, a reliance on foreign borrowing with its consequent future interest costs, or both. The only solution was to achieve some combination of a marked increase in the private saving rate or a turnaround in the government budget from deficit to surplus. Indeed, this pessimistic interpretation was validated in the numbers for a year as recent as 1993, when the net national saving rate reached a postwar low of 3.4 percent of GDP, down from a peak of 12.1 percent in 1965, and net domestic private investment was only 4.5 percent, down from 11.3 percent in 1965 (see Figure 3.5).

Those who had predicted that an ending of government deficits would stimulate private investment were vindicated, as the 1993–2000 increase in the investment ratio of 4.2 percentage points absorbed much of the increase in the government budget surplus over the same period of 7.1 points. The increase in national saving made possible by the budget turnaround was, however, almost entirely offset by a decline in the private saving ratio of 6.3 percent, requiring added borrowing from abroad (an increase in the current account deficit of 3.4 percent) to finance the extra investment.[18] Since these ratios are linked by definitional relationships, there is no sense in which these movements can be linked by attributions of cause and effect. It would be just as accurate to say that everything that changed after 1993 was an indirect effect of the New Economy and accompanying technological acceleration which (a) boosted the government budget through income growth and capital gains, (b) created new incentives for private investment, (c) raised imports more than exports by boosting domestic income growth compared to foreign income growth, and (d) caused private saving to erode as stock market gains boosted the growth of domestic consumption beyond that of disposable income.

---

[16] The identity governing the relationship in Figure 3.4 is that the government budget surplus $(T - G)$ equals the current account surplus $(X - M)$ plus the difference between domestic private investment and domestic private saving $(I - S)$. During most of the period between 1974 and 1995, the government budget surplus was a larger negative number than the current account surplus, implying that investment was substantially less than saving. After 1996, this relationship reversed sharply.

[17] Using the notation in the previous footnote, national saving equals total investment, domestic and foreign: $S + T - G = I + X - M$.

[18] The data compare 1993 with 2000:Q3 and are taken from the *Economic Report of the President*, January 2001: 312–3, Table B-32. Private saving is taken as the printed number plus the statistical discrepancy, and the government surplus is derived as a residual $(T - G = I - S + NX)$.

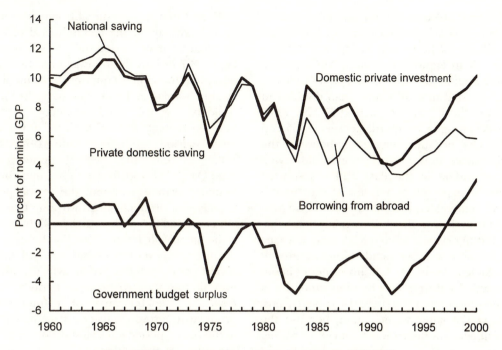

Figure 3.5 Components of net saving and investment, 1960–1999.

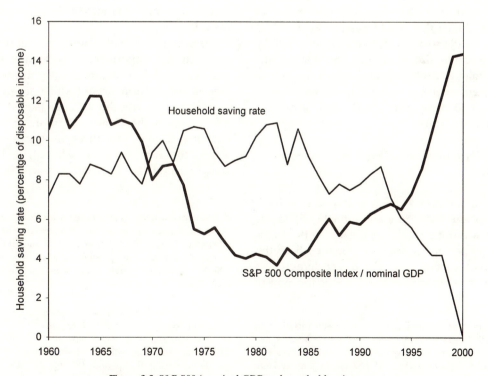

Figure 3.6 S&P 500/nominal GDP vs. household saving rate.

The final element in this chain of causation, the link between the stock market boom and the collapse of household saving, is illustrated separately in Figure 3.6. If we relate the Standard & Poors (S&P) 500 stock market index to nominal GDP, this ratio more than doubled in the four short years between 1995 and 1999, after declining by two-thirds between 1965 and 1982. The negative correlation between the stock market ratio and the household saving rate is evident in the data and is just what would be expected as a result of the "wealth effect" embedded in Modigliani's original 1953 life cycle hypothesis of consumption behavior. Putting Figures 3.5 and 3.6 together, we see that in the late 1990s rapid economic growth was fueled both by an investment boom financed by foreign borrowing and by a consumption binge financed by capital gains. Both of the latter were related, because the current account deficit was financed by willing foreigners eager to benefit from profits and capital gains in the buoyant U.S. economy; a reversal of the stock market could cause all of this to unravel, including an end to the excess of growth in consumption relative to growth in disposal income, as well as a withdrawal of foreign funds that would push down the U.S. dollar. While some worried that private indebtedness would also emerge as a problem if the stock market declined, ratios of consumer and mortgage debt had actually increased little in relation to income and had fallen greatly in relation to wealth.[19]

3.2.3. Productivity, Real Wages, and Income per Capita

Thus far we have examined several manifestations of the U.S. economic miracle of the late 1990s without focussing explicitly on the single most important factor which made all of this possible, namely the sharp acceleration in productivity growth that started at the end of 1995 and that was presumably caused entirely or in large part by the technological acceleration that we have labeled the "New Economy." Figure 3.7 divides the postwar into three periods using the standard quarterly data published by the Bureau of Labor Statistics (BLS), the "golden age" of rapid productivity growth between 1950:Q2 and 1972:Q2, the dismal slowdown period extending from 1972:Q2 to 1995:Q4, and the revival period since 1995:Q4.[20] The top frame shows that for the nonfarm private economy, the revival period registered a productivity growth rate that actually exceeded the golden age by a slight margin, while the middle frame shows that for manufacturing there never was a slowdown, and that the revival period exhibits productivity growth well over double the two previous periods.[21] As a result of the buoyancy of manufacturing, productivity growth outside of manufacturing in the revival period fell well short of the golden age although also exhibited a recovery from the slowdown period. Subsequently we examine the contrast between a technological acceleration inside manufacturing, primarily in the making of computers, with the absence of any parallel acceleration in technological change outside of manufacturing.

Perhaps no measure of well-being in the U.S. economy has experienced more of a revival than the growth in real wages, for this was the measure of performance for which progress was most dismal during the 1972–95 period. Table 3.1 compares the growth of nonfarm private output per hour with three measures of real wages, the first two of which deflate hourly compensation by alternative price indexes.

---

[19] The ratio of outstanding consumer credit to GDP rose from 1987 to 2000:Q3 only from 14.2 to 14.8 percent, and total outstanding mortgage debt only from 63.2 to 67.8 percent. See *Economic Report of the President*, January 2001, Tables B-77 (p. 366) and B-75 (p. 374), respectively.

[20] These precise quarters are chosen because they have the same unemployment rate of about 5.5 percent. The unemployment rate in the final quarter, 2000:Q1, was 4.1 percent, and we discuss below the possibility that some of the post-1995 productivity acceleration may have been a temporary cyclical phenomenon.

[21] The reference above to pessimism based on productivity growth of "barely one percent" during the 1972–95 period refers to data that were revised upward in October, 1999. The average annual growth rate of nonfarm private output per hour during the period 1972:Q2–1995:Q4 is 1.42 percent in the newly revised data.

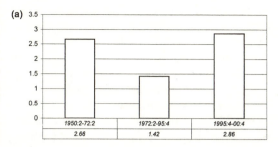

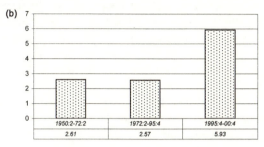

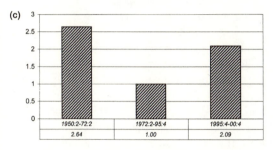

Figure 3.7 (a) Output per hour, nonfarm private business, annual growth rates by interval. (b) Output per hour, manufacturing, annual growth rates by interval. (c) Output per hour, nonfarm manufacturing, annual growth rates by interval.

Shown in line 2a is real compensation deflated by the deflator for the nonfarm private sector;

this measure would grow at the same rate as productivity if the share of compensation in nonfarm private output were constant, which is roughly true in the long run. Line 2b records a slower growth rate of the real consumption wage, slower because during the postwar period the price index of consumption goods and services has increased faster than the price index for nonfarm private output, a difference due primarily to the falling prices of many types of machinery and equipment, especially computers, relative to the prices of consumer services. The most pessimistic measure of all, shown in line 3 of Table 3.1, is also the most inaccurate, because it counts only part of compensation and uses a deflator (the CPI) which is biased upward to a substantially greater extent than the PCE deflator used in line 2b. The pessimistic measure in line 3 implies that the real wage in 2000:Q3 was only 17.7 percent above that in 1959 (an annual growth rate of only 0.4 percent), whereas the measure in line 2b implies that over the same period the real wage more than doubled (an annual growth rate of 1.78 percent per year). Both measures imply a sharp acceleration of almost 2 percentage points when the last five years are compared with the previous eight years.

A more comprehensive measure of well-being, per capita real income, allows us to illustrate the progress that the U.S. economy has made in the last few years relative to the two other largest industrialized nations, Germany and Japan. Using measures that have been adjusted for the differing purchasing power of other currencies, U.S. per capita income was 25

TABLE 3.1

Output per Hour and Alternative Real Wage Concepts, Nonfarm Private Business Sector, Alternative Intervals 1959–2000:Q4 (Percentage Growth Rate at Annual Rate)

		1959–1972 (1)	1972–1987 (2)	1987–1995 (3)	1995–1999 (4)
1.	Output per hour	2.83	1.52	1.38	2.87
2.	Real compensation per hour				
	a. Deflated by nonfarm nonhousing deflator	3.14	1.55	0.92	2.66
	b. Deflated by personal consumption deflator	2.99	1.23	0.38	2.26
3.	Average hourly earnings deflated by consumer price index	1.87	−0.66	−0.56	1.24

Sources: Economic Report of the President, January 2001, Tables B-7, B-10, B-11, B-47, and B-49.

percent higher than Germany in 1999, compared to margins of 21 percent in 1995, 16 percent in 1990, and 15 percent in 1980. Japan's rapid economic growth continued to 1990 and then stalled, and so it is not surprising that the U.S. margin over Japan widened from 22 percent in 1990 to 31 percent in 1999. However, those who would interpret these comparisons as evidence of U.S. technological success, or even more broadly as evidence that the United States has the "best" economic system, are reminded that growth rates of per capita income between these countries are not comparable. Only the United States measures the prices of computers with a hedonic price deflator, and this difference in measurement methodology alone over the 1995–9 interval adds about half a percent per year to per capita U.S. real income growth and, as stated above, subtracts about the same amount from U.S. inflation.[22] But this lack of comparability should not be overstated. Some comparisons of U.S. economic performance with leading foreign nations, for example, those showing that the U.S. unemployment rate has declined faster and stock market valuations have increased faster, are unaffected by which technique is used to deflate computer expenditures.

3.2.4. Interpreting the Dismal Slowdown Years, 1972–95

Before turning to a more detailed review of the role of IT in creating the post-1995 U.S. productivity growth revival, we should ask how the United States could have experienced such a long period of slow productivity growth between 1972 and 1995, particularly in light of the many structural advantages of the U.S. economy that became apparent after 1995. However, decades of fruitless research on the sources of the post-1972 slowdown suggest that this is the wrong question. First, the question is wrong because the U.S. slowdown was not unique, but rather with differences in magnitude and timing was shared by the rest of the

industrialized world. Second, in a more important sense the question should be flipped on its head to ask not why productivity growth was so slow after 1972, but rather why productivity growth was so fast for so long before 1972.

Every major industrialized country experienced a sharp slowdown in productivity growth after 1973, and the extent of the slowdown in most countries was greater than in the United States. During 1960–73 growth in productivity in the 15 countries of the European Union was double and in Japan quadruple that in the United States. In the 1970s and 1980s productivity growth slowed down everywhere, but later than in the United States, and by the first half of the 1990s productivity growth in Europe and Japan had converged to that of the United States. Thus, the productivity slowdown was universal in the developed world rather than being unique to the United States.

The timing of the previous "golden age" of rapid productivity growth had also differed. Following a universal experience of slow productivity growth in the nineteenth century, the U.S. "golden age" began first around 1915 and extended until 1972, whereas the golden age in Europe and Japan did not begin in earnest until the postwar reconstruction of the 1950s. Stated another way, the percentage degree of superiority of U.S. per person GDP and of U.S. productivity began to accelerate around the turn of the century, reached its peak in 1945, and then steadily fell until the early 1990s, when the degree of superiority began to increase again (as discussed above in the context of Figure 3.8).

The post-1972 slowdown in the United States, Japan, and Europe can be traced back to the sources of the "golden age" which began around the time of World War I in the United States (Gordon, 2000a). A set of "great inventions" of unprecedented scope and importance, including electricity and the internal combustion engine, had been developed during the Second Industrial Revolution of 1860–1900 and began the process of diffusion through the structure of the economy and society soon after the turn of the century (Gordon, 2000c). The productivity acceleration of the "golden age" occurred as the electric

---

[22] In addition the U.S. national accounts were revised in 1999 back to 1959 to include investment in software which is partly deflated with a hedonic price index.

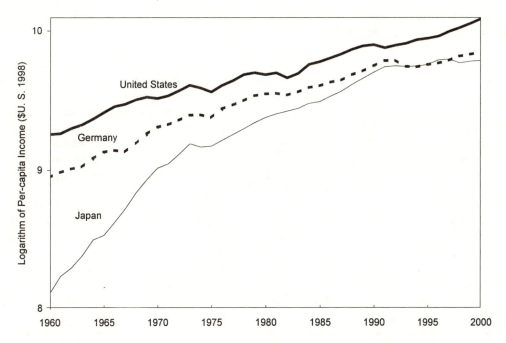

Figure 3.8 Per capita income for Germany, Japan and the United States, 1960–2000.

motor revolutionized manufacturing, as the internal combustion engine revolutionized ground transport and allowed the invention of air transport, and as other innovations in chemicals, petroleum, entertainment, communication, and public health transformed the standard of living in the United States between 1900 and the 1950s. In addition to the original advantages of the United States, particularly economies of scale and a wealth of natural resources (Wright, 1990), the dislocation of the two world wars and the turbulent interwar period delayed the diffusion of many of these innovations in Europe and Japan until after 1945, but then the rich plate of unexploited technology led to a period of rapid catch-up, if not convergence, to the U.S. frontier.

This interpretation explains the post-1972 productivity slowdown as resulting from the inevitable depletion of the fruits of the previous great inventions. The faster productivity growth in Europe and Japan during 1950–72, and the greater magnitude of their slowdowns, and the delayed timing of the slowdown into the 1980s and 1990s, is explained by the late start of Europe and Japan in exploiting the late nineteenth century "great inventions." Of course

this story is too simple to account for the differing fortunes of individual industries; as Europe and Japan recovered and caught up, they did so more in some industries than others, so that by the late 1970s and early 1980s the U.S. automobile and machine tool industries seemed more obviously in the "basket case" category than pharmaceuticals or software.

3.3. The Role of Information Technology in U.S. Economic Success

How important has the New Economy and IT revolution been in creating the U.S. productivity revival which appears directly or indirectly to be responsible for most other dimensions of the U.S. economic miracle of the late-1990s? Fortunately we do not need to explore this question from scratch, since recent academic research has produced a relatively clear answer which is summarized and interpreted in this section. The basic answer is that the acceleration in technical change in computers, peripherals, and semiconductors explains most of the acceleration in overall productivity growth since 1995, but virtually all the progress has been concentrated in the durable manufacturing sector, with surprisingly little spillover to the rest of the economy.

To provide a more precise analysis we must begin by distinguishing between the growth in output per hour, sometimes called average labor productivity (ALP), from the growth of multifactor productivity (MFP). The former compares output growth with that of a single input, labor hours, while the latter compares output with a weighted average of several inputs, including labor, capital, and sometimes others, including materials, energy, and/or imports. ALP always grows faster than MFP, and the difference between them is the contribution of "capital deepening," the fact that any growing economy achieves a growth rate of its capital input that is faster than its labor input, thus equipping each unit of labor with an ever-growing quantity of capital.[23]

In all official BLS measures of MFP and in all recent academic research, both labor hours and capital input are adjusted for changes in composition. For labor the composition adjustment takes the form of taking into account the different earnings of different groups classified by age, sex, and educational attainment, and for capital it takes the form of taking into account the different service prices of long-lived structures and different types of shorter-lived producers' equipment. Composition-adjusted growth in labor input is faster than in standard measures of labor input, since educational attainment has been increasing, whereas composition-adjusted growth in capital input is faster than the real stock of capital, since there has been a continuous shift from long-lived structures to shorter-lived equipment, and within equipment to shorter-lived types of equipment, especially computers.[24]

3.3.1. The "Direct" and "Spillover" Effects of the New Economy

How have computers and the New Economy influenced the recent productivity growth revival? Imagine a spontaneous acceleration in the rate of technological change in the computer sector, which induces a more rapid rate of decline in computer prices and an investment boom as firms respond to cheaper computer prices by buying more computers.[25] In response, since computers are part of output, this acceleration of technical change in computer production raises the growth rate of MFP in the total economy, boosting the growth rate of ALP one-for-one. Second, the ensuing investment boom raises the "capital deepening" effect by increasing the growth rate of capital input relative to labor input and thus increasing ALP growth relative to MFP growth.

In discussing the New Economy, it is important to separate the computer-producing sector from the computer-using sector. No one denies that there has been a marked acceleration of output and productivity growth in the production of computer hardware, including peripherals.[26] The real issue has been the response

---

[24] A short-lived piece of equipment like a computer must have a higher marginal product per dollar of investment to pay for its high rate of depreciation, relative to a long-lived hotel or office building. Composition-adjusted measures of capital input reflect differences in the marginal products of different types of capital and thus place a higher weight on fast-growing components like computers and a lower weight on slow-growing components like structures.

[25] As stated above, in the U.S. national accounts computer prices are measured by the hedonic regression technique, in which the prices of a variety of models of computers are explained by the quantity of computer characteristics and by the passage of time. Thus, the phrase in the text "decline in computer prices" is shorthand for "a decline in the prices of computer attributes like speed, memory, disk drive access speed and capacity, presence of a CD-ROM, etc."

[23] Technically, the growth rate of ALP is equal to the growth rate of MFP plus the growth rate of the capital/labor ratio times the elasticity of output with respect to changes in capital input. Virtually all research on the sources of growth uses the share of capital income in total national income as a proxy for the unobservable elasticity of output to changes in capital input.

[26] In this chapter we emphasize computer hardware, rather than the universe of computer hardware, software, and telecommunications equipment, because the BEA deflators for software and telecommunications equipment are problematic, exhibiting implausibly low rates of price decline, as argued by Jorgenson and Stiroh (2000).

of productivity to massive computer investment by the 96 percent of the economy engaged in using computers rather than producing them.[27] If the only effect of the technological breakthrough in computer production on the noncomputer economy is an investment boom that accelerates the growth rate of capital input, then noncomputer ALP growth would rise by the capital-deepening effect, but there would be no increase in noncomputer MFP growth. Let us call this the "direct" effect of the New Economy on the noncomputer sector. Sometimes advocates of the revolutionary nature of the New Economy imply that computer investment has a higher rate of return than other types of investment and creates "spillover" effects on business practices and productivity in the noncomputer economy; evidence of this "spillover" effect would be an acceleration in MFP growth in the noncomputer economy occurring at the same time as the technological acceleration in computer production.

3.3.2. The Role of IT in the Productivity Growth Revival

What is the counterpart of the New Economy in the official output data? The remarkable event which occurred at the end of 1995 was an acceleration of the rate of price change in computer hardware (including peripherals) from an average rate of 12 percent during 1987–95 to an average rate of −29 percent during 1996–8.[28] Computers did not become more important as a share of dollar spending in the economy, which stagnated at around 1.3 percent of the nonfarm private business economy. The counterpart of the post-1995 acceleration in the rate of price decline was an acceleration in the rate

of technological progress; apparently the time cycle of Moore's Law shortened from 18 months to 12 months at about the same time.[29]

We now combine two different academic studies to assess the role of IT in contributing to the economy-wide acceleration in ALP and MFP growth since 1995. First, we use the recent results of Oliner and Sichel (2000, 2001) to compute the contribution of computers and semiconductors both to capital deepening and to the MFP acceleration in the overall economy. Second, we summarize my recent study (Gordon, 2000b) that adds two elements to the work of Oliner and Sichel. First, it uses official BLS data to "strip" the overall economy of the contribution of the ALP and MFP acceleration that is located within durable manufacturing, so that we can assess the extent of any spillover of IT in the 88 percent of the economy located outside of durables. Second, it updates my previous work on the cyclical behavior of productivity, which shows that there is a regular relationship between growth in hours relative to the trend in hours, and growth in output relative to the trend in output. We can use this statistical relationship based on data going back to the 1950s to estimate the trend of output and productivity growth during 1995–2000, given the trend in hours, and thus extract the remaining cyclical component, that is, the

---

[27] In 1999 nominal final sales of computers and peripherals plus fixed investment in software represented 3.5 percent of nominal GDP in the nonfarm nonhousing private business economy. Thus, the "noncomputer part of the economy" represents 96.5 percent of nonfarm nonhousing private business output. Final sales of computer hardware is an unpublished series obtained from Christian Ehemann of the BEA; the other series in this calculation appear in the *Economic Report of the President*, February 2000, Tables B-10 (p. 320) and B-16 (p. 326).

[28] The numbers in the text refer to the annual rate of change of the BEA implicit deflator for investment in computers and peripherals between 1995:Q4 and 1998:Q4. One way of dramatizing the rate of price decline is to translate it into the ratio of performance to price when 1999:Q4 is compared with 1993:Q4. The BEA's implicit deflator for computer final sales implies an improvement over that six-year period by a factor of 5.2. Improvements in performance/price ratios for individual computer components are substantially larger, by a factor of 16.2 for computer processors, 75.5 for RAM, and 176.0 for hard disk capacity. See "Computers, then and now," *Consumer Reports*, May, 2000: 10, where the published reported comparisons in 1999 dollars have been converted to nominal dollars using the CPI.

[29] Moore's law states that the number of transistors on a single computer chip doubles every eighteen months. The reduction in time from eighteen to twelve months is based on a conversation between Gordon Moore and Dale W. Jorgenson, related to the author by the latter.

TABLE 3.2
Decomposition of Growth in Output Per Hour, 1995:Q4–2000:Q4, Into Contributions of Cyclical Effects and Structural Change in Trend Growth (Percentage Growth Rates at Annual Rate)

		Nonfarm private business (1)	*NFPB excluding durable manufacturing* (2)	*Effect of durable manufacturing* (1) − (2)
1.	Actual growth	2.86	2.20	0.66
2.	Contribution of cyclical effect	0.40	0.48	−0.08
3.	Growth in trend (line 1 − line 2)	2.46	1.72	0.74
4.	Trend, 1972:Q2–1995:Q4	1.42	1.13	0.29
5.	Acceleration of trend (line 3 − line 4)	1.04	0.59	0.45
6.	Contribution of price measurement	0.14	0.14	0.00
7.	Contribution of labor quality	0.01	0.01	0.00
8.	Structural acceleration in labor productivity (line 5 − 6 − 7)	0.89	0.44	0.45
9.	Contribution of capital deepening	0.37	0.37	0.00
	a. Information technology capital	0.60	0.60	0.00
	b. Other capital	−0.23	−0.23	0.00
10.	Contribution of MFP growth in computer and computer-related semiconductor manufacturing	0.30	−0.00	0.30
11.	Structural acceleration in MFP (line 8 − 9 − 10)	0.22	0.07	0.15

Sources: Updated version of Gordon (2000b, Table 2). Lines 9 and 10 come from Oliner and Sichel (2001).

difference between actual productivity growth and trend productivity growth.[30]

The results displayed in Table 3.2 allow us to assess the direct and spillover effects of computers on output per hour and MFP growth during the period between 1995:Q4 and 2000:Q4. The first column refers to the aggregate economy, that is, the NFPB sector including computers.

[30] The equations estimated are those developed in Gordon (1993).

[31] The price measurement effect consists of two components. While most changes in price measurement methods in the CPI have been backcast in the national accounts to 1978, one remaining change—the 1993–4 shift in medical care deflation from the CPI to the slower-growing PPI—creates a measurement discontinuity of 0.09 percent. The fact that other measurement changes were carried back to 1978 rather than 1972 creates a further discontinuity of 0.05 when the full 1972–95 period is compared to 1995–9. The acceleration in labor quality growth reflects the fact that labor quality growth during 1972–95 was held down by a compositional shift toward female and teenage workers during the first half of that period.

Of the actual 2.86 percent annual growth of output per hour, 0.40 is attributed to a cyclical effect and the remaining 2.46 percent to trend growth, and the latter is 1.04 points faster than the 1972-95 trend. How can this acceleration be explained? A small part in lines 6 and 7 is attributed to changes in price measurement methods and to a slight acceleration in the growth of labor quality.[31] All of the remaining 0.89 points can be directly attributed to computers. The capital-deepening effect of faster growth in computer capital relative to labor in the aggregate economy accounts of 0.60 percentage points of the acceleration (line 9a) and a 0.30-point acceleration of MFP growth in computer and computer-related semiconductor manufacturing account (line 10) sum to an explanation of 0.90 points, compared to the 0.89 acceleration in trend that needs to be explained. Because noncomputer capital makes a negative contribution of −0.23 points to the capital-deepening effect, there is a remaining 0.22 points left over as the residual, which represents faster MFP growth outside of computer manufacturing.

To locate where this remaining MFP growth revival has occurred, column (2) of Table 3.2 repeats the exercise for the 88 percent of the private economy outside of durable manufacturing. The MFP revival at the bottom of column (2) is a trivial 0.07 percent outside of durable manufacturing, and the difference between columns (1) and (2) indicates that durable manufacturing other than the production of computers accounts for the remaining 0.15 percent acceleration of MFP growth in the private economy.

Thus, the verdict on the "New Economy" is decidedly mixed. The productivity revival is impressive and real, and most of it is structural rather than cyclical. The productivity revival has spilled over from the production of computers to the use of computers. The evident effect of new technologies in reducing transaction costs and facilitating a surge in trading volumes in the securities industry is one of many ways in which the use of computers has contributed to the productivity revival, and all of this fruitful activity is encompassed in the 0.60 percent per year contribution of "capital deepening" listed in line 9a of Table 3.2.

However, the productivity revival is narrowly based in the production and use of computers. There is no sign of a fundamental transformation of the U.S. economy. There has been no acceleration of MFP growth outside of computer production and the rest of durable manufacturing. Responding to the accelerated rate of price decline of computers that occurred between 1995 and 1998, business firms throughout the economy boosted purchases of computers, creating an investment boom and "capital deepening" in the form of faster growth of capital relative to labor. But computer capital did not have any kind of magical or extraordinary effect—it earned the same rate of return as any other type of capital.

The dependence of the U.S. productivity revival on the production and use of computers waves a danger flag for the future. Consider the possibility that the accelerated 29 percent rate of price decline for computers for 1995–8 does not continue. Already in the year ending in 2000:Q4 the rate of price decline slowed from 29 to 12 percent, the same as between 1987 and 1995. If in response the growth rate of computer investment were to slow down to a rate similar to that before 1995, then the main source of the productivity revival identified by Oliner and Sichel (2000) would disappear, and with it much of the U.S. economic miracle.

3.3.3. The Puzzling Failure of the Internet to Shift the Demand Curve for Computers

While the invention of the Internet is usually treated as revolutionary, a simple analysis of the supply and demand for computer hardware may suggest a more limited role for the Internet. We have already seen that the rate of decline of prices for computer hardware, including peripherals, accelerated sharply after 1995. This fact is shown in the top frame of Figure 3.9, which plots the price and quantity of computer characteristics since 1960. The implicit price deflator for computer hardware, including peripherals, declined from 61,640 in 1961 to 33 at the end of 2000 (with a base 1996 = 100), for an annual rate of decline of 19.4 percent per annum. There has been a corresponding increase in the quantity of computer attributes, and both the rate of price decline and quantity increase accelerated after 1995 (as indicated by the increasing spaces between the annual price and quantity observations starting in 1995).

While the rate of price change has varied over time, the notable feature of rapid price decline does not distinguish the New Economy from the 1950–80 interval dominated by the mainframe computer or the 1980–95 interval dominated by the transition from mainframe to PC applications prior to the invention of the Internet.[32] Throughout its history, the economics of the

---

[32] Existing computer price deflators fail to take account of the radical decline in the price per calculation that occurred in the transition from mainframes to PCs (which have been studied only separately, not together). Gordon (1990: 239) calculates that the annual rate of price decline between 1972 and 1987 would have been 35 percent per annum rather than 20 percent per annum if this transitional benefit had been taken into account. This consideration further reduces the uniqueness of technological advance created by the New Economy.

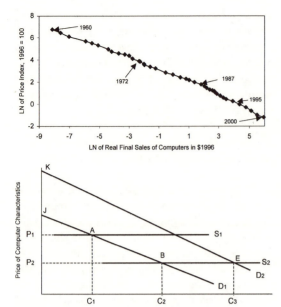

Figure 3.9 The price and quantity of computer characteristics. *Source:* Nominal final sales of computers and peripherals from BEA, linked to Producers' Durable Equipment for computers prior to 1987. Implicit Deflator from BEA back to 1972; for 1960–72 from Gordon (1990: 226, Table 6.10).

computer has featured a steady downward shift in the supply curve of computer attributes at a rate much faster than the upward shift in the demand for computer services. In fact, the story is often told with a theoretical diagram like the bottom frame of Figure 3.9, in which the supply curve slides steadily downwards from S_1 to S_2 with no shift in the demand curve at all.[33] Ignoring the possibility of a rightward shift in the demand curve from D_1 to D_2 (we return to this possibility below), the second distinguishing feature of the development of the computer industry is the unprecedented speed with which diminishing returns set in;

while computer users steadily enjoy an increasing amount of consumer surplus as the price falls, the declining point of intersection of the supply curve with the fixed demand curve implies a rapid decline in the marginal utility or benefit of computer power.

The accelerated rate of price decline in computer attributes has been accompanied since 1995 by the invention of the Internet.[34] In perhaps the most rapid diffusion of any invention since television in the late 1940s and early 1950s, by the end of the year 2000 the percentage of U.S. households hooked up to the Internet reached 50 percent.[35] Surely the invention of web browsers and the explosive growth of e-commerce should be interpreted as a rightward shift in the demand curve in the bottom frame of Figure 3.9 from D_1 to D_2. Such a rightward shift in the demand curve would imply an increase in the benefits provided by all computers, both old and new.[36]

However, if there had been a discontinuous rightward shift in the demand curve for computer hardware due to the spread of the Internet, we should have observed a noticeable flattening of the slope of the price–quantity relationship in the top frame of Figure 3.9, as the rate of increase of quantity accelerated relative to the rate of decline in price, but we do not. The rate of change of price and quantity both accelerate after 1995 (as indicated by the greater spacing between annual observations) but the slope does not change appreciably, suggesting that the spread of the Internet is a byproduct of rapid technological change that is faster than in previous decades but not qualitatively different in the relationship between supply and demand than earlier advances in the computer industry.

[33] Three examples of this graph applied to computers exhibiting no shift in the demand curve are Brynjolfsson (1996: 290), Gordon (1990: 46) and Sichel (1997: 17). The supply curves in this graph have been drawn as horizontal lines, both to simplify the subsequent discussion of consumer surplus and because there is no evidence of a rising marginal cost of producing additional computer speed, memory, and other characteristics at a given level of technology.

[34] Here to simplify the presentation we take the Internet as being synonymous with the World Wide Web and the invention of web browsers, although the use of the Internet for e-mail, at least in the academic and scientific community, dates back at least to the early 1980s.

[35] This projection is made by Henry Harteveldt, Senior Analyst at Forrester Research, in communications with the author.

[36] In terms of elementary economics, there is an increase in the consumer surplus associated with the lower supply curve S2 from the triangle JP2B to the larger triangle KP2C.

The data on the price and quantity of computer characteristics have previously been used to "map out" the demand curve (Brynjolfsson, 1996: 290). In fact, the slope of the price–quantity relationship was appreciably flatter during 1972–87 than during 1987–95 or 1995–9. If the demand curve has not shifted, the inverse of these slopes is the price elasticity of demand, namely -1.96, -1.19, and -1.11 in these three intervals, which can be compared with Brynjolfsson's (1996: 292) estimated price elasticity of -1.33 over the period 1970–89. The apparent decline in the price elasticity is consistent with the view that the most important uses of computers were developed more than a decade into the past, not currently.

3.4. The New Economy and the Sources of Technological Change

Our macroeconomic analysis has reached the paradoxical conclusion that the New Economy, interpreted as an acceleration of the rate of price decline of computer hardware and peripherals, is responsible for most of the acceleration of U.S. ALP and MFP growth, at least the part that cannot be attributed to a temporary cyclical effect. In the major portion of durable manufacturing devoted to producing goods other than computer hardware there appears to have been considerable technical dynamism, with a substantial acceleration in MFP growth and no apparent contribution of temporary cyclical effects. Yet there does not appear to have been a revival in MFP growth outside of durable manufacturing, and the acceleration of labor productivity growth in the rest of the economy seems to be attributable to the benefits of buying more computers, not any fundamental technological advance that goes beyond a return on investment in computers similar to the return on investment in any other type of capital equipment.

Albeit narrowly based in computer hardware, at least in the official statistics, the apparent "rupture" or discontinuity in the rate of technical change in the mid-1990s forces us to inquire as to its sources and lessons for understanding the economic history of the United States and

other nations. The United States is now almost universally believed to have surged to the forefront in most of the IT industries, and even a substantial correction of the stock market will still leave U.S. hi-tech companies dominating the league table of the world's leaders in market capitalization. While our detailed quantitative analysis of the U.S. productivity revival has emphasized computer hardware, our overview of the U.S. performance focusses more broadly on software, telecommunications, pharmaceuticals, and biotech.

3.4.1. National Technological Leadership: General Considerations

The discontinuity of technical change in the United States in the mid-1990s was not predicted in advance, although its significance was spotted almost immediately by *Business Week* and some other astute observers.[37] A decade ago it was "Japan as Number One", and briefly the market value of Japanese equities exceeded that of U.S. equities. Rosenberg (1986: 25) perceptively generalizes about the difficulty of forecasting the consequences of inventions in advance: "A disinterested observer who happened to be passing by at Kitty Hawk on that fateful day in 1903 might surely be excused if he did not walk away with visions of 747s or C-5As in his head." The great success of Japanese firms in dominating many leading technologies in the 1980s did not appear to give them any head start in dominating the new technologies of the 1990s. Rosenberg points to the failure of carriage makers to play any role in the development of the automobile, or even the failure of steam locomotive makers to participate in the development of the diesel locomotive. Thus, it is perhaps not surprising that Japanese electronics companies did not participate to any great extent in the particular interplay of chip-making technology and software development that created the Internet and the post-1995 technical acceleration in computer hardware. We -return below

---

[37] Most notably Edward Yardeni, now the Chief Economist of Deutsche Banc, and Alex Brown, who early in the 1990s predicted both the stock market boom and the revival of productivity growth.

to some of the possible causes of U.S. leadership in the technical developments of the 1990s.

Many inventions initially created to solve a narrow problem (for instance, the steam engine was initially invented to pump water out of flooded mines) turn out to have widespread further uses that are not initially foreseen. Major inventions spawn numerous complementary developments; while the initial motivation for the internal combustion engine was to improve the performance-to-weight ratio of the steam engine, it made possible not only motor transport and air transport, but such complementary developments as the suburb, supermarket, superhighway, and the tropical vacation industry. In turn, the complementary inventions raise the consumer surplus associated with the invention, and this may continue for a long time. The invention of the Internet is just one of many byproducts of the invention of electricity that raise the consumer surplus of that initial major invention.[38]

The literature on technology distinguishes between the initial invention and its subsequent development and diffusion. A longstanding puzzle in the retardation of British economic growth after the 1870s is the fact that many inventions initially made by British inventors were brought to commercial success in the United States, Japan, and elsewhere. This issue of who captures the fruits of innovation suggests that the British were not alone in losing out. The U.S. invention of videotape was followed by exploitation of the consumer VCR market that was almost entirely achieved by Japanese companies. The Finnish company Nokia took over leadership in mobile phones from Motorola. Within any economy there are winners and losers as upstart companies (Intel, Microsoft) seize the advantage in developing technology while leaving older competitors (IBM, Wang, Digital Equipment, Xerox) behind.

While predicting technological developments in advance is exceedingly difficult, there is an ample literature which points to particular national characteristics that help to explain, at least in retrospect, why particular inventions and industries came to be dominated by particular countries.[39] Perhaps the one generalization that spans most industries is the role of the product cycle. No matter what the causes of initial national leadership, technology eventually diffuses from the leading nations to other nations that may have lower labor costs. It is beyond the scope of this discussion to explain why some nations, for example, Korea, Taiwan, and Singapore, seem to have done so much better than other nations, for example, Brazil or India, in combining technological duplication with an advantage, at least initially, in labor costs, in industries ranging from automobiles to chip, computer, and disk-drive manufacturing.

3.4.2. Sources of U.S. Technological Leadership

3.4.2.1. The Traditional Sources of U.S. Advantage According to the standard data compiled by Maddison and others, the level of income per person in the United States moved ahead of that in the United Kingdom in the late nineteenth century and has remained in first place among the major developed nations ever since. An extensive literature on the sources of U.S. superiority (e.g., Wright, 1990) identifies national advantages both in the supply of resources and in national characteristics of demand. The United States achieved initial leadership in petrochemicals in part because of its abundant supply of cheap domestic petroleum, while its leadership in machine tools was the result of its early adoption of mass production methods, which in turn reflected its relative scarcity of labor and its large internal market. In turn mass production, together with long distances, cheap land, and the low density of urban development help to explain why the United States achieved such an enormous early lead in automobile production and ownership in the 1920s. In turn, the mass market for automobiles fed back into a rapidly increasing demand for gasoline and stimulated further

---

[38] An explicit analysis of the effect of complementary inventions on the consumer surplus of the initial invention is provided by Bresnahan and Gordon (1997: 7–11).

[39] The generalizations in the next several paragraphs are selected from the more important points made by Mowery and Nelson (1999a).

developments in petroleum and petrochemical manufacturing.

However, it is less clear that the United States' large domestic market provided a universal source of advantage throughout the history of technological development over the last two centuries. Between 1870 and 1914, flows of goods, capital, and immigrants were notably free, and trade could create international markets on the scale of the U.S. domestic markets, as demonstrated by German dominance in chemicals. After 1960, Japan rose to prominence and even domination in one industry after another, with export markets providing the scale that was lacking, at least initially, at home.

3.4.2.2. Educational Attainment and University Research

Close integration of industrial research and development (R&D) and university research is credited with German domination of the chemical products industry between the 1870s and early 1920s, as well as German and Swiss leadership in the development of pharmaceuticals in the early part of the twentieth century. More generally, a rise in educational attainment is one of the sources of rising output per hour. While the first cited role of the education system in technological development is the rise of the German chemical industry after 1870, a set of relatively uncoordinated policies at the state and local level resulted in the United States achieving the first universal secondary education between 1910 and 1940 (Goldin, 1998) and the highest rate of participation in college education after World War II.

Even in the dismal days of U.S. pessimism during the years of the productivity slowdown, it was widely recognized that the United States' private and state-supported research universities were its most successful export industry, at least as measured by its lead over other countries and its appeal for students from the rest of the world. The interplay among these research universities, government research grants, and private industry was instrumental in achieving U.S. leadership in the IT industry, and it was no coincidence that Silicon Valley happened to be located next to Stanford University or that

another concentration of IT companies in the hardware, software, and biotech industries was located in the Boston area near Massachusetts Institute of Technology and Harvard.

A U.S. educational advantage of possible importance is its early development of the graduate school of business and its continuing near-monopoly in this type of education. The mere existence of business schools did not provide any solution to the productivity slowdown of the 1970s and 1980s, and indeed the ongoing superiority of Japanese firms in automobiles and consumer electronics elicited the cynical joke in those years that "the secret advantage of the Japanese manufacturers is that they have no world-class business schools." While U.S. business schools were indeed weak in teaching such specialities as manufacturing production and quality control, they excelled in finance and general management strategy. These skills came into their own in the 1990s and interacted with the rise of the venture capital industry and Internet start-up companies; in the United States more than elsewhere there was a ready supply of thousands of well-educated MBAs, both knowledgeable about finance and receptive to a culture of innovation and risk-taking. Further, U.S. business schools have provided a wealth of talent to further develop U.S. worldwide dominance in investment banking, accounting, and management-consulting firms.

3.4.2.3. Government-funded Military and Civilian Research

Ironically for a country that has been suspicious of government involvement, it is the United States that appears to demonstrate the closest links between government policy and technological leadership. Research support from the National Institutes of Health is credited with postwar U.S. leadership in pharmaceuticals and biomedical research. Defense-funded research and government-funded grants is credited with the early emergence of U.S. leadership in semiconductors, computers, software, biotech, and the Internet itself. Government antitrust policy is credited with the emergence of a software industry largely independent of computer hardware manufacturers.

There are notable differences between the U.S. method of supporting higher education and research and that found in European countries like France, Germany, and the United Kingdom. First, the U.S. mix of private universities and those financed at the state and local level promotes competition and allows the top tier of the private university sector the budgetary freedom to pay high salaries, fund opulent research labs, and achieve the highest levels of quality, in turn attracting many top faculty members and graduate students from other countries. Second, much of U.S. central government research support is allocated through a peer-review system that favors a meritocracy of young, active researchers and discourages elitism and continuing support for senior professors whose best ideas are in the past. In Europe, a much larger share of central government support to universities and research institutes goes to general budgetary support that tends to result in a more equal salary structure less prone to reward academic "stars" and also relies less on the periodic quality hurdle imposed by peer review. This set of differences is in addition to specific national shortcomings, for example, the hierarchical dominance of senior research professors in Germany.

3.4.2.4. *Other Government Policies*

Explicit government policies to encourage the development of specific industries by trade protection and financial subsidies may have been successful in helping to accelerate the rise of Japan and Korea to industrial success, but they have been less successful in the United States and Europe and indeed may have backfired in Japan in the past decade. The relevance of particular government policies, from protection to defense spending to antitrust, differs sufficiently across industries as to discourage generalizations. In the industries of most concern to us in this chapter—semiconductors, computer hardware, and computer software, the most important aspect of public policy appears to have been the relatively unfocussed support of research and training by the U.S. government. The literature on the U.S. resurgence in semiconductor production as well as its continuing dominance in software also

emphasizes the role of private enforcement of intellectual property rights and regulation of licensing agreements (see Bresnahan and Melerba, 1999; Mowery, 1999). The U.S. pharmaceutical industry initially gained an advantage through massive government support during World War II, health-related research support during most of the postwar period, and a long tradition of strong U.S. patent protection—patent protection was also strong in parts of Europe, but not in Italy and also not in Japan. U.S. drug companies were also able to make high profits, much of which was reinvested in R&D, as a result of high rents earned in the face of a fragmented health care system with no attempt by the government to place price or profit ceilings on drug companies (see Pisano, chapter 14).

Another set of U.S. policies could be interpreted as "enforcement of benign neglect." The U.S. government took no action to arrest the erosion of state sales tax revenues as Internet e-commerce merchants sold items without charging any sales tax to customers. In effect, the freedom of e-commerce transactions from the burden of sales taxes amounted to government subsidization of shipping charges, since for e-commerce these usually amounted to roughly the same surcharge on listed prices as sales taxes at traditional bricks and mortar outlets. The U.S. government also maintained a zero-tariff regime for trade in electronic components, fostering large trade flows in both directions and a large U.S. trade deficit in IT manufacturing.

3.4.2.5. *Capital Markets*

In the 1980s, U.S. capital markets seemed to be a source of U.S. industrial weakness, with their emphasis on short-run profit maximization, and there was much envy of the access of Japanese firms to low-cost bank capital that played a role in the temporary period of Japanese domination of the semiconductor industry. But the U.S. capital market turned out to be a blessing in disguise. A long tradition of government securities regulation that forced public disclosure and information and of access of equity research analysts to internal company information had fostered a large and active market for public offerings, and this together with the relatively recent emergence of the venture capital industry provided ample finance for start-up companies once the technological groundwork for the Internet was laid in the mid-1990s.[40] Lerner (chapter 13) identifies a critical policy change as fostering the relatively recent rise of the U.S. venture capital industry, namely a ruling that allowed pension funds to invest in venture capital firms.

3.4.2.6. Language and Immigration

The literature on technological leadership omits two sources of U.S. advantage that are surely not insignificant. While language has little to do with domination in computer hardware (where indeed many of the components are imported), it is surely important for the U.S. software industry that English long ago became the world's leading second language in addition to being spoken as a first language by a critical mass of the world's educated population. Another oft-neglected factor that should be discussed more often is the longstanding openness of the United States to immigration and the role of immigrants from India, East Asia, and elsewhere in providing the skilled labor that has been essential to the rise of Silicon Valley.

Another aspect of U.S. advantage and disadvantage is also perhaps too little discussed. The technology literature summarized above places heavy emphasis on the unique role of U.S. research universities in providing a competitive atmosphere geared to the attraction of the best faculty performing the best research. Yet every year another set of test results is announced in which the United States score far down the league tables in math and science when compared to numerous countries in Europe and Asia. Those who wring their hands about

the state of U.S. elementary and secondary education might better spend their energies lobbying Congress to increase the immigration quotas for highly educated individuals with skills in those areas where some Americans are weak, science and engineering. And those who would argue that loosening of high-skilled quotas should occur at the cost of a reduction in low-skilled quotas are urged to consider the many benefits of immigration in general, including the provision of new workers to ease the strain of overly tight labor markets, the revitalization of many central cities, and the postponement forever of any so-called Social Security "crisis."

3.5. Comparisons with Other Countries

In most comparisons among the leading industrialized nations, the United Kingdom (and sometimes Canada) occupy a central ground between the extremes of American exceptionalism and the opposite tendencies of the continental Europeans and Japanese, whether concerning the level of unemployment, employment protection or the lack thereof, the degree of inequality, and the extent of government spending. Yet in comparing the extent of U.S. technological leadership with other countries, the story is not one of extremes, and the balance of advantage varies widely by industry.

The United States dominates most strongly in microprocessors and in computer software. As documented by Langlois (chapter 10), the extent of Intel's domination of the worldwide market for microprocessors is perhaps unprecedented in industrial history, and the same could be said for Microsoft. However, the U.S. advantage in computer hardware is qualified by the role of Asian countries in providing components like memory chips, hard drives, and laptop screens. In fact the United States runs a large trade deficit in computer hardware and peripherals, both because of component imports from Asia and because a substantial share of production by U.S. companies like Intel and Dell takes place not just at home but also in foreign countries like Ireland. In mobile

---

[40] As usual there are interconnections between the various sources of U.S. advantage. For instance, the best U.S. private universities have been a critical source of U.S. technological leadership and their wealth and power have been further augmented by their recent investments in U.S. venture capital firms. For instance, in 1999 Harvard made roughly a 150 percent return on its venture capital investments and a return of over 40 percent on its entire endowment which now totals almost U.S.$20 billion.

telephones, the United States has been handi-capped by regulation that favored too much competition and allowed multiple standards, thus allowing the dominant producers of GSM equipment and infrastructure (Nokia and Erics-son) to run away with the worldwide mobile phone market. The U.S. pharmaceutical indus-try also faces strong competition from U.K., German, and Swiss firms.

Nevertheless, several sources of systemic U.S. advantage stand out, most notably the mixed system of government- and private-funded research universities, the large role of U.S. government agencies providing research fund-ing based on a criterion of peer review, and the strong position in a worldwide perspective of U.S. business schools and U.S.-owned invest-ment banking, accounting, and management consulting firms. By comparison, Germany seems particularly weak in its failure to reform its old-fashioned hierarchical university system, its bureaucratic rules that inhibit start-up firms, its reliance on bank debt finance, and its weak-ness in venture capital and equity finance (see Siebert and Stolpe, chapter 5). France suffers from over centralized government control, a system of universities and research institutions which places more emphasis on rewarding those with an elite educational pedigree rather than those currently working on the research frontier, and a culture (with its frequent strikes by farmers and government workers) which is relatively hostile to innovation and change (see Messerlin, chapter 6).

Until its structural reforms and privatizations of the 1980s and 1990s, the United Kingdom shared with France and Germany a labor market dominated by strong unions. While the strong unions are gone, the United King-dom continues to suffer from handicaps that date back a century or more, including a short-fall of technical skills among manual workers and a lack of graduate management training and business-oriented culture among highly educated workers. Where the Untied Kingdom does well, as in investment banking or as a desti-nation of inward foreign investment, it relies on a relatively narrow set of advantages, including the traditional role of the City of London as a financial center, and the same advantage that

the English language provides, that is, as a comfortable place for Asian firms to build plants, to the United States, Canada, Ireland, Australia, and other parts of the former British Empire.

3.6. Conclusion

The outstanding performance of the U.S. econ-omy in the late 1990s raises the danger of a resurgent U.S. triumphalism, perhaps symbo-lized by an imaginary *Arc de Triomphe* erected over Sand Hill Road at the border between Palo Alto and Menlo Park, CA, the heart of the venture capital industry that has funded many of the start-up companies of the New Economy. But while the disastrous aftermath of the glorious inflation-free growth of 1927–9 is very unlikely to follow the glowing economic conditions of 1997–2000, we should be careful about extrapolating the successes of the recent past or in pretending that success has been universal.

While the fruitful collaboration of govern-ment research funding, world-leading private universities, innovative private firms, and a dynamic capital market set the stage for U.S. domination of the industries that constitute the New Economy, these preconditions did not prevent the United States from experien-cing the dismal 1972–95 years of the productiv-ity growth slowdown and near-stagnation of real wages, and they do not give the United States an advantage in many other industries. A quarter century after the invasion of Japanese auto imports, the quality rankings of automobiles still are characterized by a bimodal distribution in which Japanese and German nameplates (even those manufactured in the United States) dominate the highest rankings and U.S. name-plates dominate the lowest.[41] The United States shows no sign of regaining leadership in the manufacturing of computer peripherals or machine tools.

The rapid rate of output growth in the U.S. economy between 1995 and 2000 was facilitated

[41] See *Consumer Reports*, April, 2000, and the latest J. D. Powers initial quality rankings.

by two unsustainable "safety valves," the steady decline in the unemployment rate and the steady increase in the current account deficit. Since neither can continue forever, growth in both output and in productivity are likely to be less in the next five years than in the last, and the likely adjustment in the stock market may cause at least part of the U.S. economic miracle to unravel. Further, a basic finding of my recent research as summarized earlier in this chapter (see Table 3.2) is that the dominant source of the post-1995 productivity growth revival was an acceleration in the growth of computer investment, which boosted productivity growth both through the direct effect of making the computers and the indirect benefits of using the computers. If the growth of computer investment should slow down in the next five years to a rate more similar to the years before 1995 than the years since then, half or more of the productivity growth revival might disappear.

This chapter has emphasized the production and use of computers and the spread of the World Wide Web as the main channel by which technology has contributed to the U.S. productivity revival and economic miracle of the late 1990s. Much less has been said about telecommunications and biotechnology. Telecom connections have been essential to the networking effects of the web and to creating the demand for ever-more powerful computer hardware. But existing government price deflators for telecom equipment do not decline at anything like the rates registered by computer hardware, and so, simply as a matter of arith-metic, the producers of telecom equipment do not contribute to the growth of real GDP and productivity in amounts remotely approaching the contribution of computer hardware.

For biotechnology, the measurement failure is more complete and harder to repair. Benefits of biotech innovations in prolonging life or reducing pain are not included in GDP and are simply missed in our national accounts and productivity statistics. Advances in medical technology, to the extent that they are produced by the government or in the nonprofit hospitals and universities, are excluded by definition from the core sector covered by the productivity statistics, namely the nonfarm private business sector. Like many benefits of the "New Economy," biotech research may boost consumer welfare without having any measurable impact on productivity. But this is an old story—the great old inventions like electricity and the internal combustion engine delivered unparalleled increases in consumer welfare in the early and mid-twentieth century as electric light lengthened the day, consumer appliances reduced household drudgery, air conditioning made the South habitable, and motor cars, not to mention airplanes, produced flexible travel patterns and large savings of time. The fruits of innovation in telecom and biotech are both wondrous and partly unmeasured, and exactly the same could be said, with even greater emphasis, of all the great inventions dating back to the dawn of the first industrial revolution in the late eighteenth century.

4

Japan

Adam S. Posen

4.1. Introduction

The Toyota Commemorative Museum of Industry and Technology gives its visitors much to ponder. Established at the site in Nagoya where in 1911 Sakichi Toyoda founded his automatic loom factory, the basis of the family fortune which later funded his son Kiichiro's development of automobile production, the museum was opened on June 11, 1994, on the 100th anniversary of Toyota's birth. It is a popular stop on field trips for Japanese schoolchildren, who are required to study the automobile industry in the third grade. The messages which Toyota wishes to instill in its young visitors are the importance of "making things" and of "creativity and research." And confronting all museum visitors upon entry, having central place in the vast and largely empty first room of the exhibits, is Sakichi Toyoda's one-of-a-kind vertical circular loom.

As described in the Museum's catalog, "Even in the closing years of his life, [Sakichi Toyoda] continued to work to perfect the [vertical] circular loom. To symbolize this unfailing spirit of his, we are proud to exhibit the only circular loom he developed that is still in existence." This first "Symbolic Exhibit in the Museum,"

I am extremely grateful to Robert Gordon and Benn Steil for extensive, detailed comments which prompted a major revision of this chapter, and to the Council on Foreign Relations for sponsorship of this project. I am also indebted to numerous Japanese officials and economists, especially Nobuyuki Arai, Norihiko Ishiguro, Takashi Kiuchi, Mikihiro Matsuoka, Kazuyuki Motohashi, Masahiro Nagayasu, Masao Nishikawa, Tetsuro Sugiura, Tatsuya Terazawa, Yuko Ueno, and Kazuhiko Yano, for their generous sharing of data and information. All opinions expressed, and any remaining errors, in this chapter are mine alone.

whose distinctive outline serves as the Museum's logo, was manufactured in 1924. Although Toyoda first applied for a patent in 1906 on a circular loom design, and eventually held a patent in eighteen countries for the concept, and although the circular loom is quieter than flat looms (meaning it is also more energy efficient), and able to produce longer bolts of cloth without seams, the circular loom was never produced in volume. In fact, no sales, let alone profits, were ever made from this innovation. In 1924, Toyoda also perfected the Type G Automatic Loom, a flat "non-stop shuttle changing loom"—embodying an incremental but significant improvement on previous loom technology—which became Toyota's all-time bestseller in the sector. The Type G Loom, however, is not the Museum's symbolic first exhibit or logo; instead, it takes its place chronologically back in the succession of exhibits.

Why does one of Japan's, and the world's, leading manufacturing corporations choose to feature an innovative product, which was never brought successfully to market nor became any sort of technological standard, as the emblem of its tradition of industry and technology? Neither corporate public relations efforts, nor Japanese culture, are generally known for their sense of deliberate irony. Neither is known for rewarding quixotic individual quests of little practical value to the larger purpose, either. Whether intentional or not, perhaps the message is the one given at face value: that technological innovation is its own reward, and should be appraised on its own noncommercial merits. While the process of innovation is certainly related to a corporation's profitability, there is no easy one-to-one relationship between the best innovation and the best economic results, beyond the fact that people driven to innovation over the long-run have the fundamental potential for success.

What is true about innovation and performance for Toyota may well be true for Japan as well. The story of Japan's miraculous economic development after World War II is engrained in the world's memory. No other large country had ever come so far, so fast. No other country from Asia (or anywhere else outside of Europe's direct lineage) had attained Western levels of technology and wealth, was treated as an equal or even feared as an economic competitor by the United States, nor had taken leadership in many advanced industrial sectors. No other country in history had racked up so many consecutive years of positive income growth. By the end of the 1980s, with the relative decline of American economic performance, and the influence of Japanese investors felt worldwide, scholars and pundits alike were advancing a "Japanese model" of economic management. This model included supposedly distinctive aspects of Japanese policy and corporate practice, including industrial policy, an emphasis on incremental innovation of industrial processes, relationship banking between business firms and their "Main Banks," and export orientation. There seemed to be a clear message that Japan, as part of this model, had assembled a "national innovation system" which conferred significant advantages for growth.

Ten years later, the economic world has been turned upside down. It is the United States whose system is now held up as a model for economies around the world, which has run several years of strongly positive growth in a row, and which is considered the home of cutting edge technologies in the most attention-getting sectors, like information technology and biotechnology. It is Japan which is now caught in the midst of an economic malaise which it cannot seem to understand, let alone shake. This nearly complete reversal of fortune in Japan would seem to be a critical case study for understanding the determinants of national economic performance. Especially given the fear on the part of some American commentators and officials lasting into the mid-1990s that

Japan was building an insurmountable lead in "critical technologies,"—as exemplified by the pressures for Sematech—it is important to distinguish perception from reality in both technological and economic performance.

From the perspective of 2001, after 10 years of slow or negative growth in Japan, there is reason to wonder whether Japanese technical prowess evaporated for some reason, whether national innovation systems can be somehow appropriate for capitalizing on particular waves of technological development and not others, or whether perhaps technological innovation alone is insufficient to guarantee good economic performance. On this last point, it should be recognized that the bulk of the Japanese economy conducts its business largely independent of high-tech or anything resembling technological innovation. In this, however, Japan is completely normal, not distinctive—all advanced economies, including the United States, have vast shares of their resources employed in retail, service, governmental, and even manufacturing activities where technical change does not significantly alter productivity. There are only so many papers an academic can produce, so many patients a nurse can tend, so many students a teacher can teach, and so many 747s skilled mechanics can assemble, even as the IT revolution proceeds. A technological change must be very great in effect, or unusually wide in applicability as well as diffusion, to change a country's overall economic performance.[1]

In that light, it is worth emphasizing just how serious the Japanese economic downturn of the last decade has been as compared to the growth seen in the previous three decades in Japan or to the performance of the other industrial democracies. In the post-war period, no developed country lost as much growth versus potential in a recession as Japan did from 1990 to the present (a cumulative output gap in excess of

---

[1] This is in a sense the message of Oliner and Sichel (1996), that to that point, investment in computers and related equipment was simply too small a share of the U.S. economy to explain much in the way of swings in American growth. Oliner and Sichel (2000), by contrast, updated their results once there had been sufficient investment for the IT sector to matter.

15 percent of a year's gross domestic product (GDP)[2]), and no developed country's banking crisis imposed as high a direct cost to its citizens (upwards of 15 percent of a year's GDP in bad loans requiring public bailout, and still rising—compared to the entire U.S. Savings and Loan clean-up which cost less than 3 percent of a year's GDP). Corporate bankruptcies have been at all time highs, and unemployment has risen to levels never before seen in Japan, with no end to either trend in sight. Understanding this remarkable deterioration of Japanese national economic performance has to be a central concern of any assessment of the roles of various factor in economic growth, and, given the size of the change, thereby sets a very high bar for the degree to which technological innovation must have changed in this instance to have played a leading role.

This chapter is organized around the relationship between Japanese technological innovation and the sustained decline in Japan's growth rate in the 1990s as compared to the previous two decades (the very high growth rates of the catch-up period in the 1950s and 1960s are assumed to have been unsustainable). Examination of the huge shift in Japanese economic performance raises three aspects of the relationship between innovation and growth for consideration. The first aspect is how macroeconomic performance can radically change without any accompanying change in the inputs to the innovative process. Japan's national system of innovation is largely unaltered in the 1990s from the system that existed during Japan's glory days, with a few minor alterations probably including improvements in innovative capacity.[3] The second aspect is the possibility that maintenance of a sustained high level of technological innovation can continue even as the economy surrounding the national innovation suffers. In today's Japan, the production of

high-tech patents and high-end exports, that is, the measurable output of innovation, continues largely undiminished despite the erosion of macroeconomic conditions. It is usually assumed that, during harder economic times, financing and long-term investment for innovation are harder to come by, yet in the case of Japan in the 1990s that constraint appears not to have arisen.

The third aspect is how, in an industrial democracy with free flows of information, advances in productivity can remain in a limited number of sectors without diffusing across the economy. This is both a question of social organization and of the nature of the technology in question. It has long been known, for example, that Japan has a "Dual Economy" with a gap in technical achievement between the highly competitive export sector and the backwards domestic manufacturing, retail, and service sectors; this gap was true during the years of the Japanese miracle, and remains true if not widening today. In the United States, by comparison, there is an open debate whether the current such gap will persist. Gordon (chapter 3) argues that most of the technical advancement in the United States in the 1990s was confined to the manufacture of information technology, because of the limited nature of the IT revolution. On the other side, the Council of Economic Advisers (CEA) (2001) argues that IT actually diffused into use much more widely in the U.S. economy than previously believed, both because it is a "transformative" technology (applicable throughout the economy) and because the U.S. form of economic organization is prepared to take advantage of such a technology; that report explicitly contrasts U.S. flexibility in technological adoption to the barriers to the reallocation of capital and labor in the Japanese economy. Even if valid, such a characterization of Japan emphasizes that the link between technological innovation and national economic performance is intermediated by factors which have little to do with innovativeness per se, and which may affect national productivity more broadly as much as they interfere with technical diffusion.

These three aspects of the Japanese experience—that innovation inputs and outputs

---

[2] See Posen (1998: Appendix 1; 2001) for discussions of various means and results for estimating the Japanese output gap.

[3] A similar observation can be made with reference to the United States, which underwent little change in the structure of the innovation system, but a radical change in performance, between the 1980s and 1990s.

remained unchanged even as national economic performance varied widely, and that factors outside the national innovation system as traditionally defined have to be invoked to make technology play a leading explanatory role—could be troubling if one insisted on believing that technological innovation and national economic performance are intimately related. The experience of Japan would seem to indicate that such a belief should not be too tightly held. Accepting an imperfect, or at least very long-term, connection between the two is to be preferred to making a circular argument, as some do, that the reason Japanese economic performance is poor is because the entire national innovation system that once worked for Japan is "inappropriate" for today's world and technology, and the reason that we know the innovation system is inappropriate is that performance is poor. There are many other factors that determine a national economy's macroeconomic performance over periods of several years besides its technological capabilities, including economic management of the business cycle and the financial system, and there are many factors determining the ability of a country to innovate, beyond its growth rate. The inability of Japan's world-beating process innovation and productivity in its export manufacturing sectors to limit the downward swing of the rest of the Japanese economy is an important reminder of just how independent or exogenous technological development is from most of what economics is about—as was the case for Sakichi Toyoda's circular loom.

4.2. The Facts of Japanese Growth Performance: Ongoing Decline in Growth, Sharp Fall-off in the 1990s

4.2.1. What Happened in Japan

The decline of economic performance in Japan in the 1990s was a sharp and lasting contrast to what went before. From 1990 to 1997, first there was a fall in asset prices, then corporate fixed investment, then in housing starts, then inventories, and then finally consumption. The stock market peaked in December 1989, and land

prices reached their height a year later. The OECD has estimated that the net wealth lost in the asset price declines of 1989–97 was on the order of 200 percent of a year's GDP, with 50 percent of those losses borne directly by households (at least on paper). Officially, the recession began in February 1991, and lasted until October 1993 (see Table 4.1). As Motonoshi and Yoshikawa (1999) observe, corporate investment was the key variable, with the fall in investment in 1992–4 and in 1998 more than two standard deviations in size from the 1971–90 average year-on-year movements. Small and medium enterprises were particularly hard hit as the 1990s wore on, arguably due to a credit crunch as liquidity and credit standards tightened in the second half of the decade.[4] Size aside, this is actually the usual sequence of movements in demand components for a business cycle downturn following a bubble. What is unusual among the demand components listed in Table 4.1 is the persistent flatness and in fact decline in consumption growth once things turned sour.

The contrast was striking with the outstanding growth performance of the Japanese economy in the post-war period up until 1990, although every decade showed a slowdown in average growth rate (see Table 4.2). In both the 1970s and 1980s, real GDP averaged 4.0 percent or more annually, as opposed to the 1.5–2.5 percent a year growth seen in most of the other OECD economies including the United States. Despite claims by some about Japanese households' reluctance to consume, prior to 1990, private consumption growth was positive, in fact more than comparable to the growth in residential investment, and even

---

[4] MITI *White Paper on International Trade* 1999 characterized matters: "[T]he lack of depth in capital supply—for example in the setting of interest [rate] levels in line with risk—in terms of the various capital intermediation routes obstructs the smooth supply of capital to companies with credit ratings below a certain level, such as middle-ranked and small and medium companies [as well as credit for] new businesses, all of which have limited physical mortgage capacity." And the Japanese banking system which depended upon land collateral as the basis for all credit assessments, ceased to lend when the real estate market collapsed, except to rollover bad debt to borrowers who had only land as repayment.

TABLE 4.1
Contribution of Demand Components (percentage of GDP)

	GDP growth	Consumption	Housing investment	Fixed investment	Inventory investment	Public consumption	Public investment	Exports	Imports
1980	2.8	0.6	−0.6	1	0	0.3	−0.5	1.4	0.7
1981	3.2	0.9	−0.1	0.5	0	0.5	0.3	1.2	0
1982	3.1	2.6	0	0.2	0	0.3	−0.2	0.1	0.2
1983	2.3	2	−0.3	0.2	−0.3	0.3	−0.2	0.5	0.2
1984	3.9	1.6	−0.1	1.5	0	0.2	−0.3	1.5	−0.8
1985	4.4	2	0.1	1.7	0.3	0	−0.5	0.6	0.1
1986	2.9	2	0.4	0.7	−0.2	0.5	0.2	−0.7	−0.1
1987	4.2	2.5	1.1	0.9	−0.1	0.2	0.5	−0.1	−0.7
1988	6.2	3.1	0.7	2.3	0.6	0.2	0.3	0.6	−1.6
1989	4.8	2.8	0.1	2.4	0.1	0.2	0	0.9	−1.6
1990	5.1	2.6	0.3	2	−0.2	0.1	0.3	0.7	−0.8
1991	3.8	1.5	−0.5	1.2	0.3	0.2	0.3	0.6	0.3
1992	1	1.2	−0.3	−1.1	−0.5	0.2	1	0.5	0.1
1993	0.3	0.7	0.1	−1.9	−0.1	0.2	1.2	0.2	0
1994	0.6	1.1	0.4	−0.9	−0.3	0.2	0.2	0.5	−0.8
1995	1.5	1.2	−0.3	0.8	0.2	0.3	0.1	0.6	−1.4
1996	5.1	1.7	0.7	1.8	0.4	0.2	0.8	0.8	−1.3
1997	1.4	0.6	−0.9	1.2	−0.1	0.1	−0.9	1.4	−0.1
1998	−2.8	−0.6	−0.6	−2.1	−0.1	0.1	0	−0.3	0.9
1999	0.6								
2000	1.9								

Source: Motonishi and Yoshikawa (1999: Table 1).
Note: 2000 GDP Growth is OECD Forecast, November 2000.

TABLE 4.2
Long-Term Performance of the Japanese Economy

	Average annual real growth rate (percent)			
	1961–70	1971–80	1981–90	1991–7
GDP	10.2	4.5	4	1.7
Private consumption	9	4.7	3.7	2
Public consumption	4.8	4.8	2.5	1.9
Residual investment	16.8	3.2	3.9	−1.8
Business fixed investment	16.6	2.8	8.1	0.6
Public investment	14.4	5.9	0.8	4.9
Exports	16.1	9.7	5.4	5.1
Imports	14.7	5.9	6.3	4.3
Employee compensation	11.1	5.8	3.7	2.1
Disposable income	9.5	4.8	3	2.2

Source: OECD Economic Survey 1997–8.

meeting or exceeding the rate of growth in disposable income from 1971 to 1997. Meanwhile, exports rate of growth slowed every decade. The presumptive bubble can be seen in the 8.1 percent growth in business fixed investment from 1981 to 1990, especially when one considers that Japan was in recession up to the end of 1984, meaning most of that investment was concentrated in just five years.

Looking a bit more descriptively, it is possible to follow Yoshikawa (2000) and break up postwar Japanese economic development before 1990 into two periods. From 1955 to 1972, the Japanese economy grew by an average 10 percent a year. Like continental Europe during its period of post-war rebuilding, the Japanese workforce started with extensive technological skills and other human capital close to the U.S. level (Goto and Odagiri, 1997). Like continental Europe, there was a rapid shift of households from rural to urban areas, of production from agricultural to industrial products, increasing the number of households. And, like in postwar continental Europe, rising real incomes fed and were fed by demand for new consumer durables. The similarity with Germany up to the first oil shock is especially close; Japanese industry made rapid technical progress in chemicals, iron and steel, paper and pulp, and in transport machinery. Japan, like Germany, accumulated a great deal of capital with its high savings rate, and ended up having a capital-to-labor ratio of almost twice that in the U.S., despite the ongoing increase in manufacturing hours worked.

From 1972 to 1990, Japanese growth continued at higher than American or even European rates, but slowed noticeably. There is some dispute over whether this limited slowing can be attributed to the oil shocks as a *deus ex machina* in Japan, the way the oil shocks seem to have been associated with the decline in productivity growth in the United States and elsewhere around the mid-1970s.[5] In any event, there were other factors at work, just as in the United

States it became clear that the actual productivity decline began before the oil shock. At some point in the 1970s, Japan reached the technological frontier in many advanced manufacturing sectors, having "caught up" to the United States, or even surpassed it in some areas considered high-tech. Also, the shift of employment from agriculture to manufacturing, and the shift in residence from rural to urban, was largely completed. Both of these contributed to a decline in the "easy" ways to add growth.

Meanwhile, Japan actually adapted well to the aftermath of the oil shock, exporting large quantities of more fuel efficient machinery and autos to both the West and to newly developing east Asia. By the mid-1980s, people believed that the price of land could never go down in Japan, that Japanese exporters would dominate world markets in many leading industries on an ongoing basis, and that Japanese investors would acquire significant ownership over much of the world's prized assets. These were the days of "Japan as Number One".

The current sense of crisis in Japan and abroad about the Japanese economy did not arise until after the aborted recovery of 1996—in fact, until then positive perceptions about the Japanese economy remained prevalent on both sides of the Pacific. This was understandable given the not unprecedented nature of the 1991–5 slowdown, the ability to blame it temporarily on the yen's rise, and the apparent signs of recovery in 1996 following one program of true government fiscal stimulus. The severe but normal downturn of the 1990s only persisted and got worse due to the government ignoring mounting financial fragility and pursuing pro-cyclical monetary and fiscal policies (Posen, 1998). In particular, the combination of a consumption tax increase in April 1997 and the contractionary effects of the Asian Financial Crisis, as well as a mounting pile of bad bank loans in excess of 10 percent of GDP, cut off a nascent recovery which started in 1996.[6] The surprise collapses in November

---

[5] The leading figures in this debate over the causes of Japan's first slowdown were Dale Jorgenson on the oil shock side and Angus Maddison arguing against such an attribution.

[6] Boltho and Corbett (2000) note that 35 percent of Japanese exports went to the crisis countries before mid-1997, and these declined by 27 percent after the crisis hit, a direct loss of 1.5 percent of Japanese GDP.

TABLE 4.3
Monetary and Financial Developments in the 1990s (Annual Percentage Change)

	GDP deflator	CPI	WPI	Real yen/ U.S.$	Land price	Stock price
1991	2.89	2.3	−1.29	72.2	0.55	2.38
1992	0.94	2.08	−1.69	67.4	−5.11	−32.03
1993	0.44	0.91	−4.07	62.4	−5.13	16.91
1994	−0.62	0.5	1.25	58.5	−3.82	0.47
1995	−0.38	0.07	−0.06	61.5	−4.3	−4.9
1996	−2.23	0.3	−0.33	71.2	−4.43	5.47
1997	1	2.23	1.42	79.4	−3.62	−20.85
1998	0.17	−0.32	−3.64	76.8	−4.38	−15.37
1999	−0.79	0	−4.12	76.9	−5.67	23

Source: Bernanke (2000: Tables 7.1 and 7.2).

Notes: Real yen/U.S.$ rate is computed with January 1979 = 100. Land price is from index of commercial buildings in urban areas. Stock price is percentage change in Topix index. CPI: Consumer Price Index; WPI: Wholesale Price Index.

1997 of Yamaichi Securities, one of four major securities houses in Japan, and of Hokkaido Tokashokku Bank, the dominant bank on the north home island and one of the top twenty banks—despite the efforts of regulators at the time to maintain a convoy system keeping all banks afloat and all problems hidden—fed a financial near-panic among Japanese savers, as well as among counterparties with Japanese banks. The official recession lasted from June 1997 to December 1998.

From mid-1997 through the first quarter of 1999, there was a breakdown in Japanese financial markets, with credit growth collapsing, the banks subject to very high "Japan premia" in interbank markets (when they could borrow at all), a rise in the public's holdings of currency relative to bank deposits (indicating disintermediation from the banking system), and a deflationary trend on all available measures that continues today[7] (see Table 4.3). Land prices declined unremittingly throughout the period, while the stock market declined by double digit amounts in two of the last three years (and has again in 2000 to date). The combination of deflation and financial fragility created a vicious

cycle of mounting real debt, foreclosed but unsold collateral, and adverse selection in credit markets.[8] The situation only stabilized with the implementation of major financial reforms and recapitalization of part of the banking system in the first quarter of 1999—but no more than stabilized—with over half of the Japanese banking system still inadequately capitalized, with nontransparent accounting of nonperforming loans, and therefore rolling over bad loans while making risky choices with new credits (gambling on resurrection).

On the real side of the economy, Japanese unemployment has risen to exceed that in the United States beginning in mid-1998, going from 2.3 percent in 1990 to 4.9 percent in mid-2000. While the American unemployment levels are likely to rise again as the cycle turns down, Japan is estimated to have sufficient "hidden" unemployment, that is, employees officially still on the payroll of firms who do little productive work and who in some instances are not even paid, to double the national unemployment rate. Changing exchange rates make it difficult to compare levels of wealth and income between countries, but real per capita GDP measured on domestic data has grown at only a 0.6 percent compound rate since 1990 in Japan, while the rate of growth in U.S. real per

[7] In Japan, as in all economies using standard baskets to compute deflators, there is an inherent positive bias in the consumer price index (CPI) and other price indices. This bias is on the order of 1.0–1.5 percent in Japan, according to the Bank of Japan's own calculations, meaning effective deflation arguably has been present since 1992.

[8] See the chapters by Bernanke, Glauber, Shimizu, and Posen in Mikitani and Posen (2000).

TABLE 4.4
General Government Deficits (Excluding Social Security) and Gross Debt (National Accounts Basis)

	Deficit (percent of GDP)	Gross debt (percent of GDP)		
	Japan	Japan	United States	Germany
1983	6.2			
1984	4.6			
1985	3.4			
1986	3.9			
1987	2.4			
1988	1.6			
1989	0.7			
1990	0.6			
1991	0.8	57.9	71.4	40.1
1992	2	59.3	74.1	43.4
1993	4.8	63.7	75.8	49
1994	5.1	68.8	75	49.2
1995	6.4	76.2	74.5	59.1
1996	6.9	80.5	73.9	61.9
1997	5.9	84.6	71.6	62.8
1998	7.1	97.4	68.6	63.3
1999	8.9	105.3	65.1	63.5
2000	8.5	112.8	60.2	63.5
2001	8.1			

Source: OECD Economic Outlook. Note: 2000 and 2001 are projected values.

capita income has been nearly three times as great (1.7 percent compound annual rate) over the same period. In the two major "Global Competitiveness Surveys," Japan's position has declined throughout the 1990s.[9]

As of writing, Japanese annual household savings have risen to 13 percent of GDP, while in the United States, the share of private savings out of annual income have sunk towards or

[9] The IMD survey ranked Japan as the most competitive economy in the world through the early 1990s, downgraded it to fourth in 1995, and to seventeenth in 2000; the World Economic Forum had already dropped Japan to thirteenth by 1996, and the economy fell further in the rankings to twenty-first in the 2000 survey.

[10] It should be noted, however, that Japanese government net debt is not necessarily or even obviously on an unsustainable path since all of the debt is denominated in Yen, less than 6 percent of the debt is held abroad, and close to a third of the government debt is held by public agencies themselves.

even below zero. Of course, public sector savings in the two countries have shown divergences in the opposite direction over the decade, with the U.S. Federal Government moving into surplus, and the Japanese government exceeding Italy and Belgium in terms of high gross debt-to-GDP ratios[10] (see Table 4.4). This erosion of the Japanese government's balance sheet has more to do with declining tax revenues in a time of declining growth than with any ambitious public spending or tax cut programs (always far more promised than implemented, with the exception of September 1998).

4.2.2. What this Means for Japan

The mainstream macroeconomic explanation for Japanese economic decline in the 1990s is a combination of a normal negative demand shock, an excessive financial multiplier due to

TABLE 4.5

Real Interest Rates (Government Long Bond Yield Minus
Expected Inflation)

	1990–1	1994–5	1998–9
Japan	4.9	3	1.8
United States	4.2	4.6	3.8
Germany	4.5	4.3	3

Source: Boltho and Corbett (2000: Table 3).
Note: Expected inflation taken from OECD's year-end inflation forecasts.

TABLE 4.6

Changes in Business Start-ups and Closures (Annual Average Rate of Change)

	Start-ups	Closures
1975–78	5.9	3.8
1978–81	5.9	3.7
1981–86	4.3	4
1986–91	3.5	4
1991–96	2.7	3.2

Source: Management and Coordination Agency, Statistical
Survey of Business Establishments and Enterprises.

bad loans feeding back into the broader economy through connected lending and regulatory
forbearance, and severe fiscal and monetary
policy missteps turning that into debt deflation.
Consistent with this view, there has been no
decline in Japanese purchasing power or
terms-of-trade (see Table 4.3). Unemployment
has risen, and capacity utilization has declined,
while prices have fallen. Real interest rates have
declined, despite the deflation, consistent with
a lack of demand for investment (see Table 4.5).
The rate of business creation has declined in
Japan, with the number of start-ups now growing more slowly than the number of business
bankruptcies and closures. In fact, that imbal-
ance was already true even in the bubble years
of the late 1980s, when the number of business
closures per year increased more rapidly than
the number of business start-ups (see Table
4.6). The trends in "creative destruction" in
the Japanese economy display no sharp break
with long-run trends, especially given the cyclical downturn.

In short, there is no evidence of a direct hit to
Japanese productive capability or to the basic
structures of the economy from what it was
when it was idolized in the late 1980s. There is
no question that productivity growth has
declined in Japan in the 1990s (see Tables 4.7
and 4.8). According to the *MITI White Paper on
International Trade 1998*, total factor productivity
(TFP) stagnated from 1990 to 1997, after growing by 1.0 percent a year in the 1980s. But
measured productivity performance is pro-cyclical in most economies, because when there is
an economic slowdown, firms do not shed labor
as rapidly as output falls.[11] In Japan, firms have

proven especially reluctant to let workers go
even as production has been cut, exacerbating
this effect. It is worth noting that the estimates
of both Wolff (1999) and OECD (2000) indicate
that the difference between Japanese and U.S.
(or German) labor productivity growth only
widens starting in 1995, after the American
boom and the Japanese second recession/
financial breakdown began (see Table 4.8).

Furthermore, for a large, diversified, and
developed economy, like Japan, a negative
supply shock (i.e., a decline in productive capacity rather than an idling of extant capacity)
should be reflected in a shift in the relative
productivity of differing sectors. While there is
ample evidence of an ongoing and substantial
difference between the average productivity
levels of the Japanese export manufacturing
sector and of the rest of the economy (discussed
at more length later), there is no evidence of a
change in those relative levels in the 1990s, or an
abrupt shift in any Japanese sector's competitiveness versus the rest of the world. As seen in Table
4.7, the difference between average annual TFP
growth rates in the manufacturing and nonmanufacturing sectors in the 1990s (2.1 percent)
fell between the difference seen in the 1980s
(1.6 percent) and in the 1970s (3.1 percent),
and this was not the first decade in which
nonmanufacturing productivity stagnated.

Returning to the fundamentals of growth as
seen in the Solow growth model, extended by
later endogenous growth researchers, provides

[11] See the discussion of the importance of cyclical factors in
the upswing in productivity in the United States in chapter 3.

TABLE 4.7

Factor Analysis of Growth Rate of Real GDP of Japan

	Average annual growth rate (national accounts data)			
	1960s	*1970s*	*1980s*	*1990–7*
All industries				
Capital stock	6.9	3.8	2.8	1.9
Labor supply	0.4	0	0.4	−0.3
TFP	2.7	1	1.4	0.2
GDP growth (total)	10	4.8	4.6	1.8
Manufacturing				
Capital stock	7.2	2.7	2.1	0.5
Labor supply	1.4	−0.5	0.6	−1.2
TFP	5.9	3.1	2.4	2
GDP growth (total)	14.4	5.2	5.1	1.2
Nonmanufacturing				
Capital stock	6.4	4.5	3.3	2.3
Labor supply	0.2	0.2	0.3	−0.1
TFP	2.2	0	0.8	−0.1
GDP growth (total)	8.8	4.6	4.4	2.1

Source: MITI, *White Paper on International Trade* (1998).

the necessary perspective on stories of Japanese decline. In the recent literature on economic growth, such factors as initial GDP per capita (as a measure of convergence), schooling and life expectancy of workers (as proxies for human capital), national savings, rule of law and democracy (as measures of respect for property rights), and inflation and government consumption (as distortions or discouragements of investment) are significant predictors of countries' growth rates. Writing in 1996, the noted free market economist Robert Barro predicted a 3.2 percent annual real per capita growth rate for Japan for 1996–2000, on the basis of his main cross-sectional panel estimates, and Japan's high initial scores, on these growth fundamentals.[12]

Although such a result might lead one to be skeptical of the practical utility of the current state of economic growth research, it underlines just how difficult it is to say that Japan has bad, let alone declining, "fundamentals" for growth. The combined Solow and endogenous growth models take into account the supply of physical capital, of human capital (i.e., the quality adjusted supply of labor), the starting level of technology, the state of government, and the social structure. Since economic growth is composed of capital inputs, labor inputs, and technological progress, this would seem to about cover it.[13] Writing a few years later, and with the benefit of a few more years data, Hartnett and Higgins (2000) still find that Japan scores high on all of these except government policy (see Table 4.9). The particular government policy measures which they identify, however, include monetary policy and the organization of the central bank, hardly deep structures (and ones on which Japan has shifted noticeably since April 1998).

The OECD has correctly emphasized the ability of structural reform, particularly in the financial, retail, and utilities sectors, to raise Japan's long-term growth rate (e.g., OECD, 1998b), much as it has advocated liberalization for many other countries. Noting this opportunity for efficiency gains, however, does not explain why the same Japanese financial system did not appear to be a binding constraint on Japan's

---

[12] See Barro (1997). His forecasts had a 2 percent (two standard deviation) margin of error; the U.S. forecast was almost that much below Japan's, and Japan's exceeded almost all other OECD forecasts.

[13] There is some popular concern that Japanese demographics are working against growth, with the world's most rapidly aging population. While this is of course literally true, given that growth in labor supply is one of the components of economic growth, it should not be a focus of this discussion. For one thing, there are a number of currently untapped resources for Japanese labor (such as underemployment of women, and relatively early retirement ages given high life expectancies), as well as possibilities for allowing guest workers or limited immigration, which could rapidly respond to any labor constraint. Another issue is that from the point of view of economic welfare, our concern is with per capita real income growth, which is actually usually enhanced by a declining population. In any event, for the period ten years prior and ten years after the present day, Japanese net population growth is projected to be effectively zero, so talking about changes in aggregate growth and in per capita income growth are equivalent.

TABLE 4.8
Comparative Rates of Growth and Productivity Growth

		1973–9	*1979–89*	*1989–94*
Comparative annual growth rate (Wolff, 1999: Table 1, Panel II)[a]				
Japan	GDP	3.33	4	2.11
	TFP	0.72	1.79	0.91
	Labor productivity	3.35	3.45	2.81
United States	GDP	2.28	2.68	1.82
	TFP	− 0.21	0.47	0.57
	Labor productivity	0.12	0.68	0.98
Germany	GDP	2.45	1.87	2.47
	TFP	2.24	1.19	1.66
	Labor productivity	3.72	2.1	2.77

Comparative labor productivity growth (average percentage annual change in output/employee; OECD, 2000a)

	1980–90	*1990–5*	*1995–8*
Japan	2.8	0.9	0.9
United States	1.2	1.2	2.1
Germany	1.9	2.4	1.9

Comparative TFP growth rates (average percentage annual change in multifactor productivity; Gust and Marquez, 2000)

	1990–5	*1996–9*
Japan	1.31	0.85
United States	0.79	1.47
Germany	1.02	1.07

[a] GDP in 1990 U.S.$; capital is gross fixed private investment; West German data in all periods.

higher growth rate in the 1950–89 period.[14] In other words, the closer one looks at the 1990s in Japan, the more it becomes apparent that although the macroeconomic performance declined sharply and persistently, the causes were limited to the demand side and macroeconomic and financial policy mistakes.

The costliest recession in an advanced economy since 1950 does not indicate a long-term, structural decline in potential output—let alone technological regress. If it did, the output gap in Japan would be rapidly closing as growth has picked up to around 2.0 percent in 1999–2000, but instead unemployment continues to rise, wages and prices continue to fall, and capacity remains unused, all of which indicates the opposite (see Table 4.10).[15] There is no obvious evidence of a structural break from the Japan that put up stellar macroeconomic performance in the 1970s and 1980s, and historically unprecedented growth

[14] Weinstein and Yafeh (1998) convincingly argue that Japan succeeded in the post-war decades despite the drag of an inefficient "Main Bank system," and Hoshi and Kashyap (2001) provide a great deal of evidence on the development of Japanese corporate finance consistent with this view. While improvements in the Japanese financial system are sufficient to improve growth, they are not necessary to do so, and therefore lack of such improvements cannot be to blame for the Japanese growth slowdown (except in the different sense that a mismanaged financial crisis had high costs, which is not a statement about potential growth).

TABLE 4.9
Current Capital and Labor Fundamentals for Growth

	Private investment	Gross FDI inflow	Stock market capitalization	Average corporate tax rate	Labor growth	Secondary school (percent)	Tertiary school (percent)	Life expectancy
Japan	28.8	0.04	107.5	34.5	−0.3	100	43	80.3
United States	17.9	1.77	265.3	40	0.9	96	81	77.4
Germany	21	0.53	60.8	53	−0.2	95	47	77.8
Korea	32.9	0.78	75.8	28	1.1	100	68	73.5
Singapore	35.1	9	216.4	26	0.7	76	39	78.1

Source: Hartnett and Higgins (2000).
Notes: Columns 1–3 are as a percentage of GDP; investment and FDI are 1995–8 averages; stock market capitalization and corporate tax rate are 1999; labor growth is 1998–2000 average; school enrollment percentages are 1997; life expectancy is 1998.

TABLE 4.10
Labor Statistics 1985–99

	1985	1990	1995	1996	1997	1998	1999
Unemployment rate	2.6	2.1	3.2	3.4	3.4	4.1	4.7
Age 20–24	4.1	3.7	5.7	6.1	6.2	7.1	8.4
Men 60–64	7	5.1	7.5	8.5	8.3	10	10.2
Employment rate (male)	81	81.1	81.9	82.1	82.4	81.6	81
Employment rate (female)	53	55.7	56.5	56.8	57.5	57.2	56.7
Real wage index	89.9	100	103.2	104.9	105.3	103.1	102.4

Source: Ministry of Labor, *Handbook of Labor Statistics.*

prior to catching up and urbanizing in the 1950s and 1960s, once technological convergence and the transition to a modern economy are controlled for. This raises important puzzles about the relationship between technological innovation and economic growth in the Japanese context.

[15] It should be noted that an average of thirty-eight different predictions of Japan's long-term potential growth rate compiled in 1999 by the high-level Prime Minister's Committee for Strategic Economic Priorities was 2.1 percent per annum (see *Nihon Keizai Saisei eno Senryaku (The Strategy for Reviving the Japanese Economy)*, 1999), not much changed from a few years before. Meanwhile, both the OECD and the Bank of Japan have recently downgraded their estimates of Japanese potential, to 1.25 percent and 1.0 percent, respectively. Posen (2001) offers an argument for why potential growth actually rose in Japan in 1998–2000, and some explanation for why alternative methods might come to the opposite conclusion.

4.3. Independence of Macroeconomic Performance from Innovation Inputs?[16]

4.3.1. Clarifying the Image of the Japanese National Innovation System

The Japanese system of innovation and economic development had become the stuff of legend by the time that Japanese national income per capita approached American levels at the end of the 1980s. The vast literature which emerged to study it, on both sides of the Pacific, identified several key attributes of the system, many of which were exaggerated

[16] The distinction made between "inputs" to innovation in this section, and "outputs" in the next, is based on distinguishing between institutional frameworks that determine which R&D activities get pursued, and the amount of innovative products and processes that come out of these activities.

in the more popular press. Goto and Odagiri (1993, 1997) give the mainstream list of the major characteristics that can be documented. The primary emphasis of the Japanese system is on continuous improvement of production processes as well as of products in publicly identified important or strategic industries, of which steel, automobiles, and electronics were the most notable. Creation of wholly new products or lines of business was not considered to be a primary goal (although more entrepreneurship did arise than is often credited; Johnstone, 1999). This improvement in the selected industries generally began with the importation of key technologies from abroad and the setting of ambitious industrial standards by the Japanese government and industry.[17]

The approach never amounted to "picking winners" of specific companies by the powerful Ministry of International Trade and Industry (MITI) or other agencies in the sense that American observers sometimes believed. Both government contracts and trade protection were employed at early stages of development in a few chosen sectors to provide a minimum market size, but usually for a number of domestic companies. MITI would encourage, with some limited public seed money, joint research and development efforts among those invited companies. Personnel management within these companies and the Japanese educational system encouraged the training of broadly qualified engineers (rather than specialized research scientists), and the seniority system with lifetime employment emphasized the retention and transmission of specialized skills relevant to the company's products. The move-

ment of these engineers between line production and management encouraged their bringing of incremental practical improvements into corporate awareness and eventual company-wide implementation.[18] In the words of the National Industrial Technology Strategy Development Commission set-up by the Japanese government:

> Until recently, Japanese enterprises achieved and maintained competitiveness by introducing basic industrial technologies from Western nations to achieve "process innovation" (i.e., technically enhancing manufacturing processes), which dramatically upgraded productivity and product quality. Underlying this success were uniform standards of education, high workforce morale, long-term investment in human resources, and teamwork between manufacturing employees and management. In short, Japan made full use of the strengths of Japanese society and Japanese business management systems.
>
> (National Industrial Technology Strategy Development Committee, 1999: 8)

These practices on the part of government and industry to promote innovation easily coexisted with the more general principles of corporate organization in Japan: relationship financing of corporations through long-term bank lending, "lifetime" employment for many workers and limited labor mobility for all workers (with the attendant pros and cons), flexible shop floor teamwork and just-in-time inventory, widespread government regulation limiting entry and exit of businesses from various sectors, and primacy of insider stakeholder relationships over transparent accounting and shareholder value. From the perspective of the United States in 2000, for most observers these would all sound like disadvantages (with the exception of worker teams and just-in-time inventory, whose adoption is seen as contributing to the rise in U.S. productivity); what is important is that these broader characteristics of Japanese industry were just as prevalent in the glory years of 1950–80 as they have been in the 1990s.[19]

---

[17] Lee and Kantwell (1998) argue that (mostly domestic) two-way interaction between user firms and Japanese capital goods producers fed innovation through integration and specialization.

[18] Nonaka and Takeuchi (1995) claim that it is as much tacit knowledge within an organization as explicit, and therefore appropriable, knowledge which gives corporations creativity. Procedures and manuals only take one so far in producing new technologies, but Japanese companies also benefit from workers with broad internal experience that cumulates by transmission, and results in innovation.

What has recently come to light about the post-war Japanese innovation system is the degree to which *domestic competition* among firms in high-tech sectors occurred and even was encouraged, despite the status quo biases of the system. Individual entrepreneurship, while hardly encouraged, was a also significant factor in Japanese technological development. For example, Fransman (1999) documents the start of what he calls "controlled competition" in the electronics and telecommunications industry in the efforts of the Imperial Ministry of Communications in the 1920s and 1930s to have multiple, albeit chosen, suppliers for Japan's developing telecomms infrastructure (as opposed to the United States' de facto monopoly for Western Electric). The big four Japanese electronics and telecomms companies of today (NEC, Hitachi, Toshiba, and Oki) trace their roots to the late nineteenth century, but really were the result of mergers, the entry and exit of foreign joint ventures (with Siemens and Western Electric, for example), and shifting government contracts from the telephone monopoly NTT.[20]

The history of the Japanese automobile industry, home to some of the world's greatest production innovations, is one of great competition, of corporate entry and exit and re-entry, and of individual inventors and entrepreneurs, despite government activism to develop auto production. Ten domestic firms tried to get into the auto business before the end of the 1920s, and failed, with only the government-supported (through Army purchases) Dat staying in, and still Ford and General Motors dominated the Japanese market.[21] In 1932, the predecessor of MITI urged three specific companies to begin new efforts, resulting in the survival of one firm (Isuzu), and several not sponsored by MITI also emerged. Toyota Motors, funded by Toyota Looms, began as a small scale non-zaibatsu firm responding to a risk-taking entrepreneur's vision, without government support. After 1950, both Honda and Suzuki became major automotive producers after their individual owners branched out from motorcycles, and did so without any public-sector encouragement (let alone foreign exchange credits to purchase technology, or government procurement contracts). Meanwhile, Daihatsu eventually was acquired by Toyota in an example of competitive mergers. Mitsubishi Motors entered and re-entered the Japanese automobile market repeatedly as both a government favorite and a member of a major keiretsu family, and still failed to gain a leading domestic market share, let alone a major piece of the export market.[22]

What probably left the greatest impression on outside observers of the Japanese government picking winners in technologies and companies, were the attempts of MITI to create coordinated research efforts in the electronics industry, backstopped by trade policy. The perceived success of the efforts in the cases of the Japanese mainframe computer industry and of the development of very-large scale integrated circuits (VLSI) technology gave rise to the calls in the United States for the Sematech and HDTV government-led research programs (which themselves eventually were deemed failures).

Even in these instances, however, the reality was less coordinated and government directed than the common perception. As Nakayama et

---

[19] Hoshi and Kashyap (2001) make an interesting historical argument that what they call "Keiretsu financing," the Main Bank relationship financing of industry, was a post-war creation.

[20] In his introduction, Fransman (1999: 14) cites approvingly an apparently self-translated passage from a 1994 Japanese language research volume on "The Industrial Policy of Japan" which reads: "All of participants in this [multi-author] project recognized that, excluding the brief period immediately after the end of the war, the foundation of rapid growth was competition operating through the price mechanism and a flourishing entrepreneurial spirit. In opposition to the 'Japan, Inc.' thesis, it can even be said that the history of industrial policy in the principal post-war periods (in particular the 1950s and 1960s) has often been that the initiative and vitality of the private sector undermined the plans of government authorities to try to utilize direct intervention in the nature of 'controls.'"

[21] See Goto and Odagiri (1993).

[22] Michael Porter's discussion of Japan in *The Competitive Advantage of Nations* gives additional anecdotal evidence about the importance of domestic competition to Japanese technical progress and performance, arguing that Japan's export success only came as a result of this competition.

al. (1999) describe, in the early 1960s, Japan had six players in the computer industry, all but one of which were partnered with a U.S. firm. The innovative IBM System 360 and System 370 mainframe computers wiped out the competition in both the United States and Japan. The MITI Computer Systems Project of 1966–72 to build a Japanese competitor or successor to the 360 did not function as planned. "[S]kepticism pervaded the engineering staffs from the [six selected] competing companies. It often happened in national projects like this that MITI's endorsement was used to persuade corporate management to support in-house R&D, but technological exchange among [participating] companies was minimal."[23] Eventually Fujitsu and Toshiba emerged as viable competitors to IBM in the computer hardware market, but three of the other six firms participating in the project got out of the computer business entirely, while a fourth stayed in only with the support of government purchases and never was an innovative player.

Japanese firms did come to dominate the market for RAM and other integrated circuits on semiconductor chips in the 1990s, although control of the microprocessor market went back to the U.S. producers, Intel, Motorola, and others, by the mid-1990s (and most RAM chip production moved offshore from Japan).[24] This dominance is often attributed to the success of MITI's VLSI Project of 1976–80, based on the forecast that 1 megabit memory chips for general purpose computers would be a key electronics market segment. Even within the "Research Association" framework, MITI pursued a relatively decentralized course. Three laboratories (Computer Lab, NEC-Toshiba Information Systems Lab, and the VLSI Joint Lab) were set up, with the participation of an initial five companies (and a couple more added later). The brief of the joint work was to emphasize fundamentals, which in practice meant a focus on lofty far off projects (like

the development of electron beam equipment). The truly practical next generation technologies, like photolithography methods for etching circuits on chips, were tightly held within the participating companies. In fact, the biggest impact may have been on those Japanese companies, like Canon and Nikon, which were not directly involved in the VLSI Project, but received demanding requisitions for equipment to create inputs (like aligners for circuits).

In any event, this was to be MITI's last major success of this kind in the electronics industry (at least to date).[25] There were smaller Research Association-type projects pursued since 1980, but "difficult[ies] arose for MITI with the diversification of the electronics technology, the maturation of Japanese industry, and the uncertainty of emerging technologies." (Nakayama et al., 1999: 47). The trend of government subsidies for private R&D research was already on a downwards trend from 1960 through 1980, further indicating that the end of these projects was not a major difference between the Japanese innovation system of today and the recent past.[26] Writing in 1993, when the Japanese system was still believed to be a model, Goto and Odagiri gave a very measured description of industrial policy's role in promoting R&D:

> [F]or MITI, Research Associations have been a convenient way to distribute its subsidies to promote the technologies MITI (and particular firms) believed important, most notably semiconductors

---

[23] Nakayama et al. (1999: 44).

[24] See chapter 10 on innovation in the semiconductor industry.

[25] The "Fifth Generation Computer Project" which MITI started in 1981 as the next new technological goal was shut down a few years later with no visible results

[26] Only a miniscule share of government spending in Japan is spent on industrial policy, let alone on promotion of innovation. The vast bulk of public spending is on keeping dead sectors like agriculture and rural construction firms alive (and Diet members from the LDP re-elected). The waste of public funds on redundant or useless infrastructure projects cannot be exaggerated (see Posen, 1998), but also cannot be called in any way a subsidy of technical innovation—the way some defense spending in the United States can.

and computers, and have been used to avoid favoring particular firms and to minimize the cost of supervising the use of subsidies. From this viewpoint, it is not surprising that only two of the 87 associations had [actual] joint research facilities; in all other cases, each member firm simply took its share of research funds and carried out the research in its own laboratory. Therefore, how coordinated the research really was among particular firms within each Research Association is doubtful except for a few cases. The effectiveness of these Research Associations in generating new technologies is also doubtful … Research Associations' productivity as measured by the number of patents divided by its R&D expenditures was considerably lower than that of [private] industries …."

(Goto and Odagiri, 1993: 88)

Moreover, even in electronics, individual entrepreneurship played at least as great a role as government intervention in the development of Japanese capabilities. Throughout most of its rise, Toshiba had been an outsider as far as NTT's procurement went, not becoming a member of the telephone monopoly's equipment provider "family" until NTT's privatization in 1985; Fujitsu only entered and stayed in the computer industry due to the efforts of a strong corporate chairman overruling the concerns of his upper management and board. Johnstone (1999) gives numerous examples of individual Japanese electronics entrepreneurs, not all that far removed from the garages of Hewlett and Packard, or Jobs and Wozniak (although probably more crowded). As Johnstone documents, numerous Japanese physicists working in the electronics industry undertook their own trans-Pacific exchanges and education efforts, and created both innovations and companies. The paradigmatic example is, of course, Sony, which began life as Tokyo Telecommunications Research Laboratories, with twenty employees in May 1946. Starting with a small contract for recording equipment from NHK, and inspired by visits to the United States in the early 1950s, Sony's two founders built the largest consumer electronics company in the world. Sony was one of many companies worldwide to license Western Electric's transistor technology in 1953, but was the only one to gamble on creating transistor radios (which required the innovation of phosphorus doping the transistor to get reception in the radio frequency range).[27]

One important exception to the general characterization of the Japanese national innovation system as largely unchanged in the 1990s, and as less interventionist (and more competitive) than usually thought, may be the area of trade protection. By all appearances, Japan did engage in some rather aggressive infant industry protections and export promotion policies for autos, computers, and other domestic industries. And whatever the intent behind earlier barriers, there is no question that Japanese trade protection has declined in recent years through a combination of international trade agreements and U.S. pressures. It is possible that while Japanese industrial policy may not have succeeded in directing innovation or picking winners consistently, earlier industrial policy efforts might still have given benefits by granting sufficient scale to exporters of manufactured goods.

The more careful evidence, however, points in the other direction. Lawrence and Weinstein (1999) show rather conclusively in a multi-year panel of industries that trade protection interfered with sectoral TFP growth in Japan (and Korea). Imports had a salutary effect on TFP in those Japanese industries where they were allowed in, with the resulting increase in competition and learning significantly feeding innovation as long as Japan was behind the technological frontier. In other words, trade protection did not nurture internationally competitive firms in Japan in the pre-1973 period, imports did. Meanwhile, Lawrence and Weinstein show that export success by industry is significantly correlated with productivity gains, not with protection or other industrial policy measures. It is still possible that economies of scale could

[27] In fact, MITI refused to give Sony the foreign exchange credits for the license, and Sony had to come up with the money on its own.

emerge in a virtuous circle with high export growth. The key is that controlling for protection by industry or firm takes away nothing from the explanatory power.

This result is consistent with the experiences of the auto and electronics industries, those being the two most important and successful Japanese export industries, and clearly industries who developed by importing technology and facing competition. So even if the Japanese government's ability to engage in trade protection and export subsidization has declined in the 1990s versus earlier decades, that shift cannot be the source of a negative change in the national innovation system because the most innovative sectors (as measured by TFP growth) were the industries which were not subject to these policies.[28] Thus, in terms of the Japanese institutional framework for supporting innovation, the first puzzle of declining macroeconomic performance, despite unchanging innovative inputs, holds.

4.3.2. Measurable Innovation Inputs Also Remain Steady

The description of the unchanging framework of the Japanese national innovation system only takes us so far. Thinking in terms of the measurable building blocks for innovation—funds devoted to research and development, supply of technically skilled workers, communications and educational infrastructure, private sector leadership in R&D allocation—allows us to also

track whether Japan has kept the same innovation framework, but dedicated fewer resources to it, or used those resources in more wasteful ways. A drop off in innovation inputs prior to the economic downturn of the 1990s might help to explain the decline in growth, or a cutback in the funding and promotion of R&D as the downturn took hold might explain the persistence of slow growth. This remains plausible, although its importance must be limited given the aggregate level evidence outlined in the first section on why technical regress appears to be inconsistent with recent developments.

The measured inputs to innovation in Japan, however, appear to have remained steady between the 1980s and the 1990s, along with the framework for utilizing them. Japan's rate of R&D investment, as a percentage of GDP, has consistently been higher than that of Germany or the United States, running 2.80 percent on average from 1987 to 1997 (see Table 4.1, and the more detailed year by year comparisons given in chapter 1). In other forms of research and development infrastructure, such as the number of internet hosts or personal computers per capita, Japan does lag behind the United States (see Table 4.11)—but that should be consistent with a rise in the American growth rate (through IT capital deepening) in the most recent years, not a decline in the Japanese one. Germany which lags similarly behind the United States on these metrics saw its trend growth rate undiminished, although the relative growth gap widened. If "internet readiness" of the broader citizenry is the issue, the much higher Japanese use of mobile phones per capita—many of which now add wireless internet services in Japan—should at least partially compensate for the lower level of PC usage.

Japanese R&D funding, especially private corporate R&D funding, has continued to grow in the 1990s, even as total private investment has fluctuated, and for the most part steeply declined. As seen in the third panel of Table 4.12, which shows the year-over-year percentage changes, both total and private sector R&D investment declined somewhat in 1993 and 1994, immediately following the hit of the bubble's burst, but grew strongly over the next

[28] Some earlier papers by David Weinstein and co-authors, on domestic industrial policy and on the Japanese financial system, advance the argument that the Japanese economy grew despite counterproductive government interventions implemented during the high growth years, as Lawrence and Weinstein (1999) conclude with regard to trade protection specifically. Posen (1998: chapter 6) takes much the same "success despite" view of the earlier periods of Japanese development, but also extends a similar argument to the Japanese decline in the 1990s, concluding that the decline was largely caused by new mistaken policies, not by long-standing institutions that were present through times good and bad. See also McKinsey (2000: 1), "Surprisingly, we found that the Japanese economy was never as strong as it appeared to be during its glory days. In fact, today's woeful economic performance is not so much a reversal of fortune as a revelation of the holdovers of Japan's success in the 1980s."

TABLE 4.11
Current Technological Fundamentals for Growth

	R&D expenditure	Internet hosts per 10,000	PCs per 1,000	Mobile phones per 1,000	Nobel prizes per capita
Japan	2.8	163.75	237.2	374	0.032
United States	2.63	1508.77	458.6	256	0.703
Germany	2.41	173.96	304.7	170	0.329
Korea	2.82	55.53	156.8	302	0
Singapore	1.13	322.3	458.4	346	0

Source: Hartnett and Higgins (2000).
Notes: R&D expenditure is average percentage of GDP, 1987–97; Internet hosts is 1999; PCs and phones is 1998; Nobel prizes is per million population as of 1999.

four years. R&D funding in the public and university sectors was hit harder initially and responded more weakly, but showed a similar upwards J-curve. A far greater share of Japanese R&D is funded by the private sector than in the United States, despite the fact that the total share (in GDP) of R&D investment is consistently higher in Japan than in the United States. This differential is of long-standing, and not merely the reflection of the lack of defense spending in Japan. This bears out the picture of MITI and other government sponsored "research associations" playing a relatively small role in the encouragement and direction of Japanese innovation versus the role played by private corporations given above.

Considering the comparative distribution of R&D funds in the G3, Japan and the United States are actually reasonably similar in their relative weightings of basic versus applied research, with German R&D funding being more oriented towards basic research than either of the others (see Table 4.13, as well as the discussion of the biases of German research networks in chapter 5). Interestingly, research conducted in the Japanese university system tends to put a lower emphasis on basic research relative to applied engineering than in the United States or Germany. This is not a necessary result of the greater public (including defense) funding of research in the United States, since the larger share of self-funded private research in Japan could just as easily have freed up the universities to pursue more

academic projects. What is clear is that in both source of funds and orientation of their use, Japanese R&D has been at least as focused on practical private-sector industrial problems as German or American R&D.[29]

What makes this bias towards private funding, and towards applied research even in universities, particularly odd for Japan, is the absence of a patenting or licensing framework for universities to get revenues from inventions, or for universities and companies to set up partnerships. Such profitable registrations and relationships have been common in the United States, especially since the passage of the Bayh-Dole Amendment in 1983 reducing the licensing fees and allowing universities to keep revenues from patents developed on government contracts. In Japan, after much discussion, such a law was passed in April 1998, as part of an effort to promote more cooperation between industries and universities. For the purposes of the present discussion, however, the key point is that Japanese R&D funding did not become increasingly diverted from industrial concerns in the 1990s versus the earlier post-war period.

[29] National Research Council (1999) documents that these differences between the United States and Japan in emphasis on basic research, on public versus private R&D funding, and on university–corporate cooperation are of long standing. See also the narrative discussions in Goto and Odagiri (1997), Fransman (1999), and Nakayama et al. (1999), all of which give a similar description of a Japanese R&D focus on very applied engineering problems, even in the universities, to that seen in these numbers.

TABLE 4.12
Research and Development Expenditures 1992–8

Fiscal year	Total					By private firms						By public research organization					By university				
	R&D total	Wages	Material	Physical stock cash flow	Others	R&D total [1]+[2]+[4]+[5]	Wages [1]	Material [2]	Physical stock depreciation [3]	Physical stock cash flow [4]	Others [5]	R&D total	Wages	Material	Physical stock cash flow	Others	R&D total	Wages	Material	Physical stock cash flow	Others
100 million yen (current prices)																					
1992	137091	63575	21471	19108	32938	90536	39620	16928	9194	10254	23734	18968	5973	2844	4835	5316	27587	17982	1698	4019	3888
1993	135960	64990	21620	17061	32290	89803	40224	16805	8756	9343	23430	18632	6148	3115	4522	4847	27526	18617	1700	3195	4013
1994	144082	67199	23042	19706	34136	93959	41672	17912	8674	10135	24239	20302	6319	3261	5216	5506	29822	19208	1869	4354	4391
1995	149022	68649	25483	18642	36248	98813	42529	20072	8625	10508	25702	20078	6470	3549	3935	6124	30131	19650	1861	4198	4422
1996	150793	69875	25604	18683	36631	100584	43755	20194	8673	10550	26085	20078	6470	3549	3935	6124	30131	19650	1861	4198	4422
1997	157415	72094	26948	18972	39401	106584	45329	21107	8968	11571	28577	20239	6617	3890	3444	6289	30592	20148	1951	3957	4536
1998	161399	74160	26500	19383	41356	108001	46654	20891	11185	10648	29808	21170	6821	3545	4072	6732	32229	20685	2064	4664	4816
Share (percent)																					
1992	100.0	46.4	15.7	13.9	24.0	100.0	43.8	18.7	–	11.3	26.2	100.0	31.5	15.0	25.5	28.0	100.0	65.2	6.2	14.6	14.1
1993	100.0	47.8	15.9	12.5	23.7	100.0	44.8	18.7	–	10.4	26.1	100.0	33.0	16.7	24.3	26.0	100.0	67.6	6.2	11.6	14.6
1994	100.0	46.6	16.0	13.7	23.7	100.0	44.4	19.1	–	10.8	25.8	100.0	31.1	16.1	25.7	27.1	100.0	64.4	6.3	14.6	14.7
1995	100.0	46.3	17.0	12.4	24.3	100.0	43.5	20.1	–	10.5	25.9	100.0	32.2	17.7	19.6	30.5	100.0	65.2	6.2	13.9	14.7
1996	100.0	45.8	17.1	12.1	25.0	100.0	42.5	19.8	–	10.9	26.8	100.0	32.7	19.2	17.0	31.1	100.0	65.9	6.4	12.9	14.8
1997	100.0	45.9	16.4	12.0	25.6	100.0	43.2	19.3	–	9.9	27.6	100.0	32.2	16.7	19.2	31.8	100.0	64.2	6.4	14.5	14.9
1998																					
Year to year change (percent)																					
1992																					
1993	–1.4	1.9	–7.5	–2.2	–3.1	–5.3	0.9	–10.0	–1.8	–17.6	–5.4	7.0	2.9	–0.1	27.0	0.9	7.1	3.9	9.1	22.5	7.2
1994	–0.8	2.2	0.7	–10.7	–2.0	–0.8	1.5	–0.7	–4.8	–8.9	–1.3	–1.8	2.9	9.5	–6.5	–8.8	–0.2	3.5	0.1	–20.5	3.2
1995	6.0	3.4	6.6	15.5	5.7	4.6	3.6	6.6	–0.9	8.5	3.5	9.0	2.8	4.7	15.4	13.6	8.3	3.2	10.0	36.3	9.4
1996	3.4	2.2	10.6	–5.4	6.2	5.2	2.1	12.1	–0.6	3.7	6.0	–1.1	2.4	8.8	–24.6	11.2	1.0	2.3	–0.4	–3.6	0.7
1997	4.4	3.2	5.2	1.5	7.6	6.0	3.6	4.5	3.4	9.7	9.6	0.8	2.3	9.6	–12.5	2.7	1.5	2.5	4.8	–5.7	2.6
1998	2.5	2.9	–1.7	2.2	5.0	1.3	2.9	–1.0	24.7	–8.0	4.3	4.6	3.1	–8.9	18.2	7.1	5.4	2.7	5.8	17.9	6.2

Source: MITI via author's communication.

TABLE 4.13
Comparative Allocation of R&D Funds

	Total			Industrial			University		
	Basic	*Applied*	*Development*	*Basic*	*Applied*	*Development*	*Basic*	*Applied*	*Development*
Japan	15	24.6	60.5	6.8	22.2	71.1	54.2	37.1	8.7
United States	17.3	23.2	59.5	5.9	22	72.2	67.1	25.2	7.6
Germany	21		79	5.7		94.3	73.4		26.6

Source: MITI, *White Paper on International Trade* (1997).
Notes: Japan data are FY94, United States data are FY95, Germany data are FY91; German data do not distinguish between "Applied" and "Development".

If any change had occurred, it would have only pushed Japanese R&D further in what we would today consider the right direction of private funding and applied usefulness.

A similar point can be made about Japan's patent laws more generally. The extent of patent protection for innovators is a critical component in the willingness of companies to undertake large and risky investments needed for technological progress. In the post-war period, patent protection in Japan has been relatively weak as compared to American standards (although certainly much stronger than in most of the rest of Asia, and than in some other OECD countries). In Japan, patent applications are made public within 18 months of filing, allowing competitors to copy and reverse engineer, even though the granting of patent rights can take years longer. The pendency period is only seven years, and the legal code puts a narrower scope on the claims owners can make about what their invention covers. Since the Uruguay Round of trade negotiations concluded in 1994, Japanese patent protection was extended to twenty years, English language applications for Japanese patents deemed acceptable, and the Japanese patent model has converged on international norms.[30] As in other aspects of the Japanese innovation system, on this measure of patent rights, Japan exhib-

[30] The acceptance of English language patent applications is doubly important – of course, it eases the ability of foreigners to make claims for patent protection of their innovations in Japan, but it also eases the process of application for most scientists, given the use of English as the language of work in most technical fields.

ited little variation over the periods of high and low performance, and what change occurred was in what would be considered the constructive direction.

Even taking into account the large gross amount of finance provided for R&D in Japan, and the fact that it is largely provided by private-sector sources, the efficiency of the way that capital gets allocated to specific projects, and whether that changed over time, is still an open question. Of particular concern is the flow of funds to newer firms and start-ups. Although there have been examples of important businesses arising from individual or partnerships of entrepreneurs in post-war Japan, such as Sony and Honda, most observers of the Japanese economy have expressed concern about the willingness of the "Main Bank system" of Japan to shuttle funds to small and medium enterprises (SMEs). SMEs unaffiliated with supplier networks to larger firms, let alone keiretsu, are thought to be often shut out, even though such independents are probably the source of many innovative advances. And like almost every other developed economy, the culture and practice of venture capital in Japan is thought to exhibit far less vitality than in the United States.

The flip side of who gets the finance is how borrowing firms get monitored in their activities. The OECD (1995) analysis of *National Systems for Financing Innovation* gives a good description of the widely perceived differences between American-style "short-termism" and a Japanese or continental European "corporate governance" on both sides of the allocation/

monitoring coin.[31] The Japanese monitoring approach was held to have the benefit of maintaining funding through a firm's temporary liquidity problems, because involved stakeholding lenders are more able to see the actual promise of current investments beyond current cash-flow; it was also hoped that the relationship banking approach would preclude some excessive risk taking on the part of borrowing firms, in which those firms funded largely by (collateral and monitor free) equity might engage.[32] These claimed advantages were not only offset by the putative lending biases against new entrants, listed above, but also the difficulties of firms making a liquid exit when needed from a web of cross-shareholdings and large scale lending, where merger activity was largely absent.

In practice, the system of corporate finance in Japan is the aspect of the Japanese economic system to have undergone the most profound—although still partial—transformation in the last twenty years.[33] Interestingly, it has been mostly in the direction of greater liberalization and securitization, starting with a round of deregulation in 1984–6, which has allowed major nonfinancial firms to issue bonds and commercial paper (rather than to depend upon banks), and given a broader range of companies better access to capital markets. Between 1984 and 1990, the share of bonds in corporate liabilities doubled (from 4 to 8 percent), while the amount of bank lending remained stable at around 60 percent (see Table 4.14). This aggre-

TABLE 4.14

Financial Liabilities of Japanese Non-Financial Corporations (percentage shares, some categories omitted)

Year	Bank loans	Bonds
1980	56.5	3.4
1981	57.1	3.5
1982	59.5	3.8
1983	59.6	3.8
1984	59.8	4
1985	62.2	5.4
1986	64	5.8
1987	60.8	6.5
1988	61.8	6.7
1989	61.1	7.8
1990	60.7	8
1991	60.5	8.7
1992	62.1	8.7
1993	62.8	8.3
1994	62.3	8.3
1995	60.8	6.8
1996	59.6	7.4
1997	59.2	8.2

gate picture of the corporate sector masks an enormous distributional shift, with the biggest corporations radically cutting back their dependence on bank loans, and hundreds of nonkeiretsu affiliated SMEs getting new access to bank credit on the basis of land collateral rather than evaluation of credit worthiness (OECD, 1995; Shimizu, 2000).

This partial deregulation led to deposit rich banks losing their highest quality corporate borrowers. The banks' diversification of their loan portfolios declined along with average quality as the SMEs all offered the same form of collateral, and similar correlations with the business cycle. With both banks and nonbank enterprises using loans based on land price increases to purchase equities, the partial deregulation of Japanese banks was a major source of the land and stock market bubble of the late 1980s, and was the primary cause of Japan's eventual banking crisis in the 1990s. For the purpose of this chapter's investigations, what is worth noting is that from 1984 until the credit crunch came in 1997 when banks' cost of loanable funds and level of nonperforming

---

[31] A cautionary reminder is in order, that as late as 1992, the *Harvard Business Review* and MIT's Made In America project, as well as the U.S. Government's Competitiveness Policy Council, were emphasizing the purported advantages of "patient" Japanese corporate finance through bank lending, as opposed to the "short-termism" of American stock market based financing. This was held to be especially true for allowing investment to take a long-term perspective on such matters as research and development.

[32] Aoki and Patrick (1994) make the academic case in favor of the Japanese Main Bank system.

[33] A much more detailed account of the developments summarized in this and the following paragraph can be found in Hoshi and Kashyap (2001) and Mikitani and Posen (2000).

loans rose sharply, availability of credit to new firms rose, and the cost of capital to established firms fell. If anything, there was *over-investment* in capital projects in corporate Japan, right through the mid-1990s when bad loans were repeatedly rolled over (rather than foreclosed and written down) due to moral hazard on the part of below-adequacy or even negatively capitalized banks.[34]

Thus, even though the Japanese bank-based financial system clearly did great harm to the macroeconomy as a whole in the 1990s, and probably was not helpful in prior years,[35] it would seem to have been at least as supportive of *financing innovation* in recent years as it was in the past. Living up to some of the claims made for benefits of a long time-horizon for investment from relationship banking put forward during Japan's heyday, major Japanese corporations sustained the financing of R&D activities throughout even the investment and growth downturns of the 1990s. It is clear that, given the limited share of innovative activities in economic performance, and the costs of rolling-over unproductive investments, on balance such a financial system is a drag on the economy, even if R&D funding is stabilized by it.

Moreover, the experience of the 1990s has demonstrated the continued bias of relationship lenders in the Japanese financial system in favor of those who have already borrowed, and against outsider firms. Even as the pool of

those who were on the inside, and able to gain financing, rose in membership and declined in quality from 1984 onwards, the criteria for lending were biased backwards to SMEs with previously accumulated assets (particularly land) and relationships (e.g., as suppliers to established firms). Start-ups with intangible assets and future customers associated with new products or ideas were shut out (in contrast to the venture capital industry and the high price/earnings ratios for new firms in the United States). Thus, there is still potential for missed innovative investment opportunities in Japan, even while overall R&D spending is maintained through economic downturns. Japanese bankruptcy law, which as one would expect puts a great deal of power into the hands of debt holders, and gives strong incentives not to declare bankruptcy, additionally constrains risk-taking behavior by lenders and by potential heads of start-ups.[36]

Japan has consistently had a lower rate of both business start-ups and bankruptcies than the United States, which sets the benchmark for the pace of corporate "creative destruction." From 1981 to 1996, an annual average of 4–5 percent of the total number of business establishments in Japan were started, and a comparable number were closed[37] (Tanaka, 2000); in the United States over the same period, business openings ranged from 13 to 15 percent of the total number of establishments every year, and closures ranged from 11 to 13 percent. Of course, this turnover of business firms in the United States consists mostly of small service and retail sector companies (restaurants, frame shops, contractors), not high-tech start-

---

[34] Even though aggregate investment did clearly decline in the early 1990s (see Table 4.1), the fact that problem loans were rolled over rather than called for the most part meant that capital losses were not recognized at the borrowing firms, and so their investments did not decline anywhere near as much as they should have. Moreover, because the largest firms had already largely left the banking system for their major financing needs, and the application of tighter lending standards/bank recapitalization has only been extended to part of the Japanese banking system, SMEs have been the major recipients of this largess.

[35] Why else would so many strong nonfinancial firms, when given the opportunity to exit banking relationships in the mid-1980s, have done so? Why else would so many SMEs take advantage of new opportunities to borrow if they had not been credit constrained in the past? See Hoshi et al. (1990) and Weinstein and Yafeh (1998).

[36] Among the more off-putting aspects of Japanese bankruptcy law are that: creditors holding more than 10 percent of equity can declare for the firm, on the condition that the creditors believe the debtors will be unable to pay; there is only limited relief from creditors during reorganization, and no official receiver is appointed until the reorganization is complete; and the scope of the debtors' assets protected from confiscation is very narrow, limited to clothing, furniture, and other everyday items.

[37] Table 4.6 shows the growth rates in these numbers, with bankruptcies increasing faster than start-ups in both the 1980s and 1990s.

TABLE 4.15
Comparative Venture Capital: Japan and United States (1996 data)

	Japan	United States
Outside sources of new venture funding (percent)[a]		
Pension funds	0	40
Endowments	0	20
Domestic corporations	26	18
Financial sector	49	5
Individuals	1	8
Overseas investors	4	2
Venture funding (percent) by stage (years from founding)		
<1	2	5
1–5	20	46
6–10	20	32
11–20 (Japan), 11–15 (United States)	25	12
21+ (Japan), 16+ (United States)	32	5

	Japan	United States	Percentage Japan/United States
Overall venture capital environment (1996 data)			
Venture capital companies	165	699	24
Annual total investment	¥231 billion	$10 billion	21 (at ¥109/U.S.$)
Total new established	¥105.5 billion	$6.6 billion	15
Newly public companies	168	755	22 (at ¥109/U.S.$)
Total companies on OTCs	752	5568	14

Source: Weitzman (1999).
[a] Does not sum to 100 percent due to missing responses.

ups and failures, and similarly for Japan. So a steady rise in the amount of firms being allowed to exit from the Japanese business sector is probably a healthy development for the economy as a whole.[38] For innovation, the question is how many risky bets get backed to start up, even if that is a small proportion of total new businesses.

As already mentioned, the Japanese venture capital situation is far less developed than that of the United States. In 1996, for example, 75 percent of the outside funding for new ventures came from the banking system or other established companies in Japan and none from pension funds or endowment investors, while in the United States 60 percent came from those latter two sources (the more traditional angels of equity) and only 23 percent came from established corporations or banks (see Table 4.15). A survey in 1999 by Japan's National Life Finance Corporation found that family, friends, and relatives provided 42 percent of the total initial finance for start-ups, and financial firms and established corporations 35 percent (i.e., 57 percent of the outside funding). As seen in the second and third panels of Table 4.15, the Japanese venture capital sector, in addition to playing a smaller role, also tends to get in much later in a

[38] "Allowed to exit" is used consciously, given the legal, public, financial, and informal networks which constrain the free entry and exit of businesses from sectors in Japan. Ideally, this would be an impersonal market outcome, not a set of conscious decisions, but that is not yet the case for much of the economy.

company's development (77 percent of funding occurs after five years, versus 49 percent in the United States), and this has resulted in a much smaller number of new firms making it all the way to over-the-counter (OTC) stock market listings (14 percent as many in Japan as in the United States, while the Japanese economy is now less than 40 percent the size of the U.S. economy).

The underdevelopment of venture capital is an acknowledged concern by various Japanese government agencies. The New Business Promotion Department of MITI notes (2000) disapprovingly that in FY1999 the average amount of a given venture capital stake given to a start-up was Yen 45million in Japan, or about U.S.$400,000, while the average stake put up by an American venture capitalist was twelve times as much, or U.S.$4.9 million. This is attributed in part to the absence of pension funds and the like engaging in any investment, or in venture capital specifically in Japan. "If Japan's pension funds invested 2–3% of their total managed assets in venture capital investments on par with the U.S. situation in the 1980s, it would create Yen 5trillion [about 1% of a year's GDP] in venture capital, or five to six times more than the total amount of outstanding venture capital funds [in Japan] today."[39] While this emphasizes the sense of innovative opportunities missed by the Japanese financial system, it again raises an issue which cannot be said to have changed for the worse as a prelude to or concurrent with the slowdown in the 1990s, or makes Japan noticeably different from other OECD economies. On the availability of venture capital, it is the United States which is a (positive) outlier.

The final measurable input into the previously described Japanese national innovation system is that of labor and human capital. This is the one area where it could be argued that the quantity of a necessary factor in the production of innovation, in this case, of appropriately skilled labor, has declined in the 1990s. Japanese primary and secondary education remains of high quality and essentially universal.[40] The number of students going on to higher education has risen in recent years, rising from 36.1 percent in 1987 to 47.3 percent in 1997, a ratio comparable to that in the United States; graduate education, however, lags behind with the number of graduate students in Japan amounting to only 6.6 percent of the number of undergraduates, as opposed to 13.2 percent in the United States.[41]

Turning specifically to training for technological innovation, the Japanese university system curriculum in science and engineering is consistent with its use of R&D funds, described above; very applied studies are given relative weight over training in basic science, but connections with the private-sector are scarce. This is also the mirror image of most science and engineering education in the United States. In fact, private industry's funding of university research almost completely stopped in the 1970s, and the government took active steps to encourage its limited revival in the 1990s (many Japanese scholars and students jealously observed Japanese businesses' funding of research laboratories and university programs in U.S. science and engineering schools).

Perhaps as a result, the old system of each professor as an autonomous unit (*koza*) has survived, which keeps graduate students and junior faculty as disciples for long periods, and encourages incremental progress on the full professor's oft-lagging ongoing research agenda (Nakayama et al., 1999). Faculty members are recruited for the top schools from within, with no value put (and probably some sanction) on outside work or consulting experience in the private sector, while the lower

---

[40] In 1997, 96.8 percent of Japanese students aged fifteen and older went on to (three-year) high school, and were taught the rigorous nationally approved curriculum. It is beyond the scope of this essay to consider whether the common portrayal of Japanese education as rigid, emphasizing memorization and conformity, and stifling creativity holds true, and how much this detracts from the wide range of knowledge conveyed to students.

[41] Ministry of Education, Science, Sports and Culture data from *Comparison of International Educational Indices* (Japanese data are from 1995, U.S. data are from 1992).

[39] New Business Development (2000).

tier schools tend to hire faculty from the higher ranking universities when they retire.[42]

It is therefore no wonder that most Japanese firms believe they have to offer a year or more of "relevant" training after hiring to even Masters of Engineering graduates. Meanwhile, given the age profile of the faculty, the lack of corporate relationships, and the status quo bias, it should come as no surprise that the Japanese universities are significantly behind their American counterparts (and the Japanese private sector) in working on new IT technologies. The University of Tokyo, the nation's most prestigious school of higher education, does not even have an IT department, and MITI projects a shortage of 200,000 information/computer technology engineers in the coming years.[43]

Of course, the U.S. education system has also left the American economy short of skilled engineers and scientists, and the government has responded to business demands by increasing the number of immigration visas for such workers to the hundreds of thousands per year. Japan has begun down that road, but the number of foreign engineers in Japan in 1999 totaled only 15,700 (up from only 3,400 in 1991). It is in the area of skilled labor that Japan's innovation inputs may indeed be falling short in the 1990s, although this should still further explain the inability to keep up with U.S. advances rather than a decline of innovation (unless we believe IT innovation to be the only field where major advances can be made at present). The ongoing lack of both skilled and unskilled labor inputs, likely to worsen as Japan gets older, is a constraint on high-technology production as well as on the economy as a whole. Of course, greater utilization of women in the Japanese work force, and the raising of

the retirement age for already very long-lived and healthy Japanese workers, could combine with increased immigration or guest-workers to address this shortfall.

4.4. Independence of Innovation Outputs from Macroeconomic Performance

The relationship between technological innovation and national economic performance is likely to be a two-way street. While most of the traffic goes from advancements in technology and productivity to growth, there is also some flow in the other direction from growth providing the environment and resources for innovation. In the case of Japan, we have already seen that the national innovation system and more measurable innovation inputs were essentially unchanged over the period of Japan's rapid post-war growth from the 1960s to the mid-1980s, the bubble economy period of 1985–90, and even after the persistent economic slowdown of the 1990s. If we believe that variations in national economic performance are tightly tied to changes in technological innovation, over time-spans as short as business cycles, this is a disturbing result. Of course, inputs are just that, inputs, and what generates changes in productivity are innovation *outputs*, such as actual patents, high-value-added exports, and technological leadership in advanced industries. Perhaps a close association between innovation and performance in the Japanese post-war experience, including the reversal of economic performance in the last decade, can be found in the quality and quantity of Japanese innovation.

There is a plausible case to be made that although the Japanese national innovation system was largely unchanged in its structures, practices, and inputs from the 1950s through the 1990s, the world and technology changed around it, making the same system less effective at producing innovation in the 1990s. The assessment of the declining relevance of technical higher education in Japan given in the previous section bears some resemblance to this view. This interpretation that the technological world is moving past Japan could be the

---

[42] This cascade of older professors is recognized and encouraged by the differing retirement ages for faculty across universities. University of Tokyo and Tokyo Institute of Technology at the top have a retirement age of sixty, the remaining quality public universities have a retirement age of sixty-three, and the private universities have a retirement age of seventy or more.

[43] "Japan finds the powerhouse empty of skilled IT workers," Michiyo Nakamoto and Alexandra Harney, *Financial Times*, August 10 (2000: 12).

case even if the assessment of the previous section is correct, that the Japanese system permitted far more competition, with far less research coordination and picking winners, than often thought. Such a mismatch hypothesis could be true even if all of the major changes that occurred in the Japanese innovation system would have to be classified as improvements in encouraging innovation. The mismatch between Japanese economic organization and the global technology shift (to the creativity required for software and biotech, for example) would simply have to outweigh these positive factors. Such an explanation would of course allow the decline in Japanese national economic performance in the 1990s to be attributed, at least in part, to technical change after all.

This position was partly advanced by Lincoln (1988) for Japanese industrial and commercial practices more broadly, not specifically innovation, in his argument that a mature—meaning wealthy and technologically "caught-up"—Japan, having exhausted foreign technology, would have to adapt its structures to remain within acceptable political bounds on trade competition and still grow. In terms of economic analysis of growth rates, however, this argument would seem to imply that Japan should have slowed down more than the average estimated effect of convergence which occurs to all countries as they approach the technological frontier and the accumulation of advanced levels of human and physical capital, and this was not the case.[44] The declines in TFP growth of Japan throughout the post-war period seen in Tables 4.7 and 4.8 are in line with what growth economics would predict, or if anything *lower* than one would expect based on convergence.[45] This would also seem to imply that the Japanese rate of innovation should have abruptly declined upon losing easy targets for reverse or improvement engineering, which we will examine.

The idea that the unchanged Japanese innovation system no longer works given current changes in the pace or nature of technology has also been asserted more pointedly in recent years specifically with regard to technical development, although in much looser form than

Lincoln. For examples among responsible observers inside and outside Japan, see OECD (1998b), "More generally, weak business performance has led some to question the appropriateness of the Japanese corporate system in an environment which requires rapid decision-making and calculated risk-taking to achieve higher rates of return." MITI's *White Papers on International Trade* of 1998–2000 call for structural reform to converge on the U.S. model because of the gap with the United States in ICT, software, and biotechnology; and the NITSDC (1999) states, "The targets of technological innovation were clear enough in the catch-up years when Japan was achieving rapid economic growth due to increased demand. [As opposed to the present,] such targets as building a product image concept or fulfilling requirements specified were easy to identify." The popular business press is, of course, filled with strong claims that Japan is not entrepreneurial or flexible or creative enough to take advantage of new industries like those in information technology fueling the U.S. boom, because they require start-ups and lack of conformity. Again, if these assertions were true, the measurable innovative inputs marshaled by the unchanged Japanese innovation system should be of declining value, and the measurable outputs in terms of technologies and competitiveness should decline as a result.

Data are readily available on whether innovation outputs of technologies and competitive

[44] Specifically, this would mean that using the sort of cross-country panel estimated by Barro discussed in the first section to make a prediction about growth rates, controlling for other fundamentals as well as convergence (proxied by initial per capita income), Japanese growth would come in below predicted levels starting sometime in the late 1970s or early 1980s. Japan, however, remained a positive outlier in such growth regressions until the 1990s.

[45] One could also point out that the Japanese growth rate actually speeded up for several years in the mid-1980s, Japanese income levels approached American levels, and when growth slowed, it was as Japanese income levels have declined in relative terms throughout the last decade. Even such multiyear swings are probably best seen as too short-term to be determined by convergence issues, which is precisely the point against the simple catch-up hypotheses.

TABLE 4.16
Comparative Shares of Academic Research

	Percentage share of world articles[a]	Percentage share of world citations[a]	Academic papers[b] (× 10,000)		Academic citations[b] (× 10,000)		Quality ratio: citations/papers[b]	
			1986	1996	1986	1996	1986	1996
Japan	9.6	8	7.7	9.9	6.6	7.8	0.86	0.79
United States	36.2	52.3	37.5	34.6	54.6	51.6	1.45	1.49
Germany	8.1	9.2	7.8	8.5	6.6	9.9	0.85	1.16

[a] *Source:* Science Citation Index Database, computed in MITI (1997), 1994 data.
[b] *Source:* OECD (1998: Table 33).

industries are declining in Japan during the period of Japanese economic decline. Turning first to measures of the academic research produced in the sciences, Japan, of course, does continue to lag behind the United States in the capture of Nobel Prizes (see Table 4.11), and does not produce the amount of academic papers or citations proportional to its share of world population or wealth. As seen in the first panel of Table 4.16, Japan and Germany have essentially equivalent shares of articles and citations listed in the Science Citation Index (SCI) database for a representative sample year (1994), despite the German economy and population being two-thirds the size of Japan's, and the United States has several-fold more articles and citations.[46] This is a statement about comparative levels, however, not about whether Japan's share has suffered a sustained decline in recent years, and there is no evidence of that.

The second panel of Table 4.16 presents OECD (1998) data taken from the SCI in 1986 and 1996. The gap between the U.S. and Japanese number of papers published, and the number of total citations to published articles, actually closes over the decade, and in absolute terms both the number of refereed published technical papers by Japanese authors, and the

number of citations to Japanese authors rises (by 22 percent and 18 percent, respectively). It must be noted that Japan's "quality ratio" (defined as number of citations per paper) declines slightly (by 8 percent) over the decade, while the American quality ratio is essentially unchanged. So despite the concerns about the basic research capabilities of Japan as the global cutting edge technologies shifted in the 1990s, there is no evidence of a sharp decline, rather some of an improvement.

Turning to actual patents applied for and received, the evidence is also that Japanese innovation has kept up with the times. As noted previously, the 1994 Uruguay Round of the GATT led to some standardization of patent protection and procedures across countries, as well as some specific changes in the Japanese framework. This makes longitudinal comparison of data before and after 1993 somewhat problematic, but makes easier the comparison of developments across countries since that time.[47] What can be seen is that Japan has in recent years had the lion's share of patent and utility model applications worldwide. In 1997, for example, Japan filed 9.4 percent of the world's patent applications, versus 5.2 percent for the United States and 4.3 percent for

---

[46] The SCI article and publication numbers, while the best available measure, inherently understate the actual contributions of Japanese researchers because many publish some or all of their work in Japanese, which of course limits their outlets and readership (as might publishing in English as a second language, for a given quality of research). There is unfortunately no way of estimating the size of this effect.

[47] Additionally, in 1987 Japan changed its "model application" for patent protection, revising the multiple claim system which previously obtained, resulting in a steady increase in the number of patents applied for within Japan since 1988. This, too, makes analysis of the long-term pattern of Japanese patent data problematic.

Germany.[48] Of patent rights owned worldwide in 1997, the United States held 1,113,000, Japan held 871,000, and Germany held 337,000. Unlike academic papers, Japan carries a share of patents much larger than its proportionate share (as compared to the United States or to the world total) based on population and wealth. The U.S. National Research Council/Japan Society for the Promotion of Science joint task force (1999) observed that basic research conducted by Japanese corporations has been undiminished through the 1990s, while corporate basic research has actually declined in the United States. Another indication in line with the discussion under inputs, that Japan's system does maintain long-term investment, and that even if that has predictably positive effects on innovation, those do not necessarily outweigh other factors on growth (including some potentially harmful ones directly from low returns on capital).

In line with Japan's on-going production of patentable technologies, the country's balance of technology trade has improved over time. Up until the mid-1970s, Japanese firms were heavily dependent upon technological imports from the United States and Europe. As Japanese private sector R&D activities increased in the late 1970s and the 1980s, technological exports increased, first to the developed economies, and in the 1990s increasingly to affiliates or operations of Japanese multinationals in the emerging Asia. As MITI (1998) notes, the value of Japanese technological imports from Western countries remained steady in the 1990s—Japan's overall technology trade deficit has ranged between 1 and 4 percent of GDP since 1980, with no pattern of expansion in the last 10 years. This would appear to be inconsistent with a world in which new technologies emerged outside Japan that were of particularly high value added, such that Japanese firms would be incapable of producing the goods (at least in part) themselves, or of finding other technologically advanced goods to trade

for them. It is an undeniable reality that Japan has shortfalls in the production of ICT, software, and related services, especially as compared to the United States, but these are not the only high-tech goods in the world.[49] Even if investment in these technologies may have special spillover benefits for growth, that is a matter of the economy as a whole adopting them, and *not of producing* those products themselves. In other words, the willingness of the Japanese economy to do necessary capital deepening as new transformative technologies arise is likely to be independent of whether Japan has the technical capacity to produce high-tech goods; this point is discussed further in the next section.

In fact, according to the U.S. Patent and Trademark Office, the five fields generating the most patents annually since 1995 are active solid-state technologies, optics, computerized control systems, semiconductor manufacturing processes, and pharmaceuticals. Japanese companies are among the world leaders in the first four of these, and nearly control the markets for optical and active solid-state technologies.[50] In the last five years, patents granted to Japanese inventors and corporations have averaged 19 percent of the total annual patents granted by the U.S. Patent and Trademark Office, twice the proportion of twenty years

---

[48] Policy Planning and Research Office (2000), from WIPO and MITI data. Annual patent and utility applications from Japan consistently stay within the range of 39,000–46,000 per year.

[49] "Japan continues to import technologies from Europe and the United States in the fields of telecommunications and electronics, and, while relying less than before on foreign sources for hardware, depends increasingly on foreign software ... Looking at service industries, Japan ranks first in service trade deficit among major countries, and is weak in international competitiveness owing to low service export intensity." (MITI, 1998: 14).

[50] In Fransman's (1999) assessment of the ICT industries, "four out of the world's top ten computer companies are Japanese (Fujitsu, NEC, Hitachi, Toshiba); two out of the top ten telecommunications equipment firms are Japanese (NEC and Fujitsu); and six out of the top ten semiconductor companies are Japanese (NEC, Toshiba, Hitachi, Fujitsu, Misubishi Electric, and Matsushita) ... [these firms] dominated global markets in areas such as memory, semiconductors, optoelectronic semiconductors, microcontrollers and LCDs ... [they have been] significantly less successful outside Japan in crucial markets such as mainframe computers, workstations, servers, personal computers, microprocessors, packaged software, and complex telecommunications equipment."

TABLE 4.17
Leading Companies in Total U.S. Patents

	Rank in total new patents granted in that year				
	1999	*1998*	*1997*	*1996*	*1995*
IBM	1	1	1	1	1
NEC	2	3	3	4	4
Canon	3	2	2	2	2
Samsung	4	6	16	18	21
Sony	5	5	9	9	11
Toshiba	6	8	8	7	6
Fujitsu	7	7	5	8	12
Motorola	8	4	4	3	3
Lucent	9	13	11	34	na
Mitsubishi Electric	10	11	7	6	5

Source: U.S. Patent and Trademark Office.
Note: Japanese firms are shown in bold typeface.

ago.[51] As shown in Table 4.17, six of the top ten patenting companies with the U.S. Patent and Trademark Office in 1999 were Japanese, and every one of those six had been in the top ten either four or all five out of the five years 1995–9. The *Business Week* "Info Tech 200" list for 2000 puts 148 of the world's top ICT companies in the United States, while Japan has only 17 which make the list – but that 17 is good enough for second place in the national statistics, with Canada (5), Taiwan (5), and Sweden (3) rounding out the top five locations. Again, this is difficult to reconcile with a belief that recent technological advances have left Japan behind,

or that a mature Japanese economy is incapable of advancing the technical frontier. That these years coincided with the worst macroeconomic performance by the Japanese economy since 1950 is an especially striking indication of the apparent independence of Japanese innovative outputs from economic performance.[52]

4.5. The Disjuncture between High-tech Innovation and Broader Productivity Trends in Japan

Obviously, the fact that Japan has steady investment in R&D, ongoing success in generating innovation, and competitive high-tech industries has been insufficient to maintain a high level of national economic performance. This could be due to the fact that in the medium-term of even a decade such factors as macroeconomic policy and financial market efficiency, as well as external shocks, predominate in swings of growth.[53] Yet, the importance of technology to economic performance should not be entirely discarded, even for the swing in Japa-

[51] U.S. Patent Trademark Office data cited in "The Alchemy of Innovation," Conrad de Aendle, *International Herald Tribune*, September 23 (2000: 13)

[52] In a provocative empirical paper, Edward Wolff (1999: 12) groups industries by their R&D intensity of production, and by their growth rates, and analyzes whether Japan specialized in the wrong industries as compared to Germany and the United States. He concludes "... that generally speaking [in 1970–1989] Japan's industrial structure moved towards industries experiencing higher growth rates ... In the 1989–94 period, by contrast, the overall output growth rate is insensitive to the choice of output weights. This result indicates that the slowdown in aggregate growth over this period is due to the decline of output growth across the full range of industries in Japan, rather than to a shift in output towards slower growth industries.".

[53] Posen (1998: chapter 6) makes an argument to this effect as a warning to premature judging of "national economic models" as determinative of swings in economic growth, let alone as cohesive wholes.

nese growth of the last two decades; it is arguable that the major contribution of innovation to national economic performance is in how it is used and implemented across a national economy, rather than in capturing the benefits of innovation itself.

It is well known that the bulk of the Japanese economy, in fact practically the entire economy outside of the export-oriented manufacturing sectors, is beset by very low productivity, extreme inflexibility, and long-term stagnation (except where government patronage directly increases demand). There has been a complete lack of diffusion of either technical progress or labor productivity from the high-tech sector to the rest of the Japanese economy in the last forty years. This bears some resemblance to the assessment made by Gordon (in chapter 3) that, in the United States in the 1990s, the bulk of the productivity gains were made in the computer equipment industry, and were not seen (as yet) in the rest of the manufacturing sector, let alone the rest of the American economy. It would appear that technical progress can be very localized in its benefits, if the nature of the technology is simply to make production of one product (here, computers) cheaper.

Council of Economic Advisers (2001), however, argues that much of the American "New Economy" was due to the benefits of adoption of IT in sectors outside of IT production because it is a "transformative" technology; just-in-time inventory through computerization, greater tailoring of financial and other business services, more decentralized production schemes for workers, and so on, emerge out of IT usage. That report offers the first rigorous empirical evidence that productivity gains in the American economy in the 1990s can be linked to the diffusion of IT across firms. The argument is far from settled, however, and not only because we must wait to see what productivity gains survive the American downturn beginning in the last quarter of 2000. Cohen et al. (2001) note that many changes in U.S. corporate practices, particularly in dealing with their workforces, defining the boundaries of the firm, and increasing flexibility of production—the same practices which Council of Economic Advisers (2001) point to as critical to U.S. improvements in productivity—began to be adopted in the mid-1980s, timed to observable changes in labor demand, and well before IT investment was large or widespread.

What is relevant for understanding the Japanese experience from this American discussion is that, to whatever one ascribes the U.S. productivity gains, the Japanese economy already had it, at least in part; the efficiencies of production of IT components are in industries where Japanese firms and licensed technologies play a key role; the share, level, and growth of business investment in IT is higher in Japan than in any other advanced nation except the United States;[54] the high performance work organizations, including total quality management and team production, as well as just-in-time inventory were prevalent in Japanese manufacturing, and were a model for U.S. adoption. So it is striking that the overwhelming majority of Japanese economic activity has not benefited from these attributes the way that the American economy has. A persistently dual economy to the degree it exists in Japan is really rather odd.

Even putting aside supposedly transformative technologies like ICT and the internet, the idea that there could be so little spillover benefit or seepage of knowledge about productive practices from the advanced sectors in whatever technology to the rest of the Japanese economy for so long goes against some of our common ideas about technical progress. We usually assume that information or knowledge is nonrival and difficult to completely appropriate, that is, that the original innovator's using it does not constrain my also benefiting from it, and that it is difficult for that innovator to keep the knowledge completely to him-/herself. Put bluntly, patent protection is rarely impervious to efforts at copying, stealing, or reverse engineering of a product, technique, or process. This is especially true for the broader or more organizational innovations, for example, the concept of just-in-time inventory, and the methods for

---

[54] See Fujitsu Research Institute (1997), OECD (2000), and Tanaka (2000) for data on total IT investment.

implementing it, or the idea of the video cassette recorder, which tend to be quickly emulated by the innovator's competitors.

The usual qualification to this assumption is that what we refer to as development, or the detailed implementation and utilization of the knowledge in a specific product is where the profits really come from. It is true that workers can move from place to place, and learning by doing in one product line or with one client or supplier can spill over to others. It is also true that such things as brand names, client relationships, specialized design, management and especially shop floor skills permit a firm, whether the innovator or a follower, to maintain some property rights. So Toyota can watch manufacturing firms around the world adopt just-in-time inventory and quality circles, but its workers (and the training of them) allow Toyota to garner the benefits of more successfully implementing the same innovations; Sony and Phillips can both create the video recorder, find that every other consumer electronics company has their own competing model within months, and be forced to make their profits from their brand names and additional features or quality, not from coming up with the innovation itself.

For the purposes of this discussion, the key implication is that technological innovations should diffuse, both across borders within the same industry, and across industries within the same country, given sufficient human and financial capital to take advantage of the innovation. This diffusion is part of what lies behind the story of conditional macroeconomic convergence in the Solow growth model, seen in the cross-national evidence. A belief in the power of this diffusion is what underlies the many stories of Japan growing through reverse engineering and conscious "catch-up" with Western products. For an industrial sector to remain technologically backwards within a country that has good universal education, free flow of information, and some minimum mobility of workers and capital, usually some government policy (like public ownership, protection of interest groups from competition, or discrimination) is at work to reduce the incentives to improve productivity.[55]

The Japanese dual economy of forty years and counting—clearly the result of excessive government protection of particular interest groups—illustrates just how powerful such government and social disincentives can be even when more productive practices are literally around the corner. McKinsey Global Institute (2000) goes into painful detail documenting how the tightly controlled distribution network for products, the prevalence of mom-and-pop retail stores, the legal environment preventing the adoption of economies of scale in either distribution or stores, the lack of transparency in pricing for consumers, and the political connections of the small store owners to the Liberal Democratic Party, combine to increase the costs and decrease the efficiency of all purchasing in Japan; and, of course, this has implications for the economy as a whole given that consumption is 65–70 percent of Japanese GDP.[56] Hoshi and Kashyap (2001) document how the "convoy system" for Japanese banks and securities firms on the part of Japanese regulators—a much greater moral-hazard inducing version of "too big to fail"—interacted with connected lending relationships and barriers to competition to induce inefficient financial practices. Even manufacturing for domestic use or in lower-technology products in Japan suffers from over capacity and fragmented production due to lack of competition and a network that supports small companies.

The fact that these disincentives have co-existed with the Japanese national innovation system's success in producing technical progress, the Japanese world-beating export companies in high-tech sectors, and the years of both feast and famine in Japanese national economic performance, demonstrates that technological innovation on its own terms is a

[55] The existence of geographic pockets of backwardness in wealthy societies is another matter.

[56] At the margin there have been some changes in this backwards retail system in recent years, through changes in the retail stores law, the existence of internet shopping, and the creation of some discounters, but these small changes so far have not had much of a discernable impact on the Japanese economy.

TABLE 4.18
Comparative Cost Structure for Business (1997 data; Japan = 100)

	Japan	United States	Germany	Korea	Singapore
Energy					
Petroleum	100	67	117	152	53
Industrial power	100	77	81	44	38
Transport					
Railway	100	61	67	24	
Coastal shipping	100	131		40	
Port charges	100	90		47	53
Airfreight (international)	100	55	73	98	80
Telecoms					
Local calls	100	97	155	52	29
Long distance	100	48	65	23	
Real estate					
Commercial development	100	11	24	28	38
Office rental	100	55	52	56	70
Corporation tax					
Effective rate	100	82	100	65	54

far less powerful force in determining the fate of national economies than one might have thought. The regulatory structure of the economy (not specific to technology), along with macroeconomic and financial policy (as argued in the first section), may have much more to do with economic growth over any meaningful time horizon for policy than innovation does.[57] Of course, this assumes that the economy in question is at a sufficient level of development, wealth, popular education, and rule of law to allow innovation to occur where the specific protections do not apply.

[57] These sorts of interest group protecting regulations have not been classified here as an aspect of how the government treats innovation, or as part of a country's capacity to innovate. For one thing, so doing would extend the definition of innovation to be anything to do with productivity increases of any kind, and would erode any significance to the technological aspect. For another, these regulations are not directed against innovation, and their removal would directly enhance growth even if technical innovation halted. Finally, it is almost tautological to point out that protectionism, be it domestic or foreign, inhibits the flow of new technologies.

In Japan, unfortunately, the specific protections apply to almost the entire nontraded (i.e., without import competition) portion of the economy: services, retail, utilities, transportation, real estate, local construction, and so on. Table 4.18 gives the comparative costs to business in Japan and four other economies, including the United States, for various services or inputs to production. In every activity, with the exception of coastal shipping, American business costs are lower: 23–33 percent lower for energy, 39 percent lower for railway shipping, 45 percent lower for air freight shipping, 52 percent lower for long distance telecommunications, and 89 percent lower for the development of commercial real estate. Germany, Singapore, and South Korea also have meaningfully lower business costs than Japan in just about all of these categories. The high costs in each category represent either a regulation (limiting land uses), or a public monopoly (until recently on petroleum), or a government price support program of some sort (NTT on long distance services by wire) protecting an

TABLE 4.19
Diffusion Rate of Personal Computers and Networks (percentage of those surveyed)

	Japan			United States		
	Home PC	Office PC	Networks	Home PC	Office PC	Networks
1994	8.6	11.3	28	36.4	41.1	73
1995	11.1	14.1	35	39.8	46.5	82
1996	14.7	19.8	44	43.4	53.4	86
1997	21.6	27.8	48	47.4	59.1	90

Source: Industrial Policy Bureau (1998).

TABLE 4.20
Share of Information-Related Investment in Private Fixed Capital Investment (percent)

	1993	1994	1995	1996	1997	1998	1999
Japan	16.6	19.6	22.4	24.9	26.4	29.5	34.4
United States	26.8	27.7	29.7	31.9	34.1	37.3	42
Difference	10.2	8.1	7.3	7	7.7	7.8	7.6

Source: Tanaka (2000).
Note: Information-related investment includes medical and scientific equipment.

interest group, and therefore removing the incentive to increase productivity.

Consistent with this view, Agrawal et al. (1996) found that the productivity of capital in Japan is only two-thirds that in the United States, but the income share of capital is the same. This inefficiency can be attributed to Japanese corporate management underutilizing available resources, accepting local sourcing of equipment rather than searching globally, and demanding a relatively low financial return

TABLE 4.21
Foreign Direct Investment to and from Japan (Yen trillion in fiscal year)

	Inward	Outward
1994	0.4	4.3
1995	0.4	5
1996	0.8	5.4
1997	0.7	6.6
1998	1.3	5.2
1999	2.4	7.4
2000 (Jan–Jun)	1.9	na

Source: Ministry of Finance, author's communication.

on capital. For services in Japan, the picture is just as bleak. According to estimates from the Economic Planning Agency of Japan, the average price of services has quadrupled since 1970, while the retail value of manufacturing has only gone up by 70 percent. This is related directly to the productivity differential between the two sectors.

Meanwhile, the successful high-tech or high-value-added export companies in Japan, like electronics and automobiles, have shifted production overseas and cut domestic factories and employment, in an ongoing effort to stay competitive with additional productivity gains (Japan Development Bank, 1996). The irony of firms like Sony and Toshiba announcing cost-cutting and restructuring programs in 1998, while the construction industry in Japan continued to add 1000s of workers through the largesse of the Liberal Democratic Party majority in the Japanese Diet, cannot be overstated. Yet, the differential in productivity just keeps growing.

McKinsey Global Institute (2000) found that Japanese exporters in such industries as autos, steel, machine tools, and consumer electronics are still "bettering any and all [international] competitors' productivity by 20%," but those sectors only employ 10 percent of the Japanese workforce (no more than the legendarily unproductive construction sector alone). On McKinsey's (2000) estimates, the remaining 90 percent of the Japanese economy is only half as productive, with such sectors as retail, food processing, home construction, and health care running at around 60 percent of U.S. productivity levels in the same sectors. Even under the pressure of Japan's harshest recession, when real estate, wholesale and retail trade, agriculture and fisheries, finance and insurance, and construction are clearly underperforming, the already weak Japanese stock market, and their industries worldwide (Matsuoka and Calderwood, 1999)—and when the more productive Japanese firms continue to be recognized in financial markets, and to lead by example—there is no diffusion of more productive practices to be seen.

4.6. Conclusion: Accepting the Independence of Technological Innovation and National Economic Performance in the Japanese Case (and Beyond?)

Technological innovation is the ultimate source of any sustained economic growth. One can differentiate between truly revolutionary innovations, such as the steam engine or air conditioning or the transistor, and incremental improvements in production processes or products, such as Toyota's Type G loom or the video recorder or better semiconductor chip inscription.[58] The revolutionary technologies improve our well-being as well as our wealth, and can even alter political systems and the international balance of power; but all technological innovations, even the most minor, contribute to economic growth by enhancing

our productivity. As a result of such visible power, there is a temptation to ascribe much of the variation in national economic performance across countries, over time, to differences in national innovation systems. Getting beyond the statements, however, that investment in innovation is good, and that having a society that respects property rights and education helps innovation, to issues of real relevance for economic policy in the industrialized democracies takes a bit more doing.[59]

Judged on its direct results, the Japanese national innovation system must be deemed a success. Over the last half-century, Japan went from being a defeated country with a devastated economy to the world's largest net creditor nation with technological leadership in many advanced industries, as well as in many manufacturing processes. From the late-1970s to the mid-1990s, the Japanese economic model—including its emphasis on R&D and the utilization of technology—was hypothesized, described, and then idealized as an exemplar for emulation.

It turns out that with the benefit of a few more years of hindsight and of academic analysis, the elements of Japanese economic success were not all that mysterious (universal high education, high savings and investment during catch-up, low inflation, commitment to R&D, export orientation in key manufacturing sectors). It also turns out that many of the distinctive aspects of the Japanese model were as much hindrances as help (relationship banking instead of transparent securitized finance, protection of domestic sectors from competition, bureaucratic stewardship of a vast share of household savings). The politics of how this system emerged and held together are not trivial, as can be seen by the difficulties of other emerging markets achieving Japanese income levels despite explicit efforts to emulate the "model"; nevertheless, for our understand-

---

[58] Mokyr (chapter 2) and Gordon (chapter 3) to some degree debate whether the recent developments in IT and the Internet constitute such a transformative technology or not.

[59] Successful implementation of such policies as universal education and protection of property rights are very real issues in developing countries, but for the industrial democracies constitute no more than appeals to motherhood and apple pie.

ing of the role of technological innovation in national economic performance, the messages are clear.

One important conclusion is that the successful Japanese innovation system was less odd and interventionist than it was often perceived to be by American eyes, and therefore also less puzzling in its reasons for success. A consistently high level of R&D investment, funded and allocated for the most part by the private sector, adequate property rights, and excellent utilization of teamwork and specialized worker training in production, combined with domestic competition in high tech and key manufacturing industries and an insufficiently recognized degree of individual entrepreneurship, led to ongoing innovation. But as the mystery of Japan's ongoing success in innovation strictly defined recedes, other notable aspects of the relationship between Japanese innovation and growth come to the fore.

The swings in Japanese economic growth in the post-war period would be truly puzzling if the relationship between technological innovation and national economic performance were particularly tight. Japan's economic growth rate slowed from seemingly miraculous levels in the 1950s and 1960s, to simply tops among advanced economies in the 1970s and 1980s, to outright stagnation in the 1990s. Through this entire period of wide variation in economic growth, the Japanese national innovation system remained essentially unchanged, with both the institutional framework (including such matters as the role of the private and public sectors in the allocation of R&D funding) and the inputs (such as patent rights and access to credit for innovators) stable or turning slightly more favorably towards innovation in the 1990s.[60] Throughout this entire period of wide variation in economic growth, the outputs of the Japanese innovation system—in terms of scientific research, patents, net trade in technology, and competitiveness in high-tech

sectors—remained consistently impressive, and (like the inputs) either unchanged or slightly improved during the downturn of the 1990s. The measurable onwards march of Japanese innovation refutes the circular argument that the reason for Japan's poor economic performance in the 1990s must have been a shortfall in technical progress. In advanced economies, there are factors in performance much more significant than technological innovation.

Clearly, there were and are many severe structural problems affecting most parts of the Japanese economy outside of the most innovative sectors. These problems, mostly due to direct or indirect Japanese government protection of various domestic interest groups from domestic competition, have manifested themselves in the creation of a truly dual economy. There has been little or no diffusion of technological progress or productivity enhancing practices from the 10 percent of the Japanese economy that is export competitive to the 90 percent of the Japanese economy that is not—even while corporations and countries around the world have imported or implemented Japanese advances (think of the transformation of American auto industry work and supply practices). Although there are large parts of the United States and other industrialized nations that display similar backwardness relative to the high-tech sectors, in degree and depth of this disjunction, Japan stands alone among the developed economies.

While the protections that give rise to this division are not themselves directed against technological diffusion per se, and do not appear to directly interfere with technological innovation in Japan, they nonetheless do limit Japan's potential growth rate. It would stretch the meaning of "technological innovation" beyond useful recognition, however, to state that these inefficiencies should be considered failures of Japanese innovation policy just because they constrain productivity growth. Furthermore, the drag on the Japanese economy from these inefficiencies and impediments to markets have a much greater *direct* effect on Japanese economic performance than they do through obstructing the adoption of IT or other innovations. A true and complete liberalization

---

[60] The one exception being Japanese graduate science and engineering education, where there may have been a change for the worse in recent years, as discussed in section 4.2.

of the Japanese financial, retail, and telecommunications sectors would result in an increase in growth of 3 percent or more a year, according to OECD (1998), a number at least double the 1.0–1.5 percent increase in American productivity in the 1990s (which may not be entirely attributable to IT investment in any event). So it is to some degree misleading to cast the need for performance-enhancing change in Japan as a matter of increasing the receptivity of the economy to adoption of innovation—although, certainly, that would be an additional and worthwhile element of reform.

Of course, there still remains a great deal of room for Japan, as for any country, to improve its capacity for innovation and the diffusion of technical change through targeted reform efforts. As mentioned previously, the state of Japanese university research and education in the sciences is poor, and, as in most countries outside the United States, the institutions for venture capital and a culture of corporate start-ups are undeveloped. Even for an advanced economy which does maintain its position at the technological frontier in international competition, more encouragement of innovation is better. Various groups within the Japanese government and business leadership have grown concerned with their country's lagging behind the United States in such growth industries as information technology and biotechnology, while the emerging markets close the gap in manufacturing efficiency (reflected in Japanese manufacturers' "hollowing out" of domestic production).

The Japanese government's NITSDC (1999) report on "National Industrial Technology Strategies in Japan," for example, lists eight sources of concern: few homegrown technologies; lagging behind in intellectual property rights and standards; few start-ups; increasing difficulty of handing down work techniques in traditional Japanese fashion; differences between the skills of university graduates and those demanded by industry; differences between the research emphases of universities and scientific institutions, and those of industry; "foreign institutional ties" in research; and few "Nobel-prize level results." These clearly are more oriented towards increasing innovation inputs and

outputs as defined here, and not with easing the adoption of technology in the rest of Japanese society. This reflects an explicit sense of relative decline on the part of Japanese officials in the ability of Japan to "compete" in the leading industries. On my analysis, however, this may be a misguided priority, not only because Japan actually is doing well on innovation outputs, and not only because bigger gains to economic performance may be found in broader economic reforms, but also because the technologies that will be "leading" or "critical" in years ahead may not necessarily be ones which seem important today or where Japan is not already on the path to competitiveness.[61] Of course, such efforts at improving the Japanese innovation system can only help the Japanese economy— so long as they do not come at the expense of other reforms, and are of benefit to general innovative capacity (not targeted towards achieving goals in specific technologies).

The Government of Japan also has taken the view that lagging in IT and biotechnology marks a relative decline in Japan's innovative capacity. A new "Science and Technology Basic Law" passed in 1995 was intended to encourage collaboration between industry, academia, and government-funded research institutions, to begin reforming universities, to increase the creativity of students, and to increase the flexibility of government relationships with industry. As always in Japanese economic policy, however, a whole series of successor laws and programs with the same stated intention were announced before the first publicized effort was ever implemented, even in part. The most prominent in the area of innovation system reform since 1995 have been:[62]

---

[61] One need only remember how the U.S. economic bureaucracy saw the American economy as perhaps irretrievably behind the Japanese economy in the "critical" technologies of HDTV and semiconductors in the early 1990s, and took that as a verdict on its national innovation system, only later to find that HDTV was a dead-end and semiconductors had become a commodity product. Meanwhile, Japan has potentially leading technologies in optics and in wireless communications which are emerging today, although those are not acknowledged as criteria for judging the effectiveness of the Japanese innovation system, given the present fashions for biotech and IT.

- the "Science and Technology Basic Plan" of July 1996, supposed to increase the mobility of researchers by investing in postdoctoral scientific training, by enhancing the transfer of patent rights in collaborative university research, and by improving the fairness of evaluation of applications for government research grants;
- a promised increase in government R&D investment of Yen 17 trillion (U.S.$155 billion) over 1997–2002, none of which has been funded as of this writing;
- an "Educational Reform Programme" of August 1997 specifically proposed to reform the universities at both the undergraduate and graduate levels;
- an April 1998 law, actually passed, to emulate the U.S. Bayh-Dole Amendment, reducing the licensing fees for university researchers working on patentable technologies supported government grants;
- an "Action Plan for Economic Structural Reform" from MITI in October 1998, which stressed the goal of creating new industries through measures like enhanced roles for venture capital and OTC stock listings, freer labor mobility and use of outsourcing, increasing IPR protection and joint research, and investments in ICT infrastructure;[63]
- and most recently, on December 1, 2000, the Japanese government announced an "Action Plan for New Economic Growth," which "contains a wide range of policy measures to promote continuing economic reform and deregulation in Japan," including "measures to upgrade the foundation for creative research and development."

As could be expected as the result of a government initiative, these last two "Action Plans" serve many objectives at once. Both combine targeted initiatives "to maximize the utilization of IT and to induce demand and capital investment, especially in IT-related fields …" while also recognizing the more general need to reassess "… the extent to which existing systems have served to redistribute resources from high- to low-productivity sectors …."[64]

Leaving aside the questions of the Japanese government's willingness to implement such

plans, it should be noted that the stated impetus for these Japanese government proposals is much the same as concerns expressed in continental Europe, particularly in Germany, in recent years, where no abrupt fall from economic grace comparable to that of Japan in the last decade has occurred. Just as the United States was stimulated to improvement by the relatively better performance of Japan in the 1970s and 1980s, it may be inevitable for democratic market countries to compare their innovation capabilities to those of the contemporary leader in productivity. Thus, if this concern constitutes a recognition that an economy should always try to improve its potential growth rate through improvement of its innovation system, no matter how successful that system has been, this would be as healthy development in Japan as it would be elsewhere.

If, on the other hand, an attempt to precisely replicate the current American innovation system is based on a mistaken assessment that Japan's failure to be a leader in biotech and IT

---

[62] The Japanese government has announced, and in a few important (but certainly not most) cases implemented, a much broader structural reform agenda for the economy beyond the area of technological innovation. See Tanaka (2000) and Nishiyama (2000) for brief advocatory summaries of this agenda.

[63] "The government will concentrate its efforts on the development of a business environment for fifteen industries expected to grow in the future … At the same time, it will cope with various problems related to 'funds', 'human resources', 'technology', and 'information and telecommunications', all of which are indispensable for fostering new industries." (Industrial Policy Bureau, 1998: 8) The specification of target industries sounds like the old image of picking winners, but given that it is fifteen, and they include such broad areas as "Info and telecomms," "Distribution and logistics," "Environment," "Human resources," and "Aviation and space (civil)", the government's priorities seem not all that confining.

[64] Quotations taken from the overall government Action Plan of 2000 (a complete English language outline of this report can be found at http://www.miti.go.jp/english/index.html); the MITI Action Plan of 1998, which was a precursor to this plan, has similar language and multiple objectives. Interestingly, to stave off the type of cynicism engendered by this list of previous "action plans," the English summary notes that "Almost half of the 260 measures [contained in the Plan] will be carried into effect in one year."

indicates that the Japanese national innovation system is the source of Japanese economic decline, it may be unhealthy. Such an effort could divert economic policy attention from the truly pressing needs of addressing debt deflation and financial fragility in Japan, and of liberalizing the 90 percent of the Japanese economy mired in low productivity. Whether intentionally or not, that would shift the blame for Japanese economic stagnation in the 1990s from the factors that truly deserve it. And the Japanese public would in that case eventually be disappointed by its government putting too great a reliance on a close relationship between technological innovation and national economic performance – one that its own country's post-war experience indicates holds loosely at best when other factors such

as macroeconomic policy and financial shocks are taken into account. Even if the true advantages for national economic performance from technical innovation come from how widely and well a country uses technology, rather than simply how much innovation it produces, that would lead Japan to a much broader structural reform agenda to enhance competition and reallocation of productive factors, than one which strictly speaking focuses on the national innovation system. If such wide-ranging liberal reforms were ever enacted in Japan, the benefits to growth would largely be felt directly in the efficiency gains in the sectors in question - although the additional gains from the increased flexibility in adopting new technology would certainly be seen throughout the economy as well.

5

Germany

Horst Siebert and Michael Stolpe

5.1. Introduction

Germany remains Europe's largest and most diversified source of new technology, but still lags in the fastest growing areas of today's high technology. After World War II, West German policy on technology sought to rebuild the institutions which had supported Germany's leadership in the high-tech industries of the early twentieth century—automobiles, machinery, electrical engineering, chemicals, and pharmaceuticals. Increasingly, however, those institutions are seen as failing to respond to new technological stimuli. In addition, Germany's bank-centered capital and inflexible labor markets have long limited the opportunities of innovative firms for equity-based growth and the incentives for academic brains to set up in private business. Promising changes in technology policy and capital market conditions can be observed only since the mid-1990s.

The following sections expand on these themes. They deal with quantitative indicators of economic performance and policy issues for the 1970–2000 period (section 5.2), with the role of technology in explaining performance (section 5.3), and with the policies and institutions that Germany has used to harness technological change (section 5.4). West German industry has shown an impressive capacity to utilize new technology that enhances the efficiency of existing operations, raises the quality of established product lines and opens new market niches. However, Germany's technology system as a whole has not yet fully met the challenge of innovation in today's fast moving high-

tech industries, where success depends as much on speed as on a close link to cutting edge academic research. It appears that Germany's expansive institutions for research and technology transfer, which had been deployed as a substitute for missing or malfunctioning markets in the postwar area and which continue to absorb a large part of Germany's science and engineering talent, may have begun to impose undue inertia by crowding out, instead of substituting for, market forces in the allocation of resources towards innovative activities. More detailed policy lessons are discussed in section 5.5.

5.2. Performance and Policy Issues in Germany (1970–2000)

5.2.1. Macroeconomic Phases

Germany's macroeconomic performance over the past three decades cannot be explained exclusively in terms of technological change. It has rather been shaped by a mixture of influences common to all Western industrialized countries, of developments related to the creation of Europe's common market, and of events that were unique to Germany (West Germany until 1990 and reunited Germany thereafter). After the catching-up process in the 1950s and 1960s, the oil price shock of 1973 led to stagflation, a combination of persistent inflation of around 5 percent and mass unemployment at about 4 percent of the labor force, thus ending the period of extreme labor scarcity which had prevailed in West Germany since the early 1960s. The 1980s, beginning with a second massive increase in oil prices, saw successful

We thank Richard Nelson, Benn Steil and David Victor for helpful comments on an earlier draft of this paper.

monetary stabilization, crowned by an even slightly negative rate of consumer price inflation in 1986 when the oil glut cut producer prices significantly. But the 1980s also saw the gradual transformation of growing numbers of unemployed into structural unemployment as the West German economy became more service oriented and the mismatch between labor demand and the skills offered by displaced workers from declining industries became increasingly evident.

The 1990s saw a jigsaw of changing conditions. German re-unification and the policy of massive fiscal transfers from West to East first boosted demand and growth. But this boom was ended by a sharp recession in 1993 from which the economy has only slowly recovered in the latter half of the 1990s, with annual growth rates below 2 percent. Unemployment even continued to climb to 4.5 million in 1997, well above 11 percent of the labor force. Moreover, the influx of labor from eastern Germany and eastern Europe may have slowed down West German productivity growth in the early 1990s, but since the mid-1990s, substantial employment cuts and corporate restructuring have led to annual labor productivity gains of up to 8 percent in the manufacturing sector (OECD, 1998d).

5.2.2. Technological Phases

In the 1970s, the oil price shock encouraged the West German government in its drive to develop nuclear energy as a viable alternative to oil for power generation. Wage inflation at the same time prompted the private sector to search for labor-saving process technologies that would help to maintain international competitiveness in the production of tradable goods. Because input substitution was at least partially at the expense of total factor productivity, the rising relative prices of oil and labor did play an important role in the productivity slowdown (Siebert, 1992). The 1980s saw a cycle of booming exports, stimulated by the temporary rise of the U.S. dollar, and of incremental technological improvements along established trajectories, which mainly benefited the export-oriented automobile,

machinery, and chemical industries. But several attempts by large German corporations to enter newly emerging fields of high technology ended with disappointment, such as the Siemens-Nixdorf saga in computers and the early foray of Hoechst into biotechnology. With respect to computers, German producers of mainframes were at first ill-prepared for the advent of the PC. Moreover, the German adoption of decentralized computerization was slow because the required corporate restructuring, in addition to individual retraining, was delayed as many German firms gave priority to meeting the booming export demand for their established product lines in the 1980s and to the eastward expansion after German re-unification in the early 1990s. With respect to biotechnology, public technophobia, born from many years of antinuclear campaigning, and a very strict law on genetic engineering placed such narrow constraints on experiments that several projects were halted in the courts even after substantial investments had been made by private firms.

The 1990s brought a change in technological priorities. First, there was the task of upgrading the technological base in the remnants of East Germany's industries that were not immediately closed down after reunification. Second, there was the task of clearing the way for the entry of business start-ups into the fast growing international software and biotechnology industries, where the U.S. example had shown lively start-up activity to be a key to economic success. Progress in the East has been hampered by excessive wage deals and high unemployment so that labor productivity growth has merely reflected capital deepening, rather than gains in total factor productivity. However, the eventual deregulation of Germany's telecommunications industry, substantial change in Germany's capital markets and new priorities in government support policies did prepare the ground for a wave of software and biotechnology start-ups, many of which were listed in Germany's *Neuer Markt* stock market segment for technology-based growth companies created in 1997.

5.2.3. Macroeconomic Policy

Stability has been a mainstay of West Germany's economic policy throughout the postwar period. The persistent unemployment and inflation that characterized the years after the 1973 oil price shock in many industrial countries had more moderate effects in West Germany than in any comparable continental European country, except Switzerland and Sweden. At their respective peaks in the 1970s, West German inflation was at 7 percent (in 1974) and unemployment was at 4 percent (in 1975 and 1976). Moreover, the Bundesbank's tight monetary policy was spectacularly successful in bringing down inflation during the 1980s. At the same time, however, the cyclical unemployment of the 1970s turned into a persistent level of structural unemployment, so that total unemployment hovered around 8 percent after 1982 and remained unabated by significant employment growth in the expanding service economy during the 1980s. According to OECD estimates, the share of unemployment that was long-term, defined as a period of one year or more, increased from 12.8 percent in 1981 to 32.6 percent in 1988 and has since remained at one-third. During the same period the level of structural unemployment increased to 9.5 percent of the labor force, or 85 percent of total unemployment, in 1997.

Despite much anti-Keynesian government rhetoric, Germany's fiscal policy of the 1980s achieved no more than a stabilization, relative to gross domestic product (GDP), of the public debt that had accumulated as a result of expansionary policies to fight unemployment in the 1970s. So, the Bundesbank remained the main pillar of macroeconomic stability and gained considerable credibility in international markets, which in turn afforded the Bundesbank leverage to fight off inflation without raising interest rates as much as most other central banks had to do. As a consequence, bond yields remained lower than those in most European economies and debt finance continued to carry a relatively low cost of capital for private firms in Germany. This picture of relative macroeconomic stability was complemented by large

current account surpluses, exceeding 4 percent of GDP in the second half of the 1980s, and by a relatively modest level of public debt compared to many other European countries (Table 5.1).

In 1990, German re-unification changed this picture dramatically as both the current account and the public budget balance turned sharply negative and the public debt began to increase dramatically. Interest rates, both long and short term, shot up, yet—as another testimony to the Bundesbank's credibility—not as much as during the early 1980s, when central banks first became serious about fighting the inflationary legacy of the 1970s. The cause of the sudden current account swing in 1990 was Germany's enormous re-unification-induced demand for capital, an increase in absorption relative to production, which outstripped the supply of domestic savings by a wide margin (Table 5.1). Not only was it politically inopportune at the time to raise the level of domestic savings through official measures, but also the poor state of Germany's capital markets implied that the established western industrial corporations and financial intermediaries controlled the flow of available savings and largely channeled them into low-risk investments of the kind long practiced in West Germany. As a consequence, reinforced by new distortionary tax credits in favor of eastern Germany, not all socially profitable investment opportunities that arose from re-unification translated into appropriate signals and privately profitable openings for individual investors. Much of the limited additional savings that were mobilized from individuals went into cleverly marketed real estate developments in eastern Germany, which promised immediate tax savings but generated huge overcapacity and disappointing returns over the longer term.

As a further constraint, Germany's pay-as-you-go pension and health care systems already extracted a heavy toll from the working population; thus, the supply of private savings was bound to be inelastic with respect to rising interest rates. The current account surpluses before re-unification were a sign that a large portion of domestic savings went abroad, ostensibly for lack of profitable investment opportunities at

TABLE 5.1
Key Macroeconomic Data for Germany (from 1991 All Germany)

	1988	1989	1990	1991	1992	1993	1994	1995	1996	1997
Annual labor productivity change (percent)	2.9	2.1	2.7	−11.7	4.1	0.6	3.4	2.2	2.7	3.7
Gross fixed investment (percent of GDP)	20.1	20.6	21.1	23.0	23.3	22.3	22.4	22.2	21.6	21.2
Output per employee (Index for 1995 = 100)	93.1	95.0	97.6	100.0	104.1	104.7	108.3	110.6	113.6	117.7
GDP at market prices (DM billion)	2301	2384	2520	2853	2916	2882	2960	3014	3055	3121
GDP deflator	91.1	93.3	96.3	100.0	105.6	109.8	112.4	114.8	115.9	116.7
Household saving (percent of disposable income)	12.8	12.4	13.8	12.9	12.8	12.2	11.6	11.3	11.4	10.9
Labor force, total (million)	29.6	29.8	30.4	39.2	38.8	38.6	38.7	38.4	38.3	38.3
Unemployment rate	7.6	6.9	6.2	6.7	7.7	8.8	9.6	9.4	10.3	11.4
Monthly contractual pay rates	87.8	90.2	94.1	100.0	111.0	118.2	121.7	127.0	129.9	131.7
Balance on current account	88	107	79	−30	−30	−23	−33	−33	−21	−2
German direct investment abroad[a]				38	29	28	31	56	76	70
German portfolio investment abroad[a]	72	50	25	30	76	53	84	33	54	161
Foreign direct investment in Germany[a]				8	3	1	12	17	8	17
Foreign portfolio investment in Germany[a]	7	46	19	71	123	236	45	85	141	151
Total exports, fob (DM billion)	568	641	646	666	671	604	681	728	772	887
Chemicals exports	77	83	82	85	85	79	92	98	102	117
Manufactured materials exports	103	117	114	113	111	98	110	121	119	134
Machinery and transport equipment exports	273	312	319	326	333	299	336	361	383	440
Total R&D expenditure (percent of GDP)	2.9	2.9	2.9	2.8	2.6	2.5	2.4	2.3	2.3	2.3
R&D as percent of GDP in business enterprise sector	2.6	2.6	2.6	2.5	2.3	2.2	2.1	2.0	1.9	

Source: OECD (1998d).

[a] DM billion, from July 1990 including East Germany. Data are from the Sachverständigenrat (2000) based on German balance of payments statistics, which counts as direct investments share holdings of more than 20 percent in a foreign firm.

home. After re-unification, large inflows of foreign capital complemented the limited domestic supply of savings and allowed the German government to raise huge amounts of capital in the bond market, where liquidity remained high. However, the extensive fiscal and social security transfer program, which was politically motivated to reduce incentives for East–West migration, meant that the larger part of western transfer payments to eastern Germany actually went into consumption, as well as private housing and public infrastructure renovation, while private investment in new plants and equipment remained below the optimistic expectations of many commentators in the early 1990s. To the extent that western transfer payments inflated the prices of local resources, eastern Germany suffered a re-unification-induced Dutch disease; the output of nontradables expanded at the expense of the tradables sector.

Relatively low rates of nonresidential capital formation have been a drag on the West German (and later Pan-German) economy since the early 1980s, interrupted only by somewhat more expansionary investment during the late 1980s and early 1990s. From 1989 to 1992, gross fixed investment in relation to GDP rose by roughly three percentage points to 23.3 percent and has since declined by more than two percentage points. Germany's now endemic problem with private sector investment mainly reflects a rate of return which, since the re-unification boom, returned almost to the abysmally low level of the early 1980s before beginning to rise slightly in the latter half of the 1990s. In a revealing contrast, German firms have since the mid-1980s become increasingly willing to make direct investments abroad in other industrial countries and in developing countries. Although bringing the marketing and sales force closer to customers has been the dominant motive, the quest for lower labor costs and the enhancement of firms' in-house capacity to innovate have also been important considerations. In the 1990s, between 20 and 30 percent of German direct investments shifted to the newly emerging market economies of Eastern Europe, many of which offered a sufficiently skilled labor force to be in direct locational competition with eastern Germany. Advances in information and communication technologies appear to have been crucial in facilitating the effective management of foreign production subsidiaries and research and development (R&D) laboratories in an increasing array of industries. Annual statistics on the flows of direct foreign investments, such as those provided by the Sachverständigenrat (2000), are volatile because they are often influenced by large individual transactions, like the acquisition of Rover by BMW in 1994 or the acquisiton of Mannesmann by Vodafone in 2000.

In tandem with globalization, trends in technological innovation have contributed to considerable structural change within the manufacturing sector. Via technology's role in determining comparative advantages, technological change is bound to have a larger effect on industrial structure in the German economy than in the Japanese and U.S. economies since Germany, with its central European location, is much more open to and dependent on international trade. Yet, in terms of revealed comparative advantage (RCA), the technological position of the German economy has long been something of a paradox. At the aggregate level, Germany is not only Europe's leading producer and exporter of investment goods and consumer durables embodying new technology, but also home to a well-trained labor force with one of the world's highest propensities to patent industrial innovations. In 1997, for example, Germany took out more patents from the European Patent Office in proportion to the size of the labor force than any country with the exception of Switzerland and Sweden. At a disaggregate level, however, only a relatively small share of German exports comes from industries regarded as genuinely high-tech, like the science-based pharmaceutical, computer and software industries. Instead, the bulk of Germany's persistent export success is attributable to the technological sophistication of a broad range of continuously upgraded products from well-established industries, like automobiles, chemicals and machine tools, which may be labeled engineering-based. It is in these areas that Germany's capacity to innovate has long been a source of welfare gains from endogenous comparative advantages; the entry of newly industrializing countries into the world market has gradually begun to erode these gains in some areas.

5.2.4. German Technology Policy

In different guises, public debate about Germany's ability to innovate has been going on for the past three decades. It has been fed by a recurrent fear that Germany is not only losing its traditional strengths, but is also missing out on new opportunities, especially in those high-tech industries where RCAs arise from the spatial concentration of activities subject to economies of scale—the Silicon Valley phenomenon. In some sense, the German debate is only a new verse to an old song whose historical origin has largely been forgotten. Yet, much of German technology policy still rests on the ideas of List (1841) who developed a comprehensive and highly influential strategy for economic catch-up with the United Kingdom, the undisputed technological leader of the industrial revolution in the early nineteenth century. After its defeat in World War II, Germany again found itself in technological backwardness, this time vis-à-vis the United States; not only had the Nazis forced many of the best academics out of their jobs and into emigration, but also research priorities of the Nazi period with potential military applications, such as aerospace, became obsolete for political reasons. Moreover, the technological paradigm of mass production arrived much later in Germany than in the United States where it flourished under the uniquely favorable conditions of the 1920s, described in Rosenberg (1994). In West Germany's postwar setting, the adoption of often superior U.S. technology and public support for the diffusion of best practice throughout the economy were natural and complementary choices.

In the past three decades, the basic diffusion orientation of the German system of innovation has remained intact, despite several changes in official government funding priorities. The essence of the system is not found in the various government schemes that provide financial support for specific new technologies. Rather the essence is found in the institutional set-up of public research and technology transfer and in the historically prevailing conditions in Germany's capital and labor markets which determine how resources are allocated towards innovative activities and how the associated risks are shared. These conditions have helped the private sector create the absorptive capacity that allows existing firms to adopt new technologies and build on recent findings of academic research, in line with the learning role of firms' own R&D that was pointed out by Cohen and Levinthal (1989).

In the allocation of *capital* and in the governance of industrial corporations, public stock market transactions have traditionally played a much smaller role in Germany than in the Anglo-Saxon system. The largest part of established firms' external finance has often been provided in the form of negotiated debt to a so-called *Hausbank*, to which a typical industrial firm is married for virtually all its life. However, since banks often shy away from financing intangible investments, the private sector's own contribution to R&D funding typically comes from retained earnings, a second-best solution that is unavailable to most start-ups. In the *labor* market, the German system has encouraged intensive on-the-job-training and the accumulation of firm-specific human capital, which is most effectively exploited if workers stay with their employers for a long time. The diffusion-oriented education system emphasizes broad technical training at almost every level, from vocational schools to the world-famous technical universities. Diffusion is also a primary goal of Germany's proliferating institutions for the transfer of knowledge and new technology from public research into private industry. Indeed, the established paradigm of German technology policy can be interpreted as providing public institutions to substitute for missing market transactions in the diffusion of knowledge and technology. Within the scope of these institutions, there has been ample support for incremental innovations along established trajectories but relatively little incentive for radical moves into entirely new areas of technology.

This institutional heritage from the heyday of Germany's established industries has been slow to adapt to today's changing technological opportunities and constraints, such as the increasing codification of knowledge and the lost comparative advantage of large established firms in the most dynamic fields of high technology. Indeed, the inertia in Germany's science and technology institutions and in its capital and labor markets appear to have been the most important reason for Germany's lack of competitive players in biotechnology and information technology until recently. Public technophobia and the overregulation of markets, which certainly did play a role in the failure of German biotechnology activities in the 1980s, appear to have been partially overcome. The application of biotechnology in pharmaceuticals is now generally welcome, but genetically modified foodstuffs are still finding few buyers when brought to market on an experimental basis, as in the case of Nestlé's "butter-finger" candy bar.

To some extent, the technological inertia of the institutional and private sectors has been recognized long ago and the German government has repeatedly tried in the past to balance this inertia with missionary programs to develop selected technologies—like the fast breeder nuclear reactor, the Airbus family of wide-bodied aircraft and the Transrapid magnetic levitation train—which were thought too large, too complex or too much of a departure from existing technological paradigms to be manageable by private firms on their own. While the German government may have sought to emulate similar French initiatives with some of these programs, the German public has always shown much less enthusiasm for state-sponsored mega-technologies than the French, and sometimes even outright hostility. With hindsight, the mission-oriented elements of German technology policy have indeed done more harm than good, with the fast breeder long abandoned, the Airbus project at the center of recurrent trade disputes over subsidies and the Transrapid apparently too expensive for a viable commercial line even between Germany's two largest cities. Except as a drain on the public purse, these missionary technology projects have never had a significant impact on Germany's macroeconomic performance.

5.3. The Role of Technology

5.3.1. Technological Change—What Changes are we Talking about?

Since imperial Germany's successful catch-up with U.K. technology and productivity in the nineteenth century, the German innovation system has built and improved on its capacity to absorb new technology and diffuse it rapidly throughout the economy. German productivity growth has evidently not depended on a record of trailblazing domestic inventions but rather on a technological infrastructure that helps private firms to apply smoothly within the context of existing industries whatever new technology becomes available. In the 1980s, for example, West Germany adopted computer integrated manufacturing more rapidly than most other countries. In the 1990s, the technological upgrading of old firms in eastern Germany was swift wherever those firms were privatized and acquired by established western firms; as a result, more than three-quarters of today's industrial plants in eastern Germany have been installed after 1990, with heavy involvement by West Germany's leading corporations in the automobile, machinery, electrical, and chemical industries.

The initial development of these industries in the nineteenth and early twentieth centuries was associated with a wave of fundamental innovations many of which originated in Germany's new technology-based firms of that time. Some of these, like the Otto and Diesel engines used in automobiles and the pioneering designs of Werner von Siemens in electricity generation, have defined the technological trajectories on which these industries have expanded until today. The discovery of the painkiller Aspirin by Felix Hoffmann of Bayer in 1897 established a research model subsequently applied in the synthesis of many ethical drugs. The economic success of the highly organized search for new substances in the pharmaceutical industry's laboratories has influenced patterns of innovation elsewhere, although incremental tinkering is still an important feature of the innovation process in Germany's automobile and machinery industry. Product and process innovations as well as the organization of R&D in these and other industries has increasingly taken advantage of the new information technologies since the 1980s. The absorption of these radical innovations within the context of established product lines has been aided by the finely tuned excellence of many German automobile, machinery, and electrical equipment manufacturers as system integrators. Only in the 1990s, however, did the search for efficient applications of the new information technology prompt the restructuring of entire businesses and industries.

One way to assess the technological position of Germany's manufacturing sector via-à-vis other countries is to look at international trade. German exports command a share of one-third in GDP and overwhelmingly go to similarly endowed economies, the EU partners and other advanced industrialized countries. For this reason, the net trade flows associated with specific industries often tend to indicate the acquired technological strengths and weaknesses as distinct from comparative advantages due to Germany's more fundamental endowment with factors of production. In 1997, for example, German exports accounted for 20 percent of world trade in machinery and automobiles, but for less than seven percent in information technology, with intermediate shares for chemicals, electrical engineering products, professional instruments and aerospace (Bundesministerium für Bildung und Forschung (BMBF), 2000).

In order to distinguish comparative advantage from changes in the overall balance of trade, Balassa (1965) introduced the measure of RCA which is defined here for each industry as the logarithmic ratio of that industry's share of German exports to its share of German imports, multiplied by 100. Positive values indicate a relative export strength, while negative values indicate a weakness in the balance of trade in a particular product category compared to Germany's overall trade balance in a given year. Table 5.2 highlights selected long-term trends which confirm Germany's long-standing export strength in industries making relatively *intensive* use of R&D services (see also Table 5.3, last column). But unlike in Japan, the United States and the United Kingdom, only a relatively small share of Germany's exports comes from the *most* R&D intensive industries, including biotechnology (discussed further below) and semiconductors, as well as computing and telecommunications equipment, where Germany has long been a net importer, taking advantage of the innovative prowess of the United States and other countries which began much earlier to liberalize their own domestic telecommunication industries.

Germany's main contribution to the international division of labor continues to lie in exports from the upper segments of mature technology, in particular from the automobile, chemical, and machine tool industries, which tend to have a medium level of R&D intensity. (According to a commonly used classification of manufacturers, proposed by the *Fraunhofer-Institut für Systemtechnik und Innovationsforschung*, a medium R&D intensity implies a share of R&D in sales between 3.5 and 8.5 percent; whereas manufacturers with an R&D intensity above 8.5 percent are considered high technology.) Machinery and transport equipment together accounted for almost 50 percent of total German exports in 1997, and chemicals for another 13 percent, much of which is intra-industry trade between advanced countries. These long established industries with substantial product differentiation offer rich opportunities for exploiting economies of scale and scope, as described by Chandler (1990). Large portions of these industries are not science-based in the sense that new products and processes are a direct consequence of the latest advances in academic research. Science and engineering methods have rather helped to make routine the process of incremental innovation in long-established, often highly specialized R&D laboratories. Given its broad range of long-standing export strengths, Germany's most important rival on

TABLE 5.2
Selected Trends in Germany's RCAs

		1961	1970	1980	1990	1995	1999
53	Dyeing, tanning and coloring materials	93.2	115.1	102.3	85.9	84.7	85.9
54	Medicinal and pharmaceutical products	58.7	48.9	12.6	20.9	17.1	34.9
56	Fertilizers, manufactured	221.4	79.8	−19.7	−62.0	−27.7	3.6
57	Explosives and pyrotechnic products	82.7	40.5	5.4	−22.3	−18.1	−94.2
65	Textile yarn, fabrics, made-up articles, related products	−122.4	−51.5	−53.5	−24.2	−17.3	−12.7
67	Iron and steel	3.1	−14.5	10.0	−8.6	−10.6	−0.3
68	Nonferrous metals	−171.0	−140.8	−65.6	−56.9	−45.4	−23.2
69	Manufacturers of metal, n.e.s.	88.9	42.7	22.6	16.9	5.3	10.2
71	Power generating machinery and equipment	45.0	63.9	58.0	33.1	33.9	3.9
72	Machinery specialized for particular industries	75.5	89.3	94.2	95.7	106.9	97.9
73	Metalworking machinery	60.7	81.4	77.5	41.2	76.0	51.4
74	General industrial machinery and equipment, and parts	64.1	59.8	63.6	54.4	60.7	56.2
75	Office machines and automatic data processing equipment	−51.2	−39.9	−49.9	−75.4	−79.7	−90.3
76	Telecommunications and sound recording apparatus	71.8	25.5	−15.4	−56.9	−26.4	−14.7
77	Electrical machinery, apparatus and appliances n.e.s.	51.7	8.5	10.0	7.4	0.0	−1.6
78	Road vehicles (including air-cushion vehicles)	150.2	76.0	75.4	50.8	37.0	48.7
79	Other transport equipment	48.5	−53.3	−32.4	−32.9	16.9	−6.0
87	Professional, scientific and controlling instruments	55.2	33.5	13.8	27.5	33.2	37.3
88	Photographic apparatus, optical goods, watches	48.6	8.7	−34.8	−27.4	−19.7	−17.0
95	Arms, of war and ammunition	−53.4	−17.2	79.1	−42.3	15.6	−31.2

Source: OECD, International Trade by Commodities (ITCS), Rev. 2, and authors' computations; West-Germany until 1990, thereafter all Germany.

$RCA_{i,t} = \ln[(X_{i,t}/M_{i,t})/(\sum_i X_{i,t}/\sum_i M_{i,t})] \times 100$ where $X_{i,t}$ (respectivley $M_{i,t}$) is Germany's exports (imports) in product category i and year t.

the world market is Japan, but in some of Germany's export industries, there is also strong competition from Switzerland, Sweden, France, and Italy.

Over time, the pattern of Germany's export specialization has remained rather stable. Germany's most successful export industries, automobiles and industrial machinery, have held their world market shares and in the late 1990s even increased them; particularly impressive has been the rising export strength in specialized machinery. By contrast, there has been a gradual erosion of Germany's traditional strengths in chemicals and electrical machinery. With respect to high technology, the following *changes* are notable. Germany's relative export share in the telecommunications equipment industry, which had been in long-term decline

TABLE 5.3

Relative Size of R&D intensive Manufacturing Industries, Germany

	1995–7				1997			
	Value added percent[b]	Employees percent[c]	Value added percent	Employees	Foreign sales	Share of employees	Share of total sales	Share of foreign sales
R&D intensive manufacturing[a]	3.7	−3.2	5.4	−3.0	14.3	45.1	45.3	65.1
High technology	6.8	−3.5	8.6	−4.8	22.1	7.6	8.3	11.8
Pharamceutical specialities	−4.8	−3.5	−4.7	−5.2	12.2	1.7	1.8	1.9
Computing equipment	17.9	−6.9	20.7	−4.3	24.3	0.5	1.1	1.2
Telecommunications equipment	14.2	−3.2	11.4	−7.2	25.9	1.1	1.5	2.3
Aerospace	−2.5	−4.9	0.5	−2.1	40.3	0.9	1.0	1.9
Medium technology	2.8	−3.2	4.5	−2.6	12.7	37.5	37.1	53.2
Plastics	5.7	−3.4	10.0	−5.3	15.9	1.1	1.7	2.9
Machine tools	1.7	−3.1	1.2	−4.0	−0.1	1.9	1.4	2.0
Electrical switches	1.9	−4.0	2.1	−4.1	9.5	3.0	2.6	2.6
Automobile	4.8	0.7	5.3	3.2	16.4	6.2	9.9	17.2
Non–R&D intensive manufacturing[a]	0.7	−3.5	3.3	−3.2	10.1	54.9	54.7	34.9
Total manufacturing	2.2	−3.4	4.4	−3.1	12.8	100	100	100

Source: Sachverständigenrat (1998).
[a] Classification of industries according to Niedersächsisches Institut für Wirtschaftsforschung.
[b] Average annual percentage change.
[c] One year percentage change.

for many years, has increased slightly since the mid-1990s. A comparison of changes in labor input and added value between R&D intensive industries and non–R&D intensive manufacturing, provided in Table 5.3, indicates that the computing and telecommunications industries have seen the largest productivity advances, despite their persistent export weakness, in the late 1990s. In pharmaceuticals and agrochemicals, the most R&D intensive sectors within the chemical industry, Germany has lost much of its traditional strength in exports—a loss that is closely related to Germany's protracted entry into the modern biotechnology industry. In addition, the German pharmaceutical industry, once considered the world's pharmacy, has suffered from increased competition from generic drugs. Germany's former export strength in photographic apparatus, optical goods and watches was already lost

during the ascent of Japan's industry on the world market in the 1960s and 1970s, but Germany held on to its strong export position in scientific instruments. Not reflected in the official trade data is the rise of a more competitive German software industry in the 1990s, which seems to be growing beyond niche markets and beginning to compete successfully in the global market for business applications.

5.3.2. How Technical Change is Created: a Bird's Eye View

Several empirical studies have suggested that the research productivity of the German innovation system is high in comparison with most European countries. In one recent econometric study, using data on R&D workers and patenting from twenty-one OECD countries during 1988–90, Eaton et al. (1998) estimate that

West German research productivity was exceeded only by some of the relatively small countries in Scandinavia as well as by Switzerland and Austria. Moreover, they argue that Europe's income elasticity with respect to the employment of additional R&D scientists and engineers is largest if these are employed in Germany, because technological innovation in Germany tends to create the largest knowledge spillovers for other European economies.

Thus, the overall technological strength suggested by Germany's large share of world exports in R&D intensive manufacturing goods is confirmed through more direct measurement of innovative activities such as resources devoted to formal R&D or output measuress like patents. A summary of statistical evidence is provided in BMBF (2000). Of the approximately U.S.$500 billion spent on R&D in all OECD countries in 1997, Germany held a share of 8.5 percent, in third place behind the United States and Japan. But in proportion to GDP, Germany's relative position vis-à-vis the other OECD countries has declined during the 1990s. With total R&D expenditures at almost 3 percent of GDP, West Germany was still one of the most R&D intensive OECD economies in 1989. But since re-unification, the Pan-German R&D intensity has declined to less than 2.4 percent while that of most other OECD countries has either increased or stayed constant. The decline in the R&D intensity of Germany's private business sector from 2.9 percent in 1989 to 1.9 in 1996 was even more pronounced; only in the final years of the 1990s has the private business sector's R&D expenditure returned to an expansionary path.

In spite of changes in R&D intensity, the mixture of funding sources has long been rather stable and reflects Germany's fiscal federalism and distributed responsibilities for science and technology policy. Almost two-thirds of total R&D expenditures in Germany in the 1990s was funded by the private sector; government paid the remaining one-third, within which the federal government held a share of two-thirds. The other one-third of public sector funds was supplied by the sixteen federal states which are constitutionally respon-sible for the institutional funding of Germany's public universities. The Federal Ministry for Research and Education spends about 20 percent of its funding on research in universities and public sector research institutes, about 29 percent in the private business sector, and more than 40 percent in private nonprofit, often para-public research institutions. Ten percent of federal funds go to international institutions, including the European Union and the European Space Agency.

Within Germany, the federal government uses three main channels to distribute the funds: institutional funding, direct project grants, and indirect as well as the so-called indirect-specific funding (Table 5.4). The latter is targeted at certain preselected areas of technology, like computer integrated manufacturing, or socio-economic tasks, like health care and renewable energy sources, and funds within such programs are awarded on the merits of pertinent research proposals from eligible parties in the public and private sectors. Institutional support for public research institutes and private nonprofit organizations accounted for 40 percent, direct grants towards selected research proposals for 42 percent and the indirect and indirect-specific programs for 4 percent of federal R&D spending in 1996 (Klodt, 1998). Most project support for private R&D is granted upon application, conditional on the evaluation of research proposals and progress reports. Only a relatively small share of federal R&D expenditure is distributed as indirect and indirect-specific project support, in spite of the fact that these channels are especially tailored for Germany's many small and medium sized enterprises seeking to innovate in a targeted, albeit sometimes rather narrow, field of technology. And despite the variety of channels used for the distribution of federal funds, it has been estimated that only about 20 percent of private R&D projects receive any federal co-financing at all (Klodt, 1998).

Of all the R&D performed by Germany's business enterprise sector in 1993, government funding accounted for only 11 percent (Table 5.5). But the federal share was much larger in some industries and smaller in others: While the federal share was a staggering 68 percent

TABLE 5.4
Federal R&D Funds by Type of Expenditure

		1981		1990		1996	
		Million DM	Percent	Million DM	Percent	Million DM	Percent
1.	Institutional support	3563	34.0	5161	33.6	6813	40.9
1.1.	Research-funding institutions			1346	8.8	2184	12.4
1.2.	National research centers			2396	15.7	2615	14.8
1.3.	Federal research agencies			966	6.3	1363	7.7
1.4.	Other institutions			496	3.1	913	5.2
2.	Project support	5940	56.7	8321	54.2	7470	44.8
2.1.	Direct			7930	52.1	7425	42.2
	thereof:						
	Minister of Science and Technology			3309	21.7	3559	20.2
	Minister of Defense			3090	20.3	2894	16.4
	Minister of Economics			699	4.6	357	2.0
2.2.	Indirect and indirect-specific			353	2.3	677	3.8
3.	International cooperation	708	6.8	1459	8.8	1566	9.6
	Total	10484	100.0	15361	100.0	16272	100.0

Source: BMBF (1996, 1998) and Klodt (1998).

TABLE 5.5
R&D Expenditures of German Business Enterprises by Industry, 1993

	Total		Government funded	
	Million DM	Percent[a]	Million DM	Percent[b]
Energy	177	0.2	29	16.4
Mining	322	1.0	109	33.9
Manufacturing	48194	4.3	4446	9.2
Chemical industry	9664	6.1	98	1.0
Rubber and plastics	728	2.5	29	4.0
Stone and clay	474	1.6	42	8.9
Iron and steel	329	1.1	42	12.8
Nonelectrical machinery	5135	3.1	219	4.3
Motorcar industry	10467	5.2	93	0.9
Aircraft and space	3259	24.4	2789	85.6
Electrical machinery	12439	6.5	717	5.8
Instruments	778	4.9	102	13.1
Fabricated metal products	877	1.2	97	11.1
Wood, paper and printing	229	1.1	25	10.9
Textiles and apparel	279	2.0	57	20.4
Food and beverages	317	0.6	21	6.6
Other industries	2028	1.1	560	27.6
Total	51236	3.6	5658	11.0

Sources: Stifterverband für die Deutsche Wissenschaft (1995) and Klodt (1998).
[a] Share in sales of R&D-performing companies.
[b] Share in total R&D expenditures.

in aerospace, it was only 1 percent in the chemical industry and even below 1 percent in the automobile industry. Also notable among the recipients of above-average support for their R&D activities are the professional instruments, fabricated metal products, iron and steel industries as well as the textile and apparel industry. Outside the manufacturing sector, the share of government funding in total business R&D expenditures has also been high, namely about 16 percent in energy, 34 percent in mining, and 28 percent in other nonmanufacturing industries. There is thus a sharp contrast between government priorities and the private sector distribution of R&D expenditures in Germany. The main performers of business sector R&D, the chemical industry, electrical and nonelectrical machinery as well as the automobile industry, which together account for almost three-quarters of all business sector R&D expenditures, received only 20 percent of federal government funding in 1993. As Klodt (1998) notes, this mismatch between government and business spending is probably due to bureaucratic inertia and vested interests in the administration and distribution of government funds. Indeed, the sectoral structure of public R&D subsidies has remained rather stable over time, regardless of changes in the *official* priorities of technology policy which have been announced every few years.

While the level of aggregate R&D *inputs* has seen a relative decline, Germany has held its relative position vis-à-vis the other large industrial countries with respect to *output*, when measured in terms of patenting activity. Indeed, Germany has fully participated in the upsurge of patenting which has been observed throughout the OECD countries since the mid-1990s. Several factors probably explain why patenting has risen much faster in the second half of the 1990s than industrial R&D budgets (BMBF, 2000). First, regulatory reforms in a number of countries have lowered the costs of international patenting. Second, firms whose shares are traded in the stock market have discovered that systematic patenting can serve as a defense against hostile takeovers by increasing shareholder value. Third, organizational restructuring and the growing use of information and communication technologies may have increased the efficiency of formal R&D activities in the business enterprise sector by reducing the need for technical support staff. Indeed, the share of academically trained scientists and engineers among all R&D workers in the German business sector has increased since 1989 (BMBF, 2000).

Since many manufacturing industries display a stable relationship between their aggregate R&D activities and patent counts in the fields of technology to which they contribute, patenting trends have been widely used to assess structural changes in the output of innovation in the business enterprise sector. In these studies, patent count data are used to compute an indicator of revealed technological advantage (RTA), similar to the RCA indicator introduced by Balassa (1965), across different fields of technology in which patent applications are classified by the patent offices. On this indicator, Germany's technological specialization is indeed closely related to its trade specialization (see, for example, Stolpe, 1995; Casper et al., 1999; BMBF, 2000). While Germany can muster only a relatively weak patenting record in many of the fast-paced areas of today's high technology areas, especially in biotechnology, information technology, telecommunications, semiconductors and audiovisual technologies, it has a relatively strong record in many longer established and more slowly growing fields of technology, such as nuclear power, civil and mechanical engineering, engine and environmental technology as well as conventional pharmaceuticals.

On the input side, until the mid-1990s Germany's private business had sharply reduced investment in R&D and (less sharply but still significantly) cut current spending on R&D; these trends have only gradually begun to be reversed. At the same time, structural change in the output composition of German manufacturing has favored the more R&D intensive industries. Gross capital formation has shown divergent trends across industries in the second half of the 1990s. It has increased by almost 50 percent in the R&D intensive industries and while remaining constant elsewhere (BMBF, 2000). Notable also has been the trend towards increased outsourcing of R&D services in the business sector, which reached 10 percent of total business R&D spending in 1997. Cooperative R&D ventures within the private business sector, which may include competitors, customers and suppliers, accounted for two-thirds of external R&D spending in 1997. However, the share of universities and other public research institutes in the private business sector's external R&D spending was small and declined to ten percent in 1997 (BMBF, 2000).

One reason for this decline appears to be a partial mismatch between the technological specialization of business sector R&D and the research specialization of the academic sector across science and engineering disciplines. In the latest government report on Germany's capacity for technological innovation (BMBF, 2000), the profile of academic specialization is assessed in terms of the publication record of German research institutes in the Science Citation Index. Based on publications from the 1996–8 period, Germany's academic research is more strongly concentrated in nuclear physics, optics, computing, medical technology, organic chemicals and biotechnology than the index of German patent specialization based on European patent applications during 1995–7. At the same time, the publication record suggests weaknesses in process and environmental technology, machinery and civil engineering where Germany has a relatively strong patenting record. Certain long established areas of technological strength in terms of patent counts, like professional instruments, polymers, basic chemicals and materials science, are matched by a relatively strong academic publication record. But in some of the fastest growing areas of science-based technology, above all in pharmaceuticals and telecommunications, Germany's record is relatively weak in terms of *both* publications and patents. However, there is one piece of evidence to suggest that public sector research may at least partially be moving closer towards technologies with potential applications in the private business enterprise sector: All institutional subsectors within the public research system have increased their patenting activity significantly during the 1990s.

5.3.3. How Technical Change is Created: Public Research and Technology Transfer

Germany has developed one of the world's most extensive infrastructures for academic research, much of which is intended to serve private industry despite falling largely within the public sector. The public research sector is subdivided between institutes oriented towards basic research and others with a more applied focus to facilitate the transfer of knowledge from Germany's science base to industry. Among the former, university research in the natural sciences is often secondary to the research carried out by Germany's prestigious *Max Planck Institutes* and, in some fields, to the research carried out by more than eighty other large and medium sized institutes on the so-called Blue List, now named *Wissenschaftsgemeinschaft Gottfried Wilhelm Leibniz (WGL)*. Major science, which often requires an interdisciplinary approach as well as very large-scale equipment, is mainly performed by the member institutes of the *Hermann von Helmholtz Association of National Research Centers* with a combined staff of roughly 22,000. Their activities are concentrated in environmental, energy, health, materials science, information and communication and in aviation, space and other key technologies, which the private sector is thought to neglect in its drive for short-term profits. Ninety percent of the current total annual budget of about DM 4 billion is funded by the federal government, and only 10 percent on average comes from the states in which a particular institute is located.

Among the institutes with a more applied focus, the *Fraunhofer* Institutes forms the largest and most successful organizational network. The *Fraunhofer* Society currently maintains about fifty institutes across the country with a total staff of almost 5000 scientists and engineers. Each institute is focused on a clearly defined field of technology with special relevance to particular industries and thus serves as an intermediary for the transfer of technology between Germany's science base and the business enterprise sector, a demand which is mainly met through contract research. The *Fraunhofer* Society's postwar origin, described by Trischler and vom Bruch (1999), lay in Bavaria which, after the dissection of Prussia, Bavaria's arch-rival, by the allied powers in post-war Germany, seized the opportunity to lure research and engineering talent from Prussia's main science and technology activities in Berlin. Bavaria's capital, Munich, which had seen little innovative activity before the war duly became one of West Germany's preferred locations for technological innovation in a variety of industries, including in the 1960s and 1970s for electrical and electronic engineering (Siemens), and, in the 1980s and 1990s, Germany's re-emerging aerospace industry (Messerschmidt-Bölkow-Blohm) and software and biotechnology.

Germany's public system of research and technology transfer features a variety of players with a special mandate to support technological innovation in small and medium sized *Mittelstand* firms, which often cannot afford to maintain their own in-house R&D departments. The most widely dispersed of these players is the *Arbeitsgemeinschaft industrieller Forschungsvereinigungen* (AiF), a network of industrial research associations which support and carry out *cooperative* research by small and medium-sized enterprises. Moreover, Germany's many regional universities and *Fachhochschulen* (polytechnics) offer and seek opportunities for collaborative R&D under contract with private firms at the periphery of the science and technology landscape. Probably the most successful regional model is the *Steinbeiss* Foundation which maintains a network of technology transfer and consulting centers based in Baden-Württemberg's *Fachhochschulen.*

The division of labor between basic research and applied research is reflected in the mix of funding sources for the different branches of Germany's innovation system (Mason and Wagner, 1999). For example, the Helmholtz, Max Planck and Blue List Institutes are predominantly financed via institutional support from the federal and state governments. But this source of funding has accounted for no more than one-third of the income of a typical *Fraunhofer* Institute with another third coming from government-sponsored projects, usually carried out in collaboration with private busi-

ness partners, and the remaining third from commercial contract research for private sector clients. This balanced mix of funding sources has helped the Fraunhofer Society to maintain a degree of flexibility that is unusual for a bureaucracy of its size. Not only has it been able to mobilize resources for new institutes in surprisingly short time, it has also demonstrated its flexibility in closing down institutes whose area of research had become obsolete. It is for these virtues that the federal government has decided to incorporate the *Gesellschaft für Mathematik und Datenverarbeitung* (GMD), the Helmholtz center for research in information technology with a total staff of more than 1,300, into the Fraunhofer Society, whose own software expertise recently led to the invention of the MP3 data compression format now widely used for music distribution on the Internet. However, the government plan has met with considerable resistance among the research staff at the GMD who fear for their autonomy in setting research priorities and do not want to be involved in more research with commercial applications.

It is part of a more general problem that the management of individual *Fraunhofer* institutes remains constrained by Germany's general labor market rigidities and by the many specific employment rules which the government imposes as implicit and explicit conditions for its institutional funding of *Fraunhofer's* basic research activities. Mason and Wagner (1999) have therefore voiced doubts whether Germany's applied research institutes will be able to keep up with the speed at which research priorities change in today's fastest growing areas of high technology, software and biotechnology in particular. They may become less attractive research partners for private firms and also lose their attractiveness as partners for university-based researchers as the constraints of public funding rules fail to adjust to the rapidly rising private sector wages for the best scientists and engineers in some of the most dynamic fields of technology. Thus, Germany's applied research institutes ironically appear least likely to succeed in those fields of technology where the relative advantage of private firms' in-house R&D may be declining fastest, because the codification of an ever increasing portion of technological knowledge and falling communication costs in electronic networks have made new modes of research feasible which rely on rapid diffusion and on a deeper division of labor, including the outsourcing of R&D services (David and Foray 1995).

5.3.4. How Technical Change is Created: Established Industries

Germany's largest technology-based industries, electrical engineering, chemicals, machinery and automobiles, were formed in the late nineteenth and early twentieth centuries. Their subsequent growth and development has been closely linked to the making of Germany's national system of industrial innovation, whose elements are not only the institutions of public research or the official funding priorities in technology policy, but include the entire set of market and non-market institutions which determine the opportunities for innovation as well as the conditions for the diffusion of knowledge and the application of new technology throughout the economy.

Market structure in all of Germany's established industries has been quite stable over long periods of time and has effectively supported a pattern of cooperative research and innovation which often helped to internalize knowledge spillovers of the kind identified by the new growth theory (Grubel and Weder, 1993). Many small and medium sized supplier firms, often privately held, are securely placed in niche markets around dominant players, such as Siemens in electrical engineering, Daimler-Benz and Volkswagen in the automobile industry (Casper, 1997), BASF, Bayer and Hoechst in chemicals—the latter recently merged with Rhône-Poulenc of France into Aventis—and Linde, Mannesmann and a number of others in machinery. Historically, this pattern of industrial organization has provided an important source of stability in the mechanisms for diffusing new knowledge and process innovations as long as these were complementary and not disruptive to an industry's technological trajectory. Only where disruption was forced on a firm through path-

breaking technological innovation or unraveling changes in its business environment, as in the case of Hoechst's failure to manage the transition to biotechnology in two of its core businesses (agrochemicals and pharmaceuticals) did the merger with an equal-sized and even foreign firm become desirable.

On closer inspection, there are important differences between Germany's large established industries. In the electrical industry, Siemens is the giant survivor of a historic rivalry with AEG dating back to the beginnings of electric power generation, transmission and lighting in the second half of the nineteenth century. Siemens' scope today extends to applications of electrical technology as diverse as solar power, computer chips, medical equipment, household appliances and automotive engineering. Although Siemens is no longer the ground-breaking technological pioneer in its current areas of business that it was in its early days, it has nevertheless defended a position among the leaders in many markets through the introduction of countless incremental innovations, an efficient production system and the globalization of its operations. In the late 1990s, the Siemens management began to take advantage of improved capital market conditions for partial spin-offs in Siemens' more dynamic areas of business— creating the separately listed Epcos and Infineon subsidiaries in telecommunications components and chip technology—in an effort to accelerate restructuring, improve managerial incentives and raise additional equity capital.

In the German chemical industry, two of the three pioneering firms of the late nineteenth century, Bayer and BASF, still dominate alongside the German operations of Aventis. And this is in spite of the limitations which the wars and financial crises of the early twentieth century placed on the scope for the German chemical industry's diversification. Many technological opportunities were missed. World War I cut Germany off from overseas supplies of oil and the expropriation of foreign assets effectively ended the prospect of an internationally competitive oil and petrochemical industry, which had been nascent before that war (Chandler, 1990). The 1920s saw the comprehensive cartelization of Germany's chemical industry under I.G. Farben and, as a consequence, the rapid bureaucratization of decision making. In the 1930s, the Nazi regime made autarky a political priority and enlisted the chemical industry in the search for alternative fuels derived from coal as well as in other technological dead ends for military purposes. Hoechst's decision in the late 1990s to spin off its industrial and consumer chemical units and merge its core business in agrochemicals and pharmaceuticals with Rhône-Poulenc of France, in the hope of exploiting more effectively the opportunities in modern biotechnology, is a radical break with Hoechst's history as an unfocused conglomerate. Also radical was BASF's decision in 2000 to sell its pharmaceutical business to Abbott Laboratories in the United States.

Germany's most spectacular success of the postwar period was the automobile industry, which ascended to technological leadership in Europe while preserving a unique diversity of organizational models. At one end, there is Volkswagen, Europe's largest volume producer with production plants around the world. At the other end is Porsche, an engineering specialist, that is best characterized as a designer of luxury goods rather than a mere car producer. In between are the craft-based producers of performance cars, BMW and Mercedes. A somewhat less important role is played by the German subsidiaries of GM and Ford, volume producers which have rarely been in the vanguard of product technology but have often displayed the benefits of imported process and organizational innovations. The postwar success of the German automobile industry is in striking contrast to Germany's pre-war failure to capitalize on its early lead in engine technology from the pioneering days before World War I. The early German automobile manufacturers fell behind soon after Henry Ford introduced mass production in the United States, and in the 1920s Germany went through a decade of financial crises, inflation, political instability, stagnant incomes, and eventual mass unemployment. This persistent war burden prevented the emergence of an affluent middle class with the ability to pay for automotive

mobility and also crippled the German capital market so that raising sufficient amounts of equity to finance the manufacturing capacities for mass motorization was infeasible for Germany's domestic producers. Indeed, mass production techniques made their appearance only with the influx of foreign direct investment, as in the case of GM's takeover of Opel in the late 1920s. However, it was a domestic government initiative on which Germany's largest volume producer to this date, Volkswagen, was founded in the 1930s when Hitler revived plans from the 1920s that included public investment in the necessary infrastructure, including the *Autobahnen*, to make the automobile a popular means of transport. Henry Ford supplied the production equipment for Volkswagen's first plant on a greenfield site halfway between Hannover and Berlin, mainly used to produce military vehicles until the end of World War II. After the war Volkswagen's Beetle, designed in the 1930s by Ferdinand Porsche, became a symbol of West Germany's reconstruction and eventually even outsold Ford's Model T to become the world's best-selling car by the early 1970s.

In West Germany, the automobile industry soon became a driving force of export-led growth and technological catch-up with the United States. Reliance on foreign technologies was gradually reduced as German producers themselves began to pioneer important product innovations, such as the anti-lock braking system and the airbag in the 1970s. Many of these innovations were the result of close cooperation with component suppliers, such as Bosch. Also in the 1970s, Volkswagen and leading players in the component industry began to globalize their own production through direct foreign investments, largely financed from retained earnings in the German market where a variety of nontariff barriers to trade kept prices high.

A different strategy was pursued by Germany's luxury producers, Daimler-Benz, BMW and Porsche, which continued until the 1990s to serve foreign markets only through exports. The internationalization of production, it was thought, would compromise technological leadership or its perceived basis in Germany's uniquely skilled labor force. Instead, Daimler-

Benz in the 1980s fooled itself into an expensive diversification creating an unfocused technology champion, along the lines of Japanese conglomerates, when the firm acquired the bankrupt electrical giant AEG as well as several aerospace firms. But this strategy of increasing scope failed, and Daimler-Benz also eventually sought to expand the *scale* of its automobile production through direct foreign investment, building its Alabama plant in 1996, merging with Chrysler in 1998 and acquiring a large minority stake in Mitsubishi of Japan in 2000. Similarly, BMW sought to combine its own internationalization of production with a corporate transformation from a small-scale luxury producer into a European volume producer when it acquired the U.K.'s Rover in 1994. However, that takeover failed because BMW was ostensibly unable to implement its superior know-how of high-quality, flexible and efficient production techniques rapidly enough at Rover, where workers lacked the appropriate training and experience, to overcome the disadvantage of a rising exchange rate for the U.K. pound. Porsche, finally, chose to build its first foreign production plant in Finland, a member of Europe's Monetary Union, and has since benefited from the Euro's depreciation vis-à-vis the currency of its main export market, the United States.

Germany's diversified machinery industry provides yet another example of how the national system of industrial organization and corporate governance played an important role in shaping the country's dominant pattern of incremental innovation along established technology trajectories (Casper et al., 1999; Tylecote and Conesa, 1999). Many of Germany's mostly small and medium-sized engineering firms have established themselves in market niches with significant scope for adding value. Prominent examples are Linde in refrigeration, Heidelberger in printing presses and Jungheinrich in fork-lift trucks. Indeed, the systematic exploitation of a firm's core technology in a variety of niche markets appears to be a defining feature of Germany's machinery industry, which rarely generates blockbuster products to create entirely new markets. The greatest risk to this niche strategy is that unforeseen technological change could destroy an entire market segment and render obsolete a wealth of very specific knowledge, accumulated by a highly trained workforce over time. This happened, for example, to Linotype-Hell, a leader in typesetting technology until it failed to anticipate the rise of desktop publishing in the early 1990s.

Despite its inherent risks, the niche strategy has in the past proved profitable for many firms under the constraints set by Germany's labor and capital markets (Soskice, 1997). Lifetime employment has often helped to preserve the technology-specific knowledge accumulated by a firm's workers over many years of learning-by-doing. Works councils and codetermination, which are legal requirements depending on firm size, have often smoothed and speeded up the implementation of new process technologies by forcing a consensus along a firm's established technological trajectory, although worker participation has, at times, delayed the formulation of new business strategies and thus impeded more radical changes. For example, producers of household appliances faced a crisis in the late 1980s when numerical control and fuzzy logic first made their appearance in Japanese products. However, once the Germans started adopting this new technology, they did so with a vengeance and quickly regained quality leadership. More generally, German machine tool manufacturers may have been among the first to include advanced numerical controls as product features but often lost market share by pushing the prices for their highly specialized products beyond those charged for the more standardized Japanese ware. There is a long-standing tendency towards over-engineering in the German machinery industry, which is often attributed to insufficient communication and coordination between product designers and production engineers. Germany's bank-centered financial system, described below, has also generally been supportive of the incremental innovation model by providing the sort of long-term, low-risk external financing required by the long-term strategies that are typical of many engineering firms with rather large and specific investments in machinery and equipment.

5.3.5. Recent Experiences with High Technology: Software

Software firms, like biotechnology enterprises, have found relatively little specific support in Germany's traditional institutional environment when measured against the institutional conditions widely thought responsible for the huge success of software firms in the United States (Casper et al., 1999). Managerial flexibility and speed of response is what successful innovation in software primarily requires, given that the prospect of supernormal rates of return from blockbuster products is marred by particularly high risks. But German institutions have long imposed a variety of constraints on the speed and flexibility of German firms. For example, most employment contracts are unlimited in duration so that the creation of new competencies has become almost like an irreversible investment making it rational to wait and see where the market moves (Dixit and Pindyck, 1994). Moreover, Casper et al. (1999) have argued that established firms rarely want to provide the high powered incentives for individual managers which are commonly used in U.S. high-tech firms because the Germans fear such incentives could undermine consensus decisions and alienate important long-term stakeholders in their firms. Thus, in spite of the legalization of stock options as a managerial incentive and the generally improving access to equity capital, the inter-firm mobility of mid-career scientists and engineers has remained low and thus continues to constrain the ability of start-ups to move quickly into new fields of technology or to expand the scope of their operations when growing rapidly. Many of the start-ups which have transformed Germany's software industry since the mid-1990s actually appear to have discovered market niches which are more compatible with Germany's established model of innovation than the scale-intensive market segments in which U.S. firms continue to dominate the race for blockbuster products (Casper et al., 1999).

The history of software development in Germany has also been shaped by the changing technological opportunities and global industry trends on which the dominant U.S. software market has had the largest influence. In tandem with a series of revolutions in computer hardware technology, the focus of software innovation has shifted from delivering programming services for mainframe computers in the 1960s and 1970s, via churning out packaged software products for PCs in the 1980s to building client-server applications for local networks in the 1990s and, since then, to designing software applications for global communications, the Internet, and electronic commerce. German firms have made contributions to each of these phases. However, neither in programming services for mainframes, nor in mass-market software products for PCs has the German software industry played nearly as large a role as the U.S. software industry. Most German users of mainframe computers, whether in business, government or academia, have hired their own specialist programmers so that a separate market for large-scale suppliers of such services never really took off, as it did in the United States, the United Kingdom and France.

German PC users have overwhelmingly relied on the operating systems and standardized productivity software offered by dominant U.S. firms. The only domestic publisher of office productivity software to make a noticeable impact on the German market, Hamburg based StarDivision, was recently bought by U.S. based Sun Microsystems, which now offers StarDivision's technologically advanced, object-oriented products as a free download on the World Wide Web. In general, independent German publishers of PC software tend to be specialists for some well-defined niche market, often industry-specific business applications, in which they may enjoy a large domestic market share and considerable export revenue from other European markets. In part due to the worldwide success of SAP's enterprise resource planning software, the German software industry has played a much larger role in the era of client-server computing. And the 1990s, amid rapid change in the capital market, have seen a wave of business start-ups dedicated to developing software for the Internet and electronic commerce.

A crucial regulatory issue for the software industry has been the protection of intellectual property, implemented mostly through weakly enforced copyrights. While legal practice in the United States has gradually moved towards patent protection of software related inventions, software has remained unpatentable in the European Union, although this may change in the near future. In response to weak official protection of intellectual property rights, the software industry everywhere has developed its own strategies for protecting innovations against imitators and pirates (Stolpe, 2000). The most basic and most widely adopted technical strategy lies in the distinction between the software's source code, which developers write and manipulate and which most commercial publishers keep secret, and software's machine-readable compilation, which is distributed via media, like diskettes and CD-ROMs, or via the Internet.

Unfortunately, secret source codes not only provide weaker protection than patents, but also do so without requiring the publication of all the technical specifications pertaining to the innovation, which is an essential part of patents. With hindsight, published source codes might have saved a significant share of the resources which actually went into socially wasteful parallel R&D by competing software publishers and attempts at reverse engineering the secret source code of successful software, sometimes only for the purpose of linking a new software product to a hidden interface. The widespread adoption of the open source Linux operating system in the late 1990s has not only demonstrated the opportunities for productive interaction in the development of this particular product, but has also suggested novel forms of cooperative development at the design stage of other kinds of software, if their publishers were to adopt the open source model. In a pioneering quantitative study of one of the oldest U.S. repositories for the Linux open source project, Dempsey et al. (1999) have found that contributors' demographics reveal a strikingly strong European influence within the Linux community, with German residents being by far the most prolific group of all non-U.S. based contributors identifiable by their email country suffix.

Moreover, there is evidence to suggest that small and medium sized firms in Germany have a higher propensity to use open source software, for example on their Internet servers, than large German corporations and U.S. firms of all sizes (Lutterbeck et al., 2000).

By helping the large established software publishers to monopolize the opportunities for upgrading and further developing their core products, secret source codes may have had a distorting influence on market structure in many segments of the software industry. It is often alleged that Microsoft has thrived on this strategy with respect to its MS-DOS and Windows operating systems and has therefore come to exhibit too much vertical integration. The rule of secret source codes in most parts of the existing software industry has magnified the importance of rapid market penetration, with large returns from appropriating the static and dynamic economies of scale that ensue. U.S.-based software publishers who took advantage of their huge and fast growing home market for speedy diffusion and market penetration automatically gained valuable credibility with software users and potential customers around the world. They thus won a bigger prize for early success in the most scale-intensive segments of software than any of the smaller markets in other countries could possibly offer. The prevailing intellectual property rights regime has thus combined with the economic characteristics of software technology, like network externalities, in not only boosting the incentives for *early* innovators to define and conquer markets for the very scale-intensive software categories, like operating systems and standard productivity applications, but also in influencing the international playing field.

Non-U.S.-based software publishers have faltered and failed in the most scale-intensive segments of the software market. German software publishers, for example, quickly abandoned attempts to market their own operating systems for PCs in the early 1980s. And in 1997, Siemens-Nixdorf sold most of its software business to Baan, a start-up in the Netherlands, when it became clear that Germany's electrical and computing conglomerate could not create the right incentives for successful in-house development of standard application software. Even today the German software industry remains highly fragmented, encompassing many thousands of firms of various sizes. They often serve niche markets which emerged after the demise of mainframe computing and the rise of the PC created a mass market for standardized software products and a separate market for computer consulting services dedicated to customizing and integrating hardware and software. As Casper et al. (1999) have pointed out the institutional requirements of the IT service segment are more compatible with conditions in Germany, where large corporations have long performed many business services in-house instead of buying them from external providers: The technology is cumulative, built on experience and the providers' ability to re-use solutions, algorithms and software code from earlier projects. Indeed, the largely firm-specific knowledge, experience and networking of employees account for the major part of a firm's capital in IT services, while the financial risk is relatively low. Consulting services for decentralized PC users have therefore not only accounted for a large part of the German software industry, but have also provided the basis for many new ventures in the product-based software segment.

SAP, whose enterprise resource planning software make it one of today's most successful software publishers in the world, provides an example of the kind of technological strategy adopted by many smaller German software firms. In fact, SAP's main product, R/3, is an example of software straddling both the product and the IT service segment of the software market; the implementation of R/3 requires a considerable service input to meet the specific needs and parameters of client firms. Besides enterprise resource planning software, German publishers have also successfully marketed computer-assisted software engineering tools and standardized software products for production planning and work flow management, architectural graphics, electronic commerce and document management, both at home and in export markets, making the German software industry the strongest in Europe.

The business history of SAP (Meissner, 1997) highlights how Germany's institutional set-up tends to constrain the early growth of new technology-based firms, especially when compared with Microsoft, the leading U.S. software publisher. Despite being several years older than Microsoft, SAP's growth was initially much slower. After its foundation in 1972 by a group of former IBM employees, SAP could not afford to purchase a (mainframe) computer of its own on which to write and test its programs under development in the 1970s. Programmers worked at night on the mainframe of SAP's first client, the German subsidiary of the U.K. chemical giant ICI to whom they sold custom programming and consulting services by day. SAP bought its first computer only in 1979. The initial public offering of SAP shares on the German stock market came in the fall of 1988, when equity capital was sought for an international expansion. This IPO took place much later in the firm's history than Microsoft's debut on the NASDAQ in 1985.

Whereas Microsoft hit straight into the most scale-intensive opportunity in software development when the IBM PC was launched, SAP implicitly protected its software from imitation by making it rather complex. In fact, SAP pursued the initial development of a PC version of its main software, R/3, only as a sideshow to its continuing mainframe activities in the late 1980s. Nevertheless, SAP's R/3 software became a de facto standard for enterprise resource planning when the client-server model was widely adopted, not only by firms replacing mainframes, but also by a wave of first-time adopters of business computing. After passing this threshold in market growth and penetration, SAP has played a special platform role for the German software industry, similar to Microsoft's role in the U.S. software industry. They both created a standardized program which opened up new opportunities for developers of auxiliary programs and other applications software, which in turn have made SAP's R/3 system more valuable for users, just as third-party applications increased the value of using Microsoft's Windows.

Since the mid-1990s, conditions for software-based start-ups have greatly improved, and venture capital has become widely available in Germany. Many start-ups now compete in scale-intensive Internet applications and e-commerce software for global markets. One of the best-known examples of this new type of firm is Intershop, a software publisher founded in 1992 and still largely based at Jena in eastern Germany. With venture capital support, Intershop has been able to grow rapidly and establish its e-commerce software as a potential global de facto standard for online shops. According to industry analysts, Intershop held third place in terms of global market share at the beginning of 2000. Unlike SAP some twenty years earlier, Intershop used an early initial public offering on Germany's Neuer Markt in 1998, only six years after the firm's foundation, to break free from the dominance of its first large customer, Deutsche Telekom. Being a publicly held firm helped to build valuable credibility among new clients and potential strategic allies with respect to the prospect that Intershop would remain a potent independent supplier of e-commerce software and upgrades.

Deutsche Telekom, the former state mono-poly for telecommunications services in Germany, has long been an important client for the communications equipment and soft-ware industries. Moreover, the firm has been a significant player in the German corporate venture capital market. But it did not adopt an explicit strategy to buy German software as part of an industrial policy, not even before its partial stock market flotation in 1997. Nor did other parts of Germany's vast government sector, which includes federal and state govern-ments as well as local authorities and Germany's state-controlled universities, display any signifi-cant procurement favoritism towards German software. Regardless of whether decisions were fully decentralized at the institution actually using the software or centralized at the state government level, as in some federal states (Länder), procurement decisions have gener-ally been risk averse in the sense of sticking to the market leader in the software category under consideration.

As a monopoly, Deutsche Telekom made an important contribution in terms of hardware investment, particularly in the provision of country-wide ISDN and cable networks. Deutsche Telekom also developed a proprietary online service named BTX in the 1980s which was technically comparable with France's Mini-tel, but never really caught on in Germany. One reason was initial problems with data security which were quickly exposed by members of Germany's ill-famed Chaos Computer Club who gained illegal access to online bank accounts of third parties. Despite its own failure in the market, BTX was important as the precurser to t-online, now Europe's largest Internet service provider. Apart from poor marketing and security problems, the adoption of the BTX service by consumers was also slowed down by the high level of Deutsche Tele-kom's monopoly prices for telecommunications services, which exceeded those of comparable countries well into the 1990s.

After German reunification, Deutsche Tele-kom's monopoly was maintained for longer than the former state monopolies in telecom-munications elsewhere, partly for the political purpose of financing the building of a modern telecommunications infrastructure in eastern Germany from Deutsche Telekom's retained monopoly earnings. However, the delayed deregulation, which was eventually forced upon Germany by the European Union, imposed a heavy toll in terms of missed oppor-tunities. In mobile telecommunications tech-nology, for example, Sweden and Finland appear to have gained a significant technologi-cal lead over Germany. Most recently, Deutsche Telekom has used its remaining monopoly power from owning the last mile of end users' network access in pushing its own services, espe-cially a flat rate scheme of Internet access; and there are claims of price discrimination from those rivals who, for lack of proprietary infra-structure, can only resell services purchased at wholesale prices from Deutsche Telekom.

5.3.6. Recent Experiences with High Technology: Biotechnology

Germany's slow start in the modern biotechnol-ogy industry is not just another consequence of the country's pattern of industrial organization and corporate governance but, in contrast with the software case, also reflects major weaknesses in Germany's university system as well as hostile regulation. Developments in the past twenty years fall into two distinct phases in which the most immediate beneficiary of biotechnology in Germany, the country's well-established pharmaceutical industry, played very different roles. The initial phase, in the 1980s, was driven by strategic investments from Germany's large chemical conglomerates into pharmaceutical and agrochemical activities and was accompanied by political antagonism which culminated in the introduction of a rather restrictive law on genetic engineering in 1990; this was somewhat relaxed in 1993. The often irrational public hostility towards biotechnology—which informed the law and had, even before its enactment, led to a series of anti-biotechnology court decisions—amounted at least partially to a denial of property rights in private biotechnology investments. In the 1980s Hoechst, for example, struggled for many years with the authorities and the courts to put a newly built plant for artificial insulin into operation, while imports from Hoechst's Danish and U.S. competitors took over the German market. Towards the end of the 1980s, Germany's large chemical and pharmaceutical firms seemed to be giving up on biotechnology made in Germany and invested directly in the United States, then the undisputed biotechnology leader, where they acquired start-ups and built their own large-scale laboratories.

Since biotechnology innovation continues to be driven by entrepreneurial start-ups even after more than twenty years of industry growth in the United States, the development of biotechnology appears to require a set of institutions not easily reconciled with Germany's traditional system of industrial organization and corporate governance (Casper et al., 1999). The discovery of new drugs requires highly specialized skills and fragmented scientific knowledge of the sort which can only be obtained and maintained through close links with basic research (Zucker et al., 1994). Hence, small start-ups, especially those with their origin in academic research programs, appear not only to offer the best opportunity for university researchers to become involved

in the commercial development of biotechnology, be it through employment or temporary consulting, but also to have an enduring comparative advantage with respect to innovation. Large pharmaceutical firms, by contrast, continue to hold the specialized assets for the development, clinical testing and marketing of new drugs and thus can still appropriate much of the pecuniary payoff even from innovations found in cooperation with biotechnology start-ups. Indeed, it was partly for the purpose of becoming a more potent and attractive research partner for biotechnology start-ups that Hoechst and Rhône-Poulenc recently merged and concentrated their pharmaceutical and agrochemical activities in Aventis.

The late 1990s have seen a wave of biotechnology start-ups in Germany. At the end of 1999, there were 279 new biotechnology firms with fewer than 500 employees (VCI, 2000). As a group, they achieved annual increases in employment, patents and sales of more than 30 percent in the last two years of the 1990s. R&D expenditure even increased by more than 50 percent annually in 1998 and 1999, reaching 640 million Deutschmark. Total sales of these firms reached more than one billion Deutschmark for the first time in 1999. However, the economic significance of biotechnology start-ups still pales if compared to the situation in the United States. Moreover, many of Germany's new biotechnology firms are even small by European standards. In 1999, 20 percent of European biotechnology firms with fewer than 500 employees were located in Germany, but these accounted for only 15 percent of European employees and less than ten percent of sales, according to a study of Ernst and Young (2000).

Taking a closer look at the German biotechnology scene, Casper et al. (1999) have identified two distinct market segments within biotechnology which have fared rather differently under the influence of Germany's broader innovation system. Relatively few German start-ups are in the "therapeutic segment" doing drug discovery research. By way of contrast, what Casper et al. (1999) call the platform technology segment—firms that create the research tools used in therapeutics—is more active and more in line with the German system of innovation. Indeed, the platform technology segment has given the main impetus to biotechnology's second phase in Germany, beginning in the mid-1990s, and includes start-up ventures in genetic sequencing and engineering as well as the application of information technology and automation technologies in drug screening. For example, one of Germany's most successful new biotechnology firms, Qiagen, appears to hold a strong technological lead as well as a dominant and profitable market position as a supplier of cheap consumable kits that replace labour intensive processes in DNA filtration. Platform technologies of this kind are not directly targeted at consumer markets, do not themselves introduce genetically modified substances and therefore have created much less controversy and public hostility than, for example, genetically modified foods.

Casper et al. (1999) have emphasized the distinction between platform technologies and the therapeutics segment because their distinct economic characteristics can help explain the differential success of firms under the incentives and constraints set by Germany's innovation system. The discrete nature of technology in the therapeutics segment and the short time horizon of individual research programs makes a frequent reorientation of a firm's research strategy necessary. Research may become obsolete whenever a competitor wins a patent or an unexpected technological obstacle occurs, and biotechnology firms must constantly be on the alert and move with speed when entering or leaving a particular field in the therapeutics segment. Success at that game requires a frequent turnover of employees with highly specialized human capital, which is difficult to accommodate within Germany's tightly regulated labor market. Moreover, there are also high financial risks because the failure rate of many therapeutics research programs is high, time to market tends to be long, and the percentage of cost devoted to R&D can be extreme. On top of this, there is the unique risk of meeting regulatory testing and approval requirements, which is often hard to predict in terms of timing and probability.

Platform technologies, by contrast, possess the characteristic that their development usually relies on cumulative rather than discrete technologies. Research scientists and engineers therefore need much more firm-specific knowledge than is typically acquired within therapeutic firms. By improving employees' incentives to invest in firm-specific skills, the long-term employment contracts which are standard in Germany's labor market can actually give German firms a competitive advantage over foreign rivals in the platform technology segment. Compared to the therapeutics segment, the share of R&D in total costs appears to be lower, technological failure is less likely and innovations have to meet fewer regulatory approval and testing requirements. Moreover, Casper et al. (1999) have observed that key inventions can often be leveraged into new markets through follow-up R&D and continued close interaction with users, most of which are other biotechnology or pharmaceutical firms. For all of these reasons, the financial risks of investing in platform technologies are much lower than those in the therapeutics segment, and new firms have found Germany's underdeveloped market for private equity less of a constraint. Many start-ups in the platform technology segment have actually relied on state subsidies for their initial R&D investment and used retained earnings to finance subsequent R&D, while building their standing with a Hausbank to prepare for an initial public offering of equity shares.

The 1990s saw some significant and novel government initiatives aimed at closing the gap vis-à-vis the United Kingdom and the United States in biotechnology. In recognition of systemic interdependencies at the regional level, which had become a hot subject in academic discussions, the German government in 1995 announced a contest, named BioRegio, for the allocation of regionally targeted subsidies. The idea was not to award subsidies to individual firms selected on their own merit, but to select the one region with the best prospects of accommodating a vibrant biotechnology industry. Criteria for selection were the level of commercial biotechnology activity already established within the region and the specific merits of a regional plan to further develop and improve conditions for the transfer of technology from universities to private firms as well as for inter-firm cooperation within the region. In the end, three regions were awarded funds totaling 150 million Deutschmark, disbursed over the course of five years. The winners include the region around Cologne, the Rhein-Neckar triangle and Munich where the Max Planck Institute for Biochemistry with almost 500 research scientists has been an important center of academic research. Within three years of announcing the contest, the number of biotechnology firms in Germany tripled; but, of course, even with hindsight it is hard to tell how much of this burst of activity was related to the BioRegio contest rather than to the creation of the Neuer Markt stock market in 1997 or to other pertinent improvements in financial market conditions in the second half of the 1990s.

5.4. How Germany Develops and Harnesses Technological Change

5.4.1. Regulatory Issues: Capital Markets

Germany's capital market, for a long time aptly described as bank-centered, has seen the development of much broader and more liquid equity markets in the 1990s. The market capitalization of shares of domestic firms traded on Germany's main stock exchange, the Deutsche Börse in Frankfurt, quadrupled between 1990 and the end of 1999, while the value of domestic bank credits and the market value of bonds barely doubled. There have been several events behind this, including Europe's monetary union, which has intensified foreign competition for Germany's financial intermediaries, and technological change, which lowered the costs of financial market transactions while increasing the demand of innovative private firms for public equity issues. In a broad historical picture, the German capital market has come almost full circle, since it was private equity provided by banks and wealthy individuals that fueled Germany's industrial revolution in the nineteenth century. It was no

coincidence at the time that a member of the Siemens family headed the Deutsche Bank and steered the allocation of capital in the emerging electrical industry (Gall et al., 1995). Indeed, the private banks founded during the boom years of Germany's industrial revolution after 1850 often acted much like venture capitalists and investment banks today. But that earlier emphasis on equity finance was lost during the long series of financial crises which followed in the wake of Germany's failed military ambitions in the first half of the twentieth century. Hyperinflation in 1923, the stock market crash of 1929 and the subsequent depression caused so much financial loss, economic disruption and political disaster that risk aversion did not only become widespread among the German people but also dominant in the official regulation of banks and financial markets.

Today, the total stock market capitalization as a percentage of gross domestic product (GDP) is much smaller in Germany than in the United Kingdom or the United States. According to data from the International Federation of Stock Exchanges (FIBV), the market capitalization of listed domestic firms was only 51 percent of GDP in Germany at the end of 1998, approximately one-third of the U.S. ratio, less than one-third of the U.K. ratio and even less than one-fifth of the ratio in Switzerland. Also the number of publicly listed domestic firms remains relatively low; at the end of 1999, shares of only 851 German firms were traded in Deutsche Börse's regulated market segments, far fewer than the 2274 U.K. firms whose shares were traded on the main and parallel markets of the London stock exchange. The total number of domestic firms with a public listing on a German stock exchange was 966, up from 776 in 1990, according to the Deutsches Aktieninstitut, a private organization advocating greater political support for public equity in Germany.

Amid booming stock markets of the 1990s, even the Germans began to take a less cautious stand on equities, and the number of German shareholders reached five million in 1999, according to a survey conducted by Infratest on behalf of the Deutsches Aktieninstitut. But at the end of 1997, the private household sector's holdings of equity shares, excluding its even less significant holding of investment funds, accounted for only 8.3 percent of all liquid assets held by private households in Germany. They still held much larger shares in saving deposits (22 percent), life insurance schemes (22 percent) and fixed income securities issued by the government, by Germany's state banks or the large private banks (21 percent) (Deutsches Aktieninstitut, 1998). Moreover, because Germany's compulsory pay-as-you-go pension scheme is comprehensive, only about 20 percent of the limited number of shares in circulation was held by institutional investors, such as insurance firms, pension and other investment funds, against 70 percent in the United Kingdom. For lack of a competitive brokerage industry, most outside investors' access to the securities markets is effectively controlled by banks; even institutional investors rarely have their own trading desks. Revealingly, Germany's large private banks still own 80 percent of Deutsche Börse which runs the Frankfurt stock exchange. A number of regional stock exchanges also continue to exist.

Although the stock market has greatly gained in importance during the 1990s, Germany's financial system must still be considered as basically bank-centered. It is a system, however, which has long defied a simple classification as credit-based, because German banks tend to play a dominant role not only in the allocation of credit, but in the provision of external finance in general (Christensen, 1992). Banks and insurance firms have also retained their traditional roles as supervisors of many publicly held firms through seats on supervisory boards and through proxy voting rights. Conversely, most German firms still rely on banks or retained earnings to finance investments. However, while banks are often willing to offer long-term financing for tangible capital, they do not normally finance R&D. Credit constraints for intangible investments are significant despite the ability of German industrial firms to extend long-term commitments to their own stakeholders, including employees and the firm's Hausbank, which is seen as motivating banks' long-term commitment of credit in general (see Casper et al., 1999). Because of

their long-term relationship with client firms, banks can often monitor the status of their investments more closely than other outside investors. Germany's universal banks may lack the expertise to monitor investment in new technology, but reputational monitoring has often helped to overcome that deficiency in the past.

Within the banking industry, there is a clear segmentation of markets between the big private banks, which mainly cater for large corporations, the state-owned Landesbanken, which have a mandate to finance regional development regardless of firm size, and last, but not least, the numerous cooperative banks and municipal savings institutes (Sparkassen), where most consumers keep their savings and where the small, privately held Mittelstand firms find the cheapest and most readily available loans. Together, the public sector banks (i.e., the Landesbanken and municipal savings institutes), hold a share of almost 50 percent in the German banking market, measured in terms of either balance sheet totals or business volume (Sinn, 1997). While the five major private banks hold only a relatively small share of Germany's retail banking market and also neglect Mittelstand firms with less than five million Deutschmark in annual sales, they have long dominated the market for corporate clients and have recently been gearing up to compete in the fast growing markets for corporate restructuring, asset securitization and the underwriting of public share offerings. Yet, they are still frequently outdone by the large U.S. investment banks with German subsidiaries which have successfully used their own home market experience, global presence, and sheer size as a leverage in the German market.

On the other hand, Germany's major private banks also face stiff competition from the Landesbanken which are subsidized in a variety of ways by their respective state government owners and mostly act like any universal bank, lending freely in national and international markets and holding shares in many German industrial firms. At the behest of Germany's private banks, the state subsidies, mainly in the form of unlimited government guarantees for the liabilities incurred by the Landesbanken, are currently under review by the European Commission. The municipally owned savings institutes still provide the backbone of external financing for Germany's numerous small and many medium-sized Mittelstand firms, except for high-tech start-ups which cannot offer collateral and thus do not qualify for debt finance. The municipal savings institutes are barred from holding equity in private firms and thus cannot play the venture capital game. Throughout much of the postwar period, the cost of capital for German firms has appeared to be low in comparison with other countries mainly because the obstacles for small and new firms seeking to raise external equity have defied measurement and have thus long been ignored.

The absence of effective public equity markets has probably had a decisive impact on the rate and direction of technological innovations pursued by German industry. Some of the leading technology firms, such as Bosch and Carl Zeiss, are still privately held through foundations with the express purpose of keeping the firms independent from outside interference. These protected holding constructions may not only have adverse effects on the quality of corporate governance, but also effectively rule out these firms from venturing into fast-growing new markets that require large-scale investment in new technological competencies outside their traditional core technologies. However, in new technology-based industries, the lack of access to public equity markets has been hardest on newcomers so that, for example, in telecommunications Mannesmann, an old steel and engineering conglomerate, enjoyed a head start in terms of financial resources even if the firm wasted many of these resources during its internal transformation into a telecommunications business. That it was taken over by the purebred U.K. mobile communications operator Vodafone after a hostile battle in 1999 merely confirmed Mannesmann's lower firm value for being an anachronistic conglomerate in the high-tech world.

In the 1990s, new guidelines for regulatory harmonization within the European Union, set out in the Investment Services Directive, prompted significant changes in Germany's securities market legislation and for the first time created a federal agency to oversee securities trading in Germany. Insider trading became a punishable offense in 1994. The Corporation Control and Transparency Act, which took effect on May 1, 1998, allows share buybacks using distributable capital and simplifies the regulation of stock option programs for employees of private firms. Such programs are often seen as vital for liquidity-constrained start-ups in high-tech industries seeking to attract and motivate appropriately qualified and experienced managers; however, established firms also have made wider use of stock option programs since their partial deregulation. In one of the most important measures introducing best practice and international standards in German equity markets, issuers are no longer required to generate consolidated financial statements under German law when they are already obliged by overseas laws to use foreign or international standards for their financial statements. A law regulating corporate takeovers and mergers is currently being prepared.

The reforms of the 1990s in the regulation of securities trading were matched by private reform initiatives at the Deutsche Börse which owns the all-important Frankfurt stock exchange. As elsewhere in Europe, adoption of new information and communication technologies to automate trading and settlement has had a pervasive impact on equity markets. Not only has Deutsche Börse's continuous, order-driven electronic trading with intermittent auctions generated huge network externalities and enhanced stock market liquidity, but also the accuracy and speed in the settlement of stock market transactions has been improved. The latter is provided by Clearstream, the settlement specialist partly owned by Germany's large private banks. The main reason that outside investors' explicit trading costs remain much higher than the implicit trading costs determined by Deutsche Börse's trading technology is that Germany's universal banks still dominate brokerage and have so far defended their position as effective gatekeepers to the stock market (Domowitz and Steil, 2001).

In terms of impact on the wider economy, the most important achievement in Germany in the

1990s has been the creation of the Neuer Markt segment for small growth stocks in March 1997 which, in contrast to a previous attempt at creating a regulated market for small caps in the 1980s, attracted a large number of initial public offerings of shares from new technology-based firms. The total market capitalization in the Neuer Markt grew within three years after its start to more than 120 billion Euro, and included more than 200 listed firms at the end of 1999; there were even 338 listed firms with a total market capitalization of 115 billion Euro at the end of 2000, according to a press release by Deutsche Börse. Germany's Neuer Markt thus accounted for 50 percent of Europe's combined market capitalization of fast growing small-caps listed in the various new market segments of national stock exchanges. With stringent disclosure requirements, the Neuer Markt has sought to replace an issuer's long-established reputation for financial stability by transparency as the main key to outside investor confidence. Moreover, each newly listed firm is required to name two designated sponsors responsible for providing matching share offers and bids at any time, although such market making activity to maintain liquidity in thinly traded stocks would probably occur spontaneously in the continuous trading that is practiced by the Neuer Markt. While banks which appear to use market making as a loss leader also dominate the IPO market as underwriters, IPOs can in principle be introduced by other financial intermediaries as well. By creating an attractive option of exit via an initial public offering of shares, the Neuer Markt has certainly improved the refinancing conditions for venture capitalists in Germany.

In policy initiatives predating the creation of the Neuer Markt, the German government has made support of venture capital for new technology-based firms a top policy priority in the 1990s. In one scheme, for example, the Kreditanstalt für Wiederaufbau and the Deutsche Ausgleichsbank, the national development banks, guarantee 65 percent of the potential loss of equity participations which they have co-financed for a period of up to ten years. In addition, individual federal states grant targeted subsidies and subsidized loans for small- and medium-sized enterprises. Many obstacles to the growth of venture capital, some of which were originally introduced to avoid tax evasion, have indeed been substantially relaxed (OECD, 1998d). For example, capital gains are now tax free after only one year of share holding, it is no longer required to take ventures public within ten years, the minimum number of shareholders has been reduced and majority holdings in individual firms are now possible for up to eight years. However, more needs to be done, especially in the tax system and with respect to inflexible labor market regulations.

While Germany's venture capital industry remains small in comparison with that of the United States, it has recently grown much faster than the venture capital industries in most European countries. In 1998, approximately 30 percent of all European venture capital investment in the early stages of start-up firms was made by German venture capitalists, according to data gathered by the European Venture Capital Association. Relative to GDP, however, the German venture capital market reached only a level of 0.7 percent, including a level of 0.25 percent for early stage deals, in 1998. These levels are still small compared with the United States (2.3 and 0.75 percent), the Netherlands (1.7 and 0.5 percent), Belgium (1.1 and 0.7 percent) and Finland (1.0 and 0.6 percent). Nevertheless, with a much larger emphasis on early stage investments than in the larger U.K. venture capital market, the German venture capital industry seems to have embarked on a promising learning cycle. Indeed, there are signs of an increasing specialization of investments in software, Internet and biotechnology related ventures—which demand a particularly large share of intangible investment and where the comparative advantage of venture capital vis-à-vis other forms of financial intermediation is greatest. This ongoing learning cycle should soon begin to raise the efficiency of the screening, selection and management support services provided by venture capitalists for new technology-based firms in Germany. Moreover, the increasing depth and improved functioning of Germany's stock market is likely to benefit new technology-based firms in a variety of other ways.

In particular, by promoting the independence of small firms from dominant customers—as venture capital might have done in the case of SAP in the early 1970s had it been available—venture capital may also facilitate the freer flow of knowledge via more varied user–producer relationships and by enhancing the mobility of people across small, fast-growing firms.

5.4.2. Regulatory Issues: Labor Markets

The German labor market suffers from a plethora of regulations and rigidities that make life difficult for innovators who want to start a new business. Many of these regulations were originally introduced to protect workers from dismissal and unfair treatment by established employers. But the rigidities have an adverse effect on Germany's capacity for innovation by reducing the mobility of workers across regions and industries, by reducing workers' incentives to form human capital and by making the formation of new firms unnecessarily risky for entrepreneurs. High unemployment means that many people do not participate in the learning process. Low rates of employment among the less skilled imply inter alia an underdeveloped service sector. Moreover, people do not move easily between firms because it is risky for new firms to hire people; the opportunity costs of leaving the corporate sector or the university sector to start a new firm are exacerbated.

Wages are determined through autonomous negotiations between the trade unions and the employers associations of broadly defined industries; negotiated wages are protected by a set of legal rules. For example, it is illegal to offer a job contract to a union member that deviates from the collective wage agreement unless the deviation improves the worker's situation by paying a higher hourly wage or by granting a reduction in hours worked. But a reduced risk of losing the job is not considered to be a legal improvement of a worker's situation by the German labor courts. Moreover, decentralized bargaining at the firm level is legally permissible only if it is explicitly provided for in the industry-wide wage contracts. The law thus provides strong protection of the cartelized

bargaining process, not least because firms tend to apply the negotiated wage to non-union members as well. As a consequence, Germany's unemployed have effectively lost the opportunity to enter the labor market at a wage below the industry-wide negotiated wage.

As an implication of labor market rigidities, the unemployment rates of West Germany's states became more diverse over the period 1975–90, while the regional wage structure remained largely constant (Siebert, 1994; Table 7.1). Moreover, the wage structure with respect to qualifications has also remained constant during the last twenty years, although there has been a massive shift in labor demand at the expense of less qualified workers (Sachverständigenrat, 2000: 343). This created excess levels of unemployment among the less qualified and lowered their incentives and opportunities to build up the human capital required for a more active participation in the economy's innovation process. To the extent that the constant wage structure has followed from resistance to allow higher wages for skills in strong demand, there have also been insufficient incentives for qualified workers to extend and further improve their human capital in response to changing demand in the German labor market. In the 1990s, for example, acute scarcities developed in the labor market for computer specialists.

In an important contrast to the rigid wage structure, Germany has achieved much more flexibility with respect to working time in the past decade. A large number of more flexible working time arrangements were negotiated at the firm level, between management and workers' councils who chose to ignore the industry-wide wage contracts on these points. In exchange for their cooperation, a firm's workers were usually given a guarantee against layoffs for some specified number of years.

Siebert (1997) provides a comprehensive description of the institutional arrangements affecting the performance of Germany's labor market. Besides the market process, layers of rules governing wage formation, the legal system and the system of nonemployment income have adversely affected labor market performance, because the cumulative effect of these rules has made the German labor market ever more rigid since the late 1960s. The tax wedge widenened, pressure on the unemployed to accept job offers was lowered as the replacement ratio rose and rules of reasonableness were introduced. Sick leave payments were raised to 100 percent of regular pay for six weeks for all workers in 1969. Employment schemes financed by the government were introduced which paid 90 percent of the previous net wage.

Looking at the impact of Germany's present labor market regulations on innovation, it can be argued that they tend to favor established firms seeking only to expand along well-established trajectories. The main point is that long-term commitments to firm-specific human capital are credible. People do not have to fear that they will be sacked unless the firm as a whole sinks. Moreover, codetermination can at least in principle be interpreted as a safeguard against a strategic reorientation which might devalue the sort of firm-specific human capital which employees have accumulated over time and which have made German firms competitive in some traditional industries. But such an incentive structure comes at a high cost: fundamental changes with a new innovative path become less likely. Risks are less likely to be taken. Actually, the German government now plans to update the law relating to the rules that must be adhered to in firms (Betriebsverfassungsgesetz) intending to give worker councils an even larger say. An important area to be included is retraining for workers whose skills have become obsolete due to new technological developments. To what extent worker councils may try to resist retraining schemes and thus may stifle firms' innovative capacity in the future remains to be seen.

Layoff constraints represent another institutional aspect affecting technological advance. This is especially relevant for research personnel. For firms, these restraints are costly by forcing them either to keep research workers with low productivity or to pay high severance to make them quit voluntarily. Given that public funding generally rules out severance pay for the public and semi-public research sector and for tenured positions in the universities, there is

an even worse problem of adverse selection there; the less productive researchers tend to stay within the system and reduce spontaneity and inventiveness.

5.4.3. The University System

A major weakness of the German innovation system is the organization of its universities, which are steered by administrative processes, and largely shielded from competition. This may be rooted in the many protective attitudes in German society. Moreover, reform of the German university system has been slowed down politically by an implicit agreement that all major changes must be coordinated through committees at the federal level although the constitutional responsibility for education and science rests with the individual federal states. In particular, the conference of science and education ministers from the sixteen states acts as an effective cartel by suppressing any unilateral change in the organization of schools and universities which might affect the accessibility of educational institutions in one state for students from another.

Lack of competition and the absence of a price mechanism in the allocation of academic resources are at least partly to blame for massive overcrowding, poor teaching quality, high withdrawal rates and prolonged study periods before a fraction of the initially enrolled students eventually graduates. In their external relations, German universities often appear sluggish and inflexible. Changing demands of the labor market tend to have little impact on the content and methods of teaching; entirely new fields of study are developed and introduced only very slowly. The system of degrees is incompatible with the U.S. model where a first degree is regularly awarded after four years of college education. In Germany, by contrast, most students need at least five years before obtaining their first university degree, despite having spent thirteen years in primary and secondary education. Another five years of study is now the rule for a doctoral degree, although that does not yet qualify for independent academic teaching. Anyone seeking a career as a university teacher needs to earn another degree, the Habilitation, for which no equivalent exists in the United States. While a doctoral degree is primarily awarded in recognition of demonstrated originality of research, the Habilitation is thought to recognize precision and breadth of knowledge as well.

Many of the current deficiencies of the German university system are a legacy of political priorities in the postwar reconstruction and subsequent expansion of higher education. Due to demographic change, general economic progress and changing labor market conditions, demand for university studies began to rise rapidly in the late 1960s and state governments primarily aimed at a quantitative expansion of supply. In addition, there was some relaxation of the administrative control by state governments, but instead of using market mechanisms and competition, new rules of democratic decision making were introduced which involve students and administrative staff in many internal university decisions, thus limiting the traditional authority of academic teachers. Nonetheless, state governments retained ultimate control over budgets, the hiring of personnel and strategic choices about future directions of research as well as broad areas of teaching. Despite the expansion and democratization of the past three decades, the basic structure of the German university system still reveals its historic origin in the early nineteenth century.

The origin of the modern German university can be precisely dated because it was the foundation of Prussia's Berlin reform university by Wilhelm von Humboldt in 1810 which marked a clear break from the prior practice of universities as mere teaching colleges as well as from the French model of specialized higher education where each school trained students only for a particular industry or profession. In the era of European enlightenment, research was separate from teaching and primarily conducted by individuals or private academic societies. The task of universities was merely to categorize and preserve the state of knowledge and to pass it on to the next generation of scholars. The separation between basic and applied research, which plays such a prominent role in technology policy today, only began to be practiced in the nineteenth century, after Wilhelm von Humboldt had made the unity of basic research and teaching a central tenet of his Berlin reform university. When Germany was unified under Prussia's leadership in 1871, education and research policies remained the responsibility of individual state governments, establishing a principle that continues to hold until today. At the same time, however, the imperial government in Berlin assumed responsibility for setting standards and patent legislation, and this assignment endowed the imperial government with responsibility for certain areas of technology-related research.

Germany's first imperial research institute in the area of high technology, founded in 1887 under the name Physikalisch-Technische Reichsanstalt, was devoted to research in the new field of electrical engineering and was led by the prominent physicist and physician Hermann von Helmholtz. At that time, the Physikalisch-Technische Reichsanstalt, with its focus on industrial applications, was a center of excellence, a playground for the best scientists and engineers, whereas university teaching was considered a suitable occupation for less qualified academics. The private industrial research laboratories which emerged in Germany's chemical and electrical industries of the late nineteenth century also acquired a high status and established a new pattern of applied research which in turn influenced the organization of research in the university sector and in publicly funded academies.

Prussia took the lead in devising a science policy which used private sector funds but remained under the influence of the state with respect to its strategic orientation. In line with these policies, the Kaiser-Wilhelm-Gesellschaft zur Förderung der Wissenschaften was founded in 1911 as a private association controlled by the government. Within its first three years, the Kaiser-Wilhelm-Gesellschaft established five research institutes, devoted to chemistry, physical chemistry, coal, biology and medical science, which were directed by powerful representatives of their respective discipline who were chosen for their academic reputation. Many of the activities of the Kaiser-Wilhelm-Gesellschaft were directed not towards basic research but towards applied research which proved extremely useful in the chemical and electrical industries.

After World War I, Germany's academic research found itself in a serious crisis. Not only did private funding cease to flow, but many international contacts also ceased. In an emergency response, leading scholars founded the Notgemeinschaft der Deutschen Wissenschaft in 1920, which later became the Deutsche Forschungsgemeinschaft. Their primary purpose was to fend off the imminent exploitation of academic research for narrow political or commercial ends and to establish the principle that the scientific community should decide for itself how to distribute the funds it acquired from private and government sources. As an instrument for the acquisition of funds from private industry, the Stifterverband der Notgemeinschaft der Deutschen Wissenschaft was founded in December 1920, and all donations thus received were duly passed on to the Notgemeinschaft der Deutschen Wissenschaft. In addition, substantial funds flowed in from abroad, above all from the Rockefeller-Foundation in the United States. Throughout the 1920s, the appropriate influence of private industry on the priorities in academic research was the subject of intense discussions and the Helmholtz-Gesellschaft became a competing model with a much stronger influence of industrial financiers than was tolerated by the Notgemeinschaft der Deutschen Wissenschaft.

After World War II the institutes of the Kaiser-Wilhelm-Gesellschaft were transformed to become the new Max-Planck-Gesellschaft zur Förderung der Wissenschaften (MPG). The Max Planck Institutes were now dedicated to basic research. Within the university sector, the initial postwar decade was devoted merely to the reconstruction of teaching activities. But in the 1960s there was a public debate about the appropriate scale of university education in an advanced industrial country. In light of the rapidly expanding college education system in the United States, the numbers of enrolled students in higher education in Germany seemed totally inadequate. There was much talk about an educational crisis which would strangle efforts by the German economy to

catch up with the United States. So towards the end of the 1960s and throughout the 1970s, the German university sector embarked on an ambitious quantitative expansion of teaching activities. Not only did the teaching staff at existing universities expand with the opening of new faculties, but also new regional universities were built in several West German states. Initially, that expansion aimed at creating capacity for 200,000 students in West Germany; after a revision in the 1970s, capacity was expanded to 900,000 students, but in 1990, there were actually one million students in West Germany alone.

The strong quantitative expansion came largely at the expense of high-quality research. Indeed, the university system's transition away from applied research after World War II now appears to have been a key factor in the economic stagnation that has overtaken Germany. After the war, universities became skittish about applied research for a variety of reasons—including the ambiguous moral issues that emerged during the Nazi regime, the "brain drain" and flight of many talented scholars to the United States, and the lack of resources that accompanied a damaged infrastructure. The unity of research and teaching that had defined the pre-World War II era was lost and along with it much of the university sector's role in Germany's economic progress.

The neglect of research is also beginning to affect the development of Germany's dense network of technical universities, whose name already indicates their ambition to be as comprehensive as the more established humanistic institutions. Technical universities need a critical size, which Berlin, Aachen and Munich already achieved in the nineteenth century. But some state governments no longer heed this lesson and have recently created small new technical faculties in old humanistic universities where the prospects for research will be very limited. In addition, the postwar period has seen the institutional innovation of Fachhochschulen—comparable to polytechnics or universities of applied science—which emphasize teaching but do almost no original research. Instead they use consultancy work to bring students into contact with business practice. Fachhochschulen thus represent an important stepping stone on the way towards an increasing separation of teaching and research.

Research within the proper university system is also thought to be hampered by statutory limits on non-academic income-generating activities of a university professor (Nebendienstverordnung) which can make it difficult to set up in business to commercialize inventions and other findings of prior academic research. In a peculiar contrast, German professors are allowed to acquire patents on their own account even if they are based on official university research (Hochschullehrerprivileg). But this is now to change because in the past, many professors did not exploit their patenting opportunities efficiently, concentrating instead on furthering their academic publication record. According to current government plans, property rights in future academic research are to be held by the respective university and the share of its inventor-employees is to be limited to one-third of all license income, still much higher than in the private sector. Another factor that hinders research lies in the Beamtenrecht which has long prevented the employment of foreign academics as tenured professors in German universities.

One way of measuring the international competitiveness of the German university system is by looking at the number of foreign students it attracts to spend part or all of their study period at a German university. Public perception is that the numbers have been declining, and comparisons are often made with the early years of the twentieth century when overall student numbers were small and a relatively large portion of privileged students from the United States came to Germany for advanced studies.

Recent data on the number of foreign students, presented in Tables 5.6 and 5.7, reveal distinct patterns for source countries, depending on their location in Europe, Asia, the Americas or Africa. While most students from developing countries in Asia and Africa appear to be coming for full courses of studies, largely concentrated in engineering and the sciences, students from the Americas appear to be coming primarily as exchange students for a spell of one year or less, to study the German language and culture in the humanities. Among European students, the proportion of temporary exchange students has declined since the opening of Eastern Europe led to an influx of students who sought to study full courses at German universities in order to obtain a German degree, with a strong preference for the humanities, social sciences, law, and business studies.

One question for policy makers is whether foreign students can make up for an increasing mismatch between the qualifications of German graduates and the changing structure of labor market demand. Indeed, the steady supply of German engineering and science graduates has begun to dwindle in the 1990s under the impact of unfavorable demographics and a declining quality of high school education in mathematics and the sciences. However, unlike in the United States, foreign students have neither arrived in sufficient numbers to fill these gaps, nor are those from developing countries normally allowed to compete in the German labor market after their graduation.

More general comparisons with the United States and other countries are difficult for a number of reasons. Student flows are not only influenced by the expected academic quality of the chosen host university, but also by the costs of study (including the costs of living and tuition which is generally free in Germany) as well as by students' language skills. But in a revealing contrast with the U.S. system, participation rates of foreigners are at their lowest among doctoral students in Germany, whereas in the United States, the share of foreigners is at its highest among doctoral students. While this surely reflects on the strength of research in U.S. universities, there is also a financial reason: Foreign doctoral students in Germany often cannot take up positions as teaching assistants because of language problems and legal barriers.

5.4.4. Other Microeconomic Issues of Innovation Policy

As an example of excessive product market regulation and mismanagement which has stifled innovation, the German railway system stands out, especially in comparison with neighboring

TABLE 5.6
Foreign Students in Germany (percentage of beginners in parentheses)

Locus of nationality	Winter term					
	1975–6	1980–1	1985–6	1990–1	1995–6	1998–9
Europe	22730 (24.7)	29086 (24.7)	39670 (21.4)	53151 (26.9)	87455 (30.2)	104368 (29.6)
Africa	3249 (19.9)	3884 (17.8)	4310 (16.6)	6441 (21.8)	13555 (15.9)	16500 (18.0)
Americas	5451 (39.5)	6572 (34.9)	7600 (35.4)	8455 (36.4)	9084 (34.3)	8972 (39.3)
Asia	14408 (17.1)	17056 (16.5)	21667 (14.8)	30051 (17.2)	34051 (13.8)	34390 (18.7)
Other	1460 (20.1)	1115 (18.7)	1327 (19.1)	1662 (22.0)	2326 (15.8)	1764 (18.6)
Total	47298 (23.6)	57713 (22.9)	74574 (20.6)	99760 (24.3)	146471 (25.1)	165994 (26.6)
Bildungsinländer[a]					48082 (17.8)	57209 (16.5)
Percentage share of foreign students in all students	5.7	5.6	5.6	6.3	7.9	9.2
Percentage share of foreign students minus Bildungsinländer in all students					5.3	6.0
Percentage share of foreign beginners in all beginners	6.8	6.8	7.4	9.6	14.0	16.8
Percentage share of foreign beginners minus Bildungsinländer in all beginners					10.7	13.2

Source: Statistisches Bundesamt, Hochschulstatistik, authors' calculations.
[a] Bildungsinländer are legally considered foreign, but they have graduated from a high school in Germany, in most cases because they were brought up by foreign parents living in Germany.

TABLE 5.7
Major Fields Chosen by Real Foreign Students[a] in Germany in the Winter Term 1998–9 (percentage of nationality group in parentheses)

Locus of nationality (total number in parentheses)	Social sciences, law and business studies	Humanities	Engineering studies	Sciences	All others, including arts, sports, medicine and agriculture
Europe (59584)	17608 (29.6)	20727 (34.9)	7644 (12.8)	6483 (10.8)	7122 (11.9)
Africa (14460)	2528 (17.4)	2033 (14.1)	5269 (36.4)	3172 (21.9)	1458 (10.1)
Americas (7555)	1501 (19.9)	3195 (42.3)	945 (12.5)	876 (11.6)	1038 (13.7)
Asia (26129)	4763 (18.2)	5730 (21.9)	5660 (21.7)	4731 (18.1)	5245 (20.1)
Other (1057)	155 (14.7)	195 (18.4)	275 (26.0)	185 (17.5)	247 (23.4)
Total (108785)	26555 (24.4)	31880 (29.3)	19793 (18.2)	15447 (14.2)	15110 (13.9)
Percentage share of real foreigners in all students	4.7	7.7	6.5	5.7	6.1

Source: Statistisches Bundesamt, Hochschulstatistik, own calculations.
[a] After subtracting Bildungsinländer, i.e. students born to foreign parents in Germany.

France, a world leader in the implementation of advanced railway technology. This is not to deny that the German railway equipment industry has established a strong patenting record over time. But throughout the postwar period, German infrastructure investment has been biased in favor of the automobile. In sunset industries, disincentives for innovation have often been caused by massive subsidies which tend to protect long obsolete products and processes. As a general problem, low rates of capital formation, at least partially induced by the tax system, have adversely affected technology adoption in many industries. Moreover, Germany differs from many other advanced countries in refusing to grant a general R&D tax credit.

The current tax reform, which has been approved by both houses of parliament in 2000 and is to take effect in 2001, once again reveals a mistrust of capital markets as a guide for the allocation of investments in the economy. The tax reform is rightly intended to improve the private incentives for investing in physical capital by lowering taxes on earnings. However, while tax rates are indeed lowered, the depreciation period is reduced so that the private user costs of capital may actually be increased for many firms. On balance, it appears the net effect will be improved invest-

ment incentives for most firms. What is clear, however, is that the tax reform discriminates against new firms by introducing a split tax rate for earnings retained in the firm and those paid out to its owners. New firms, especially those based on new technology with high fixed costs of R&D before the product launch, often do not have retained earnings and thus cannot benefit from such a tax privilege. By the same token, the tax reforms also reduce the influence of the capital market on firms' investment decisions. Because retained earnings are to be taxed at a lower rate than distributed profits, self-financing becomes relatively more attractive than raising equity externally, for example, by issuing public shares on the stock market. What is more, the tax reform will penalize investments in human capital because the returns from these are to be taxed at the much higher personal tax rate and do not benefit from the reduced tax rate on retained earnings.

5.5. Summing Up

What policy lessons can be derived from the German experience? Germany certainly has developed a set of fine institutions which have successfully supported industrial innovation in

Germany's traditional areas of technological strength. Some, like the Fraunhofer institutes of applied research, are now being copied and adapted in many industrial countries, such as France, and have even been imported in the United States and Singapore. But outside Germany's traditional areas of strength, economic performance has probably been hampered mainly by two factors: by a failure to innovate in the university system, which has reduced the quality of teaching and research, and by over-regulation of markets, which has distorted incentives and inhibited the free flow of knowledge in many sectors. More flexibility is needed foremost in the labor market. While heavy investment in public infrastructure to facilitate the transfer of technology may have its merits under conditions of incremental technological change in an established industry, it may impose undue inertia when new opportunities emerge in entirely new areas of technology.

Above all in industries with skill shortages, it may be counterproductive for the government to promote the technology transfer by setting up special centers that directly compete with private firms for skilled labor. A better strategy might be to set incentives for people to move between firms in the private sector and the universities. Many of the necessary reforms can be introduced in a piecemeal fashion; there is no need for central planning and coordination through political committees. In practice, however, frictions between the different interest groups in Germany's corporate system are often invoked as an excuse for arranging round-table talks at the highest level. But such talks rarely achieve any significant reform. They rather give the participants a high-profile opportunity to present their views, and so they effectively reinforce the corporate system that is at the root of Germany's difficulties with reform.

Our analysis suggests that Germany's problems with technological innovation are based less on market failures, but rather on missing markets. In the past, technology policy has invested in institutions that were meant to substitute for some of the missing markets. With an accelerated pace of change in today's high-tech industries, that strategy is becoming increasingly obsolete. However, Germany has begun to move in the right direction in recent years, when it began to place greater trust on the market in allocating resources towards innovative activities. The biggest remaining problem is the labor market.

In a far cry from the infant industry argument of trade policy first formulated by List (1841), protectionism for high technology is no longer seriously considered, except in the aircraft industry. Instead, policy makers are now urged towards greater openness and market flexibility so as to improve the capacity of an economy to seize some of the enormous opportunities in today's most dynamic industries. These urges appear to be particularly relevant for Germany which already has many of the assets needed for a leading role in knowledge-based industries, like software and biotechnology, but which—for reasons we have explored—has often been tardy in entering newly emerging fields of technology with sufficient vigor to actually establish a leading position.

6

France

Patrick A. Messerlin

6.1. Introduction

The case of France illustrates the costs of a fragmented innovation system. Skill production is fragmented, with no cross-fertilization between the narrowly specialized Grandes Ecoles and the universities, and the primary education system lagging well behind in performance. The flaws in the latter inhibit the propensity and capability to innovate in a large proportion of the population. Innovation production is fragmented, with almost no flows of skilled labor between the public and private laboratories, and excessively narrow specialization in outputs. Innovation funding is fragmented, with little overlap among funding sources and chronic difficulties in attracting new funding. Reducing the costs of such fragmentation, in terms of the barriers it imposes to the continuous efficient re-allocation of limited resources necessitated by the unpredictable course of modern technical progress, is the central aim of this chapter's policy conclusions.

The balkanization of the French innovation system was (and still is) largely due to the dominant role of the government (and of the military innovation subsystem, France being one of the best illustrations of a "military-industrial" complex). Moreover, the government's dominance has increased anti-competitiveness and collusion in the French innovation system (in both output *and* input markets) to an extent rarely seen in other industrial countries, with its unholy alliances of private monopolies and public bureaucracies in international *and* domestic markets. (This is a major difference with Japanese policy which encouraged internal competition; Ostry and Nelson, 1995.) Reducing the fragmentation of the French innovation system will require profound regulatory reforms to achieve a much more flexible innovation system largely—but not entirely—driven by markets.

This chapter adopts an historical perspective to capture the impact of economic performance on the French innovation system. An innovation system, as defined by Nelson (1993), requires years to reveal its strengths and weaknesses. The problem with the French innovation system is that its initial successes (assuming that they have been real successes, a debatable proposition as shown below) have been perceived as resulting from its intrinsic qualities, while in truth they have been mostly the outcome of "happy circumstances" (see section 6.2). Indeed, this misperception has delayed the much-needed reforms.

The degree of openness of the economy is a key evolutionary factor for the domestic innovation system. Closed economies are unlikely to offer much-needed breathing space to the domestic innovation system (despite the government's good intentions), as best shown by France during the immediate postwar period. Open economies shift competitive pressures to innovation-intensive products, thus stimulating the productive capacity of the domestic innovation system, as illustrated by France during the 1960s. Largely open economies allow a substantial vertical disintegration between innovation production and the rest of the production process, as suggested by France during the 1990s: in addition to trading innovations through products or patents, one "trades" them through direct foreign investment in innovation facilities. Such an evolution is not so surprising: it simply mirrors a better use of the domestic comparative advantages in innovation activities, making them less dependent on domestic production activities per se.

This chapter is organized as follows. Sections 6.2 and 6.3 present the interactions between economic performance and innovation (once again focusing on the impact of performance on the innovation system) for three different periods: the Uncertain Years (1945–56), the Glorious Years (1957–74), and the Wavering Years (from 1975 to date). Section 6.4 examines the currently pending and most pressing regulatory issues in the French innovation system (in capital markets, labor markets for scientists and education, public policies, and firms and market structures). Section 6.5 describes two very different illustrations of French economic performance and technological innovation—Minitel and hypermarkets. Section 6.6 concludes the chapter.

6.2. From the Uncertain Years to the Glorious Years (1945–74)

These periods share a common feature: France's economic performance and innovation interact essentially within the limits of the French *domestic* economy. But they also differ strongly: the France of the earlier period still looks quite uncertain about its economic and technological future, whereas the France of the later period looks overly confident of its ability to create an original economic and technological "model."

6.2.1. The Uncertain Years (1945–56)

During this period, French growth was strong enough to allow a profound restructuring of the French economy. But France's average GDP growth rate (5.4 percent), and her growth rate of its industrial value-added (5.8 percent) were not as high and stable as one could have expected from a country just emerging from fifteen years of massive war damage and severe economic depression. These rates were substantially lower than the growth rates of Germany, an arch-rival elevated to the status of *the* reference country. Indeed, this difference in growth rates was a source of major concern for most French during this time, who were still afraid of potential conflicts

with Germany. More importantly, French growth was not high enough to improve profoundly and durably social relations in France, leaving the social environment of the French economy unstable for decades to come (again in contrast with the German "social-market economy").

Two reasons explain this difficult "catching-up." First, in 1945, France was considerably impoverished in terms of capital stock. The 1930s had led to an estimated decline of the French net equipment and building capital of 24 percent and 15 percent, respectively; the Second World War had further reduced net capital by an estimated 16 and 14 percent, respectively: more than during the First World War, but less than during the 1930s (Villa, 1993). Massive investment was necessary, but international capital flows, which were limited to the Marshall Plan funds, could not satisfy the need. Nor could it be provided by private funds: French firms and households were subjected to severe liquidity constraints and to a systematic policy of financial repression.

As a result, the fate of France's growth during this period depended on two forces, labor mobility and public investment. The labor market was highly flexible: the period witnessed the silent migration of almost three million unskilled workers from farms to industrial plants. This movement was a key source of growth (and a sharp decline of the hidden unemployment in the farm sector during the 1930s).

By contrast, public investment (mostly in the form of equipment subsidies) had imposed a drag on the French economy during the period because it was concentrated too much on infrastructure (in particular, coal, electricity, and railways) and housing (Sicsic and Wyplosz, 1996). The share of the cumulated public subsidies granted to these privileged sectors between 1947 and 1956 was higher than the corresponding shares of these sectors in the French total capital in 1950. The rate of return from such highly capital-intensive sectors was low, thereby exerting a drag on growth. Such a concentration could have made sense if these investment subsidies had been passed on to consumers through lower prices. But, during the period

1950–8, the price of value-added in the energy sector increased while the corresponding prices in the other manufacturing sectors decreased, and the price of value-added in the housing sector increased more than the corresponding prices in the other services. As all the sectors favored by public investment were run by public institutions or firms (except housing, to a limited extent), these price movements strongly suggest that public investment was largely dissipated into wasteful choices and/or rents captured by the public firms involved.

The large-scale misallocation of public capital reflects the costs of the quasi-command economy regime that was established in France after the Second World War, and that prospered behind high tariffs and numerous quantitative restrictions during this period. The prices of all the key products, almost all the interest rates, the wages of unskilled workers in manufacturing, and the social costs of all the workers (during the period, labor costs were more expensive in France than in Germany) were totally regulated by the government. Nationalized banks and firms, closely controlled by the authorities, could influence large chunks of the economy, as best illustrated by the wage and social policy of Renault (the nationalized French car producer), which had an impact on the whole industrial sector. In this context, the goal of "catching up" with more advanced industrial countries was conceived in rudimentary terms, ignoring the notions of comparative advantages and market forces. Rather, it relied on "indicative planning;" that is, a consensus between the French bureaucracy and the major French public and private decision-makers on which strategic choices, already made by more advanced economies, would be replicated by France under the banner of "modernization" (indeed, following successful foreign "models" was a consistent approach of French economic policies until the late 1990s).

In this context, France's economic performance suggests looking at technological innovations from two perspectives—the use and production of innovations. The growth rate of the period was large enough to favor the *use* of the many innovations developed in France *before*

the war and not yet introduced because of the lack of investment during the 1930s—as best illustrated by the car sector: the Beetle was already produced in large scale in Germany before the war, at a time when its French equivalents, the Citroen 2CV or Renault 4CV, remained at the model stage.

But the Uncertain Years did not witness the *production* of major technological innovations in France. This situation may be due the fact that the period was short and that the period was devoted to the creation of a series of public laboratories from Centre National de la Recherche Scientifique (CNRS), to Commissariat à l'Energie Atonic (CEA), etc., which constituted the core of the French innovation system until the 1990s. It was difficult to expect research outcomes in 1958 from labs established only in the early 1950s. But there is also an *economic* explanation to this lack of innovations. Most of the sectors in which public investment was concentrated were not intensive in new technologies so that they could not generate strong incentives for new innovations. In fact, the total factor productivity (TFP) annual growth rates of the sectors that benefited most from public investment during the period (energy, construction, and transport) were the lowest (with the exception of the food industry) of the economy (2 percent, 2 percent, and 2.9 percent, respectively), comparing poorly with the average TFP growth of 3.6 percent for the whole economy (Sicsic and Wyplosz, 1996).

The building of a French innovation system around public laboratories deserves a final comment. On the one hand, it has undoubtedly improved French innovation capacity. During this period, public laboratories had relatively easy access to the only source of capital, public grants and subsidies. They were also able to recruit skilled labor unable to find equivalent jobs in the few private and poor laboratories or in the universities. The French university was so much entrenched and confined in its old system of centralized and bureaucratic rules that it would have been unable, even if its endemic poverty had been alleviated, to provide a better alternative to the system of public laboratories. In fact, the biggest public laboratory (CNRS) was largely created as a reaction against

TABLE 6.1
The French Economic Performance: Annual Growth Rates, 1948–99

	1948–1958	1958–1974	1975–1999	1975–1990	1990–1999
GDP	5.4	5.5	2.2	2.4	1.7
GDP per capita	4.5	4.5	1.6	1.9	0.9
Industrial value-added	5.8	7.5	1.4	1.4	1.2
Total factor productivity	3.6	3.6	–	1.8[a]	1.1[b]
Labor productivity	–	4.8	2.6	3.3[a]	2.0[b]

Sources: INSEE, Sicsic and Wyplosz (1996) and Accardo et al. (1999).
[a] 1977.
[b] 1997.

the way the French university had mismanaged research and innovation during the first half of the century.[1] On the other hand, the French innovation system was barely used during the period, if only because the public investment policy favored innovation *non*-intensive sectors. The only sizable exception was the railway electrification, which benefited from public investments in electrification and transport, and which relied on a large stock of engineers working in the two largest public firms, SNCF (the railway company) and Electricité de France. As a matter of fact, the *use* of the state-related innovation system emerged only during the next period of the Glorious Years.

6.2.2. The "Glorious Years" (1956–74)

In a short period (1957–8), France drastically changed both its trade and its macro-economic policies. By signing the Treaty of Rome, founding the European Economic Community (now known as the European Union, or E.U.) in 1957, it renounced her staunch protectionist

[1] At this time, the other pillar of French high education, the Grandes Ecoles, much richer than the university, was simply not interested in producing innovation. It was attracting promising students, but mostly interested in a traditional career in the French administration. Nevertheless, the "pantouflage" practice (the shift of senior engineers from R&D activities to public management activities, more lucrative and closer to the decision-making centers) allowed the few students of the Grandes Ecoles interested in innovation to begin their career in public laboratories, and to finish it in the administration.

policies of the earlier period (Adams, 1989; Messerlin, 2001). This dramatic change was amplified, a few months later, by the adoption of a new macroeconomic policy based on budgetary balance and monetary stability (with the U.S. dollar as the anchor). These essential trade and macroeconomic commitments were well fulfilled during the period, despite some difficulties between 1962 and 1964 (due to uncertainties on the anti-inflation policy at the end of the Algerian war, and doubts regarding European integration during the negotiations on the Common Agricultural Policy) and in 1969–70 (the aftermath of the 1968 social troubles).

This period witnessed France's best economic performance of the entire twentieth century, with a stable average GDP growth rate of roughly 5.5 percent, an average growth rate of industrial value-added of 7.8 percent, and an unemployment rate of less than 2 percent (see Table 6.1). GDP growth was not only higher, but it was more stable than in most other OECD countries, while French industrial growth was as volatile as that in the other OECD countries, a stability achieved by an active counter-cyclical monetary policy. As the French economy was running under strict capital controls during the whole period, the use of monetary policy as the dominant counter-cyclical instrument did not translate into serious external imbalances and exchange rate instability (until the very early 1970s, the real exchange rate between the U.S. dollar and the French franc was quite stable, although delays in nominal corrections after periods of high inflation gave the impression of crises more serious than they really were).

The new course of trade and macroeconomic policies was essential for the innovation system inherited from the earlier period. In particular, trade liberalization enlarged the size of the innovation-intensive markets so much previously constrained. New and large markets requiring more innovation-intensive products than their traditional colonial markets became accessible to French exporters; within five years, the share of French trade with former colonies declined by one-third (from 37 percent in 1958 to 21 percent in 1962), while the share of French trade with the rest of the European Union increased almost symmetrically (from 22 percent in 1958 to 37 percent in 1962). These massive changes in the French trade pattern by *country* reflected substantial changes in the French trade pattern by *product*. Between 1958 and 1975, the share of "simple" consumer goods, from textiles to clothing to leather, in French total exports declined sharply, while the share of innovation-intensive consumer and equipment goods, from pharmaceuticals to machinery to transportation equipment, greatly increased.

The Treaty of Rome did much more than open the French economy to the other E.U. member states; it was an instrument of liberalization to the *whole* world. First, defining the E.U. common tariff as the simple average of high (Italian and French) and low (Benelux and German) member state tariffs has automatically reduced the protection of the French economy with respect to the world. Second, as Germany could hardly accept a permanent increase of its pre-1958 tariffs on manufactured goods (a consequence of averaging the member state tariffs for getting the E.U. common tariff), the European Union concluded the GATT Dillon and Kennedy Rounds, which led to further reduction of the E.U. common industrial tariff. In the mid-1970s, the E.U. common tariff was equal to the German pre-1958 tariff, meaning that, in less than two decades, the average tariff imposed on French imports from the non-E.U. world decreased from 17 percent to 6 percent (and of course, from 17 percent to 0 percent on imports from the European Union).

The role of trade liberalization was important all the more because the quasi-command economy regime inherited from the earlier period was dismantled very slowly and imperfectly during the period. This retreat was limited to the *product* markets, and it was slow enough to generate a "soft-command" economy, characterized by a progressive erosion of direct government controls on product markets *without* the emergence of strongly competitive markets. If price controls became old fashioned in the early 1970s, they were really dismantled by the Barre government only in 1978, *after* the end of the Glorious Years, and even then, many regulated prices (production prices of farm products, retail prices of pharmaceuticals, and many other "essential" goods) remained in place. Moreover, the tight web of public firms, the intricate relations between the bureaucracy and the public *and* private business decision-makers inherited from the "indicative planning" mechanism, and the almost non-existent competition policy, allowed the survival of many collusive practices in many deregulated product markets during the whole period.

The deregulation of product markets was not only slow, but was also counterbalanced by an evolution in the opposed direction in the *labor* markets. After the 1968 social troubles, the minimum wage was extended from the manufacturing sector to the whole economy (a coverage three times larger than during the earlier period), and it was increased in constant terms; unemployment benefits were boosted and labor laws were solidified, shifting away from a contractual basis and toward a centralized and political mechanism. Meanwhile, the public grip on domestic capital flows was relaxed only marginally, whereas inward and outward foreign investments remained subjected to controls as severe and discriminatory as those before.

Changes between 1956 and 1974 in the relative prices of goods brought about by the opening of the French economy were strong enough to generate factor reallocations, the labor market becoming rigid only at the very end of this period. Sicsic and Wyplosz (1996) estimated that capital allocation contributed strongly, almost one-third, to the economy-wide TFP growth of the period, while the contribution by labor allocation declined to one-tenth of the global TFP growth, reflecting the end of migration flows from rural to industrial activities in the early 1960s and the late stabilizing of the labor markets.[2] Moreover, if the TFP growth rate for the whole economy during the period remained similar to the growth rate observed for the previous period (3.6 percent), then the TFP growth rates by *industry* differed substantially between these two periods; the rates increased in manufacturing and transport sectors, and decreased in services.

The innovation system established in the late 1940s, and in particular the core of public laboratories, had no problems in adjusting to the new economic environment for several reasons. First, the fact that macroeconomic stabilization was mostly ensured by monetary policy, and not by budgetary policy, did not threaten the dominant financial source of French innovation (public subsidies). In fact, public labs "improved" their access to "capital:" France's better economic performance made it possible for the government to "invest" (subsidize) much more heavily in innovation activities, as illustrated by the increase in domestic R&D spending from less than 1 percent of GDP in 1959 to 2 percent in 1969. Second, public laboratories were not severely hurt by the increasing rigidity of the labor markets at the very end of the period. They were still able to recruit young skilled labor unable to find positions in the closed university system, and remained attractive places immune to sclerosis at the end of the period. Lastly, the trade liberalization of the 1960s generated a demand for innovation-intensive products relatively similar to those favored by the French infrastructure-related investments made during the previous period or to those required by military activities; for example, transport, energy and certain types of telecommunications.

In sum, France's political will to keep some influence in the world has been easily translated into the "necessity" to be at the forefront of certain technological races—hence the long series of "grands programmes" in many "dual-use" goods, such as oil extraction, nuclear energy, aircraft and rockets, computers, and radar telecommunications. These grands programmes were based on large public commitment and tight cooperation between French public and private firms. They had four major features: they were based on military-dominated funding, provided in massive amounts and for long periods; the funding was managed by a few agencies (Direction Générale de l'Armement) and operated by few research institutions (CNRS, CEA, etc.); they were operated by the largest French private firms (for instance, Dassault and Matra); and they tended to react slowly to market forces because all this "military-industrial complex" typically relied on a non-competitive market structure (a monopoly for the innovation buyer and a duopoly for the innovation producers), which was also prone to being captured by public and private vested interests.

The problem was that French decision-makers understood the "happy coincidence" between France's high growth and grands programmes during the Glorious Years as a proof of the efficiency of the French innovation system *per se*. As a result, little attention was paid to the intrinsic weaknesses of the French innovation system—and no measure was taken. First, the system was unable to cope in a satisfactory manner with the "exit" problem. Every new grand programme and project was seen as requiring a new innovation structure, whereas the old structures were left in place whether they reached their objectives or not.[3] This inability to reallocate the resources devoted to

---

[2] They estimated that, during the period 1945–56, capital allocation contributed negatively to the economy-wide TFP growth, whereas labor allocation (the migration from agriculture to industry) contributed substantially (one-fifth) to the economy-wide TFP growth. This symmetry with what has occurred during the Glorious Years fits in well with the relative level of deregulations.

[3] If, in the very long run, innovation capacities contributed to shape comparative advantages, the causality was less clear in the medium run (say within a decade or two). Between 1958 and 1974, the relative endowment of total human capital in the French economy (hence of innovation capacities) grew slowly (at least, in relative terms). Moreover, a large proportion of this human capital stock could have been considered as "specific" to industries (engineers in electronics could hardly switch to nuclear energy, and vice-versa).

innovations led to an ever increasing tendency to "dredge" (*saupoudrer*) public funds over increasingly numerous objectives—a policy that became less and less efficient because of the ever-stricter limits on the public budget. Second, the dominant role of military aspects gave tremendous power to very few decision-makers for choosing the innovation projects and the operating agencies, public laboratories and private firms, of the grands programmes. Over time this concentration of power made the decision-making process increasingly subject to vested interests blocking each other, and therefore chaotic and inefficient (Cohen and Bauer, 1985).

Thirty years later, none of the major programs of this period emerged as a clear success, as illustrated by the following examples. Concorde has recently shown its technical limits (its only serious accident in 2000 has been enough to severely downgrade it in terms of safety, because Concorde flies much less frequently than the other types of planes), having been a commercial failure since its birth. The computer program (Plan Calcul) was unable to keep a French producer in the supercomputer market, and its focus on large machines generated a long-lasting misapprehension in France regarding the major trends in the electronic and information technology sectors for the 1980s and later. Even the nuclear electricity program is far from a clear success: it did not disconnect the French energy prices from world prices, contrary to what was incorrectly expected by successive governments, and its *domestic* profitability (unimpressive by the usual standard) is hard to estimate in the absence of an adequate assessment of safety risks; in sum, benefits are certain only for those foreign consumers of French nuclear electricity who are unlikely to be hurt by dominant winds in case of a major accident.

More importantly, all these massive programs severely restricted resources, such as skilled labor and capital, for alternative innovations that could have been developed in France, such as more demand-oriented aircrafts (Airbus instead of Concorde), more flexible sources of energy (natural gas instead of nuclear energy), a more decentralized information system (based on personal computers, rather than on huge centralized machines). Unfortunately, there is no available estimate of such costs.

6.3. The "Wavering Years" (1975–2000)

The 1975 recession (GDP declined by 0.3 percent, and industrial value-added fell by 4.1 percent) broke with the long series of high positive growth rates of the earlier period, and opened a new era. Between the Golden and Wavering Years, the average GDP growth rate fell by almost two-thirds (from 5.5 percent to 2.1 percent), while the average growth rate of industrial value-added fell by almost 80 percent (from 7.5 percent to 1.2 percent). Between 1975 and 2000, there were two years with negative GDP growth rates (1975 and 1993) and nine years with negative growth rates of industrial value-added. Last but not least, the unemployment rate increased by a factor of five (from less than 2 percent to an average 11.2 percent for the 1990s). This section begins by describing the overall impact of this faltering French economic performance on the innovation system and then examines the productivity growth by sector and technological innovation in France during the period.

6.3.1. The Impact of the French Economic Performance on the Innovation System

The decade following the 1975 recession witnessed so many U-turns in macroeconomic, structural and foreign policies that it can be nicknamed the Lost Decade—particularly compared to the dramatic and decisive changes in U.S. and U.K. policies.

On the macroeconomic front, the reaction to the first oil shock (1974–7) focused on income stabilization (accommodating the inflationary shock); as a result, it amplified the oil price increase in France with the resulting depreciation of the French franc, in sharp contrast with what happened in Germany. The Barre government (1977–81) returned to pre-1974 macroeconomic policies, with a much less accommodating policy for the second oil shock combined with the choice of the German Mark as the anchor. During its first three years, the Mitterrand presidency reverted to income stabilization, with a demand-driven macroeconomic policy relying on budgetary and monetary expansion. This policy, which did not prevent a drop of the growth rate and a sharp increase in the rate of unemployment, ended in the exchange rate debacle of 1983. Only then did the Socialist governments realize that the openness of the French economy could not be reversed without huge economic, and therefore political, costs. The key decision to stay within the European Union was taken with much tighter monetary *and* budgetary policies that have characterized the last fifteen years of this period (1985–2000).

Contrary to what happened during the Glorious Years, the policies of the Wavering Years badly damaged the existing French innovation system in several respects. First, the restrictive budgetary policy damaged the main financial source of the French innovation system. Cuts in public funds during the late 1970s and stagnating public funds during the 1980s further slowed the already insufficient reallocation of resources among innovation activities. Stable funds were increasingly absorbed by the labor costs of existing staff, and public laboratories increasingly behaved as social fortresses for insiders. Second, the tighter monetary policy decreased the capacity of private and public firms to invest. For instance, the lax treatment of the first oil shock (in 1974) essentially consisted of transferring French firms' profits to foreign producers' rents, triggering a sharp decline of the profit/ national income ratio (from 38 percent in 1972 to 33 percent in 1975) and of the investment/ GDP rate (from 28 percent in 1973 to 21 percent in 1985). A decade later, an ever increasing public debt (from 21 percent of GDP in 1977 to the peak of 59.3 percent in 1998) created a crowding out effect of the private firms in the undeveloped French capital markets of the 1980s and early 1990s. Of course, private investments in risky innovation activities were among the first casualties.

U-turns in "structural" policies were also an impediment to a smooth evolution of the French innovation system. First, the nationalization of a few large industrial firms in the "high-tech" sector (in particular electronics) led to an indirect nationalization of their laboratories, reversing the evolution of the 1960s and 1970s that had witnessed a slow move to a more diversified research structure. It exacerbated the conflicts between the "old" and "new" public laboratories fighting for a common pool of reduced public funds. Second, the key commitment to stay within the European Union, and specific circumstances such as the oil crisis, further opened the French economy: the share of exports and imports in French GDP increased from 30 percent in 1970, to 37 percent in 1975, to 47 percent in 1981, and to 55 percent in 1997.[4] As a result, the French innovation system was becoming increasingly constrained and rigid precisely at the time when pressures for upgrading products (including more innovations) increased. Third, the liberalization of the French capital markets made accessible new opportunities for higher and quicker profits to private *and* public firms and households. Although this initiative was a logical step toward a more open economy, it occurred in a general context unfavorable to the French innovation system—generating additional and powerful disincentives to invest in long-term and/or risky innovations projects, all the more so because the Stock Exchange success story (so key for Socialist governments) offered an altewrnative source of short-term profits.[5]

---

[4] This evolution owes much to trade with non-E.U. countries: for instance, the E.U. share of French product exports declined from 65.4 percent in 1988 to 62.8 percent in 1997, while the non-OECD share increased from 18 percent to 22 percent during the same period.

[5] In particular, the French Stock Exchange has rapidly become a politically useful source of good economic results, at a time when traditional indicators of economic performance (growth and employment rates) have been consistently bad. The successive French governments did not oppose to the implementation of the OECD and E.U. measures liberalizing capital flows—though France remained one of the few E.U. member states, with Germany, to have noticeable reservations on the OECD code of liberalization on capital movements until the late 1990s (Single Market Review, 1997: 78).

Last, U-turns in foreign policy were costly for the military base of the French innovation system. The military was dominant until the 1970s, with most of the French innovation successes of the Golden Years derived from military projects. The ostensible opposition of the Mitterrand presidency during its first years to the French military-industrial complex led to the subsidization of initiatives in the "civilian" sector, such as TV sets, video-cassette recorders, Minitel, and so on, under ongoing nationalization. When almost all of these initiatives failed a few years later, the support for arms production was renewed. But so many successive inconsistencies in a centralized innovation system as the French one, and the remaining doubts about the direction of the French foreign policy, made it very difficult for private and public firms to determine long-term innovation strategies.

The years 1985–2000 witnessed a healing of the consequences of all these economic and political U-turns, but at a very slow rate. Successive governments, from left and right alike, took measures to relax constraints on the labor market and to limit public intervention in market forces. But, the generalized capture of the French government by all kinds of vested interests and lobbies (farmers, trade unions, truckers, etc.) induced successive governments to act in incremental and opaque ways—making it hard for *outsiders* to have a feel for the dominant trend of French labor policies and regulations. Not only could such a covert and piecemeal supply-side policy hardly get quick results (much more open and drastic supply-side policies implemented in other OECD countries have been slow to get results), but it also generated very costly distortions between those able to understand the new course of the economic policy (i.e., the insiders), and those unable to do so.

6.3.2. French Economic Performance: a Sectoral View

Table 6.2 presents a breakdown by sector of the overall trends of the Wavering Years summarized in Table 6.1.[6] To keep the focus on the interactions between economic performance and technological innovation, the table provides a sectoral indicator of technological innovation intensity (defined as the R&D expenses as a percentage of production value). The four sectors with a "innovation intensity" index larger than 2.5 percent correspond to the "high-tech" sectors as often defined in policy debates (electronics, motor vehicles, aircraft-ships-arms, and chemicals-pharmaceuticals).[7] Table 6.2, which is based on unweighted averages (results based on value-added weighted averages are very similar), suggests five points centered on these four relatively innovation-intensive sectors.

First, the four innovation-intensive sectors represent a small share of the French value-added (columns 2 and 3): roughly 11.2 percent in 1997. However, this share increased substantially over the period (from 9.1 percent in 1975: i.e., an increase of one-fourth). Interestingly, the two sectors driving this increase are electronics and chemicals-pharmaceuticals; that is, two sectors where innovations are coming mostly from the rest of the world.

Second, the four innovation-intensive sectors show better-than-average economic performance (columns 4 and 5). Between 1975 and 1990, the average growth rate of their value-added was higher than the average for the whole economy, and it declined by less between 1990 and 1997. The telecom–post service sector deserves a remark: it exhibited by far the highest growth between 1975 and 1990, reflecting the huge investment in fixed telephony following the oil crises. But during the 1990s, its growth rate also substantially declined, although slightly less than the growth rate of the whole economy.

---

[6] The 31 sectors cover the whole French economy, except farming, from less than 4 percent of GDP in the mid 1980s to 2.5 percent in the late 1990s, and non-market services, roughly 16 percent of GDP.

[7] The "high-tech" nature of the arms sector is a highly debated issue. It is often said that the military version of goods insists more on reliability on the battlefield than on really high-tech features. If correct, this argument underlines the high risks taken by the French authorities when pushing for the civilian "version" (really high tech) of military products, and may explain the corresponding high costs of these civilian programs.

Third, the four innovation-intensive sectors represent a substantial share of the French exports and imports (not shown): roughly 30 percent in 1975, 37 percent in 1990, and 43 percent in 1997 (see Table 6.7 for more disaggregated figures). However, there are noticeable differences between the four sectors: electronics and chemicals-pharmaceuticals show increasing shares in both exports and imports, whereas the export share of aircraft-ships-arms sector is stable, as are the export and import shares of the car sector. Only three of these four sectors have, on average, "revealed comparative advantages" (RCAs, see columns 6 and 7), whereas the electronics sector exhibits negative RCAs (meaning that this sector is not among the set of industries for which France has some comparative advantage, vis-à-vis the rest of the world). A word of caution is necessary: the correlation observed between innovation intensity and revealed comparative advantage in the three sectors exhibiting high RCAs may reflect more the importance of French public intervention (particularly subsidies and public procurement in the aircraft-ships-arms sector), than market forces at work.[8]

Fourth, during the 1990s (there is no comparable data for the period 1975–90), the French economy showed an increase in the capital/labor ratio (column 8).[9] This evolution can be observed for almost all the sectors, hence suggesting a general lesson: such an increase does not support the fear of a negative impact of trade on wages (it makes sense only if wages are increasing relative to the rate of return), and it echoes the substantial rigidity

of the French labor markets.[10] The four innovation-intensive sectors show some interesting differences. Only the car and chemical-pharmaceutical sectors exhibit a high increase—reflecting the high level of competitive pressures during the 1990s in these sectors, which have high RCAs. The changes in the capital-labor ratio in the aircraft-ships-arms and electronic sectors are much more limited, possibly reflecting state intervention (aircraft) and low RCAs (electronics).

Lastly, Table 6.2 presents the most recent estimates of the evolution of French TFP by sector in France between 1975 and 1997 (Accardo et al., 1999).[11] Table 6.2, with columns 9 and 10 based only on the TFP estimates unadjusted for the changes in labor skills during the whole period (skill-adjusted estimates mostly magnify changes in trends without modifying the broad picture) provides two key observations. First, the TFP growth rates for the innovation-intensive sectors are higher than the economy-wide average (except for the car industry). Second, the TFP growth rates for

---

[8] RCAs for industry i are defined as $\ln[(Xi/Mi)/(X/M)]*100$, where Xi and Mi are the French exports and imports of industry i, and X and M the French total industrial exports and imports. There are RCAs for the service sectors because of available data and because trade in services has a much more important investment component than trade in goods.

[9] Capital is defined as the net fixed capital, according to the French National Accounts (expenses necessary for re-creating the existing fixed capital as it is), and labor is defined as the number of men-hours (wage-earners weighted by the average annual working time).

[10] The two exceptions are coal and steel (under a drastic policy of adjustment and contraction during the period) and electricity-gas-water, which has such a high capital-labor ratio in the French economy in 1990 (twelve times the French average) that it has needed some industrial adjustment.

[11] The Accardo et al. (1999) study is based on a traditional Solow "accounting" approach: a change in TFP is thus the weighted average of the observed labor and capital productivities (Cobb-Douglas function under perfect competition), the weights used being the observed labor and capital shares in factor incomes. However, the Accardo et al. study takes into account three main adjustments, two for capital and one for labor. Capital is measured as the stock of capital available, that is, the existing capital stock adjusted for its (average) rate of utilisation during each period. Labor is measured by the number of hours worked, adjusted for labor qualification (in order to take into account the fact that the skilled labor share has increased from 13 percent in 1975 to 28 percent in 1997). The adjustment for qualification consists in calculating an "unskilled labor equivalent" based on relative wages (for three levels of skills). Unfortunately, the Accardo et al. study does not include the farm sector, making it difficult to catch the possible impact of innovations (from fertilizers to bio-technologies) in this sector. Other available studies on labor productivity (Duchêne et al., 1997; Duchêne and Jacquot, 1999) tend to confirm the conclusions of the Accardo et al. study.

TABLE 6.2
Innovation intensity, Growth, Revealed Comparative Advantages, Changes in Factor Proportions and Estimated Total Factor Productivity in France, by Sector (1975–97)

Sectors (French industrial classification "T")	Innovation intensity index	Sector share in total value-added (percent)		Average growth rate of value-added (percent)		Revealed comparative advantages in manufacturing (index)		Change in capital labor ratio (percent)[a]	Total factor productivity[b] (unadjusted for labor quality)	
	1986–91	1975–90	1990–7	1975–90	1990–7	1990	1997	1990/80	1975–90	1990–7
	1	2	3	4	5	6	7	8	9	10
2 Meat and milk	–	1.4	1.5	2.2	2.6	34.5	41.9	1.5	0.9	3.1
3 Other agrobusiness	–	4.0	3.1	0.6	1.8	19.6	10.2	12.2	–1.4	2.2
4 Coal, etc.	–	0.4	0.1	–7.0	0.6	–219.6	–260.2	–37.6	8.3	10.7
5 Oil and natural gas	–	3.1	3.2	0.0	0.2	–170.9	–169.4	14.3	–1.9	1.6
6 Electricity, gas, water	–	2.4	2.6	5.6	2.4	166.3	261.6	–2.1	2.1	2.2
7 Iron and steel	0.8	1.0	0.8	0.5	0.9	14.5	8.8	–21.4	4.8	4.8
8 Non-ferrous minerals and metals	0.6	0.5	0.7	5.3	0.3	–26.8	–42.0	26.6	1.8	2.0
9 Construction materials	0.2	1.8	0.9	–0.4	–1.7	–20.0	–14.9	27.1	1.2	0.3
10 Glass	1.1	0.5	0.4	1.8	1.4	33.1	26.5	20.0	2.4	3.0
11 Basic chemicals, fibers	2.5	1.3	1.7	3.7	2.1	3.5	–3.9	28.2	4.1	3.5
13 Foundries	0.3	3.3	2.6	1.2	0.8	–6.0	–3.2	18.2	1.5	2.3
21 Paper, cardboard	0.2	0.8	0.7	2.1	–0.5	–43.6	–33.1	24.2	1.5	–0.2
23 Rubber, plastics	2.4	1.3	1.2	2.3	0.3	–1.1	–1.1	23.7	1.8	0.6
14 Mechanical construction	1.2	3.7	2.8	1.2	0.0	–6.8	0.3	26.7	2.2	1.3
15 Consumer electronics	7.6	3.3	5.6	4.4	4.9	–15.1	–7.8	10.5	2.8	6.0
16 Motor vehicles	2.6	3.1	2.2	0.6	–0.1	25.7	26.4	40.3	1.0	0.4
17 Aircraft, ships, arms	14.4	1.3	1.1	2.0	–0.4	77.6	73.5	8.4	3.5	1.8

12 Chemicals, pharmaceuticals	4.7	1.4	2.3	4.8	3.6	47.2	50.0	36.3	3.0	2.4
18 Textile, clothing	0.1	3.0	1.3	-0.7	-3.3	-22.7	-36.6	35.9	2.2	1.1
19 Leather, shoes	0.1	0.7	0.2	-3.0	-4.7	-48.5	-57.6	10.8	-0.1	0.1
20 Wood, furniture, other manufacture	0.1	1.4	1.5	1.5	-0.3	-29.4	-32.5	18.6	1.4	1.6
22 Press, publishing	0.4	1.9	1.5	2.3	0.7	-25.9	-24.7	24.1	0.5	0.8
24 Construction	-	12.1	7.6	0.9	-2.3	-	-	6.6	2.0	0.0
25 Trade	-	16.8	15.8	2.3	0.6	-	-	15.0	0.0	-0.3
31 Transport services	-	6.0	6.8	2.9	1.9	-	-	4.4	1.9	1.4
32 Telecom, post	-	2.0	6.0	9.0	3.6	-	-	18.9	5.5	4.0
29 Auto repair	-	2.5	1.8	1.2	-0.6	-	-	22.0	-0.6	-2.0
30 Hotels, cafes, etc.	-	3.5	3.0	1.9	0.1	-	-	14.4	-2.3	-2.1
33 Business services	-	9.5	12.1	4.4	0.8	-	-	67.9	1.7	-2.4
34 Consumer services	-	6.1	8.8	4.5	2.2	-	-	33.0	-1.2	-1.9
Innovation-intensive sectors (unweighted)	Avg 7.3	Sum 9.1	Sum 11.2	Avg 3.0	Avg 2.0	Avg 33.8	Avg 35.5	Avg 23.9	Avg 2.6	Avg 2.7
All sectors (unweighted)	2.3	100.0	100.0	1.9	0.6	-	-	17.6	1.7	1.6
All sectors (weighted)	-	-	-	2.6	1.0	-	-	-	1.8	1.1

Sources: Column 1, Iung and Lagarde (1998); columns 4, 5, 9, 10, Accardo et al. (1999); other columns, author's computations.

Note: "Innovation Intensity Index" is the ratio of R&D spending (constant francs) to production (constant francs), multiplied by 100.

[a] Net capital per man-hour (see text).

[b] Based on material capital, adjusted for utilization rate (see Accardo et al, 1999). –, not available.

TABLE 6.3
The French Contribution to Fundamental Research

	1983	1990	1991	1992	1993	1994	1995
Shares (percent) of French publications in fundamental research							
In the world	4.3	4.7	4.7	4.8	4.9	5.0	5.1
In the European Union	14.5	15.6	15.6	15.6	15.7	15.7	15.6

Comparison with selected other countries in 1995, index[a]					
United Kingdom	Germany	Italy	Japan	United States	France
145.0	105.0	–	75.0	100.0	100.0

Source: OST (1998) and NSF (1998).
[a] Index is the number of publications weighted by GDP (France = 100).

the innovation-intensive sectors follow the general pattern of a decline over the period—with the exception of electronics, which exhibit the highest increase among the sectoral TFP growth rates. As expected, the TFP growth rate for the telecom-post sector is also large but declining.

6.3.3. Technological Innovation in France (1975–2000)

The opening of the French economy deeply influenced not only its economic performance but also the relations between economic performance and technical innovation. During the last decade, this opening has reached such a level that it may have (a) loosened the relations between French economic performance and innovations (French economic performance relying on ever more unrestricted sources of foreign innovations) and (b) strengthened the relations between *foreign* economic performance and *French* sources of innovations (French innovators looking increasingly at foreign economies as "natural" outlets for their ideas, goods, or services).

These two evolutions may have led to a "vertical disintegration" between domestic productive and innovation structures. In particular, it may have favored the emergence of "specific" comparative advantages of the French innovation "sector," which would not necessarily correspond to the comparative advantages of the French sectors *integrating* innovation and

production. These evolutions may have been favored by the rapid internationalization of large French firms and the role of their foreign subsidiaries in innovation activities during the 1990s.

The following review of a few key aspects of French technological innovation during the period aims at providing evidence of this possible loosening of the relations between French economic performance and technological innovation, and of the emergence of French comparative advantages in innovations distinct from those in production *per se*.

6.3.3.1. The Contribution to Scientific Research

A first measure of the French innovation system is its contribution in terms of scientific research, as estimated by the number of French papers published in academic journals. Table 6.3 shows that the share of French papers in a worldwide set of scientific publications (provided by the international database available in such publications) has increased since 1983, and substantially more rapidly in the 1980s than in the early 1990s. When compared to the other E.U. member states, the share of French papers also increased, but only in the 1980s; it has stagnated in the 1990s.

Table 6.4 presents the share of French papers in world scientific publications by topic and by decreasing order of importance of the topics in 1995. French scientists seem to enjoy some "revealed comparative advantage" (i.e., showing a performance higher than the overall aver-

TABLE 6.4

The French Contribution to Scientific Progress: Share (percent) of French Publications in Fundamental Research, by Scientific Topic (shown in decreasing 1995 rank)

	1982	1990	1995	1990/82 (percent change)	1995/82 (percent change)
Mathematics	4.2	6.1	7.1	145	169
Biology, fundamental	4.8	5.2	5.5	108	115
Chemistry	4.8	4.7	5.3	98	110
Physics	5.3	5.0	5.2	94	98
Sciences of the universe	3.9	4.6	4.9	118	126
Medical research	4.1	4.5	4.8	110	117
Biology, applied	3.1	3.3	4.0	106	129
Sciences for engineers	3.2	3.5	3.8	109	119
All scientific fields	4.3	4.7	5.1	109	119

Source: OST (1998).

age during the whole period) in four topics; namely, mathematics, fundamental biology, chemistry and physics—though these two last topics do not show a clear trend (the late 1980s and early 1990s witnessed a slowdown in French production). It is worth noting that there is no clear overlap between the four innovation-intensive sectors defined in Table 6.2 and these four topics, except (maybe) for fundamental biology.

Combined, Tables 6.3 and 6.4 suggest an increasing divergence in the French innovation system: "fundamental" science has prospered relatively well during the last twenty years and has performed better than "applied" science (the four bottom topics in Table 6.4). What follows tests the robustness of this apparent opposition between a relatively successful French "fundamental" science and an apparently laggard French "applied" science.

6.3.3.2. The Contribution to Technological Progress
In a period of fast and relatively cheap information, a good record in scientific research is neither a sure recipe nor a necessary condition for a good record in industrial research measured by patents, because patents require many other conditions, related to market structure and firms' strategies, and not just a good scientific basis. The following shows that the

French record in terms of patents has been increasingly poor in recent years.

Before providing such evidence, it is important to note that data on patents may underestimate the French contribution to technical progress in an international setting for two reasons. First, because the French innovation system focused so much on "dual-use" innovations—that is, on activities close to military topics from aerospace to arms to nuclear energy—that incentives and the possibility to patent such "sensitive" activities may have been low compared to countries specializing in purely "civilian" innovations. Second, the French innovation system was largely based (and still is, to a large extent: see below) on public laboratories having contacts (and contracts) with a limited number of administrations or large private firms, and largely dependent on public money. Such an institutional structure tends to make the non-patenting approach less costly because it provides alternatives to patents: for instance, the government may guarantee the "ownership" of the innovations and the availability of the necessary direct technology transfers, if any. The attraction of these alternatives depends on the types of innovations: it may be greater for short-lived innovations, for which the risks that the government changes its mind and its

TABLE 6.5
The French Contribution to Technological Progress: French Patents, 1987–96

	1987	1993	1996	1993/87	1996/87
Shares (percent) of French patents (in the E.U. patent regimes)					
In the world	8.5	7.9	7.0	92.9	82.4
In the European Union	17.2	17.9	16.2	104.1	94.2
Shares (percent) of French patents (in the U.S. patent regime)					
In the world	3.8	3.5	3.1	92.1	81.6
In the European Union	15.7	17.6	17.2	112.1	109.6

Sources: INPI, OEB and USPTO. OST-CHI computations.

policy are smaller, than for innovations having a long life-time, for which there are serious risks of a "spoliation" of the intellectual property rights because the government can change its policy. Lastly, the possible gap between French and foreign incentives to patent may be less important over time during this period because of the relative stagnation or decline of public funds and dual-use programs.

Table 6.5 looks at the French shares in both the European patent regimes and the U.S. patent regime. These regimes are different enough to trigger different behavior for firms willing to patent innovations. In the European context, the share of French patents exhibits a noticeable decline, both with respect to the world and with respect to the European Union alone. In the U.S. context, the French decline is confirmed with respect to the world but not with respect to the European Union. However, the U.S. patent regime may induce a lower level of declaration than the E.U. regimes (its first-to-invent rule makes a non-patenting

policy a reasonable option if one can provide enough evidence of the date of invention). As a result, European data may better reflect the negative evolution of the French record in terms of technological progress. It is interesting to underline that the rate of decline seems larger since the early 1990s.

A logical conclusion of Table 6.5 is that French producers should increasingly find the innovations they need outside France by buying foreign patents or foreign products that embody technical progress. Indeed, the patent balance drawn from the balance of payments suggests a long-term deterioration trend, with some interesting sectoral specifics. Table 6.6 suggests that France is increasingly becoming a net importer of patents in the industrial sectors, which are the only ones really open to world trade during the period examined. Indeed, more detailed data than that shown in Table 6.6 suggest that half of the patent "deficit" in manufacturing results from pharmaceuticals (Banque de France, 1999). This sector is highly regulated in France (drugs are subjected

TABLE 6.6
The French Technological Balance, FFR million, 1998

	Patents: sales and purchases			Royalties on patents			Information technology services		
	Total	Industry	Services	Total	Industry	Services	Total	Industry	Services
Revenues	795.3	671.5	123.8	6825.8	3241.7	3584.1	4526.2	470.3	4055.9
Expenses	542.0	75.7	466.3	8378.4	5768.8	2609.6	3694.0	1926.7	1767.3
Net balance	253.3	595.8	−342.5	−1552.6	−2527.1	974.5	832.2	−1456.4	2288.6

Source: Banque de France (1999).

TABLE 6.7

The French Contribution to Technical Progress: Patent Shares, by Industrial Sector, 1990 and 1996

	In the world[a]		In the world[b]		In the European Union[a]		French exports of goods and services[c]		Innovation Intensity Index[d]
	1996	1996/90	1996	1996/90	1996	1996/90	1989	1994	1995
Aerospace	16.0	−16.0	10.4	18.2	36.6	13.0	12.6	17.0	19.1
Electronics	5.6	−10.0	2.1	−34.4	18.7	−12.0	3.9	3.3	12.2
Equipment goods	7.1	−19.0	3.0	−14.3	16.0	−7.0	5.8	5.7	11.0
Pharmaceuticals	6.6	−5.0	5.1	6.3	18.2	11.0	10.2	9.7	7.2
Chemicals	5.2	−7.0	3.4	−2.9	12.7	−2.0	7.2	7.7	2.6
Land transportation	11.4	−12.0	3.0	−26.8	18.8	−8.0	6.9	7.2	2.6
Resource intensive sectors	7.2	−22.0	3.2	−20.0	15.1	−17.0	7.6	7.5	0.6
Labor intensive sectors	8.3	−25.0	3.2	−25.6	15.5	−15.0	5.1	4.6	0.3
Total	7.0	−18.0	3.1	−16.2	16.2	−8.0	6.4	6.3	2.8

Sources: INPI, OEB, Chelem. OST computations.

[a] Share (percent) of French patents based on European patent regimes.

[b] Share (percent) of French patents based on U.S. patent regime.

[c] Share (percent) of French exports of goods and services in world markets.

[d] R&D spending as a percentage of production (see Table 6.2).

to price cap regulations from the French Social Security and to many regulations imposing *de facto* monopolies in wholesale and retail distribution hence depressing production prices). In these circumstances, it is no wonder that French multinationals have established close links with non-French multinationals having substantial research capacity outside France.

In sharp contrast to what happened in the manufacturing sector, France maintained a positive balance of patents in services which remained protected by all kinds of regulations and cultural barriers (such as language) during the whole period.

6.3.3.3. The Contribution to Commercial Advances
This aspect can be analyzed by looking at the relationships between three indicators: patenting, innovation intensity indexes (Table 6.2), and export performance. For example, is there any relationship between the French share of patents and the French share of innovation-intensive exports? What follows concentrates exclusively on industrial sectors because information on services is too scarce.

Table 6.7 suggests three main conclusions. First, there is only a loose relationship between patent performance and innovation intensity.

Of course, there are sectors with high innovation intensity and high patent performance, as best illustrated by the aircraft industry. But there are sectors, such as the pharmaceutical sector, much more active in patenting than sectors with a higher innovation intensity (the latter are less likely to focus on patenting to achieve a head start on their rivals). Second, the relations between patent shares and export performance are also relatively loose. In particular, patents are an important instrument for the two sectors where French export shares have decreased (pharmaceuticals and electronics). Lastly, Table 6.7 shows a declining patenting performance during the first half of the 1990s spread over all the French industrial sectors (at this level of aggregation). Again, the main exceptions are the pharmaceutical and aircraft industries.

Because it is based on an industrial classification, Table 6.7 may be subject to an aggregation problem: "averaging" may have blurred divergent evolutions between more disaggregated sectors. To address this, Table 6.8 provides a breakdown of patents by "key technological domains", which are defined by a much more detailed and technology-oriented classification. Unfortunately, export performance and innova-

TABLE 6.8
The French Contribution to Technical Progress: Patent Shares by Key Technical Domain, 1990 and 1996

	In the world[a]		In the European Union[a]	
	1996	*1996/90*	*1996*	*1996/90*
Biotechnology	6.4	120.8	21.8	124.6
Transportation	12.1	114.2	22.2	121.3
Industrial processes	6.5	100.0	14.6	83.0
Environment	12.1	98.4	19.4	99.5
New materials	7.8	94.0	18.0	83.3
Information technology	4.9	92.5	28.9	113.8
Drugs	6.6	89.2	25.8	9.8
Telecoms, audiovisuals	5.3	79.1	20.0	120.5
Electronic components	5.0	69.4	17.4	68.5
Instruments	7.2	66.1	18.3	80.6
Construction	5.8	52.7	16.9	81.6
All key technologies	7.2	85.7	20.2	93.5

Source: Ministere de l'Industrie (1995).
[a] Share (percent) based on European patent regimes.

tion intensity are unavailable at this level of disaggregation. There are 136 domains (only the 11 more important are reported in Table 6.8), of which 88 domains have generated more than 50 French patents during the period 1980–96.[12] Table 6.8 suggests increasing French patent shares in biotechnology and transportation, but decreasing shares in almost all the other domains, including telecoms, audiovisuals, and electronic components—the major components of the IT sector.

The poor French performance in the IT sector, with only 23 percent of households equipped with a computer and 7 percent of households with an Internet address in 1999, calls for two comments.[13] First, the protection granted to certain industries (micro-computers) or services (fixed telephony) has kept prices high for key components of the IT

sector (particularly because revenues from the high telephone prices charged by France Telecom have been transferred to the French government for subsidizing the inefficient French computer industry over the last two decades). For instance, basic personal computers, those that individual consumers tend to buy, were roughly 40 percent more expensive in France than in the United States until the mid 1990s, and telephone charges in France were almost 50 percent higher than the average charges in three other European countries (United Kingdom, Finland and Sweden) until 1998 (Messerlin, 2001). All these costs reduced or eliminated the benefits of the massive public investment program in telephone lines during the 1970s. Second, the emergence of strong intellectual property rights (IPRs) following the Uruguay Round Agreement on Trade-Related Intellectual Property Rights (TRIPs) may represent a serious danger by making future innovations by non-incumbents more expensive. This negative evolution for French newcomers could be exacerbated by public measures. For instance, following a similar measure already imposed on blank video-cassettes, the minister of culture recently suggested imposing a tax (representing 6–10

[12] The definition of the domains is interesting *per se*: it implicitly reveals the view of the French authorities about what counts in technology.

[13] For comparison's sake, the equipment rates are, respectively, 33 percent and 10 percent (United Kingdom), 37 percent and 26 percent (United States), and 45 percent and 25 percent (Canada), all for the year 1998. For an depth comparison, see Rexecode (1998).

percent of the entire computer price) on hard-disks to compensate singers and actors, for revenues foregone owing to possible IPR infringements by the future owners of the computers. If enacted, this measure will further slow the expansion of the IT sector in France, and far from deterring piracy, it may increase it, thereby harming the interests of audiovisual producers.

6.4. Regulatory Reforms in the French Innovation System: "Reforming the Dinosaur"

The Schumpeterian view associating innovations with large firms or laboratories was shared by almost all the French public authorities, public and private firms, and public opinion from the 1970s to the late 1990s. That no strong evidence supported this Schumpeterian perception even before the so-called "new" economy (Carlton and Perloff, 1990) is largely unknown to French decision-makers. Today, this view still remains dominant. Although the "start-up" phenomenon of the new economy has raised some doubts about it, the current slowdown in the world and French IT sector may help to restore it rapidly. The reliance of innovations on relatively small-scale initiatives, possibly developed in a competitive context created *within* a firm or a laboratory, and on transitory cooperation between complementary skills, flies in the face of two entrenched traditions in French research: large public *agencies* as mere aggregations of small but fiercely independent innovation *units*. For instance, it is little known that the largest public innovation agency (CNRS) employs 14,000 researchers working in more than 1,300 research units, with each of these units being difficult to reshuffle. Change occurs almost exclusively by voluntary resignation or retirement. These two features constitute a hostile environment for the fast and relatively unpredictable course of modern technical progress, leading a minister of education and research (Claude Allègre) to use the image of a dinosaur to describe the CNRS and the French innovation system.

The necessary regulatory reforms have been delayed by the "happy circumstances" of the Golden Years. The costs of these delays have been huge in certain cases. For instance, financial constraints and rigidities, and behind-the-scene links with the bureaucracy that one expects in such a centralized and closed system, may have played a major role in the rather dubious behavior of the Institut Pasteur with regard to protectionist measures taken against foreign innovations for decontaminating HIV-infected blood in the mid-1980s. These measures led to many deaths among people receiving blood transfusions and created a major political scandal in the area of health safety in the early 1990s. This section describes the regulatory reforms recently undertaken to make the French innovation system more flexible.

6.4.1. Capital Markets

From the 1970s to the mid-1990s, there were no significant French mechanisms that specialized in investment in R&D and innovation. By the mid-1990s only a handful of companies provided the risk capital for innovation. They pertained to the banking sector (CDC-Innovation) and manufacturing (Thomson-CSF Ventures). As shown in Table 6.9, the annual total amount of risk-capital invested in the mid 1990s was still very small (FFR 1.5 billion). These investments were concentrated in two or three sectors—two of them pertaining to the IT sector that ended up as a failure in the French innovation system as discussed earlier.

TABLE 6.9
Investment (million francs) in Joint-Ventures

	1995	1996
Information technology	568	420
Telecoms	74	367
Medical research	260	319
Electronics	201	175
Biotechnology	174	131
Chemicals, new materials	69	34
Industrial robots	48	2
Energy	37	1
Total	1431	1449

Source: AFIC, quoted in Guillaume (1998).

TABLE 6.10
Type of Investors, All Investments (million francs)

	1995	1996
Banks	2361	1872
Pension funds	631	838
Private persons	56	651
Insurance companies	636	630
Industrial firms	385	584
State institutions	117	309
Universities	0	201
Others	144	235
Total	4330	5320

Source: AFIC, quoted in Guillaume (1999).

Moreover, these modest data deserve a word of caution: risk-capital investments in France in the mid-1990s included relatively mature operations, as best illustrated by the small *and* declining population of "angel" investors in the very early, risky stages of innovation ventures (from 19 projects registered in 1993 to 4 in 1996). Table 6.10, however, may suggest a more optimistic view, with the total amount of innovation-related capital (*capital-investissement*) reaching FFR 4–5 billion in 1996. This figure, however, does not distinguish between the investments strictly related to high-tech projects and those related to more general development. As a result, the most important finding from Table 6.10 may be the emergence of new types of investors: pension funds, almost all of them from the United States, private persons and, in a dramatic and hopeful departure from a two century tradition, universities.

Even the evidence provided by Table 6.10 does not suggest an important role for capital markets in financing French innovation efforts until the mid-1990s—less than 3 percent of total French R&D expenditure. Recent initiatives for developing French capital markets have thus been taken, based on two new stock exchange markets: the Nouveau Marché and the Brussels-based EASDAQ. In October 1997, the capitalization level of the Nouveau Marché amounted to FFR 10 billion, with 35 firms (out of which 4 have dual quotations) able to raise on average FFR 50 million. In late 1997, the EASDAQ capitalization level

amounted to FFR 5 billion, with 23 firms involved. But these two markets, in addition to serious growth troubles, exhibit a common feature already visible in Table 6.10: they show a limited involvement of *French* financial firms and institutions. Only 15 percent of the funds raised by the Nouveau Marché have been financed by French financial firms, compared to 33 percent by private persons, and 50 percent by non-French financial institutions (which own 40 percent of the French assets quoted on the main market in Paris). Only 5 French brokers operate on EASDAQ (now NASDAQ-Europe), and 3 U.S. brokers account for the largest share of trading on the market.

6.4.2. Education and Human Capital Markets

Human capital issues are very different depending on whether one is considering the higher education system that provides the skills necessary for *producing* innovations, or the lower education system that produces the skills needed for *using* recent and future innovations.

The French higher education system is well known for its antiquated and segmented structure. On the one hand there are the "Grandes Ecoles," relatively rich, each recruiting an annual flow of a few hundred students at most, and sitting in small niches transformed into fortresses. On the other hand there are a hundred universities, poor, living on annual subsidies without any wealth component, in charge of the rest of the students (about 2 million). However, during the last decade this system began to evolve because of rising competition from foreign universities (particularly from U.S. universities), which induced both the Grandes Ecoles and the French universities to develop new strategies, including joint initiatives, for keeping students.

Until the 1980s, the Ecoles limited their activities to their narrow and closed "reserved" markets in the administration or in the Army (Chesnais, 1993). The fact that many students with a science diploma from the Grandes Ecoles were immediately going to better-paid careers in public or private *management* meant that the public investment in generating these scientific skills was largely a waste from the *innovation*

TABLE 6.11
Education and Researcher Output, 1975–95

	United Kingdom	Germany	Italy	Japan	United States	France	Share in France (percent)[a]
Indexes of diplomas in exact sciences among 24 year olds (100 = France)							
1975–85	145.0	170.0	–	235.0	200.0	100.0	2.0
1994–5	170.0	116.0	–	128.0	108.0	100.0	5.0
Indexes of researchers per 1000 active workers (100 = France)							
1981	–	122.2	63.9	150.0	172.2	100.0	0.36
1993–5	86.7	98.3	53.3	138.3	123.3	100.0	0.60

Source: MENRT, OECD and NSF (1998).
[a] Share of total French diplomas or total French workers (percent).

point of view (in most of the Ecoles, students do not pay the full costs of their studies). Such a highly segmented and monopolistic system also imposed a severe drag on the development of a large and flexible technological innovation system in France. However, since the 1980s, because of the increasingly stagnating careers and budgetary constraints in the administration and the more profitable job opportunities in private or formerly public firms, the Grandes Ecoles have shown an increasing interest in innovation activities, even if their students still tend to go to the reserved markets carefully monopolized by their alumni.

Things have also changed for the universities. If the Golden Years did not witness reforms of the innovation system *per se*, they witnessed dramatic changes in the university education regime. Following the 1968 demonstrations, massive investments were made in the university system—the first of such magnitude since the late nineteenth century. These efforts in terms of staff and equipment have (very slowly and imperfectly) eroded the very bureaucratic regime in place in the French universities since the late nineteenth century, and they have increased the number of students in higher education. The French lag in scientific and engineering skills has been reduced over the last twenty years. Table 6.11 shows that, since the 1970s, the percentage of diplomas in exact sciences among French 24 year olds has increased relative to the corre-

sponding percentages in other large industrial countries, except for the United Kingdom; it more than doubled between the two periods, although it is still the lowest among the countries included in Table 6.11.

As many students from Grandes Ecoles have a diploma in sciences yet make their careers as administrators—not scientists—the percentage of researchers per active worker may be a better indicator of the *effective* production of scientists by the higher education level. Table 6.11 shows that the French situation has also improved in this respect, relative to the countries for which data are available.[14]

It may now be useful to examine some evidence on the evolution of French high-level diplomas by scientific discipline. Looking at the stock of PhD theses in 1997, two promising fields of innovations, information technology and biotechnology, were represented by 40 percent of the total stock of PhD theses, an increase of 27 percent with respect to 1992. This is somewhat more than the average increase for all topics. One-quarter of these

[14] One could argue that the relative change in the French share may flow from the fact that changes in the working population have been greater in France than in the other countries—because France has experienced a higher increase in unemployment between the two periods considered than any other country included in Table 6.11. However, though this factor reduces the magnitude of the effective "catching up" process ongoing in France, it is not significant enough to reverse the basic trend.

PhD theses were completed by foreign students, roughly the same percentage as for all scientific PhD theses. This evolution is interesting because it suggests a healthy reaction from PhD students to market-based incentives (i.e., the rise of the IT and biotechnology sectors). However, available data on the 1997 stock of students in the first year of French PhD progammes ("Diplôme d'études approfondies" or DEAs), which give a crude estimate of the outflow of PhD theses in the years 2001–2, do not confirm the above-observed reallocation of PhD theses: they show a decrease of 7 percent of DEA students in information technology and biotechnology, compared to 1992.

There is a final interesting aspect to examine in the higher education segment, namely "skill mobility;" that is, the imbalances between the *production* of skills by the domestic education system and the *use* of skills by domestic producers. Comparing France and the United Kingdom in this respect suggests substantial differences between the two countries. Table 6.11 shows a U.K. "specialization" in producing scientific diplomas: in 1994–5, the United Kingdom had the highest rate of "producing" diplomas and the lowest rate of "using" researchers per active worker among the five countries for which there is enough available information (the United Kingdom, Germany, Japan, the United States, and France). In other words, the United Kingdom has the capacity to attract students from the rest of the world, to import skills, but not the capacity to keep them as researchers or innovators. In contrast, Table 6.11 suggests a French education system that is less attractive, but that is comparatively better at keeping educated skilled graduates. This feature may be due to general factors, such as the lack of mobility owing to language problems—a barrier that is rapidly disappearing.

Lower education is the key for nurturing higher education. It is also essential for generating a large work force familiar with current innovations, and not afraid to use future innovations in their jobs. The French lower education system is often praised for its quality: schoolchildren leaving French lower education and going to foreign higher education are often considered well prepared. However, this observation relies on "successful" French schoolchildren. It ignores the fact that 45 percent of French schoolchildren leave school having completed only mandatory school years (compared to less than 20 percent in Germany) (Möbus and Sevestre, 1991). This high proportion of *de facto* drop-outs reveals an important inefficiency of French lower education, with significant consequences for the whole economy, since unskilled workers constitute one-third of the unemployed. It also suggests that a substantial proportion of the French labor force has not received an adequate stock of human capital, and is thus unlikely to be inclined to be aware of and interested in new innovations, and therefore cannot introduce or use them.

6.4.3. Labor Markets for Scientists

In all countries, labor markets for scientists are segmented by skills so that they tend to be thin. The French innovation system is characterized by three additional sources of segmentation that do not exist in large OECD countries, at least to any great extent.

First, there is the segmentation between the labor markets for public and private R&D researchers (Chesnais, 1993). In the late 1990s, the labor market for "private" scientists (estimated on the basis of a census relying on firms having more than 20 wage-earners) involved roughly 80,000 high-level staff (researchers and engineers), while the labor market for "public" researchers amounted to 80,000 people (two-thirds in the universities and one-third in public laboratories).[15] The largest public laboratories are CNRS, covering all topics (14,000 staff); CEA (7,700 staff), specialized in nuclear research, but diversifying

---

[15] Figures on the number of high-level staff in private laboratories differ noticeably according to the source: the figure quoted is from the Ministry of Research, while other estimates go up to 110,000 (Commissariat Général du Plan). However, there is an agreement on the trend—with the proportion of researchers in private laboratories rising from 40 percent in the early 1980s to at least 50 percent in the late 1990s.

rapidly; Institut National de la Récherché Agronomique (INRA, 2,400 staff), specialized in agriculture; and, lastly, Institut National de la Santé et de la Récherché Médicale (INSERM) and Institut Pasteur, specialized in medical research and biotechnology (2,800 researchers total). The key point is that the public and private scientist labor markets are almost the same size, and have little contact: in 1995, less than 2 percent of researchers in the private labor sub-market came from the public labor sub-market, and even this minute flow seems to have decreased (Guillaume, 1998: 43).

There is a second source of segmentation: the age pyramid of the researchers, which is very different between the two sub-markets (of course, this difference is made possible by the absence of interactions between them). The average age of researchers in the public sector is high (47 years old on average), and it is still increasing. This situation reflects the principle of "research for life" adopted in the public laboratories, and the fact that employees are generally civil servants behaving as bureaucrats à la Niskanen (1971), able to capture the bureaucratic rigidities for their own profits. In sharp contrast, not only are researchers in private firms younger (41 years old on average), but this average age is also declining: 17 percent of these researchers are less than 30 years old (compared to 11 percent of white collar workers in private firms), and half of these have worked in the same enterprise for 10 years or less. In fact, research jobs in private firms tend to be taken over by students at the end of their studies, with many researchers shifting to non-research jobs after a decade or more in the labs. There will thus be a crucial issue of replacing the rapidly aging population of researchers and engineers, in particular in the public laboratories, which have mandatory retirement at 65 years old. This "generation" replacement will be so massive and costly, particularly for the best scientists,[16] that it is likely to impose a

major reorganization of the working conditions in public laboratories, moving toward a much greater flexibility.

The last source of segmentation specific to the French innovation system comes from the fact that innovation activities within French firms have less contact with the rest of the firm than is the case in firms in other large OECD economies. In the labor markets, this feature is aggravated by the profound differences between engineers coming from Grandes Ecoles (with the school diploma or with a PhD thesis done within the Grande Ecole) and those having a university PhD. Not only do engineers from Grandes Ecoles benefit from better conditions in terms of formation (the spending per student is several times greater in a Grande Ecole than in university), but they are more often and earlier in contact with firms: almost 33 percent of the PhDs from Grandes Ecoles have seen their thesis financed by a firm, against only 11 percent in the case of university PhDs. These features give a considerable and ever-lasting advantage to the students from Grandes Ecoles over students from the universities, although this situation is slowly changing under the competitive pressures of the foreign university diplomas.

Of course, labor markets for scientists operate under the general constraints existing in all French labor markets (see section 6.3). In this context, one observation is essential. As shown in Table 6.12, the gap between the wages for skilled and unskilled labor (in terms of the wage of unskilled women) has narrowed over the past 25 years. In particular, the wage for skilled men has deteriorated substantially and without interruption. This evolution may reflect the increase in skilled jobs allowed by the greater capacity of the education system to produce skills. But it may also mirror the impact of regulatory measures taken in favor of unskilled labor, such as successive large increases of the statutory nation-wide minimum wage since the 1970s. In such a context, benefits from education are increasingly limited to the fact that skilled labor has a much lower rate of unemployment than unskilled labor. However, if such benefits could indeed be observed until

---

[16] This is best illustrated by the case of Professor Luc Montagnier, a HIV specialist, who had to leave his laboratory at the age of 65, and who immediately got a research position in the U.S. university system.

TABLE 6.12
Evolution of Relative Wages, by Qualification, 1970–93

	1970	1977	1985	1993	1993/70 (percent)
Men[a]					
Without diploma	137	136	125	126	92.0
Technical diploma[b]	190	177	157	158	83.2
Baccalaureat	273	247	215	202	74.0
Baccalaureat + 2 years	296	230	212	218	73.6
More than Baccalaureat + 2 years	476	405	334	326	68.5
Women[a]					
Without diploma	100	100	100	100	100.0
Technical diploma[b]	129	127	125	124	96.1
Baccalaureat	170	171	152	148	87.1
Baccalaureat + 2 years	184	179	166	166	90.2
More than Baccalaureat + 2 years	273	229	204	215	78.8

Source: Goux (1996).
[a] Index 100 = women without diploma.
[b] BEP, CAP.

TABLE 6.13
Evolution of Jobs and Unemployment by Level of Education, 1970–93

	1970	1977	1985	1993
Men[a]				
Without diploma	−4.2	−2.4	−2.0	−2.8
Technical diploma[b]	−0.4	−0.6	−1.6	−0.9
Baccalaureat	2.9	−0.2	2.5	1.7
Baccalaureat + 2 years	5.3	11.2	4.4	7.0
More than Baccalaureat + 2 years	6.5	1.6	4.7	4.1
Women[a]				
Without diploma	−1.6	−1.9	−0.2	−1.2
Technical diploma[b]	2.3	0.4	−1.2	0.4
Baccalaureat	6.1	0.5	4.4	3.6
Baccalaureat + 2 years	1.6	12.7	3.5	6.0
More than Baccalaureat + 2 years	8.7	5.3	6.0	6.6
Unemployment rate, men and women[c]				
Without diploma	2.0	4.5	14.5	16.5
Baccalaureat and above	1.0	2.0	2.5	6.0

Source: Goux (1996).
[a] Average annual rate of change.
[b] BEP, CAP.
[c] Percent of labor force unemployed.

1991, they were substantially eroded during the 1993 recession, with the unemployment rate peaking at 6 percent for skilled labor (see Table 6.13). This situation seems to have been a turning point in the behavior of French students: an increasing number of newly skilled students are emigrating to the United States (students in technological activities) or other European countries (students in business activities).

6.4.4. R&D Public Funding

The French national spending in R&D slightly increased in the early 1980s, but it stagnated during the late 1980s and has declined since then (see Table 6.14). However, the French catching up, in terms of spending, between the 1960s and the early 1980s was large enough to keep the overall French situation better than that in the rest of Europe during the 1980s and 1990s—but not better than in the United States and Japan. This overall indicator, however, is not the most important. In particular, it misses the two major features of the French innovation system, again pointing to strong elements of segmentation.

First is segmentation in terms of public-private funding. As shown in Table 6.14, the share of public funding is much larger in France than in other countries, *including* the United States, despite the special importance of military innovation in that country. However, this feature has been less obvious since the first half of the 1990s: the decline of public funding in France explains the relative increase in other countries. Table 6.15 provides more complete information over a longer period: the relative weight of public funding has decreased in two steps (the late 1970s and the early 1990s), separated by a long period of relative stability (the 1980s) characterized by massive industrial subsidies to public "national" champions. Table 6.15 also shows that the "operating/financing" ratio has continuously increased for public agencies, while continuously decreasing in the private sector, thus echoing the high segmentation of these two parts of the French innovation system. But the most important evidence comes from Table 6.16, which provides an "input-output" description of the various flows between the *source* of funds (public civil and military, private, and foreign source) and the *use* of these funds (universities, public civil and military labora-

TABLE 6.14
R&D Spending, and its Public And Military Components, 1970–96

	Germany	Italy	Japan	United States	France (index)	France (percent of GDP)
National R&D spending share of GDP (index 100 for France)						
1970	–	–	–	–	100.0	1.91
1981[a]	122.9	44.5	107.7	122.9	100.0	1.98
1991[a]	108.6	54.9	117.4	118.2	100.0	2.40
1996	98.3	–	122.0	112.9	100.0	2.32
Of which: public R&D funding share of GDP (index 100 for France)						
1991	75.2	54.7	32.1	84.7	100.0	1.37
1996	84.4	64.2	51.4	85.3	100.0	1.09
Of which: R&D military credit share of GDP (index 100 for France)						
1991	22.4	10.2	4.1	140.8	100.0	0.49
1996	31.3	9.4	9.4	159.4	100.0	0.32

Sources: MENRT, OECD.
[a] Domestic R&D spending.

TABLE 6.15
R&D Finance and Operations, 1971–96

	1971	1978	1981	1988	1991	1996
Finance sources (billion francs)						
Public institutions	10.6	17.2	36.1	64.5	86.9	89.3
Private firms	6.2	12.6	26.5	48.6	76	93.8
Operating agents (billion francs)						
Public institutions	7.3	11.8	25.7	46.7	62.8	70.1
Private firms	9.3	18	36.8	66.5	100.3	112.1
Operation/finance ratios (percent)						
Public institutions	68.9	68.6	71.2	72.4	72.3	78.5
Private firms	150.0	142.9	138.9	136.8	132.0	119.5

Source: MENRT.

tories, private laboratories, and foreign use). Table 6.16 clearly reveals three major clusters of the French innovation system, largely independent from one another in terms of source and use.

The second source of segmentation of the French innovation system derives from the crucial role of military innovation, which contributes to the fragmentation of the whole system. Table 6.14 has already shown the huge gap in this respect between France and the other countries examined—except for the United States and, to a much lesser extent, the United Kingdom. In fact, the narrowing gap with the United Kingdom may be due to the steep decline in French military spending, which reflects a host of issues ranging from budgetary difficulties to an increased uncertainty about the future direction of French foreign policy in a world much less threatened by large worldwide conflicts, and more vulnerable to regional conflicts requiring rapid, and costly, logistics. Table 6.17 shows the main features of this dramatic evolution of French military innovation during the 1990s: the number of enterprises involved in military R&D has been reduced by two-thirds, funding by public institutions halved, and internal funding reduced by one-third. The firms involved in these innovation activities are increasingly operating with their own finances, echoing the evidence drawn from Table 6.15. Such a situation has important consequences in the long run for the level and type of innovation done, and for

TABLE 6.16
R&D Finance and Operations, FFR billion, 1994

Origin of funds	Universities and CNRS	Public civil labs	Military labs	Firms	Foreign cooperation
Public civil	27.4	21.1	0	9.3	4
Public military	0.1	1.5	12.9	11.7	
Firms	0.9	2.3		79.6	
Exports of R&D		1		8.3	
Total	28.4	25.9	12.9	108.9	4

Source: OST, quoted in Guillaume (1998).

TABLE 6.17
The Collapse of Military R&D in French Firms, FFR billion, 1991–7

	1991	1994	1997	1997/91 (percent)
1. Firm own funds	45.1	38.0	30.3	−33.0
2. Public funding	17.1	11.7	9.1	−46.9
3. Public-based subcontracting	2.7	2.0	1.2	−56.9
Ratio 2/(1 + 2) (percent)	27.5	23.6	23.1	−16.0
Number of enterprises	331	120	129	−61.0

Source: CGP (1999: 398).

the level of fragmentation of the French innovation system.

6.4.5. *Firms and Market Structures*

The private firms and market structures involved in the French innovation system present two major features. First, and unsurprisingly, French public funding is concentrated on large firms, as Table 6.18 suggests. More surprisingly, this concentration is more marked for the firms working on civilian contracts than for those pertaining to the military-industrial complex. The main reason for such a situation is the few but particularly large grands

programmes, such as TGV (high-speed trains) and nuclear electricity.

Second, French multinationals began to substantially change the location of their innovation activities during the mid-1990s. This evolution is hard to precisely document because, at the time of writing, there are no systematic data about French multinationals in this regard, but only limited information from the countries in which their subsidiaries are located. For instance, U.S. sources suggest that in 1994, the U.S. subsidiaries of French multinationals spent roughly FFR 10 billion on R&D (three times more than in 1990) and employed 10,000 people (CGP,

TABLE 6.18
Breakdown of Public Contracts, by Firm and Contract, 1994

	Firms benefiting from public contracts (million francs)			Firms without public contracts (million francs)	Firms benefiting from public contracts (percent)			Firms without public contracts (percent)
	A1	A2	B	C	A1	A2	B	C
Aerospace	5431	6346	27	0	23.4	27.4	0.1	0.0
Electronics	833	756	253	63	3.6	3.3	1.1	0.3
Equipment goods	4985	1397	429	48	21.5	6.0	1.8	0.2
Chemicals	340	53	153	43	1.5	0.2	0.7	0.2
Other industries	12	35	828	249	0.1	0.2	3.6	1.1
Services	129	202	569	6	0.6	0.9	2.5	0.0
Total	11729	8789	2259	409	50.6	37.9	9.7	1.8

Source: MENRT-DGRT, OST computations, quoted in Guillaume (1998: 211).
Notes: A1, the 120 firms under public defense contracts; A2, the same 120 firms and their public civilian contracts; B, the 660 firms under public civilian contracts representing more than 5 percent of their R&D expenses; C, the 2700 firms which undertake R&D and do not benefit from public contracts.

1999). These resources are smaller than those invested by the U.S. subsidiaries of U.K. or German firms (FFR 17 billion), but they represent 5–6 percent of the costs of the France-based innovation activities and the stock of scientists based in France. Available information suggests that the subsidiaries of French multinationals spent roughly FFR 7–10 billion in the other E.U. member states in 1994. As a result, all foreign subsidiaries of French multinationals spent roughly FFR 17–20 billion outside France, a figure close to the expenditure by foreign multinationals in French research and development.

6.5. Minitel and Hypermarkets

This section focuses on two very different innovations. First is the typical grand programme: Minitel, a forerunner of the Internet. The choice of such a case (instead of successful examples based on private efforts in very traditional French exports, such as wines) was motivated by the importance of the government role in the French innovation system. The second case is in services: the creation of a specific type of large store, or "hypermarket," by French retailers. The choice of such a case was motivated by the fact that France may have more comparative advantages in services than in goods, and because innovation is a more global concept than R&D.

6.5.1. The Minitel Case

The Minitel program established in the very late 1970s and implemented in the mid-1980s is a good illustration of all the errors made in the French innovation system, which depends too heavily on the choices of public institutions (which are *de facto* the choices of a *handful* of decision-makers in the French bureaucratic system). It is particularly interesting because Minitel is not a civilian extension of a military program, such as Concorde or nuclear energy. There is a striking difference between these dual civil-military *grands programmes* and Minitel. In the *grands programmes*, the proponents largely ignored the demand side. (The demand for

Concorde has always been tiny, and if there is large demand for energy, there is not a demand for nuclear energy as such.) In sharp contrast, the Direction Générale des Télécommunications (DGT) of the French Ministry of Telecommunications had, with the Minitel, the *right* instinct about the potential demand to emerge during the following decades. Online services of all types based on interactive telephony were set to grow dramatically. In sum, all the reasons for the failure of Minitel are located on the supply or innovation side, and that is what makes the case interesting for this chapter.

The first important reason for failure was the DGT's desire to make the Minitel a completely French instrument, ignoring the huge international potential of telecom-related activities in both hardware and software. The software was French, the Minitel was based on the first French-made chip, and the actual machine (a telephone equipped with limited interactive capacity) was conceived by DGT and three firms led by Alcatel. As a result, the technological risk was huge: if one element of any of the basic Minitel components failed or became outdated, it would be difficult to rely on foreign sources to salvage or upgrade the system. (In fact, the system became quickly outdated, slow and rigid, compared to the Internet.)

The second source of failure was the highly noncompetitive environment of the whole program, which relied on a very naïve view of scale economies. DGT granted the entire production of the Minitel machines to three firms, with Alcatel as the dominant player. The key service operator was France Telecom, the then-public telephone monopoly. More than 4 million machines were granted *free* to French households between 1981 and 1988, on the basis that "more machines will allow the development of services." But the *effective* use of all these machines remained greatly constrained by very high telephone call rates (telecom deregulation was seen as evil by the DGT). Moreover, economically speaking, a machine given away for free may not be used at all as it may have no real value for the beneficiaries. It is thus not so surprising that the Minitel became for many French—much like the revered family deities in Roman times—a (ugly) thing sitting enthroned in the entrance or dining room for welcoming visitors, but never used because it was too unpredictable.

In 1989, the French Cour des Comptes provided interesting evidence about the failure of the program. It concluded that between 1981 and 1987 the accumulated costs of the Minitel for the Treasury were roughly FFR 8 billion, whereas the estimated cumulated benefits, in the form of increased phone traffic and savings on printed phone books, amounted to less than FFR 3 billion. In 1988, the administration estimates of the Minitel benefits and costs from its origin until 1995 suggested net costs of roughly FFR 4 billion still to be expected by 1995. Following the Court's auditing, the DGT decided to impose a user tax on Minitels introduced after 1991, thereby reducing the subsidy effect. Meanwhile, the French administration worked hard to make the Minitel use *de facto* compulsory for many essential administrative tasks, such as the enrolment to baccalauréat (the key exam in the French academic cursus) or the application to universities. However, the bulk of Minitel services were always positioned in a very narrow range of services: getting phone numbers, making railway (not airlines) reservations, and, by far the largest segment of the Minitel-derived demand, getting sex-related services.

The Minitel experience was the source of a third failure that is crucial for the history of regulatory reforms in European telecoms and other services under the 1992 Single Market Program. It showed the limits of the French Napoleonic legal and regulatory regime— more precisely, the practical impossibility for an administration (France Telecom) to correctly handle the legal, financial, and accounting complexities of a telephone-based network (Cour des Comptes, 1989: 39–41). This failure played an important role in the French decision to decouple operators and regulatory agencies, a decision not easily taken within the framework of the French legal system.

In a typical French way, the "death certificate" of the Minitel had to be given by a prime minister: in 1998, Lionel Jospin officially announced that French consumers should turn

to the Internet. The global cost of the Minitel experience is hard to evaluate, all the more so because it should take into account opportunity cost: many observers argue that Minitel was a key cause of the French lag in investment in modern IT.[17]

6.5.2. Hypermarkets "à la Française"

Innovations do not consist only in physical goods: they may consist in successful ideas in services, as illustrated by the concept of the hypermarket "à la française." In the mid-1960s, French retailing relied almost completely on a dense network of small "mom-and-pop" stores. The only exceptions were department stores located in the centers of large towns, and less than a handful of mail-order firms. In the late 1950s, a few entrepreneurs (who were small shop-keepers at this time) introduced in France the "supermarket" concept already operating in the United States. A supermarket is a store (often, but not necessarily) larger than the average "mom-and-pop" store; its main feature is to offer lower prices on a relatively narrower set of goods, carefully chosen—mostly basic food products, with a few essential maintenance goods.

The rapid success of the supermarket formula led the French entrepreneurs to go one step further; that is, to create their own

[17] In 1975, this investment was negligible in France, whereas in the United States it already represented 1.9 percent of the value added. In 1996, this situation was not much better, with 0.8 percent in France, compared to 3.4 percent in the United States (this picture is striking all the more because the share of total private investment is higher in France than in the United States for the period covered: 16.8 percent in France vs 13.9 percent in the United States in 1975, and 14.1 percent in France vs 13.7 percent in the United States in 1996). However, these figures deserve a caveat: the gap between the two indicators may have been amplified by differences in accounting methods (French accounts treat investments in software as intermediate consumption). But according to INSEE, taking into account these differences would have increased by at most 15 percent the value of French investments in IT in 1992 (Boyer and Didier, 1998: 106). As a result, such differences in accounting methods are unlikely to reverse the broad picture.

hypermarket concept, different from the U.S. formula. A hypermarket is not merely a very large supermarket (to give an order of magnitude, supermarkets range from 400 to 1500 square meters, whereas hypermarkets range from 2500 to 12000 square meters). In the French concept, it also sells *all* possible goods—with the consumers paying at the *same* cashier for food *and* non-food products. Since the start of the French hypermarket formula, the range of non-food products available on the shelves has been defined widely, from clothing to consumer electronics to pleasure goods, and it was continuously expanded until the early 1990s, transforming the hypermarket into a mini mall on its own.

The challenge of the hypermarket was the optimal trade-off between the varieties of the goods to put on shelves (certain non-food products, such as clothing, can be diversified ad infinitum) and the logistics necessary for managing the flows and stock of so many different products (and related services). The solution to the flow issue came from the "bar code" innovation, with the scanners attached to the cash registers allowing, two decades later, an almost instantaneous inventory of the inflows and outflows of products in the hypermarket. The solution to the stock problem was the timing of the payments between the retailers and the producers of the goods: the French retailers running hypermarkets have benefited from favorable delays of payments which, in addition, have induced all the operators (from producers to retailers) to keep stocks as small as possible. This delicate trade-off was not achieved immediately. Mistakes have been made: certain hypermarkets reached such a gigantic size (more than 24,000 square meters) that they had to be divided subsequently into different stores.

The success of this formula allowed French hypermarket retailers to overcome all the barriers erected by the associations of small shop-keepers in France, and to expand rapidly during the 1970s and early 1980s. In fact, these legal barriers now protect the existing hypermarkets against new entrants. During the 1980s and early 1990s, French retailers exported their formula to other European countries, first in southern Europe, and then in central Europe. The 1990s have seen a few firms (such as Carrefour and Promodes) expanding first into the emerging markets in Latin America (i.e., Brazil and Argentina) and in Asia (i.e., China and Taiwan, where they had to adjust their formula due to the lack of space in Asian towns, to accommodate multi-floor stores), and then to the highly regulated markets of certain rich countries such as Japan.

6.6. Conclusion

This chapter has focused on the major problem of the French innovation system: its inability to coordinate and allocate available resources, such as capital and skills, efficiently; that is, quickly enough to take advantage of the relatively unpredictable course of modern technical progress.

The conclusion is obvious: more flexibility is required, and this suggestion could be developed in many ways. The lower education level should be improved in order to "produce" a more innovation-friendly population, an evolution that requires relationships between secondary schools and firms. The various components of the higher education level (Grandes Ecoles and universities, including foreign universities) should be induced to cooperate more in developing competitive strategies and in generating challenging market entry by newcomers into niches currently controlled by incumbents. The same should be done by the various components of the innovation system: the laboratories, financing agencies, and so on. In particular, an in depth reform of the CNRS, which represents roughly 9 percent of the entire French innovation capacity, should be undertaken to limit its overall scope to purely scientific matters; the other activities, such as social sciences, which have anyway always had a difficult life within the CNRS, should be transferred to the universities. The current narrow definition of the principle of "research for life" in public laboratories should be revised. Lastly, because the French innovation system is suffering particularly from a lack of competition and collusive practices, France would greatly benefit from efforts to enforce the pro-competition clauses included in the TRIPs Agreement, signed under the multilateral negotiations of the Uruguay Round, so that the anti-competitive effects of this Agreement are minimized.

These objectives cannot be achieved without the dismantling of many existing regulations. However, this approach does not mean that the government's role should become negligible. Rather, it should become indirect, creating the appropriate legal environment for the development of independent initiatives by the private and public participants in the French initiation system. In particular, the government should grant more freedom to the various public operators, particularly the universities, financially "endowing" these operators (universities, laboratories, etc.) to induce them to make their own long term choices and develop their own long term strategies. This devolution of power *and* wealth, certainly the most difficult regulatory reform to undertake for a French government, is much more important for the future of the French innovation system than the current piling-up of often small and scattered subsidy schemes.

The United Kingdom

Stephen Nickell and John Van Reenen

Over the period since 1970, The United Kingdom has improved its relative productivity performance, but there remains a significant gap in market sector productivity between The United Kingdom and both Continental Europe and the United States. Much of the gap between The United Kingdom and Continental Europe is due to lower levels of capital intensity and skill. However, even taking these into account, there remains a significant gap between The United Kingdom and the United States. This reflects not just a weakness in high tech areas but an inability to absorb best-practice techniques and methods in wide swathes of the market sector. Part of this is due to a weakness in technological innovation despite a high quality science base. This includes comparatively low and falling levels of R&D and patenting as well as a distinct lag in the diffusion of innovations relative to other countries.

7.1. Introduction

In the 1970s, The United Kingdom was widely known as the "sick man of Europe." Why? During the European Golden Age, which stretched from the post–World War II recovery to the first oil shock in 1973, The United Kingdom had been overtaken by the major countries of Continental Europe in terms of gross domestic product (GDP) per capita despite having been far ahead in 1950. Furthermore both unemployment and inflation had been rising steadily since the mid-1960s. Then, on top of

this, the first oil shock itself was a disaster. By the end of 1974, unemployment was rising rapidly, inflation was heading towards 25 percent and the stock market had fallen in real terms to its level in 1920.

Performance continued to be relatively weak until the early to mid-1980s since when there has been some catch up with Continental Europe in terms of GDP per capita, unemployment has fallen substantially and inflation has stabilized at a relatively low level. Nevertheless, even today there is a significant productivity gap, with business sector productivity (output per hour worked) probably around 20 percent below that in France and Germany, and 30 percent below the United States.

So where does technological innovation fit into this story? Technological innovation across the world is one of the driving forces behind productivity advance. However, it is hard to argue that technological innovation, or the lack of it, in The United Kingdom is an important factor in explaining the vicissitudes of the last fifty years. The unemployment/inflation story has only the most tenuous connection with technological advance. Even the large fluctuations in productivity and GDP per capita relative to other countries have less to do with technological innovation, per se, and more to do with the extent to which U.K. companies utilize best-practice methods. These are, of course, intimately related to technology but the fundamental problem is more organizational than technological.[1] And the basic questions concern the incentives to utilize best-

We are most grateful to Richard Nelson, Benn Steil, and David Victor for helpful comments on an earlier draft and to the Leverhulme Trust Programme on The Labour Market Consequences of Technological and Structural Change.

[1] The matched plant studies carried out in the 1980s and 1990s by the National Institute of Social and Economic Research bring this home vividly (Steedman and Wagner, 1987).

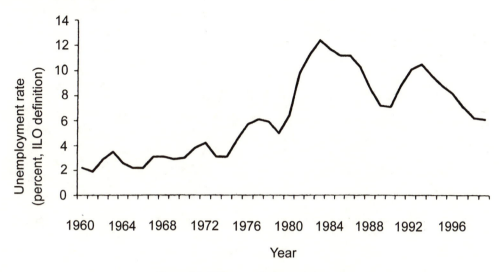

Figure 7.1 U.K. unemployment (percent).

practice methods and the barriers against doing so. These are, of course, big issues[2] which we only discuss tangentially in what follows. Here, we focus on the role of technological innovation although this, inevitably, leads us to touch on how innovations are used.

The remainder of the chapter is set out as follows. In section 2, we provide a picture of the economic performance of the United Kingdom over the past three decades, the main focus being on productivity. This is followed in section 3 by a detailed review of technological innovation in the United Kingdom over the same period. The overall picture reveals that after a long period of falling behind, U.K. productivity performance over the last twenty years has been relatively good with some degree of catch-up on the major competitor countries. However, there remains a productivity gap. With regard to technological innovation, the U.K. performance in basic science has been good but the innovation performance in the market sector is weak.

In the light of these overarching facts, in section 4 we discuss various aspects of the environment in which U.K. companies operate in order to shed some light on their productivity and innovation performance. Then, in the

concluding section, we set out our understanding of what has been happening with regard to technological innovation in the United Kingdom. Our basic story is one of a weakness in the United Kingdom in the commercial application of technological innovations despite the high quality science base. Major reasons for this are poor educational standards outside the top third of the ability range, lack of (and low valuation of) general management skills and low levels of product market competition in many sectors. Attempts are now being made to address these problems but there is some way to go.

7.2. The Economic Performance of the United Kingdom (1970–2000)

As we have already noted, the dramatic fluctuations in unemployment and inflation in the United Kingdom since 1970 have only the most tenuous relationship to technology, so after a very brief overview of the main macroeconomic indicators, we focus on GDP per capita and productivity.

7.2.1. Basic Macroeconomic Indicators

Since the 1960s, the U.K. economy has been on a bit of a roller-coaster ride. In Figures 7.1–7.3

---

[2] McKinsey (1998) presents a comprehensive analysis of these questions.

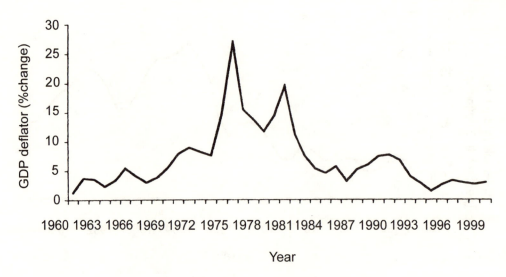

Figure 7.2 Inflation (GDP deflator) (percent per annum).

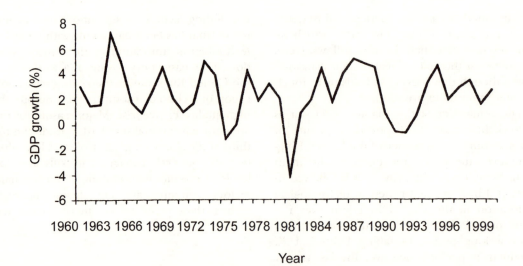

Figure 7.3. GDP growth (percent per annum).

we report on unemployment, inflation and GDP growth. During the 1960s unemployment and inflation were low and GDP growth was high. Indeed GDP probably grew by more in the 1960s than in any other decade in U.K. history. However, by the end of the 1960s unemployment and inflation were both starting to rise and by the early 1970s they had both reached their highest level since 1950. After the first oil shock, GDP growth fell and inflation and unemployment rose to new heights. After Mrs Thatcher came to power in 1979, macroe-

conomic policy was significantly tightened and with the onset of the second oil shock, the United Kingdom had its worst recession since the 1930s. A slow recovery followed but, assisted by macropolicy relaxation in the latter half of the 1980s, a big drop in commodity prices and financial deregulation, this turned into a dramatic boom. This was immediately followed by an equally dramatic slump as monetary policy was tightened in response to rising inflation. However, since the exit from the European Exchange Rate mechanism in 1992, monetary

TABLE 7.1

Rates of Growth of GDP per Capita (percent per annum)

	1860–1914	1920–39	1951–73	1974–95	1995–9
United Kingdom	1.04	1.56	2.24	1.87	2.03
France	0.96	0.78	4.92	1.63	1.93
Germany	1.47	2.91	5.11	2.01	1.89
United States	1.70	0.86	1.54	1.72	2.74

Source: Crafts and Toniolo (1996: Table 1.10); Eurostat and *OECD Economic Outlook.*

policy has been placed on a sound footing (based on inflation targeting) and this has assisted in creating a stable and rather benign state of affairs which has lasted until the present day. However, it is clear that the period from 1970 to 1995 was one of great volatility relative to previous decades.

7.2.2. GDP per Capita, Productivity and Labor Input

In the mid-nineteenth century, the United Kingdom was the richest country in the world. Table 7.1 presents a brief summary of what has happened since. As a consequence of their superior growth rates, first the United States and then Germany had overtaken the United Kingdom by 1914. However, two world wars and the economic upheavals of the inter-war years changed things somewhat, so that by 1950, both France and Germany[3] were over 30 percent below the United Kingdom in terms of GDP per capita and the United States was nearly 70 percent above (see Table 7.2).[4] Then, during the European Golden Age (1950–73), the forces of convergence assisted by the Common Market (1959) enabled Continental Europe to grow at an unprecedented rate, so that by 1973 France and Germany had overtaken the United Kingdom which, in its turn, had caught up slightly with the United States. Until the early 1980s, the United Kingdom fell further behind its European competitors but since then it has

[3] In the post-war period, Germany refers to West Germany.

[4] Note both France and (West) Germany had recovered from World War II by 1951 in the sense that GDP per capita was by then higher than in any pre-war year (Crafts and Toniolo, 1996: Table 1.2).

been catching up so that by 1996 GDP per capita in the United Kingdom is fairly close to that of its European partners while still being well behind the United States. Finally, it is worth noting that there is no sign of any dramatic improvements in growth rates in the late 1990s outside the United States.

In order to understand more clearly what has been happening in the post-war period, it is important to divide GDP per capita into GDP per hour worked (productivity) and hours worked per capita (labor input). The reason for doing so is that there have been dramatic changes in labor input in some countries since 1973, which are shown in Table 7.3. The key feature is that while in 1973, the labor input (hours × employment/population) was of the same order of magnitude in all the countries except Japan, since that time it has fallen by over 20 percent in France and Germany, by over 10 percent in the United Kingdom whereas it has risen by over 10 percent in the United States. Bearing this in mind, we now look at productivity growth rates in the post-war period in Table 7.4. Here we see that after 1973, growth rates in output per hour are considerably higher than those for GDP per

TABLE 7.2

GDP per Capita (United Kingdom = 100)

	1950	1973	1996
United Kingdom	100	100	100
France	69.7	110.2	105
Germany	63.3	104.7	113
United States	167.4	151.6	137

Source: Bean and Crafts (1996: Table 6.2); O'Mahony (1999: Table 1.1).

TABLE 7.3

Labor Inputs

	1973	1979	1983	1990	1996	1999
Employment/population ratio (age 15–64)						
United Kingdom	71.4	70.8	64.3	72.4	69.8	71.7
France	65.9	64.4	60.8	59.9	59.2	59.8
Germany	68.7	66.2	62.2	64.1	64.5	64.9
United States	65.1	68.0	66.3	72.2	72.9	73.9
Japan	70.8	70.3	71.1	72.6	74.1	72.9
Annual Hours Worked Per Worker						
United Kingdom	1929	1821	1719	1773	1732	1720
France	1904	1813	1711	1668	1644	1604
Germany	1868	1764	1733	1611	1668	1556
United States	1924	1905	1882	1943	1951	1976
Japan	2201	2126	2095	2031	1955	1842

Source: OECD *Employment Outlook* (various issues).

capita for the European countries, reflecting the decline in labor input. Moving on to total factor productivity growth rates, most noteworthy is the fact that in the United Kingdom there is hardly any decline after 1973, in contrast to all the other countries which exhibit dramatic falls. This reflects the fact that the decline in labor productivity after 1973 was much lower in the United Kingdom than elsewhere allied to the United Kingdom's generally lower investment rates (see Table 7.10 in the next section). The interesting question of why labor productivity growth in the United Kingdom was so much higher relative to the other countries after 1973 than it was before, despite

the roller-coaster ride of the macroeconomy, has been the subject of much research (Layard and Nickell, 1989; Nickell et al., 1992; Bean and Crafts, 1996). Key factors include the transformation of industrial relations, the dramatic decline of unions in the private sector and the increase in product competition market following extensive privatization, and the introduction of the European Single Market.

The consequences of all these differences in growth rates led to the picture in 1996 which is set out in Table 7.5. Once we control for the differences in labor input we see that the United States, France and Germany are relatively close to each other but there remains a

TABLE 7.4

Productivity Growth Rates (percent per annum)

	Output per hour		Total factor productivity	
	1950–73	1973–96	1950–73	1973–96
United Kingdom	2.99	2.22	1.74	1.65
France	4.62	2.78	3.10	1.62
Germany	5.18	2.56	3.76	1.67
United States	2.34	0.77	1.49	0.38
Japan	6.11	3.06	3.57	1.33

Source: O'Mahony (1999: Tables 1.2 and 1.5).

TABLE 7.5
Levels of Productivity, 1996

		United Kingdom	France	Germany	United States	Japan
1.	GDP per capita	100	105	113	137	113
2.	GDP per person engaged	100	126	126	129	102
3.	GDP per hour	100	132	129	121	90
4.	Market output per hour	100	120	131	128	81
5.	TFP (1995), whole economy	100	118	109	112	77
6.	TFP (1995), market sector	100	108	115	119	76
7.	TFP (1995), skills adjusted, market sector	100	N/A	104	116	N/A

Source: O'Mahony (1999: Tables 1.1, 1.4 and 1.5).

significant productivity gap between these countries and the United Kingdom. If we focus on the market sector, in which output measures are more reliable, there is a 30 percent labor productivity gap between the United Kingdom and Germany and the United States (see row 4). These gaps are, however, different in nature. Once we control for capital intensity and labor quality (in row 7), the gap between the United Kingdom and Germany all but disappears. However, the gap between the United Kingdom and the United States remains at 16 percent. It is possible to "explain" this gap by including the stock of R&D in this analysis, because the United States has a substantially larger stock of R&D per unit of output than the United Kingdom (see Crafts and O'Mahony, 2000: Table 7.5). The remaining gap of 16 percent between the United Kingdom and the United States would then simply be down to lower levels of "innovation." This is rather simplistic, however, since it sheds no real light on the underlying process. This is what McKinsey (1998) sets out to explain and concludes that the gap is fundamentally due to the low levels of competitive intensity in the United Kingdom, the high level of product market regulation and the lack of exposure to best practice. Looking at it from the viewpoint of technological innovation, the problem in the United Kingdom is the lack of effective use of technology in major sectors of the economy.

7.2.3. Productivity Growth in Different Sectors

The trends outlined in section 2.2 can be broken down by sector. Table 7.6 shows that the produc-

TABLE 7.6
Total Factor Productivity by Sector in the United Kingdom

	Levels of TFP in the United States relative to the United Kingdom, 1995	TFP growth (percent per annum) 1973–95
Agriculture	100	2.92
Mining	140	−2.15
Utilities	115	2.87
Manufacturing	142	1.85
Chemicals	112	2.10
Metals	129	2.02
Engineering	166	2.02
Textiles, etc.	132	1.29
Food, etc.	166	0.18
Other	99	1.89
Construction	84	2.15
Transport/ communication	111	3.06
Distributive trade	135	0.43
Financial services	122	0.98
Personal services	135	1.21
Nonmarket services	–	0.17
Total	112	1.65

Source: O'Mahony (1999: Tables 2.9, 2.13).

tivity gap relative to the United States is not fundamentally driven by any particular sectors. Compared to the United States, the United Kingdom's position is generally unfavorable. An exception is in agriculture where total factor productivity (TFP) was much higher in the United Kingdom than in France, Germany or Japan. U.K. TFP is also relatively strong in the utilities and construction compared to the other countries of the European Union.

The United Kingdom's performance in manufacturing is generally worse than her relative position in the total market economy. However, even in the service sectors the United Kingdom does not enjoy a TFP advantage. The United Kingdom's TFP gap in financial services is large relative to Germany (41 percent), and her gap is large in personal services relative to the United States (35 percent). Looking over time, the United Kingdom's relative decline in market services compared to Germany owes much to the decline in her relatively favorable position in services. Relative to the United States, the productivity gap was closed proportionately less in services than in manufacturing.[5]

7.2.3.1. High Tech Sectors

In policy debates there is often a focus on "strategic high tech" sectors. The OECD statistics classify these as the following: aircraft (ISIC 3845), office and computing (ISIC 3825), drugs and medicines (3522), radio, TV and communication equipment (3832).[6] Across the OECD these industries are characterized by having relatively high shares of skilled workers, high levels of productivity and high shares of trade. They have also had much higher than average growth rates of skilled workers, productivity and trade. Although the manufacturing sector as a whole has declined, high tech sectors

enjoy an increasingly large share of this sector at the expense of low tech industries.

It is important to bear in mind that these sectors are small relative to the economy as a whole. For example, even within manufacturing the high tech sectors (including electricity machinery and instruments) employed only 20 percent of U.K. workers in 1994 relative to 16 percent in 1970 (OECD, 1997). About a fifth of manufacturing workers were also employed in these high tech sectors in the rest of the G5.

Looking at TFP growth by broad sector, manufacturing actually had slower growth over 1973–95 than the utilities (electricity, gas and water), transport and agriculture, forestry, and fishing. Within manufacturing, however, it is the case that the relatively high tech chemical sector has enjoyed faster TFP growth than the relatively low tech textiles and food sectors.

7.2.4. Summary

U.K. labor productivity is lower than the United States, France and Germany. Most of the productivity gap with France and Germany can be accounted for by different factor usage. Relative to Germany, for example, the United Kingdom invests less in physical and human capital. Even accounting for this, there remains a substantial TFP gap with the United States of the order of 16 percent. The United Kingdom made some improvement in closing this gap, especially in the 1980s. For this reason, the OECD-wide post–1973 TFP slowdown appeared much less severe in the United Kingdom than in other countries. This improvement, however, was not primarily driven by better performance in the more technologically advanced parts of the economy. We now turn explicitly to U.K. innovation performance.

7.3. Technological Innovation in the United Kingdom (1970–2000)

As we have seen, the relative productivity performance of the United Kingdom has improved over the last two decades particularly given factor inputs. Over this period, TFP growth has been among the highest in the G7.

---

[5] Although the caveats regarding measurement problems in the service sectors should be born in mind.

[6] For example, OECD (1999: Annex 1). The classification is based on R&D performed and R&D "acquired' from other industries. Medium–high tech includes instruments, vehicles, electrical machinery, chemicals, other transport and nonelectrical machinery.

TABLE 7.7

Indices of Papers and Citations per head (1981–94) (United Kingdom = 100)

	Papers	Citations
United Kingdom	100	100
France	70	58
Germany	64	53
United States	96	114
Japan	45	32

Source: U.K. Office of Science and Technology.

TABLE 7.8

GERD as a Percentage of GDP

	1981	1985	1990	1995	1997
United Kingdom	2.4	2.2	2.2	2.0	1.9
France	2.0	2.3	2.4	2.3	2.2
Germany	2.4	2.7	2.8	2.3	2.3
United States	2.4	2.9	2.8	2.6	2.7
Japan	2.1	2.6	2.9	2.8	2.9
OECD	2.0	2.3	2.4	2.2	2.2

Source: OECD (1999a: Table 3.1.1).

In this section, we focus on the record of technological innovation in the United Kingdom over the same period. We start with the performance of the science base and then work outwards.

7.3.1. The Output of the Science Base

The United Kingdom has a relatively strong position on indicators of the science base. With only 1 percent of the world's population the United Kingdom produces 8 percent of the world's scientific research papers (Table 7.7). The share of citations stands at 9 percent. This is ahead of all other E.U. countries and Japan. Other indicators of elite science are also strong. For example, in winning science prizes in excess of U.S.$200,000 the United Kingdom is second only to the United States and well ahead of third placed Germany.[7]

These figures need to be interpreted with care, however, as they may partially reflect the fact that English is the dominant language of science. It is no surprise that the United States is ahead of the United Kingdom in these measures of the scientific base, but rather more surprising that Canada (although not Australia) has a higher share than the United Kingdom of scientific papers and citations.

Not only is the United Kingdom strong in elite science it also produces a high proportion

of graduates in science and engineering. In 1995 the flow of these graduates as a proportion of total employment was higher than any other G7 country (see OECD, 1999a: Table 2.6.1). This is important in terms of stimulating technology transfer. A large proportion of these graduates, however, end up working outside the scientific sector, for example in finance or consultancy.

7.3.2. General Innovative Performance

7.3.2.1. R&D

Looking at the OECD as a whole, gross expenditure on R&D (GERD) as a proportion of GDP rose substantially in the 1970s and 1980s, but stabilized or fell in the 1990s (see Table 7.8). Much of the 1990s fall was due to government cutbacks in R&D especially in countries where there was a high military spend on R&D as a result of end of the Cold War. There has also been a general move away from direct government subsidies to R&D (and a increase in fiscal subsidies such as tax credits).[8]

The United Kingdom stands out as having the lowest general R&D and business R&D (BERD) intensity of the G5 countries. It is also one of the very few countries to have cut its R&D expenditure as a proportion of GDP

---

[7] An often heard boast is that there are more scientific Nobel prizewinners in Trinity College, Cambridge than in France.

[8] See Bloom et al. (1999). The United States, Canada and France have relatively generous tax breaks for R&D compared to the United Kingdom and Germany. The United Kingdom introduced an R&D tax credit for small firms in April 2000.

TABLE 7.9
R&D Expenditure and Funding

	United Kingdom	France	Germany	United States
1981				
GERD as a percentage of GDP	2.4	2.0	2.4	2.4
BERD as a percentage of GDP	1.5	1.1	1.7	1.7
Percentage of BERD financed by industry[a]	70.0	75.4	83.1	68.4
Percentage of BERD financed by government	30.0	24.6	16.9	31.6
Industry-financed BERD as a percentage of GDP	1.1	0.8	1.4	1.2
1996				
GERD as a percentage of GDP	1.9	2.3	2.3	2.6
BERD as a percentage of GDP	1.3	1.4	1.5	1.9
Percentage of BERD financed by industry[a]	90.5	87.3[b]	91.0	83.6
Percentage of BERD financed by government	9.5	12.7	9.0	16.4
Industry-financed BERD as a percentage of GDP	1.2	1.2	1.4	1.6

Source: Main Science and Technology Indicators, OECD (1998). *Notes*: GERD, gross domestic expenditure on R&D, which covers all R&D carried out on national territory and therefore includes government intramural expenditure on R&D, expenditure by the higher education sector on R&D and BERD. BERD, business enterprise expenditure on R&D.
[a] Includes domestic and foreign industry, and also "other" which is a very small category.
[b] Latest figures available for France is for 1995.

since the early 1980s. Furthermore, even if we focus on business performed R&D, stripping out R&D performed in government labs, universities and elsewhere in the public sector, the United Kingdom stands out as one of the only countries where business enterprise R&D fell in the 1980s.

The falling relative R&D intensity in the United Kingdom since 1981 is not really explained by change in the industry mix (such as the relatively fast rise of the low R&D service sectors in the United Kingdom). It is mainly a "within industry" phenomenon (see Van Reenen, 1997).[9] Interestingly, in the early 1970s, the U.K. general R&D intensity was second only to the U.S. level amongst G7 countries, and even in 1981 the GERD/GDP ratio was 2.4 percent, similar to the United States and Germany (see Table 7.8).

Part of the story is that the proportion of

R&D performed by business but *funded* by government has fallen more dramatically in the United Kingdom than in other countries. The share of BERD funded by the U.K. government fell by from 30 percent to 10 percent between 1981 and 1996 (see Table 7.9). Industry funded BERD as a proportion of GDP has been broadly stable in the United Kingdom and in Germany and has risen in the United States and France (and most other OECD countries). This is a result of explicit U.K. government policy to move away from funding "near market" R&D.

Interestingly, of all the G7 countries only Canada has a higher proportion of its R&D performed by smaller companies (under 500). It appears to be the larger U.K. firms who are failing to invest in R&D as much as other countries (see OECD, 1999a: Table 5.4.1).

7.3.2.2. Investment in Tangible Capital
As we noted in section 2, investment in tangible capital is low compared to other OECD countries (see Table 7.10 and Bond and Jenkinson, 1996). Disaggregating the types of

[9] A more recent decomposition analysis of business R&D intensity in manufacturing 1990–7 (OECD, 1999: 143) also reveals that the 0.6 percent fall in U.K. intensity was all within industry.

TABLE 7.10
Investment as a Percentage of GDP, 1960–95

	United Kingdom	France	Germany	United States
Gross fixed capital formation	17.9	22.2	22.3	18.3
Gross fixed capital formation excluding residential construction	14.2	15.5	15.7	13.6
Gross fixed capital formation: machinery and equipment	8.3	8.8	8.7	7.5

Source: OECD *Historical Statistics*, 1960–95, 1997 edition.

TABLE 7.11
U.S. Patents Granted (1963–93)

	Percentage of total (G7)			Percentage of total (G7 excluding Japan)		
	1963–79	*1985*	*1993*	*1963–79*	*1985*	*1993*
United Kingdom	4.2	3.5	2.3	4.5	4.3	3.0
France	2.8	3.3	3.0	3.0	4.0	3.9
Germany	7.2	9.4	7.0	7.6	11.4	9.1
United States	71.2	55.2	54.1	75.4	67.2	70.0
Japan	5.6	17.8	22.7	–	–	–

Source: U.S. Patent and Trademark Office, Patenting Trends in the United States, 1963–93.

investment is instructive. The United Kingdom invests about 8.3 percent of GDP in plant and equipment which is the OECD average. The poor position is mainly driven by very low investment in public infrastructure and in residential construction.

On the other hand, the United Kingdom has successfully attracted the largest volume of foreign direct investment in the OECD. In 1997 inward investment was 2.8 percent of GDP compared to an E.U. average of 1.4 percent and OECD average of 1.1 percent (see OECD, 1999a: Table 6.1.3). This internationalization of investment is equally true of R&D—the United Kingdom had 15 percent of its R&D funded from abroad in 1997, which was the highest proportion in the OECD. Some of this position is simply due to financial flows—outward investment is also exceptionally high. Part of the FDI numbers, however, do reflect genuine new plant; but here the numbers are not so dramatic. The share of foreign affiliates[10] in manufacturing production, for example, is about equal to that in France (30.5 percent in United Kingdom, 25.8 percent in France)

although higher than Germany (7.1 percent) or Italy (10.2 percent).

Overall investment in "knowledge" (defined by OECD to be the sum of R&D, software and public spending on education) was 8.3 percent in 1995. The European Union and OECD averages were 7.9 percent (United States spent 8.4 percent, Germany 8.1 percent and France 10.2 percent).

7.3.2.3. Patents

R&D is only a measure of the inputs to the science base. What about the outputs? The United Kingdom has a lower share of patents than other G5 countries (see OECD, 1999a: Table 11.2.1). Furthermore, this share has declined over time (whether one uses U.S. or E.U. patents) even if we exclude Japan which has had an enormous increase (see Table 7.11 for U.S. patents). This is particularly disappointing given that the United Kingdom's R&D spend is concentrated in pharmaceuticals

[10] To be a foreign affiliate there has to be a greater than 50 percent holding in the establishment by a parent company.

TABLE 7.12
Expenditure on Innovation as a Share of Sales, 1996

	Manufacturing	*Services*
United Kingdom	3.16	4.02
France	3.92	1.25
Germany	4.12	2.95

Source: OECD (1999a: Table 5.5.1).

TABLE 7.13
ICT Expenditure as a Percentage of GDP, 1997

	IT hardware	*IT services and software*	*Telecom*	*Total*
United Kingdom	1.5	3.4	2.7	7.6
France	0.9	3.3	2.2	6.4
Germany	0.9	2.4	2.3	5.6
United States	1.7	3.4	2.7	7.8
Japan	1.1	2.7	3.6	7.4
OECD	1.3	2.8	2.8	6.9

Source: OECD (1999a: Table 2.3.1).

which have a relatively high propensity to patent.

7.3.2.4. Innovation

E.U. innovation surveys (CIS) give an alternative measure of innovative output. On this measure, U.K. manufacturing firms spent less of their turnover introducing new products and processes than those in France and Germany (Table 7.12). This appears mainly due to larger firms' lower spend. The position is reversed, however, in services.

The problem with the CIS is that the concept of innovation is somewhat vaguer than R&D where the OECD Frascati definition is more precise. Furthermore, whereas the response rates for the R&D surveys are close to 100 percent (they are confidential and compulsory in many countries), the CIS survey has a much lower response rate. In the United Kingdom, response rates were about 43 percent.[11] Thus, one must be careful in drawing any strong conclusions from the innovation survey.

7.3.2.5. Diffusion

The main productivity benefits from innovation are only reaped as it becomes spread around the economy. Measuring the spread of a new technology is no easy task, however. Which technology do we choose to measure? Do we have internationally comparable data examining the same technology? Is this measured in a consistent way over time? Finally, the technological innovations may be less important than the organizational innovations that may accompany the new technology.[12]

7.3.2.5.1. ICTs Data sources are richest on information and communication technologies (ICTs). The United Kingdom seems to perform relatively well on these measures. Of the G7 countries, the United Kingdom is second only to the United States in ICT expenditure as a proportion of GDP in 1997 (according to Table 7.13). Secure web servers for e-commerce stood at 1.4 per 100,000 inhabitants in August 1998 which was higher than France, Germany and Italy, but below Canada and the United States. Eighteen percent of the U.K. population were regular internet users in 1998 compared to 37 percent in the United States, 11 percent in Japan, 10 percent in Germany and 11 percent in France (OECD, 1999a). The United Kingdom has some advantages in these areas because of a good IT infrastructure. Telecommunication prices are relatively low compared to other E.U. countries, due to tough competition.

7.3.2.5.2. Other Indicators Vickery and Northcott (1995) review a number of national surveys of the diffusion of advanced manufacturing technologies and microelectronics. The traditional S-shaped diffusion curve is observed. The United Kingdom does appear to be a laggard in the take up of these new technologies for both indicators (see

---

[11] See Craggs and Jones (1998) for a description of the U.K. CIS.

[12] See Bresnahan et al. (1998) for a study suggesting that the failure to introduce complementary organizational changes alongside computerization harms productivity.

TABLE 7.14

Specialization Profiles in Science, 1981–6 Based on Citations

	United Kingdom	France	Germany	United States	Japan
Clinical medicine	1.17	0.78	0.68	1.07	0.72
Biomedical	0.96	0.96	0.93	1.11	0.92
Biology	1.25	0.64	0.81	0.89	0.95
Chemistry	0.89	1.34	1.58	0.67	1.92
Physics	0.70	1.53	1.55	0.86	1.19
Earth and space	0.93	0.87	0.71	1.19	0.33
Engineering/technology	0.65	0.82	1.18	0.94	1.86
Mathematics	0.90	1.39	1.16	0.97	0.67

Source: CNR-ISRDS.

Vickery and Northcott, 1995: 259), although it eventually catches up. This would be consistent with the notion that poor workforce skills delay the introduction of new technologies.

The cross-national pattern in organizational innovations is less clear. According to Ruigrok et al. (1999), the picture mirrors that of technical diffusion. For example, 10.2 percent (17.9 percent) of all European firms sampled has introduced "extensive decentralisation of strategic decisions" in 1992 (1996). In the United Kingdom, the figures stood at only 8 percent and 13.6 percent. The most comprehensive is probably the European Union's 1996 EPOC survey covering 33,000 European establishments (OECD, 1999e). On a number of indicators the United Kingdom appears average or above average (team-based work organization, delayering of management, employee involvement).[13] Of course, it is controversial as to how innovative these organizational forms are, or how important they are in stimulating productivity growth.

7.3.3. Innovation Performance by Industry

7.3.3.1. Science Base

As we can see in Table 7.14, the U.K. Science Base is particularly specialized in the medical-

biological sector and is notably weak in chemistry, physics and engineering, exactly the opposite of Germany and Japan. In the United States, the research effort is much more evenly spread with the notable exception of the weakness in chemistry.

7.3.3.2. Industry Specifics

R&D intensity in manufacturing is lower than the G5 average in every industry except the chemicals, metal products and pharmaceuticals industries (see Figure 7.4). U.K. R&D is particularly low in the lowest tech industries (textiles, paper and wood products). The strength of pharmaceuticals is striking. About a quarter of all U.K. business R&D is located in this sector, and U.K. R&D intensity is well above average.

The United Kingdom has the strongest biotech sector in Europe and is second only to the United States in the OECD. There are more biotech firms in the United Kingdom than any other E.U. country. Despite the setbacks over the backlash against genetically modified (GM) foods, the drugs related sector is forecast to have high worldwide growth. The strength of the sector rests in its close relation to the academic science base (clusters around universities such as Cambridge) and the presence of sophisticated capital markets in the United Kingdom. These may also have been factors behind the success of the pharmaceuticals industry. In fact, corporate venture capital from the companies in this sector is another advantage enjoyed by U.K. biotech

---

[13] Thirty-three percent of U.K. workplaces with at least 50 employees used team-based organization compared to 30 percent in France, 28 percent in Italy and 20 percent in Germany. Denmark was the highest at 40 percent.

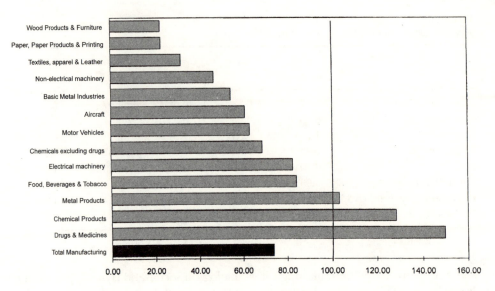

Figure 7.4. R&D intensity in U.K. manufacturing 1995 (relative to G5 average = 100). *Source:* OECD.

firms. The absence of a significant manufacturing component is probably an advantage given U.K. weakness in intermediate skills (see section 7.4).

7.3.4. Some Notable U.K. Innovations

A picture seems to be emerging of a strong science base but weaknesses in translating scientific innovations into marketable and profitable products. This picture is worth illustrating with a few notable U.K. inventions.

- *The Computer.* The 1500 valve, programmable Collosus computer was completed in 1943 in Bletchley Park in order to decode communications between Hitler and his generals encrypted using the Lorenz cipher. Built by Tommy Flowers based on a design of Max Newman and Alan Turing, it operated successfully until the end of the war after which it was destroyed, along with all the blueprints, on the orders of the U.K. government and those who worked on it were forbidden to talk about it!
- *The X-Ray Scanner.* The most significant advance in radiology since the discovery of X-rays, it was invented by Geoffrey Houndsfield at EMI. Houndsfield won a Nobel prize but EMI lost so much money in disastrous

attempts to manufacture and market the scanner that its medical electronics division ceased to exist.

- *The Structure of DNA.* This discovery in 1953 by Crick and Watson at Cambridge laid the foundation of the biotechnology industry. Like penicillin, it was not patented.
- *Zantac.* This anti-ulcer drug generated such gigantic profits that it turned Glaxo from a small player to the largest pharmaceutical company in the world (after the merger with Smithkline/Beecham). Zantac was not even the first in the field (Tagamet was first), but its world domination was essentially a marketing triumph.
- *The Proof of Fermat's Last Theorem.* The most famous mathematical discovery of the latter part of the twentieth century. Of no known commercial value.

7.3.5. Summary

The United Kingdom has a relatively strong academic science base. Inventiveness and the position of elite science continues to be impressive. The reasons for this are a complex mixture of culture, the fact that English is a global language and the ensemble of institutions around the universities.

The United Kingdom has been weak at translating this science base into innovation and industrial performance. Some high tech industries, such as pharmaceuticals, closely connected to the thriving biomedical science base have also done well, but these are the exceptions to the rule. Business R&D and patenting are low (and falling) by international standards. Diffusion of innovations around the economy appears to lag behind other countries, although this may be less true of the current wave of ICTs than in the past.

There remains, however, an apparent contradiction. As we have seen, since the early 1970s, the United Kingdom's innovation performance in terms of R&D and patents has weakened relative to that of its main competitors. And yet, TFP growth has risen relative to these same competitors over the same period. So what is the explanation. Basically, we would argue that the good performance of TFP reflects catch-up, the process being driven by the factors discussed in section 2.2. Nevertheless, there remains a TFP gap (see Tables 7.5 and 7.6) and the fundamental reasons underlying this have already been discussed at the end of section 2.2. But one of the more immediate factors relates to the picture of technological innovation which we have drawn, namely strong basic science but weak commercial follow-up. This reflects a weakness in the ability of the commercial sector to absorb basic innovations, with this weakness being directly related to low levels of R&D. It is known that R&D investments help firms absorb innovations (see Griffith et al., 1999, for strong evidence) including the output of basic science. To pursue this, and related issues, further, we turn next to the overall environment within which U.K. firms operate.

7.4. The Environment in which Firms Operate

As we have seen, the level of technological innovation in U.K. companies is comparatively low and this is one of the factors behind the TFP gap between the United Kingdom and its main competitors. In order to see why this is so, we look at a number of features of the environment within which U.K. firms operate. In turn, we consider the capital market, the labor market, education, macroeconomic policy, industry structure, property rights, openness to trade and government policies more generally.

7.4.1. The Capital Market

Overall, these are deep and liquid being very well integrated into global markets with London being one of the top three financial centers in the world. Two aspects of the capital market are particularly important for innovation, namely equity markets and the venture capital sector.

7.4.1.1. The Equity Market

This is again very liquid and is dominated by institutional investors. It is driven by shareholder value and it is structured so that mergers and acquisitions are relatively easy to undertake. There is a very active market for corporate control with "deal-making" being one of the main activities of corporate chief executives. To provide a picture of this, we present an analysis of public takeovers in Table 7.15 which reveals that the proportion of hostile takeovers in the United Kingdom is massively higher than elsewhere. What are the consequences of this? First, there is a direct consequence. Managers have a very strong incentive to avoid a hostile takeover because, in 90 percent of cases, the top management of the target company is replaced within two years (Franks and Mayer, 1992). What, then, do managers do when under threat of takeover. Basically they institute changes to improve total factor productivity and they reduce investment expenditure, particularly if the threat is hostile (Bond et al., 1998; Nuttall,

TABLE 7.15
Number of Public Takeovers (1990–4)

	Non-hostile	Hostile	Total	Percent hostile
United Kingdom	285	68	353	18
France	492	4	496	1
Germany	51	2	53	4
United States	831	27	858	3

Source: AMDATA; McKinsey Analysis in CBI (1996: Exhibit 23).

1998). This latter result might, at first sight, be interpreted as supporting a short-termist view of takeovers. However, when combined with the result on TFP, it might equally support a disciplinary view of takeovers where the hostile threat reduces managerialist overinvestment.

Despite this argument, there is no question that many commentators in the United Kingdom think that pressure from the equity market induces managers to behave in a short-termist fashion and that this explains the weakness of the R&D performance of U.K. firms. Thus, in 1986, Nigel Lawson, U.K. Chancellor of the Exchequer, remarked "The big institutional investors nowadays increasingly react to short-term pressure on investment performance ... they are unwilling to countenance long-term investment or sufficient expenditure on R&D." However, hard evidence in favor of this view is in short supply. R&D or capital expenditure announcements tend to raise stock prices (McConnell and Muscarella, 1985) and the apparently decisive econometric results in Miles (1993) are undermined by his less than convincing modelling of the risk premium. What about measures of the cost of capital? Major international studies include McCauley and Zimmer (1989) and Coopers and Lybrand (1993) and some results are reported in Table 7.16. Taking the numbers at face value certainly indicates that the cost of capital in the United Kingdom tends to be on the high side, particularly for R&D. This is partly a result of the high weight of equity relative to debt in U.K. investment funding and partly the absence of any tax breaks for R&D. However, these are average measures of the cost of capital, not marginal measures, so how revealing they are is not clear.

A final piece of evidence concerning the supply of capital to U.K. firms is the fact that the sensitivity of firm-level investment to cash flow is stronger in the United Kingdom than in Continental European countries (e.g. Bond et al., 1997, 1999). This fact could be interpreted as evidence of more severe financial constraints in the United Kingdom than elsewhere. There are alternative explanations, however. For example, current cash flow may be simply a proxy for better future demand opportunities and the greater sensitivity of U.K. firms an indication of their flexibility rather than their inability to finance projects.

Overall, U.K. managers are under considerable pressure from the stockmarket and they do appear to face somewhat higher levels of the cost of capital than their foreign counterparts. However, there is no strong evidence that this is a significant factor in explaining low levels of R&D expenditure.

7.4.1.2. Venture Capital

The U.K. has a strong venture capital sector, the largest in the European Union. However, very little U.K. venture capital goes into early-stage companies (17 percent as opposed to nearly 30 percent in Germany and the United States). Survey evidence shows that 20 percent of U.K. companies reported delay, cancellation or prevention of innovation projects. Of these, sources and cost of finance was an important

TABLE 7.16
After Tax Cost of Capital (percent)

	McCauley and Zimmer		Coopers and Lybrand
	Plant/machinery (20 year life) 1988	R&D (10 year payoff lag) 1988	1991
United Kingdom	9.2	23.7	19.9
Germany	7.0	14.8	17.5
United States	11.2	20.3	15.1
Japan	7.2	8.7	14.7

Source: Coopers and Lybrand (1993), McCauley and Zimmer (1989: Table 2).

factor in around half the cases (around twice the E.U. average). High tech businesses were more likely to encounter financial constraints. So there is some evidence of a "finance gap" for new high tech projects, although this may currently seem hard to believe, in the light of the number of new dot.com companies which have been able to raise equity capital at minimal cost.

7.4.2. The Labor Market

7.4.2.1. General Issues

The U.K. labor market is, and always has been, relatively lightly regulated. The major change since the 1970s has been the progressive disappearance of trade unions from the private sector, where union density is currently below 20 percent, having been above 50 percent in 1979. Furthermore, trade unions are now generally cooperative with regard to innovation whereas in the 1970s they were frequently hostile. Indeed, overall, trade unions are far less adversarial than they were in the 1970s as evidenced by a dramatic decline in industrial disputes. The reasons underlying this include anti-union legislation in the 1980s, increased product market competition and changes in industrial structure. Since the early 1980s, there is no reason to believe that the labor market has been an important factor in explaining the poor innovation performance of the U.K. market sector.

7.4.2.2. The Managerial Labor Market

The key feature of the labor market for the brightest and the best in the United Kingdom was dramatically expressed by Sir John Harvey-Jones, former chairman of ICI (at that time the largest manufacturing company in the United Kingdom) on a BBC Radio 4 program on the City (January 5, 1995), "When I was chairman of ICI all the advisers that we used, advisers mark you, were all paid more than I was, be they the auditors, be they the merchant banks, be they the City solicitors. Now I ask you, in realistic national terms, who is likely to have the biggest impact on the fate of the bloody country?" (reported in Owen, 1999: chapter 9).

Thus, the starting salary in GBP (percentage

growth rate over first five years) for 1995 U.K. graduates was 23K (5.5) in merchant banking, 20K (7.0) in IT consulting, 17.5K (8.2) in accountancy and 14.5K (2.0) in blue-chip engineering.[14] One of the consequences of this structure is that U.K. management is not, on average, up to the quality of that of its main competitors. Thus, for example, in a comparison of domestically owned U.K. plants with U.S.-owned U.K. plants in comparable sectors, the U.S.-owned plants have a 32 percent value-added advantage. Of this 32 percent, 18 percent is down to extra capital and higher quality labor and the remaining 14 percent is down to better management (see study by National Institute of Social and Economic Research, 1998). The managers in U.S. plants are more likely to have been trained in a "best-practice" environment.

7.4.3. Education

The U.K. education system works very well for the top 30 percent of the ability range and this is reflected in the performance of the science base. However, it is weak in both the mid-range of abilities and at the bottom end. Considering the latter first, the International Adult Literacy Survey (1994–5) shows that 23 percent of the U.K. labor force is at the lowest level in quantitative literacy (e.g., unable to check their change in a shop) compared with 21 percent in the United States and 7 percent in Germany. In the mid-range, relative to both Germany and the United States, there is a distinct weakness in education after the age of 16 in the United Kingdom for those who are not going on to degree level (see Steedman, 1999).

The upshot of this implies that science, engineering and quantitative disciplines produce high qualified manpower at a rate comparable to other OECD countries. There are, however, distinct shortages at the technician and craft level. Furthermore, because of the structure of demand, the long-term prospects of those highly qualified in science and engineering are far better in finance and consultancy than

---

[14] IDS Management Pay Review: Pay and Progression for Graduates 1995/96.

in industry. Thus, for example, in a survey of 1980 U.K. graduates, by 1987 those who worked in science and engineering tended to be rather badly paid whereas those with science and engineering degrees were, on average, rather well paid. The difference was due to those scientists and engineers who migrated to the financial sector.

7.4.4. Industry Structure

Concerning the basic industrial structure, a key feature is the very rapid decline of the proportion of employment in industry and the equally rapid rise in services since 1973. As we can see in Table 7.17, this change has been far quicker than elsewhere. More specific and perhaps relevant features of the U.K. product market environment are the following. First, the United Kingdom has had a relatively weak competition policy over the post-war period. This has allowed low levels of competition to exist in many sectors, a situation exacerbated by a desire to create national champions. Second, privatization and the consequent regulatory framework introduced in the 1980s has led to some increase in competitive intensity.

Third, the fact, as we have seen, that one of the main methods by which firms grow is via mergers and acquisitions[15] imposes substantial real resource costs as well as weakening competition in many cases. Overall, the low level of product market competition in the United Kingdom has probably been detrimental to

TABLE 7.17
Percent of Total Employment

	Industry		Services	
	1973	1994	1973	1994
United Kingdom	43	26	55	72
France	40	27	49	68
Germany	47	38	45	59
United States	33	24	63	73
OECD	37	28	52	64

Source: OECD Employment Outlook, 1996, Table D (the missing sector is agriculture).

TFP growth and, more specifically, to innovation (Geroski, 1990; Nickell, 1996).

7.4.5. Openness

The United Kingdom has a low level of trade barriers although its membership of the European Union means that it suffers from E.U.-wide trade barriers which have adversely affected both U.K. agriculture and the automobile sector by reducing competitive pressures. It is worth noting that recent research indicates an important relationship between trade openness and the rate of cross-country sectoral productivity convergence. Furthermore, R&D intensity and human capital also speed up convergence by raising the rate at which imported technology is absorbed (Proudman and Redding, 1998; Griffith et al., 1999).

7.4.6. Macroeconomic Policy

From the first oil shock in 1974 until the United Kingdom's ejection from the European Monetary System in 1992, it is safe to say that macroeconomic policy in the United Kingdom was not a great stabilizing force.[16] Over this period, U.K. firms faced more volatility than at any time since the 1930s. However, since 1992, with the onset of inflation targeting, the economy has been increasingly stable. However, whether this has impacted on productivity performance,

[15] Amazingly enough, U.K. companies spent more on foreign mergers and acquisitions than U.S. companies in 1998 (around U.S.$128 billion as opposed to U.S.$123 billion) (OECD, 1999: Table 8.2). Of course, the quantity of foreign assets available to U.S. companies is much less than that available to U.K. companies. Indeed more U.S. assets were purchased by non–U.S. companies than were purchased in the remainder of the G7.

[16] This is not a particular criticism of U.K. policy makers. The same situation applied in most countries, in part because of the size of the shocks and in part because of the lack of experience in dealing with large supply shocks. Here, the United Kingdom was notably badly placed because in 1973 it had been persuaded, by Milton Friedman, among others, that the best way to deal with shocks was to index wages. While this is fine for nominal demand shocks, for large imported commodity price shocks it is, of course, disastrous because to return to equilibrium, the real consumption wage must fall.

which improved strongly in relative terms in the early 1980s, is a moot point.

7.4.7. Government Policies

Some recent policy changes and nonchanges are relevant to some of the above. In summary, we have:

- A strong current emphasis on basic education in order to improve literacy and numeracy. Intermediate vocational education remains weak although reforms are promised.
- A new Competition Act came into force on the March 1, 1998 and this promises to be much tougher on anti-competitive practices than has been the case hitherto. This should help to raise levels of competition in the United Kingdom.
- The regulatory regimes in the utilities, telecom/IT and the financial sector are generally well thought out and tend to be focused on encouraging competition. However, there have been some notable exceptions such as the recent problems with British Telecom in unbundling the local loop.
- Labor market regulations currently strike a reasonable balance between employer and employee although the act of complying with some of the increasingly complex rules (e.g., the E.U. working time directive) imposes substantial real resource costs per employee particularly on small firms.
- Planning and building regulations are overbearing and tend to be insensitive to economic costs and benefits.
- Broadly the policy has generally been opposed to wide-ranging tax breaks in favor of innovation although an R&D tax break has, in fact, just been introduced for small firms (April, 2000). Indeed current policy is moving towards special help for SMEs, the rationale being that they face financial constraints particularly in the high tech sector. However, there is a danger here of ineffectual tinkering with complicated measures which cost little, and probably have correspondingly small effects.

7.4.8. Two Examples

To illustrate the implications of some of these features of the environment in which U.K. firms operate, we present two mini-industry studies. The first deals with the highly successful U.K. pharmaceutical sector (Box 1), the second looks at the distinctly less successful U.K. automobile industry (Box 2).

Box 1: *The U.K. Pharmaceutical Industry*

The pharmaceutical industry is a U.K. success story. Despite having only 3 percent of the world's market, almost 10 percent of world R&D in this sector is located in the United Kingdom. The R&D to value added ratio (in 1997) was higher in the United Kingdom than any other G7 country. In 1998, 22 percent of all U.K. business R&D was performed by the drugs industry, a higher share than any of the other fourteen major OECD countries. Not only is the level of R&D high, so is its productivity. For example, the ratio of first patent filings of new molecular entities (NMEs) to R&D is higher in the United Kingdom than any other major OECD country. The industry has been dominated by three players: Glaxo-Wellcome, Smithkline-Beecham and Astra-Zeneca. A remarkable number of the world's best selling drugs have come from U.K. laboratories: Tenormin (ICI), Tagamet (Smithkline), Zantac (Glaxo), Zoviraz (Wellcome) and most recently Viagra (Pfizer's R&D lab in Sandwich, Kent).

What are the reasons for success in this field, but not in other science-based sectors such as computers and semiconductors? There are basically four factors to consider: regulation, foreign investment, the academic base and an "absence of negatives." Historically, many writers have pointed to the United Kingdom's regulatory system as an enabling factor. There are two aspects to this—price and quality regulation. The Pharmaceutical Price Regulation Scheme (PPRS) [17] allows firms to launch at prices of their own choosing subject to a rate of return cap (with generous allowances for R&D spend). The advantages of the PPRS have been in its stability—its precursor was introduced in 1957—and its voluntary nature.

The U.K. drug licensing authority was one of the first (1967) requiring drugs to pass an efficacy test as well as a safety test. Regulatory approval is faster than most other European countries. This combination of fast access to market for highly effective drugs and a reasonable rate of return meant U.K. companies focused their efforts on developing world-class drugs (Thomas, 1994). The systems in France, Italy and Japan rewarded firms who develop "me too" drugs sold on the local market and penalize more innovative firms with low reimbursement prices and unstable regulation. It is noticeable that countries that have more flexible price controls and tougher quality regulation (United States, United Kingdom, Switzerland and Germany) also tend to also have a stronger pharmaceutical industry. [18]

A second argument (Owen, 1999) stresses the importance of foreign direct investment (mainly by U.S. and Swiss firms) in the 1940s and 1950s. This exposed U.K. companies to competition from innovative world leaders. [19] By contrast, many other industries were protected in the 1950s and 1960s by high tariffs or procurement policies. The National Health Service (founded in 1948) provided stable and high demand, support for clinical trials, and unlike many European systems did not discriminate between national and international suppliers. Fortunately, there was no attempt to create "national champions" in pharmaceuticals.

All these arguments may explain *historically* why the U.K. industry has grown strong, but inertia apart, they can no longer be the main reason why the industry continues to be an important R&D base. There are no strong reasons why drug discovery, clinical trials, or even manufacturing (within the European Union) need to be located in markets where regulation is better or the market is larger.

A more compelling explanation of why the United Kingdom remains a popular location for R&D is the strong tradition of biomedical research (see Table 7.14). Scientific labor is less mobile than capital, so the proximity to research centers enables companies to capture both skilled labor and new ideas. This is particularly important for world class scientists, but also for the steady flow of pharmacology graduates. The strong academic science base would also explain why foreign firms locate their R&D laboratories in the United Kingdom.

The United Kingdom also has more biotechnology firms than any other E.U. country. This industry is reliant on a strong academic science base in biomedicine—for example, the cluster around Cambridge. The presence of sophisticated capital markets and corporate venturing by the larger pharmaceutical firms are also factors in success.

Finally, the industry has been largely free of the negatives affecting other U.K. industries. The manufacturing aspect is minor compared to the R&D and marketing aspects. Thus the United Kingdom's traditional weakness in manufacturing due to poor intermediate skills, labor relations troubles and delayed entry into the European Union [20] were relatively unimportant.

---

[17] See Bloom and Van Reenen (1998) for a more extended discussion.

[18] Of course the causality may be reversed. Lobbying by strong indigenous drugs companies could result in more favorable regulations.

[19] This was hardly welcomed by the locals. The CEO of Glaxo, Sir Harry Jephcott, concluded a 1957 study with the grim warning "having regard to the weight of certain US companies in men and money it is only a matter of time before the British firms were swamped out of existence ..." (Owen, 1999: 371).

[20] The European market is far more fragmented in pharmaceuticals due to different national regulations.

Box 2: *The U.K. Automobile Industry*

A Brief Post-war History
In the 1950s, the U.K. car industry was booming. Output rose from 523 thousand units in 1950 to 1353 thousand units in 1960 and had risen to close on 2 million by the mid-1960s (Owen, 1999: chapter 9). This level was maintained until the early 1970s, then halved over the next decade. From the mid-1980s there has been a significant recovery.

In the 1950s, the U.K. industry was dominated by three domestically owned companies, BMC, Rootes and Standard, and two American owned companies, Ford and Vauxhall (GM). By the end of the 1960s, there was one domestically owned company, British Leyland (BL), the "national champion." At the present time (2000), the national champion (Rover) has all but disappeared but three Japanese manufacturers (Nissan, Honda, Toyota) are major players, and Ford and Vauxhall remain strong. So we have a post-war history of two phases, a significant decline from the 1960s to the 1980s followed by a strong recovery.

Why the Decline?
(i)   The United Kingdom's failure to join the European Common Market in 1958. From 1958 to 1972, when the United Kingdom joined, the U.K. car industry faced substantial barriers to trade in what was then the fastest growing and most competitive mass car market in the world.
(ii) The creation and subsequent mismanagement of British Leyland. More or less all the nonforeign owned U.K. car firms were merged in 1968, essentially because the then Labour government believed that the way to strengthen U.K. industry was to create "national champions." This turned out to be a disaster, reducing domestic competition while creating a disparate and ramshackle entity which was, apparently, impossible to manage.
(iii) Finally, the whole of the U.K. car industry, foreign and domestically owned, was beset by very poor labor relations.

The upshot of these factors was that by 1980, the U.K. car industry produced less than one-third of the cars produced in either France or Germany. The engineering skills were there and cars like the Mini, the Land-Rover and the Jaguar E-type were designed, produced and sold in large numbers. But the techniques, management skills and effort required to compete success-fully in the high volume sector of the market were missing, partly because of the absence of strong enough incentives. Given this dire situation, why did things get better?

Why the Recovery?
By the late 1970s, it had become clear to car makers around the world that the Japanese had invented a system for designing and making cars which was vastly more effective than any used elsewhere. When Bill Hayden, head of manufacturing in Ford of Europe, went to Japan in 1978, he remarked subsequently that he could not believe the magnitude of the productivity gap (Owen, 1999: 246). The methods used by the Japanese manufacturers became widely known within a short space of time and every car manufacturer in the world now uses them to some degree.

As a consequence, the U.K. car industry benefited greatly from the fact that Nissan, Toyota and Honda all built car plants in the United Kingdom in the 1980s. This Japanese invasion had a substantial positive impact both on the other foreign-owned car producers and on the supplying industries. For example, in 1992 the average rejection rate of parts from Nissan's U.K. supplier base was 1,180 per million. By 1995 it was down to 190 per million (McKinsey,

1998). The introduction of efficient new plants in the United Kingdom and the consequent spill-over effects has meant that car production is now getting close to its 1960s peak.

Yet the impact of the new Japanese car plants (which produce around one-quarter of U.K. cars) should not be overstated. On average, these Japanese transplants in the United Kingdom remain around *twice* as productive as the remaining plants. So why do the latter not simply adopt global (Japanese) best-practice methods? It is not because of any lack of high tech automotive engineering skills in the United Kingdom. For example, nearly all Formula 1 racing cars are made in the United Kingdom and most racing teams are based there. In fact, the basic problem is that the non–Japanese plants do not have a big enough incentive to undertake what is a complex and time consuming activity (switching to best practice). Voluntary trade restrictions limit Japanese manufacturers' share of U.K. (and other big European) export markets. These restrictions encourage Japanese manufacturers to maintain their prices in line with domestic producers rather than using their productivity advantage to cut prices and increase market share. This has obviously weakened the competitive pressure on non–Japanese domestic producers, resulting in persistently low productivity, with the high price umbrella enabling the relatively unproductive plants to continue operating as they are. This situation contrasts with that in the United States, where domestic car manufacturers have been subject to unrestrained Japanese competition and have, as a consequence, improved their productivity performance by substantially more than their U.K. counterparts.

The Overall Picture

The U.K. car industry presents a typical example of some widespread problems in the U.K. economy. The fact that the United Kingdom dominates the world in the construction of specialized racing cars shows its excellence at high tech automotive engineering. But this excellence does not translate into the ability to use best practice in mass vehicle manufacture even when examples of such best practice are just around the corner. One of the reasons is that for a substantial part of the post-war period, the U.K. car industry has not been subject to the full blast of international competition—in the 1960s because the United Kingdom was outside the European Common Market, in the 1980s and 1990s because of Japanese quotas. Furthermore, domestic competition was deliberately emasculated by the misguided desire to create a national champion. This lack of competition severely restricted the incentives for the domestic companies to go through the difficult process of adopting best-practice techniques.

7.5. The Final Picture

Over the period from 1970, the United Kingdom has improved its relative productivity performance, but there remains a significant market sector productivity gap between the United Kingdom and both Continental Europe and the United States. Much of the gap between the United Kingdom and Continental Europe is down to lower levels of capital intensity and skill. However, between the United Kingdom and the United States, there remains a signifi-cant gap even if these are taken into account. These gaps cover all sectors and reflect not just a weakness in high tech areas but an inability to absorb best-practice technology and methods into wide swathes of the market sector. Underlying causes here include low levels of product market competition, high levels of product market regulation and general lack of exposure to best-practice methods and technology.

Part of this story is a weakness in technological innovation despite a high quality science base. This includes comparatively low and falling levels of R&D and patenting as well as a distinct lag in the diffusion of innovations. Specific factors underlying this weakness in the commercial application of technology innovations include the following:

- There is some evidence that financing constraints are important despite a thriving venture capital sector. Many also consider short-termism to be a significant factor but there is little hard evidence to support this commonly held view.
- While the education system is excellent for those at the upper end of the ability range, the structure in place for post-school vocational education is weak and this leads to a noticeable shortfall in technician skills which holds back the absorption of innovations.
- General management skills are not as highly valued as skills in finance, accounting and consultancy in the U.K. labor market, so the brightest graduates (science or arts) tend to go into the latter areas. Furthermore,

because a large proportion of U.K. companies are not operating at the frontier of best practice, the majority of managers learn the job in a non-best-practice environment. This, of itself, inhibits the generation and absorption of innovations.
- Until the early 1980s, the rising power of trade unions and their adversarial nature sometimes militated against innovation. This problem no longer applies.
- Underlying the above has been an overall weakness in competitive intensity in the U.K. economy in many sectors. This weakness is gradually being eroded with deregulation in various product markets, privatization and strengthened legislation against anti-competitive practices. In some sectors, however, there is a good way to go.
- Finally, in recent years, the macroeconomy has been far more stable than of late and the structure of both monetary and fiscal policy is geared to maintaining this stability. This should help the overall investment climate for firms.

8

The Nordic Countries

Matti Virén and Markku Malkamäki

8.1. Introduction

The Nordic countries—Denmark, Finland, Norway, and Sweden—offer an interesting case for the analysis of technological innovation and economic performance. In these countries, technological innovations have clearly affected the economy and society as a whole. They have also, for the first time, had an effect on world markets. Four out of ten mobile phones are produced in these countries, with a similar level of dominance on the infrastructure side.

Although the Nordic countries are, at least from the non–European viewpoint, very similar, there are substantial differences between them, particularly with respect to innovation systems. These differences make it possible to distinguish critical factors for technological change.

The Nordic countries (Denmark, Finland, Norway, and Sweden) have much in common: political institutions, the legal system, religion, living standards, and even language to some extent. At one point in time they even belonged to the same kingdom.[1] As for economics, all the countries are small open economies and all are typically characterized as generous welfare states. Indeed, the Nordic countries, Sweden in particular, have often been cited in international comparisons as extreme examples of the size of the public sector and the welfare system. Another typical feature of these countries is the power of trade unions. Union membership has been among the highest in the world. Although some changes have taken place, the Nordic countries can be characterized by strong collective trade unions and extensive welfare systems.

A large public sector and high taxes have not been the only factors that have affected market conditions in the past. Perhaps the most important factor is capital market regulation and credit rationing. In Finland, Norway, and Sweden capital markets were heavily regulated until the mid-1980s (in Denmark most controls were abolished in the 1970s). Regulation took the form of interest rate ceilings and quantitative credit rationing schemes. This served to strengthen old-fashioned firm–bank relationships (in contrast to the Anglo-Saxon financial market approach). After the abolition of domestic capital market controls and restrictions on capital movements, financial markets in the Nordic countries started to develop very quickly. Overall efficiency increased, thereby lowering the cost of funding. Also, the discriminatory border between "new" and "old" firms has largely disappeared, and within the financial sector an intensive search for new technically advanced operating techniques has begun (providing a major boost to telebanking, for example). In the case of Finland, Norway, and Sweden, quite severe banking crises (comparable to the U.S. Savings and Loan bank crisis) in the early 1990s also contributed to this development.[2]

We are grateful to Erkki Koskela, David Mayes, Richard Nelson, Benn Steil and David Victor for very useful comments and Ville Haukkamaa and Heli Tikkunen for research assistance.

[1] Since the mid-1950s the Nordic countries (the above-mentioned countries plus Iceland) have had a common labor market and citizens have been able to move from country to country without passports. All of the countries are members of the Nordic Council and this has perhaps made the biggest contribution in the area of harmonization of civil laws.

[2] The banking crisis can be regarded as a consequence of financial market liberalization. Macroeconomic shocks and policy as well as failures in financial supervision also contributed to the crisis.

TABLE 8.1
Some Basic Features of the Nordic Countries

	Denmark	Finland	Norway	Sweden
Population (millions)	5.4	5.2	4.4	8.9
GDP per capita (U.S.$)	23300	20100	24700	19700
Size of public sector[a]	57.4	50.0	51.0	56.8
NATO/EU/EMU membership	NATO EU	EU EMU	NATO	EU
Exports/GDP (percent)	35.7	37.6	40.8	38.9
Union membership as percentage of total workforce[b]	76	81	58	91

[a] General government taxes and nontax receipts as a percentage of GDP. *Source:* http://www.odci.gov/cia/publications/factbook. The data are for 1998.
[b] The U.S. number is only 13.5.

A summary of some basic statistics on the economies of the Nordic countries is given in Table 8.1.

Recently there have been some striking differences in the economic performance and growth prospects of these countries. Finland, which lagged far behind the other three countries in the early 1970s, both in terms of living standards and technological development, caught up with the other three in the 1990s and become a technology leader in Europe and to some extent globally. Sweden has also made remarkable progress in terms of technological innovations, while the other two countries have not made significant progress in this area. To some extent, the differences are even larger than between, say, the United States and Germany. Clearly, these different development patterns warrant an examination of the causal factors. In the case of the Nordic countries, we can trace back to the most important policy choices and other economic determinants to explain why such large differences have emerged among the Nordic countries, and why Finland and Sweden (as opposed to Denmark and Norway) have been so successful in developing the "new economy" over the last ten years. The main argument is that both Finland and Sweden have undergone deep structural change, partly due to the problems of the early 1990s, which represents an interesting example of so-called "creative destruction."

To obtain some perspective on the performance of the Nordic countries, we compare these countries' indicators with those of Germany, the United Kingdom and the United States. Germany represents continental Europe while the United Kingdom represents a mixture of the U.S. and continental European models.

In some cases, the data do not allow for a complete comparison of these seven countries, and we have to concentrate on the Nordic countries only. In some cases, we focus on Finland and Sweden alone because of lack of data and also because we want to examine in most detail the cases where technological innovations have been of substantial importance.

8.2. Performance of the Nordic Countries

This section reviews developments in some basic indicators of economic performance in the Nordic countries. The indicators mainly consist of output, consumption and productivity, thus emphasizing developments on the real side of the economy. Given these indicators, we make a preliminary assessment of the role of technological innovation in growth in these countries. A more detailed review of the technological innovations is presented in section 8.3.

On a practical level, the performance of the Nordic countries is illustrated by the following indicators:

- growth in gross domestic product (GDP)
- (private) consumption per capita
- labor and total productivity

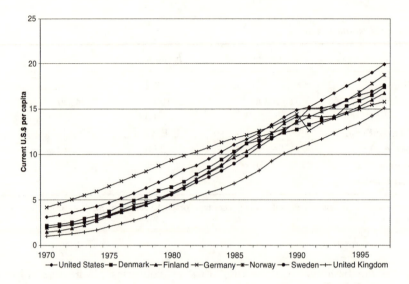

Figure 8.1 Private consumption per capita, 1970–1997. *Source:* OECD Main Economic Indicators. The data correspond to private consumption at current U.S.$ market prices divided by mid-year population.

• stock market capitalization rate.

The evolution of (private) consumption per capita, labor productivity and stock market capitalization rates is illustrated in Figures 8.1–8.3 and a summary of the other indicators is given in Table 8.2.

Starting with the per capita consumption figures, there were not many dramatic changes

over the thirty-year period. The most striking was German reunification, but in the case of the Nordic countries very little happened. In the early 1990s, Finland experienced an exceptionally severe depression, which is reflected in a substantial output gap and exceptionally high unemployment for most of the 1990s. Although the other Nordic countries also experienced economic difficulties at the same time, none

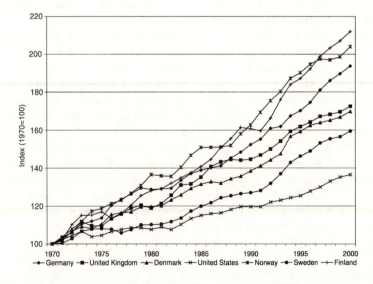

Figure 8.2 Labor productivity, 1970–2000, 1970 = 100. *Source:* OECD National Accounts.

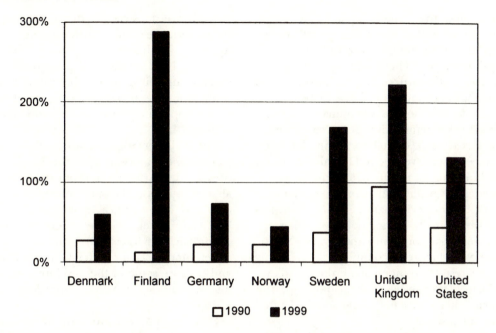

Figure 8.3 Stock market capitalization as a percentage of GDP, 1990 and 1999. *Source:* Bloomberg L.P. data bank.

suffered from substantial output losses. Thus, for instance, Norway had quite favorable growth throughout the whole decade, which explains the current high living standards.

For the period from 1970 to 1998, Norway had the highest growth rate and Sweden the lowest. To some extent these growth rates reflect convergence of GDP (per capita) levels. This convergence is particularly evident for

Finland, which also shows some acceleration of growth towards the end of the 1990s.

The growth rate differences do not, however, tell the whole story regarding the growth performance. A look at the productivity figures reveals a great deal about the rate of efficiency and the technological channel. Thus, in the case of Norway, labor productivity growth is very high but TFP clearly lags behind Finland,

TABLE 8.2
Growth Performance of the Nordic Countries 1970–98

	Denmark	Finland	Germany	Norway	Sweden	United Kingdom	United States
GDP growth	2.22	2.71	2.29	3.44	1.71	2.15	2.87
GDP growth 1995–9	2.74	4.19	1.96	3.08	2.42	2.29	3.36
Employment growth	0.46	0.20	0.09	1.07	0.17	0.33	1.84
Productivity growth	1.76	2.51	2.21	2.36	1.54	1.82	1.04
GDP per capita growth	1.96	2.21	1.16	3.13	1.29	1.99	1.84
SD of GDP growth	1.88	2.99	1.82	1.73	1.90	2.14	2.14
Total factor productivity (TFP) growth	1.47	3.25	1.31	0.41	2.08	1.80	1.30
TFP growth 1996–9	0.31	3.70	1.07	1.13	1.32	0.95	1.80

All numbers are percentage values.
Source: OECD data CD. The TFP values for 1996–9 are derived from Gust and Marquez (2000). Swedish data are 1996–8.
Notes: Except for the standard deviation (SD) of GDP growth, the numbers are the average growth rates of the respective variables for the period 1970–98 (for GDP and TFP, also 1995/6–9).

Sweden and the United States. This simply reflects the fact that Norwegian growth is very much related to the oil industry being highly capital intensive. Thus, high growth and a high living standard cannot be attributed to technological change in the case of Norway.

Finland is just the opposite in that growth has been achieved mainly without increasing physical inputs (in fact, capital deepening has been negative for some years), and this also shows up in all indicators of technological innovation.

Sweden is somewhat similar to Finland although the performance figures are less impressive. Finally, Denmark has it own story, which has less in common with the other Nordic countries and more in common with Germany and the rest of continental European.[3] Thus, productivity growth has in fact slowed down in Denmark, in contrast to Finland and the United States, for instance.

At this point, we also take a brief look at the financial dimension of development by examining movements in stock prices, namely the stock market capitalization ratios for the countries in our sample. Figure 8.3 shows that the Nordic countries fall into two categories: Denmark and Norway forming one group and Finland and Sweden the other. In the case of Sweden and—even more so—Finland, the growth of the information and communication technology sectors is evident in market expectations of high future growth rates.

8.3. The Record of Technological Innovation

On the basis of the TFP figures we would expect to find that Denmark and Norway have quite a low profile in terms of technological innovation, while Finland and Sweden have made important advances in this area. To see whether this or a related hypothesis is true, we scrutinize a relatively large set of indicators of technological innovation. We start with indicators that

characterize the structure of the economy and the importance of the information and communication technology sectors. Indicators comprise both volume and price data. Sector-specific and firm-specific indicators are not dealt with here although we comment on the most important specific developments in section 8.4.

The indicators used to illustrate the record of technological innovation in the Nordic countries are: the structure of production; the overall development of communications technology; and the technical developments in the financial markets. We pay special attention to the financial markets, partly because they are of key importance for both Finland and Sweden and because some of the developments are of interest outside the Nordic countries and even Europe.

First we report some descriptive statistics for the structure of economy (see Table 8.3 and Figures 8.4–8.6). We use a fairly simple measure for this purpose: the share of high-tech industries in total manufacturing industry. Two definitions (a narrow one and a broad one) for high-tech industries are used here. This is, of course, a somewhat old-fashioned measure because it only focuses on manufacturing and does not include services. Consequently, a broader measure is also introduced later. In addition to production shares, we focus on a specific "export specialization index" in which we compute export shares in relation to average values from the OECD (see Table 8.3 and Figure 8.7).[4]

---

[3] An obvious question in this connection is how much of the accelerated growth in Finland and Sweden is due to high-tech. In Finland, a typical estimate is one-third (of the growth rate of, say, 5 percent). The Swedish estimates point in the same direction although they are somewhat lower.

[4] The export specialization indexes are computed using the following comparative advantage indexes: $R_{ij} = (X_{ij}/X_i)/(X_j/X)$ where R_{ij} is the export specialization index for country i in commodity j (here high-tech); X_{ij} is the exports from country i of commodity j; X_i is the total exports from country i; X_j is the total OECD exports of commodity j; and X is the total OECD exports. If $R_{ij} > 1$, country i has some comparative advantage in terms of commodity j and vice versa. As the United States dominates so heavily in high-tech exports, we have also computed the index so that instead of X_j/X we use the country average of this ratio for the OECD area. The values are quite different because the country average of export shares for the OECD is (in 1996) is 19.2 while the corresponding total export share is 24.3 percent.

TABLE 8.3

Indicators of the Growth of R&D Intensive Industries

		Denmark	Finland	Germany	Norway	Sweden	United Kingdom	United States
Total output	1978	5.83	4.11	12.14	5.53	8.89	10.97	12.75
	1996	7.47	14.69	14.12	6.10	15.85	9.37	18.06
Value-added	1978	8.47	5.59	15.77	8.70	11.96	13.77	16.32
	1996	8.47	16.77	15.41	6.99	12.04	10.44	20.52
Employment	1978	8.78	6.88	16.39	7.44	12.94	14.96	17.50
	1996	8.70	16.16	18.28	8.14	13.78	13.19	18.16
Exports	1978	10.74	4.56	15.61	5.17	13.05	17.97	25.38
	1996	16.16	22.00	20.03	10.62	24.84	30.25	38.05
Export specialization index (EXS)	1978	1.17	0.50	1.69	0.56	1.41	1.95	2.76
	1996	0.84	1.15	1.04	0.55	1.26	1.58	1.88
Export specialization share (EXSS)	1978	0.70	0.30	1.02	0.34	0.85	1.18	1.66
	1996	0.67	0.91	0.82	0.44	1.00	1.25	1.48

Source: OECD STAN database.

Notes: Values denote the percentage share of production, value-added, employment and exports of high R&D intensity industries in total manufacturing industry. EXS and EXSS denote the export specialization indexes (explained in footnote 4): for EXS the point of comparison is the country average of export share while EXSS is the export share of total exports of OECD countries. The high R&D industries are defined according to the following ISIC categories: 3825 (office machinery and computers); 383 (electrical machinery); 3845 (aerospace); and 385 (scientific industries).

In trying to describe the R&D or "high tech" intensive industries and the information and communication technology sectors, we face several conceptual and measurement problems. First, all classifications are typically based on quite broad sector aggregates. Thus, when we speak about R&D intensive sectors, we have to include production which is not necessarily R&D intensive or high-tech (and at the same time disregard such production in other sectors). Typically, this classification assumes that the whole of the aerospace industry is

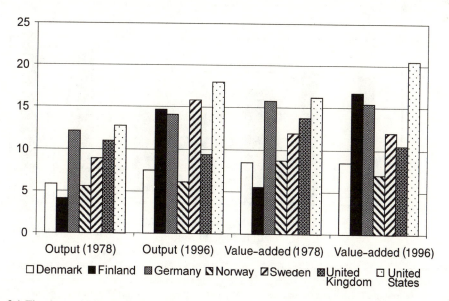

Figure 8.4 The share of R&D intensive sectors as a percentage of total output. Source: OECD STAN database.

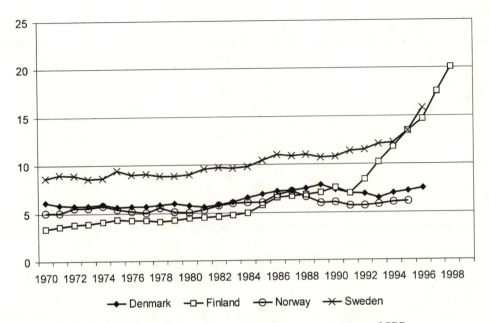

Figure 8.5 Production in R&D intensive sectors as a percentage of GDP.

R&D intensive and belongs to the high-tech sector, which may be a bit misleading. Because this industry is very large in some countries (especially in the United States and the United Kingdom) and almost nonexistent in other countries (Denmark and Norway), the indicators reflect the role of the airspace industry very (too?) strongly.

Another problem is related to the basic definition of the information and communication technology sector. What is to be included: only production, or services as well? Here we follow some alternative routes, reporting values (for the Nordic countries only) which correspond to the whole of the (ICT) sector (Figure 8.10). Alternatively, we report values which reflect

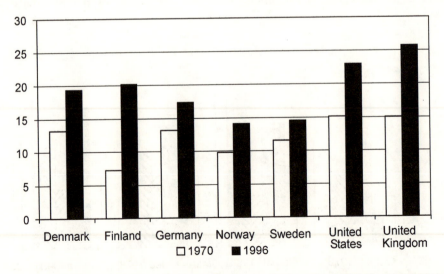

Figure 8.6 The share of R&D intensive sectors (broad definition) as a percentage of GDP. The high R&D industries are defined according to the following ISIC categories: 342, Printing and publishing; 3533, Drugs and medicine; 3825, Office machinery and computers; 383, Electrical machinery; 3845, Aerospace; 385, Scientific industries. *Source:* OECD STAN database.

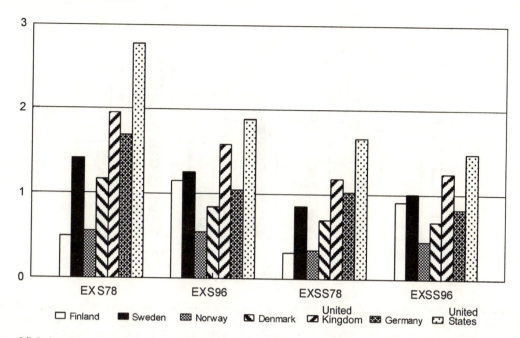

Figure 8.7 Index of export specialization of R&D intensive sectors (see Table 8.3 and footnote 4 for definitions). *Source:* OECD STAN database.

expenditure (investment) on information technology only (and a separate value for the size of the telecommunications sector; see Figure 8.9).

All the indicators convey a very similar message: Finland, which lagged well behind all the other Nordic countries and the other three comparison countries for almost two decades, 1970–90, has become either a technology leader or at least a country which is very close to the leading edge.[5] Sweden, which started from a relatively high level, has managed to maintain its high position and even to improve in many respects, although in relative terms (relative to Finland) its position has deteriorated somewhat. By contrast, Denmark and, even more so Norway, have almost stagnated. Because of the very high standard of living, these countries have some favorable indicators of technological innovation (computer, internet and mobile phone densities), but in general their position in all production-related indicators is quite poor.

The indicators for the share of the R&D and "high-tech" sectors show that Finland and Sweden differ quite clearly from Denmark and Norway. In the latter countries there is no visible sign of any change in the role of R&D intensive sectors.[6] A similar outcome emerges when we examine the data for high-tech patents (Figure 8.8). In this respect, Finland and Sweden have a clear lead over all other countries. With all patents, there seems to be no clear pattern that is invariant over time.[7]

[5] The most recent (1998) Finnish values are quite impressive. Thus, Y98 = 20.08, VA98 = 21.96, E98 = 16.21 and Ex98 = 30.05.

[6] More generally, Finland seems to differ from the sample countries in terms of persistence of the overall structure of industrial production. Thus, when regressing the 1997 industry shares of production with the 1970 shares, R^2 turns out to be 0.52 while in other countries this statistic varies between 0.80 and 0.96 (Germany and the United States have the highest values).

[7] Thus, data for 1997 differ considerably from the 1998 data (Finland and Sweden have the highest values and Denmark and Norway by far lowest values). In addition to these timing problems, one should be aware of the problems and limitations of using patents as indicators of innovative activity. A more accurate description of the state of the art could be obtained by using copyright data as supplementary information (concerning the ICT service sector, in particular).

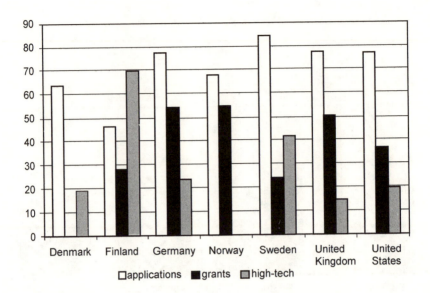

Figure 8.8 Applications for and grants of patents 1998. Applications denote patent applications filed by residents (per 100,000 inhabitants). Grants are defined similarly while the high-tech patent applications are related to one million inhabitants. Data for Denmark and Norway are somewhat deficient. *Data source:* WIPO IP/STAT/1998/A/Patents and Eurostat.

In the case of information technology expenditure and the size of both the telecommunications sector and the entire information and communications technology sector, the country differences are smaller, probably because the concept is too broad for our purposes (see Figures 8.8 and 8.9). Notice, however, that the country ranking seems to be quite systematic and that Norway is again far behind the other Nordic countries.

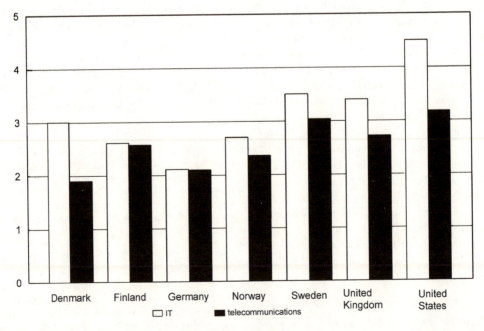

Figure 8.9 Expenditure on information technology (IT) and communications as a percentage of GDP. *Source:* European Information Technology Observatory (1999) and Telecommunication Statistics (1999).

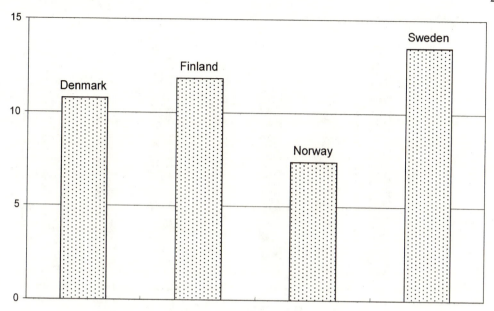

Figure 8.10 The GDP share of the information and communication technology sector in the Nordic countries as a percentage of GDP. *Source:* Nordic Council of Ministers (1998).

A clearer picture emerges when we examine the density of computer and Internet hosts (Figure 8.11). Finland and Sweden are quite close to the United States while the other comparison countries (Germany and the United Kingdom) are at a substantially lower level. The same pattern emerges in the case of mobile telephones, where Finland is a market

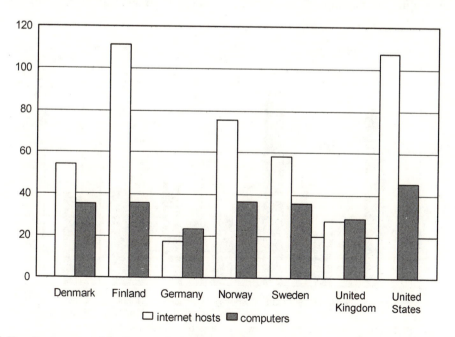

Figure 8.11 Use of computers and the Internet. *Source:* Telecommunication Statistics (1999) and The World Competitiveness Yearbook (1998). Computers per 100 inhabitants and Internet hosts per 1000 inhabitants.

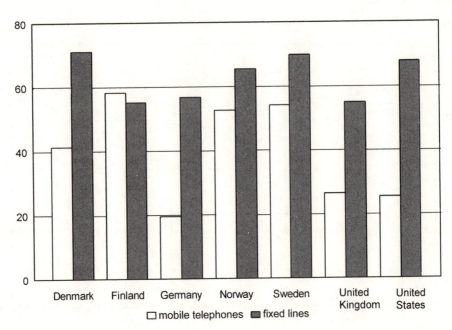

Figure 8.12 Telephone subscribers (per 100 inhabitants). *Source:* Telecommunication Statistics (1999).

leader (Figure 8.12). Not only are the volumes (densities) high in Finland, but prices are also very low (both mobile telephone charges and data communication charges). Obviously these two factors are interrelated (Figures 8.13 and 8.14). Here one might imagine that some sort of economies of scale argument can explain the data; for example, increased volumes are reflected in lower marginal costs. The data for computers, mobile phones and so on obviously reflect the consumption side of high tech; as the cases of Denmark and Norway show, consump-

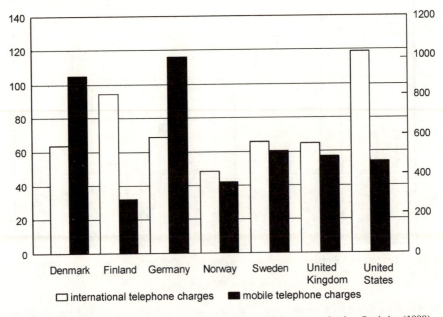

Figure 8.13 Index of telecommunication charges. *Source:* Telecommunication Statistics (1999).

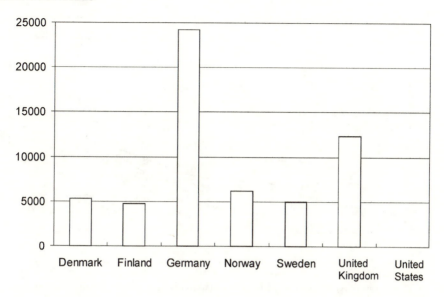

Figure 8.14 Index of data communication charges. *Source:* Telecommunications Statistics (1999). Data for the United States were not available.

tion and production do not necessarily develop in a similar manner.

The Nordic countries' good performance in information and communication technology indicators does not necessarily extend to other areas of technological development. Thus, for instance, biotechnology has not made similar progress, although there have been some serious research and development efforts. One

reason is simply time: interest in biotechnology has arisen, only very recently.

Finally, the evolved structure of the capital markets and developments in payment systems and banking technology merit some comment. The technical sophistication of the payment system is typically measured by the extent of cash used in transactions; that is, the more cash used, the more old fashioned the system

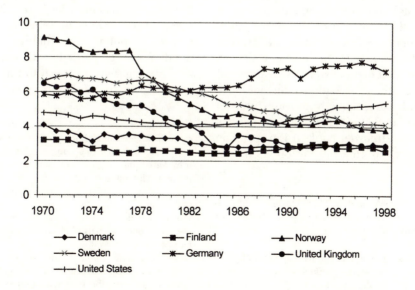

Figure 8.15 Currency outside banks as a percentage of GDP. *Source:* BIS (1998).

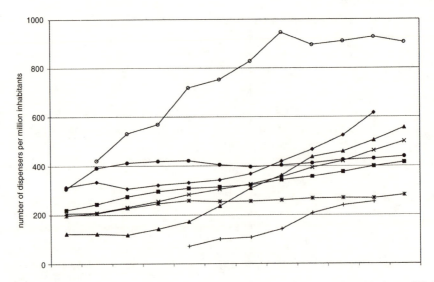

Figure 8.16 The density of ATMs and cash dispensers (total number per million inhabitants). *Source:* BIS (1998).

tends to be. Another measure is the extent to which devices such as ATMs and cash dispensers are used instead of bank offices.

We do know the extent to which cash is used in transactions. We measure this by the amount of cash in circulation outside banks; that is, cash held by the public. Figure 8.15 shows that cash outside banks in relation to GDP is very low in Finland, which is an indication that other means of payment are widely used.[8] Analogously, we find that the number of cash dispensers and ATMs in relation to population is much higher in Finland than in other sample countries (see Figure 8.16). In fact, the Finnish figures already show signs of decline, which, in turn, suggests that many customers have started to use more advanced banking facilities. All major Finnish banks already provide Internet banking services.[9] Merita-Nordbanken is actually the leading Internet bank in Europe. The vast majority of its Internet customers are in

Finland, where all big banks have offered price incentives to encourage the use of new banking technologies (see European Central Bank, 1999; Salomon et al., 1999; Warburg et al., 2000).[10]

8.4. Identification of the Factors Behind Technological Innovations

In this section we address the question of why the four Nordic countries have followed such a different course in terms of technological innovation. To put it a bit differently—why have Sweden and, in particular, Finland succeeded in achieving such high growth through techno-

---

[8] In the case of Germany and the United States, a considerable part is held by foreigners, but that probably does not explain the whole difference.

[9] Unfortunately, we do not have comparable figures for the use of telebanking and Internet banking services. Given the fragmentary evidence that we do have, we believe that Finland is also a market leader in this respect.

[10] The scale of e-commerce is obviously one interesting indicator of the level of technological innovation. Recent data (although somewhat deficient) suggest that Nordic countries have quite high penetration rates (Denmark 0.20 percent, Finland also 0.20 percent, Norway 0.26 percent and Sweden 0.68 percent). In fact, the Swedish figures well exceed the U.S. figures (0.48 percent). See OECD (2000a) for details. The figures presented above reflect just one (concrete) part of electronic commerce. A recent Finnish survey showed that 80 percent of (Finnish) enterprises have some form of sales via the Internet which suggests that the importance of electronic commerce is much larger than the reported business to consumer e-commerce penetration rates.

logical innovation and successful adaptation of innovations in production? In answering this question, we cite a rather lengthy list of factors to provide different viewpoints in identifying the critical elements. We are also interested in factors or explanations which do not explain the differences in technological progress.

We argue that the good performance of Finland and Sweden (and not so good performance of Denmark and Norway) is no surprise. We expect the answers to be found in changes in the market environment, investment in R&D, and government policies, which have all contributed to successful structural change. Although we find some fascinating stories of innovation and the growth process at the company level, the main lines of development can still be traced back to these (macroeconomic) fundamentals. Moreover, it seems well-founded to characterize the process which changed the Finnish and Swedish production systems as "constructive destruction."[11]

Next we discuss in a little more detail the country evidence using this hypothesis as a starting point, with particular emphasis on the Finnish experience, which represents a clear-cut example in terms of policy changes and changes in the market environment. The Swedish story is similar in many respects, while Denmark and Norway require some different arguments.

8.4.1. Capital Markets

In the Nordic countries, the most important event in recent history was the abolition of capital controls and the introduction of modern contestable financial market regulation in the mid-1980s. All major restrictions on capital movements were then abolished in all the Nordic countries. Figure 8.18 shows that investment flows out of and into these countries expanded many-fold, Sweden and Finland being the most active investors and destinations

for investment. Foreign ownership of listed companies has increased being highest in Finland, where foreign investors held about 74 percent of the total market value and 41 percent of the total number of shares of listed companies at the end of 2000. Since then, the Nordic countries have been able to benefit from relatively competitive and efficient capital markets. One indication of this process is the fact that interest rates gaps vis-à-vis major European countries (e.g., Germany) have shrunk to practically zero.[12]

The change has dramatically affected the structure of financial markets and corporate governance. The traditional bank-centered system was largely replaced by market-driven instruments and control mechanisms. Bank deposits have lost their dominant role; they now represent only about 10 percent of financial claims in, for example, Finland. The role of the stock market has increased because of large issues and a sharp rise in stock indexes. This development has also changed the behavior of firms with regard to investment and risk-taking, with a switch in favor of new areas and products at the cost of traditional production.

The changes in capital markets are evident in the dramatic growth of direct investment and portfolio investment in the 1990s (see Figure 8.18). In all four countries, inward portfolio investment has increased more than outward portfolio investment. Here, too, Finland is an extreme example of such flows, especially considering the size of the economy. This development is reflected in the share of foreign ownership. While in the 1980s Nordic firms were typically domestically owned, foreign ownership is now significant in large Finnish and Swedish firms. Foreign ownership has also improved corporate governance, which used to be bank-dominated before capital market liberalization and the banking crisis.

Foreign direct investment is perhaps the most important factor that helps technology transfer between countries and firms. Another way to transfer is a technology alliance in which two or more firms cooperate in technological devel-

---

[11] One may quote here the chief executive of Nokia, Jorma Ollila, who says: "The deep recession at the start of 1990s forced us to restructure for the new economy much earlier than other European countries. We had to be radical." (*Financial Times*, May 11, 2000).

[12] Interest rate developments obviously reflect changes in inflation and exchanges rates (see Figure 8.17).

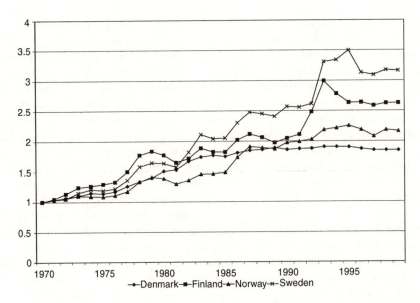

Figure 8.17 Exchange rates vis-à-vis the German Deutschmark (1970 = 1). *Source:* Bank of Finland database.

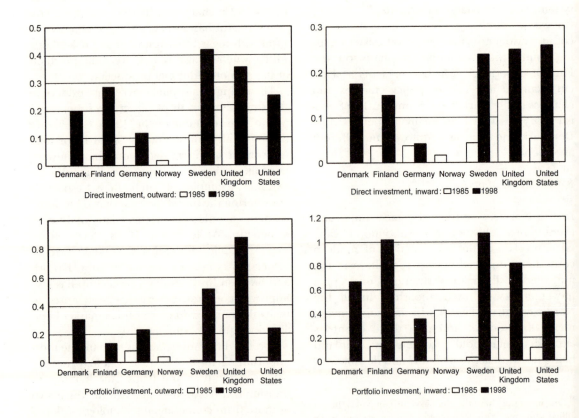

Figure 8.18. Direct and portfolio investment: outward and inward investment, 1985 and 1988. *Source:* International Financial Statistics. All figures are expressed as GDP ratios. In the case of Norway, only 1990 values are available and for Germany, the 1998 values have been replaced by 1997 values.

opment (and possibly also in production and marketing). Data on these alliances suggest that Sweden has succeeded rather well in this respect. Thus, for instance, there are about the same number of U.S.–Swedish technological alliances as U.S.–Italian alliances. Finland is much behind Sweden in this respect, while Denmark and Norway are even further behind (Pajarinen et al., 1998). Clearly, small open economies can greatly benefit from globalization, which is so often forgotten when discussing the harmful consequences of this phenomenon.

Adoption of new banking technologies has been a common feature in all the Nordic countries. The Finnish banks are the technology leaders within this country group and perhaps also in the global context, as was seen from Figure 8.16. They have succeeded in encouraging their retail customers to use remote electronic services. This has enabled them to cut the number of physical branches by about 50 percent and to halve the number of employees in less than ten years. At the same time, their profitability has increased remarkably, and is among the highest in the world. Thus, the return on equity in banks in Finland increased from 6.1 percent in 1990 to 27.4 percent in 1998. In Sweden, the comparable change was from 9.4 percent to 15.6 percent, while in Denmark the returns actually decreased from 20.0 percent to 15.5 percent.

These drastic developments are due to a number of factors. First, Finland was over-banked in the early 1990s. It had the highest density of bank branches and cash dispensers and ATMs. Second, the severe banking crisis forced the banks to cut costs. Third, the new technology enabled capacity reductions in the traditional service channels; that is, branches and personnel. However, the biggest cost savings were made possible by multipurpose ATMs and Internet banking in the mid- and late-1990s. Fourth, banks differentiated pricing of bill payments and money transfers so as to create strong incentives for retail customers to start using electronic remote services. Fifth, Internet penetration and use in Finland are the highest in Europe. Consequently, it is

feasible for the banks to provide services over the Internet.

In fact, Finland and Sweden have the highest levels of Internet banking and broker penetration in the world. In this respect, Denmark and Norway are quite close. The leading banks in this area, the Finnish–Swedish Merita-Norbanken and the Swedish SEB bank, have penetration rates close to 25 percent of their client base, which is far above the average penetration rates of, say, Germany and the United Kingdom, where the corresponding rates are 2–4 percent. Until recently, the Nordic banks (and Internet broker specialists) have not tried to expand aggressively outside the home market, but now the tide seems to be changing and they may well benefit from the technology leadership in the Central European and U.K. markets.

8.4.2. Labor Markets and Education

The labor force in the Nordic countries has been almost stagnant over the last two or three decades. Population has increased very little (typically the population growth rate in all Nordic countries has been less than half a percent per annum). Moreover, female labor force participation has not changed much since the 1970s; female labor force participation has traditionally been among the highest in the world.[13] Thus, the labor force has grown very slowly and employment actually declined in the 1990s.

The mirror image of this development is, of course, an increase in unemployment. The Nordic countries, which in the early 1970s had unemployment rates well below the European average (and below U.S. unemployment rates at the time), now have quite high unemployment rates. There are many reasons for this, but clearly we cannot exclude the fact that Nordic labor markets do not function particularly well. The very high unionization rates, extensive

---

[13] Currently, the rates are at the same level as in the Unites States (somewhat above 70 percent). A big difference between the Nordic and U.S. labor markets is the age structure. Thus, for instance, the share of people aged 50–64 of all working age people is 26 percent for the Nordic countries and 21 percent for the United States.

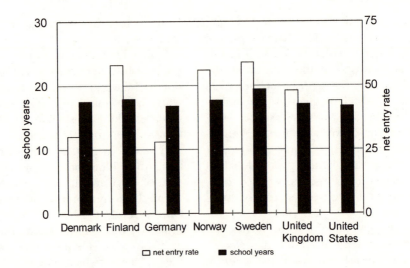

Figure 8.19 Net entry rates to universities and average schooling years. Net entry rate (right scale) indicates the percentage of population that net enters tertiary (university) education. School years (left scale) indicate the current (1998) school expectancy in years. *Source:* OECD (2000).

labor market legislation, generous unemployment benefit systems and relatively high overall labor costs may well support the view that labor markets are the Achilles heal of the Nordic countries (see OECD, 1994, 1999h; UNICE, 1999).

Looking at the prerequisites for technological innovations, the functioning of labor markets in the Nordic countries would seem to be the single most important obstacle to innovations and growth.[14] The reason why this obstacle has not been of crucial importance is perhaps the fact that most new jobs have been created in sectors outside those dominated by traditional labor market institutions.[15] This shows up in the fact that average wages in the ICT manufacturing sector are not notably higher than in rest of manufacturing industry. In the ICT services sector, however, the difference is quite substantial, being of the magnitude of 10–25 percent. The fact that wages in the ICT (manufacturing) sector reflect only weakly increased demand and higher skill requirements may be explained by the fact that the age structure of employment is quite different from the rest of the economy. Thus, the share of employees below 35 years is much higher in the ICT sector. In Finland, for instance, the share is 44 percent in the ICT sector and 32 percent in the rest of the economy.

One area where a lot has changed is the level of education. The share of university graduates in the respective age cohort in the Nordic countries is one of the highest in the world. Similarly, the average duration of education is clearly higher than the OECD average. Not surprisingly, this is also evident in spending on education. A look at Germany and the United Kingdom, for instance, again helps to explain why Finland and Sweden have outperformed these two countries in the area of technological innovations (see Figures 8.19 and 8.20; Kreuger and Lindahl, 2000). Not only has the overall educational attainment improved over time, but also the number of people who have diplomas in the area of information technology has increased considerably. Thus, for instance, in Finland the share of secondary and tertiary education diplomas in this area was 0.3 percent

---

[14] (Some) politicians seem to be conscious of this problem which shows up for instance in the fact that more favorable tax treatment is granted to foreign experts (in Denmark and Finland) with limited time contracts. Thus, the tax rates would be 25–30 percent instead of the general 50–60 percent.

[15] A recent survey among Finnish ICT firms indicates that the unionization rate varies between 10 and 50 percent compared with the overall rate of 80 percent.

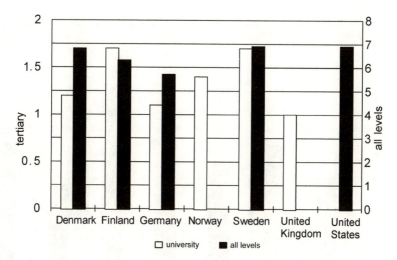

Figure 8.20 Expenditure on education. University (left scale) indicates educational expenditure from public and private sources for tertiary (university) education as a percentage of GDP. All levels (right scale) indicate corresponding expenditure for all levels of education. *Source:* OECD (2000). Some data for Norway, United Kingdom and United States are missing.

in 1971, whereas in 1997 this had increased to 5.0 percent.

Although differences in educational expenditure and schooling expectancy are noticeable, perhaps more important differences exist between subject categories in higher education. Thus, in the Nordic countries the share of social sciences, business and law is just one half of the U.S. figure. By contrast, the share of engineering, physical sciences, mathematics, statistics and computing is much higher (being at the same level as in Germany).[16] This heavy concentration on science and engineering gives Finland and Sweden a clear advantage in expanding production in the ICT sector.

The educational requirements are clearly higher in the ICT sector than in the rest of the economy. This also shows up, for instance, in the share of university graduates among all employed persons. In the whole economy, the share is about 10 percent while in the ICT sector it varies between 15 and 20 percent.[17] Clearly the ICT sector is relatively knowledge-intensive, and hence an increase in the overall educational attainment helps increasing output in this sector.

8.4.3. R&D Investment

The data for R&D investment clearly show that the countries that occupy the top places in technological innovation have the highest R&D investment rates. Changes in the investment rate reinforce this view. Thus, for instance, Finland used to spend very little on R&D in the early 1970s, when the growth of the economy was largely factor-intensive (see Figure 8.21). A quite different picture emerges for the 1990s, when productivity growth was largely achieved by technological innovations and improved efficiency. R&D investment rates were then three times higher than in the early 1970s.

Along with the increase in overall R&D investment rates, the way in which such investment is financed has also changed. Particularly striking

[16] The share of social sciences, business and law is only 23.5 percent in Finland and 25.2 percent in Sweden while the U.S. figure is 41.4 percent (OECD, 2000a). The share of engineering and other sciences is 30.5 percent in Finland which is quite close to the German figure (32.1 percent). In Sweden the share is somewhat lower, and in Denmark and Norway much lower (in fact, approaching the U.S. figures). See OECD (2000a) for more details.

[17] There is no big difference between manufacturing and services, in this respect.

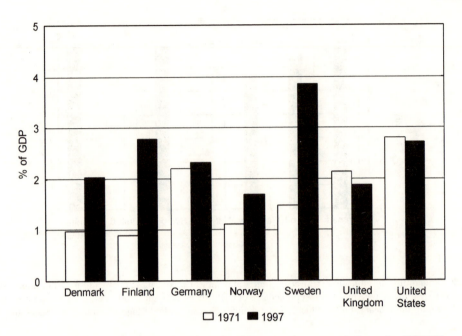

Figure 8.21 R&D Expenditure, 1971 and 1997. *Source:* OECD *Main Science and Technology Indicators I and II* (1997) and National Statistics.

is the increase in the share that is financed by private firms (as public funding decreased). This is clearly shown in Table 8.4. These figures also reflect the more important role of R&D intensive (or high-tech) industries.[18]

The structure of financing affects the role of universities, in particular. Thus, typically more and more research funding comes from

outside universities, which in the Nordic countries are—with a few exceptions—all public.[19] In Finland and Sweden, the share of regular public funding of research activities is much lower than in other Nordic countries. This is obviously a healthy situation as regards orienting research activities into more productive directions. As for (academic) research subjects, there is not much difference among the Nordic countries (except perhaps between Norway and the other countries) in the share of sciences and engineering.

8.4.4. Characteristics of Firms and Industry

Perhaps the most important change that has affected firms in the Nordic countries is related to capital market liberalization and the lifting of capital controls. The bankruptcy wave which swept the Nordic countries forced firms to adopt a completely new attitude towards the choice of business and business practice. As can be seen from Figure 8.22, bankruptcies hit Sweden and Finland particularly hard, while in Denmark the phenomenon can hardly be discerned. The Swedish figures are very high indeed, but they do partly reflect the nature

---

[18] The role of government subsidies to R&D investment might deserve closer scrutiny. It is only that the magnitude of subsidies is so small that their economic importance can be questioned. Thus, in Finland where the R&D subsidies are the largest, they only represent about 0.15 percent of GDP. Unfortunately, the effectiveness of these subsidies has not been thoroughly examined. Some analyses suggests, however, that public sector subsidies do not foster growth in sales or employees, neither does it increase R&D or productivity in subsidized companies (see, e.g., the study by Klette and Moen (1999) based on the Norwegian data). Still, it is widely believed that these schemes (like the Finnish National Technology Agency (TEKES)) are useful in helping the start-up of new ICT enterprises.

[19] According to IMD (2000) Finland and Sweden perform very well in international rankings of technological cooperation between business firms and between universities ands business firms. (Finland is the leading country in the IMD comparison.)

TABLE 8.4
R&D Expenditure in the Nordic Countries

	Denmark	Finland	Norway	Sweden
Total research expenditure in 1987 (percent of GDP)	1.38	1.75	1.67	2.98
Total research expenditure in 1997 (percent of GDP)	1.94	2.78	1.68	3.85
Share of public research funding in 1987 (percent)	46	39	47	37
Share of public research funding in 1997 (percent)	38	31	43	26
Private sector R&D expenditure (U.S.$ million)	1467	1777	1047	4827
– of that high-tech sectors	654	1094	331	2305
Public sector R&D expenditure (U.S.$ million)	391	379	302	233
Universities R&D expenditure (U.S.$ million)	530	537	490	1381
– of that financed by public sector (percent)	69	50	68	50
Share of research expenditure in universities in sciences and engineering, 1997 (percent)	57	48	42	53
Share of research expenditure in universities in medicine, 1997 (percent)	14	25	27	29
Share of research expenditure in universities in social sciences, business and law, 1997 (percent)	29	27	31	18

Source: Analyseinstitut for Forsking (2000).

Nordic Silicon Valleys

Although the Nordic Silicon Valleys are not so well known as their American counterpart, they have profoundly affected industry standards in the Nordic countries. In Sweden, there is Kista (a suburb of Stockholm) while in Finland there are at least two centers, Espoo and Oulu, near the Technical University (of Espoo and Helsinki) and the University of Oulu, respectively.

In Kista, there is a huge collection (about 375) of high-tech companies, which together with some service companies have a workforce close to 30,000. Companies include both Swedish (Ericsson, of course) and most international IT companies such as Intel, Microsoft, Nokia, etc. The Royal Institute of Technology has set up a dedicated IT university in Kista which will expand to 10,000 students in a few years.

The Finnish Center of Oulu has expanded together with the University of Oulu. Currently, there are more than 7000 job in high-tech enterprises. The interesting thing in the technology center of Oulu is the location. The city is in northern Finland, which has suffered badly from declining industries and emigration to the southern part of the country. The technology center has probably been the decisive factor that has made Oulu, almost unknown outside Finland ten years ago, one of the fastest growing and prosperous cities in the entire country. Another interesting feature in the Center of Oulu is the close university–company cooperation. Nokia was the first company in the area, but many new enterprises have now moved there. The premises of the companies and the university facilities are located in the same place; there are close personal ties in research projects and other activities, and most of the research money comes from the private high-tech enterprises.

The apparent success stories of Kista and Oulu have obviously had a deep impact on higher education, regional policies and firms' choice of location in the Nordic countries. Not surprisingly, a large number of Nordic cities have tried to create a similar center, but with more modest success.

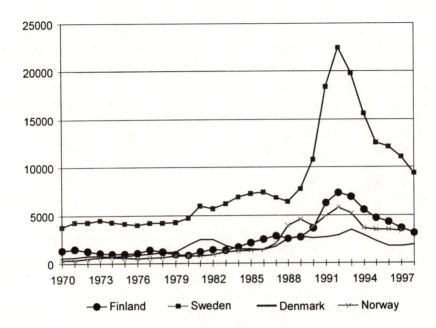

Figure 8.22 Total number of bankruptcies in the Nordic countries. *Source:* National Bankruptcy Statistics.

of (financial) firms.[20] Thus, if one scrutinizes the credit losses for the same period, the values for the four countries are similar. In Denmark, the maximum credit losses per year are 1.6 percent of GDP, while in Finland and Norway the corresponding figure is 3.1 percent and in Sweden 3.9 percent.[21]

One can with reason speak about "constructive destruction," at least in the case of the Finnish (and to a somewhat lesser degree Swedish) corporate sector. Firms which relied on products that seemed to be safe from competition (such as merchandise in trade with the Soviet Union) experienced major difficulties in adjusting to a new market environment where competition was present everywhere and new products appeared continuously (at the same time as demand for old products could simply vanish overnight). In the case of more traditional industries (such as consumer

electronics and heavy industry), firms faced serious problems and far-sighted entrepreneurs therefore tried to find completely new areas and goods for production. Electronics, or more generally, ICT, was (in retrospect) an obvious choice.[22]

There has been a lot of discussion on the question of whether depressions (bankruptcies) are good or bad for new innovations (see e.g., Caballero and Hammour, 2000 for a review of the main arguments). One way of thinking about the propagation mechanism is to assume that the opportunity costs of some productivity

---

[20] The number of firms is quite different in the Nordic countries. Thus, in 1998/1999 the number of active (reporting) firms was estimated to be 61,000 in Denmark, 33,000 in Finland, 64,000 in Norway, and 194,000 in Sweden.

[21] In Norway, the credit losses were mainly caused by consumer debt.

[22] As mentioned earlier Finland experienced a very severe depression in the early 1990s (partly due to the collapse of Soviet trade in 1991). GDP decreased (cumulatively) by almost 15 percent and the unemployment rate increased up to 20 percent. The recession had a particularly severe impact on low-tech sectors such as shipbuilding, textiles, and food production. The banking sector also experienced a major crisis. All this showed up in an exceptionally large restructuring of production and employment (see footnote 6 and Bradburg (1999) for a comparison). Although the depression had some beneficial effects via constructive destruction that does not, of course, mean that we should adopt some sort of "liquidationist" school of thought in business cycles and economic policy, in particular (see De Long, 1990 for discussion on the related experiences of the Great Depression).

improving activities falls in a recession, which has a long-term positive impact on output. However, depressions should on average not last longer or be more frequent, since the expectation of future recessions reduces today's incentives for investment and growth.

One may also formulate the problem in terms of the customer relationship. Newly established firms often try to secure their market position by building up a base of loyal customers. While recessions may not destroy technological leadership, they may be harmful for such firm–customer relationships. Without such customer bases, these firms find themselves more vulnerable to attacks by competitors. Hence, recessions might be good for growth since they weaken the incumbent firm's position, and thereby stimulate research by outside firms.

In the case of the Nordic countries, the opportunity cost argument is, of course, quite appealing. The recession of the early 1990s did not only affect traditional firm–customer relationships and market structures but more important changes were caused by the more or less contemporaneous elimination of (financial and nonfinancial) trade barriers which created new incentives to investment in R&D. Generally, underdeveloped and badly functioning institutions are a major impediment to well-functioning markets, creating a destruction process and resulting in technological sclerosis and spurious reallocation. In the case of the Nordic countries, this problem did not exist; the problem of recurrent crises, another major obstacle for creative destruction, also did not exist. In Finland and Sweden, the depression of the early 1990s was the first real recession after World War II.

If we compare the other Nordic countries in this respect, we see that Sweden experienced somewhat similar problems as Finland, partly due to the recession in early 1992 and also due to deteriorating profitability of its heavy metal industries. Given relatively high labor costs, there were not many options for new production possibilities, and the high-tech sector turned out to be a good candidate. In addition, Sweden has a relatively long tradition in the manufacture of machinery and consumer electronics.[23]

As for Denmark and Norway, they faced similar problems in terms of structural adjustment.

In Denmark, the structural crisis occurred in the early 1980s, and since then Denmark's macroeconomic performance has been reasonably good. Hence, there has been no compelling reason for the country as a whole or Danish firms, in particular, to find new products or branches of production to survive in international competition.[24] Basically the same argument also applies to Norway. Norway experienced some problems towards the end of the 1980s due to oil price fluctuations and the aftermath of financial market liberalization (which was reflected in a quite severe but relatively short-lived banking crisis at the end of the 1980s). In the 1990s there were no major macroeconomic problems in the Norwegian economy. Oil has been the driving force of the whole economy and there have been no active efforts to diversify the structure of the economy or to foster the birth of new firms or branches. With some slight exaggeration, the Norwegian problem can perhaps be described as "too affluent for innovations."

One might expect the growth of technological innovation to be related in some way to the size distribution of firms. A look at Figure 8.23 suggests, however, that the relationship is not very straightforward. Thus, the existence of big firms is by no means a prerequisite for innovation. This seems natural given that many high-tech firms are completely new and literally start from zero. Although they grow at a very rapid (even astronomical) rate, it takes time before they reach the size of conventional big firms.

[23] Here we might cite such firms as Asea, Ericsson, SKF, and Alfa Laval. See Edqvist and Lundvall (1993) for a more thorough (comparative) analysis of Danish and Swedish innovation systems.

[24] Denmark has traditionally relied on the agroindustrial complex, which has actually been very efficient and successful in the European Union. Thus, production and exports have specialized heavily in agricultural products. Going from agriculture to high-tech would under these circumstances be rather difficult. Even so, one should not, completely nullify the Danish efforts in keeping pace with Finland and Sweden. For instance, the transformation of former industrial cable producer NKT into one of biggest high-tech firms in the Nordic countries shows that Danish firms still have a lot possibilities and advantages.

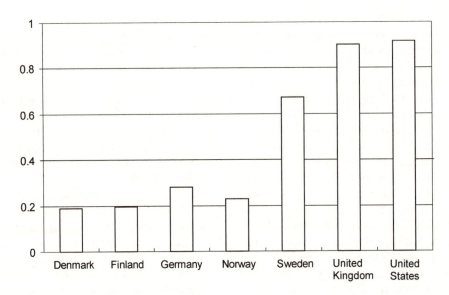

Figure 8.23 The FT Global 500 firms (per million inhabitants). *Source: Financial Times (http://www.ft.com/ftsurveys/q36666.htm).* The firms are ranked according to market capitalization.

This shows up in the size distribution of firms, which is relatively even especially in the ICT services sector. Thus, firms with less 100 employees represent about 50 percent of total employment in ICT services. In ICT manufacturing, the share is much lower, representing about 65–85 percent of total employment (Finland and Sweden have the higher values, obviously due to Nokia and Ericsson; see Nordic Council of Ministers (1998) for further details).

8.4.5. Intellectual Property Rights

The general opinion among Nordic managers of high-tech firms is that intellectual property rights is not a crucial issue.[25] The main reason for this attitude is an apparent awareness that in this area firms cannot succeed in the market by stealing other firms' ideas. This, in turn, follows from the fact the product cycle is so short that if you just imitate others' ideas your products will always be outdated and obsolete.

Until now, Europe has differed from the United States in the sense that patents have not been granted for computer software. Now the attitude seems to be changing (following a recent German Supreme Court decision which will probably lead to E.U.-wide changes in legal practice). Both in Europe and the United States, it is still a much debated question whether stronger patent protection affects R&D investment positively or negatively (see e.g., the arguments of Besson and Maskin (1999) who suggest that the latter might be true).[26]

Everybody agrees, of course, that property rights must have reasonable minimum legal protection to avoid problems of piracy and theft, for instance. In general, the Nordic countries do perform well in all international comparisons of such variables as the security of property and contracts, tradition of law and order, the government's propensity to repudiate contracts, and the quality of bureaucracy.[27] Moreover, indicators of software piracy are also

[25] Even so, the share of the high-tech sector's patent applications is increasing rapidly also in the Nordic countries. Thus, for instance, in Finland, the respective share was about 5 percent in 1985 while in 1999 it was 25 percent.

[26] In this area, copyright laws may, in fact, be more relevant and important (see Miles et al., 1999, for further discussion).

[27] If we use, for instance, the International Country Risk Guide (ICRG) data, the values of the composite index are quite close to the United States (ranging from 86 to 93 compared with 88 for the United States).

reasonably low for the Nordic countries.[28] Software piracy is an interesting indicator because there is some evidence of an inverse relationship between piracy and R&D investment (see e.g., Marron and Steel, 2000).

8.4.6. Macroeconomic Policies

Macroeconomic policies have certainly been of some importance in creating a more stable environment for business activity. During the immediate postwar era, macroeconomic policy in all the Nordic countries was predominantly directed towards boosting economic growth. Thus, the public sector had a large structural surplus that was used to finance private sector investment activity. Furthermore, monetary policy was relatively loose, both in order to keep real interest rates down and to accommodate various shocks. The stance of monetary policy was clearly evident in the devaluation of exchanges rates, in which regard Finland and Sweden had a notorious record (see the nominal exchange rates vis-à-vis Germany in Figure 8.17). This environment helped the economy to grow quite rapidly but at the same time it provided very few incentives for structural reforms and efforts to increase the efficiency of production.

Policies changed gradually in the 1980s, when inflation was brought under control. Another factor that contributed to this course of development was an increase in government indebtedness. In all the Nordic countries, government finances deteriorated markedly in the late 1970s (especially in Denmark and Sweden) and in the early 1990s (Finland). The change effectively prevented the government from increasing its involvement in production activities. By contrast, governments have been (have had to be) quite active in cutting subsidies, for instance for agriculture (see section 8.4.7), enhancing competition by changing legislation and implementing privatization programs, especially in Finland.

The current policy setup—notably Finnish membership in European economic and monetary union—means the end of old policies, and firms are being forced to find alternatives to capital and labor-intensive growth. European Monetary Union (EMU) membership may be important, especially for small countries which have a rather dubious record in anti-inflation policies. One should not, however, exaggerate the importance of membership: Finland and Sweden's different choices in terms of EMU membership do not seem to have significantly affected the growth of the IT sector in these economies.

8.4.7. Structural Policies

In the 1970s, governments actively pursued structural policies, which were very often intended to boost heavy industries. Moreover, government policy was often quite orthodox in preserving government (and national) ownership and control. After some failures in government enterprises, interest in this kind of policy decreased markedly. The deterioration in government finances was also a contributory factor.

Currently, governments' structural policies have quite a low profile, and their goals represent an almost complete U-turn compared with the ideas of the 1970s.

One sign of this change is the elimination of subsidies. The latest figures for 1996–8 show that government support to industry in the Nordic countries is clearly below the E.U. average (which is 1.12 percent of GDP). The figure for Denmark is 0.94, for Finland 0.47, and Sweden 0.78.[29] Policies nowadays tend to be geared towards heavy investment in education.

---

[28] The piracy rates (in percentage terms) for the Nordic countries turned out to be 41 for Denmark, 46 for Finland, 52 for Norway and 50 for Sweden (compared with 28 for the United States). See Business Software (1997).

[29] In early 1990s, the figures clearly exceeded 1 percent (for instance, 1.2 percent for Finland in 1993). A the same time the share of R&D support out of total support has somewhat increased: 11 percent in Denmark, 30 percent in Finland and 7 percent in Sweden. The German values are 1.45 percent (of GDP) for total support and 4 percent for the share of R&D support. See European Commission (2000).

Perhaps even more important is privatization policy, which has been quite actively pursued, notably by Finnish and Swedish governments during the recent past. This policy has had some very important consequences, especially in the telecommunications sector, but also in the paper, chemical, and metal industries. In Finland, for instance, the Sonera corporation, which was previously a state-owned telecommunications company, was listed in late 1998. It has reshaped itself and invested in mobile telephone technology. At one point in time, it became the second largest listed company in Finland in terms of market value. The Swedish authorities have been more cautious in privatizing their public telecommunications company, Telia (that finally took place in mid-2000). The Norwegian authorities have been even more cautious, delaying the privatization process of Telenor until late 2000. In Denmark, Tele Danmark was privatized much earlier, in 1994, which is perhaps explained by the fact that government involvement in business has been quite modest in Denmark in comparison to the other Nordic countries.[30]

8.4.8. Other Government Policies

Overall, government policies in the 1990s had a beneficial effect in the Nordic countries, as they (1) increased competition, (2) eliminated distorted taxes and other obstacles, (3) led to investment in the infrastructure of technological innovations, and (4) helped create common standards and cooperative agreements between firms.

It can be argued that policies of this kind have been most successful in Finland. As pointed out above, membership of the European Union (and EMU), cuts in subsidies, an extensive

privatization program, and reforms of the tax system have had a profound effect on the market environment and prerequisites for innovations and new enterprises.[31] It should also be noted that the motivation and need for major and effective government action were also very high in Finland because of the very deep recession and heavy indebtedness of the country in the early 1990s.

The Finnish government and Bank of Finland have also made a significant contribution, together with the banks, to developing payment and settlement systems and securities market infrastructure. The early introduction of postal giro (1939) and bank giro (1942) and the early agreement on cooperation in this area (1948) made credit transfers the main payment vehicle instead of checks. The Bank of Finland took an active part in the introduction of prepaid cards (1993) and electronic purses (1994) through its ownership of the leading company in this technology. The company was sold in the late 1990s to a group of leading commercial banks operating in Finland. The central bank was also a majority owner of the Helsinki Money Market Center, which started to operate in 1992. The system is now merged with all the other securities market infrastructure companies in Finland, including the Helsinki Stock Exchange. These efforts are examples of cooperative effort between the authorities and market participants. It should be stressed that the operational efficiency of payment and securities market systems can be increased by cooperative efforts of this kind. Central banks and governments in other Nordic countries have likewise been centrally involved in investment in securities market infrastructure. All in all, these government policies seem to have been beneficial in the Nordic countries.

---

[30] Tele Danmark became completely private in 1997 which also makes it different from other Nordic telecommunication companies. As for companies in general, in Finland almost all state companies have been either totally or partially privatized. Sweden lags somewhat behind in this respect (the number of state companies was 74 in 1998) although state ownership is now clearly below 10 percent of GDP. In Norway, there have been only weak attempts to privatize, for example, the very large oil industry. Finally, in Denmark, state ownership is currently almost nonexistent.

[31] One sign of this changing attitude was a complete overhaul of corporate taxation in 1990 whereby complicated double-taxation systems were replaced by the current avoir fiscal system with a one of the lowest tax rates within the European Union.

The Story of Nokia

The history of Nokia goes back to 1865 when the company was established as a forest industry enterprise in south-western Finland on the Nokia river (after which the town of Nokia is named) by a mining engineer called Frerik Idestam. This was not a particularly remarkable event as numerous forest industry enterprises existed in Finland at the time. Later, Nokia came into contact with two enterprises that were outside the traditional forest industry. These firms were the Finnish Rubber Works Ltd (founded in 1898) and the Finnish Cable Works Ltd (founded in 1912). The gradual concentration of the ownership of these companies led in 1966 to the establishment of Nokia Corporation, into which all the above-mentioned companies were merged.

Nokia grew fairly rapidly in the 1970s and 1980s, partly because of the then-flourishing (bilateral) Soviet trade, which was boosted by the oil crises in 1973 and 1980. When the Soviet trade collapsed in 1991, Nokia ran into difficulties (partly because of the collapse in trade per se, partly because of the general economic recession in Finland and partly because of problems Nokia had with its traditional production lines). Serious consideration was given to selling Nokia in its entirely to the Swedish company Ericsson, but the merger did not materialize. Nokia's solution to the crisis was to concentrate on the production of electronics (and thus to abandon the production of paper and pulp, tires, rubber boots, cables and so on), to invest massively in R&D and to adapt a new management strategy that relied extensively on domestic and foreign subsidiaries and subcontractors. Nokia also actively sought to become a genuinely international firm.

By Finnish standards, the management strategy was really revolutionary because previously companies had tried to be as self-sufficient as possible in production (the biggest firms even had their own power companies). Nokia decided to concentrate solely on the final product and on the high tech end of production. Nokia's new strategy also involved investment in R&D. Besides investing heavily in research and development, Nokia created a very useful network of research contacts between universities and itself. This cooperation has been of great benefit to both Nokia and Finnish universities.

Currently, Nokia accounts for more than 20 percent of Finland's total exports and its growth contribution (in terms of the Finnish GDP) is estimated at 1.5 percent. Nokia alone accounts for about 40 percent of the R&D expenditure by private enterprises in Finland. Moreover, it accounts for 70 percent of the stock market value of the Helsinki Stock Exchange (and most of Finland's millionaires).

Almost 60 percent of Nokia's workforce is currently outside Finland (the total number of employees is relatively small: about 1 percent of total employment in Finland, while the share of value added is about 4 percent). Its success shows up most dramatically in its earnings and market capitalization values. Thus, in 1999 Nokia's profits equaled the combined profits of its two main rivals Ericsson and Motorola, and its market capitalization was over U.S.$200 million, almost twice Finland's GDP.

For data sources, see Ali-Yrkkö et al. (1999) and Statistics Finland (1999a,b).

8.5. Conclusions

The chapter has demonstrated that favorable changes in the market environment can have a profound effect on technological innovation and economic growth. Especially the case of Finland attests to the benefits of "creative destruction," which enables the economy to have "a new start" without the burden of old structures and restrictions. The experiences of

Denmark and Norway show the outcome of a contrasting development, where the old structures continue to dominate the economy.

A "new start" nevertheless requires heavy inputs in terms of human capital and substantial investment in R&D. In addition, markets must function effectively and the government must not act in a distortive way. Of course, it is even better if the government helps to create better functioning markets, contributes to the accumulation of human capital and plays a positive role in increasing cooperation and establishing common standards between firms and other market players. Something like that has happened in Finland and Sweden, and these countries have succeeded relatively well in benefitting from technical progress in spite of some problems due to large government and relatively rigid labor markets.[32]

The experience in the Nordic countries also shows that technological innovations can boost economic growth in spite of a relatively rigid and extensive welfare state. They may also produce completely new solutions for regional development problems. This suggests that recent advances in growth theory are indeed useful in evaluating different countries' growth potential.

[32] In 1986–7 OECD arranged a set of reviews of national science and technology policy in the Nordic countries (see OECD 1987, 1988). It is interesting to compare the recommendations of these reviews with the past developments. The recommendations rightly emphasized increased cooperation between universities and private enterprises, higher R&D investment rate, the benefits of global technology transfer and more flexible university funding and salary systems. The reviews did, however, emphasize the role of government in overseeing and (directly) supporting the R&D activities.

Part III

INDUSTRY STUDIES

9

The Internet

David C. Mowery and Timothy Simcoe

9.1. Introduction

The Internet is the world's largest computer network—a steadily growing collection of more than 70 million computers that communicate with one another using a shared set of standards and protocols. The evolution of this network is the story of a variety of innovations in fields ranging from computing and communications to utility regulation, business and finance. In the roughly thirty years since its invention, the Internet has evolved from the publicly funded research project of a small group of U.S. computer scientists into a global phenomenon that has spurred massive private investments. Together with the World Wide Web—a complementary software innovation that dramatically increased the accessibility of the network for many users—the Internet helped stimulate a communications revolution that has changed the way that individuals and institutions use computers in a wide variety of activities.

The Internet and World Wide Web jointly comprise a General Purpose Technology (GPT). Together, they are an invention with the potential to transform the dissemination of information in a global economy that relies ever more heavily on knowledge.[1] As with other GPTs, it has taken some time for the Internet to diffuse into a wide array of applications, and the process appears to be far from over. This extended diffusion period reflects the important role of a host of complementary innovations—technological and organizational improvements that adapt the network to the needs and uses of a wide variety of institutions. Still, the rate of adoption of the Internet (measured in terms of the number of hosts, users, applications, total traffic, or available content) has been rapid, exceeding the adoption rates of other postwar GPTs such as computers or semiconductors. The network has spawned considerable economic activity and wealth creation in a relatively short time period. Although the evidence on the "economic impact" of the Internet, especially at the macroeconomic level, is uncertain, the economic effects of the Internet may well exceed those of other GPTs at a similar point in their evolution.

The emergence of a dominant set of technical standards is a critical part of the Internet's story. The term "Internet" is derived from the expression "inter-networking," used by early researchers to describe the idea of connecting several different computer networks. The earliest inter-networking efforts represented a fundamental shift in researchers' thinking about computer networks, as they realized that it would be more useful to create a "network of networks" than to create a network of computers. The distinction turns on the idea of open standards. By adopting a set of publicly available protocols and ensuring that any suitably constructed network can communicate with any other using those standards, the Internet allows network users to share information and applications despite idiosyncratic differences in local computing and communications technology.

Research for this paper was supported by the Andrew Mellon Foundation and the Alfred P. Sloan Foundation. We are grateful to the editors and to Richard Nelson for useful comments on earlier drafts.

[1] Lipsey et al. (1998) use four criteria to define a technology as a GPT—the ability to make dramatic technical improvements, the existence of a variety of technological complementarities, and the breadth and scope of applications for the technology. Although they argue that Information Technology represents a single GPT, we feel that these criteria apply equally well to the Internet.

Scientists and engineers from around the globe have made important contributions to the invention of the Internet, including the creation of the technological core of the World Wide Web. Similarly, the adoption of the Internet has occurred on a global scale, with especially rapid diffusion occurring in the United States and in several Nordic countries, including Sweden and Finland. Nevertheless, the development and widespread application of the Internet and the exploitation of its economic possibilities occurred first and have proceeded most rapidly in the United States. We devote considerable attention to explaining this U.S. lead in the development and diffusion of the Internet.

The institutions and policies associated with the postwar U.S. "national innovation system" figure prominently in the development of the Internet. Research universities, defense-related R&D and procurement, antitrust policy, new entrant firms, and R&D investments by established firms all made important contributions to the development and adoption of the Internet in the United States, just as they did in the postwar development of the semiconductor, computer hardware, and computer software industries (see Mowery and Nelson (1999), as well as Bresnahan and Malerba (1999), Langlois and Steinmueller (1999), and Mowery (1999)). Federal R&D funding played a key role in the creation of an "infrastructure" of trained researchers and related institutions, including universities; federal antitrust and procurement policies tended to weaken any nascent market power held by established firms in related industries; and new firms were central to the commercialization of a variety of applications. The large size of the U.S. domestic market, especially the large "installed base" of desktop computers and computer networks, as well as regulatory reform in telecommunications, accelerated the domestic adoption of the Internet.

An important difference between the development of the Internet and the emergence of other postwar U.S. information technology industries is the central importance of governance institutions in the development of the Internet. As a network of networks, the Internet's very existence depended on the creation

of open standards that accommodated rapid growth without reinforcing the market power of any particular innovator. The growth of the Internet also depended on the ability of these institutions to coordinate investments in improved communication protocols and other component technologies. These institutions relied on government and nongovernment funding, and operated in a "quasi-academic" style that utilized industrial, as well as government and academic, expertise. They appear to have effectively managed a difficult series of tradeoffs among open and closed standards.

The Internet's development in an era of global markets and technology flows illustrates vividly the enduring national elements of large-economy innovation systems such as that of the United States. At the same time, the Internet's development extends well past the end of the Cold War era of heavy federal investments in defense-related R&D and procurement that proved to be indispensable to the creation of the U.S. information technology industries. But the Internet's development and diffusion during the 1990s have been aided by a set of "post-Cold War" institutions that may figure prominently in the development of other high-technology industries in the twenty-first century.

In view of the feverish rhetoric of the late 1990s and beyond about the role of the Internet as a catalyst for the creation of a "New Economy" in the United States, this chapter briefly considers the broader economic impacts of the Internet. Since the widespread commercialization of Internet applications has occurred only recently, this discussion is necessarily brief and speculative. Nevertheless, many of the issues that figure prominently in our discussion of the "economic impact" of the Internet are anything but novel. Students of the ongoing debate over the productivity effects of information technology are familiar with the difficulties of measuring nonmanufacturing output, the complex issues related to quality and productivity measurement in technology industries, and the important role of complementary investments in technology and organizational innovation. Indeed, the very concept of a "New Economy," populated by new firms in new industries, distorts the likely channels and causal relationships through which the productivity and economic effects of the Internet will be realized. This major innovation, like most before it, will be adopted widely in mature as well as new industries, and its productivity effects are likely to be present (and difficult to measure) throughout the economy.

Section 2 provides a short history of the technological development of the Internet that focuses on the sources of key innovations. Section 3 describes the contributions to the Internet's development of the various institutions and policies that are central to "the U.S. national innovation system." Section 4 examines the global diffusion of the Internet, discussing the influence on this diffusion process of the availability of infrastructure and the structure of the telecommunications industries in the United States and other industrial economies. Section 5 reviews the limited evidence on the economic impacts of the Internet, and Section 6 briefly discusses a few of the many public policy issues raised by its extensive adoption. Our approach covers a great deal of material in a small number of pages. It is our hope that the various parts of this story are complementary, so that like the many small networks that comprise the Internet, the whole chapter will amount to more than the sum of its parts.

9.2. The Development of the Internet

The evolution of the Internet from an experimental network connecting three U.S. research facilities that transferred data at top speeds of 56 thousand bits per second to a global network with over 72 million hosts and a backbone capacity in excess of 2 billion bits per second relied on a series of technical and organizational innovations.[2] The key component technologies in any computer network are the computers or

terminals, often called nodes, that lie at the edges of the network, the wires and switches that comprise the network infrastructure, and the shared protocols that allow devices attached to the end of the network to communicate. Since the invention of the computer, the technical performance of each of these network components has advanced rapidly, driven by innovations in semiconductor technology that have improved the capacity and performance of memory and central processor components, software engineering, signal processing, and communications theory. By significantly lowering the costs of computing technology, these improvements have driven large-scale adoption of desktop computers, creating a huge domestic installed base within the United States that opened up a mass market for hardware and applications. In addition to creating enormous economic opportunities, these technological improvements enabled engineers to design increasingly complex applications for the network that linked more and more of these individual computers. It is difficult to overstate the importance of this sustained improvement in the performance of its components to the evolution of the Internet.

But the evolution of the Internet is more than a purely technological phenomenon. As a collection of independent but interconnected computer networks built and managed by a wide variety of different institutions, the Internet has also relied on a number of organizational innovations. As the Internet evolved from its origins in a U.S. Department of Defense research project to a novel tool for educational and research organizations and subsequently, to a vast collaboration among public and private sector institutions, the network drew on a number of formal and informal governance mechanisms to coordinate its standards and infrastructure. Perhaps because of its development and early application in an academic and "quasi-academic" environment, the Internet retained many of the characteristics of an informal and widely distributed collaboration, even as it grew exponentially and made the transition from a public to a privately managed and financed infrastructure. Decisions on issues of network infrastructure, standards, interoper-

[2] A bit represents a single one or zero—the fundamental unit of digital information. The term "backbone" refers to the fiber-optic cables and high-speed switches at the center of a network that carry large quantities of data aggregated from many thousands of simultaneous users. For a simplified guide to the networking terminology of bandwidth and capacity, see Appendix B.

ability, conduct and content were made by a variety of organizations serving different constituencies. Whether and how these diverse entities can maintain their historic roles in managing the Internet as it becomes a central feature of the global regulatory, political and market environment are open questions (Lessig, 1999).

Our history of the Internet divides its development into two phases. From 1960 to 1985, computer scientists and engineers made many of the fundamental theoretical and technical contributions to its development. During this period, the Internet remained a loosely organized communications technology used largely by the research community. The number of users and applications grew throughout this period, and the technical and organizational challenges shifted from inventing the network to expanding its core infrastructure and establishing a framework for connectivity that could accommodate the growing demand service. From 1985 to 2000, the Internet made a lengthy transition from public to private management and, during the final five years of the twentieth century, experienced explosive growth. This period began with the introduction of NSFNET, the National Science Foundation (NSF)'s "backbone" for the national Internet (see below for further discussion). NSFNET launched a period of sustained growth, particularly within the academic community. The privatization of NSFNET, completed in early 1995,[3] occurred almost simultaneously with the development of HTML and the introduction of the first widely used "browser." Both developments accelerated Internet and World Wide Web adoption within the private sector. Although we do not discuss it as a separate phase, it is possible to discern the outlines of a third phase in the evolution of the Internet in the late 1990s that is focused on developing new commercial content and applications that take advantage of the rapidly growing network.

9.2.1. 1960–1985: Early Computer Networks

9.2.1.1. Packet Switching

Research on computer networking started in the 1960s, nearly fifteen years after the advent of the computer itself. This early research was motivated primarily by the desire to promote sharing of the scarce computing resources located at a few research centers, a motive that also led to the development of timesharing. Like many of the early academic and industrial efforts in computing technology, networking research was funded largely by the U.S. Department of Defense (DoD). Although the DoD sought to exploit a number of these new technologies in defense applications, it supported "generic" research on the theory that a viable industry capable of supplying defense needs in computer technology would also require civilian markets (Langlois and Mowery, 1996).

During the early 1960s, two researchers, Leonard Kleinrock at MIT and Paul Baran of RAND, independently developed the basic theory of packet switching.[4] Packet switching offered performance and efficiency advantages for data networks. A packet-switched architecture also allowed computer science researchers to experiment with new networking protocols outside of the circuit-switched network infrastructure operated by the Bell System.[5] From its inception, the fundamental innovation underpinning the Internet thus tended to weaken the market power of the dominant provider of telecommunications services in the United States.

By the late 1960s, the theoretical work and early experiments of Baran, Kleinrock and

---

[3] www.merit.edu/merit/archive/nsfnet/transition/950205.update.html

[4] Packet switching is fundamentally different from circuit switching—the method used to connect an ordinary telephone call. On a circuit switched network, each communication is allocated its own connection. On a packet-switched network, information is broken up into a series of discrete "packets" by a sending computer. The packets are sent individually, and reassembled into a complete message on the receiving end. With packet switching, a single circuit may carry packets from multiple connections, and the packets for a single communication may take different routes from source to destination.

[5] The researchers did, however, lease the long-distance phone lines used to carry their data from AT&T.

others led the Department of Defense Advanced Research Projects Agency (DARPA) to fund the construction of a prototype network. In December 1968, DARPA granted a contract to the engineering firm of Bolt, Beranek and Newman (Cambridge, MA) to build the first packet switch.[6] The switch was called an Interface Message Processor (IMP), and linked computers at several major computing facilities over what is now called a wide-area network. A computer with a dedicated connection to this network was referred to as a "host." The entire project was known as ARPANET, and is widely recognized as the earliest forerunner of the Internet (National Research Council, 1999a: chapter 7).

The first "killer application" developed for the ARPANET was electronic mail (e-mail), released in 1972. A 1973 ARPA study showed that within one year of its introduction, e-mail generated 73 percent of all ARPANET traffic. E-mail was the first example of an unanticipated application rapidly gaining popularity on the network—a pattern that would be repeated many times in the history of the Internet.

9.2.1.2. TCP/IP

ARPANET—the entire collection of computers running NCP and attached via an IMP to the DARPA network backbone—grew quickly throughout the 1970s.[7] By 1975, as universities and other major defense research sites were linked to the network, ARPANET had grown to more than 100 nodes. In 1973, two DARPA-funded engineers, Bob Kahn and Vint Cerf, developed an improved communications proto-

col to replace NCP. They called their new protocol the Transmission Control Protocol (TCP). TCP allowed physically distinct networks to interconnect with one another as "peers" in order to exchange data. Special hardware, called gateways, connected the various networks. The idea of an open architecture that allowed for network-to-network connectivity was a key intellectual advance in computer network design.[8] Kahn and Cerf first published their TCP specification in the *IEEE Transactions on Communication* in 1974, effectively placing this key technical advance in the public domain, and the first tests of the protocol were run a year later.

The TCP protocol eventually was split into two pieces and renamed Transmission Control Protocol/Internet Protocol (TCP/IP). The protocol was rapidly adopted, for several reasons. First, it was highly reliable and fixed many of the problems associated with first-generation network protocols. Second, it was implemented as an open standard—a complete description of TCP/IP was freely available to the networking community along with several different implementations.[9] Finally, TCP/IP arrived just as the computing research community began to standardize on a common platform—IBM or DEC hardware running the

---

[6] Bolt, Beranek and Newman was an early MIT "spin-off," founded in 1948 by MIT Professors Bruce Bolt, Leo Beranek, along with a graduate student named Robert Newman (Wildes, 1985). Populated as it was in its early years by a mixture of recent graduates, professorial consultants, and other technical employees with close links to MIT research, BBN is a good example of the "quasi-academic" environment within which many Internet-related innovations were developed.

[7] DARPA's support for ARPANET applications and extensions reflected a broader shift during the 1970s in the R&D programs overseen by the agency toward near-term research and the development of stronger links with industry (National Research Council, 1999a:, chapter 4).

[8] In addition to implementing inter-networking, Kahn and Cerf's protocols improved network performance in a variety of new ways. TCP did away with the need for an IMP, since the interaction between the protocol and distributed routing hardware ensured packet delivery. If packets were lost en route, the protocol would trigger a re-transmission. TCP also separated the physical layer of the network from the transmission layer, which administered to addresses and the routing of packets. This meant that gateways, situated between different networks, could handle the details of passing packets between one type of physical network architecture and another.

[9] In software development, standards refer primarily to the specification of an interface—a set of commands that can be used by other programmers to write new software. These interfaces simplify the complex task of writing a program from scratch. With open standards, the developer of an interface places the set of commands—and generally the source code used to create them—into the public domain. This allows other developers to improve and extend the interface, and encourages programmers to adopt the commands contained in it as a true industry standard.

Unix operating system—and the TCP/IP protocols became an integral part of that de facto standard.[10]

As networking evolved over the fifteen years following the introduction of TCP/IP, a number of proprietary network architectures and protocols were introduced. But the free, reliable, and open characteristics of TCP/IP supported its emergence as an ideal "glue" for integrating networks built on a variety of different platforms and protocols. Following an extended period of multiprotocol networking, TCP/IP emerged in the early 1990s as the dominant protocol for most applications, and now is virtually synonymous with the technical definition of the Internet. Although there have been many modifications to the standard, Kahn and Cerf's innovation remains the dominant networking protocol.

9.2.1.3. Early Coordination Efforts
In addition to technological innovations, the diffusion of the Internet relied on the creation of a set of flexible and responsive governance institutions. Most of these institutions can trace their origins back to an informal correspondence process called Request for Comments (RFC), which was started in 1969 by Steve Crocker, a UCLA graduate student in computer science.[11] The use of RFCs grew quickly, and another UCLA student named Jon Postel became the editor of the series documents, an

informal yet influential post that he would hold for many years. RFCs were distributed over the nascent computer network, and quickly became the standard forum for ARPANET's growing technical community to communicate new ideas, comments and refinements to existing proposals. RFCs combined open dissemination and peer review—features characteristic of academic journals—with the speed and informality characteristic of an e-mail discussion list.[12] The documents were used to propose specifications for important new applications such as Telnet (used to control networked computers from a remote terminal) and File Transfer Protocol (FTP, used to transfer files between networked machines), as well as to refine the development of major standards like TCP/IP (Request for Comments #318, 1972).

The first formal governance organizations associated with Internet began to appear during the early 1980s, as it became apparent that the Internet was entering a period of infrastructure consolidation and rapid expansion. Several federally funded networking initiatives were underway, including ARPANET, efforts by NASA and the Department of Energy, and CSNET, the NSF-funded precursor to NSFNET. These networks shared much of their infrastructure, and efforts to further rationalize resources led to the creation of a set of organizations, funded by NSF and DARPA, to oversee the standardization of the backbone on TCP/IP. The Internet Configuration Control Board (ICCB) was established in 1979 by Vint Cerf, who was running the DARPA network at the time. The ICCB and its successors drew their leadership from the ranks of computer scientists and engineers who did much of the early government-funded networking research, but membership in the organization was open to the community of Internet users. In 1983, the year that ARPANET switched over to TCP/IP, the ICCB was reorganized and renamed the Internet Activ-

---

[10] The Unix operating system was invented by Kenneth Thompson and Dennis Ritchie at Bell Laboratories in 1969, and is another example of the power of an open standard. AT&T originally licensed the Unix source code to universities for a nominal fee because of a 1956 consent decree that restrained them from competing in the computer industry mandated the licensing of patented technology. The licensing policy had several offsetting effects. Research users, including computer scientists at UC Berkeley, developed modifications that significantly improved the operating system (including the bundling of TCP/IP), but developed several incompatible versions of the program. AT&T's subsequent efforts to commercially exploit Unix failed in the presence of free and arguably superior, albeit incompatible, competing versions of the operating system. (http://www.datametrics.com/tech/unix/uxhistry/brf-hist.htm).

[11] Host Software, RFC 001, April, 1969.

[12] Indeed, the RFC process of widely distributed problem-solving individuals and teams that discovered and fixed technical flaws in the network technology anticipates some of the key features of "open source" software development, an activity that depends on the communications and interactions made possible by the Internet (see Lee and Cole, 2000; Kuan, 2000).

ities Board (IAB). The IAB was composed of two primary subgroups, the Internet Engineering Task Force (IETF), which managed the Internet's architecture and standard-setting processes including editing and publishing the RFCs, and the Internet Research Task Force (IRTF), which focused on a longer-term research agenda. The IAB and its progeny coordinated the infrastructure and connectivity boom that took place in the next decade.

By the early 1990s, the costs of managing the Internet infrastructure began to exceed the available federal funding, and in 1992 the Internet Society (ISOC) was founded with funding from a variety of private and public sector sources. ISOC helped coordinate the activities of a number of loosely affiliated institutions including the IAB, IETF, IRTF, and the Internet Assigned Numbers Authority (IANA). The informal organizations governing the growth of the Internet made a number of architectural and standards decisions that contributed to the remarkable growth in scale and technical performance of the overall network. Their track record owes much to their informal "quasi-academic" style of organization and their ability through much of this period (one during which the commercial possibilities of the Internet were largely unanticipated) to develop open standards in an environment free of the pressures of standard setting for proprietary technologies. Partly from sheer luck in the timing of various advances in its development, and partly because of the academic venue within which much of its development occurred, the Internet benefited from a standard-setting process that produced open standards, but did so in a relatively timely fashion.

9.2.2. 1985–2000: Internet Explosion

Although the use of the Internet grew during its early years, through at least 1985 its use was limited to researchers, computer scientists, and networking engineers. During the next fifteen years, however, the infrastructure created from the ideas developed during the earlier phase of the Internet's evolution was tested by phenomenal expansion in the number of new networks and users. Figure

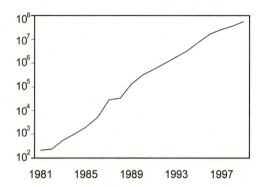

Figure 9.1 Total internet hosts. *Source:* Internet Software Consortium.

9.1, which depicts growth in total Internet hosts between 1981 and 2000, illustrates the rapid growth in Internet use.

9.2.2.1. Infrastructure Growth
In 1985, the NSF, by then one of several federal agencies managing the national "backbone" of the Internet, made the first in a series of policy decisions that encouraged the standardization of Internet infrastructure and promoted the widespread diffusion of the network. The 1985 decision required any university receiving NSF funding for an Internet connection to provide access to all "qualified users," and mandated the use of TCP/IP on its network. Standardization around TCP/IP encouraged interoperability and supported the creation of a large pool of university-trained computer scientists and engineers skilled in use of the protocol. In the same year, all of the federal agencies operating networks—DARPA, NSF, DOE and NASA—collaborated to establish the Federal Internet Exchange (FIX), a common connection point that allowed them to share their backbone infrastructure. The "peer to peer" model for exchanging traffic represented by FIX became a fundamental feature of the core Internet infrastructure. The process of network rationalization concluded with the decommissioning of the original ARPANET in 1990 and the transfer of its users and hosts to the new NSFNET. As had been the case with federal support for the early development of other computer technologies, DoD policymakers appear to have been more than willing to turn over the Internet

infrastructure created under their sponsorship to a broader academic user community.[13]

The accelerating growth of both regional networks and the NSFNET backbone in the late 1980s inspired a number of technical innovations. Increasing demand for capacity on the network backbone led to a continual stream of more efficient routers and bridges—specialized switches that control the flow of data at branching points in the network. The speed of the NSFNET backbone was upgraded from 56K (57,600 bits/s) in 1985 to T1 (1.5 million bits/s) in 1988 and to T3 (46.1 million bits/s) in 1991. Another technology made necessary by the growth in Internet infrastructure was the Domain Name Server (DNS), introduced in 1984. A DNS is a file, maintained on particular computers with known physical addresses, that contains a map from Internet domain names (e.g., haas.berkeley.edu) to the numerical network address scheme utilized by TCP/IP. The DNS provides a real-time concordance between machine-readable and humanly recognizable Internet addresses, something that is indispensable to the growth of a public network such as the Internet. A third important technological contribution was the creation of a hierarchical classification scheme for subnetworks. The creation of this classification system was indispensable to preventing saturation of the IP address space, a critical constraint to the growth of the Internet.[14]

These innovations were incorporated into networking hardware and software products whose market grew exponentially throughout the 1990s. The firms that came to dominate the market were not the large systems vendors such as IBM, DEC or Sun. Instead, a group of smaller firms, most of which were founded in the late 1980s, rose to prominence by selling multiprotocol products that were tailored towards the open platform represented by TCP/IP and Ethernet. Cisco, Bay Networks and 3Com, all new entrants into the industry, built large businesses selling products based on this open network architecture.

As the public network continued to grow, commercial enterprises expanded their role in its management. In 1987, NSF contracted with Merit Computer Networking for the management of the NSFNET backbone, and Merit formed a technical partnership with IBM and MCI to monitor and upgrade the infrastructure. The NSF also began encouraging universities to collaborate with commercial partners to create regional computer networks that could be connected to the larger NSFNET (Chinoy and Salo, 1997). The NSF supported this process by funding the creation of a series of Internet Exchanges (IXs) and Network Access Points (NAPs).[15] These facilities provided a physical location for regional networks to connect to the NSFNET's inter-regional network backbone using long-distance lines leased from telecommunications providers.[16] The increased involvement of private firms in development and management of the growing public network contributed to the growth of substantial private-sector expertise and served as an "incubator" for many of the entrepreneurs who founded Internet-based service firms and "dot.coms" in the 1990s.

Despite increasing private-sector participation in the management of the Internet, the NSF maintained an Acceptable Use Policy (AUP) that prohibited use of NSFNET for

---

[13] In the case of early technological advances in computing technology, DoD research sponsors sought the broadest possible dissemination of the underlying technical developments, in the expectation that the long-term national security benefits from such broad diffusion would exceed those associated with the exploitation of the technologies by defense-related researchers and firms (Langlois and Mowery, 1996).

[14] Class A IP addresses were reserved for large national networks, Class B for regional networks, and Class C for the growing number of smaller LANs.

[15] The terms NAP and IX emphasize different aspects of the backbone infrastructure. Originally, NAPs were the location where university subnets could connect to the NSFNET, while IXs were locations where commercial networks exchanged traffic. Because interconnect and peering are commonly located in the same physical facilities on the contemporary Internet, we use the terms interchangeably throughout.

[16] By this time the U.S. telecommunications system was well into the middle of its lengthy transition from regulated monopoly to competitive service provision, a development that aided in the competitive provision of Internet infrastructure.

"commercial purposes" until 1991. In practice, this meant that commercial users could access the NSFNET as a research tool, but were prohibited from using it to conduct business. As more commercial users attached to the network, on their own or in partnership with academic institutions, they increasingly lobbied the NSF to abandon the AUP. Private-sector demand for commercial-use inter-networking was fed by the growth in local-area networking, which had been developing since the late 1970s. As Unix workstations and microcomputers (PCs) began to overtake the minicomputer, and as demand for these machines was fueled by the creation of "killer-applications" such as document processing and spreadsheets, the number, size and scope of corporate networks began to grow. Growth in the demand for networking services was also spurred by the spread of the client/server computer architecture for distributed computing. NSF formally ended the AUP in 1991.

An important catalyst for the privatization of the Internet backbone was the creation of the Commercial Internet Exchange (CIX)—modeled on the federal agencies' FIX—in 1991. CIX was an alliance among a new group of companies called Internet Service Providers (ISPs), which leased lines from the large telecommunication companies to construct their own networks for carrying data. The major "backbone ISPs" that emerged in the late 1980s included California Education and Research Federation network (CERFnet), founded in 1988 and named in honor of Vint Cerf, PSINET (founded in 1989) and Alternet/UUNET (founded in 1987) (Zakon, 2000). In 1995, the transition of the core network infrastructure into private hands was completed when the NSF transferred control of its four major Network Access Points to Sprint, Ameritech, MFS, and Pacific Bell.

9.2.2.2. Origins of the Consumer Internet

Our discussion thus far has focused on the co-evolution of commercial and academic computer networking. Another important type of networking, centered on individual rather than institutional users, also emerged during the 1980s. The process began in 1975 with the introduction of the first "personal computer," the MIPS/Altair, an innovation that created a mass market for computer hardware, software, and services. Hobbyists quickly put this power to a variety of uses, including connecting personal computers to the telephone network through modems that enabled communication with other PCs. Compuserve launched the first commercial "bulletin board" or BBN service in 1979, the same year that Hayes Incorporated introduced a U.S.$400 modem for microcomputers that transmitted data at 300 bits per second.[17] Although Compuserve quickly gained thousands of subscribers, most bulletin boards remained local affairs run by hobbyists. Establishing a BBN required little more than a PC, a phone line, and a small modem bank. These services were largely bulletin boards and "chat rooms" where users with a variety of interests could meet and carry on a live conversation using e-mail. Online service providers could not offer their customers access to the broad portfolio of applications already available on the Internet.

Several companies followed Compuserve into the market, and the entire group became known as online service providers. The three largest on-line service providers—Prodigy, Compuserve and America Online—became household names. Prodigy was a joint venture between IBM, Sears and CBS Television (which exited the venture after two years) launched in 1984, while AOL was founded by Steve Case in 1985. These companies built their own networks that initially were independent of the NSFNET infrastructure. Over time, however, the core infrastructure of online service providers' networks grew to resemble and often coincide with the packet switches and leased lines of the larger ISPs.[18]

---

[17] Compuserve, was a small Ohio computer company founded in 1969 that happened to be among the first enterprises to spot the potential of microcomputer networking.

[18] The proprietary online services and the broader Internet utilized different technologies to link users' personal computers to the network. Since most PCs were not capable of running TCP/IP using a dial-up connection, they communicated with online service providers using modem protocols such as v.22 and v.32.

During the early 1990s, many small ISPs used dial-up connections to replicate the features of academic computer networks (Greenstein, 2000a). These small ISPs benefited from the distance-sensitive pricing of long distance telecommunication services that created opportunities for entry by ISPs into local markets, the focus of larger ISPs on high-density urban locations, and the fact that no more than a few hundred customers were needed to provide sufficient revenues to fund a modem pool and high-speed connection. At the same time, many of the larger online services hesitated to provide unrestricted Internet access, which they saw as diluting the value of their proprietary applications. In a classic illustration of the power of network externalities, the rising number of Internet hosts and users compelled the major online service providers to offer e-mail connectivity and later, browsing, in order to keep their customers.

The evolution of online service providers' offerings and the growing utilization of the Internet were also affected by the regulatory reform of telecommunications that began with the 1984 breakup of AT&T and by the Telecommunications Act of 1996.[19] The competition among telecommunication service providers that resulted from the 1984 Modified Final Judgment and the 1996 Act led to declines in prices for leased lines and long-haul services, key components of Internet infrastructure. Increased demand and entry by new service providers led to rapid investment in new capacity, particularly in major metropolitan areas, and brought telecommunications service providers into direct competition with national and regional ISPs. Incumbents like AT&T, Sprint and MCI have merged or now compete in a number of markets with new telecommunications carriers (Qwest, WorldCom, Level One), national ISPs (AOL, UUNET) and an army of regional ISPs. The PC networks that evolved from bulletin boards into online service providers were a significant source of Internet growth and competition in the market for access.

9.2.2.3. World Wide Web

In May 1991, Tim Berners-Lee and Robert Cailliau, two physicists working at the CERN laboratory in Switzerland, released a new document format called Hyper-Text Markup Language (HTML) and an accompanying document retrieval protocol called Hyper-Text Transfer Protocol (HTTP).[20] HTML was based on a well-known document formatting language known as Standard Generalized Markup Language (SGML), but added two key innovations. First, HTML incorporated a basic set of multimedia capabilities that allowed document authors to incorporate pictures and graphics into the text of their documents. Second, HTML was an implementation of hypertext—authors could specify particular words, phrases or images within a document as HTTP "links" that directed readers to another HTML document. Together, HTML and HTTP turned the Internet into a vast cross-referenced collection of multimedia documents. The collaborators named their invention the "World Wide Web" (WWW). The Web proved to be another Internet "killer application" and accelerated the emergence of the Internet as a global social and economic phenomenon.

In order to use the World Wide Web, a computer needed a connection to the Internet and the application software that could retrieve and display HTML documents. Although it was not the first functional Internet "browser," a free program called Mosaic that was written by Marc Andreesen, a student working at the University of Illinois' National Center for Supercomputing Applications, launched the Web on a rapid growth trajectory. During 1993, the first year that Mosaic was available, HTTP traffic on the Internet grew by a factor of 3416. By 1996, HTTP traffic was generating more packets than any other Internet application.

---

[19] According to the FCC's web site, "The goal of this new law is to let anyone enter any communications business—to let any communications business compete in any market against any other." (www.fcc.gov/telecom.html).

[20] The development of these important technical advances was motivated by Berners-Lee and Caillau's interest in facilitating the ability of physicists to archive and search the large volumes of technical papers being transmitted over the Internet as it then existed.

The HTML standard evolved considerably following its introduction, incorporating extensions that allowed programmers to add new features to web pages that facilitated multimedia capabilities, searching, purchasing and other complex interactions between the Internet user and a web site. A relatively informal Internet-based standard setting body, the World Wide Web Consortium (W3C), proved effective in maintaining a common standard for HTML, even in the face of the competitive battle between Microsoft and Netscape over their respective browsers (see Cusumano and Yoffie (1999), for an account of the "browser wars"). The W3C was founded in 1994 by Tim Berners-Lee at MIT in collaboration with CERN. The organization, which received support from DARPA and the European Commission, developed a set of technical specifications for the Web's software infrastructure that promoted openness, interoperability and a smooth evolution for the HTML standard.

The Web's popularity can be attributed to several factors. Adding visual content to documents opened up a new world for users who were not inclined to wade through pages of text on a computer terminal. Hypertext was also an effective way to organize and reference information when combined with a good browser. The simplicity and user-friendliness of HTML helped create an increasing-returns dynamic among early adopters. As users became familiar with the Web, many created their own documents and added them to the growing collection. As the amount and variety of information available started to take off during the early 1990s, still more users were drawn to the Web. As Greenstein (2000a) has pointed out, the explosive growth of the Web during the 1990s also benefited from the long period of gestation and refinement that the Internet infrastructure had enjoyed. By the early 1990s, the basic protocols governing the operations of the Internet had been in use for nearly twenty years, and their stability and robustness had improved considerably. The rapid diffusion of the innovation represented by the World Wide Web thus reflected the fact that it utilized a relatively mature infrastructure technology.

Although HTML and HTTP were not invented in the United States, the historic investments by the federal government and private industry in long-term research and infrastructure had created the conditions for its rapid domestic adoption and development. As a result, U.S. researchers and entrepreneurs were among the pioneers in developing commercial applications of the Web, despite the fact that their efforts relied on the non-U.S. inventions of HTML and HTTP. This successful inward transfer and exploitation of foreign inventions echoes a key feature of U.S. technological development during the late nineteenth and early twentieth centuries (Mowery and Rosenberg, 1998).

9.2.2.4. Commercial Applications: 1995–Present

The Web served as a major catalyst for the creation of commercial content that complemented the Internet's privatized infrastructure. Changes in the relative proportions of top-level "domain names" (the three-letter suffix to Internet addresses) provide an indication of the rise of commercial Internet content. In 1996, the commercial ".com" and ".net" domains contained roughly 1.8 times as many hosts as the educational .edu domain. By 2000, the term "dot com" had become a popular expression for fledgling Internet businesses, and the .com and .net domains accounted for more than 6 times as many hosts as the .edu domain. Where the commercialization of network infrastructure had occurred gradually in response to the ponderous forces of regulatory reform and investment flows, commercial use of the Internet grew explosively during the late 1990s. And although access to the Internet has diffused internationally with remarkable speed, U.S. firms retain a dominant position in the commercial exploitation of the Internet.

If there was a defining moment that marked the start of the manic commercialization of Internet content, it was the initial public offering (IPO) of Netscape in August of 1995. Netscape hoped to commercialize a version of the Mosaic browser, but at the time of its IPO, had made no profits and owned assets consisting largely of Mr Andreesen and a rapidly growing user base. Nevertheless, the offering was a spectacular success, and sparked a surge in entre-preneurial activity centered on applications of the Internet, much of which focused on imple-menting various forms of e-commerce. The level of enthusiasm for almost any business opportunity related to the Internet can be judged by the growth in the late 1990s in the stock-market valuations of Internet start-ups, the number of IPOs, or the amount of venture capital made available to Internet entrepre-neurs throughout the late 1990s. In 1995, there were a total of 657 information technol-ogy-related venture capital financings worth U.S.$3.3 billion. In 1999, four years later, there were more than 1,600 deals with a combined valuation in excess of U.S.$20 billion.[21]

Much of the entrepreneurial enthusiasm surrounding the Internet focused on business opportunities in the area of electronic commerce. Broadly defined, e-commerce is the use of the Internet as a medium for conducting transactions. A variety of traditional business activities have flourished on the Inter-net, including the retailing of consumer goods such as apparel, books, videos and recordings, and travel and event tickets. A number of more innovative transaction mechanisms including auctions, barter, and reverse-auctions (where buyers name the price that sellers can accept or decline) that are less common in traditional business environments have also grown rapidly in the e-commerce environment. Consumer-oriented e-commerce markets, such as online retailing, content delivery and auctions have generated high visibility and a number of recog-nizable "Internet brands" like Yahoo!, Amazon.-com and eBay, but the use of the Internet for intermediary or business-to-business transac-tions appears to have grown even faster.[22]

In the business-to-business environment, just as with consumer e-commerce, the Internet is streamlining established tasks and supporting innovative applications. Companies have found that applications running on an open network architecture and accessible through a browser can streamline a variety of traditional business processes, such as procurement, reim-bursements, shipping, and customer service. Internet-based applications are typically more flexible than the proprietary legacy software that they replace in back-office and logistics applications. The Internet's open architecture has also encouraged innovation. Many compa-nies now have "opened up" their supply chain by replacing bilateral transactions with virtual markets where suppliers and purchasers can meet to post bid and ask prices and exchange information. New online auction markets in commodities ranging from communications bandwidth to fresh fish, steel and computer programmers are an indication of the breadth of the Internet's potential impact on business and the economy.

9.3. The Internet and the U.S. Innovation System

The Internet resembles many postwar innova-tions in information technology in that it was invented and commercialized primarily in the United States. The invention, diffusion and commercialization of computer networking technology illustrate the operation of the unusual mix of institutions and policies that characterize the post-1945 U.S. "national inno-vation system" (Mowery and Rosenberg, 1993, 1998). Federal agencies such as the DoD and NSF played a critical role in funding the devel-opment and diffusion of early versions of the technology. Federal spending on R&D and procurement was complemented by the R&D investments of large corporations and the many start-ups that quickly appeared in Inter-net-related industries. These small firms often drew on expertise developed in U.S. research universities or in large corporations and bene-fited from the regulatory and antitrust policies of federal agencies such as the Federal Commu-nications Commission and the Justice Depart-ment. In this section, we examine the

---

[21] www.ventureone.com

[22] There are a number of estimates of the total volume of U.S. and global e-commerce prepared by private firms, but no commonly cited public statistics. Forrester Research placed the figure at U.S.$660 billion for 2000, but the figures presented by a variety of forecasting firms vary dramatically.

influence of these institutional components of the U.S. national innovation system on the development and adoption of the Internet.

9.3.1. The Role of Government-Sponsored Research

Federal R&D spending, much of which was defense-related, played an important role in the creation of an entire complex of "new" post-war information technology industries (including semiconductors, computers, and computer software) in the United States. The origins of the Internet can be traced back to these efforts. Internet-related projects funded through the DoD include Paul Baran's early work on packet switching, the ARPANET, and research on a variety of protocols, including TCP/IP. These public R&D investments in networking technology were preceded by a fifteen-year DoD investment in hardware and software technology that began with the earliest work on numerical computing. Federal R&D investments strengthened U.S. universities' research capabilities in computer science, facilitated the formation of university "spinoffs" like BBN and Sun, and trained a large cohort of technical experts who aided in the development, adoption, and commercialization of the Internet.

We lack the necessary data to estimate the total federal investment in Internet-related R&D. Even were such data available, the complex origins of the Internet's various components would make construction of such an estimate very difficult. Nevertheless, federal investments in the academic computer science research and training infrastructure that contributed to the Internet's development were substantial. According to a recent report from the National Research Council's Computer Science and Telecommunications Board, federal investments in computer science research increased fivefold during the 1976–95 period, from U.S.$180 million in 1976 to U.S.$960 million in 1995 in constant (1995) dollars. Federally funded basic research in computer science, roughly 70 percent of which wsa performed in U.S. universities, grew from U.S.$65 million in 1976 to U.S.$265 million in 1995 (National Research Council, 1999a: 53).

Langlois and Mowery (1996) compiled data from a variety of sources that indicate that between 1956 and 1980 the cumulative NSF funding for research in "software and related areas" amounted to more than U.S.$250 million (1987 dollars). Most of this funding went to U.S. universities. DARPA R&D funding from its Information Processing Techniques Office (IPTO), which went to both universities and industry, averaged roughly U.S.$70 million annually (1987 dollars) between 1964 and 1980, before growing sharply to more than U.S.$160 million in 1984–5. Between 1986 and 1995, the NSF spent roughly U.S.$200 million to expand the NSFNET (Cerf et al., 2000). The investments of NSF and DARPA in almost certainly constituted a majority of Internet-related R&D funding, especially in academia. These federal R&D expenditures were sizeable and importantly, contributed to both research and training of skilled engineers and scientists. Nevertheless, the scale of these investments pales in comparison with the investments by private firms in information technology during the 1990s (see below).

In addition to their size, the structure of these substantial federal R&D investments enhanced their effectiveness. DARPA's research agenda and managerial style gave researchers considerable autonomy and the agency spread its investments among a group of academic "centers of excellence" (MIT, UC Berkeley, Stanford, Carnegie-Mellon, the University of Utah, and UCLA).[23] DARPA frequently funded similar projects in several different universities and private R&D laboratories. Moreover, the DoD's procurement policy complemented DARPA's broad-based approach to R&D funding.[24]

---

[23] DARPA's early strategy in information technology R&D, beginning in the late 1950s, focused on the development of strong academic research institutions, rather than on peer-reviewed awards to individual investigators. Although DARPA research grants typically were made to individual researchers, this remarkably successful program did not adhere strictly to the norms of peer review that now are widely viewed as indispensable to research excellence (Langlois and Mowery, 1996).

[24] DARPA was strictly a defense R&D agency, and did not engage in large-scale procurement.

Contracts were often awarded to small firms such as BBN, which received the contract to build the first IMP. This policy helped foster entry by new firms into the emerging Internet industry, supporting intense competition and rapid innovation.

Another factor in the success of federal R&D programs was their "technology-neutral" character. U.S. research programs avoided the early promotion of specific product architectures, technologies, or suppliers, in contrast to efforts in other industrial economies, such as the French "Minitel" program, or celebrated postwar U.S. technology policy failures, such as supersonic transport or the fast-breeder nuclear reactor (Nelson, 1984). The NSF, for example, focused on funding a variety of academic research projects, largely through grants to university-based computer scientists. NSF support, dating back to the late 1950s, literally laid the foundation for the formation and growth of many U.S. universities' computer science departments, a key component of the research and training infrastructure that supported the development and diffusion of the Internet. In addition to their research contributions, university computer science departments and CSNET formed the core of the early Internet.

The diversity of the federal Internet R&D portfolio reflected the fact that these federal R&D investments were not coordinated by any central agency (even within the Defense Department), but were distributed among several agencies with distinct yet overlapping agendas. NASA and the DoE, for example, pursued their own networking initiatives in parallel with ARPANET during the 1970s, and DoD spending paralleled and occasionally duplicated NSF grants. In fact, the NSF's greatest single contribution to the diffusion of the Internet was the NSFNET program, which was initiated and carried out during a period of declining defense-related R&D investments in information technology. In an environment of technological uncertainty, this diversified and pluralistic program structure, however inefficient, appears to have been beneficial.

Despite considerable publicity, the Clinton Administration's initiatives in the "National Information Infrastructure" (NII) area involved modest new funding and consisted primarily of loose coordination among federal agencies of their programs in the computing and information technology areas (Kahin, 1997). The NII initiatives' most significant contributions may lie in their support for the pro-competition provisions of the 1996 Telecommunications Act, rather than in any R&D or investment funding. In some respects, the various advisory and interagency groups that comprised the Clinton Administration's NII may represent an interesting innovation in "post-Cold War" technology policy. Rather than allocating federal R&D investment funds or committing these funds to a particular technological architecture, these groups provided a forum for consultation and limited coordination among federal agencies and between the public and private sectors. These efforts primarily focused on promoting the development of the Internet infrastructure that by the mid-1990s was already expanding rapidly due to private investments.

The Internet's loosely organized governance institutions were another beneficiary of federal funding. Internet standard-setting largely avoided the long delays frequently associated with committee-based processes and the market power that the de facto creation of proprietary standards has produced in other sectors. Some of this success was fortuitous, as standards policies emerged during a period in which the commercial possibilities of the Internet were not apparent. However, the heavy involvement of academic and "quasi-academic" researchers in the standard-setting process, along with the largely public sector applications then envisioned for the Internet, contributed to the open processes that prevailed. These standard-setting processes resulted in relatively rapid technical decisions under conditions of great uncertainty and yielded protocols and standards that proved to be both technically robust and free to the technical community.[25]

---

[25] The federal government did not back individual platforms, but major "governance" decisions (e.g., the standardization of the ARPANET/NSFNET backbone on TCP/IP) favored the use of open standards.

9.3.2. Other Federal Policies

The role of the federal government in the development and diffusion of the Internet was not limited to its financial support for R&D, but also worked through federal regulatory, anti-trust, and intellectual property rights policies. The overall effect of these (largely uncoordinated) policies was to encourage rapid commercialization of Internet infrastructure, services and content by new, frequently small firms.

AT&T's failure to capture a large share of the computer networking market is a good illustration of the important role played by federal regulatory and antitrust policy. The Department of Justice's 1949 antitrust lawsuit against AT&T was settled by a 1956 consent decree that was modified in the 1982 conclusion to the federal antitrust suit against AT&T that was filed in 1974. The FCC hearings, "Computer I and II," (decided in 1971 and 1976, respectively) declared that computing lay outside the boundary of AT&T's regulated monopoly (Weinhaus and Oettinger, 1988). The 1956 consent decree and the FCC hearings imposed significant restrictions on AT&T's activities outside of telecommunications services. As a result, several of Bell Laboratories' major information technology innovations, including both Unix and the C programming language, were licensed on liberal terms and diffused extensively. Unix in particular was widely adopted within the academic community and played a major role in the diffusion of TCP/IP.

Federal telecommunications policy, particularly the introduction of competition in local markets following the 1984 break-up of AT&T, also affected the evolution of the Internet in the United States. The 1984 Modified Final Judgment stipulated that Regional Bell Operating Companies (RBOCs) would not be allowed into long distance until they established competitive local markets. This meant allowing Competitive Local Exchange Carriers (CLECs) to connect to the network infrastructure on reasonable terms that would allow them to compete in various retail markets. The spread of local competition promoted the widespread availability of affordable leased lines that allowed commercial ISPs to connect their networks to IX points, long-haul carriers, and one another. The Telecommunications Act of 1996 reinforced competition in markets for broadband data communication.

State and federal regulations in the pricing of telecommunications services also aided the domestic diffusion of the Internet. State regulators have long enforced low, time-insensitive rates for local telecommunications service, in order to encourage the broadest possible access to local phone service. Regulators extended this time-insensitive pricing policy to ISPs. Most ISPs established their modem banks within the local loop and were classified by the FCC as "enhanced service providers." This classification was reaffirmed in the FCC's May 1997 "Access Reform Order," and ensured that ISPs did not have to pay the same per minute access charges that long-distance companies pay to local telephone companies for use of the network. Unmetered local access for residential telephone services encouraged the growth of the ISP industry in local markets and the widespread diffusion of the network among residential customers in the United States.[26]

U.S. intellectual property rights (IPR) policy also affected the evolution of the Internet, although the influence of IPR policy is less obvious and direct than that of antitrust policy or telecommunications deregulation. Many of the key technical advances embodied in the Internet (such as TCP/IP) were placed in the public domain from their inception. This relatively weak intellectual property rights regime reflected the network's academic origins, the Defense Department's support for placing research into the public domain, and the inability of proprietary standards to compete with the open TCP/IP standard. The resulting widespread diffusion of the Internet's core technological innovations lowered barriers to the entry by networking firms in hardware, software and services. Although patent rights in the United States have been strengthened significantly since 1980, this policy shift did not initially affect

---

[26] As we note below, metered pricing of local telephone services is associated with lower penetration rates for the Internet in other industrial economies.

the software-based architecture and protocols at the heart of the Internet.[27] Intellectual property rights for Internet-related software and services now appear to be somewhat stronger, as a result of federal judicial decisions and other developments, and they are likely to exercise a greater influence over the future evolution of the Internet.

9.3.3. *The Role of the Private Sector*

Our emphasis thus far on the numerous examples of successful publicly funded R&D in Internet-related technologies should not be construed as suggesting that private R&D and related investments were unimportant to the development and diffusion of the Internet. Private-sector institutions played important roles in inventing, diffusing and commercializing the Internet. Privately financed research led to the development of several basic networking technologies, including networking hardware, Unix and the Ethernet protocol.[28] Start-up firms were crucial to the commercialization of Internet-related innovations. And perhaps most importantly, U.S. industry invested heavily in information technology during the 1980s, supporting the rapid diffusion of the TCP/IP network during the 1990s.

Although we lack data on the size of corporate R&D investments in the development of Internet-related technologies, several firms made major contributions to networking research. Two of the standards contributed by the corporate research community, Unix and Ethernet, arguably were as influential as TCP/

IP in supporting the diffusion of the Internet.[29] The proprietary network architectures and protocols developed during the 1980s by a number of large firms, such as IBM's SNA architecture, remain significant. Interestingly, very few of the corporate developers of these advances, most of whom were large firms, reaped significant profits from their innovations. The growth and stock market performance of open-architecture entrants such as 3Com rapidly outstripped those of larger incumbents that focused on proprietary solutions.

Small firms and start-ups, many of which had close links to U.S. university researchers, also played an important role in commercializing networking technology. Beginning with BBN's contract to build the first IMP, small private firms commercialized a number of important Internet-related innovations. Start-ups contributed to the development of the basic Internet infrastructure (BBN, Novell, 3Com) and expanded the market for Internet service (AOL, Prodigy, Compuserve). The importance of new firms in networking and Internet services echoes their importance in other postwar U.S. information technology industries, such as semiconductors and software.

A third major contribution of private sector institutions was their sustained level of investment in the information technology that provided the foundation for the domestic adoption of the Internet. Data from the U.S. Department of Commerce indicate that expenditures on software and information technology accounted for 24 percent of total U.S. private fixed investment in 1970, U.S.$8.31 billion in constant 1996 dollars. IT's share of annual private sector investment flows grew during the next thirty years, exceeding 30 percent throughout the 1980s and remaining above 40 percent during the 1990s, reaching U.S.$542.2

---

[27] The Internet helped to spawn the Free or Open Source software movement, which has taken an extremely strong stance against the use of patents and copyright in the software industry.

[28] Ethernet was developed by Robert Metcalfe at the Xerox Palo Alto Research Center (Xerox PARC) in 1972. It is the most widely used protocol in the many corporate, academic and institutional Local Area Networks (LANs) that comprise the Internet. Unlike TCP/IP, which operates through gateways to connect different networks, Ethernet governs the operation of computers on a single network that share a physical connection.

[29] Both Unix and Ethernet were developed within the private sector, but quickly became part of the public domain. Critics who note that Xerox failed to capture most of the surplus generated by the invention of Ethernet tend to overlook the link between openness and the success of the standard, as well as the complementary relationships between Ethernet and other Xerox-owned technologies in fields such as laser printing.

billion in constant 1996 dollars by 1999. This investment in computing power created a huge installed base of hardware that could be attached to the network, an attribute shared by few other industrial nations. Moreover, much of this hardware was already attached to some type of network, whether an office LAN running Ethernet or the Wide Area Network of an online service provider. Adoption of the Internet involved little more than connecting these various networks and installing TCP/IP on each of the computers.

9.3.4. Internet Commercialization and the Changing U.S. Innovation System

The commercial exploitation of the Internet that began in the 1990s drew on federal investments in network infrastructure that originated in the Cold War era. Many of the institutions that contributed to the development of the Internet also played a role in its explosive commercial growth, but the role of others declined in importance during the post-Cold War period of the 1990s. This shift reflected both the maturation of the technology and change in the structure of the U.S. innovation system. Although antitrust and deregulatory telecommunications policies remained influential, defense spending on basic R&D came to be overshadowed by private sector R&D investment. Commercialization was fueled by the

availability of capital in a healthy macroeconomic environment and the unique opportunities associated with a large and technologically sophisticated domestic market.

As the population of Internet users continued to grow throughout the 1990s, many businesses quickly moved online, producing a dramatic surge in the number of.com hosts and in the visibility of the 30-year-old network. U.S. financial markets played a key role in the commercialization of the Internet by ensuring a robust supply of equity and venture-capital financing for new firms (Gompers and Lerner, 1999). Figure 9.2 shows the growth in U.S. venture capital funding of technology start-ups between 1995 and 2000. The important role of venture capitalists in supporting the creation of new firms for commercial exploitation of the Internet parallels their roles in the development of the semiconductor, computer, and biotechnology industries in the postwar U.S. economy (Mowery and Rosenberg, 1993, 1998).

The large size of the U.S. domestic market and its heavy investments in information technology also accelerated Internet commercialization. The diffusion of personal computers in the home and workplace established a large domestic market that was standardized around two desktop computing platforms (Apple and the IBM-PC). This led to the growth of private fortunes in packaged software as well as the creation of a homogeneous, large domestic

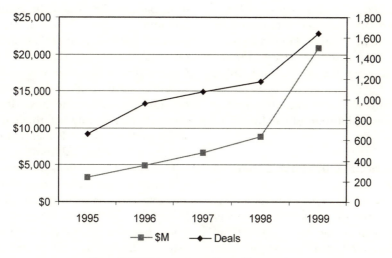

Figure 9.2 VC investments. *Source:* Venture One.

market for the commercialization of consumer Internet applications, including e-commerce. As a result, U.S. firms were first movers in many hardware, software and networking applications and products. Many of these firms took advantage of the scale economies characteristic of both hardware and software products to gain large leads in supplying the global market for Internet-related products and services.

The Internet explosion of the 1990s in the United States relied on close university–industry links, an abundant supply of venture capital, an increasingly active antitrust policy, and a deregulatory posture in telecommunications. Most if not all of these policy elements have been important factors within the U.S. innovation system since 1945, although the type of intragovernmental and public–private coordination exemplified by the NII contains some novel elements within civilian technology policy. Defense-related procurement, which played a prominent role during earlier stages of the Internet's development, was not an important factor during the 1990s. Defense-related R&D investment in Internet-related fields, such as computer science, also declined modestly throughout the decade, although cutbacks in DoD R&D investments in computer science were more than offset by increased investments from other federal agencies such as NSF and the Department of Energy (National Research Council, 1999b: 83–4). The relatively open intellectual property rights regime that typified the development of Internet infrastructure also appears to have shifted towards a "pro-patent" posture. Finally, the shift in U.S. macroeconomic policy from its destabilizing posture during the 1970s and 1980s toward greater stability assuredly contributed to the capital investment boom that underpinned the domestic diffusion of the Internet.

9.4. The Internet in Other Industrial Economies

Although the United States was consistently at the forefront of networking research, computer scientists from around the world played an important part in the effort and made a number of significant contributions to the development of the Internet. European academic accomplishments often rivaled those of U.S.-based computer scientists, but the lack of a common public platform as large as ARPANET or NSFNET meant that many European countries lagged the United States in the early stages of Internet development and adoption. The persistence of state telecommunications monopolies, the scarcity of technical talent, and the dominance of English language content on the Internet also contributed to a lag in European adoption. Nevertheless, the Internet has diffused globally with remarkable speed. Nearly every nation on the planet can now access the Internet in some capacity, and counts of new Internet hosts indicate that most developing economies are experiencing the exponential growth trajectory already traversed by many industrial economies. Moreover, current measures of Internet adoption indicate that parts of Europe have caught up to or surpassed the United States. This section reviews the historical and statistical evidence on the international diffusion of the Internet.

9.4.1. History

From its beginning, computer networking research was an international endeavor, and a number of European countries established experimental networks during the early years of ARPANET. In 1967, the British networking pioneer Donald Davies (who invented the term packet) developed the National Physical Laboratory Data Network in Middlesex, England. In 1972, Louis Pouzin led a French effort to build an ARPANET replica called CYCLADES. Experimental packet-switched networks were developed and tested throughout Europe during the next decade, but the research community on the continent never developed a unified networking platform comparable to the ARPANET.

During the early 1980s the first links between U.S. and European networks were established and experiments in intra-European and U.S.-European collaboration began. In 1982, the first international ARPANET nodes were established at University College in London and at NORSAR, a research laboratory in Norway, and two new European research networks, the European Unix Network (EUNet) and the European Academic and Research Network (EARN), were launched. EUNet ran the Unix to Unix Copy Protocol (UUCP) and EARN ran a protocol called Network Job Entry (NJE). These networks offered basic services similar to those of ARPANET, such as e-mail and file transfer, to the European academic and research community. Nevertheless, the standards adopted by these European networks did not achieve the widespread success of the TCP/IP protocol suite, and the European networks grew more slowly than the TCP/IP-based Internet.[30]

Perhaps the best-known European networking experiment of the 1980s was the French Minitel service, launched in 1981. In many ways, Minitel was a precursor of the World Wide Web, offering users a variety of services ranging from computer dating to government services, travel reservations, banking and telephone directories. Despite its qualified success within France, however, Minitel did not achieve the success of its eventual successor, the World Wide Web. Although some of Minitel's limitations were technological, the system was based on a proprietary architecture, rather than the open architecture characteristic of the Internet. Its closed architecture meant that development of new applications for Minitel was more difficult than was true of the Internet, and the smaller commercial opportunities provided by the Minitel further discouraged such development activity. Nevertheless, Minitel was a farsighted, early attempt to bring the benefits of data networking to a large group of users (OECD, 1998).

Computer users from industrial economies outside the United States began to attach to the NSFNET infrastructure in large numbers towards the end of the 1980s. In 1988, Canada, Denmark, Finland, France, Iceland, Norway, and Sweden connected to the NSFNET. They were followed in 1989 by Australia, Germany, Israel, Italy, Japan, Mexico, Netherlands, New

Zealand, and the United Kingdom. Around this time, Reseaux IP Européens (RIPE) was created by the fledgling European ISP industry to provide the administrative and technical coordination needed to establish a European IP Network. Although RIPE was founded shortly after the major U.S. backbone service providers PSI, UUNET and CERFnet had created CIX, Europe lacked the important complementary factors that propelled rapid growth of hosts and users in the United States during the early 1990s. These complements included an extensive academic network operating on a common platform, a large regional LAN infrastructure, a commercial online services industry, a strong domestic base of network equipment manufacturers, and a huge private investment in computing infrastructure.

The structure of regional telecommunications markets also slowed the development of an ISP industry and the growth of Internet-based commercial business models throughout much of Europe and Japan. The widespread persistence of local telecommunications monopolies and the use of metered access charges for local telephony limited Internet usage and restricted entry by ISPs. Figure 9.3 illustrates the lag in telecommunications deregulation of many OECD countries relative to the United States. As late as 1997, fewer than half of the OECD member economies had significant domestic competition in telecommunications services. Figure 9.4 shows the relationship

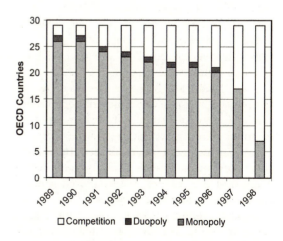

Figure 9.3 OECD telecom regulation. *Source:* OECD.

---

[30] Ironically, the decision to use TCP/IP as the standard for the rapidly growing NSFNET was made in 1985 with the help of Dennis Jennings, who came to the NSF from Ireland to help coordinate the transition from ARPANET to NSFNET.

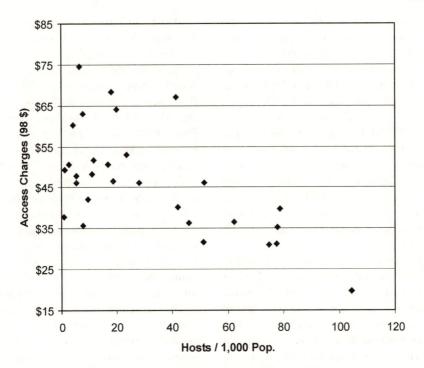

Figure 9.4 Pricing and Internet hosts. *Source:* OECD.

between Internet access charges and adoption rates for the OECD countries. Not surprisingly, the figure shows a downward sloping "demand" for Internet services (i.e., higher access charges are associated with slower diffusion rates for the technology). Additional evidence on the relationship between telecommunications pricing and network diffusion is provided by the high penetration of both Internet hosts and secure servers in Australia, Canada, New Zealand and the United States, the four OECD countries with unmetered pricing of local telecommunications services (OECD, 2000: 30).

Despite the apparently slower pace of Internet adoption in some European economies, by the late 1980s, the Internet had been widely adopted throughout the industrial economies. Slight lags in infrastructure development or the adoption of new services can easily be overcome in an environment characterized by double-digit compound growth rates in both investment and use. Indeed, international statistics on Internet adoption suggest that several European countries had surpassed the United States in various measures of Internet penetration by the late 1990s. Nonetheless, these

economies appear to lag the United States in the adoption of e-commerce (see below).

9.4.2. International Adoption and Diffusion Patterns

The data on Internet hosts used to construct Figure 9.1 and several of the other statistics presented below are from a census of Internet hosts originally run by Network Wizards and now maintained by the Internet Software Consortium. This project tracks Internet hosts dating back to the first computers on the original ARPANET, and is one of the best-known sources of data on network growth and diffusion. Although these data provide measures of aggregate adoption that extend back to the formative days of the Internet, meaningful international comparisons are not available until the 1990s, when the network had been widely adopted in the largest and wealthiest economies. Even as the Internet penetrated more nations, however, its growth remained very rapid in the regions that originally had dominated its adoption. This section discusses the diffusion of the Internet during the 1990s, supplementing direct measures of network

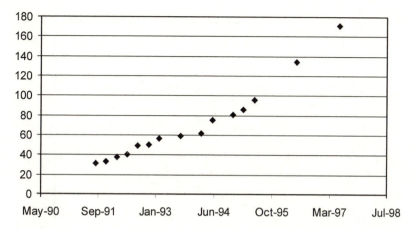

Figure 9.5 Country-specific top-level domains. *Source:* Internet Software Consortium.

adoption with a variety of telecommunications infrastructure indicators collected by national regulatory authorities and the OECD.

One measure of the international diffusion of the Internet is the number of countries with Internet access, proxied by the number of country-specific top-level domains, such as.uk (United Kingdom) or.de (Germany). Figure 9.5 shows the rapid growth in country-specific top-level domains between 1991 and 1997. All of the OECD countries were connected to NSFNET prior to 1991, and much of the developed world was connected to the network by 1993. The rapid growth after 1994 is associated with growth among late-adopting African and Asian countries as well as a number of smaller nations. By 1997, with a few exceptions, the Internet had reached every corner of the globe.

Host counts provide another indication of the relative intensity of Internet use within different regions.[31] Figure 9.6 depicts growth in the total number of Internet hosts for five

major geographic regions during the 1986–2000 period on a logarithmic scale. Within each of these regions, the number of Internet hosts grew exponentially during this period. The roughly parallel growth trends for each region depicted in the figure suggest that the United States and Canada are about one year ahead of Europe and as much as four years ahead of Asia in overall Internet adoption, with the rest of the world lagging considerably behind. The continuing rapid growth of the network in North America makes it difficult to predict when or whether this international "adoption gap" will begin to close. Infrastructure indicators, such as the global distribution of Internet Exchange points (IXs) shown in Figure 9.7, provide a similar picture of the size of regional networks.[32]

Host counts and IX counts indicate the absolute size of regional networks but do not provide a useful metric for international comparisons of the intensity of utilization in different regions; nor do they provide a basis on which to predict future growth. Per capita measures of computer and Internet penetration and statistics on infrastructure investment are needed to address these questions. The per capita host counts in Figure 9.8 were

---

[31] The top-level domain of each host computer provides a good indication of that host's country of origin. Although many top-level domain names indicate the country of origin directly (e.g., .de for Germany or .uk for England) this is problematic for a few countries—notably the United States—where the majority of hosts have a "generic" top-level domain, such as .com or .edu. There is, however, a limited amount of information on the domain name registration system that allows allocation of these generic top-level domains (gTLDs) among countries. We have chosen to allocate gTLDs based on the gTLD registration data for 1998 published by Imperative, Inc. and published in the OECD Communications Outlook (1999c).

[32] The number of IXs around the world—and particularly in the United States—is now growing so rapidly that there is a reasonable level of uncertainty about the figures, but across various counts, the relative size of regional networks appears fairly consistent regardless of the specific sources.

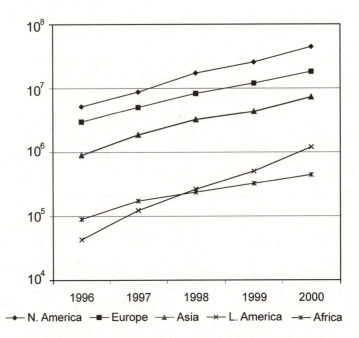

Figure 9.6 Regional Internet diffusion. *Source:* Internet Software Consortium.

constructed by the OECD using data from Network Wizards. This comparison indicates that several Nordic countries have achieved higher rates of penetration of the Internet than the United States and Canada, which lead the rest of the industrial economies. The relatively high levels of Internet penetration in countries like Finland may be associated with that nation's historically competitive telecommunications industry structure, in addition to

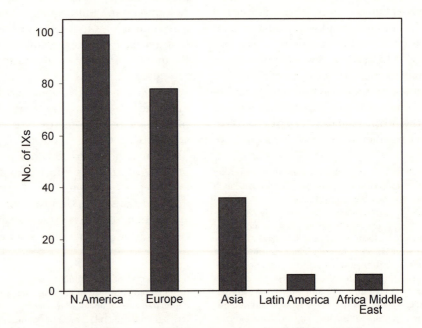

Figure 9.7 Regional Internet exchanges. *Source:* Telegeography (1999).

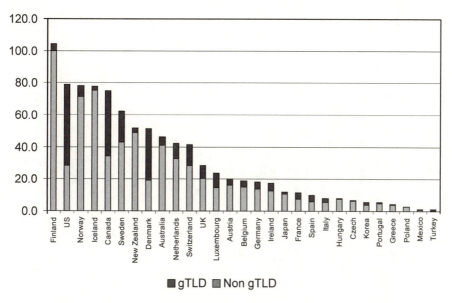

Figure 9.8 Hosts per capita (gTLD generic top-level domains). *Source:* OECD.

high levels of domestic adoption of personal computers, currently the most common method of Internet access, within these nations.[33] One measure of the potential for future Internet growth in various national economies is the extent of network penetration relative to PC ownership (Figure 9.9). The United States and several Nordic countries have achieved relatively high levels of per PC connectivity, indicating that short-run network growth opportunities may be greater in other large European countries that currently have lower shares of their large domestic PC installed base connected to the Internet.

Another indicator of the potential for future Internet growth is the worldwide investment in data networking capacity. Investments in bandwidth are necessary for the growth of Internet infrastructure, and promote Internet adoption through the downward pressure they exert on prices for telecommunications services. Investments in bandwidth also reflect investors'

expectations of growth in the demand for capacity required to link new devices, applications, and users to the global network. Figure 9.10, which shows FCC projections of the total available trans-Atlantic and trans-Pacific bandwidth originating in the United States, illustrates the dramatic surge in bandwidth that will accompany the arrival of several new fiber-optic lines during 1999 and 2000. OECD forecasts of capacity and pricing trends around the world also suggest that declining prices for leased lines will continue to encourage the expansion of the Internet and electronic commerce (OECD, 1999b: 5).

In addition to evidence on the growth and regional penetration of the Internet, more limited data illustrate global trends in Internet use, especially the commercialization of Internet content during the late 1990s. The share of different top-level Internet host domains (".edu," ".com," ".gov," etc.) is one indicator of change over time in Internet content within the global network. Figure 9.11 shows the total number of Internet hosts within the six major generic top-level Internet domains between 1996 and 2000. Hosts within the.edu and.org domains correspond to the academic institutions and quasi-academic governance organizations that were the earliest adopters of the

---

[33] With the rapid adoption of Internet-capable cell telephones and other handheld electronic devices, PC connectivity is likely to become a less reliable indicator of Internet penetration. Adoption of some of these devices, such as Internet-capable cell phones, is occurring more rapidly outside of the United States.

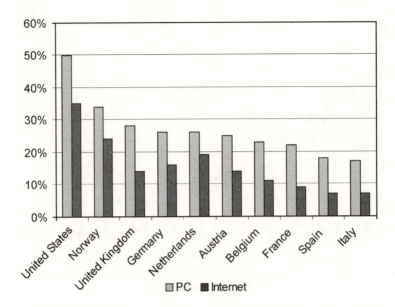

Figure 9.9 PC and Internet penetration. *Source:* IDC/Goldman Sachs (1999).

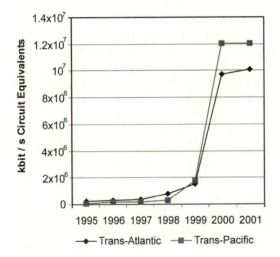

Figure 9.10 U.S. network capacity expansion. *Source:* FCC.

Internet, and the majority of.com and.net hosts are owned by commercial organizations and private network service providers. The rapid growth of.com and.net hosts and domain name registrations illustrate the explosion of commercial Internet content discussed above.[34]

[34] This figure understates the actual growth in commercial Internet content because it fails to account for the many non-U.S. commercial sites registered under country-specific top-level domains (e.g., www.amazon.de).

A clearer picture of contrasts in national adoption of e-commerce applications is provided by data from a census of Secure-Sockets Layer (SSL) servers conducted by Netcraft and published by the OECD (1999). SSL is a protocol used by commercial websites to encrypt sensitive information, such as credit card numbers, before transmitting it over a network. The number of Internet hosts using SSL therefore is a reasonable proxy for the number of e-commerce sites within a given domain. Figure 9.12 shows the number of SSL servers per capita as calculated by the OECD for member nations. The figure highlights the fact

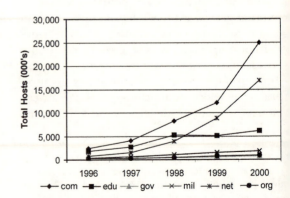

Figure 9.11 Hosts by top-level domain. *Source:* Internet Software Consortium.

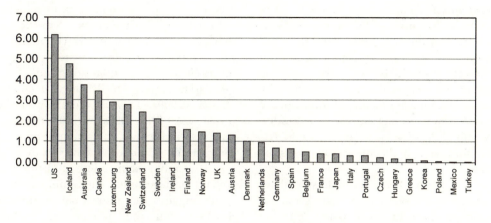

Figure 9.12 Secure servers per capita (per 1000 population). *Source:* OECD.

that the United States appears to be the world leader in adopting e-commerce, based on the per capita level of encryption-enabled Internet servers.[35] Surprisingly, this measure suggests that the Nordic states with high Internet penetration rates have been slower to adopt e-commerce than other nations, such as New Zealand and Australia.

As a whole, these statistics on Internet adoption underscore the importance of the relationships among domestic telecommunications regulation, telecommunications infrastructure, and Internet adoption. Although the United States arguably is no longer the indisputable leader in Internet utilization, the United States appears to be a leader in e-commerce applications. These statistics also reinforce the central statistical fact about the Internet as a general purpose technology—its remarkable rate of growth. In spite of the significant national and regional differences in the adoption of network infrastructure and applications, the Internet has grown and continues to grow at an exponential pace within the global economy.

9.5. The Economic Impacts of the Internet

9.5.1. Macroeconomic Impacts

"You can see the computer age everywhere but in the productivity statistics" (Solow, 1987). Robert Solow's now famous quote summarizes the "productivity paradox" debated by economists for the past twenty-five years. Annual labor productivity growth in the business sector declined from an average rate of 3 percent during the 1948–73 period to roughly one-half that during 1973–90 (Council of Economic Advisers, 2000). Paradoxically, this measured decline in productivity growth coincided with a revolution in information technology that many believed was having a profound and positive impact on the productivity of individual workers throughout the economy. Solow and other economists puzzled over this apparent contradiction throughout the 1980s.

Beginning in the early 1990s, however, the American economy entered a period of sustained growth with low unemployment and inflation that seemed to signal a recovery in the rate of long-term growth. Labor productivity

---

[35] This indicator of e-commerce adoption is not without problems. In particular, U.S. statistical leadership may simply reflect the much larger number of U.S. websites—the United States almost certainly leads among industrial nations in the number of ".com," ".edu," and ".gov" sites per capita. But the available alternative measure of e-commerce adoption, the ratio of "SSL Hosts/Total Internet Hosts" on a per country basis, is difficult to interpret. SSL servers constitute an extremely large share of total hosts in small countries (e.g., Poland) with relatively few overall Internet hosts. Pornographic sites also exercise a disproportionate influence within simple counts of e-commerce hosts. We believe that the per capita SSL host count is the best available measure of e-commerce adoption within individual nations.

growth during 1995–9 increased to an average of 2.8 percent per year in the business sector of the economy (Council of Economic Advisers, 2000: 26). During the same period, rapid growth in equity prices, the decline in rates of unemployment to levels not seen since the 1960s, and relatively stable prices all gave rise to characterizations of the U.S. economy of the 1990s as a "New Economy," in which new industries would flourish, equity prices would rise without limit, and the business cycle would be repealed.

At least a few of these sunny illusions have been clouded by events (especially events in the equity markets) during 2000 and 2001, but the coexistence of the Internet's rapid diffusion and the remarkable performance of the U.S. economy during the past decade are taken by some observers as a measure of the Internet's aggregate economic impact. One interpretation of these events is that networking technology served as the catalyst that unleashed the long-awaited productivity gains of information technology. Nevertheless, measuring the effects of the Internet and e-commerce on growth in incomes and productivity is difficult, reflecting a number of factors that have impeded measurement of the aggregate economic effects of information technology more generally (a good recent survey of these general problems is provided in David, 2000).

Among the most important of these difficulties is that of measuring output. The Internet and information technology more generally have supported the creation of new products or dramatic improvements in the quality of established products. Neither of these sources of economic benefit is measured well in the public statistical data. Indeed, much of the reported productivity impact of computers can be found in the computer industry, in large part because only this sector of the U.S. economy has benefited from a systematic effort by U.S. public statistical agencies to adjust measured output for quality improvement. In addition, many Internet and information technology applications affect the productivity or creation of new products in the nonmanufacturing sector, where output measurement has always been poor and no attempts have been made by the U.S. public statistical agencies to adjust measured output for quality improvement.

In a recent review of the "New Economy" debate, the OECD points out that the 1990s were characterized by a pattern of growing divergence in gross domestic product (GDP) per capita among OECD member economies (OECD, 2000). This divergence, which spans the decade of the 1990s, was caused by a simultaneous reduction in unemployment and increase in labor productivity within a few OECD economies, including the United States, Ireland, and Australia. The timing of the divergence suggests that more than the Internet is involved, but the accelerating multifactor productivity (MFP) growth between 1995 and 1997 among the OECD economies that include the most rapid adopters of the Internet is striking. The OECD concludes that these divergent trends reflect a changing relationship between innovation and economic growth,[36] and argues that information technologies, including the Internet, have played a key role in facilitating these developments.[37] Moreover, the report argues that divergence among member economies in their performance during the late 1990s could prove to be enduring. In this view, the first-mover advantages enjoyed by U.S. firms in exploiting the Internet rely in part on demand-side scale economies within a global information technology marketplace. Certainly, the evidence provided earlier on the differential rates with which commercial applications of the Internet have been adopted in various industrial economies suggests that the United States remains a leader in this field. Nevertheless, there is very little basis on which to evaluate this assessment of the Internet's aggregate economic impact.

In seeking evidence of the economic impacts of the Internet, it is important to keep in mind

[36] "… innovation has become more market-driven, more rapid and intense, more closely linked to scientific progress, more widely spread throughout the economy." (OECD, 2000: 8).

[37] The OECD report also acknowledges that the economic effects of the large-scale adoption of the Internet cannot yet be observed in aggregate economic data (OECD, 2000: 56–7).

the fact that widespread commercial exploitation of this technology is scarcely five years old, a relatively short period during which to anticipate measurable impacts on the overall economy. Moreover, many applications of the Internet will require significant complementary investments in physical capital and related technologies, as well as significant organizational innovations, before they realize their productivity-enhancing potential. Consequently, we can anticipate that the investments and experimentation that necessarily precede productivity impacts will take a significant amount of time. As David (2000) points out, realization of the productivity benefits of electric power in the U.S. economy took more than forty years, largely because of the need for these complex complementary investments and organizational innovations. Information technology generally, and the Internet in particular, are likely to involve similar complementary investments and innovations, and the realization of any productivity or growth impacts of the Internet will take considerable time.

9.5.2. Firm-level Impacts

In light of these measurement challenges, as well as the relatively short time during which the Internet has been applied on a large scale, it is hardly surprising that evidence on the aggregate economic impacts of the Internet is lacking. Nevertheless, a small number of studies of the Internet's impact on individual markets and industries have been conducted, and their results suggest that even at this level the effects of the new technology are complex. For example, Smith et al. (2000: 106) review the empirical evidence on pricing in e-commerce markets and find that there is relatively little consensus. Contradictory results are obtained from different studies of "the effect of e-commerce" on price levels and demand elasticities, even for relatively simple commodities such as books and recorded music. Contrary to the popular wisdom that e-commerce will lead to uniform pricing with rapid competitive adjustments, the three papers surveyed by these authors indicate that online retail markets lead to increases in price dispersion. There is some evidence that

these results reflect consumers' retailer brand-awareness, trust, and the quality of the shopping experience. The increased information provided by the Internet thus appears to have complex effects on consumer behavior that are not yet fully understood.

In another survey examining the case study and empirical literature on the firm-level productivity effects of information technology, Brynjolfsson and Hitt (2000) point to "organizational complements such as new business processes, new skills, and new organizational and industry structures as a major driver of the contribution of information technology." They review evidence from a number of case studies and from empirical examinations of the relationship between information technology investment and financial market performance and between information technology and organizational change. While each approach has its weaknesses, the sum of the evidence points towards information technology having a measurably positive impact on economic performance at the firm level that is amplified by the presence of organizational complements, a finding that is nearly as old as information technology itself (a review of this older evidence may be found in Cyert and Mowery, 1987). These recent findings on the effects of information technology thus are consistent with much prior evidence, but none of these studies separates the firm-level effects of the Internet from those of information technology more generally.

A number of important aspects of the economic importance of the Internet have yet to be addressed within the academic literature. Most of the studies cited above, for example, focus on the impact of the Internet at the retail level. The Internet's effect on business-to-business transactions remains largely unexplored. A common hypothesis is that the network will encourage "disintermediation" in business-to-business supply chains, the replacement of specialized brokers, dealers, and marketing agents by direct transactions between customer and supplier. While the importance of reputation and related nonprice features within Internet-based retail markets suggest the importance of some types of intermediary (e.g., intermediaries that guarantee delivery schedules and product quality) much more than that of others (e.g., those providing pricing information), very little empirical research has been conducted to evaluate such speculative observations. More generally, the importance of intermediaries is likely to depend on the idiosyncrasies of particular markets and transactions.

In addition to its flimsy empirical foundations, the popular mythology of a "New Economy" that is powered by the Internet suffers from a major conceptual flaw. New economy enthusiasts often presume a sharp divide between the firms and industries likely to benefit from spectacular productivity gains, and those that are consigned to "Old Economy" stagnation. In actuality, the Internet, like semiconductors or electrical power, is a pervasive technology that will be adopted by "Old" and "New Economy" firms alike. Much of the eventual (possibly measurable) productivity impact of the Internet is likely to be realized through its application by well-established firms in traditional industries to streamline supply chains and enhance marketing activities. These activities will not be the exclusive province of new firms in entirely new industries. Like the division between "high-technology" and "low-technology" industries or "sunrise" and "mature" sectors of the economy, the implicit conceptual division between an "Old Economy" and a "New Economy" is fallacious. Technologies flow across industry boundaries, and their application by established industries—a process that consumes considerable time, learning, and investment—is an important source of aggregate growth in productivity, income, and welfare.

Reconciling the discrepancies between measures of the impact of information technology on aggregate economic performance and estimates of the impact of this technology at the firm level is an important research task on which there has been surprisingly little progress, given the effort devoted to this issue. Moreover, distinguishing between the productivity effects of the Internet per se and those of information technology more generally poses an additional forbidding intellectual challenge. The limited evidence that is currently available should inspire caution, rather than hyperbole,

among the proponents of a "New Economy" powered by the Internet. As with other general purpose technologies, it will take time for the Internet and its many associated applications to diffuse, for complementary technical and organizational innovations to occur, and for the cumulative effects of these changes to be understood and ultimately measured.

9.6. Internet-related Public Policy Issues

One area in which the effects of the Internet are apparent is in the challenges created by its international and domestic adoption and its commercial applications in myriad economic activities for public policy. In the limited space available to us, we can do little more than highlight several of these: (1) the causes and economic consequences of unequal access to the Internet; (2) the new issues raised by the Internet for competition policy; and (3) the interaction between the Internet and the growth of new forms of intellectual property protection in the United States. This review only scratches the surface with respect to Internet-related policy issues, but it provides a sense of the technology's extraordinarily broad and diverse implications.

9.6.1. Unequal Internet Access

Despite its rapid global diffusion, the Internet reaches fewer than half of the households in even the most wired countries. Large-scale commercial applications of the Internet are likely to be limited by the level and pace of its adoption, and substantial income-related differences in adoption rates will affect the distribution of the Internet's benefits. Studies by the U.S. Department of Commerce's National Telecommunications and Information Administration indicate that income, education, and race are significant predictors of computer and Internet use within U.S. households.[38] The NTIA finds that even when income is held constant, there are statistically significant gaps

---

[38] "Falling Through the Net" http://www.ntia.doc.gov/ntia-home/fttn99/

of eight to ten percent in computer penetration between white and black households. The survey also indicates that white households are more likely to have home Internet access than Black or Hispanic households are to have any kind of network access. But the NTIA study also indicates that computer and Internet use is spreading quickly within all demographic groups, suggesting that the long-term domestic "digital divide" could decline in severity.

Whether long-term declines in differential access to and use of the Internet will offset the consequences of these current domestic inequalities is an issue that goes far beyond the scope of this chapter. From a global perspective, however, the digital divide is just one manifestation (and arguably not the most important one) of the broader inequalities that deprive eighty percent of the world's population of access to a telephone. Extending the benefits of the Internet and information technology to this large majority of the world's population is an important challenge. Internet access may be less important to the quality for these groups, however, than (equally unavailable) clean drinking water, a fact that should temper the more sweepingly optimistic assessments of the Internet's potential effects on global economic welfare.

9.6.2. The Internet and Competition Policy

The proper scope of antitrust and competition policy in the information technology industries attracted a great deal of attention during the 1990s. Many of these debates over competition policy focus on the Microsoft antitrust lawsuit. (Articles by Fisher, Davis and Murphy, and Hall in the May, 2000 *American Economic Review* provide a good overview of the case.) The Microsoft trial includes a variety of complex issues, but a central concern is the relationship between desktop computer operating systems and the Internet. The U.S. Department of Justice asserted that Microsoft abused its monopoly position in the market for PC operating systems in order to prevent the Internet browser from becoming an effective competitor. Microsoft's response has been that the company should be free to pursue innovations that its customers demand, such as tighter integration between its browser and the operating system. The company has also suggested that it is unnecessary to pursue aggressive antitrust actions in the rapidly changing information technology market, where technological competition will provide sufficient discipline for companies with market power.

Microsoft's arguments concerning the appropriate role of antitrust policy in technology-intensive industries have wide-ranging implications. The final judicial response to these arguments (which may well come from the U.S. Supreme Court) will influence much more than this giant software firm. For example, there is a debate over whether the owners of residential cable television lines should be subject to the same common-carrier provisions that force local telephone operators to lease their infrastructure to third-parties. This issue, which figured prominently in the 2000 review by the Federal Trade Commission of the merger between America Online and Time Warner, has major implications for the provision of high-speed Internet access. The cable companies' argument—that competition between the cable and telephone platforms will discipline their pricing—resembles Microsoft's position. The networks, network externalities, and rapid innovation that characterize these industries present a number of challenges to regulators who want to balance the benefits of competition against the risk of reducing the rate of technological innovation in nascent industries. The outcome of the FTC's review of the AOL–Time Warner merger, which mandated that Time Warner provide access to other providers of Internet content, suggests that (as in the Microsoft case), federal authorities are likely to press for relatively liberal access by the providers of complementary technologies to the "platforms" created by dominant infrastructure or operating system firms.

9.6.3. Intellectual Property Policy

As we noted earlier, the Internet developed and diffused rapidly in an environment of relatively weak formal intellectual property rights covering its architecture and networking protocols.

With the expansion of business applications of the Internet, however, this situation has changed significantly. The "pro-patent" posture of the federal judiciary, especially the U.S. Court of Appeals for the Federal Circuit (CAFC), has increased the value of patents on Internet-related "business methods." On August 23, 1998, the CAFC validated a controversial software patent in *State Street Bank v. Signature Financial Group* that covered a method for computing the closing prices of stocks for mutual funds.[39] Since the *State Street* decision, "business-methods" patenting has expanded rapidly—the number of applications to the USPTO for such patents doubled from 1285 in 1998 to 2600 in 1999, and more than 600 patents on business methods issued in 1999.

Like all new technology fields, business methods patent applications create great challenges for the U.S. Patent and Trademark Office's examiners. Examination of patents for their validity and nonobviousness typically relies heavily on searches by examiners of patent-based "prior art," patents issued to other inventors. But in a new technology field, such "prior art" may be lacking. Moreover, the business methods field is especially controversial, because the CAFC's decision in *State Street* extended patent protection to an area in which developers have been active for some years. The recent flurry of business methods patent applications thus may include applications covering technical methods long in use, but not previously patented. This situation is made worse by the tendency for technical advances in software and Internet technologies to be highly cumulative—thus, inventors may be unwittingly infringing on intellectual property that has suddenly been protected by a patent.

Patenting and patent litigation in the business methods area have grown in the wake of *State Street*. Several firms have filed patent applications for "one-click" Internet ordering techniques, and the Internet vendor of books and other products, Amazon.com, has threatened to sue other Internet firms for allegedly infringing its patent on "one click" order methods. Priceline.com, another Internet marketing firm, has sued Microsoft over the latter's alleged infringement of its patented "reverse auctions."

The long-term implications of this wave of patenting and litigation are uncertain, but the reliance on litigation within the U.S. patent system for determining patent scope and validity means that the growth in business methods patents could result in an atmosphere of litigious paralysis. In a series of speeches in the Spring of 2000, USPTO Commissioner Dickinson announced that the Patent Office would expand its efforts to examine "prior art," in order to reduce the patenting of nonnovel business methods (see Graham and Mowery, 2000). The USPTO also announced a "Business Methods Patent Initiative" that among other things will seek to improve the training of patent examiners and expand searches of nonpatent prior art. Moreover, the flurry of business methods patent applications themselves should over time provide a much more extensive body of patent-based prior art for such searches. The ultimate economic significance of business methods patents, however, will almost certainly be determined by the reactions of European and other OECD nations' patent offices to similar applications. The e-commerce activities that are covered by such these patents are very footloose, and a business methods patent that is valid only in the United States may prove to be of little commercial value.

Among other things, the challenges raised by the Internet for U.S. intellectual property rights policies underscores the fact that the Internet may have far-reaching consequences for the structure and performance of the U.S. national innovation system. The "business methods" patent controversy illustrates another characteristic of national intellectual property rights regimes that is frequently overlooked by economists and other scholars who wish to treat these policies as exogenous. In fact, national IPR systems and national economies and innovation systems "co-evolve" in a complex, path-dependent, and interactive fashion. The Internet is only the latest illustration of this long-established historical tendency.

[39] 149 F.3d 1368 (CAFC, 1998).

9.7. Conclusion

The Internet's development began nearly forty years ago, and continues to evolve in a dynamic and unpredictable fashion. It is impossible to forecast the ultimate effects of this "general purpose technology" on incomes, economic growth, and the conduct of our daily lives. The rapid diffusion of the Internet during a period of strong U.S. economic performance has fueled speculation about its role in creating a new economy. But the full economic impact of the Internet will not be felt for some time, and its effects may never admit of easy measurement. Nevertheless, preliminary indications are that the Internet's effects on all of these areas are likely to be profound. The network of networks that is the Internet began as a small publicly funded experiment run largely by academics, but it has grown into a global enterprise requiring major private investments in infrastructure and applications, spurring a host of technological and commercial innovations.

Among the important "nontechnological" innovations spawned by the Internet was an unusually informal, yet responsive, set of institutions to manage its evolution and, in particular, to establish technical standards. The ability of these institutions of governance to develop open standards and to adapt these standards rapidly to meet new technical and economic challenges was remarkable, and contributed powerfully to the rapid diffusion of the Internet. The success of these standard-setting institutions may have implications for the governance of related innovations, because of the central importance of technical standards for technological development and market structure in the information technology sector.

Although it drew on important technical advances from foreign sources, the development of the Internet was primarily a U.S.-based phenomenon, and drew on many of the same institutions and policies of the postwar U.S. "national innovation system" that were influential in other postwar high-technology industries. The prominent role of Defense Department funding and procurement in the development of the Internet and related technologies is in many respects an artifact of the Cold War era, and DoD funding is likely to play a smaller role in the future evolution of these technologies. The strength and breadth of formal intellectual property rights, whose relative weakness in Internet-related technologies arguably supported the Internet's rapid development, have also been extended considerably since the early 1980s, with uncertain effects on the future development of the Internet and related technologies. Other elements of the postwar U.S. "national innovation system," however, such as the vibrant equity-finance system and the historically close relationships between U.S. industry and universities, have changed the era of the Internet. Venture capital finance appears to have played a greater role in the commercial exploitation of the Internet, and the focus of many university–industry formal research relationships emphasizes patenting and licensing of faculty inventions to a greater extent than historically was the case (Mowery et al., 2001). Although many other industrial economies now seek to emulate the remarkable success of U.S. firms in commercializing the Internet, the "transferability" of the web of U.S. policies and institutions, not least the scale of the U.S. domestic market, may limit the diffusion of these business models. In a global economy that is more and more tightly integrated, many of the institutions and policies characteristic of the U.S. national innovation system remain unusual, if not unique, by comparison with those of other industrial economies.

For all its novelty, the development and diffusion of the Internet closely resemble those of other "general purpose technologies," such as the much broader area of information technology or electric power, or such important yet more limited technologies as the airplane. Like all of these major innovations, the Internet underwent a prolonged period of "gestation" that dates back more than thirty years (the first "node" was inaugurated in 1969). Although the current Internet relies on the same basic protocols and principles as its predecessor of more than thirty years ago, the ease of use and performance of the current Internet have dramatically improved, due in no small part to the remarkable advances in the complementary technologies on which the Internet relies. We confidently predict that this period of incremental refinement and improvement will continue for some years to come. Another hallmark of the Internet, like radio, is the profound uncertainty over its economic applications and effects. The "dot.com depression" of 2000 should give pause to anyone claiming to understand "best practice" for commercial applications of the Internet. Both this uncertainty over applications and the prolonged period of incremental improvement and refinement are hallmarks of virtually all major innovations, and means that the economic effects of the Internet, like those of these other major technical advances, are likely to be realized gradually and through a process of trial and error.

Like other major innovations, the Internet also raises profound challenges to policy in a number of areas. We have noted the complexities created within intellectual property rights by the recent surge of Internet-related "business methods" patents; but this example is only one of many policy issues raised by the Internet, ranging from encryption technologies to privacy and equality of access to the Internet (the so-called "digital divide"). These policy issues will challenge governments in the industrial and industrializing nations alike. For example, further commercialization of the Internet by U.S. firms is likely to require the resolution of policy conflicts among the United States and other industrial economies in areas such as intellectual property and personal privacy. The ability of the Internet to overcome the "tyranny of distance" means that its global diffusion is likely to add to the growing pressure for harmonization of the many policies that affect various national innovation systems. This process will be slow, conflict-ridden, and uneven, not least because of the enduring national uniqueness of many such policies in the United States and other industrial economies. Ultimately, however, the computer network's impact in the policy arena, as in business and technology, will reflect the tremendous breadth and scope of application inherent in this important general purpose technology.

Appendix A: An Internet Timeline (adapted from Hobbes' Internet Timeline by Robert H. Zakon) www.zakon.org/robert/internet/timeline

1957	USSR launches Sputnik, first artificial earth satellite. In response, United States forms the Advanced Research Projects Agency.
1961	Leonard Kleinrock, MIT: *Information Flow in Large Communication Nets*, first paper on packet-switching theory.
1964	Paul Baran, RAND: *On Distributed Communications Networks*, packet-switching networks; no single outage point.
1965	ARPA sponsors study on "cooperative network of time-sharing computers"—MIT Lincoln Lab and System Development Corporation (Santa Monica, CA) are directly linked (without packet switches) via a dedicated 1200 bps phone line. Digital Equipment Corporation (DEC) computer at ARPA later added to form "The Experimental Network".
	Donald Davies, NPL: *Proposal for the Development of a National Communications Service for On-line Data Processing*, first NPL network plan.
1966	Lawrence G. Roberts, MIT: *Towards a Cooperative Network of Time-Shared Computers*, first ARPANET plan.
1967	ARPANET design discussions held by Larry Roberts at ARPA IPTO PI meeting in Ann Arbor, MI.
	First design paper on ARPANET published by Larry Roberts: *Multiple Computer Networks and Intercomputer Communications*.
	National Physical Laboratory (NPL) in Middlesex, England develops NPL Data Network using 768 kbps lines.

1968   Request for proposals for ARPANET sent out in August; responses received in September.
        University of California Los Angeles (UCLA) awarded Network Measurement Center contract in
        October.
        Bolt Beranek and Newman, Inc. (BBN) awarded Packet Switch contract to build Interface Message
        Processors (IMPs).
1969   ARPANET commissioned by DoD for research into networking.
        Nodes are stood up as BBN builds each IMP (Honeywell DDP-516 mini computer with 12K of
        memory); AT&T provides 50 kbps lines.
        Node 1: UCLA (30 August, hooked up 2 September).
        Node 2: Stanford Research Institute (SRI) (1 October).
        Node 3: University of California Santa Barbara (UCSB) (1 November).
        Node 4: University of Utah (December).
        First Request for Comment (RFC): *Host Software* by Steve Crocker (7 April).
        First packets sent by Charley Kline at UCLA as he tried logging into SRI. The first attempt resulted in
        the system crashing as the letter G of LOGIN was entered (October 29).
1970   First publication of the original ARPANET Host-Host protocol: C.S. Carr, S. Crocker, and V.G. Cerf,
        HOST-HOST Communication Protocol in the ARPA Network, in AFIPS Proceedings of SJCC.
        ARPANET hosts start using Network Control Protocol (NCP), first host-to-host protocol.
        First cross-country link installed by AT&T between UCLA and BBN at 56 kbps.
1971   Ray Tomlinson of BBN invents e-mail program to send messages across a distributed network.
1972   Ray Tomlinson (BBN) modifies e-mail program for ARPANET.
        Larry Roberts writes first e-mail management program (RD) to list, selectively read, file, forward, and
        respond to messages.
        International Conference on Computer Communications (ICCC) demonstration of ARPANET
        between forty machines organized by Bob Kahn.
        International Network Working Group (INWG) formed in October as a result of a meeting at ICCC
        identifying the need for a combined effort in advancing networking technologies.
        Louis Pouzin leads the French effort to build CYCLADES.
1973   First international connections to the ARPANET: University College of London (England) via
        NORSAR (Norway).
        Bob Metcalfe's Harvard PhD Thesis outlines idea for *Ethernet*.
        Bob Kahn poses Internet problem, starts internetting research program at ARPA. Vinton Cerf sketches
        gateway architecture in March on back of envelope in a San Francisco hotel lobby.
        Cerf and Kahn present basic Internet ideas at INWG in September at University of Sussex, Brighton,
        UK.
        ARPA study shows e-mail composing seventy-five percent of all ARPANET traffic.
1974   Cerf and Kahn publish *A Protocol for Packet Network Interconnection* which specified in detail the design of
        a Transmission Control Program (TCP) (*IEEE Trans. Comm.*).
        BBN opens Telenet, the first public packet data service (a commercial version of ARPANET).
1976   Unix-to-Unix CoPy (UUCP) developed at AT&T Bell Laboratories and distributed with *UNIX* one year
        later.
1978   TCP split into TCP and IP (March).
1979   Meeting between University of Wisconsin, DARPA, *National Science Foundation* (NSF), and computer
        scientists from many universities to establish a Computer Science Department research computer
        network (organized by Larry Landweber).
        ARPA establishes the Internet Configuration Control Board (ICCB).
1981   Computer Science NETwork (CSNET) built by a collaboration of computer scientists and University of
        Delaware, Purdue University, University of Wisconsin, RAND Corporation and BBN through seed
        money granted by NSF to provide networking services (especially e-mail) to university scientists with
        no access to ARPANET. CSNET later becomes known as the Computer and Science Network.

Minitel (Teletel) is deployed across France by France Telecom.

RFC 801: *NCP/TCP Transition Plan.*

1982   Norway leaves network to become an Internet connection via TCP/IP over SATNET; University College London does the same.

DCA and ARPA establish the Transmission Control Protocol (TCP) and Internet Protocol (IP), as the protocol suite, commonly known as TCP/IP, for ARPANET.

European UNIX Network (*EUnet*) is created by EUUG to provide e-mail and USENET services. Original connections between the Netherlands, Denmark, Sweden, and UK.

Exterior Gateway Protocol (RFC 827) specification. EGP is used for gateways between networks.

1983   Name server developed at University of Wisconsin, no longer requiring users to know the exact path to other systems.

Cutover from NCP to TCP/IP (1 January).

CSNET/ARPANET gateway put in place.

Desktop workstations come into being, many with Berkeley UNIX (4.2 BSD) which includes IP networking software.

European Academic and Research Network (EARN) established. Very similar to the way BITNET works with a gateway funded by IBM.

1984   *Domain Name System* (DNS) introduced.

Number of hosts breaks 1000.

1986   NSFNET created (backbone speed of 56 kbps)

Internet Engineering Task Force (IETF) and Internet Research Task Force (IRTF) comes into existence under the IAB.

The first Freenet (Cleveland) comes on line.

1987   NSF signs a cooperative agreement to manage the NSFNET backbone with *Merit Network, Inc.*

UUNET is founded with Usenix funds to provide commercial UUCP and Usenet access.

First TCP/IP Interoperability Conference.

Number of hosts breaks 10,000.

1988   DoD chooses to adopt OSI and sees use of TCP/IP as an interim. U.S. Government OSI Profile (GOSIP) defines the set of protocols to be supported by Government purchased products.

NSFNET backbone upgraded to T1 (1.544 Mbps).

California Education and Research Federation network (CERFnet) founded by Susan Estrada.

Internet Assigned Numbers Authority (IANA) established in December with Jon Postel as its Director.

Countries connecting to NSFNET: Canada (CA), Denmark (DK), Finland (FI), France (FR), Iceland (IS), Norway (NO), Sweden (SE).

1989   Number of hosts breaks 100,000.

Reseaux IP Européens (*RIPE*) formed by European service providers.

First relays between a commercial electronic mail carrier and the Internet: MCI Mail and Compuserve.

Countries connecting to NSFNET: Australia (AU), Germany (DE), Israel (IL), Italy (IT), Japan (JP), Mexico (MX), Netherlands (NL), New Zealand (NZ), Puerto Rico (PR), United Kingdom (UK).

1990   ARPANET ceases to exist.

Electronic Frontier Foundation (EFF) is founded by Mitch Kapor.

The World comes on line (world.std.com), becoming the first commercial provider of Internet dial-up access.

Countries connecting to NSFNET: Argentina (AR), Austria (AT), Belgium (BE), Brazil (BR), Chile (CL), Greece (GR), India (IN), Ireland (IE), Korea (KR), Spain (ES), Switzerland (CH).

1991   Commercial Internet eXchange (CIX) Association, Inc. formed by General Atomics (CERFnet), Performance Systems International, Inc. (PSInet), and UUNET Technologies, Inc. (AlterNet), after NSF lifts restrictions on the commercial use of the Net.

World-Wide Web (WWW) released by *CERN*; Tim Berners-Lee developer.

Pretty Good Privacy (PGP) released by Philip Zimmerman.

NSFNET backbone upgraded to T3 (44.736 Mbps).

NSFNET traffic passes 1 trillion bytes/month and 10 billion packets/month.

Countries connecting to NSFNET: Croatia (HR), Czech Republic (CZ), Hong Kong (HK), Hungary (HU), Poland (PL), Portugal (PT), Singapore (SG), South Africa (ZA), Taiwan (TW), Tunisia (TN).

1992   Internet Society (ISOC) is chartered.

Number of hosts breaks 1,000,000.

Countries connecting to NSFNET: Antarctica (AQ), Cameroon (CM), Cyprus (CY), Ecuador (EC), Estonia (EE), Kuwait (KW), Latvia (LV), Luxembourg (LU), Malaysia (MY), Slovakia (SK), Slovenia (SI), Thailand (TH), Venezuela (VE).

1993   U.S. National Information Infrastructure Act.

Mosaic takes the Internet by storm; WWW proliferates at a 341,634 percent annual growth rate of service traffic.

Countries connecting to NSFNET: Bulgaria (BG), Costa Rica (CR), Egypt (EG), Fiji (FJ), Ghana (GH), Guam (GU), Indonesia (ID), Kazakhstan (KZ), Kenya (KE), Liechtenstein (LI), Peru (PE), Romania (RO), Russian Federation (RU), Turkey (TR), Ukraine (UA), UAE (AE), U.S. Virgin Islands (VI).

1994   NSFNET traffic passes 10 trillion bytes/month.

Countries connecting to NSFNET: Algeria (DZ), Armenia (AM), Bermuda (BM), Burkina Faso (BF), China (CN), Colombia (CO), Jamaica (JM), Jordan (JO), Lebanon (LB), Lithuania (LT), Macao (MO), Morocco (MA), New Caledonia (NC), Nicaragua (NI), Niger (NE), Panama (PA), Philippines (PH), Senegal (SN), Sri Lanka (LK), Swaziland (SZ), Uruguay (UY), Uzbekistan (UZ).

1995   *NSFNET reverts back to a research network*. Main U.S. backbone traffic now routed through interconnected network providers.

The new NSFNET is born as NSF establishes the *very high speed Backbone Network Service (vBNS)* linking super-computing centers: NCAR, NCSA, SDSC, CTC, PSC.

WWW surpasses ftp data in March as the service with greatest traffic on NSFNet based on packet count.

Traditional online dial-up systems (*Compuserve, America Online, Prodigy*) begin to provide Internet access.

Net related companies go public, with *Netscape* leading the pack.

Registration of domain names is no longer free (NSF continues to pay for.edu registration, and on an interim basis for.gov).

1996   Internet phones catch the attention of U.S. telecommunication companies who ask the U.S. Congress to ban the technology (which has been around for years).

MCI upgrades Internet backbone adding ∼13,000 ports, bringing the effective speed from 155 Mbps to 622 Mbps.

WWW browser war fought between Netscape and Microsoft.

1998   Web size estimates range between 275 (Digital) and 320 (NEC) million pages.

Network Solutions registers its 2 millionth domain on 4 May.

Appendix B. Bandwidth Terms

Network Capacity Terminology

	Bits/s	Mbit/s	Dowload time for 5 MB file
14.4 modem	14400	0.01	52 min
56K line	57600	0.06	12 min
128K ISDN	131072	0.13	5 min
T1	1536000	1.54	43 s
T2	6144000	6.3	7 s
T3	46080000	45	1 s
OC-3	155000000	150	0.5 s
OC-12	600000000	600	0.15 s
OC-48	2400000000	2400	NA
OC-192	9600000000	9600	NA

10

Computers and Semiconductors

Richard N. Langlois

10.1. Introduction

At the end of the twentieth century, it became common to talk of the "digital revolution," a historical phenomenon worthy of its place among the various industrial revolutions of the previous two centuries. Underlying the digital revolution is the technology of the semiconductor, a device that emerged at the century's half-way point. Although the digital revolution ramifies itself throughout the modern world, notably into telecommunications and consumer goods, its most signal embodiment is the digital computer, a technology born at almost exactly the same point in history.

Figure 10.1 suggests why the progress of digital technology appears so revolutionary. One very broad measure of the power of a computer is the number of so-called floating-point operations (like adding together two numbers) a machine can perform in a second. The first truly digital computer, the ENIAC of 1946, cost some U.S.$750,000 to produce—something like U.S.$6,265,000 in 1998 dollars—and could perform 5,000 calculations per second. The circa 1998 Pentium II computer on which I am writing this chapter cost about U.S.$1,500 and can perform 200 million calculations per second. That is about U.S.$1.25 billion per million floating-point operations per second (MFLOPS) for the ENIAC—and about U.S.$8 per MFLOPS for the Pentium II. This phenomenal decline is tied to the rapid improvement of the semiconductor technology on which computers now depend.[1]

Using broad strokes, this chapter sketches the intertwined history of these two industries—semiconductors and computers. In so doing, it attempts to shed light on the sources of technological change in these industries and on the complex mechanisms through which that technological change has translated into economic growth.

A distinctive theme in this history will be the emergence and significance of *general-purpose technologies* (GPTs). Such technologies (and their attendant systems of skill and knowledge) typically develop in response to specific technological puzzles or bottlenecks, but they ultimately generate principles and techniques that are applicable to a wide variety of otherwise distinct output sectors of the economy (Bresnahan and Trajtenberg, 1995; Bresnahan and Gambardella, 1998). Nathan Rosenberg (1963) described this process as *technological convergence*. Because what is learned once can be reused many times, technological convergence generates the something-for-nothing effect economists call *increasing returns*, a phenomenon at the heart of economic growth.[2]

---

[1] Data in this paragraph and in Figure 10.1 are from Kurzweil (1999: 320–1).

[2] By the concept of "returns" economists mean the following. If you double all your inputs and get exactly double the output, that is constant returns to scale. If you double your inputs and get less than double your output, that is diminishing returns to scale, the bane of economic growth feared by David Ricardo and the classical economists. If you double your inputs and get more than double your outputs, that is increasing returns to scale. Technological convergence generates increasing returns because one can double output without having to double one of the inputs (knowledge). Notice also that by economic growth economists usually have in mind intensive growth, that is, growth in real output per capita, rather than extensive growth, which is just plain growth in real output.

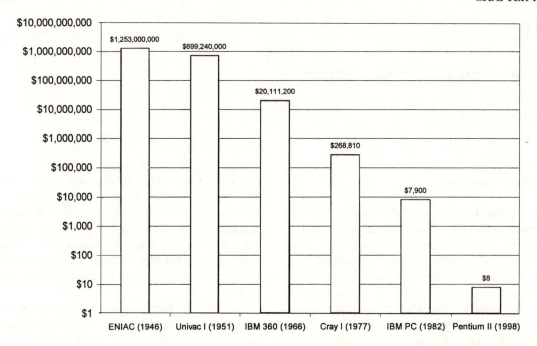

Figure 10.1 The decreasing cost of computing power (1998 U.S.$ per MFLOPS). *Source:* Kurzweil (1999: 320–1).

This chapter argues that the rapid performance improvements and price declines experienced by the semiconductor and computer industries can be traced to the status of these technologies as GPTs. Perhaps the most important GPT is the planar process, the basic technique for fabricating increasingly large numbers of transistors on a single chip. But there are other related GPTs as well, including the integrated circuit, standardized memory, the microprocessor, the von Neumann stored-program architecture of computers, and modular computer platforms.

The chapter also makes a number of more specific arguments about the sources of American success in digital technology.

- America benefited early on from federal demand for both semiconductors and computers, but the role of computer demand quickly supplanted government procurement as a driver of semiconductor technology. The two technologies codeveloped or coevolved in a virtuous cycle of technological progress, with declining costs in semiconductors driving increased demand for computers, and increased demand for

computers driving cost declines in semiconductors.

- Universities played a crucial role in the birth of the digital computer and in developing the field of computer science, a body of knowledge complementary to the computer. But universities played little role in the birth and development of semiconductor technology, which was driven by the capabilities of semiconductor firms.

- Technological advance and diffusion of both semiconductor and computer technology depended on the *lack* of broad intellectual-property protection, especially of the principles underlying fundamental general-purpose technologies.

- Like its early success, the recent resurgence of the American semiconductor industry can be traced to the synergistic effect of demand from the American computer industry, in this case the microcomputer industry. Contrary to most pronouncements at the nadir of American fortunes in the mid-1980s, American institutions and industrial structure have not proven inherently inferior to those of Japan; indeed, in its ability to spur innovation, the vertically fragmented American industry may prove the more viable long-term model.

- Government policy toward the semiconductor and computer industries around the world has had a significant effect on the development of those industries, but the actual effects were often quite different from those intended. In both Japan and the United States, policy to foster cooperative research and development never proved effective, although in both cases it had some benefit in enhancing capabilities in the semiconductor equipment, rather than directly in the semiconductor manufacturing, industry. National policies to promote a mainframe computer industry on the model of IBM diverted resources from areas of national comparative advantage and were ultimately rendered irrelevant by the development of the microcomputer.

10.2. Semiconductors and Computers: an Interwoven History

10.2.1. The Origins of Semiconductor Technology

Even though semiconductors and computers were born in the years immediately following World War II, their institutional origins were quite different. The invention of the computer involved both universities and direct government research funding. By contrast, the transistor—the basic building block of the semiconductor industry—emerged from private research at AT&T's Bell Labs. Because of its success and its secure status as the nation's telephone monopoly, AT&T was able to pursue a policy of research that, while arguably more focused toward commercial ends than basic research at universities, was nonetheless willing to indulge basic science and to envisage a research agenda quite far from commercial fruition.[3]

One of the long-run problems facing the Bell System was the expansion of a switching system

based on electromechanical relays. By the 1930s, Mervin Kelly, the research director at AT&T's Bell Labs, was voicing the opinion that electromechanical relays would eventually have to be replaced by an electronic alternative in order to handle the growing volume of traffic. William Shockley, one of the three Bell scientists to receive the Nobel Prize for the transistor, was impressed by this observation, and believed that the objective would be best realized with solid-state technology (Shockley, 1976).

Bell Labs announced the transistor in December of 1947.[4] Almost immediately transistor technology began spilling out to other firms. This was not, however, a process in which slippery knowledge leaked unintentionally to others but rather a deliberate and systematic attempt by AT&T to disseminate know-how through inexpensive licenses, technical symposia, and site visits (Tilton, 1971: 75–6; Braun and Macdonald, 1978: 54–5). The main driver of this policy was the consent decree AT&T had just signed with the Antitrust Division of the U. S. Justice Department, which specified how the company was to treat technology outside the scope of the company's primary mission.[5] But there is also reason to think that AT&T pursued the strategy of dissemination because the company saw value in taking advantage of the capabilities of others. AT&T was still primarily concerned with the usefulness of transistors to its own line of business, telephone switching. Although AT&T had developed the transistor and begun using it early in telephone devices and circuits, it was still an extremely immature technology. The company believed that if it allowed access to the transistor, telephony would reap the benefits of spillovers from the development of the capabilities of others in the electronics industry to an extent that would outweigh the foregone revenues of proprietary

---

[3] For a classic account of how the research environment at Bell Labs led to the transistor, see Nelson (1962).

[4] For detailed histories of the invention of the transistor, see Braun and Macdonald (1978), Morris (1990), and Nelson (1962).

[5] AT&T's strategy of dissemination may also have been motivated by a desire to preempt any thought the military might have had of classifying the technology (Levin, 1982: 58).

development[6] (McHugh, 1949; Bello, 1953; Braun and Macdonald, 1978: 54; Levin, 1982: 76–7).

One implication of this policy of easy access to the basic technology is that profits—or "rents," as economists would put it—would accrue not to the inventors as much as to those who could make innovative commercial improvements in the basic technology. The unintended consequence was thus to create a large cohort of entrants intent on finding ways to commercialize this new technology (Mowery and Steinmueller, 1994).

The large vacuum-tube firms, as well as Bell Labs itself, continued to be major sources of transistor innovations through the 1950s, especially in the realm of process and materials. The work of this period led ultimately to a pivotal innovation that did allow for rapid experience-based improvements and cost reductions: the *planar process*, a development arguably responsible for the increasing-returns trajectory upon which the semiconductor industry now finds itself. But the planar process was not developed by Bell Labs or by any of the established vacuum-tube firms. Instead, in what would become a pattern characteristic of the American semiconductor industry, the new approach was developed by a small start-up organization.

Among the many Bell Labs researchers who had struck out on their own in the 1950s was Shockley, who returned home to the San Francisco peninsula to found Shockley Semiconductor Laboratories. Apparently prompted by dissatisfaction with the company's orientation toward product breakthroughs at the neglect of the commercially richer area of process technology (Braun and Macdonald, 1978: 84; Holbrook, 1999), eight of Shockley's team defected in 1957, and, with the backing of Long Island entrepreneur Sherman Fairchild,

founded the semiconductor division of Fairchild Camera and Instrument Corporation. The Fairchild group mounted an ambitious plan to produce silicon mesa transistors using technology developed at Bell Labs (Malone, 1985: 88; Lydon and Bambrick, 1987: 6). In attempting to overcome some of the limitations of this transistor design, one of the eight defectors, Jean Hoerni, found a way to create a "planar" device—that is, a device created by building up layers on a flat surface (Dummer, 1978: 143; Braun and Macdonald, 1978: 85; Morris, 1990: 38). The planar structure made it easy for Fairchild to devise a way to replace the mesa's clumsy wires with metal contacts deposited on the surface.

The advantages of the planar process for transistor fabrication were overwhelming and recognized immediately throughout the industry (Sparkes, 1973: 8). It has become the basis of all semiconductor fabrication, including, of course, the integrated circuit (IC), for which the process is of critical importance. ICs are semiconductor devices containing an entire circuit of transistors and other devices on a single "wafer" or chip. The IC held out the promise of overcoming a developing bottleneck in the mass fabrication of transistor-based systems, what Braun and Macdonald (1978: 113) have aptly called the "tyranny of numbers." As systems became more complex, requiring interconnections among hundreds of transistors, assembly costs mounted; more importantly, complex systems became vulnerable to the failure of any single connection or component. By fabricating an entire circuit using the techniques of semiconductor manufacture, the "monolithic" approach could yield greater reliability.

By 1961, two Americans, Robert Noyce of Fairchild and Jack Kilby of Texas Instruments (TI), had created prototype ICs.[7] Unlike Kilby, who had started with the monolithic idea and then sought to solve the problem of fabrication

---

[6] An AT&T vice president put it this way. "We realized that if this thing [the transistor] was as big as we thought, we couldn't keep it to ourselves and we couldn't make all the technical contributions. It was to our interest to spread it around. If you cast your bread on the water, sometimes it comes back angel food cake." Quotation attributed to Jack Morton, in "The Improbable Years," *Electronics* 41: 81 (February 19, 1968), quoted in Tilton (1971: 75–6).

[7] The idea of the integrated circuit was probably first propounded in 1952 by G.W.A. Dummer of the British Royal Radar Establishment (Braun and Macdonald, 1978: 108).

and interconnection, Noyce began with a process for fabrication and metallic interconnection—the planar process—and moved easily from that to the idea of the integrated circuit. Under pressure from the industry, TI and Fairchild forged a cross-licensing agreement in 1966 under which each company agreed to grant licenses to all comers in the range of 2–4 percent of IC profits (Reid, 1984: 94–5). This practice served to reproduce and extend the technology licensing policies of AT&T, again broadly diffusing the core technological innovation to all entrants and thereby reasserting the principle that innovative rents should flow to those who could commercialize and improve upon the key innovation.

As important as the innovation of the IC was, the planar process is arguably the more important technological breakthrough, not merely because it underlay the IC but because it provided the paradigm or technological trajectory the industry was to follow.[8] By either etching away minute areas or building up regions using other materials, semiconductor fabrication alters the chemical properties of a "wafer," a crystal of silicon. Each wafer produces many ICs, and each IC contains many transistors. The most dramatic economic feature of IC production is the increase in the number of transistors that can be fabricated in a single IC. Transistor counts per IC increased from 10 to 4,000 in the first decade of the industry's history; from 4,000 to over 500,000 in the second decade; and from 500,000 to 100 million in the third decade. The ten-million-fold increase in the number of transistors per IC has been accompanied by only modest increases in the cost of processing of a wafer, and almost no change in the average costs of processing the individual IC. This factor alone has been responsible for the enormous cost reduction in electronic circuitry since the birth of the IC. Electronic systems comparable in complexity to vacuum-tube or transistor systems costing millions of dollars can be constructed for a few hundred dollars, a magnitude of cost reduction that it is virtually unpre-

cedented in the history of manufacturing. The cheapness of electronic functions has reduced the costs of electronic systems relative to mechanical ones and lowered the relative price of electronic goods in general—developments that have had a major effect on the industrial structure of the electronics and IC industries.

Langlois and Steinmueller (1999) have pointed to the critical role of end-use demand in shaping industrial structure and competitive advantage in the worldwide semiconductor industry throughout its history. In the early years, demand in the United States came first from military sources and then importantly from the computer industry. Government procurement demand proved so valuable to the development of the industry not only because of its extent but also because of the military's relative price-insensitivity and its insistence on reliability (Dosi, 1984). Commercial demand eventually grew more rapidly than military, however, and, by the mid-1970s, government consumption had declined to less than 10 percent of the market (Kraus, 1971: 91).

The American government also pushed the transistor and the IC through support of R&D and related projects. But scholarship on the subject is essentially unanimous that this activity was far less important for, and less salutary to, the industry than was the government's procurement role. All the major breakthroughs in transistors were developed privately with the military market (among others) in mind. And, although the government tended to favor R&D contracts with established suppliers, notably the vacuum-tube firms, it *bought* far more from newer specialized semiconductor producers (Tilton, 1971: 91). The pragmatic policy of awarding work to those firms that could meet supply requirements was particularly important for encouraging new entry.

A significant feature of the transition to the IC was the virtual disappearance of the vertically integrated American electronics companies that had led in the production of vacuum tubes and that had been able to stay in the race during the era of discrete transistors. The

---

[8] Canonical sources here are Abernathy and Utterback (1978) and Utterback (1979).

market shares of those firms declined in the face of new entrants and the growth of relatively specialized manufacturers like TI, Fairchild, and Motorola. Why did the vertically integrated electronic system firms do so poorly in this era? Wilson et al. (1980) point out that the new leaders were either specialized start-ups or multidivisional firms (like TI, Fairchild, and Motorola) in which the semiconductor division dominated overall corporate strategy and in which semiconductor operations absorbed a significant portion of the attention of central management. By contrast, the semiconductor divisions of the integrated system firms were a small part of corporate sales and of corporate strategy, thereby attracting a smaller portion of managerial attention and receiving less autonomy.

10.2.2. The Birth of the Digital Computer

The history of the digital computer has much in common with that of semiconductor technology, even if there are a number of important differences. Like the transistor, the digital computer was developed with a specific bottleneck in mind. But, unlike the transistor, the digital computer was developed not privately but at universities, with explicit government subsidy from the start.

During World War II, the U.S. Army contracted with J. Presper Eckert and John W. Mauchly of the Moore School at the University of Pennsylvania for a device "designed expressly for the solution of ballistics problems and for the printing of range tables"[9] (Stern, 1981: 15). By November 1945, they had produced the Electronic Numerical Integrator and Computer (ENIAC), the first fully operational all-electronic digital computer—a behemoth occupying 1,800 square feet, boasting 18,000 tubes, and consuming 174 kilowatts of electricity. Universities continued to play an important role throughout the early life of the technology, helping to create the wholly

new discipline of computer science. Indeed, Rosenberg and Nelson go so far as to call the computer "the most remarkable contribution of American universities to the last half of the twentieth century" (Rosenberg and Nelson, 1994: 331).

Like the transistor, the computer opened up wide possibilities for technological convergence.[10] In part, this convergence arose because of the falling cost of computation—attendant eventually on the falling cost of semiconductors—which allowed the device to be used in a wide range of applications requiring numerical computation and, later, information processing more generally. But a specific innovation in the design of digital computers was also central to the device's wide potential. In the summer of 1944, the mathematician John von Neumann learned by accident of the Army's ENIAC project. Von Neumann began advising the Eckert-Mauchly team, which was working on the development of a new machine, the EDVAC. Out of this collaboration came the concept of the stored-program computer: instead of being hard-wired, the EDVAC's instructions were to be stored in memory to facilitate modification. A single hardware design could thus be quickly adapted to a variety of different uses through what came to be called *software*. Von Neumann's abstract discussion of the stored-program concept (von Neumann, 1945) circulated widely and served as the logical basis for virtually all subsequent computers.[11]

Government, especially military, support for the computer remained significant throughout the 1950s, and government funding helped spur important technical developments like ferrite-core memory, which emerged from the military-funded Whirlwind project at MIT (Redmond and Smith, 1980; Pugh, 1984).

---

[10] Rosenberg (1992: 382) explicitly likens the technological convergence of the digital computer to that of the nineteenth-century machine tool industry.

[9] In the event, the end of the war reduced the urgency of this goal, and the first major task given the ENIAC was actually to perform calculations for the development of the hydrogen bomb (Stern, 1981: 62).

[11] The stored-program idea was also contained in the work of Turing in Britain, and the first functioning storable-program computer was run for the first time on June 21, 1948 at the University of Manchester.

But, as Bresnahan and Malerba (1999: 89–90) argue, government research support had little to do with the success of the *commercial* computer industry. Moreover, much of government policy, notably in the areas of R&D funding and antitrust, was actually aimed at forestalling the emergence of IBM as a dominant "national champion" in computers. As in semiconductors, however, the military's pragmatic approach to procurement favored those firms who could deliver the goods, and in computers that meant IBM (Bresnahan and Malerba, 1999: 90; Usselman, 1993).

By the mid-1960s, however, IBM found itself riding herd on a multiplicity of physically incompatible systems—the various 700-series computers and the 1400 series, among others—each aimed at a different use. Relatedly, and more significantly, software was becoming a serious bottleneck. By one estimate, the contribution of software to the value of a computer system had grown from 8 percent in the early days to something like 40 percent by the 1960s (Ferguson and Morris, 1993: 7). And writing software for so many incompatible systems greatly compounded the problem. In what *Fortune* magazine called "the most crucial and portentous—as well as perhaps the riskiest—business judgment of recent times," IBM decided to "bet the company" on a new line of computers called the 360 series. The name referred to all the points of the compass, for the strategy behind the 360 was to replace the diverse and incompatible systems with a single modular family of computers (Flamm, 1988: 96–9). Instead of having one computer aimed at scientific applications, a second aimed at accounting applications, etc., the company would have one machine for all uses. This was not to be a homogeneous or undifferentiated product; but it was to provide a framework in which product differentiation could take place while retaining compatibility.

As Timothy Bresnahan suggests, the 360 was the first major computer *platform*, by which he means "a shared, stable set of hardware, software, and networking technologies on which users build and run computer applications" (Bresnahan, 1999: 159). To put it another way, the 360 was a *modular system*, albeit one

that remained mostly closed and proprietary despite the efforts of the "plug compatible" industry to pick away at its parts. The essence of such a system is compatibility among the components, which, in the case of a computer platform, is maintained by (often de facto) interface standards (Langlois and Robertson, 1992). A large literature has arisen describing the positive-feedback character of technical standards: the more users adopt a platform, the more desirable that platform becomes to others, leading to a "virtuous circle" and pressure for the dominance of a single platform.[12] The IBM 360 did indeed become a dominant platform, a prototype form of general-purpose technology in the computer industry.[13]

As the market for computers picked up speed, the symbiosis between computers and semiconductors became stronger. In contrast to IBM, which did not begin using ICs until 1970, IBM's competitors, such as RCA and Burroughs, adopted ICs more quickly in an effort to gain an advantage (Borrus et al., 1983: 157). This led to a dynamic interaction in which competition among computer makers drove the demand for ICs, which lowered IC prices by moving suppliers faster down their learning curves, which in turn fed back on the price of computers, etc. The result was a self-reinforcing process of growth for both industries. Indeed, the falling prices of semiconductor logic fueled a second computer revolution, that of the minicomputer.

Minicomputers were smaller than mainframes and geared toward specialized scientific and engineering uses. Digital Equipment Corporation (DEC), founded in 1957, was the pioneer in the field. Among the other firms to enter the minicomputer market were Scientific Data Systems, Data General (founded in 1968 by defectors from DEC), Prime Computer, Hewlett-Packard, Wang, and Tandem (Flamm, 1988: 131).

[12] Useful entry points are David and Greenstein (1990) and Economides (1996).

[13] "The very idea of platform is associated with re-use across multiple sites, an inherent scale economy" (Bresnahan, 1999: 160).

10.2.3. Memory Races and the Japanese Challenge

The early history of innovation in semiconductors is largely an American story. But European and Japanese firms did enter the industry early, and the paths of development in those areas were guided in large part by rather different structures of end-use demand and government policy.

In terms of innovation, European firms trailed American firms in the early years of the transistor, but they nonetheless remained competitive in germanium transistors well into the 1960s by concentrating on the European market, where the dominant demand was for consumer and industrial, rather than military and computer, uses (Malerba, 1985: 75–80, 88–9). This structure of demand gave advantage in Europe to the large vertically integrated systems houses, who viewed transistors as a necessary input into electronic system products rather than as an end product. Significantly, the European firms tended to license technology almost exclusively from those American firms whom they most resembled—the large vacuum-tube firms—and almost not at all from the American merchant houses (Malerba, 1985: 65).

By the mid-1960s, Britain, France, and Germany had all begun efforts to foster national computer industries (Dosi, 1981: 27). As Bresnahan and Malerba (1999) point out, much of those European (and of Japanese) policies toward computers were aimed at forestalling IBM with preferential procurement policies as well as outright subventions. By subsidizing national computer makers, who were motivated if not constrained to buy from national semiconductor makers, the European computer initiatives thus attempted to create some indigenous demand for logic ICs. Moreover, all three countries initiated R&D programs in computers, some of which spilled over into semiconductors.[14] As Tilton (1971: 131) notes, these programs tended to favor a small number of large established firms—to a much greater extent than had American military R&D. Indeed, European government policy in this

period encouraged consolidation and rationalization. Especially in Britain and France, which did not initially have "national champions" the size of Philips or Siemens, a wave of mergers took place, both in computers and semiconductors, with government approval and sometimes government instigation. This policy of consolidation had the effect of reducing indigenous competition in the face of penetration by subsidiaries of American firms and generated "champions" that proved unfit to take on the Americans (Tilton, 1971: 131–2).

The early origins of the Japanese semiconductor industry are broadly similar to those of the European, albeit with some differences that may prove crucial in explaining the quite distinct path of Japanese development in later periods. As in Europe, the principal producers of transistors in the 1950s and 1960s were diversified systems houses, including firms that had previously produced vacuum tubes, rather than companies that were principally specialized into semiconductors. And, as in Europe, the main end-use for transistors in Japan in this period was consumer products rather than the military. At the same time, however, there were substantial differences from Europe at both the level of the firms themselves and at the level of government policy.

Japan responded to American competitive advantage with high tariffs, and in addition imposed quotas and registration requirements[15] (Tyson and Yoffie, 1993: 37). In contrast to European policies, moreover, the Japanese government essentially forbade foreign direct investment, which forced American firms to tap the Japanese market only through licensing and technology sales to Japanese firms rather than through direct investment. In addition, the rate of growth of the Japanese semiconduc-

---

[14] Several of these programs are described in Dosi (1981: 27).

[15] This is in contrast to European policy, which featured high tariffs but no prohibition on foreign direct investment. As a result, much of the European demand for semiconductors was satisfied by European subsidiaries of American companies. Japanese companies have typically supplied some 90 percent of the Japanese semiconductor market, whereas American firms—through imports or foreign direct investment—have supplied between 50 and 70 percent of the European market (Tyson and Yoffie, 1993: 34).

tor industry was much greater than that of the European simply because the Japanese started from a smaller base. And because the Japanese vacuum-tube firms were much smaller than their American or European counterparts at the beginning of the transistor era, they had less to lose in moving to the new technology. As Tilton (1971: 154) notes, the fact of rapid growth "also helped create a receptive attitude toward change on the part of the receiving tube producers by reducing the risks associated with new products and new technologies and by increasing costs, in terms of declining market shares, to firms content simply to maintain the status quo." In many ways, then, Japanese systems firms faced many of the same constraints, and adopted many of the same approaches, as the aggressive American merchant firms rather than those of the American, or European, systems houses.[16]

Despite their early success in transistors, Japanese firms found themselves in a weak position by the 1970s. These firms were slow to make the transition to batch-produced silicon devices in the early 1960s, and, when they turned later in the decade to the production of bipolar ICs, they could not compete with the likes of Texas Instruments and National Semiconductor; some Japanese firms accused the Americans of "dumping" (Okimoto et al., 1984: 14–5). After 1967, indeed, the purchase of American ICs created a Japanese trade deficit in semiconductors (Malerba, 1985: 136).

How did Japanese industry move from this weak position in the 1970s to its dominant position by the mid-1980s? Until recently, the tacit assumption of most commentators had been that Japanese success was the result of some combination of (1) Japanese industrial structure, understood as superior to American industrial structure in a very general or even absolute sense, and (2) Japanese industrial policy, understood as a highly intentional—and even prescient—system of government industry planning and control. Langlois and Steinmueller (1999)

suggests a somewhat different picture. Although both industrial structure and government policy played important roles in the rise of the Japanese semiconductor industry, the benefits of that industrial structure were far less timeless than commentators supposed, and the effects of government policy were far less intentional, and perhaps somewhat less significant, than the dominant accounts suggested.

As in the earlier rise of the American semiconductor industry, the pattern of end-use demand was crucial in shaping the bundle of capabilities that Japanese industry possessed, as well as in narrowing and limiting the choices the Japanese firms had open to them. In this case, that end-use demand came largely from consumer electronics and, to a somewhat lesser extent, from telecommunications, especially purchases by NTT, Japan's national telephone monopoly (see Table 10.1). Consumer demand helped place the Japanese on a product trajectory—namely MOS and especially CMOS ICs—that turned out eventually to have much wider applicability.[17] Moreover, Japanese firms adopted a strategy of specialization in high-volume production of one particular kind of chip—the DRAM. The DRAM, or dynamic random-access memory chip, is a technology that benefited from increasing returns to scale not only because of the volume effects of mass production but also because it is arguably a general-purpose technology of considerable importance—a device that can store digital information for a wide variety of purposes.[18]

Established American firms, accustomed to providing customized devices, were slow to recognize the cost-reduction advantages of a standardized memory chip (Wilson et al., 1980: 87; Dorfman, 1987: 193). Two new firms—National and Intel—quickly gained

---

[16] Unlike European firms, the Japanese firms sought and received licenses from Texas Instruments, Fairchild, and other American merchant firms rather than limiting themselves to arrangements with American systems houses.

[17] MOS stands for metal-oxide semiconductor, and CMOS for "complementary" MOS.

[18] DRAMs are "dynamic" in the sense that the electric charges containing the remembered information decay over time and need periodically to be "refreshed." This stands in contrast to the static RAM (or SRAM), which does not require refreshing, but which therefore has disadvantages in size, cost, and power consumption because it requires more transistors per memory cell.

TABLE 10.1
Demand for Integrated Circuits by End-use Market: United States, Japan, and Western Europe, 1982 and 1985
(in percent)

End-use	United States		Japan		Western Europe	
	1982	1985	1982	1985	1982	1985
Computer	40	45	22	36	25	20
Telecommunications	21	10	10	13	20	29
Industrial	11	10	17	6	25	19
Military and Aerospace	17	18	0	0	5	7
Consumer	11	16	51	45	25	25

Source: OECD (1985).
Note: Includes captive consumption.

advantage over their established competitors in the merchant market by moving more quickly into the production of high-volume standardized devices. Both firms were spin-offs from Fairchild—two of the first of what came to be called the "Fairchildren" (Lindgren, 1969). In pushing standardized DRAM chips, however, these firms precipitated a "memory race" in which Japanese firms were eventually to prove dominant. American firms led in the early—1K and 4K—DRAM markets. But an industry recession delayed the American "ramp-up" to the 16K DRAM, which appeared in 1976. Aided by unforeseen production problems among the three leaders, Japanese firms were able to gain a significant share of the 16K market. By mid-1979, sixteen companies were producing

DRAMs, and Japanese producers accounted for 42 percent of the market (Wilson et al., 1980: 93–4) (see Table 10.2). The opportunity opened for Japanese producers in the 16K DRAM market had proven sufficient for them to advance to a position of leadership in the 64K DRAM market. Japanese dominance accelerated in the 256K (1982) and one-megabit (1985) generations. Intense price competition, combined with the general recession in the U.S. industry in 1985, caused all but two American merchant IC companies to withdraw from DRAM production[19] (Howell et al., 1992: 29). In 1990, American market share had fallen to only 2 percent of the new generation 4-megabit DRAMs[20] (see Table 10.2).

Why did the Japanese succeed? In broad terms, circumstances had staked out for the Japanese industry a strategic path that fit well the existing competences of the firms—namely those in mass production and quality control—and supported the thrust of their final products, which, despite government efforts of to create a computer industry (Fransman, 1990), were still in consumer electronics and telecommunications.

TABLE 10.2
Maximum Market Share in DRAMs by American and Japanese Companies, by Device

Device	Maximum market share (%)	
	United States	Japan
1K	95	5
4K	83	17
16K	59	41
64K	29	71
256K	8	92
1M	4	96
4M	2	98

Source: Dataquest, cited in Methé (1991: 69)

[19] The exceptions were Texas Instruments, which produced in Japan, and Micron Technology, which produced in Idaho.

[20] These figures do not take into account the sizable captive production at IBM and AT&T.

Rather than feeling that they were on the verge of overtaking American companies, the Japanese saw their computer industry as relatively weak against IBM, and perceived that a key feature of IBM's advantage was technology, specifically its position in ICs. From the viewpoint of Japanese firms, the American IC industry was enormously innovative but did not share much of the manufacturing culture that had developed in the larger Japanese electronics companies, where quality, systematic capacity expansion, and long-term market position were regarded as key variables to control. The fact that Japanese IC producers were large companies in comparison with their American counterparts gave them one particular advantage: they were able to mobilize internal capital resources to make investments in the IC industry in a way that American companies could not.

James March (1991) has pointed out that there is a necessary tradeoff between exploration and exploitation—tradeoff between searching for new ideas and running with the old ones. As the technology leaders, the American firms found themselves with a full plate of alternatives to pursue, in both product and process technology. Sitting somewhat behind the frontier, Japanese firms could pick one item off the plate and run with it. Their morsel was the mass production of DRAMs.

10.2.4. Personal Computers and the American Resurgence

American industry and politics certainly did not let these events go unnoticed, and alarms went up as early as the 64K generation. More worrisome than the loss of the memory market was the possibility that Japanese dominance in DRAMs would be translated into equal success in other kinds of chips. Although memories constituted at most 30 percent of the IC market, many believed them to be "technology drivers" essential for continued progress in increasing the number of transistors on an IC. If American firms could n0t use DRAM production to develop and gain experience in the next generation of technology, then Japanese producers would soon be able to climb up the design-complexity ladder and challenge American positions in logic markets (Ferguson, 1985; Forester, 1993).

In 1986, Japan's overall market share in semiconductors slipped ahead of that of the American merchants. Thus, in 1988 the American industry appeared to stand on the brink of oblivion, with no haven in product or process that could be counted to insure its survival into the 1990s. But the predicted extinction never occurred (see Figure 10.2). Instead, American firms surged back during the 1990s, and it now seems that it is the Japanese who are embattled.

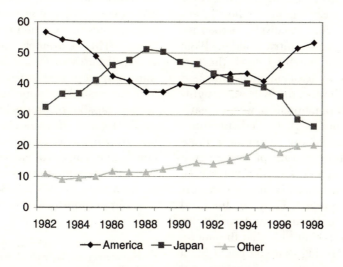

Figure 10.2 Worldwide semiconductor market shares (in percent), 1982–98. *Source:* Semiconductor Industry Association.

Langlois and Steinmueller (1999) argue that this resurgence is not the result of imitating Japanese market structure and policy but rather of taking good advantage of the distinctly American market structure and capabilities developed in the heyday of American dominance. Just as the innovation of, and the growing market for, the standardized DRAM had favored the Japanese, another semiconductor innovation, and the burgeoning market it created, came to favor the Americans. That innovation was the microprocessor, an IC designed not to store information (like the DRAM) but rather to provide on a single chip the information-processing capability of a digital computer.

In 1969, a Japanese manufacturer asked Intel to design the logic chips for a new electronic calculator. Marcian E. ("Ted") Hoff, Jr., the engineer in charge of the project, thought the Japanese design too complicated to produce. The then-current approach to the design of calculators involved the use of many specialized hard-wired circuits to perform the various calculator functions. Influenced by the von Neumann architecture of minicomputers, Hoff reasoned that he could simplify the design enormously by creating a single programmable IC rather than the set of dedicated logic chips the Japanese had sought (Noyce and Hoff, 1981) By using relatively simple general-purpose logic circuitry that relied on programming information stored elsewhere, Hoff effectively substituted cheap memory (then Intel's major product) for relatively expensive special-purpose logic circuitry (Gilder, 1989: 103). The result was the Intel 4004, the first microprocessor. A sixth of an inch long and an eighth of an inch wide, the 4004 was roughly equivalent in computational power to early vacuum-tube computers that filled an entire room. It also matched the power of a 1960s IBM computer whose central processing unit was about the size of a desk (Bylinsky, 1980: 7).

Intel gained an early lead in microprocessors that it never relinquished. Early on, Intel did not push patent protection, and, in Hoff's view, "did not take the attitude that the microprocessor was something that you could file a patent claim on that covers everything" (quoted in Malone, 1985: 144). Because the microprocessor is a general-purpose computer, there are many different ways to implement the microprocessor idea without infringing on a particular implementation. And the appropriation of rents in microprocessors has always depended on first-mover advantage rather than on patent protection for particular features of the system design or on the ability to produce a microprocessor that could not be emulated technically.

The microprocessor found uses in a wide variety of applications involving computation and computer control. But it did not make inroads into the established mainframe or minicomputer industries, largely because it did not initially offer the level of computing power these larger machines could generate using multiple logic chips. Instead, the microprocessor opened up the possibility of a wholly new kind of computer—the microcomputer.

The first microcomputer is generally acknowledged to have been something called the MITS/Altair, which graced the cover of Popular Electronics magazine in January, 1975.[21] Essentially a microprocessor in a box, the machine's only input/output devices were lights and toggle switches on the front panel, and it came with a mere 256 bytes of memory. But the Altair was, at least potentially, a genuine computer. Its potential came largely from a crucial design decision: the machine incorporated a number of open "slots" that allowed for additional memory and other devices to be added later. These slots were hooked into the microprocessor by a network of wires called a "bus." This extremely modular approach emerged partly in emulation of the design of minicomputers and partly because hobbyists and the small firm supplying them would have been incapable of producing a desirable (i.e., more-capable) nonmodular machine within any reasonable time. In effect, the hobbyist community captured the machine, and made it a truly open modular system. The first clone of the Altair—the IMSAI 8080—appeared within a matter of months, and soon the Altair's archi-

---

[21] For a much longer and better-documented history of the microcomputer, see Langlois (1992), on which this section draws.

tecture became an industry standard, eventually known as the S-100 bus because of its 100-line structure.

The S-100 standard dominated the hobbyist world. But the machine that took the micro-computer into the business world adopted a distinctive architecture, built around a Motorola rather than an Intel microprocessor. Stephen Wozniak and Steven Jobs had started Apple Computer in 1976, quite literally in the garage of Jobs's parents' house. The hobbyist Wozniak, also influenced by the architecture of minicomputers, insisted that the Apple be an expandable system—with slots—and that technical details be freely available to users and third-party suppliers. With the development of word processors like WordStar, database managers like dBase II, and spreadsheets like VisiCalc, the machine became a tool of writers, professionals, and small businesses. Apple took in U.S.$750,000 by the end of fiscal 1977, U.S.$8 million in 1978, U.S.$48 million in 1979, U.S.$117 million in 1980 (when the firm went public), U.S.$335 million in 1981, U.S.$583 million in 1982, and U.S.$983 million in 1983.[22]

Existing computer companies were slow to develop competing microcomputers, largely because they saw the machines as a small fringe market. But as business uses increased and microcomputer sales rose, some computer makers saw the opportunity to get a foothold in a market that was complementary to, albeit much smaller than, their existing product lines.[23] By far the most significant entry was that of IBM. On August 12, 1981, IBM introduced the computer that would become the paradigm for most of the 1980s.

In a radical departure, IBM decided to produce the machine outside the control of

company procurement policies and practices. Philip Donald Estridge, a director of the project, later put it this way. "We were allowed to develop like a start-up company. IBM acted as a venture capitalist. It gave us management guidance, money, and allowed us to operate on our own" (*Business Week*, October 3, 1983: 86). Estridge knew that, to meet the deadline he had been given, IBM would have to make heavy use of outside vendors for parts and software. The owner of an Apple II, Estridge was also impressed by the importance of expandability and an open architecture. He insisted that his designers use a modular bus system that would allow expandability, and he resisted all suggestions that the IBM team design any of its own add-ons. Because the machine used the Intel 8088 instead of the 8080, IBM needed a new operating system. A tiny Seattle company called Microsoft agreed to produce such an operating system, which they bought from another small Seattle company and rechristened as MS-DOS, for Microsoft Disk Operating System.

The IBM PC was an instant success, exceeding sales forecasts by some 500 percent. By 1983, the PC had captured 26 percent of the market, and an estimated 750,000 machines were installed by the end of that year. The IBM standard largely drove out competing alternatives during the decade of the 1980s. This happened in part because of the strength of the IBM name in generating network effects, principally because it created the expectation among users that the key vendor would continue to provide services long into the future and that a wide array of complementary devices and software would rapidly become available. But in large measure the "tipping" of the market to the IBM PC standard was a result of the openness of the IBM system, which could be easily copied by others, and the eagerness of Microsoft to license MS-DOS to all comers.

As it had with the 360/370 series, IBM had created a dominant computer platform. But, in the case of the PC, the dominance of the platform would not translate into a dominant market share for IBM. Because of the strategy of outsourcing and the standards it necessitated, others could easily imitate the IBM hard-

[22] Data from Apple Computer, cited in "John Sculley at Apple Computer (B)," Harvard Business School Case no. 9-486-002, revised May 1987: 26.

[23] Few people inside or outside IBM foresaw the sweeping changes the PC would make in computer markets. In April 1981, four months before the official announcement of the IBM PC, IBM gave presentations estimating it would sell 241,683 PCs over five years. In fact, IBM shipped 250,000 PCs in one month alone (Zimmerman and Dicarlo, 1999).

ware, in the sense that any would-be maker of computers could obtain industry-standard modular components and compete with IBM. A legion of clones appeared that offered IBM compatibility at, usually, a lower price than IBM. By 1986, more than half of the IBM-compatible computers sold did not have IBM logos on them. By 1988, IBM's worldwide market share of IBM-compatible computers was only 24.5 percent. IBM's choice of an open modular system was a two-edged sword that gave the company a majority stake in a standard that had grown well beyond its control. For reasons that are debated in the literature, but that likely have to do both with strategic mistakes by IBM and with the inherently strong positions of key suppliers in controlling their proprietary "bottleneck" technologies—the microprocessor and the operating system—Intel and Microsoft gained control of the standard that IBM had originally sponsored (Ferguson and Morris, 1993). The PC architecture is now often referred to as the "Wintel" (Windows/Intel) platform.

Langlois (1992) has argued that the rapid quality-adjusted price decline in microcomputers resulted not only from the declining price of computing power attendant on successive generations of Intel processors but also from the vibrant competition and innovation at the level of hardware components and applications software that resulted from the open modular design of the PC. A decentralized and fragmented system can have advantages in innovation to the extent that it involves the trying out of many alternate approaches simultaneously, leading to rapid trial-and-error learning. This kind of innovation is especially important when technology is changing rapidly and there is a high degree of both technological and market uncertainty (Nelson and Winter, 1977). Moreover, the microcomputer benefited from technological convergence, in that it turned out to be a technology capable of taking over tasks that had previously required numerous distinct—and more expensive—pieces of physical and human capital. By the early 1980s, a microcomputer costing U.S.$3,500 could do the work of a U.S.$10,000 stand-alone word-processor, while at the same time keeping track of the books

like a U.S.$100,000 minicomputer and amusing the kids with space aliens like a 25-cents-a-game arcade machine.

The personal computer grew rapidly in a niche that existing mainframes and minicomputers had never filled. Quickly, however, the microcomputer's niche began to expand to encroach on the territory of its larger rivals, driven by the rapidly increasing densities and decreasing prices of memory chips and microprocessors. In the early 1980s, a class of desktop machines called workstations arose to challenge the dominance of the minicomputer in scientific and technical applications. As in the case of personal computers, the workstation market was driven by open technical standards and competition within the framework of what was largely a modular system (Garud and Kumaraswamy, 1993; Baldwin and Clark, 1997). Initially, these workstation used microprocessors and operating systems different from those of personal computers.[24] By the early 1990s, however, the same process of increasing power and decreasing cost began pushing the Windows-Intel platform into what is today a dominance of the workstation space. At the same time, workstations hooked together (or hooked to personal computers) began to take over many of the functions of larger minicomputers and mainframes. By the 1990s, networks of fast, cheap smaller machines were widespread, a development accelerated by the spectacular growth of the Internet.[25] This growth had a significant negative effect on the makers of larger computers, notably the Boston-area minicomputer makers. Many went bankrupt; and, in

---

[24] So-called traditional workstations are built around Reduced-Instruction-Set-Computing (RISC) microprocessors and run variants of the UNIX operating system. Intel-platform workstations use high-end versions of the same microprocessors used in personal computers and typically run Microsoft's Windows NT or Windows 2000, which are compatible with Microsoft's operating systems for personal computers.

[25] In some respects, the demand for large websites created by the Internet has spurred demand for large central servers. Increasingly, however, even these servers are essentially high-powered workstations rather than traditional mainframes or minicomputers.

a telling development, the flagship maker of microcomputers—DEC—was acquired by Compaq, a maker of microcomputers. Bresnahan and Greenstein (1996, 1997) refer to this encroachment of smaller computers as the "competitive crash" of large-scale computing.

The losses incurred by the makers of large computers (including IBM) have been more than offset, however, by the growth of the personal computer industry and its suppliers. Principal among the beneficiaries has been the American semiconductor industry. The abandonment of the DRAM market by most American firms—including Intel—was a dark cloud with a bright silver lining. When Intel led the world industry in almost all categories, it and many of its American counterparts faced a full plate of product alternatives. With the elimination of mass memory as a viable market, these firms were impelled to specialize and narrow their focus to a smaller subset of choices. The areas in which American firms concentrated can generally be described as higher-margin, design-intensive chips. For such chips, production costs would not be the sole margin of competition; innovation and responsiveness would count for more. And innovation and responsiveness were arguably the strong suit of the "fragmented" American industry. As in the case of the personal computer industry, the decentralized structure of the American semiconductor industry permitted the trying out of a wider diversity of approaches, leading to rapid trial-and-error learning (Nelson and Winter, 1977). And the independence of many firms from larger organizations permits speedier realignment and recombination with suppliers and customers. Building on existing competences in design (especially of logic and specialty circuits) and close ties with the burgeoning American personal computer industry, American firms were able to prosper despite the Japanese edge in manufacturing technology (Ferguson and Morris, 1993).

The most important area of America specialization is microprocessors and related devices.[26] Between 1988 and 1994, a period in which merchant IC revenues grew by 121 percent, revenues from the microprocessor segment grew much faster than did memory

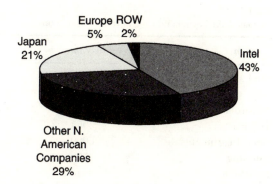

Figure 10.3 Production of MOS microprocessors and related devices in 1996 (percent). *Source:* ICE (1998).

revenues (ICE, 1998). This evolution of the product mix in the industry has strongly favored American producers. In the microprocessor segment of the chip market, American companies accounted for 72 percent of world production in 1996, compared with a 21 percent share for Japanese companies (see Figure 10.3).

The importance of the microprocessor segment has meant that a single company, Intel, is responsible for much of the gain of American merchant IC producers. In 1996, Intel accounted for 43 percent of world output in the microprocessor segment (see Figure 10.4). Intel's strategy for recovery, begun in the 1980s, has proven remarkably successful (Afuah, 1999). In the late 1980s, the firm consolidated its intellectual-property position in microprocessors by terminating cross-licensing agreements with other companies and, more importantly, began extending its first-mover advantage over rivals by accelerating the rate of new product introduction. These developments pushed Intel into the position of the largest IC producer in the world, with 1998 revenues of U.S.$22.7 billion—more than the next three largest firms combined (see Table 10.3). Although Intel dominates the microprocessor market, it is not entirely without competitors; and it is significant that its principal

---

[26] This segment includes not only microprocessors but also microcontrollers (less sophisticated microprocessors that are used in embedded applications) and related "support" chips, such as memory controllers, that are necessary to assembling a microprocessor system.

TABLE 10.3
Estimated 1998 Semiconductor Revenues ($ million)

Company	Revenues
Intel	22675
NEC	8271
Motorola	6918
Toshiba	6055
Texas Instruments	6000
Samsung	4752
Hitachi	4649
Philips	4502
STMicroelectronics	4300
Siemens	3866
Fujitsu	3866

Source: Dataquest, cited in *Electronics Times* (1999: January 11, p. 3).

competitors in microprocessors are also American companies, notably AMD and Motorola.

The success of American firms in microprocessors and related chips has been reinforced by trends in end-use demand. In 1989, computer applications took 40 percent of merchant IC sales, followed by consumer and automotive applications at 28 percent.[27] By 1996, the respective shares were 50 percent for computer and 23 percent for consumer and automotive applications. The worldwide changes have led to increasing specialization. Between 1989 and 1994, North American use of ICs for computer applications soared from 15 to 24 percent of the total value of world merchant sales, while the Japanese IC market for consumer applications fell from 13 percent to 10 percent of world merchant sales. Thus, in contrast to rough parity (15 versus 13 percent) in 1989, an enormous gap has opened between IC demand for consumer and computer applications in the Japanese and American markets. Keep in mind that these figures are in terms of revenue not physical units, and much of the reversal of American fortunes has to do with the high value per component of microprocessors and other design-intensive chips, as against the low value

per unit of the mass-produced DRAMs on which Japanese firms long rested their strategies.

Another aspect of specialization that benefited the American industry was the increasing "decoupling" of design from production. Such decoupling is in many respects a natural manifestation of the division of labor in growing markets (Young, 1928); in this case, it was abetted by the development of computerized design tools (Hobday, 1991) and the standardization of manufacturing technology (Macher et al., 1998). On the one hand, this allowed American firms to specialize in design-intensive chips, taking advantage of an American comparative advantage that arguably arises out of the decentralized and "fragmented" structure of that country's industry.[28] On the other hand, it also allowed many American firms to take advantage of growing production capabilities overseas. This "modularization" of the industry is spurring the kind of decentralized innovation from which the personal computer industry has benefited.

As globalization (broadly understood) has bolstered the fortunes of American firms, it has eroded those of the Japanese. Japanese firms were not the only ones who could understand the economics of capacity investment or productivity in manufacturing, and they were soon joined by Korean semiconductor producers and by larger American companies who matched Japanese productivity by the simple expedient of establishing Japanese plants. The result is a dilution of the control of capacity investment by Japanese producers. By the mid-1990s, a Korean firm had displaced Japanese firms as the leading producer of DRAMs in the world, and two other Korean firms had joined the top ten (see Table 10.4).

And what of the role of government policy in the American resurgence? The American response to the Japanese success of the early 1980s took two principal forms: (1) trade protection and (2) the funding of cooperative research,

---

[27] These and succeeding figures in this paragraph are from ICE (1990, 1995, 1998).

[28] Perhaps surprisingly, the mid-1980s—that dark period for American fortunes—was actually the most fertile period in history for the start-up of new semiconductor firms, by a large margin. Most of these new firms were involved in design-intensive custom devices and ASICs (Angel, 1994: 38).

TABLE 10.4

Worldwide Merchant-Market Sales of DRAMs (U.S.$ million)

Company	Country	1995	1996
Samsung	Korea	6462	4805
NEC	Japan	4740	3175
Hitachi	Japan	4439	2805
Hyundai	Korea	3500	2300
Toshiba	Japan	3725	2235
LG Electronics	Korea	3005	2005
Texas Instruments	United States	3200	1600
Micron	United States	2485	1575
Mitsubishi	Japan	2215	1400
Fujitsu	Japan	2065	1350
Others		4999	1880

Source: ICE (1998).

notably the Sematech consortium. These policy responses both arguably had some effect on competition in semiconductors, but the effects were not necessarily the ones expected.

Trade protection came in the form of the Semiconductor Trade Agreement (STA), signed in September, 1986, which established what was effectively a price floor for DRAMs and EPROMs shipped to the United States. The agreement lasted through 1991, and was replaced by a somewhat weaker version that expired in 1996. The price floor catalyzed cartel behavior among Japanese producers by giving them a mechanism with which to coordinate their prices. Prices for DRAMs stabilized by 1986 and began to rise, reaching a peak in 1988–9. The price of EPROMs followed a similar pattern. Industry officials have claimed that the rents in EPROMs generated by the STA enabled Intel to develop the microprocessor line on which its current success rests[29]—and some have even claimed that many of the largest American companies would have gone bankrupt without those rents (Helm, 1995). Constructing counterfactuals is always a tricky

business, however. What is clear is that the price rise in 1988–9 benefited Japanese DRAM producers at the expense of consumers. One estimate places these "bubble profits" (as they were called in Japan) at U.S.$3–4 billion (Flamm, 1996: 277).

As with most complex policy interventions, the STA also had some unintended consequences. Early on, critics—and even some proponents of managed trade—pointed out that Japanese firms were plowing their bubble profits into research and development, which would strengthen those firms for further rounds of competition and the much-feared push into other semiconductor markets (Tyson, 1992: 117). Moreover, as Japanese firms are more vertically integrated than American ones, Japanese computer makers would have the advantage of internal transfer prices rather than market prices, giving them an edge over Americans in the computer arena.[30] It is largely this concern, indeed, that led Mowery and Rosenberg (1989: 114) to suggest that, if "the Semiconductor Trade Agreement thus far is an example of successful 'managed trade,' it is hard to know what might constitute a failure."

In the event, however, the DRAM cartel generated a somewhat different set of unintended consequences—consequences much less happy for Japanese firms. By stabilizing DRAM prices and making that market so profitable, the cartel arrangement kept Japanese firms heavily invested in what was to become a low-margin commodity item. When the high prices attracted entry from Korea and Taiwan, prices and profits began to fall, and the cartel collapsed. By contrast, American firms like Intel were arguably well served in the medium term by their failure in DRAMs, a failure that left them free to pursue high-margin logic and specialty chips that would be in high demand by the burgeoning American personal computer market.

As we saw, much popular and professional opinion circa 1985 attributed the relative decline of American competitiveness to the

---

[29] Andrew Grove of Intel has also asserted that the pressure the STA exerted on Japan to increase the penetration of American chips led Japanese personal computer makers to adopt Intel microprocessors, which they might not otherwise have done (Siegmann, 1993).

[30] In fact, this possibility did not materialize, partly because the cartel was short lived and partly because the structural disadvantages of the Japanese computer makers far outweighed any advantages from cheaper DRAMs.

inherent inferiorities of American industrial structure relative to that of Japan. One widely touted aspect of the "Japanese model" was research coordination and collaboration in general and the much-touted VLSI Project specifically. As a result, another facet of the American policy response was an attempt to encourage cooperative research by indirect means as well as by direct subsidy.

Originally motivated by a desire to build a mainframe computer industry to rival IBM, the Very Large Scale Integrated Circuit (VLSI) Project was a pair of programs funded between 1975 and 1981 by the Japanese Ministry of International Trade and Industry (MITI) and by the Japanese telephone monopoly (NTT). These programs called for cooperative research among a number of leading Japanese semiconductor firms with the goal of improving manufacturing technology to challenge American dominance in semiconductors. Although contemporary accounts tended to heap praise on the VLSI project and to assign it most of the credit for Japanese success in DRAMs, recent scholarship has painted a rather different picture (Fransman, 1990; Callon, 1995). In planning the VLSI Project, MITI saw joint organization in a single laboratory as politically valuable, and pressed the companies to agree. This feature has attracted great attention and has been emulated in other consortia designs. It was also a feature that the companies vehemently opposed (Fransman, 1990: 63; Callon, 1995: 57). The companies reluctantly accepted MITI's joint laboratory organization as the price of the private research subsidies they really wanted (Fransman, 1990: 64). One consequence of the resistance is that only 15–20 percent of the total budget went to the joint laboratories; 80–5 percent went to private research in company laboratories (Fransman, 1990: 80). To the extent that the VLSI project contributed to the improvement in Japanese manufacturing capabilities, it did so by bolstering the capabilities of supplier firms, notably Nikon and Canon in optical lithography (Flamm, 1996: 103).

The VLSI model was directly influential in the creation of research consortia in the United States, notably Sematech. In 1987, the Defense Science Board, a committee advisory to the American Department of Defense, issued dire warnings that the decline of the American semiconductor industry would have serious repercussions for national defense. The committee proposed a manufacturing facility to be jointly owned by industry and government. In the same year, a committee of the SIA representing fourteen major semiconductor manufacturers issued a proposal for a research consortium to be funded by equal private and federal contributions. By the end of the year, the Defense Department agreed to fund such a consortium, with the fourteen firms uniting as the founding members of the Semiconductor Manufacturing Technology Consortium (Sematech). The organization was funded at a yearly level of U.S.$100 million from federal sources and U.S.$100 million from dues assessed to members.

Sematech set up shop in Austin, TX, staffed importantly by personnel on secondment from the member companies. The goal was to develop cutting-edge production technology of use to consortium firms. By 1989, a large-scale semiconductor fabrication facility had been completed at Sematech headquarters in record time. Largely because of problems of appropriability and proprietary information, however, the Sematech members were unable to agree on an appropriate research program for the facility (Grindley et al., 1994: 730). As a result, Sematech quickly reoriented its mission away from developing cutting-edge process technology for and with member companies toward improving the capabilities of the American semiconductor-equipment industry and strengthening cooperation between those firms and the semiconductor manufacturers they serve. This involved "contract R&D" with equipment suppliers, as well as programs to coordinate and set standards, in many cases through the offices of an organization called SEMI/SEMATECH that was set up at Sematech in 1987 to represent equipment makers. As in the case of the Japanese VLSI project, then, the ultimate virtue of Sematech may have lain not so much in the research it produced as in its role in reducing the transaction costs of research dissemination and in fostering closer "vertical" collaboration and coordination between manufacturers and equipment suppliers.

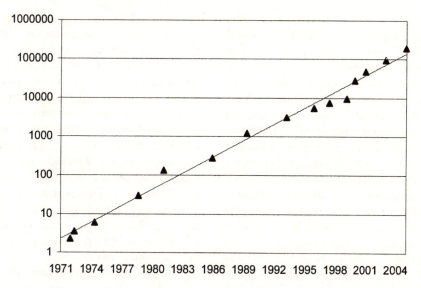

Figure 10.4 Transistors per chip in microprocessors, 1971–2005 (thousands). *Source:* Intel Corporation, Semiconductor Industry Association (1999).

10.2.5. Coda: Digital Technology and Economic Growth

Without much exaggeration, one could say that the engine of growth within digital technology derives from a single innovation, the planar process, and its logical extension, the integrated circuit. The planar approach to semiconductor fabrication created a technological trajectory of miniaturization that yielded genuinely astounding increases in the number of functions—bits of information stored or number of logical instructions processes—that could be fit on each chip, along with commensurate decreases in cost per function.[31] This phenomenon is encapsulated in the now-famous "law" promulgated by Intel co-founder Gordon Moore: that the number of functions that can be crammed on a chip doubles every 18–24 months.[32] This law of constant doubling time has held true since the beginning of IC technology, and will continue to do for the near future according to

the "technology roadmap" plotted out by the Semiconductor Industry Association (1999).

Consider the microprocessor. The Intel 4004 of 1971 contained some 2300 transistors. A Pentium III processor from late 1999 contains 28 million transistors. Figure 10.4 plots the number of transistors in a microprocessor over time using historical data for Intel microprocessors and projections from Semiconductor Industry Association (1999). The doubling time works out to a bit less than 26 months.

But there is a demand side as well as a supply side to the story. Moore's Law is limited by the extent of the market, and, as Moore himself clearly recognized, it takes a "phenomenally elastic market" to soak up all the transistors produced (Moore, 1997). What generated the demand response to the phenomenal cost decline of semiconductors? The answer is in large measure that digital technology offered a variety of general-purpose technologies—technologies that could be adapted to a wide variety of both new and existing uses.

Some of these GPTs are indeed technologies in the narrow sense. The DRAM is a concrete device that can store an infinite variety of information. Others are "technologies" in the wider sense, like the von Neumann stored-program concept, as implemented first in large compu-

---

[31] This is so because historically the cost of producing a chip has risen only about a third as fast as the number of functions per chip.

[32] Actually, Moore's original formulation claimed a doubling time of one year (Moore, 1965).

ters and then in the microprocessor. This created the possibility of a generic "brain" that could put its mind to an infinite variety of processing tasks. At another level are modular platforms like the IBM 360 or the Wintel platform, which extend demand by allowing consumers assemble exactly the components that best meet their needs. Such platforms also benefit from network effects, another source of increasing returns, as well as from the possibilities for rapid trial-and-error learning when the system is open to competition. The Internet (Mowery and Simcoe, chapter 9) is another general-purpose technology that extends the market for semiconductors and computers.

Economic historians debate whether technological change is really "revolutionary" and whether economic growth depends on such revolutions (Mokyr, 1990a). During the 1980s, this was a question of significance, as the technological manifestations of the digital revolution did not seem to translate into economic growth. In the well-known catch phrase attributed to Nobel laureate Robert Solow, "we see the computers everywhere but in the productivity statistics" (David, 1990: 355). By the end of the century, however, an almost unprecedented decade-long expansion in the United States had erased most remaining doubts about the ability of new technology to drive growth.

Gordon (chapter 3) shows that the acceleration in technical change in computers, peripherals, and semiconductors explains most of the acceleration in overall productivity growth in the American economy since 1995. In part, this acceleration reflects gains in the computer-producing sector: prices of computer hardware (including peripherals) declined at an average rate of 14.7 percent during 1987–95 and at an average rate of 31.2 percent during 1996–9. But the productivity gains also ramified themselves throughout the durable-goods manufacturing sector that uses computers.[33]

As Gordon and other authors in this volume suggest, the productivity gains experienced by the United States in recent years, especially those resulting form the adoption of computer technology, have not been as great elsewhere in the developed world. This suggests that the United States is enjoying considerable macroe-

conomic advantage from the success of its computer and semiconductor industries. As this chapter has argued, America's early—and more recent—success in both of those industries is related to the codevelopment or coevolution of the two technologies, which led to virtuous cycles of increased productivity leading to increased demand leading to further increases in productivity.[34] Why in the United States? Gordon (chapter 3) discusses some of the general reasons for American success. In the specific context of semiconductors and computers, this chapter has pointed to: (1) the absolute size of the American market; (2) the early role of the federal government as a demander of semiconductors and computers, which gave way to a relatively more laissez-faire role as the technology matured; and (3) the relatively more diverse and open structure of American industry, which allowed for more rapid experimentation and learning than in other countries.

[33] However, it appears that computers had little productivity-enhancing effect outside the durable-goods sector. As Gordon himself hints, and as other economist would insist, this may be because gains in consumer welfare are harder to measure outside the durable-goods sector. One benefit of computers in the consumer sector has been the ability more finely to tailor product characteristics to the tastes of individual consumers—so-called mass customization. To the extent that computers have allowed greater diversity and variety of products, rather than lower prices for existing products, current data-gathering techniques may not register these gains (Cox and Alm, 1998).

[34] Gordon (chapter 3) argues that increases in demand for computers have actually been increases in quantity demanded, that is, movements along a relatively stable demand curve rather than shifts in a demand curve.

Banking and Financial Intermediation

Charles W. Calomiris

11.1. Introduction

Technological improvements in the areas of banking and corporate finance are hard to measure. Inputs and outputs are not well defined, and product quality changes over time in ways that are hard to measure. Are deposits an input or an output of a bank? When more ATMs are added to a bank's network, by how much does that improve the quality of a bank deposit?

When measuring improvements in corporate finance, it is even harder to define productivity gains associated with changes in the financing structure of firms. When does a shift toward a higher or lower equity ratio connote progress (i.e., reduced costs of access to external finance)? How does one measure improvements in the ability of firms to access venture capital finance, and to place their initial public offerings (IPOs) more easily, and how does one translate those gains into productivity improvements comparable to improvements in manufacturing productivity? How does the existence of new derivative contracts (which allow firms to limit various risk exposures) reduce the cost of capital for firms?

Not only is technological change in banking and corporate finance hard to measure; it is also hard to visualize. The image of a Wall Street trader or investment banker, telephone in hand, staring at multiple computer screens amidst the buzz of the trading floor offers a concrete image of technological progress, but that image is only a small part of the picture. Despite the importance of innovations in computing and telecommunications, technolo-

Sanket Mohapatra and Woodrow Johnson provided excellent research assistance.

gical improvement in corporate finance and financial intermediation goes far beyond these tangible improvements in physical capital. In the areas of banking and corporate finance, the main sources of increased productivity are improvements in the ability to create and use information. Technological change sometimes reflects new physical technology used to process information (e.g., faster computers), but more often it results from improvements in the organization of the *market*'s information processing ability embodied in new kinds of firm-customer relationships, new kinds of financial intermediaries, and new ways to organize purchases and sales of financial instruments, which reduce information cost and enhance productivity. Thus, important technological change occurs outside the confines of innovations in physical capital used by a firm or an intermediary.

The creation of new types of financial institutions and intermediation networks and changes in the extent of competition among financial intermediaries have been extremely important in transforming the shape of the marketplace, and in producing increases in productivity associated with improvements in information creation and dissemination. These issues are the focal point of this chapter. The elimination of limits on U.S. bank branch locations and the expansion of the mix of products U.S. banks are able to offer are prominent examples of such changes. More generally, deregulation of banks and the erosion of limits on capital mobility internationally have been important for the development of efficient financial networks.

At the same time, important information-enhancing changes in industrial organization, competition, and the structure of financial networks have occurred for reasons other than deregulation. The growth of institutional investors (pension funds and mutual funds) as purchasers of securities in the 1960s and 1970s fundamentally altered the ways primary and secondary markets for securities are organized. These sorts of organizational changes have had dramatic long-term consequences for the cost of information processing in the financial sector. Borrowers and lenders, issuers and purchasers of equity, and the intermediaries that bring them together, have benefited enormously from such organizational changes.

Of course, financial product innovation, and technological progress in telecommunications and computing in general, have spurred deregulation and the growth in new intermediaries by creating greater opportunities for entry into previously protected niches. Thus, it would not be correct to view information-enhancing changes in industrial organization as exogenous to the process of technological change. My central point is, rather, that changes in the structure of intermediaries and financial networks have been important for the full realization of the gains from product and process innovation.

Given the myriad problems of defining financial sector inputs and outputs, adjusting for changes in their quality, and measuring the gains in consumer and producer surplus from financial innovation, no attempt is made to reduce financial progress to a single aggregate measure, or to explain the timing and extent of changes in such a measure. Instead, a broad range of illustrative evidence is reviewed that suggests the importance of organizational changes for producing important technological progress in finance.

Useful measures of technological progress vary according to the aspect of financial sector "production" one is studying. Improvements in financial services technology should be reflected in reductions in financial frictions. For example, if problems of adverse selection limit access to public equity markets, then an increase in the number of firms with access to equity markets is an indicator of a technological improvement in financial services. Similarly, if financial intermediaries help consumers to diversify their portfolios and to allocate savings to its best use, then the ability of capital to move

more easily across borders improves the environment for financial intermediation. In the discussion that follows, the frictions that the financial sector is designed to address are categorized, and observable manifestations of improvements are considered.

The remainder of this chapter is organized as follows: Section 11.2 reviews the financial frictions that technological change should mitigate. Section 11.3 considers evidence that financial technology has improved, and links that evidence with changes in the organization of the financial services industry. Visible improvements include: (1) reductions in the costs of operating banks; (2) a richer menu of contracts and a richer menu of services available to businesses and consumers (i.e., more complete markets); (3) an improvement in the ability of financial contracting to overcome fundamental costs of adverse selection and moral hazard, visible in the ability of firms and their agents to convince outsiders to hold junior (equity-like) positions in their firms more easily; (4) greater risk sharing domestically and internationally, visible especially in increasing international flows of claims, or in new means of broadening the holding of a particular bundle of risks through "asset securitization;" and (5) greater liquidity—that is, improvements in the ability to trade an asset on short notice at a price near its long-run fair market value. Section 11.4 concludes.

11.2. Financial Frictions and Financial Progress

Financial services are a means to mitigate "frictions" that would otherwise prevent desirable transactions from taking place. Financial service providers (1) channel savings to select investments efficiently, (2) improve the liquidity of assets, (3) facilitate portfolio diversification, (4) provide proper corporate governance and the oversight of the management of nonfinancial firms, and (5) enforce the contractual rights of creditors and debtors.

There are three broad categories of frictions that financial intermediaries and financial contract design seek to ameliorate: (1) physical transacting costs (the time and effort necessary for executing transactions in the literal physical sense, which for an intermediary may entail physical costs of bridging distances); (2) information costs (gaining accurate knowledge about the traits or behavior of clients); and (3) control costs (control presumes the availability of information about debtors, managers, and controlling shareholders on the part of bankers and asset managers, and entails the additional costs of creating and executing the necessary mechanisms to enforce contracts or otherwise control agents' behavior). Note that these three categories of cost can be incurred either at a point of contact between the final issuer and holder of a contract (the firm and its ultimate security holder), or as is more often the case, between either of these parties and an "intermediary."

When intermediaries are involved in financial transactions (as they almost always are) they add a layer of additional costs involving all three categories. Presumably, intermediaries are used because their involvement reduces the overall costs of the transaction relative to what those costs would have been without intermediation (unless intermediaries are able to extract rents from the market because of monopoly power). That is what it means for intermediaries to serve as efficient mechanisms. For example, technological improvements in intermediation that permit intermediaries to mitigate information costs (which are often associated with bank deregulation, changes in competition, and changes in bank industrial structure) should increase the scope of intermediaries and lead to a channeling of more transactions through their hands at lower cost (not necessarily, however, to an increase in their balance sheet assets).

Despite the costs incurred by intermediaries or by ultimate holders of securities from collecting information and enforcing contracts, doing so mitigates two classes of problems. First, collecting information reduces costs associated with adverse selection—the tendency of relatively informed buyers (sellers) to take advantage of relatively less informed sellers (buyers). For example, as Myers and Majluf (1984) showed, adverse-selection costs may discourage the sales of equity because uninformed buyers

impose a "lemons discount" on the purchase of shares. The inability of buyers to gauge the profitability of existing and prospective firm opportunities can be mitigated by the due diligence and marketing efforts of investment bankers, but there are substantial costs associated with those activities, as well. Here, technological improvement would be reflected in an increase in the amount of junior securities placed in the hands of outsiders, and a reduction in the costs investment banks charge for placing these securities.

Second, information and a control technology are necessary for proper enforcement of contracts to prevent moral-hazard problems between contracting parties. Moral-hazard (or agency) problems can occur between debtors and creditors, between managers and stockholders, and between controlling stockholders and minority stockholders. The moral-hazard problem of debtors is sometimes called the asset-substitution problem. After debtors have contracted with creditors they face an incentive to increase the riskiness of assets, which effectively transfers wealth from creditors to debtors (Jensen and Meckling, 1976; Myers, 1977). The agency problem between managers and stockholders revolves around the conflict of interest over several key decisions: corporate financial structure (where managers tend to favor less than optimal leverage), asset profitability and risk (where managers can be excessively risk-averse, and too willing to hold cash), effort (where managers prefer less to more), and expenditures (where managers may spend wastefully in ways that increase their private utility).

The conflict between controlling stockholders and minority stockholders can give rise to similar abuses of power, and especially to "tunneling,"—the process by which revenues are captured or valuable assets are transferred at below market prices to profit shareholders with a controlling interest in the firm at the expense of other shareholders. As in the case of adverse-selection costs, technological improvements in mitigating problems of moral hazard should be reflected in the greater willingness of outsiders to hold risky debt and equity claims on firms, which in turn should be reflected in a rising quantity of such holdings and lower investment banking costs.

Intermediaries exist primarily to generate and use information (whether they are investment bank underwriters or bank lenders), and to facilitate contractual enforcement to mitigate one or more of these moral hazard problems. Private lenders (banks and finance companies) rely on contractual rights of seniority (collateral and covenants) to use private information to mitigate problems of asset substitution. Pensions, mutuals, and private equity funds (as holders of equity) use private or public information, along with blocks of voting shares, to mitigate conflicts between managers and stockholders, or between minority and controlling stockholders. Intermediaries also mitigate physical costs associated with constructing diversified portfolios (within banks, mutual funds, pension funds, and the like), and physical costs of clearing claims (as in bank clearinghouses, futures clearinghouses, and securities exchanges).

Liquidity refers to the ability to convert a valuable asset into purchasing power. Assets may be illiquid either because of physical factors that limit their transactability (e.g., an inconvenient location, indivisibility, an absence of buyers in the vicinity with a desire to purchase the asset) or because adverse-selection problems limit the marketability of the asset. Intermediaries that provide liquidity (banks, futures exchanges, and stock exchanges) do so by engaging in a combination of activities that together reduce the costs of information production and the physical costs of transacting.

This brief introduction to the productive role of the financial sector shows how the specific frictions that give rise to particular financial contracts, legal protections (creditors' rights and minority shareholders' rights), and financial services translate into quantifiable manifestations that can be used to gauge progress in financial sector technology. The extent to which portfolios can be shown to be globally rather than locally diversified can be used to gauge the degree of success of the financial sector in overcoming a combination of physical transacting costs and delegation costs (e.g., the extent to which banks or mutual funds can be

trusted to properly construct and manage portfolios). The extent to which firms have access to particular markets or intermediaries, the extent to which markets or intermediaries can be shown to properly predict risk, the extent of market liquidity, and the degree of the effectiveness of control over debtors, managers, and controlling stockholders, are all potentially important gauges of the technological achievement of the financial sector.

It is difficult to trace improvements in the five main quantifiable areas of financial performance (lower costs of intermediation, a richer menu of contracts and services, greater marketability of junior claims, greater risk sharing, and greater liquidity) to particular reductions in one or more of the three categories of frictions (physical costs, adverse-selection costs, and moral-hazard costs). That is because the effects of performance along one of the five dimensions will often influence other dimensions of performance. For example, a liquid secondary market in equity may raise equity prices, thus making it more attractive for firms to offer equity, ceteris paribus. Positive feedback also occurs among the primary causal influences that drive reductions in frictions (e.g., improvements in physical technology, greater bank competition, and deregulation reinforce one another).

11.3. Financial Progress and its Links to Organizational Change

This section traces recent trends in financial intermediation and corporate finance and considers the extent to which those trends provide evidence of technological progress (improvements in one or more of the five quantifiable areas of financial performance). A detailed discussion is given on the highly visible transformation of the banking industry in the United States, focusing on measuring and interpreting improvements in bank productivity that were associated with those changes in industrial organization. The improvements in securities markets that have taken place in global equity markets (most notably, the increased access of small firms in industrialized countries, and

TABLE 11.1
U.S. Bank Consolidation

Year	No. of banks	No. of banks with branches	No. of unit banks	No. of bank offices	No. of bank employees	No. of new charters	No. of voluntary mergers
1970	13502	3985	9517		946497	178	146
1975	14372	5505	8867		1182791	245	84
1980	14421	6831	7590		1434290	205	126
1985	14402	7012	7390	57372	1553755	330	336
1990	12329	6849	5480	62346	1505684	165	393
1995	9921	6426	3495	65949	1470231	101	609
1999	8563	5830	2733	71664	1641710	231	421

Source: FDIC data on insured commercial banks.

firms in emerging market economies) are then described. Finally, the new financial instruments and techniques that have been developed in recent years for managing and trading risks (derivatives and securitization), and the phenomenon of increasing international capital flows are reviewed.

11.3.1. Banking System Structure and Performance, Within and Outside the United States

Table 11.1 shows that the physical structure of the U.S. banking system has undergone a remarkable transformation over the past decade as the result of consolidation. The number of banks has fallen by nearly a third. Nevertheless, it would be wrong to characterize

banking as a shrinking industry, even in the physical sense of the word. The number of bank offices (headquarters plus branches) has grown substantially over that period, and the number of bank employees has also increased.

In financial terms, Table 11.2 indicates that banks have become increasingly important in the economy (with their share of gross domestic product (GDP) rising substantially over the past thirty years), and increasingly profitable (the last several years have seen very high and relatively stable levels of return on equity). This is worth emphasizing. Despite the substantial new competition in banking, ushered in by the post–1980 era of bank deregulation, the elimination of interstate entry barriers in banking over the past twenty years, and the growth in securities

TABLE 11.2
U.S. Bank Performance

Year	Net income (U.S.$ million)	Net income (U.S.$)/ GDP (U.S.$) (percent)	Return on equity (percent)	Net interest margin/assets (percent)	Non-interest income/assets (percent)	Non-interest expense/assets (percent)
1970	4817	0.46	10.93	3.17	0.74	2.54
1975	7250	0.44	11.35	2.94	0.92	2.52
1980	13950	0.50	12.97	3.03	0.77	2.51
1985	17874	0.42	11.32	3.38	1.32	3.19
1990	15872	0.27	7.31	3.46	1.67	3.49
1995	48447	0.65	14.69	3.72	2.02	3.64
1999	71174	0.77	15.48	3.53	2.66	3.77

Sources: FDIC data on insured commercial banks, and Council of Economic Advisers.

market substitutes for bank assets and liabilities, banks have been able to *increase* their net interest margins, and have seen substantial growth in noninterest income. Interestingly, noninterest expense has risen substantially as a share of assets, too (reflecting new efforts by banks to attract customers through greater convenience and an expanding range of services).

These trends indicate that, while competition has eroded pure "rents" that banks enjoyed when they were protected from competition, bank profitability has not suffered because banks have found ways to create value for their franchises by restructuring their businesses. In part, that has taken the form of introducing new information processing technology and marketing new products and services that help them to attract profitable clients. In large part, however, it has also meant finding new ways of combining existing products and technology, and reorganizing financial intermediaries to make more productive use of information technology.

The competitive pressures U.S. banks have had to face are clearly visible in their changing liability structure, as shown in Table 11.3. From 1970 to 1999, deposits fell as a share of total assets, from 85 percent in 1970 to 67 percent in 1999. Within the category of deposits, domestic demand deposits fell even more rapidly, declining from 51 percent of total domestic deposits in 1970 to only 17 percent by 1999. These demand deposits—whose interest rates were limited by Regulation Q—were an impor-

tant source of captive rents enjoyed by banks in the first two decades after World War II.

As higher inflation eroded the purchasing power of low-interest deposits, consumers and businesses sought means for increasing the real rate of return on savings. Various innovations resulted. Commercial paper offerings (whether placed directly by corporations or issued to finance the activities of finance companies that compete with banks as intermediaries) drew funds out of the banking system, as did money market funds. Banks responded with various new bank products, including repurchase agreements, sweep, NOW, Super NOW, and MMDA accounts, all of which raised the interest cost of bank funds, and put pressure on bank profit margins. Banks, especially large banks, also relied increasingly on high-cost bonds and equity as sources of funds, particularly as new capital requirements, imposed in the 1980s, encouraged increases in those financing components.

Banks also faced new challenges in loan markets. Table 11.4 shows the effects of increasing competition in commercial and industrial lending. C&I loans fell substantially as a share of total loans, from 38 percent of loans in 1970 to 28 percent in 1999.

But rather than suffer long-term reductions in profit from the erosion of rents associated with low-interest deposit funding, and increasing competition in loan markets, banks responded with organizational changes that improved financial technology. Deregulation of entry

TABLE 11.3
U.S. Bank Liability Composition

Year	Total assets (U.S.$ million)	Deposits/assets (percent)	Domestic demand deposits/domestic deposits (percent)	Subordinated notes/assets (percent)	Fed funds purchased/assets (percent)	Equity/assets (percent)
1970	566500	85.17	51.23	0.37	2.93	7.16
1975	935827	97.87	41.17	0.47	5.58	6.82
1980	1848392	80.13	36.35	0.35	7.21	5.82
1985	2719890	77.87	25.11	0.54	8.16	6.22
1990	3369559	78.65	19.69	0.71	7.28	6.49
1995	4282783	70.69	22.41	1.02	7.62	8.16
1999	5687670	67.35	16.53	1.34	7.83	8.44

Source: FDIC data on insured commercial banks.

TABLE 11.4

U.S. Bank Asset Composition

Year	Total assets	Loans/assets (percent)	C&I loans/ loans (percent)	Loans secured by real estate/ loans (percent)	Nonfarm, domestic, commercial real estate loans/ domestic, real estate loans (percent)	Investment securities/ assets (percent)	Corporate bonds and equity/ investment securities (percent)	Trading account/ assets (percent)
1970	566500	52.26	37.65	24.51	31.80	24.90	1.97	1.00
1975	935827	53.20	34.72	26.88	34.42	23.69	4.90	0.61
1980	1848392	54.86	37.68	25.94	38.29	17.46	7.58	0.51
1985	2719890	58.38	35.02	26.61	47.65	16.08	7.57	1.49
1990	3369559	60.53	28.96	39.07	45.37	17.83	15.66	1.42
1995	4282783	58.37	25.35	41.40	34.88	18.70	13.88	5.07
1999	5687670	59.36	27.79	43.20	37.44	18.09	22.48	4.52

Source: FDIC data on insured commercial banks.

barriers, and of limits on bank products, contributed to the ability of surviving banks to find productivity-enhancing strategies for expanding their geographic reach and the bundle of services that they could deliver. Banks expanded into new kinds of lending and investing (particularly into real estate lending, leveraged buyout (LBO) financing, and private equity financing), and came to rely increasingly on trading profits and fee income from other services.

Table 11.5 shows how increases in loan market competition and improvements in technology have increased the average distance between small business borrowers and their lenders, a clear physical measure of technologi-

TABLE 11.5

Average Distance Between Locations of U.S. Small Business Borrowers and Their Lenders

Lender type	Year that lending relationship began			
	1973–9	1980–9	1990–3	1973–3
Banks	15.8	34.0	67.8	42.5
Nonbanks	235.9	221.1	280.5	251.6
Nonfinancial firms	117.3	165.9	209.2	182.5
Total	51.2	92.6	161.3	114.7

Source: Petersen and Rajan (2000: Table 1).
Notes: Distance is measured in miles.

cal improvement in bank lending. From the 1970s to the 1990s, for all lenders the average distance increased from 51 miles to 161 miles, and for banks average distance rose from 16 miles to 68 miles.

Despite the erosion of pure rents, the newly competitive, deregulated banking industry has seen substantial increases in "quasi rents" from superior use of private information, which is reflected in the rising market-to-book value ratios of universal banks. Table 11.6 reviews the sharply increasing trend in market-to-book values for the national and regional giants that have thrived from the wave of bank consolidation, and the expansion of bank powers that coincided with it.

Table 11.7 compares the number of bank offices and employees in U.S. banking with those of Japan and Western Europe. The conclusion usually drawn from this table is that the superior performance of U.S. banks (e.g., the higher return on assets shown in Table 11.8) is due to lower brick and mortar expenses in the U.S. Tables 11.7 and 11.8, however, show that while the U.S. economizes on bank offices, in comparison with Europe and Japan, U.S. banks actually have higher employment, and higher ratios of noninterest expenses to assets than the banks in other highly industrialized economies. Indeed, one interesting

TABLE 11.6
Recent Trends in Market-to-Book Value of Select Large U.S. Banks' Equity

	MVE/BE 1980	MVE/BE 1985	MVE/BE 1990	MVE/BE 1995	MVE/BE 1997	MVE/BE 1999
Chase (Chemical)	0.53	0.89	0.33	1.41	2.30	2.83
(Old) Chase	0.69	0.74	0.36			
Citicorp	0.76	0.98	0.52	1.74	2.97	
Bank America (Nations Bank)	0.74	1.59	0.80	1.50	2.04	1.90
(Old) Bank of America	1.14	0.62	0.97	1.35	2.61	
Bank of New York	0.59	1.21	0.49	1.89	4.33	5.76
Fleet Boston	0.68	1.53	0.62	1.79	2.67	2.18
(Old) Bank Boston	0.61	0.97	0.32	1.60	3.16	
First Union	0.69	1.66	0.66	1.74	2.71	1.95
Keycorp	0.52	1.24	1.05	1.70	2.99	1.54
Mellon	0.69	0.86	0.81	2.05	4.21	4.25
J.P. Morgan	0.92	1.35	1.75	1.51	1.86	1.94
Wachovia	0.72	1.75	1.51	2.07	3.23	2.43
SunTrust	0.94	1.78	1.25	1.82	2.88	2.78
U.S. Bancorp	0.77	1.02	0.98	2.41	4.69	2.39
Comerica	0.53	1.02	0.93	1.76	3.76	2.27

Notes: Values are for the end of the fiscal year, and are taken from Compustat. MVE: market value of equity; BE: book equity.

pattern shown in Table 11.8 is that the three countries with the highest return on assets (United States, United Kingdom, and Spain) also have the highest ratios of operating costs to assets, and the highest net interest margins relative to assets.

Those facts are consistent with the view that investment in quasi rent creation, not contraction in overhead, is the path to greater profitability in banking. Thus, while some noninterest costs (excessive brick and mortar expenses) probably indicate some room for cost cutting in European banking, that is not to say that

European banks need to cut expenses; rather, they need to reallocate their expenses toward more profitable pursuits.

Table 11.9 presents calculations on U.S. bank productivity growth, which indicate that, irrespective of whether bank "production" is defined narrowly or broadly, there has been substantial improvement over time in the ability of banks to provide the same "output" (measured here as quantities of assets) at lower cost. According to these calculations, annual bank productivity growth has averaged more than 0.4 percent during the 1990s.

TABLE 11.7
Cost Structure Differences in Banking Among the United States, Europe, and Japan

	Number of branches per 1,000 people			Number of employees per $1,000 in assets		
	1990	1995	1998	1990	1995	1998
United States	0.29	0.28	0.29	0.40	0.32	0.29
Japan	0.18	0.19	0.19	0.07	0.06	0.06
Euro Area	0.56	0.55	0.55	0.21	0.15	0.15[a]

Source: Bank for International Settlements, Annual Report (2000: 135).
[a] European data shown in the 1998 column are actually for 1997.

TABLE 11.8

Performance of Large Banks and Mergers for All Banks in Industrialized Countries

Country	Return on assets (percent)		Net interest margin/assets (percent)		Operating costs/ assets (percent)		No. of mergers and acquisitions		Value of M&A (U.S.$ billions)	
	1994	1998	1994	1998	1994	1998	1993–4	1997–8	1993–4	1997–8
Japan	−0.21	−0.74	0.90	1.07	0.74	1.00	8	28	18.8	4.1
France	0.17	0.27	1.60	0.63	2.04	0.95	71	36	0.5	4.0
Germany	0.52	0.56	1.82	0.98	2.06	1.65	83	45	1.9	23.2
Netherlands	0.69	0.60	2.27	1.90	2.17	2.32	13	9	0.1	0.4
Sweden	0.55	0.93	2.34	1.46	1.76	1.57	23	8	0.4	2.1
Spain	0.70	1.07	2.47	2.76	2.45	2.82	44	30	4.5	5.9
Switzerland	0.63	0.46	1.17	0.80	2.17	1.92	59	22	3.9	24.3
United Kingdom	1.22	1.19	2.45	2.18	3.02	2.41	40	17	3.3	11.0
United States	1.81	1.42	3.57	3.03	3.80	3.93	1477	1052	55.3	362.4

Source: Danthine et al. (2000).

Table 11.10 examines the relationship between scale and productivity improvement over time for U.S. banks. Over time, the advantages from scale economies appear to have risen, particularly for the largest category of banks (those with assets of greater than U.S.$5 billion). The scale economies of large banks were smaller in 1991 than in 1997, irrespective of which definition of output is used.

This evidence suggests that the consolidation wave in U.S. banking has contributed to recent growth in productivity. One explanation for the increasing advantages from large scale is the role that deregulation of entry played in promoting economies of scale. Prior to branch-ing deregulation, banks could only grow large locally, which limited the gains from diversification produced by larger size. Furthermore, deregulation of bank products likely added to improvements in scale economies; larger scale makes economies of scope larger by making the expansion of products, and the overhead costs of marketing and selling those products, more cost-effective.

Another possible contributor to productivity improvement for large banks has been their propensity to employ the Internet as a means of attracting customers, expanding sources of revenue, and reducing transacting costs. Table 11.11 shows that the larger a bank is, the more

TABLE 11.9

Productivity Growth in U.S. Banking

	Narrowest definition of bank production[a]	Narrow definition of bank production[b]	Broad definition of bank production[c]
Annual percentage productivity growth of banks over the period 1991–7	0.44	0.42	0.44

Source: This table is adapted from Stiroh (2000).

Notes: Productivity growth is estimated by Stiroh (2000: Table 3) from a pooled regression analysis of total costs, using a translog specification.

[a] The "narrowest" definition of output includes the quantity of business loans, consumer loans, and securities.

[b] The "narrow" definition of output includes the asset items in the "narrowest" definition and net noninterest income.

[c] The "broad" definition of output includes the items in the "narrow" definition and off-balance sheet items as an output.

TABLE 11.10
Increases in Scale Economies Over Time in U.S. Banking[a]

Bank size	Narrowest definition of bank production[b]			Narrow definition of bank production[c]			Broad definition of bank production[d]		
	1991	1994	1997	1991	1994	1997	1991	1994	1997
U.S.$200 million < assets < U.S.$300 million	1.056	1.042	1.069	1.062	1.067	1.065	1.055	1.045	1.076
Assets > U.S.$5 billion	0.979	0.908	0.942	0.967	0.926	0.954	0.984	0.909	0.937

Source: This table is adapted from Stiroh (2000: Table 5).

Notes: Numbers less than one imply scale economies (increases in cost less than proportional to output), while numbers greater than one imply scale diseconomies.

[a] "Expansion path scale economies," as defined originally by Berger et al. (1987), and estimated by Stiroh (2000), measure the proportional change in costs as a bank moves along the observed expansion path from one output bundle to a larger output bundle.

[b] The "narrowest" definition of output includes the quantity of business loans, consumer loans, and securities.

[c] The "narrow" definition of output includes the asset items in the "narrowest" definition and net noninterest income.

[d] The "broad" definition of output includes the items in the "narrow" definition and off-balance sheet items as an output.

likely it is to choose to become an "Internet bank" (defined as those with a transactional web site). Moreover, Internet banks also tend to rely more on fees rather than interest income, within each size category. Although causality cannot be inferred from such simple associations, the connection between noninterest income and Internet banking may indicate that the Internet is a particularly useful tool for attracting customers for nonlending purposes.

Table 11.12 provides additional insights about the potential gains from Internet banking in the United States, and about the likely growth in Internet banking over the next few years. The average Internet transaction costs the bank only 2 cents, in contrast to a branch transaction, which costs an average of

TABLE 11.11
U.S. Performance in Internet Banking for National Banks

Bank asset size	No. of banks offering internet banking	Internet banks as a percentage of national banks in that size category	Percentage increase in number of banks offering Internet banking from 1998:Q1 to 1999:Q3	Noninterest income/net operating revenue (percent) (non–Internet banks shown in parentheses for comparison)	Return on equity (non–Internet banks shown in parentheses for comparison)
Assets < U.S.$100 million	85	7.1	226.9	22.0 (14.6)	6.34 (10.13)
U.S.$100 million < assets < U.S.$1 billion	265	27.1	258.1	23.1 (16.8)	14.15 (13.03)
U.S.$1 billion < assets < U.S.$10 billion	73	61.9	82.5	36.8 (23.0)	18.26 (15.68)
Assets > U.S.$10 billion	41	100.0	95.2	40.1	15.35
All asset sizes	464	19.9	188.2		

Source: Furst et al. (2000).

Notes: "Internet banks" are defined as banks with a transactional web site.

TABLE 11.12

U.S. Trends in Internet Banking for National Banks

	Actual 1999:Q3	Planned 2000:Q4	Percent increase	Forecast 2001[c]	Forecast 2003[d]	Transaction cost
Number of Internet banks	464	1,047	125.6			
Millions of households banking on-line	5			18.3	23–32	
Type of service						
Balance inquiry and fund transactions	412	969	135.2			
Bill payment	363	853	135.0			
Credit applications	269	646	140.1			
Set up new account	170	487	186.5			
Brokerage	100	230	130.0			
Cash management	73	445	509.6			
Fiduciary	55	150	172.7			
Bill presentment	49	258	426.5			
Insurance	25	95	280.0			
Basic[a]	360	836	132.2			
Premium[b]	111	471	324.3			
Branch transaction (U.S.$)						1.07
Telephone transaction (U.S.$)						0.55
ATM transaction (U.S.$)						0.33
PC banking (U.S.$)						0.13
Internet banking (U.S.$)						0.02

Sources: For all information other than costs of transacting, see Furst et al. (2000). For costs of transacting, see Claessens et al. (2000), based on information from Goldman Sachs and Boston Consulting Group.

Notes: "Internet banks" are defined as banks with a transactional web site.

[a] "Basic" service includes balance inquiry, funds transfer, and bill payment.

[b] "Premium" service includes "Basic" plus at least three other services.

[c] The forecast for 2001 is by the Gartner Group, cited in Furst et al. (2000: Figure 7).

[d] The forecasts for 2003 are from Jupiter Communications (23), Piper Jaffray (25.2), and IDC Research (32), cited in Furst et al. (2000: Figure 7).

U.S.$1.07. In the year 2000, the number of Internet banks is projected to increase by 126 percent. The growth rate of the number of banks offering an expanded range of "premium" Internet services is expected to grow even faster (by 324 percent). While only 5 million households were banking on line in 1999, by 2003 various analysts forecast that between 23 and 32 million households will be doing so. The Internet is likely to remain a continuing source of expanded revenue and reductions in transacting costs for many years to come.

Whether other countries will share in the productivity boom that has transformed U.S. banking is more controversial. Some countries (especially the United Kingdom, Spain, and the Netherlands) increasingly are following the example of large U.S. banks, and have developed universal banks, providing retail and wholesale banking services through traditional brick and mortar networks. These banks employ cutting-edge techniques for cross-selling products, diversifying and laying off risk, and economizing on capital. Other countries (especially France and Italy) are still struggling to catch up. The new strategies include novel ways of selling products, the securitization, sale, or syndication of some loans or parts of loans, the internal use of derivatives for hedging, and the ability to supply a broad range of services to consumers and businesses (derivatives, private equity, insurance, underwriting, cash management, etc.) in addition to traditional lending and deposit taking.

With regard to Internet banking, some countries are likely to be better able to follow the U.S. lead than others. As Table 11.13 shows, Finland, Sweden, Australia, and Denmark are far ahead of other industrialized countries in the number of Internet IP addresses per 10,000 people, as of 1998. This makes Internet banking much more attractive in those countries. For example, even though 90 percent of Spanish banks are offering on-line services, far fewer of their customers are using such services, in comparison with other countries where more of the population is connected to the Internet.

Countries other than the United States are much more dependent on traditional banking as a means of intermediating capital, creating liquidity, and offering investment opportunities to savers. Nevertheless, government control and taxation of the banking sector (which is known as "financial repression") has been a constraining influence on bank development, and therefore, on economic development for nearly all developing countries since World War II (for a review of the literature on financial repression, and its effects on capital allocation and growth, see Beim and Calomiris, 2000: chapters 2–4). The recent trend toward financial liberalization has helped to undo some of the damage of financial repression, although liberalization has not always been pursued properly (Beim and Calomiris, 2000: chapters 3, 7, and 8).

Table 11.14 reviews the major changes in the size of financial intermediation in developing and developed economies since 1960. Countries are grouped according to their average real GDP levels for the period. Three clear patterns are visible in Table 11.14. First, financial depth (measured as private credit, bank credit, or liquid liabilities, relative to GDP) is higher for richer countries. Second, poorer countries tend to have a much greater ratio of central bank assets relative to GDP. Third, over the past four decades, all income classes have seen a substantial rise in credit relative to GDP, although the poorest group of countries saw a slight decline in credit relative to GDP in the 1990s.

TABLE 11.13
Internet Banking Trends Around the World

	Percentage of banks offering on-line banking	Percentage of bank customers using on-line banking	Computers with IP address connected to the Internet, per 10,000 people in 1998
The Americas			
Argentina	4	3	16
Brazil	<50	5	10
Mexico	<10	<1	9
United States	63	4	975
Europe			
Austria	75	4	163
Central Europe	35	<1	54
Denmark	60	5–10	359
Finland	85	29	996
Germany	60	2	141
Greece	40	<1	38
Italy	50	1	56
Spain	90	<2	62
Sweden	90	11	430
Switzerland	75	5	289
United Kingdom	50	2	202
Asia			
Australia	90	4	400
Hong Kong	25	<2	108
India	10	<1	0
Indonesia	0	0	0
South Korea	90	3	38
Malaysia	10	<1	18
Philippines	15	<1	1
Singapore	95	5	187
Taiwan	10	0	48
Thailand	0	0	4

Source: Claessens et al. (2000: Table 5), based on data from Credit Suisse First Boston Global Bank Team (1999) and World Bank (2000a).

This last fact suggests the persistence of a "financial repression divide" separating the poorest countries from others; in other words, the global liberalization in financial

TABLE 11.14
International Trends in Private Credit and Liquidity

	1960	1970	1980	1990	1997	1960s	1970s	1980s	1990s
Liquid liabilities/GDP									
LIG	0.20	0.18	0.24	0.23	0.25	0.18	0.21	0.25	0.24
LMIG	0.21	0.25	0.38	0.46	0.43	0.23	0.30	0.43	0.44
UMIG	0.18	0.40	0.42	0.47	0.58	0.35	0.42	0.57	0.50
HIG	0.48	0.57	0.63	0.77	0.88	0.52	0.60	0.69	0.82
Private bank credit/GDP									
LIG	0.06	0.10	0.15	0.13	0.13	0.10	0.12	0.15	0.13
LMIG	0.13	0.17	0.22	0.28	0.31	0.15	0.19	0.24	0.28
UMIG	0.11	0.20	0.26	0.30	0.39	0.14	0.22	0.33	0.33
HIG	0.33	0.41	0.48	0.66	0.83	0.37	0.44	0.54	0.73
Private credit from all financial institutions/GDP									
LIG	0.07	0.11	0.17	0.15	0.14	0.10	0.13	0.16	0.14
LMIG	0.15	0.20	0.26	0.30	0.35	0.17	0.22	0.28	0.32
UMIG	0.14	0.26	0.31	0.37	0.50	0.18	0.27	0.41	0.42
HIG	0.39	0.52	0.65	0.87	0.99	0.46	0.59	0.72	0.93
Central bank assets/GDP									
LIG	0.10	0.05	0.10	0.12	0.10	0.07	0.07	0.12	0.13
LMIG	0.08	0.09	0.12	0.18	0.06	0.08	0.08	0.17	0.11
UMIG	0.03	0.04	0.06	0.11	0.05	0.04	0.05	0.12	0.07
HIG	0.06	0.05	0.05	0.04	0.03	0.05	0.04	0.05	0.04

	1980	1990	1996
Insurance company assets/GDP			
LIG	0.08	0.03	0.03
LMIG	0.04	0.10	0.13
UMIG	0.08	0.13	0.26
HIG	0.13	0.24	0.36

Source: Beck et al. (1999).
Note: LIG, lowest income group; LMIG, lower–middle income group; UMIG, upper–middle income group; HIG, upper income group.

services in the 1990s has not taken root in the poorest countries. This is properly viewed as a failure of policy, not a failure of banks. There is a large body of research (reviewed in Beim and Calomiris, 2000) linking the financial underdevelopment of poor countries to their failure to adopt institutional changes that promote banking sector growth (legal reforms to enhance creditors' rights, liberalization of banking regulations and taxes, etc.). Banking sector growth happens rapidly when governments permit it.

Table 11.14 also reports insurance company assets relative to GDP for the four country income groups. Its pattern, across time and across country groups, follows that of banking sector development, with one notable exception: the lower–middle income group (LMIG) shows a much faster rate of growth in insurance than in banking during the 1980s. Part of the explanation for this phenomenon has to do with changes in the demand for life insurance at different phases of economic development. Life insurance is one of the first major financial assets purchased by entrants to the middle class; hence the increase over time in insurance company assets for the LMIG group relative to the lower income group (LIG) may simply reflect a demand-side effect associated with income growth.

11.3.2. The Rise of Equity: Institutional Investors and Technological Progress

Discussions of banking sector developments in the United States and elsewhere emphasize that the banking sector's transformation from a focus on traditional deposit taking and lending to global universal banking was largely a response to competitive pressures from outside banking, which pushed banks (and their regulators) to improve their scale, product mix, risk management, and marketing strategies. The result is a banking sector that serves as a platform for virtually all financial activities: lending of all kinds, private equity investing, asset management, insurance, underwriting, derivatives selling, and cash management. Banks are absorbing underwriting and asset management firms and insurance companies.

Banks have become not so much competitors with securities markets (as they were sometimes seen in the 1980s) but rather a primary means of accessing securities markets (whether in the form of derivatives transactions, securitizations of assets, underwriting, or asset management). These various new banking activities could be broadly defined as the "securitization" of the banking industry—that is, the increasing involvement of banks in a wide range of securities market transactions.

But where did these securities markets come from? Why were they more developed in the United States than elsewhere? How and why has their development accelerated in the past forty years? It is easy today to take for granted the existence of an active securities market, but its origins have a history of their own, and the current universal banking system (which combines financial markets and financial inter-mediaries in novel ways; Calomiris, 2000: chapter 6) would not have been possible without the parallel development of an improved banking structure and increasingly efficient securities markets.

Just as in the case of banking sector structural change, securities markets have a structure—a set of buyers and sellers. Innovations that improved that structure, along with improvements in information processing technology, have increasingly encouraged entry into public markets by securities issuers, and facilitated the trading of securities at declining costs of transacting.

Securities market development is usefully divided into the development of primary and secondary markets. That is not to say that these developments are unrelated. The growth of primary markets (markets for new issues) and secondary markets (markets for trading existing issues) are related in two ways. First, the same causal factors have helped to spur both primary and secondary market development. For example, the growth of institutional investors (which act both as purchasers of new offerings in the primary wholesale market, and trade actively in the wholesale "upstairs" secondary market) probably was the single greatest contributing influence to the growth of equity markets in the last forty years. Second, primary and secondary market development are related through effects that each has on the other. The trend toward greater liquidity in the secondary market (shown by Steil in chapter 12) reduces the required return on securities (the so-called liquidity premium), and thus reduces the cost of raising funds via public offerings. And, of course, deep secondary markets are not possible without sufficient outstanding securities to be traded. Thus, the development of primary and secondary markets, particularly for equity, have helped to spur each other.

The development of securities markets—especially the relatively new phenomenon of highly active markets for very junior, risky claims like new companies' stock issues and risky junk bond issues—is itself one of the major transformations of the financial sector in the past forty years. It is useful to consider how much the structure of equity markets has changed over the past decades, and how changes in structure have coincided with increased access to those markets by new classes of issuers and investors.

The growth of equity and junk bond markets has been a major triumph, a clear example of financial innovation. Risky publicly held securities, unlike privately held bank debt and stock, are especially susceptible to adverse-selection and moral-hazard problems. Potential purchasers of these securities face severe problems in identifying firms' ex ante characteristics sufficiently to warrant confidence in the value of their junior claims (the adverse-selection problem). Purchasers also may lack confidence in their ability to protect themselves from abuse ex post (i.e., the extraction of control rents by managers at the expense of minority stockholders, or increases in asset risk by bond issuers, which effectively transfer value from risky bondholders to stockholders).

Beginning in the 1960s, institutional investors have helped to mitigate these problems because they buy in bulk and because they are repeat buyers. They participate directly and repeatedly in "road shows" for stock offerings, providing reactions to the marketing efforts of investment bankers, and thus helping to price shares and to ensure sufficient buying interest for new offerings (for a review of the theoretical literature, see Calomiris and Raff, 1995). Investment bankers benefit from the reactions of institutional buyers during the road show, from their expres-

sions of interest (which reduce the risk of insufficient demand for the offering), and investment bankers face strong incentives to behave honestly with institutional investors, since they anticipate substantial repeat business with them in the future.

Institutional investors (pensions and mutual funds) became important intermediaries (in terms of their share of total assets) in the 1960s, as shown in Table 11.15, and they have grown substantially since then. As of 1999, pensions and mutuals control 37 percent of financial wealth. The involvement of mutual funds and pension funds as holders of corporate equity became significant in the 1960s, as shown in Table 11.17. As of 1999, institutional investors of all kinds held 47 percent of outstanding corporate equity. As recently as 1960, that number was only 12 percent.

The constructive role of institutional investors in primary and secondary equity markets was noted at an early date. Friend et al. (1970: vii) noted that:

These institutions, which first sparked the cult of common stocks, later attracted attention to "growth" stocks and create the fashion for instant performance. Innovative and inventive, institutional money managers have ventured into areas where older and more prudent investment men feared to tread, taking positions in the stocks of unseasoned

TABLE 11.15
Percentage of U.S. Household Assets Held in Various Investments and Intermediaries

	1946	1950	1955	1960	1965	1970	1975	1980	1985	1990	1995	1999
Deposits + money market funds	19	17	17	17	19	21	24	23	25	21	15	12
Deposits	19	17	17	17	19	21	24	22	23	19	13	10
Money market funds	0	0	0	0	0	0	0	1	2	2	2	2
Credit market instruments	15	13	12	11	9	8	7	6	8	10	9	7
Corporate equities	17	17	24	26	31	22	13	13	10	12	19	24
Mutual fund shares	0	0	1	1	2	2	1	1	2	3	5	9
Life insurance reserves	7	7	7	6	5	5	5	3	3	3	3	2
Pension fund reserves	2	3	5	7	8	10	13	15	21	23	27	28
Investments in bank trusts	0	0	0	0	0	5	5	4	4	4	4	3
Equity in noncorporate business	38	40	33	29	25	25	31	33	26	22	17	13

Source: Federal Reserve Flow of Funds Data.

TABLE 11.16
Market Values of Various Financial Instruments Held in the United States

	1945	1950	1955	1960	1965	1970	1975	1980	1985	1990	1995	1999
Money market mutual funds	0	0	0	0	0	0	3.7	76.4	242.4	493.3	741.3	1573.8
Corporate and foreign bonds	26.9	40.9	60.8	91.8	123.1	204.3	336.4	507.6	883.1	1705.7	2848.1	4610.8
Corporate equities	117.7	142.7	281.8	420.3	734.9	841.4	845.7	1494.9	2270.4	3542.0	8495.7	19576.3

Source: Federal Reserve Flow of Funds Data.

companies, setting up hedge funds, devising new types of securities.

The boom in equity issues and the growth of institutional investors were so dramatic in the 1960s that the SEC undertook a multi-volume study, published in 1971, of the role institutional investors had played in the growth of the equity market. The study concluded that, in the market for new common stock, bulk buying by these investors had fundamentally changed the technology for selling issues. The SEC (1971) found that institutional investors accounted for a large percentage of IPO purchases (24 percent) over the period 1967–70, and that they tended to hold those stocks as long-term investments. The SEC emphasized that, because of their role as wholesale buyers, institutional investors were able to economize on the costs of marketing securities, and that investment bankers' fees and expenses for placing stock had fallen significantly as the

TABLE 11.17
Percentage of Equity Held in the United States by Various Holders of Equity

	1945	1950	1955	1960	1965	1970	1975	1980	1985	1990	1995	1999
Households	93	90	88	86	84	68	59	59	47	51	48	44
State and local governments	0	0	0	0	0	0	0	0	0	0	0	1
Depository institutions	0	0	0	0	0	0	1	0	0	0	0	0
Commercial banks	0	0	0	0	0	0	0	0	0	0	0	0
Savings institutions	0	0	0	0	0	0	1	0	0	0	0	0
Institutional investors	5	7	8	12	14	29	37	36	47	41	45	47
Bank trusts and estates	0	0	0	0	0	10	11	9	8	5	3	2
Insurance companies	3	3	3	3	3	4	5	5	6	4	6	6
Life insurance companies	1	1	1	1	1	2	3	3	3	2	4	5
Other insurance companies	2	2	2	2	2	2	2	2	3	2	2	1
Private pensions	0	1	2	4	6	8	13	16	23	17	15	12
State and local government pensions	0	0	0	0	0	1	3	3	5	8	9	10
Mutual funds	2	3	3	5	5	6	5	3	5	7	12	17
Open-end	1	2	2	4	4	5	4	3	5	7	12	17
Closed-end	1	1	1	1	1	1	1	0	0	0	0	0

Source: Federal Reserve Flow of Funds Data.

TABLE 11.18

Percentage of Corporate and Foreign Bonds Held by Various U.S. Holders

	1945	1955	1965	1975	1985	1999
Households	31	8	7	19	9	15
State and local governments	0	0	0	0	1	2
Depository institutions	13	7	3	8	10	7
Commercial banks	10	3	1	3	4	5
Savings institutions	3	4	2	5	6	2
Institutional investors	51	81	86	70	64	54
Bank trusts and estates	0	0	0	3	2	1
Insurance companies	44	63	52	35	36	29
Life insurance companies	42	61	50	31	32	25
Other insurance companies	2	2	2	4	4	4
Private pensions	7	13	18	12	11	6
State and local government pensions	0	4	14	18	12	7
Mutual funds	0	1	2	2	3	11
Money market funds	0	0	0	0	0	3
Other mutual funds	0	1	2	2	3	8

Source: Federal Reserve Flow of Funds Data.

result of the growth of the wholesale market. More formal analyses of changes in underwriting costs (Mendelson, 1967; Calomiris and Raff, 1995) have concluded that costs did indeed decline markedly during the 1960s, and that the most likely explanation for that decline is the increasing importance of institutional inves-

TABLE 11.19

Percentage of Money Market Mutual Fund Shares Held by Various U.S. Holders

	1975	1985	1995	1999
Households	100	80	60	54
Nonfinancial corporations	0	6	10	12
Nonfarm noncorporate businesses	0	0	1	0
Bank trusts and estates	0	5	5	3
Life insurance companies	0	4	3	8
Private pensions	0	4	5	6
Funding corporations	0	2	16	17

Source: Federal Reserve Flow of Funds Data.

tors. A study of cross-sectional differences in underwriting costs in today's market (Hansen and Torregrossa, 1992) similarly concluded that institutional involvement tends to reduce investment banking costs.

Table 11.20 summarizes the history of U.S. underwriting fees (not including expenses) from 1913 to 1993. Calomiris and Raff (1995) argued that the decline in common stock underwriting costs in the 1940s and 1950s mainly reflected a change in the composition of firms accessing the equity market. The rise of private placements (a new form of corporate debt funding, held primarily by life insurance companies, which grew rapidly in that period) allowed smaller firms to avoid the high-cost equity market. In the 1960s and 1970s, however, equity offerings by small firms rose dramatically, as shown in Table 11.20, but average underwriting costs continued to decline. This average change reflected much larger declines in underwriting costs for smaller firms. Based on regression analysis, Calomiris and Raff esti-

TABLE 11.20
U.S. Underwriting Fees on Various Securities as a Percentage of Value Offered

	Percentage fees on bonds	Percentage fees on preferred stock	Percentage fees on common stock	Percentage fees on common stock, small manufacturing	Annual common stock issues, small manufacturing (U.S.$ million)
Circa 1913	5–10	7.5–10	20–25		
1912–3	4	8–14	>20	>20	
1925–31			9–23	14–23	
1926–9 (large only)	3.1				
1925–9 (small only)	5.2	7.1			
1935–8			16.4	17.4	43
1935–8 (small only)	3.4	8.9			
1938	2.6	10.5	20.0	13.2	28
1939	1.9	8.8	16.6	16.5	42
1940	2.1	7.4	15.9	15.9	42
1951–3, 1955	0.8	3.3	8.8	11.1	15
1963–5		2.4	7.9	10.9	27
1971–2	1.5	1.5	8.4	10.1	206
1992–3	1.5	4.1	6.7	8.7	130

Source: Calomiris and Raff (1995: Table 9).
Notes: Fees are payments to underwriters and do not include expenses. The definition of small offerings varies. For purposes of measuring the annual common stock issues of small manufacturers, issues of less than U.S.$10 million (in 1991 dollars) are included (see the details in Calomiris and Raff, 1995: Table 9). For underwriting fees measured for 1925–9, and for 1935–8, small is defined as issues less than U.S.$5 million.

mated that fees for small issuers of common stock declined from 14.2 percent in 1950 to 9.2 percent in 1971.

Since the mid-1970s, institutional investors have also helped to finance private equity markets, which provide a major source of new IPOs, and thus offer additional stimulus to public equity market development via this channel. Indeed, pension funds are the dominant source of funds for the private equity market.

TABLE 11.21
U.S. Mergers and Acquisitions and Private Equity

	1980	1988	1990	1991	1992	1993	1994	1995	1996	1997	1998	1999
Dollar value of completed acquisitions (U.S.$ billions)							137	242	352	460	650	1102
Cross-border M&A transactions for U.S. firms (U.S.$ billions)			100	44	33	50	87	182	121	121	310	480
Total funds committed to all types of private equity partnerships (U.S.$ billions)			7.8	7.9	11.0	13.6	22.8	29.2	37.8	55.1	88.5	28.5
Number of attempted hostile takeovers	5	86	18	9	8	11	37	68	51	29	19	

Source: Boswell (2000), based on data from Securities Data Co., and The Private Equity Analyst.

As such they have also become an important source of funds for LBOs. Table 11.21 summarizes recent trends in these transactions. Although hostile takeovers have declined in importance, in response to new corporate defenses against them, friendly takeovers and private equity have continued to grow in importance in recent years.

Table 11.22 summarizes data on the holdings of pension funds in other industrialized countries. It is clear from this table that pension funds in the United States, the United Kingdom and Ireland maintain unusually large proportions of their assets in the form of domestic and foreign equity in comparison with other European countries. U.K. pension funds hold 73.7 percent of their assets in equity, Irish pensions hold 59.5 percent of their assets in equity, and U.S. pensions hold 63.1 percent in equity. For other countries in Europe, equity comprises only 30.1 percent of assets. But that low level masks some high growth rates in equity investments in some countries, notably Austria and Spain, and in virtually all countries, the

TABLE 11.22

Asset Allocation of Pension Funds in Various Countries, 1999

	Cash assets (percent)	Domestic bonds (percent)	Domestic equity (percent)	Foreign bonds (percent)	Foreign equity (percent)	Loans and mortgages (percent)	Real estate (percent)	Other (percent)	Total (percent)	Average annual percentage growth in equity 1995–9
Austria	1.6	62.3	17.2	5.3	11.0	1.0	0.5	1.2	100	32.6
Belgium	3.4	23.6	20.1	14.1	32.7	0.0	4.7	1.4	100	11.1
Denmark	0.7	51.5	30.7	0.6	11.0	0.0	3.7	1.7	100	9.8
Finland	6.5	48.6	21.3	0.0	0.8	16.8	6.0	0.0	100	na
France	19.7	46.1	10.0	5.9	2.3	1.9	0.5	13.5	100	2.6
Germany	8.2	33.0	19.4	2.6	5.8	26.2	3.3	1.4	100	2.3
Ireland	6.6	16.4	27.3	7.4	32.2	0.0	5.8	4.4	100	16.9
Italy	16.3	25.4	2.7	3.1	0.3	10.0	42.2	0.0	100	−0.2
Netherlands	1.8	18.6	19.2	16.1	25.5	13.3	5.4	0.0	100	7.8
Norway	3.8	62.7	20.7	0.0	2.2	3.8	1.7	5.2	100	5.8
Portugal	7.0	39.8	22.0	10.0	13.0	0.0	6.5	1.7	100	na
Spain	13.4	44.9	16.9	10.6	8.6	0.0	0.5	5.1	100	20.6
Sweden	1.6	71.6	15.3	4.9	1.8	0.0	4.7	0.1	100	4.5
Switzerland	9.2	16.1	14.4	15.2	14.9	3.1	16.9	10.2	100	8.5
United Kingdom	3.4	10.8	50.6	3.8	23.1	0.2	4.9	3.2	100	12.3
Total Europe	4.9	19.6	34.2	7.3	19.2	4.4	7.0	3.5	100	9.8
Europe, excluding United Kingdom and Ireland	6.7	27.4	16.3	11.6	14.8	9.5	9.8	4.0	100	7.2
United States	4.7	22.7	53.1	1.1	10.0	1.5	1.9	5.0	100	16.1

Notes: Data are taken from *Financial Times*, Special Section on European Pension Provision, November 10 (2000: IV), based on data compiled by Intersec Research.

TABLE 11.23
Various Measures of Equity Market Development across Countries, by Country Income Group

	1980		1985		1990		1995		1997	
	Mean	Frequency	Mean	Frequency	Mean	Frequency	Mean	Frequency	Mean	Frequency
Stock market capitalization (SMC)/GDP										
LIG	0.04	3	0.04	6	0.08	7	0.15	11	0.12	9
LMIG	0.10	6	0.08	10	0.12	13	0.19	26	0.20	25
UMIG	0.28	7	0.24	8	0.32	10	0.45	18	0.55	13
HIG	0.22	20	0.38	26	0.49	26	0.60	30	0.75	26
Stock market turnover ratio (trading volume/SMC)										
LIG	0.01	4	0.01	6	0.01	7	0.01	12	0.03	9
LMIG	0.01	8	0.01	11	0.04	13	0.05	27	0.08	24
UMIG	0.03	8	0.03	8	0.04	12	0.09	18	0.22	13
HIG	0.08	25	0.16	27	0.34	25	0.33	30	0.71	26

Source: Beck et al. (1999).
Note: LIG, lowest income group; LMIG, lower–middle income group; UMIG, upper–middle income group; HIG, upper income group.

portfolio share of equity is rising. Thus, along-side the new global competition in banking, and the trend toward "universal banking American-style" in Europe, Asia, and Latin America, there is every reason to believe that the culture of equity investing and the institutions that facilitate it will spread increasingly throughout the world.

Table 11.23 summarizes global trends in equity markets from 1980 to 1997, measured by the changing ratio of stock market capitalization (SMC) relative to GDP, and the ratio of trading volume to SMC (turnover). Observations are divided into four income classes, as before. High-income countries have shown remarkable increases in both SMC and turnover (an increase from 0.22 SMC and 0.08 turnover in 1980 to 0.75 SMC and 0.71 turnover in 1997). All other country groups have shown pronounced increases in these ratios since 1980. For example, the lower-middle income group in 1997 had reached SMC and turnover ratios comparable to those of the high-income group in 1980. Legal limitations on shareholder protection and severe information problems in many developing economies continue to limit the growth of equity markets worldwide (see the review in Beim and Calomiris, 2000). Nevertheless, there has been remarkable progress in

spreading equity offerings and trading throughout the world in the past twenty years.

A limitation of examining progress in equity markets by focusing on changes in outstanding quantities of equity holdings is that doing so fails to distinguish between growth in equity holdings that results from internally generated equity (retained earnings) and growth that reflects new stock offerings. The distinction is an important one. In the most primitive financial systems (those where banking systems are undeveloped and the issuing of both debt and equity securities in public markets is impossible), equity holdings by insiders will be the sole means of corporate finance. Thus, a rise in outstanding corporate equity, by itself, does not constitute evidence of greater access to equity markets. To examine changes in access to equity markets, it is useful to focus on new offerings of equity.

Table 11.24 summarizes trends in U.S. securities issues of various types from 1980 to 1999. The number of offerings, and the total proceeds of offerings are given for each of the major categories of securities (nonconvertible debt, nonconvertible preferred stock, convertible debt, convertible preferred stock, seasoned common stock offerings, and initial public stock offerings). The high rate of growth of securities

TABLE 11.24
Number and Volume of U.S. Private Sector Securities Issues of Various Types, Adjusted for Inflation

	1980		1984		1988		1992		1994		1996		1998		1999	
	No.	U.S.$	No.	U.S.$	No.	U.S.$	No.	U.S.$	No.	U.S.$	No.	U.S.$	No.	U.S.$	No.	U.S.$
Non-convertible debt	418	40.9	459	51.2	746	112.6	2136	267.1	3456	306.3	7077	481.2	12689	970.3	12234	938.3
Non-convertible preferred	46	2.1	47	3.0	115	6.6	231	17.8	76	7.9	142	24.2	192	23.5	146	16.3
Convertible debt	98	4.9	66	3.9	36	2.9	65	6.0	36	3.9	62	7.3	37	5.1	52	12.1
Convertible preferred	28	1.4	27	0.9	10	0.5	51	7.2	39	4.9	36	4.4	37	6.9	27	5.6
Common stock	540	14.8	611	9.7	432	28.0	1114	63.8	1129	54.7	1646	91.2	991	93.6	1031	138.6
IPOs	149	1.5	356	3.7	290	22.3	604	33.8	645	28.0	873	39.2	398	35.2	572	56.7
Seasoned equity	391	13.2	255	5.9	142	5.7	510	30.0	484	26.7	773	52.0	593	58.5	459	81.8

Source: Securities Data Co.
Note: The value of proceeds from securities issues are adjusted for inflation by dividing by the producer price index, which has a value of 100 in 1982.

offerings is immediately apparent, particularly in the areas of nonconvertible debt and common stock offerings. Roughly speaking, the number of common stock issues in the 1990s is double that of the 1980s, and the real proceeds from common stock offerings have grown nearly an order of magnitude from 1980 to 1999.

Table 11.25 examines trends in underwriting costs (fees plus expenses) for the same categories of offerings. Consistent with the view that underwriting fees and expenses are a payment to underwriters for helping to mitigate problems of asymmetric information, which increase with the risk of the security being sold, observed costs increase as the riskiness of the security rises (from relatively senior nonconvertible debt and preferred stock to relatively junior common stock).

There is a downward trend in underwriting costs for all categories, particularly for junior securities (common stock, convertible debt and preferred stock). That observation suggests that recent technological improvements in selling securities may have disproportionately

favored the riskiest securities. This observation is consistent with the evidence that Calomiris and Raff (1995) provide for technological improvements in the 1960s, which favored small equity issuers, and likely reflects the fact that these issuers are the ones whose costs of underwriting are most responsive with respect to improvements in information technology.

One could imagine an alternative explanation of the downward trend of underwriting costs, namely that the attributes of issuers have changed since the 1980s to include a greater proportion of firms whose equity is inherently easy to sell. As Table 11.26 shows, it is true that underwriting costs vary significantly across firms, and vary with characteristics of firms that may proxy for differences in the potential for adverse selection problems. Firms that one would expect to be "information-problematic" a priori do tend to have higher underwriting costs. Underwriting costs are relatively high for small firms, firms with large R&D expenditures, riskier firms, and firms whose portfolio and financing behavior indicates high shadow costs of external finance (i.e., firms that pay

TABLE 11.25
Underwriting Costs as a Percentage of Value Offered for Securities Issues of Various Types

	1980		1984		1988		1992		1994		1996		1998		1999	
	No.	Avg	No.	Avg	No.	Avg	No.	Avg	No.	Avg	No.	Avg	No.	Avg	No.	Avg
Non-convertible debt	328	1.9	393	2.0	588	1.7	1108	1.2	630	1.3	858	1.0	911	0.9	1112	0.6
Non-convertible preferred	45	2.4	46	3.1	111	2.4	221	2.4	63	3.2	126	3.2	161	3.5	20	2.2
Convertible debt	86	4.5	65	3.7	33	5.9	63	4.0	32	3.8	48	4.1	19	2.6	7	2.5
Convertible preferred	28	7.8	22	8.0	8	6.3	49	6.3	34	8.4	26	4.8	30	8.3	7	2.5
Common stock	389	10.0	575	13.2	423	11.5	1089	9.5	1037	10.4	1534	9.2	793	8.4	850	7.9
IPOs	125	14.2	356	16.1	285	12.9	597	11.0	619	12.4	843	11.3	373	10.9	496	9.3
Seasoned equity	264	8.0	219	8.6	138	8.6	492	7.6	418	7.5	691	6.6	420	6.1	354	5.9

Source: Securities Data Co.
Note: Underwriting cost is defined as the ratio (in percent) of all underwriting fees and expenses divided by the value of proceeds from securities issues.

TABLE 11.26
Characteristics of Seasoned Equity Issuers By Size Quartiles of Underwriting Cost, 1980–94 Median Values, Standard Errors of Medians in Parentheses

	<3.0 percent	3.0–6.9 percent	6.9–11.4 percent	>11.4 percent
Underwriting cost (as percentage of proceeds)	4.5 (0.05)	6.5 (0.02)	8.5 (0.05)	14.0 (0.22)
Annual sales	718 (46)	146 (8)	61 (4)	16 (1)
Financial working capital/sales	0.11 (0.01)	0.14 (0.01)	0.13 (0.01)	0.14 (0.01)
R&D/sales	0.018 (0.002)	0.024 (0.004)	0.024 (0.010)	0.033 (0.003)
Short-term debt/long-term debt	0.052 (0.003)	0.091 (0.005)	0.113 (0.007)	0.142 (0.009)
Percentage of firms with dividends > 0	64	35	26	15
Percentage of firms with rated debt	25	8	4	2
Standard deviation of equity return	0.023 (0.000)	0.029 (0.000)	0.031 (0.000)	0.036 (0.001)

Source: Calomiris and Himmelberg (2000).

zero dividends, lack access to public debt markets, depend on short-term debt, and maintain large buffers of cash to self-insure against shortfalls in cash flow).

In the event, however, the average changes visible in Table 11.25 are not explained by changes in the composition of borrowers. In fact, smaller and younger firms have been increasingly attracted to the equity market, and so the average changes shown in Table 11.25 likely understate the reductions in the cost of underwriting. Nevertheless, given the importance of cross-sectional heterogeneity, when measuring the extent of technological change through the window of underwriting costs, it is useful to control for basic differences in firm characteristics. Table 11.27 provides a simple approach to doing so, using regression analysis.

The equations estimated in Table 11.27 are intended mainly as descriptive, rather than as a formal structural empirical model of underwriting cost (for the latter, see Calomiris and Himmelberg, 2000). They include the key control variables of firm size (market value of equity) and the size of the offering. Firm size should enter with a negative coefficient, since large firms are more mature, and thus less information problematic. Offering size should enter negatively as well, if there are fixed costs associated with offerings (or alternatively, if small offering size is an endogenous indicator of a bigger information problem).

Technological progress over time in marketing equity offerings (i.e., improvements in financial intermediaries' ability to credibly transmit information to potential purchasers of equity) is captured in the regressions by the coefficient on "Year" and by the coefficients on the interaction variables that include Year. Interestingly, the coefficient on Year changes sign depending on the inclusion of interactive effects of Year with proceeds and market value of equity. When interaction effects are excluded, the coefficient on Year is positive, indicating an increase in underwriting costs over time. But when interaction effects are included, the sign becomes negative.

The implication of this result is clear: the extent to which firm size and proceeds size affect underwriting cost has changed over time, and unless one takes account of those changes one gets a false impression about technological progress. If one allows for the possibility that the cost penalty on small firm size and small offering size has fallen over time (which the coefficients on the interaction terms indicate they have), then one also finds that, additionally, the general trend in underwriting costs has been toward falling costs over time. In other words, average costs have been falling, but the average size of issues have also been rising, in large part because of the reduction in issuing costs. Imposing a time-invariant coefficient on proceeds biases the estimated time trend coefficient, and produces the wrong (positive) sign for that coefficient. The central conclusion of this exercise is that there has been substantial improvement in the technology of underwrit-

TABLE 11.27
Underwriting Cost Regressions for Seasoned Equity Offerings, 1980–99. Dependent Variable: Log of Underwriting Cost as a Percentage of Proceeds, Coefficient Estimates, Standard Errors in Parentheses

Constant	−22.077 (1.095)	39.500 (2.257)
Year	0.013 (0.001)	−0.018 (0.000)
ln adjusted proceeds	−0.156 (0.005)	−7.208 (1.683)
ln adjusted MVE	−0.148 (0.003)	−7.447 (1.172)
(Year) × (ln adjusted proceeds)		0.0035 (0.0008)
(Year) × (ln adjusted MVE)		0.0037 (0.0006)
Number of observations	7522	7522
Adjusted R-squared	0.71	0.72

Notes: MVE, market value of equity. Proceeds and MVE are adjusted for inflation using the producer price index.

ing, that those improvements have favored small firms, and that they have tended to encourage larger issues.

11.3.3. New Financial Instruments and Increased Global Risk Sharing

Perhaps the most visible changes in the global financial system are the new financial instruments that have been created over the past twenty years, especially over-the-counter (OTC) derivative securities and asset-backed securities. These innovations rely critically on the new infrastructure of computing and telecommunications technologies that have made it possible to carve up and quantify various bits of risk attendant to any financial transaction, and to transmit those bits of risk throughout the world to the party that is most willing and able to absorb them. Carving up risk in new ways has permitted issuers and holders of securities to distribute and manage risk in a way that reduces the cost of raising funds for firms, and increases the risk-adjusted returns to portfolio holders.

Corporate and individual clients, as well as banks, can use customized derivatives to hedge risks and transfer them to other parties who have a comparative advantage in bearing those risks. Financial engineers now produce a variety of sophisticated means for accomplishing this objective (currency swaps, interest rate swaps, equity swaps, collars, options, swaptions, etc.). Hedging risk for corporations (including banks) helps them to economize on equity capital (which, because of adverse-selection costs of raising such capital, is the most expensive component of corporate financing). In essence, derivatives help corporations and individuals conserve on capital by reducing the amount of total asset risk that their capital must absorb, and conserving on capital reduces the overall costs of financing their operations (for a formal treatment, see Calomiris and Wilson, 1998; Froot and Stein, 1998; Brewer et al., 2000).

The securitization of assets expands financing opportunities for firms and permits holders of securities to purchase specific tranches of risk that match their desired portfolio holdings. That process is often embodied in a new set of financial entities, which are managed by financial intermediaries. Assets are placed into special conduits (which, legally, are trusts, separate from the entities that originate the assets). The conduits then issue various tranches of securities backed only by the assets placed in the trust. Sometimes twenty or more different classes of securities may be issued by the same trust.

Consider, for example, credit card securitization. Prior to the placement of credit card receivables in "master trusts" the banks that originated the receivables held them directly, and had to maintain minimum capital of 8 percent against these receivables, irrespective of their risk. By placing relatively high-quality receivables into trusts, the costs of financing these receivables could be reduced, since the capital needed to absorb the aggregate risk of default on the portfolio was much smaller than 8 percent. Another gain from creating securitization trusts comes from being able to better target various securities holders with customized securities that match their tastes for risk (or that respond to regulations limiting investors' ability to hold high-risk claims—as in the case of insurance company investors).

Derivatives and securitization have also spawned other related process and product changes in the financial system. The payoffs to holders of derivatives, by definition, are determined in other securities markets (e.g., in stock markets for equity derivatives), and suppliers of derivatives (e.g., banks) hedge their derivatives exposures by entering into contracts in those other securities markets. Thus, derivatives not only offer more opportunities for hedging, but they also tend to promote greater depth in securities markets. New techniques for measuring risk have also been encouraged by these financial innovations. In the case of derivatives, complex customized derivative contracts can only be priced using highly sophisticated mathematical models, which translate the risks of underlying securities into the newly constructed bundle of risks from the customized derivatives contract. In the case of securitization, holders of asset-backed securities require that third parties (dealers and rating agencies) act as agents to protect investors from problems of adverse selection and moral hazard. Issuers must

TABLE 11.28

U.S. Public Asset Backed Securities Issuance, 1985–97

	1985	1987	1989	1991	1993	1995	1997
Home equity	5	4	5	10	10	15	47
Credit cards	0	0	6	40	30	55	45
Automobile	0	5	5	20	35	20	30
Manufactured housing	0	0	2	3	3	4	12
Other	0	0	1	2	7	15	30

Source: Flanagan et al. (1998).

provide substantial information about the securities that they place in securitization conduits, and ratings agencies use that information, along with sophisticated new credit scoring techniques, to price asset-backed securities.

Table 11.28 summarizes trends in the growth of public offerings of asset-backed securities (other than government-sponsored offerings) since their origins in the mid-1980s. As the table shows, these markets have grown rapidly in the 1990s. Table 11.29 compares recent trends in securitization across different regions of the globe. While the vast majority of securitization is still confined to North America, the rapid growth that is taking place in Europe, Asia and Australia, and Latin America suggests that a decade from now, the volume of issues for the rest of the world will more than match those of North America.

Table 11.30 traces the progress in two of the new growth areas of the U.S. asset-backed secu-

TABLE 11.29

Global Securitization Issuance By Region

Year	North America	Europe	Asia and Australia	Latin America
1994	145	5	1	2
1995	155	9	2	6
1996	234	20	5	14
1997	313	46	13	6
1998	454	47	30	10
1999 (est.)	536	72	43	10

Source: Danthine et al. (2000), based on Moody's Investors Service, except for 1999 values for Europe, which are taken from *Financial Times*, November 3 (2000: 25), based on Merrill Lynch.

rities market: commercial mortgage-backed securities and small business loans. These assets have traditionally been viewed as among the most difficult to securitize, since information about their credit risk is relatively difficult to obtain and to quantify. Thus, the rapid growth in these areas in the past four years suggest that technical improvements in securitization, and market confidence in these new instruments (notwithstanding some of the dislocations that occurred in the asset-backed securities market in the aftermath of the Russian crisis of 1998) will continue to propel increasing growth in asset securitization.

Table 11.31 examines growth in derivatives contracts, including both exchange-traded and OTC contracts, from 1988 to 1998. Both sets of contracts have grown by more than ten fold in the past decade, and OTC contracts grew particularly fast in 1998. Table 11.32 summarizes data from a recent study of currency derivatives used by large U.S. corporations. That study found that 59 percent of corporations studied use some kind of derivatives, and 41 percent of them use currency derivatives. The use of currency derivatives (which was the focus of the study that produced these data) is higher for firms with large foreign currency exposures, but also varies positively with the proportion of institutional ownership, firm size and with the number of analysts following the firm. Furthermore, firms that use currency derivatives have substantially lower quick ratios (which measure liquid assets relative to short-term liabilities). These facts suggest that firms with sophisticated outside stockholders, or whose financial affairs are heavily scrutinized, see advantages to

TABLE 11.30
High Growth Areas in U.S. Asset Backed Securitization Issuance

	1994	1995	1996	1997	1998	1999
Commercial mortgage- backed securities (U.S.$ millions)			26365	36798	74332	56571
Securitized small business loans (U.S.$ millions)	202	241	642	718	1220	2312

Source: Federal Reserve Board (2000).

TABLE 11.31
Global Growth in Derivatives ($billions)

	1988	1991	1994	1995	1996	1997	1998	1999	2000
Exchange-traded contracts	1306	3523	8863	9189	9880	12202	13549		
Interest rate futures	895	2157	5778	5863	5931	7489	7702		
Interest rate options	279	1073	2624	2742	3278	3640	4603		
Currency futures	12	18	40	38	50	52	38		
Currency options	48	61	56	44	47	33	19		
Stock index futures	28	77	128	172	196	212	321		
Stock index options	44	137	238	329	378	777	867		
Over-the-counter contracts	na	4449	11303	17713	25453	29035	50997		
Interest rate swaps	1010	3065	8816	12811	19171	22291	na		
Currency swaps	320	807	915	1197	1560	1824	na		
Other swap-related	na	577	1573	3705	4723	4920	na		
Credit derivatives	0	0	0	0	10	190	340	440	800[a]

Sources: Bank for International Settlements (BIS) Annual Reports for all information other than credit risk derivatives. Credit risk derivatives are from *Financial Times*, International Capital Markets, May 19 (2000: v).
[a] Estimated by Bank Austria-Creditanstalt, according to *Financial Times*, International Capital Markets, May 19 (2000: v).

TABLE 11.32
The Use of Currency Derivatives By Large U.S. Corporations

	Currency derivatives users (154 firms)		Currency derivatives nonusers (218 firms)	
	Mean	Median	Mean	Median
Pretax foreign income/total sales	0.033	0.027	0.018	0.008
Identifiable foreign assets/total assets	0.346	0.316	0.350	0.240
Foreign loan-term debt/total assets	0.023	0.001	0.005	0.000
Total sales (log U.S.$ million)	8.24	8.26	7.13	7.13
Institutional ownership percentage	55.46	58.30	48.59	52.00
Number of analyst firms	26.16	25.00	15.43	14.00
Quick ratio	0.25	0.15	0.35	0.19

Source: Geczy et al. (1997).

TABLE 11.33

International Capital Flows to Developing Countries

	1970	1975	1980	1985	1990	1995	1997
Stocks of Outstanding Debt							
Private sector foreign debt/GDP	1.6	1.9	2.9	3.4	1.7	4.2	5.7
Latin America	7.2	6.2	6.5	9.1	2.7	5.5	8.2
East-Central Europe	0.2	0.4	1.5	1.2	0.5	2.2	3.7
East Asia	1.6	3.1	3.8	4.0	3.3	6.3	8.1
Middle East, North Africa	0.1	0.0	0.2	0.3	0.3	0.3	0.3
South Asia	0.7	0.5	0.4	0.9	0.7	1.8	2.1
Sub-Saharan Africa	0.6	0.8	2.0	2.9	2.1	3.6	2.6
Public sector foreign debt/GDP	3.9	5.6	11.7	23.0	23.9	24.2	20.1
Latin America	8.9	11.1	16.8	40.3	30.5	23.3	18.7
East-Central Europe	0.5	0.8	5.5	13.3	13.2	28.0	23.0
East Asia	2.4	5.5	10.1	17.5	20.9	16.6	15.1
Middle East, North Africa	9.2	7.3	11.7	16.6	23.8	23.9	17.4
South Asia	14.1	14.8	16.1	19.1	28.7	25.9	21.4
Sub-Saharan Africa	9.2	12.0	16.5	40.5	52.6	60.1	50.5
Flows of equity investment							
Foreign direct investment net inflows/GDP	0.2	0.4	0.2	0.4	0.6	1.9	2.5
Latin America	0.6	0.8	0.8	0.7	0.8	1.9	3.1
East-Central Europe	0.0	0.0	0.0	0.0	0.1	1.8	1.9
East Asia	0.1	0.4	0.3	0.5	1.2	3.1	3.4
Middle East, North Africa	0.7	1.0	−0.7	0.4	0.6	−0.1	0.8
South Asia	0.1	0.1	0.1	0.1	0.1	0.6	0.8
Sub-Saharan Africa	0.7	0.8	0.0	0.5	0.3	1.2	1.6
Portfolio equity inflows/GDP	0	0	0	0	0.1	0.6	0.5
Latin America	0	0	0	0	0.1	0.5	0.5
East-Central Europe	0	0	0	0	0.0	0.3	0.4
East Asia	0	0	0	0	0.3	1.1	0.5
Middle East, North Africa	0	0	0	0	0.0	0.0	0.3
South Asia	0	0	0	0	0.0	0.5	0.4
Sub-Saharan Africa	0	0	0	0	0.0	1.7	0.5

Source: World Bank (2000b).

hedging their currency risks, and that doing so helps firms to economize on liquid asset holdings (since liquid assets provide an alternative form of self-insurance against cash flow shortages produced by exchange rate swings). There is every reason to believe that the number and amount of derivatives contracts will continue to expand, and that improvements in risk management and risk sharing will continue alongside that expansion.

Finally, consider the evidence of increased global risk sharing. Global risk sharing is visible both in the rising capital being transferred among developed economies, and from developed countries to developing economies. Table 11.33 examines stocks of debt and flows of equity investment, both relative to GDP, from 1970 to 1997, by type of claim (sovereign borrowing, private sector borrowing, foreign direct investment, and portfolio equity flows), and by region. Several patterns are worth noting. First, flows have increased over time in all categories and to all regions. Second, debt remains the dominant type of flow to emerging market economies. Third, private sector debt is growing relative to public sector debt. Fourth, equity is growing relative to debt—indeed, flows of foreign direct investment and portfolio equity were virtually zero in 1980, and now represent a significant part of capital inflows. In particular, the ability to channel funds from developed countries to private sector firms in developing countries has improved substantially, despite the recent financial crises that have buffeted emerging market economies in 1995, 1997, and 1998.

A recent study by Portes and Rey (2000) of cross-border equity flows concludes that cross-country differences in factors affecting the cost of information are crucial prerequisites for cross-border equity flows among developed economies. Indeed, the authors find that, contrary to the prediction of a simple international version of the standard capital asset pricing model, international diversification opportunities, per se, do not go very far in explaining which countries' issuers gain access to international equity investors. In contrast, institutional and informational indicators are powerful predictors, including the presence of branches of foreign financial institutions, communication linkages (proxied by the frequency of international telephone calls), physical distance from securities purchasers, and the extent of insider trading in the issuing country. This study lends support to the notion that institutional networks are crucial mitigators of information costs relevant to the ability to market equities.

11.4. Conclusion

Technological progress in corporate finance and banking has multiple dimensions. Although physical product and process innovation is a crucial element of technological change, improvements in the organization of financial intermediaries and financial networks also have been important. Organizational changes have been independent contributors to technological improvement and have also helped to spur successful product and process innovation.

Financial intermediaries (especially banks) have become much more productive over the past thirty years, especially in the United States, as the result of their ability to expand geographically and to enter new product areas. With those changes have come new competition, which has been a driver in the development of new financial services and new techniques of customer relationship management, information production, risk management, and marketing.

Outside of banking, securities markets have also seen substantial improvements, which reflect reductions in physical costs, as well as lower costs that reflect reduced information and control frictions (adverse selection and moral hazard). Those cost reductions have been reflected in improvements in corporations' ability to access markets for equity and junior debt, in the development of new products which offer new means for managing and sharing risk (OTC derivatives and asset-backed securities), and in greater global risk sharing (most notably, a large increase in international capital flows to emerging market countries).

In all these cases, technological change has not been confined to technical improvements, but also reflects new rules governing competition and financial openness, and new institutions that come into being or become transformed because of political or regulatory changes or other exogenous shocks (reductions in government limits via unit banking, demographic and regulatory changes that produce growth in insurance companies, pensions, and venture capitalists). These regulatory and institutional shifters probably have been at least as important as the Internet, credit scoring, financial engineering, improved telecommunications, or other sorts of purely technical improvements for explaining improvements in the technology of banking and corporate finance over the last century.

The regulatory process and technological change are dynamically linked. Costly regulations give incentives for new products, services, and intermediaries to be developed (e.g., commercial paper, money market mutual funds, finance companies, foreign entry), which help to spur deregulation. This can be a very long-run adjustment process, and can depend on exogenous facilitators (high inflation in 1970s) to become important stimuli for technological improvement. There can be technological regress when bad shocks and bad regulatory policy combine (as during the Great Depression), but there is a certain inevitability to progress that comes from the combination of competitive markets, facilitating shocks, and general improvements in communications technology.

Securities Trading

Ian Domowitz and Benn Steil

12.1. Introduction

Much recent debate has focused on the "New Economy" drivers of equity prices. Rising price/earnings ratios and falling dividend yields over the course of the 1990s, particularly in the United States, imply a falling cost of equity in the capital markets. Yet cause and effect are not easy to isolate. The perception of improved business prospects increases expectations of returns on equity investments, and draws capital into the markets. At the same time, declining investment costs reduce investors' required returns, driving down capital costs and stimulating corporate investment and the launch of new businesses. Virtually all recent popular commentary has focused on the former effect, but we are interested in the latter.

Since the mid-1990s, the cost of trading in most of the world's equity markets has fallen considerably, with the most dramatic effect documented for the United States (Domowitz et al., 2001). One of the primary drivers of this cost reduction appears to be automation-driven disintermediation of trading (Domowitz and Steil, 1999), itself a product of the "New Economy" spread of computer technology.

Major advances in computer and telecommunications technology over the past 30 years have had a significant effect on the way corporate securities are traded. The most obvious impact is on the speed at which transactions are made, but there is a host of other economically significant *potential* effects where the direct role of trading automation is less readily observable. The most important of these effects relate to the cost of trading and the cost of corporate equity capital.

In order to deepen our understanding of the impact of technological innovation in the financial markets on the performance of the real economy, we have set out to determine what linkage might be discerned tracing from trading automation to trading costs through to the cost of corporate equity capital. In the most mundane terms, we are interested in understanding the impact of innovation in the "plumbing" of the market on the performance of the market itself, measured from the perspectives of those investing and raising capital in the market.

To address this question, we examine the major discrete links in the investment chain. After briefly reviewing the historical connection between technological development and market structure in section 2, we analyze the impact of trading automation on trading costs in section 3. In section 4, we develop cost of equity capital measurements for the United States and a range of European and Latin American countries, based on market data, which allow us to estimate the implied required returns of investors. In section 5, we then apply econometric techniques to examine the impact of trading costs on the cost of equity capital, considering the role of turnover as an intermediating variable.

We find that reductions in trading cost have an enormous stimulative effect on turnover, but that increased turnover in large capitalization issues does not itself have a material effect on the cost of equity. Rather, reductions in trading cost have a significant and direct causal effect on declines in the cost of equity. In section 6, we document the economic significance of this effect through an examination of U.S. and European trading and capital cost data from the period 1996–8. In section 7, we then analyze these findings in the context of our earlier findings on automation and trading costs. The goal of this exercise is to gauge what effect trading automation itself might have on the cost of equity. Our contribution is to demonstrate that the documented decline in the cost of corporate equity capital owes much to changes in trading market infrastructure, and that explanations based on rising public expectations with respect to firm value are incomplete.

In section 8, we summarize our work and consider its policy implications. We believe that our findings may go some way towards indicating the degree of "connectedness" between technology-driven structural changes in financial markets and the performance of the wider economy.

12.2. Technology and Market Structure: An Historical Perspective

Since the mid-nineteenth century, the state of technology has had a critical impact on the way in which trading is conducted. From 1817 to approximately 1870, the New York Stock Exchange (NYSE) ran a formal daily "call auction'" for listed stocks. An auctioneer simply called out tentative prices into the trading crowd until he arrived at the price that roughly balanced supply and demand on the floor. The tremendous growth in listed stocks and member firms in the late 1860s, however, produced an unbearable strain on this highly labor-intensive technology, and the Exchange was thus obliged to adopt continuous auction trading as a means of accommodating large numbers of stocks and traders in a single physical location (Kregel, 1992). The spread of telegraph technology during this period also served to increase the dominance of the NYSE (Stedman, 1905; DuBoff, 1983), as the rapid dissemination of quotation and price information reduced the need for independent centers of price formation.

The development of the embryonic Nasdaq market in the 1930s coincided with the spread of long-distance telephony in the United States, thus making possible decentralized share trading. Continued advances in communications technology led to a further decline

in the number of stock exchanges, from over one hundred at the end of the nineteenth century to twenty-two in 1935, and only seven today.[1] This figure would arguably be lower still were it not for the effects of the Intermarket Trading System, which the Securities and Exchange Commission instigated as a means of implementing federal legislation calling for the creation of a "National Market System" in 1975.

More recent advances in computing and communications introduced a new form of market institution, the computerized auction mechanism. Auction systems utilize communication technologies to facilitate rapid messaging between traders and a central computer system. A programmed set of rules dictates the form the messages can take and the way in which they are processed into securities transactions. One set of rules controls the type of information displayed to market participants as well as the parameters of allowable bids to buy and offers to sell. A second set governs the automated trade execution algorithm, which determines transactions prices, execution priority assignments, and quantity allocations.

The most common architecture for automated trading today is the continuous electronic auction market, or "order-driven" market. First introduced into the U.S. equity markets by Instinet, a brokerage firm, in 1969, the technology spread to Canada in the 1970s and Europe in the 1980s. Every stock exchange in Western and Central Europe, and many in Eastern Europe, currently employ a version of this architecture, which allows for automatic execution of matching buy and sell orders.[2]

In the United States, most registered exchanges still operate floor-based systems

---

[1] An alternative view is given by Arnold et al. (1999), based on listings and competition for order flow. Such competition would not have been readily possible, however, without the technological advances highlighted here.

[2] See Domowitz (1993) for a listing and taxonomy of systems, and Domowitz and Steil (1999) for updates with respect to conversions from traditional trading mechanisms to automated execution technology.

with human intermediation of trading.[3] The Nasdaq "over the counter" (OTC) market has since 1997 run a hybrid screen-based version of a dealer market (where intermediaries buy from and sell to investors) and an auction market (where investor buy and sell orders match directly, with intermediaries only acting as agents to find the counterparties). The basic architecture of the 30-year-old Nasdaq electronic bulletin board for dealer quotations is still in use, but since 1997 dealers and so-called electronic communications networks (ECNs) have been obliged to post their customer limit orders at the highest bid and lowest offer price (unless, in the case of dealers, the dealers' own prices are better). The ECNs, however, each operate electronic auction systems which can match customer orders internally, as well as route them to the Nasdaq bulletin board for execution against outside orders. U.S. market structure is, relative to Europe, both more complex and more directly influenced by regulatory intervention.[4]

12.3. Automation and Trading Costs

Organized markets around the world, regardless of their structure, have made significant investments in computer and telecommunications technology over the past decade as a means of increasing the capacity, efficiency, and reliability of their trading networks. An examination of trading automation per se, however, tells us relatively little about its impact on the securities industry and the wider economy. Such an exercise fails to distinguish between what might be termed "evolutionary" and "revolutionary" applications of automation. The NYSE, for example, has invested far more in technology over this period than any of its competitors, yet no fundamental changes

have been introduced into the way in which its trades are executed. The basic structure of floor trading remains largely the same as it has been for many decades (and, arguably, since the 1870s).

This evolutionary approach to trading automation contrasts with that taken by a number of ECNs in the United States and exchanges in Europe. These applications of technology have, to varying degrees, operated to eliminate "distance costs" and layers of intermediation. All participating traders, wherever located geographically, have direct electronic access to the trade execution mechanism, akin conceptually to being one of a restricted number of members on the floor of a traditional exchange. Importantly, these systems either eliminate the brokerage function (i.e., the intermediation of orders between investor and trading system) or reduce it to an electronic credit risk control function (i.e., ensuring the investor has the requisite funds to buy or securities to sell).[5]

In all cases, these more revolutionary applications of technology have been far less complex and costly than those of the NYSE. They are not aimed at "speeding up" traditional market mechanisms, but rather at supplanting them. As such, they are of particular interest in terms of understanding automation's impact on trading cost, turnover, and cost of capital. They represent applications of technology to building auction market structures which are not actually feasible in the absence of the technology. For our purposes, we refer to such applications of technology as "automated markets."

In the context of the U.S. markets, it is possible to compare trading costs across automated and traditional market structures by examining executions via ECNs with those consummated through the NYSE floor or "upstairs" market and the Nasdaq dealer market. To do this properly, it is important to control for critical factors such as trading style, trade difficulty, market

---

[3] This situation is beginning to change, however, commencing with the purchase of the Pacific Stock Exchange's stock trading business by Archipelago, an electronic communications network (ECN) aspiring to registered exchange status. Island ECN also is applying for exchange status.

[4] A more detailed discussion of these issues can be found in chapter 8 of Davis and Steil (2001).

[5] This does not imply that market-making activities cannot be undertaken on an electronic order-driven system. To the extent that demand for immediacy exists, market-making operations arise voluntarily within such markets. Endogenous emergence of market making is very different, however, from markets designed around dealers, or artificial market access restrictions through traditional brokerage.

TABLE 12.1

Trading Costs on Automated Systems Relative to Traditional Brokerage and Execution

	Total cost (percent)	Fees (percent)
OTC stocks	−32.5	−
Listed stocks	−28.2	−70.0

Note: Cost differences are computed as costs (as percentage of principal traded) incurred through automated execution systems, including Instinet, AZX, and Posit, relative to those incurred through traditional brokerage and execution, based on 34 brokers and dealers. Fees, including commissions, are reported for listed stocks only, given broker–dealer practices in the OTC market.

structure rules,[6] and "soft commission"[7] trades. Domowitz and Steil (1999, 2001) carried out such studies using single-institution trade data between 1992 and 1996, with benchmark corrections applied for trade difficulty. The fund manager studied was, to the best of our knowledge, the largest single user of ECNs among active money managers during this period, and had no soft commission arrangements with brokers as a matter of company policy, thus making its trade data exceptionally well suited for the study. Summary statistics are provided in Table 12.1, based on data from Domowitz and Steil (2001).

On average, total trading costs (fees and price impact) are 0.80 percent of principal for Nasdaq trades through traditional brokers, and 0.54 percent through automated systems. Exchange-listed (mainly NYSE) trading costs are 0.39 percent through traditional brokers, and 0.28 percent through automated systems.[8]

[6] Our data predate a major change in Nasdaq market structure deriving from implementation of the SEC's "order handling rules" in 1997. These rules blurred the distinction between automated and nonautomated trade execution.

[7] Soft commission trades are those allocated to a specific broker not because that broker offers the lowest cost of execution on a given transaction, but because the institutional investor is obliged to pay a minimum level of annual commissions to that broker in return for services unrelated to trade execution—in particular, company and macro research.

TABLE 12.2

Trading Costs: United States versus Europe, 1996–8

	Total (percent)	Explicit (percent)	Implicit (percent)
United States	0.37	0.07	0.30
European Continent[a]	0.38	0.31	0.07

Data source: Domowitz et al. (2001).

[a] France, Germany, Italy, The Netherlands, Spain, Sweden, Switzerland.

Thus, average trading cost savings achieved through the use of automated systems are 32.5 percent on Nasdaq trades, and 28.2 percent on trades in NYSE-listed stocks. Commissions and fees are usefully compared only for exchange-listed shares, given broker–dealer pricing practices on the Nasdaq market. Automated execution (i.e., ECN) fees are, on average, 70 percent less than those levied by traditional institutional brokers in the sample.

It is important to note that ECNs are a distinctly American phenomenon, whose growth is accounted for by a combination of market structure and regulatory idiosyncrasies. In particular, the vast majority of non–U.S. exchanges operate the same market architecture as the primary American ECNs (continuous electronic auctions), thereby severely limiting the potential size of their competitive niche outside of the United States. Thus, the results of this study should be interpreted as a reflection of the benefits of the disintermediating effects of automated trading systems, rather than a reflection of the benefits of the institution of an ECN as such.

This view is borne out by a cross-country study of trading costs over the period 1996–8 carried out by Domowitz et al. (2001). The authors find that whereas explicit trading costs in Europe

[8] When trade difficulty is accounted for, it is found that more difficult trades are more frequently executed through traditional means, but that automated executions are still generally less costly for all levels of trade difficulty. See Domowitz and Steil (1999) for results and discussion. Trade difficulty is proxied by shares per trade, market capitalization of the stock, beta, volatility, and the inverse of the share price.

were on average three to four times higher than in the United States, implicit cost advantages for the former fully offset this differential (see Table 12.2).[9] This marked discrepancy would appear to reflect a more competitive and efficient *brokerage industry* in the United States, but more competitive and efficient *trading systems* in Europe.

12.4. The Cost of Equity Capital

Domowitz and Steil (1999) provide measures of the impact of trading automation on trading costs. Domowitz et al. (2001) provide measures of trading costs in different national markets. Turnover figures are readily available from published exchange statistics. What remains to be quantified is the cost of equity capital, changes in which may logically be influenced by both trading costs and turnover.

Like the implicit cost of trading, the cost of capital in a given firm or market must be estimated; it is not simply observable, like the current yield on a bond. We apply a discounted cash flow model to calculate the cost of equity capital across different national markets—the same basic model applied by U.S. public utility regulators and featured in antitrust textbooks.[10] The cost of equity capital is estimated based on expectations of the future stream of dividends, expressed in the following form:

$$k = DIV_1/P_0 + g,$$

where k is the discount rate, or investors' required return on equity, which is equivalent to the cost of capital; DIV_1 is the expected dividend in the coming year; P_0 is the current price of a stock, or basket of stocks (an index); and g is the long-term growth rate of the dividend (a constant).

For the United States and twelve European countries, we calculate k according to two differ-

ent approximations of DIV_1. k_0 is the cost of capital using the current year's dividend (DIV_0) as a proxy for DIV_1. k_1 is the cost of capital using the following year's actual dividend as a proxy for DIV_1. In the first case, we are assuming that the current year's dividend is an unbiased estimate of the following year's dividend. In the second case, we are assuming that the market's expectation of the following year's dividend, which is unobservable, is approximately equal, on average over time, to the actual dividend paid in the following year. P_0 is based on the main market index for each country. g is calculated as the average annual growth rate of the dividend over the period 1980–98.[11] For seven Latin American countries, we have only actual dividend yields (DIV_0/P_0), and therefore have calculated k_0 only. Furthermore, g is proxied by a long-term sustainable growth rate of earnings per share estimate provided by Goldman Sachs.[12]

12.5. Trading Costs, Turnover, and the Cost of Capital

12.5.1. Correlations Between the Variables

We begin with a simple analysis of the correlations between turnover, trading costs, and the cost of capital, presented in Table 12.3. Figures are computed for the full sample, using k_0, in panel A, while panels B and C contain results for Europe and the United States, with respect to k_0 and k_1, respectively.

The evidence suggests that a decrease in trading costs reduces the cost of capital. The correlation of trading cost with cost of capital is positive and economically significant, regardless of time period, region, and precise defini-

---

[9] We take European trading cost data from the eight largest continental markets, where over half the trading volume in the main index stocks takes place on automated order books.

[10] For example, Kaserman and Mayo (1995).

[11] Malkiel (1992) uses dividend growth estimates from unnamed financial services firms as proxies for market expectations, rather than using actual historical market data, as we have, for such proxies. The Malkiel approach has the benefit of using forward-looking data, but is obviously subject to sample bias in the choice of forecasters.

[12] We are grateful to Nick Beim and his colleagues at Goldman Sachs for all the data used in the cost of capital calculations.

TABLE 12.3
Correlations of Turnover and Trading Cost with Cost of Capital Measures

This table contains simple correlation coefficients between average annual trading costs and annual turnover with cost of capital. Computations for the pooled sample are over 1996–8. Figures in columns labelled by year are computed cross-sectionally. Panel A contains correlations for the United States, Europe, and Latin America, computed with k_0, cost of capital computed using a random walk forecast of dividends. Panels B and C contain correlations for the United States and Europe, computed with k_0 and k_1, respectively, where k_1 is cost of capital computed using the actual dividend for the year following the price.

	Pooled	*1996*	*1997*	*1998*
Panel A: Correlations for the Full Sample				
Trading cost	0.176	0.254	0.078	0.250
Turnover	−0.276	−0.225	−0.225	−0.353
Panel B: Correlations with k_0 for the United States and Europe				
Trading cost	0.280	0.413	0.096	0.220
Turnover	−0.229	−0.213	−0.241	−0.228
Panel C: Correlations with k_1 for the United States and Europe				
Trading cost	0.282	0.419	0.075	0.212
Turnover	−0.225	−0.201	−0.230	−0.218

tion. Results from the sample that is pooled over time range from 0.18 to 0.28.

An increase in turnover reduces the cost of capital. This result is obtained for all regions and definitions of the cost of capital. The correlations again are reasonably large for the pooled sample, ranging from −0.23 to −0.28.

Trading costs are falling over time, while turnover is generally rising. Our estimates of the cost of capital are also falling over the period. However, the negative correlation of cost of capital with turnover, and the positive correlation with trading costs, are not due to time trends alone. The correlations for all years have the same sign as for the time-pooled sample. The cross-sectional magnitudes of the effects sometimes are even larger than those obtained in the pooled sample. Only the correlation of cost of capital with trading costs shows a substantial decline in magnitude, and for only a single year, 1997.

12.5.2. Elasticities From Univariate Regressions

We complement the simple correlation analysis by the computation of cost of capital elasticities

with respect to trading costs and turnover, in order to gain some preliminary insight with respect to relative magnitudes of effects. The elasticities measure the percentage change in cost of capital to be expected from a one percentage point change in trading costs or turnover. Elasticities computed from univariate regressions are reported in Table 12.4, together with their standard errors.[13]

The elasticities all exhibit the same signs as the simple correlations, as might be expected, despite the introduction of controls for cross-country differences. On the other hand, the effect of cost in the full sample is substantially reduced relative to what might have been anticipated, and is estimated with a large standard error. The cause of this result is traceable to financial turmoil in developing countries

[13] Controls for country-specific influences are introduced in the form of unobservable fixed effects by country. Although these variables are needed to control for cross-country differences that are unobserved, yet related to cost of capital, the magnitudes of the fixed effects are uninteresting, and therefore not reported.

TABLE 12.4
Elasticities from Univariate Fixed-Effects Regressions

This table contains elasticities, computed from univariate regressions of cost of capital on trading costs and turnover, respectively, in which all variables appear in logarithmic form. Figures in parentheses are standard errors. All regression estimates are computed using country-specific fixed effects, and annual data from 1996 to 1998. Results for the full sample include Latin America, and use k_0, the cost of capital computed using a random walk forecast of dividends. Results for the United States and Europe are derived using both k_0 and k_1, where k_1 is cost of capital computed using the actual dividend for the year following the price.

	Full sample	United States/Europe (k_0)	United States/Europe (k_1)
Trading cost	0.015 (0.063)	0.121 (0.047)	0.152 (0.055)
Turnover	−0.057 (0.038)	−0.025 (0.031)	−0.042 (0.036)

during the crises of 1997 and 1998.[14] Cost of capital in Latin America, in particular, rose 16 percent between 1997 and 1998, for reasons unrelated to trading costs.[15]

A fairer picture is painted by the results for the United States and Europe, for which crisis effects are less evident, especially relative to developing countries. Trading cost elasticities are reasonably large, and different from zero at any reasonable level of statistical significance. The elasticities range from 0.12 to 0.15, depending on the precise definition of cost of capital. In other words, a 10 percent increase in trading cost implies an increase in the cost of capital by 1.2–1.5 percent. The estimates are surprisingly precise, given the amount of noise inherent in cost of capital measures across countries.[16]

The magnitude of turnover effects on cost of capital is remarkably small, relative to what might have been anticipated from the simple correlation analysis. Estimates range from −0.025 to −0.057, depending on the definition of cost and sample. Not only are these figures economically small, they also are insignificantly

different from zero, based on standard t-statistics.

12.5.3. The Relative Contributions of Trading Costs and Turnover to Cost of Capital

Turnover and trading cost are highly correlated. Domowitz et al. (2001) further found that the causal link between them runs from trading cost to turnover, as opposed to the reverse. Fixed effects regressions of turnover on trading cost, using the samples here, yield a turnover elasticity with respect to cost of −0.78 in Europe and the United States, which is both economically and statistically significant.[17] In other words, were trading costs in Europe to exhibit the same percentage decline as witnessed in the United States over the 1996–8 period, turnover would be expected to increase by approximately 40 percent.

The high correlation between turnover and trading cost is suggestive of two possible, and related, factors in the analysis. First, the magnitude of turnover effects in the univariate examination of cost of capital may be a function of the high correlation with trading costs. Alternatively, turnover may indeed be found to intermediate the impact of trading cost on the cost of capital, once the correlation is taken into account.

[14] See Domowitz et al. (2001) with respect to cost and turnover in emerging markets during those periods, and Coppejans and Domowitz (2000) for general references to the literature with respect to recent crises.

[15] Trading costs continued to fall over the period, with only a slight increase in Asia, for example, of approximately 3 percent in 1997; see Domowitz et al. (2001).

[16] Measured t-statistics for the coefficients are 2.6 and 2.8, for k_0 and k_1, respectively.

[17] Inclusion of Latin America yields an elasticity of −0.29. The elasticities are based on the quarterly, fixed-effects regression formulation of Domowitz et al. (2001), and include market capitalization and return volatility as controls.

TABLE 12.5
Multivariate Regression Results

This table contains elasticities, computed from multivariate regressions of cost of capital on trading costs and turnover, in which all variables appear in logarithmic form. Figures in parentheses are standard errors. Regression estimates are computed using country-specific fixed effects, and annual data from 1996 to 1998. Results for the full sample include Latin America, and use k_0, the cost of capital computed using a random walk forecast of dividends. Results for the U.S. and Europe are derived using both k_0 and k_1, where k_1 is cost of capital computed using the actual dividend for the year following the price.

	Full sample	United States/Europe (k_0)	United States/Europe (k_1)
Trading cost	0.008 (0.063)	0.138 (0.044)	0.167 (0.051)
Turnover	−0.056 (0.034)	−0.004 (0.027)	−0.016 (0.031)
R^2	0.055	0.093	0.095

In order to investigate these possibilities, we estimate models of the form

$$y_{it} = \alpha_i + \beta_1 c_{it} + \beta_2 \tau_{it} + \varepsilon_{it},$$

where y, c, and τ are cost of capital, trading cost, and turnover, respectively, all measured in logs, and α_i is a country-specific effect. Estimates of the trading cost and turnover elasticities are given in Table 12.5.[18] The full sample regressions, inclusive of the Latin American countries, continue to exhibit the same sort of crisis-induced irregularities as in the univariate analysis. We restrict the discussion below to the sample consisting of the United States and Europe.

Inclusion of turnover in the models relating cost of capital to trading cost increases the trading cost elasticities across both measures of cost of capital.[19] It now appears that an increase in trading costs by 10 percent would increase the cost of capital by as much as 1.7 percent, for example. These estimates continue to be statistically significantly different from zero, despite the high correlation of trading cost with turnover.

On the other hand, the impact of turnover on cost of capital *declines* once trading costs are accounted for. The decrease in effect is precipitous, from −62 percent to −84 percent, depending on the definition of cost of capital. In fact, the effects are now not only statistically insignificantly different from zero, but also economically zero. A 10 percent increase in turnover is expected to result in a decrease in cost of capital of as little as 0.04 percent, for example.[20]

Taken together, the results imply that the effect of trading cost on cost of capital is not intermediated by turnover—at least not for the most liquid blue-chip stocks. In fact, quite the reverse is true: once the correlation between trading cost and turnover is taken into account, turnover ceases to have an economically interesting effect on the cost of capital. It would appear that declines in trading costs directly reduce the gross real returns (i.e., exclusive of trading costs) which investors demand on equities, thereby reducing the cost to companies of raising equity capital.

The results do suggest, however, that market and country factors which affect turnover, and not trading cost, would generally fail to influence the cost of capital. Turnover is often taken to be a proxy for market liquidity. Increased liquidity has indeed been proposed

[18] Interestingly, random effects estimation produces almost identical coefficients, suggesting that turnover and cost are uncorrelated with the country-specific effects, and providing higher R^2 measures of goodness-of-fit. We continue to report the fixed effects estimates for unambiguous comparisons with the univariate results.

[19] For k_0, the impact rises by 14 percent, while for k_1, the effect is slightly less, with an increase in the elasticity of about 10 percent.

[20] The elasticity in the case of k_0, for example, is only −0.004, while the alternative definition yields a percentage impact of −0.016.

TABLE 12.6

Decline in Cost of Capital Due to Trading Costs

This table contains statistics pertaining to the fraction of the decline in equity cost of capital due to trading costs for the United States and Europe. Computations are over 1996–8. The averages for Europe are market capitalization weighted by country. All numbers are in percentage terms. Δ cost is the change in total trading transaction costs over the period. Δk_0 and Δk_1 are changes in cost of equity capital by region, where k_0 is the cost of capital computed using a random walk forecast of dividends, and k_1 is cost of capital computed using the actual dividend for the year following the price. Δk_0-pred and Δk_1-pred are the changes in k_0 and k_1, respectively, as predicted by cost of capital elasticities with respect to trading costs, computed over the same period as the changes in trading cost and cost of capital. Δ due to cost (k_0) and Δ due to cost (k_1) are percentage fractions of the change in actual cost of capital due to trading costs.

	Δ cost	Δk_0	Δk_1	Δk_0-pred	Δk_1-pred	Δ due to cost (k_0)	Δ due to cost (k_1)
United States	−53.0	−9.26	−9.02	−7.31	−8.85	78.9	98.1
Europe	−16.9	−4.26	−5.47	−2.33	−2.82	54.7	51.6

as a factor reducing the cost of capital.[21] Our findings do not imply that liquidity fails to influence the cost of capital across countries. Turnover is simply a poor proxy in this context, while trading cost itself, given its implicit cost component, may be a much better indicator of liquidity in the market.

12.6. The Impact of Declines in Trading Cost on the Cost of Capital

The previous analysis demonstrates the statistical significance of trading cost on the cost of equity capital. It is arguable, however, as to whether the cost elasticities, ranging from 0.14 to 0.17, are economically important. We approach this question by examining trends in

---

[21] The proposition that increased market liquidity, or smaller associated liquidity costs, leads to a lower expected return required by investors for any level of risk, is not new; Amihud and Mendelson (2000) survey the area. There is a variety of liquidity-related factors that play a role in the potential for lower cost of capital for a firm. The size of the investor base may increase, for example, a phenomenon that bears some relationship to the Internet and its trading and information advantages; for a treatment focusing on cost of capital effects, see Brennan and Tamarowski (2000). A decrease of asymmetric information via better firm disclosure is another possibility, also aided by technology; see Botosan (2000). Both possibilities decrease the opportunity cost of trading, by building participation in the trading process, reducing search costs, and minimizing trading delays.

trading costs, and the effect of automation on such costs. The goal is to provide a range of plausible values for the fraction of the historical decline in cost of capital due to trading costs and automation of trading market structure.

Data from 42 countries, contained in Domowitz et al. (2001), indicate that total trading costs decreased by 16.4 percent on average, over the 1996–8 time period. The estimates reported in the last section then suggest that equity cost of capital should have declined by 2.26–2.74 percent due to cost alone, depending on how cost of capital is measured. We do not have cost of capital figures for such a large sample, and cannot make an exact comparison. For illustration, a 5 percent fall in global equity cost of capital would imply that trading costs account for approximately 50 percent of the decrease.

We can be more exact with respect to developments in the United States and Europe. Table 12.6 contains estimates of the fraction of the decline in cost of capital due to trading costs. Trading costs fell over the 1996–8 period by 53 and 17 percent across the two regions. In the United States, cost of capital decreases by 9.0–9.3 percent over the period, depending on the definition of cost of capital. The analogous figures for Europe are −4.3 and −5.5 percent, using market-capitalization weighted averages of figures across countries in the sample. Using the elasticities from Table 12.5, it is possible to predict the declines in cost of capital due to that in trading costs, and to compare them with figures obtained from the actual cost of capital data.

The fraction of the decline in cost of capital due to trading costs is estimated to be 52–55 percent for Europe. The figures are considerably higher with respect to trading activity in the United States: from 79 to 98 percent, depending on the cost of capital definition.

In terms of the raw figures, the differences are explainable by a combination of the disparity between the decline in transactions costs, and the differences in the percentage rate of decrease in cost of capital over the period. In absolute terms, cost of capital is falling in the United States 88 percent faster than in Europe. The commensurate decline in trading costs in the United States is three times that observed in Europe over the period.

12.7. The Impact of Trading Automation on the Cost of Capital

12.7.1. Historical Impact

Data quality questions notwithstanding, quantifying the historical impact of trading costs on cost of capital is a relatively straightforward exercise. Not so the impact of automation. To do so we must be able to quantify how much more (or less) automated a market has become over the period being studied; in our case, 1996–8. Only very rough proxies for the degree of market automation are available.

In the case of the Nasdaq market, we know that the ECN share of total volume increased from about 20 percent to 30 percent over the period 1996–8. Table 12.1 documents an estimated 33 percent cost savings from automated trading in the Nasdaq market. A 10 percentage point increase in volume should therefore have resulted in more than a 3 percent decline in trading cost across the Nasdaq market, over this 3-year period, as a direct result of automation. Applying the midpoint of our lower and upper estimate of the elasticity of cost of capital with respect to trading costs (15.5 percent), we find a decline in the cost of capital to Nasdaq listed companies over this period of approximately 0.5 percent ascribable to automation.

In the case of the major western European markets, all of these were operating automated trading systems prior to 1996 with the exception of the London Stock Exchange (LSE). Unfortunately, the LSE only went live with its SETS electronic trading system in late 1997. Our trading cost data cannot, therefore, be applied meaningfully to a discussion of automation's historical impact on European cost of capital.

The period we focus on in this paper clearly presents only a small window into the effects of trading automation on cost of capital, and the window is obviously not optimally positioned to capture trading regime changes in different markets. A forward-looking analysis is therefore necessary to capture the potential of automated trading.

12.7.2. Future Impact

There are two fundamental aspects to the automation of trading structures. The first is the use of automation to allow investor orders to interact with one another directly, without the intervention of dealers or specialists. The second is to allow investors to transmit their orders to the trading system directly, without having to pay intermediaries to do this on their behalf.

The current landscape of the U.S. markets indicates considerable potential for changes along the first dimension: the elimination of dealer and specialist intervention. For that segment of the market which is automated, however (mainly the ECN component of the Nasdaq market), direct order transmission by institutional investors is already widespread.

In the European markets, automated order-matching has long been the norm. Yet, the membership structure of the stock exchanges (there is minimal ECN presence and usage) still leaves considerable scope for disintermediation of order transmission from investor to trading system. This is reflected in the findings of Domowitz et al. (2001). As noted in section 3, whereas implicit trading costs in Europe were roughly 1/3 to 1/4 of U.S. levels (attributable to more efficient order matching structures), explicit costs were roughly 3 to 4 times higher (attributable to less efficient trade intermediation).

TABLE 12.7
Anticipated Further Decline in U.S. Cost of Capital Due to Completed Automation

	Percent of trading volume automated	Percent trading cost savings from automated trading	Percent estimated trading cost savings from completing market automation	Percent estimated cost of capital savings from completing market automation
Nasdaq	30	33	23	3.6
NYSE	5	28	27	4.2

We may then usefully inquire into the potential effects on the cost of equity capital in the United States and Europe if both markets were to "automate fully," defined as a shift to wholly disintermediated electronic order matching. This experiment involves one important and controversial assumption: that the opportunity cost of passing up immediate execution facilitated by dealer-intermediary capital is essentially zero. Although some trading cost consultants hold opportunity costs to be significant (e.g., Wagner and Edwards, 1993), their analysis is contradicted by conflicting data findings (Keim and Madhavan, 1998; Perold and Sirri, 1993). More importantly, opportunity costs are only meaningful where investors have private information, and fund managers themselves appear very rarely to believe that they have such information (Davis and Steil, 2001).[22]

Putting aside the question of opportunity costs, then, we now consider the potential impact of fully automating the 70 percent of the Nasdaq market and 95 percent of the U.S. exchange-listed market which is not currently automated. On the basis of our estimates of automated Nasdaq trading cost savings (33 percent) in Table 12.1, full automation would

imply a further 23 percent decline in trading costs. Estimated savings of 28 percent on automated exchange-listed trading imply a further 27 percent fall in NYSE and regional exchange trading costs from full automation. Applying our estimated cost of capital elasticity of 15.5 percent implies an expected reduction capital cost reduction of 3.6 percent for Nasdaq listed companies and 4.2 percent for NYSE listed companies as a direct result of completing automation of these markets. This is summarized in Table 12.7.

In the case of Europe, the benefits of automating the order transmission process would logically fall most heavily on the explicit cost of trading. Weighted by national market capitalizations, the average explicit cost of trading was 29.6 percent in Europe in 1998. Based on Table 12.1, estimated explicit cost savings of 70 percent are expected from automation of exchange-listed U.S. share trading. Applying this estimate to European explicit costs implies total trading cost reductions of 50 percent from automating order transmission—excluding any further declines in implicit costs which might also be expected to result from disintermediation.[23] The 15.5 percent cost of capital elasticity therefore implies a further 7.8 percent reduction in capital costs to European listed companies as a direct result of automating the institutional brokerage function. This is summarized in Table 12.8.

---

[22] Furthermore, new automated call market and matching systems have been designed specifically to automate large block and portfolio trading, the traditional purview of dealer intermediaries. An example outside the equity world is BondConnect, which employs special algorithms to maximize executed trade sizes. Domowitz and Steil (1999) account for trade difficulty (including trade size) in their cost comparisons, and find automated executions to be cheaper even at high levels of difficulty.

[23] See chapter 8 of Davis and Steil (2001) for a detailed explanation of how intermediation can increase trading costs by facilitating front-running of investor orders.

TABLE 12.8
Anticipated Further Decline in European Cost of Capital
Due to Automation-Driven Disintermediation

Percent estimated explicit trading cost savings from disintermediation	Percent estimated total trading cost savings from disintermediation	Percent estimated cost of capital savings from disintermediation
63	50	7.8

12.8. Summary and Conclusions

This chapter has examined the impact of technological innovation in securities trading structures on the cost of equity trading and the cost of corporate equity capital. Automation of the trading process, defined in terms of the use of computerized auction systems to match investor buy and sell orders directly, is shown to have a significant impact on lowering the cost of trading. On the basis of U.S. trading data, we believe such savings to be in the range of 28–33 percent relative to the traditional floor and dealer market structures of the NYSE and Nasdaq, respectively. Using blue-chip trading data from the United States and Europe, we further demonstrate that trading cost reductions are a tremendous stimulant to trading; each 10 percent decline in cost producing an 8 percent increase in share turnover.

Contrary to popular belief, we find that higher trading volume has no effect on the cost of equity capital for large public companies.[24] Rather, trading cost reductions have a direct and significant impact on the cost of equity capital; each 10 percent decline in trading cost producing a 1.5 percent decline in the cost of capital. Using time series estimates for U.S. cost of equity capital, we show that the halving of U.S. trading costs we document for the period 1996–8 translates directly into cost of capital savings to S&P 500 companies of approximately 7.5 percent.

Finally, we estimate that replacement of the current Nasdaq and NYSE trading structures

with nonintermediated electronic order-matching systems would result in further cost of capital savings to listed companies of approximately 4 percent. In Europe, where such trading systems already predominate, we estimate that disintermediating the exchange members who currently route buy and sell orders from investors to the exchanges would result in a decline in trading fees of roughly 70 percent, which would translate into a 7.8 percent cost of capital savings for European blue-chip companies.

The diffusion of technological innovation throughout the securities trading industry has a significant and direct impact on the cost of investing and the cost to companies of raising capital in the market. This message emerges clearly from the wide range of numerical results obtained, and has some important public policy implications.

Policy should act to facilitate the ability of automated trading system operators to offer services directly to investors, without the necessity of intermediation. As technological access limitations and distance costs are small or nonexistent in computerized markets, there is no logical necessity for investor trades to be subject to costly human intermediation. Trading system operators may choose, for wholly commercial reasons, to require outside credit validation on investor trades, but there is no public interest benefit in *mandating* the human intermediary as the central pillar of trading market microstructure. For those transactions which require intermediary liquidity provision for immediate execution, the supply of risk capital will emerge naturally from the profit incentive, regardless of market platform.

Policy should also make the demutualization of exchanges possible, and, if already possible, less costly in terms of regulatory constraints. The traditional model of an exchange as a mutual association of broker–dealers is a remnant of the pre-automation era, when trading venues were of necessity physical places rather than virtual environments. The demutualization process is already well underway among European exchanges (and globally in the case of derivatives markets). The switch to corporate for-profit structure increases the competitiveness of the trading services industry,

---

[24] An effect may exist for less actively traded stocks, but our data simply do not address the point.

and permits quicker adaptation to technological developments. There are significant costs to
be borne by investors and listed companies
from exchanges maintaining governance structures designed for an industry structure which
technology has reshaped so dramatically.

Both direct access and market demutualization require legal changes in many countries.
In some jurisdictions, exchange access is
currently restricted to broker–dealers by law.
Regulatory obligations and member privileges
can make direct competition to official mutua-
lized exchanges difficult or infeasible. The
natural emergence of for-profit exchange operations calls into question the logic of regulatory
systems which treat exchanges as quasi-public

enterprises, with significant delegated self-regu-
latory functions and powers over the wider
market.

Accurately quantifying the further impact of
the effects we document in this chapter on the
overall level of investment, productivity, and
growth is clearly beyond the bounds of feasi-
bility. Yet there are compelling reasons to
believe that the technological advances studied
here reduce costs, and that their effects are
nonnegligible and ongoing. Within this industry, at least, the Solow paradox would not
appear to hold: the computer age is visible
not only on traders' desks, but also in the
most relevant measures of the trading industry's productivity.

13

Venture Capital

Josh Lerner

13.1. Introduction

Venture capital has attracted increasing attention in both the popular press and academic literature. The recent dramatic growth in the venture capital industry in the past two decades has been accompanied by new academic research that explores its form and function. At the same time, many of the questions that are most critical to policymakers—in particular, those relating to the highly effective manner in which venture capital apparently stimulates technological innovation—remain unanswered. Thus, this chapter has a twofold role: to summarize and synthesize what we do know about the impact of venture capital on innovation from recent research, and to indicate the important questions that we cannot yet answer.

A natural first question is what constitutes venture capital. Many start-up firms require substantial capital. A firm's founder may not have sufficient funds to finance these projects alone, and therefore must seek outside financing. Entrepreneurial firms that are characterized by significant intangible assets, expect years of negative earnings, and have uncertain prospects are unlikely to receive bank loans or other debt financing. Venture capital organizations finance these high-risk, potentially high-reward projects, purchasing equity stakes while the firms are still privately held. At the same time, not everyone who finances these firms is a venture capitalist. Banks, individual investors (or "angels"), and corporations are among the other financiers of these firms. Venture capital is defined here as independently managed, dedicated pools of capital that focus on equity or equity-linked investments in privately held, high-growth companies.

Four limitations should be acknowledged at the outset. The primary focus of this chapter is on drawing together the empirical academic research on venture capital and highlighting its relevance to the innovation process. The many theoretical papers that examine various aspects of the venture capital market are beyond the scope of this chapter. Much of the theoretical literature examines the role that venture capitalists play in mitigating agency conflicts between entrepreneurial firms and outside investors. The improvement in efficiency might be due to the active monitoring and advice that is provided (Marx, 1994; Cornelli and Yosha, 1997; Hellmann, 1998), the screening mechanisms employed (Chan, 1983), the incentives to exit (Berglöf, 1994), the proper syndication of the investment (Admati and Pfleiderer, 1994), or the staging of the investment (Bergemann and Hege, 1998). This work has improved our understanding of the factors that affect the relationship between venture capitalists and entrepreneurs.

Nor do we seek to duplicate the guides that explain the intricacies of the venture financing process to practitioners. Numerous excellent volumes exist (especially Bartlett, 1995; Levin, 1995; Halloran, 1996), which document the legal and institutional considerations associated with raising venture financing at much greater depth than could be done in this chapter.

Third, the upstream relationships between venture capitalists and the institutions who provide them with capital are not considered at much length. Over the past several years, a

This chapter is based in part on the works of Gompers and Lerner (1999b, 2001), and many of the ideas and frameworks herein were jointly developed with Paul Gompers. I acknowledge helpful comments from Richard Nelson, Benn Steil, David Victor, and the Council on Foreign Relations study group members. All errors are my own.

series of research papers have given us a better understanding of how venture capital funds are structured, and how incentive issues that arise are (or are not) addressed. This topic, however, would take us too far from our central mission. The interested reader is referred to Gompers and Lerner (1999b).

Finally, this chapter focuses on the venture capital industry, and not the financial *function* played by venture capital organizations. The financing of high-risk projects have been played by many actors across history, including government leaders, corporations, and wealthy individuals. The focus on the modern venture capital industry is motivated by two considerations. First, this is a phenomenon of considerable complexity. To expand the scope of the chapter would require a book, not a chapter. Second, while (as is frequently noted in this chapter) our state of knowledge about the venture capital industry is still quite incomplete, our understanding of many of the alternative forms of financing high-risk young firms (especially "angel" investing) is far more incomplete (see the discussion in Lerner, 1998). Thus, it is premature to seek to provide a comprehensive overview of the financing of entrepreneurial projects.

The rest of the chapter is organized as follows: section 13.2 presents a brief history of the venture capital industry. The selecting of investments, structuring of deals, monitoring of firms, and exiting of investments by venture capitalists are taken up in section 13.3. Section 13.4 discusses the evidence on venture capital and innovation. The final section highlights an area that urgently needs future research: the internationalization of the U.S. venture capital industry and its implications.

13.2. The Development of the Venture Capital Industry

The venture capital industry—using the definition above—was in its initial decades a predominantly American phenomenon. Only gradually has it spread to elsewhere around the globe.

The industry had its origins in the family offices that managed the wealth of high net worth individuals in the first decades of this century. Wealthy families invested in and advised a variety of business enterprises, including the Rockefeller family (Douglas Aircraft and Eastern Airlines) and the Phipps (Ingersoll Rand and International Paper). Gradually, these families began involving outsiders to select and oversee these investments. In many cases, these entities formed the nuclei for what would ultimately become independent groups. These included J.H. Whitney & Co. (Whitney family) and Venrock Associates (Rockefeller family).[1]

The first venture capital firm satisfying the criteria delineated above, however, was not established until after World War II. American Research and Development (ARD) was formed in 1946 by MIT President Karl Compton, Harvard Business School Professor Georges F. Doriot, and local business leaders. A small group of venture capitalists made high-risk investments into emerging companies that were based on technology developed for World War II. The success of the investments ranged widely: almost half of ARD's profits during its 26-year existence as an independent entity came from its U.S.$70,000 investment in Digital Equipment Company (DEC) in 1957, which grew in value to U.S.$355 million. Because institutional investors were reluctant to invest, ARD was structured as a publicly traded closed-end fund and marketed mostly to individuals (Liles, 1977). Many of the other venture organizations begun in the decade after ARD's formation were also structured as closed-end funds.

The first venture capital limited partnership, Draper, Gaither, and Anderson, was formed in 1958. Imitators soon followed, but limited partnerships accounted for a minority of the venture pool during the 1960s and 1970s.

---

[1] These family offices are not the only antecedents to modern venture capital firms. For instance, patent agents in the United Kingdom and United States also played an intermediary role during the late nineteenth and early twentieth centuries, introducing individual inventors to wealthy potential investors. They typically did not, however, raise funds or invest their own capital into these firms. For a discussion, see Lamoreaux and Sokoloff (2000) and MacLeod (1992).

Most venture organizations raised money either through closed-end funds or small business investment companies (SBICs), federally guaranteed risk-capital pools that proliferated during the 1960s. While the market for SBICs in the late 1960s and early 1970s was strong, incentive problems ultimately led to the collapse of the sector. The annual flow of money into venture capital during its first three decades never exceeded a few hundred million dollars and usually was substantially less.

The activity in the venture industry increased dramatically in late 1970s and early 1980s. Table 13.1 and Figure 13.1 provide an overview of fund-raising by venture partnerships, highlighting the changing volume of investments over the years, as well as the shifting mixture of investors. Industry observers attributed much of the shift to the U.S. Department of Labor's clarification of ERISA's "prudent man" rule in 1979. Prior to this year, the Employee Retirement Income Security Act (ERISA) limited pension funds from investing substantial amounts of money into venture capital or other high-risk asset classes. The Department of Labor's clarification of the rule explicitly allowed pension managers to invest in high-risk assets, including venture capital. In 1978, when U.S.$424 million was invested in new venture capital funds, individuals accounted for the largest share (32 percent). Pension funds supplied just 15 percent. Eight years later, when more than U.S.$4 billion was invested, pension funds accounted for more than half of all contributions.[2]

One important change in the venture capital industry around this time was the rise of the limited partnership as the dominant organizational form. Limited partnerships have an important advantage that makes them attractive to tax-exempt institutional investors: capital gains taxes are not paid by the limited partnership. Instead, the (taxable) investors only pay taxes. Venture partnerships have predeter-

mined, finite lifetimes (usually ten years although extensions are often allowed). Investors in the fund are limited partners. In order to maintain limited liability, investors must not become involved in the day-to-day management of the fund.

The subsequent years saw both very good and trying times for venture capitalists. On the one hand, during the 1980s and 1990s venture capitalists backed many of the most successful high-technology companies, including Apple Computer, Cisco Systems, Genentech, Netscape, and Sun Microsystems. A substantial number of service firms (including Staples, Starbucks, and TCBY) also received venture financing. At the same time, commitments to the venture capital industry were very uneven. As Figure 13.1 and Table 13.1 depict, the annual flow of money into venture funds increased by a factor of ten during the early 1980s, peaking at just under six billion 1996 dollars. From 1987 to 1991, however, fund-raising steadily declined. Over the past five years, the pattern has been reversed. 1999 represented a record fund-raising year, in which over U.S.$30 billion was raised by venture capitalists. This process of rapid growth and decline has created a great deal of instability in the industry.

As Figure 13.2 depicts, returns on venture capital funds had declined in the mid-1980s, apparently because of overinvestment in various industries and the entry of inexperienced venture capitalists. As investors became disappointed with returns, they committed less capital to the industry. The recent activity in the initial public offering (IPO) market and the exit of many inexperienced venture capitalists led to an increase in returns. New capital commitments rose again in response, increasing by more than ten times between 1991 and 1999. Interestingly, while previous investment surges have been associated with falling returns, the past few years have seen a steady rise in the returns to these funds.

The question of how the venture industry will evolve over the next decade is a particularly critical one because the recent growth has been so spectacular. It is natural to ask whether the growth of private equity can be sustained. Has too much capital been raised? Is the indus-

[2] The annual commitments represent pledges of capital to venture funds raised in a given year. This money is typically invested over three to five years starting in the year the fund is formed.

TABLE 13.1

Summary Statistics for Venture Capital Fund-Raising by Independent Venture Partnerships (all dollar figures are in millions of 1992 U.S. dollars)

	1978	1979	1980	1981	1982	1983	1984	1985	1986	1987	1988
First closing of funds											
Number of funds	23	27	57	81	98	147	150	99	86	112	78
Size (millions of 1992 U.S.$)	414	469	1208	1661	2026	5289	4694	4065	4295	5217	3606
Sources of funds (percent)											
Private pension funds	15	31	30	23	33	26	25	23	39	27	27
Public pension funds	a	a	a	a	a	5	9	10	12	12	20
Corporations	10	17	19	17	12	12	14	12	11	10	12
Individuals	32	23	16	23	21	21	15	13	12	12	8
Endowments	9	10	14	12	7	8	6	8	6	10	11
Insurance companies/ banks	16	4	13	15	14	12	13	11	10	15	9
Foreign investors/other	18	15	8	10	13	16	18	23	11	14	13
Independent venture partnerships as a share of the total venture pool (percent)[b]	c	c	40	44	58	68	72	73	75	78	80

	1989	1990	1991	1992	1993	1994	1995	1996	1997	1998	1999
First closing of funds											
Number of funds	88	50	34	31	46	80	84	80	103	161	186
Size (millions of 1992 U.S.$)	3354	2431	1483	1950	2480	3582	4045	6805	8060	16933	31299
Sources of funds (percent)											
Private pension funds	22	31	25	22	59	47	38	43	40	37	9
Public pension funds	14	22	17	20	a	a	a	a	a	10	9
Corporations	20	7	4	3	8	9	2	13	30	18	16
Individuals	6	11	12	11	7	12	17	9	13	11	19
Endowments	12	13	24	18	11	21	22	21	9	8	15
Insurance companies/ banks	13	9	6	14	11	9	18	5	1	3	11
Foreign investors/other	13	7	12	11	4	2	3	8	7	13	22
Independent venture partnerships as a share of the total venture pool (percent)[b]	79	80	80	81	78	78	c	c	c	c	c

Source: Compiled from the unpublished Venture Economics funds database and various issues of the *Venture Capital Journal.*
[a] Public pension funds are included with private pension funds in these years.
[b] This series is defined differently in different years. In some years, the *Venture Capital Journal* states that nonbank SBICs and publicly traded venture funds are included with independent venture partnerships. In other years, these funds are counted in other categories.
[c] These data are only available between 1980 and 1994.

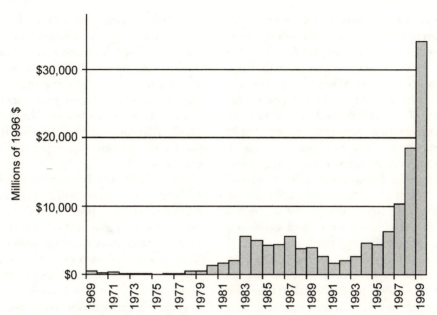

Figure 13.1 Commitments to the venture capital industry. Commitments are defined as the amount of money that is pledged to venture capital funds in that year. Amounts are in millions of 1996 U.S. dollars. *Source:* Venture Economics and Asset Alternatives.

try destined to experience disappointing returns and shrink dramatically?

These are fair questions. As highlighted below, short-run shifts in the supply of or demand for private equity investments can have dramatic effects. For instance, periods with a rapid increase in capital commitments

have historically led to less restrictions on private equity investors, larger investments in portfolio firms, higher valuations for those investments, and lower returns for investors. These patterns have led many practitioners to conclude that the industry is inherently cyclical. In short, this view implies that periods of rapid

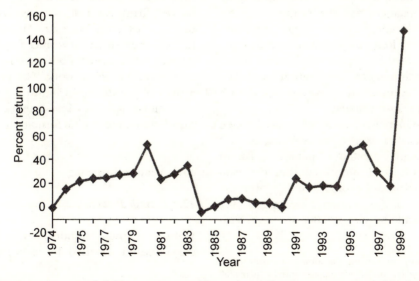

Figure 13.2 Return on venture capital. The average annual internal rate of return on venture capital funds, net of fees and profit-sharing, is plotted by year. *Source:* Compiled from Venture Economics (2000b) and their unpublished data.

growth generate sufficient problems that periods of retrenchment are sure to follow. These cycles may lead us to be pessimistic about the prospects for the industry in the years to come.

It is important, however, to consider the *long-run* determinants of the level of private equity, not just the short-run effects. In the short run, intense competition between private equity groups may lead to a willingness to pay a premium for certain types of firms (e.g., firms specializing in tools and content for the Internet). This is unlikely to be a sustainable strategy in the long run: firms that persist in such a strategy will earn low returns and eventually be unable to raise follow-on funds.

The types of factors that determine the long-run steady-state supply of private equity in the economy are more fundamental. These are likely to include the pace of technological innovation in the economy, the degree of dynamism in the economy, the presence of liquid and competitive markets for investors to sell their investments (whether markets for stock offerings or acquisitions), and the willingness of highly skilled managers and engineers to work in entrepreneurial environments. However painful the short-run adjustments, these more fundamental factors are likely to be critical in establishing the long-run level.

When one examines these more fundamental factors, there appears to have been quite substantial changes for the better over the past several decades.[3] Consider two of the determinants of the long-run supply of venture capital in the United States: the acceleration of the rate of technological innovation and the decreasing "transaction costs" associated with private equity investments.

While the increase in innovation can be seen though several measures, probably the clearest indication is in the extent of patenting. Patent applications by U.S. inventors, after hovering between 40,000 and 80,000 annually over the first 85 years of this century, have surged over the past decade to over 120,000 per year. This does not appear to reflect the impact of changes in domestic patent policy, shifts in the success rate of applications, or a variety of alternative explanations. Rather, it appears to reflect a fundamental shift in the rate of innovation.[4] The breadth of technology appears wider today than it has been ever before. The greater rate of intellectual innovation provides fertile ground for future investments, especially by venture capitalists.

A second change has been decreasing cost of making new private equity investments. The efficiency of the private equity process has been greatly augmented by the emergence of other intermediaries familiar with its workings. The presence of such expertise on the part of lawyers, accountants, managers and others—even real estate brokers—has substantially lowered the transaction costs associated with forming and financing new firms or restructuring existing ones. The increasing number of professionals and managers familiar with and accustomed to the employment arrangements offered by private equity-backed firms (such as heavy reliance on stock options) has also been a major shift. In short, the increasing familiarity with the private equity process has made the long-term prospects for investment more attractive than they have ever been before.

Many of these changes appear to have actually been driven by the activities of private equity-backed firms: for instance, venture capitalists have funded many innovative firms, which have in turn, created opportunities for new venture investments. It appears as if there is somewhat of a "virtuous circle" at work. The growth in the activity of private equity industry has enhanced the conditions for new investments, which has in turn led to more capital formation.

13.3. Venture Investing

13.3.1. Basic Patterns

Venture capital disbursements are highly concentrated. Divided by industry, about 60

---

[3] It is also worth emphasizing that despite its growth, the venture pool today remains very small relative to the overall pool of public equities, which has also grown rapidly during these years.

[4] These changes are discussed in Kortum and Lerner (1998).

TABLE 13.2
Number and Dollar Amount of Venture Capital Disbursements in the United States in the First Three Quarters of
1999, by VentureOne Industry Classification (all dollar
figures are in millions of current U.S. dollars)

Industry	Number of transactions	Total U.S.$ invested
Information technology		
Communications and networking	255	4498
Electronics and computer hardware	59	423
Information services	296	3053
Semiconductors and components	58	518
Software	489	4233
Total	1157	12726
Life sciences		
Healthcare services	47	411
Medical compounds	84	649
Medical devices and equipment	114	827
Medical information systems	44	336
Total	289	2233
Non- technology or other		
Retail and consumer products	30	227
Other companies	454	5580
Total	484	5807
Grand total	1979	20957

Source: Compiled from unpublished VentureOne databases.

percent in 1999 went to information technology industries, especially communications and
networking, software, and information services.
About 10 percent went into life sciences and
medical companies, and the rest is spread over
all other types of companies. When venture
capital disbursements are viewed geographically, a little more than one-third of venture
capital went to California. A little less than
one third went to Massachusetts, Texas, New
York, New Jersey, Colorado, Pennsylvania, and
Illinois, combined. The remaining third was
spread between the other forty-two states.

Tables 13.2–13.4 present historical information on the mixture of investments. Table 13.2
provides a detailed summary of investments in
the first three quarters of 1999; Table 13.3
presents a more aggregated summary of investments (in manufacturing firms only) over the
past three decades; and Table 13.4 provides a
summary of investments in the ten states with
the most venture capital activity over the past
three decades.

The industry results in Tables 13.2 and 13.3
highlight the continuing focus by venture capitalists on high-technology firms (e.g., communication, computers, electronics, biotechnology,
and medical/health). The percentage of
venture capital invested in high-technology
firms never falls below 70 percent of annual
investments. Industry investment composition
suggests that venture capitalists specialize in
industries in which monitoring and information
evaluation are important.

13.3.2. Why This Concentration?

Uncertainty and informational asymmetries
often characterize young firms, particularly in
high-technology industries. These information
problems make it difficult to assess these firms,
and permit opportunistic behavior by entrepreneurs after financing is received. This literature
has highlighted the role of financial intermediaries such as venture capitalists in alleviating
these information problems.

To briefly review the types of conflicts that
can emerge in these settings, Jensen and Meckling (1976) demonstrate that conflicts between
managers and investors ("agency problems")
can affect the willingness of both debt and
equity holders to provide capital. If the firm
raises equity from outside investors, the
manager has an incentive to engage in wasteful
expenditures (e.g., lavish offices) because he
may benefit disproportionately from these but
does not bear their entire cost. Similarly, if the
firm raises debt, the manager may increase risk
to undesirable levels. Because providers of
capital recognize these problems, outside
investors demand a higher rate of return
than would be the case if the funds were
internally generated.

TABLE 13.3

Number and Dollar Amount of Venture Capital Disbursements for U.S. Manufacturing Industries, by Industry and Five-Year Period

No.	Industry	1965–9	1970–4	1975–9	1980–4	1985–9	1990–6
Panel A: Venture capital investments (nos.)							
1	Food and kindred	1	9	6	23	80	93
2	Textile and apparel	4	12	9	19	27	70
3	Lumber and furniture	2	8	6	24	62	37
4	Paper	2	2	2	2	12	14
5	Industrial chemicals	1	1	1	6	18	23
6	Drugs	1	12	34	245	554	746
7	Other chemicals	1	7	8	10	52	46
8	Petroleum refining and extraction	3	3	26	92	27	14
9	Rubber products	1	5	6	19	11	7
10	Stone, clay and glass products	0	1	3	14	48	31
11	Primary metals	0	3	5	20	44	33
12	Fabricated metal products	0	0	0	2	1	2
13	Office and computing machines	39	84	108	744	641	442
14	Other nonelectrical machinery	12	12	32	254	280	162
15	Communication and electronic	23	65	60	497	736	709
16	Other electrical equipment	0	6	16	36	52	50
17	Transportation equipment	1	7	5	6	24	25
18	Aircraft and missiles	0	0	0	12	20	4
19	Professional and scientific instruments	13	37	70	383	549	544
20	Other machinery	7	14	16	62	89	98
	Total	111	288	413	2470	3327	3150
Panel B: Venture capital disbursements (millions of 1992 U.S.$)							
1	Food and kindred	4	19	7	25	212	258
2	Textile and apparel	6	15	14	27	45	186
3	Lumber and furniture	4	17	9	26	200	354
4	Paper	1	8	3	3	22	46
5	Industrial chemicals	0	1	1	41	34	33
6	Drugs	0	15	136	623	1869	3017
7	Other chemicals	1	40	4	9	155	87
8	Petroleum refining and extraction	12	6	92	359	110	29
9	Rubber products	1	3	15	28	8	18
10	Stone, clay and glass products	0	1	5	34	99	45
11	Primary metals	0	8	11	25	67	166
12	Fabricated metal products	0	0	0	1	0	1
13	Office and computing machines	67	404	288	3253	2491	1426
14	Other nonelectrical machinery	64	17	37	677	669	323
15	Communication and electronic	44	189	82	1746	2646	2627
16	Other electrical equipment	0	8	53	78	107	104
17	Transportation equipment	0	10	4	9	47	96
18	Aircraft and missiles	0	0	0	19	19	8
19	Professional and scientific instruments	13	86	114	811	1449	1509
20	Other machinery	7	28	22	113	176	350
	Total	225	874	895	7907	10423	10685

Source: Based on Kortum and Lerner (2000) and supplemented with tabulations of unpublished Venture Economics databases.

Note: The count of venture capital investments in each five-year period is the sum of the number of firms receiving investments in each year.

TABLE 13.4

Number and Dollar Amount of Venture Capital Disbursements for all Industries in the Ten States with the Most Venture Capital Activity, by State and Five-Year Period

State	1965–9	1970–4	1975–9	1980–4	1985–9	1990–6
Panel A: Venture capital investments (nos.)						
California	65	179	310	1863	2645	3380
Massachusetts	45	93	155	708	1014	1028
Texas	18	71	84	373	584	489
New York	28	90	73	311	324	276
New Jersey	15	35	47	171	291	336
Colorado	5	22	31	194	258	298
Pennsylvania	8	21	32	120	290	311
Illinois	16	29	31	133	214	312
Minnesota	12	34	42	170	186	194
Connecticut	3	20	37	136	217	210
Total, all states	302	847	1253	5365	8154	9406
Panel B: Venture capital disbursements (millions of 1992 U.S.$)						
California	218	546	691	6711	9670	13603
Massachusetts	61	155	197	1943	2829	3386
Texas	37	140	148	1161	2171	2010
New York	32	154	162	688	1404	1394
New Jersey	33	82	77	370	1214	1711
Colorado	12	50	46	493	805	951
Pennsylvania	18	41	116	370	1530	1109
Illinois	59	134	117	287	1208	1413
Minnesota	6	90	44	270	406	522
Connecticut	1	32	85	319	1463	724
Total, all states	687	1935	2259	15261	30742	37162

Source: Based on tabulations of unpublished Venture Economics databases. All dollar figures are in millions of 1992 U.S. dollars.

Note: The count of venture capital investments in each five-year period is the sum of the number of firms receiving investments in each year.

Even if the manager is motivated to maximize shareholder value, informational asymmetries may make raising external capital more expensive or even preclude it entirely. Myers and Majluf (1984) and Greenwald et al. (1984) demonstrate that equity offerings of firms may be associated with a "lemons" problem (first identified by Akerlof, 1970). If the manager is better informed about the investment opportunities of the firm and acts in the interest of current shareholders, then managers only issue new shares when the company's stock is overvalued. Indeed, numerous studies have documented that stock prices decline upon the announcement of equity issues, largely

because of the negative signal sent to the market. These information problems have also been shown to exist in debt markets by Stiglitz and Weiss (1981) and others.

More generally, the inability to verify outcomes makes it difficult to write contracts that are contingent upon particular events. This inability makes external financing costly. Many of the models of ownership (e.g., Grossman and Hart, 1986; Hart and Moore, 1990) and financing choice (e.g., Hart and Moore, 1998) depend on the inability of investors to verify that certain actions have been taken or certain outcomes have occurred. While actions or outcomes might be observable, meaning that investors know what the entrepreneur did, they are assumed not to be verifiable: that is, investors could not convince a court of the action or outcome. Start-up firms are likely to face exactly these types of problems, making external financing costly or difficult to obtain.

If the information asymmetries could be eliminated, financing constraints would disappear. Financial economists argue that specialized financial intermediaries, such as venture capital organizations, can address these problems. By intensively scrutinizing firms before providing capital and then monitoring them afterwards, they can alleviate some of the information gaps and reduce capital constraints. Thus, it is important to understand the tools employed by venture investors discussed below as responses to this difficult environment, which enable firms to ultimately receive the financing that they cannot raise from other sources. It is the nonmonetary aspects of venture capital that are critical to its success.

13.3.3. The Specific Tools

One of the most common features of venture capital is the meting out of financing in discrete stages over time. Sahlman (1990) notes that staged capital infusion is the most potent control mechanism a venture capitalist can employ. Prospects for the firm are periodically reevaluated. The shorter the duration of an individual round of financing, the more frequently the venture capitalist monitors the entrepreneur's progress and the greater the need to gather information. Staged capital infusion keeps the owner/manager on a "tight leash" and reduces potential losses from bad decisions.[5]

The research on conflicts between investors and managers discussed above suggests several factors that should affect the duration and size of venture capital investments. Venture capitalists should weigh potential agency and monitoring costs when determining how frequently they should reevaluate projects and supply capital. The duration of funding should decline and the frequency of reevaluation should increase when the venture capitalist expects conflicts with the entrepreneur.

If monitoring and information gathering are important—as models by Admati and Pfleiderer (1994), Amit et al. (1990a,b), and Chan (1983) suggest—venture capitalists should invest in firms in which asymmetric information is likely to be a problem. The value of oversight will be greater for these firms. The capital constraints faced by these companies will be very large and the information gathered will help alleviate the constraint. Early-stage companies have short or no histories to examine and are difficult to evaluate. Similarly, high-technology companies are likely to require close monitoring. A significant fraction of venture investment should therefore be directed towards early-stage and high-technology companies.

In practice, venture capitalists incur costs when they monitor and infuse capital. Monitoring costs include the opportunity cost of generating reports for both the venture capitalist and entrepreneur. If venture capitalists need to "kick the tires" of the plant, read reports, and take time away from other activities, these costs can be substantial. Contracting costs (e.g., legal fees) and the lost time and resources of the entrepreneur must be imputed as well. These costs lead to funding being provided in discrete stages.

Even though venture capitalists periodically "check-up" on entrepreneurs between capital infusions, entrepreneurs still have private information about the projects that they manage. Gorman and Sahlman (1989) show that

---

[5] Two related types of agency costs exist in entrepreneurial firms. Both agency costs result from the large information asymmetries that affect young, growth companies in need of financing. First, entrepreneurs might invest in strategies, research, or projects that have high personal returns but low expected monetary payoffs to shareholders. For example, a biotechnology company founder may choose to invest in a certain type of research that brings him/her great recognition in the scientific community but provides little return for the venture capitalist. Similarly, entrepreneurs may receive initial results from market trials indicating little demand for a new product, but may want to keep the company going because they receive significant private benefits from managing their own firm. Second, because entrepreneurs' equity stakes are essentially call options, they have incentives to pursue highly volatile strategies, such as rushing a product to market when further testing may be warranted.

between financing rounds, the lead venture capitalist visits the entrepreneur once a month on average and spends four to five hours at the facility during each visit. Venture capitalists also receive monthly financial reports. Gorman and Sahlman show, however, that venture capitalists do not usually become involved in the day-to-day management of the firm. Major reviews of progress and extensive due diligence are confined to the time of refinancing. The checks between financings are designed to limit opportunistic behavior by entrepreneurs between evaluations.

The nature of the firm's assets also has important implications for expected agency costs and the structure of staged venture capital investments. Intangible assets should be associated with greater agency problems. As assets become more tangible, venture capitalists can recover more of their investment in liquidation. This reduces the need to monitor tightly and should increase the time between refinancings. Industries with high levels of R&D should also have more frequent agency problems, and venture capitalists should shorten funding duration. Finally, a substantial finance literature (e.g., Myers, 1977) argues that firms with high market-to-book ratios are more susceptible to these agency costs, thus venture capitalists should increase the intensity of monitoring of these firms.

Gompers (1995) tests these predictions using a random sample of 794 venture capital-financed companies. The results confirm the predictions of agency theory. Venture capitalists concentrate investments in early stage companies and high-technology industries where informational asymmetries are significant and monitoring is valuable. Venture capitalists monitor the firm's progress. If they learn negative information about future returns, the project is cut off from new financing. Firms that go public (these firms yield the highest return for venture capitalists on average) receive more total financing and a greater number of rounds than other firms (which may go bankrupt, be acquired, or remain private). Gompers also finds that early stage firms receive significantly less money per round. Increases in asset tangibility increase

financing duration and reduce monitoring intensity. As the role of future investment opportunities in firm value increases (higher market-to-book ratios or R&D intensities), firms are refinanced more frequently. These results suggest the important monitoring and information generating roles played by venture capitalists. Consistent evidence regarding the actual contractual terms in these agreements is found in Kaplan and Stromberg's (1999) analysis of 130 venture partnership agreements.

Why cannot other financial intermediaries (e.g., banks) undertake the same sort of monitoring? First, because regulations limit banks' ability to hold shares, they cannot freely use equity to fund projects. Although several papers focus on monitoring by banks (James, 1987; Hoshi et al., 1990; Petersen and Rajan, 1994, 1995), banks may not have the necessary skills to evaluate projects with few collateralizable assets and significant uncertainty. In addition, Petersen and Rajan (1995) argue that banks in competitive markets will be unable to finance high-risk projects because they are unable to charge borrowers rates high enough to compensate for the firm's riskiness. Taking an equity position in the firm allows the venture capitalist to proportionately share in the upside, guaranteeing that the venture capitalist benefits if the firm does well. Finally, venture capital funds' high-powered compensation schemes give venture capitalists incentives to monitor firms more closely, because their individual compensation is closely linked to the funds' returns. Corporations, investment banks, and other institutions that have sponsored venture funds without such high-powered incentives have found it difficult to retain personnel, once the venture capitalists have developed a performance record that enables them to raise a fund of their own.

In addition to the staged capital infusions, venture capitalists will usually make investments with other investors. One venture firm will originate the deal and look to bring in other venture capital firms. This syndication serves multiple purposes. First, it allows the venture capital firm to diversify. If the venture capitalist had to invest alone into all the companies in his portfolio, then he could make many fewer investments. By syndicating investments, the venture capitalist can invest in more projects and largely diversify away firm-specific risk.

For example, a typical venture capital firm may raise a fund of between fifty and one hundred million dollars. In any one particular round, a portfolio company receives between two and five million dollars. If the typical venture-backed company receives four rounds of venture financing, any one firm might require between ten and twenty million dollars of financing. If the venture capital firm originating the deal were to make the entire investment, the fund could only make five to ten investments. Hence, the value of bringing in syndication partners for diversification is large.

A second potential explanation for syndication patterns is that involving other venture firms provides as a second opinion on the investment opportunity. There is usually no clear-cut answer as to whether any of the investments that a venture organization undertakes will yield attractive returns. Having other investors approve the deal limits the danger that bad deals will get funded. This is particularly true when the company is early-stage or technology-based.

Lerner (1994a) tests this "second opinion" hypothesis in a sample of biotechnology venture capital investments. In a sample of 271 firms, Lerner finds that in the early rounds of investing, experienced venture capitalists tend to syndicate only with venture capital firms that have similar experience. Lerner argues that if a venture capitalist were looking for a second opinion, then he would want to get a second opinion from someone of similar or better ability, certainly not from someone of lesser ability.

The advice and support provided by venture capitalists is often embodied by their role on the firm's board of directors. Lerner (1995) examines the decision of venture capitalists to provide this oversight. He examines whether venture capitalists' representation on the boards of the private firms in their portfolios is greater when the need for oversight is larger. This approach is suggested by Fama and Jensen (1983) and Williamson (1983), who hypothesize that the composition of the board should be shaped by the need for oversight. These authors argue that the board will bear greater responsibility for oversight—and consequently that outsiders should have greater representation—when the danger of managerial deviations from value maximization is high. If venture capitalists are especially important providers of managerial oversight, their representation on boards should be more extensive at times when the need for oversight is greater.

Lerner (1995) examines changes in board membership around the time that a firm's chief executive officer (CEO) is replaced, an approach suggested by Hermalin and Weisbach's (1988) study of outside directors of public firms. The replacement of the top manager at an entrepreneurial firm is likely to coincide with an organizational crisis and to heighten the need for monitoring. An average of 1.75 venture capitalists are added to the board between financing rounds when the firm's CEO is replaced in the interval; between other rounds, 0.24 venture directors are added. No differences are found in the addition of other outside directors. This oversight of new firms involves substantial costs. The transaction costs associated with frequent visits and intensive involvement are likely to be reduced if the venture capitalist is proximate to the firms in his portfolio. Consistent with these suggestions, geographic proximity is an important determinant of venture board membership: organizations with offices within five miles of the firm's headquarters are twice as likely to be board members as those more than 500 miles distant. Over half the firms in the sample have a venture director with an office within sixty miles of their headquarters.

Another mechanism utilized by venture capitalists to avoid conflicts is the widespread use of stock grants and stock options. Managers and critical employees within a firm receive a substantial fraction of their compensation in the form of equity or options. This tends to align the incentives of managers and investors, unlike large public companies, where the CEO's personal wealth typically increases by only a dollar or two for each U.S.$1000 increase in firm value.

The venture capitalist also employs additional controls on compensation to reduce potential gaming by the entrepreneur. First, venture capitalists usually require vesting of the stock or options over a multi-year period. In this way, the entrepreneur cannot leave the firm and take his shares. Similarly, the venture capitalist can significantly dilute the entrepreneur's stake in subsequent financings if the firm fails to realize its targets. This provides additional incentives for the entrepreneur. In order to maintain his stake, the entrepreneur will need to meet his stated targets.

13.3.4. Distortions to the Venture Investment Process

Until this point, this section has highlighted the ways in which venture capitalists can successfully address agency problems in portfolio firms. The argument is often made by venture capital practitioners, however, that the industry has gone through periods of disequilibrium. During periods when the amount of money flowing into the industry has dramatically grown, they argue, the valuations at which investments are made or the likelihood that certain transactions get funded can shift dramatically. If there are only a certain number of worthy projects to finance, then a substantial increase in the amount of venture fund-raising may increase the prices that are paid to invest in these companies. These higher prices may ultimately affect the returns on investment in the industry.

Sahlman and Stevenson (1987) chronicle the exploits of venture capitalists in the Winchester disk drive industry during the early 1980s. Sahlman and Stevenson believe that a type of "market myopia" affected venture capital investing in the industry. During the late 1970s and early 1980s, nineteen disk drive companies received venture capital financing. Two-thirds of these investments came between 1982 and 1984, the period of rapid expansion of the venture industry. Many disk drive companies also went public during this period. While industry growth was rapid during this period of time (sales increased from U.S.$27 million in 1978 to U.S.$1.3 billion in 1983), Sahlman and Stevenson question whether the scale of investment was rational given any reasonable

expectations of industry growth and future economic trends.[6] Similar stories are often told concerning investments in software, biotechnology, and the Internet. The phrase "too much money chasing too few deals" is a common refrain in the venture capital market during periods of rapid growth.

Gompers and Lerner (2000) examine these claims through a dataset of over 4000 venture investments between 1987 and 1995 developed by the consulting firm VentureOne. They construct a hedonic price index that controls for various firm attributes that might affect firm valuation, including firm age, stage of development, and industry, as well as macroeconomic variables such as inflow of funds into the venture capital industry. In addition, they control for public market valuations through indexes of public market values for firms in the same industries and average book-to-market and earnings-to-price ratios.

The results support contentions that a strong relation exists between the valuation of venture capital investments and capital inflows. While other variables also have significant explanatory power—for instance, the marginal impact of a doubling in public market values was between a 15 and 35 percent increase in the valuation of private equity transactions—the inflows variable is significantly positive. A doubling of inflows into venture funds leads to between a 7 and 21 percent increase in valuation levels.

The overall price index is depicted in Figure 13.3. The index is constructed such that the price level in the first quarter of 1987 is set equal to 100. The index controls for differences in the underlying deals in the venture industry. While prices rose somewhat in 1987, they declined and remained quite flat through the 1990s. Starting in 1994, however, prices steadily increased. This increase coincided with the recent rise in venture fund-raising. The regres-

[6] Lerner (1997) suggests, however, that these firms may have displayed behavior consistent with strategic models of "technology races" in the economics literature. Because firms had the option to exit the competition to develop a new disk drive, it may have indeed been rational for venture capitalists to fund a substantial number of disk drive manufacturers.

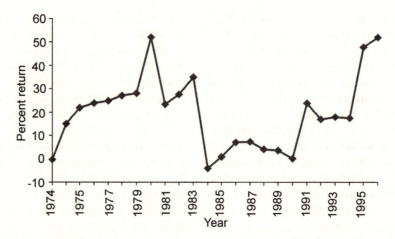

Figure 13.3 Price index of venture capital investments. The chart depicts the relative price of venture capital investments, controlling for changes in the companies funded. *Source:* Gompers and Lerner (2000).

sion results show that this rise in fund-raising is an important source of the increase in prices.

The results are particularly strong for specific types of funds and funds in particular regions. Because funds have become larger in real dollar terms, with more capital per partner, many venture capital organizations have invested larger amounts of money in each portfolio company. Firms have attempted to do this in two ways. First, there has been a movement to finance later-stage companies that can accept larger blocks of financing. Second, venture firms are syndicating less. This leads to greater competition for making later-stage investments. Similarly, because the majority of money is raised in California and Massachusetts, competition for deals in these regions should be particularly intense and venture capital inflows may have a more dramatic effect on prices in those regions. The results support these contentions. The effect of venture capital inflows is significantly more dramatic on later-stage investments and investments in California and Massachusetts.

Gompers and Lerner (2000) also examine whether increases in venture capital inflows and valuations simultaneously reflect improvements in the environment for young firms. If shifts in the supply of venture capital are contemporaneous with changes in the demand for capital, their inferences may be biased. They show that success rates—whether measured

through the completion of an IPO or an acquisition at an attractive price—did not differ significantly between investments made during the early 1990s, a period of relatively low inflows and valuations, and those of the boom years of the late 1980s. The results seem to indicate that the price increases reflect increasing competition for investment.

13.3.5. Exiting Venture Capital Investments

The final stage in the investment process is exiting. In order to make money on their investments, venture capitalists need to turn illiquid stakes in private companies into realized return. Typically, as was discussed above, the most profitable exit opportunity is an IPO. In an IPO, the venture capitalist assists the company in issuing shares to the public for the first time. Table 13.5 summarizes the exiting of venture capital investments through IPOs as well as comparable data on nonventure capital offerings.

Initial empirical research into the role of venture capitalists in exiting investments focused on the structure of IPOs. Barry et al. (1990) focus on establishing a broad array of facts about the role of venture capitalists in IPOs, using a sample of 433 venture-backed and 1123 nonventure IPOs between 1978 and 1987.

Barry et al. (1990) document that venture capitalists hold significant equity stakes in the

TABLE 13.5

The Distribution of Venture-Backed and Nonventure IPOs for the period 1978–99

Year	Number of venture-backed IPOs	Amount raised in venture-backed IPOs (U.S.$)	Total number of IPOs	Total amount raised in all IPOs (U.S.$)	Venture-backed IPOs as percent of all IPOs (number)	Venture-backed IPOs as percent of all IPOs (amount)
1978	6	134	42	485	12.50	21.59
1979	4	62	103	777	3.74	7.34
1980	24	670	259	2327	8.48	22.35
1981	50	783	438	4848	10.25	13.91
1982	21	738	198	1901	9.59	27.97
1983	101	3451	848	17999	10.64	16.09
1984	44	731	516	5179	7.86	12.37
1985	35	819	507	13307	6.46	5.80
1986	79	2003	953	23902	7.66	7.73
1987	69	1602	630	19721	9.87	7.52
1988	36	915	435	6679	8.28	13.70
1989	39	1110	371	6763	10.51	16.41
1990	43	1269	276	4828	15.58	16.29
1991	119	3835	367	16872	32.43	22.73
1992	157	4317	509	23990	30.84	17.99
1993	193	4905	707	40456	27.30	12.12
1994	159	3408	564	27786	28.19	12.26
1995	205	6251	566	36219	36.22	17.26
1996	284	10976	845	38245	33.61	28.70
1997	138	4419	628	40278	21.34	10.60
1998	78	3388	319	31075	24.45	10.90
1999	271	20757	485	56952	55.87	36.45

Sources: Barry et al. (1990), Ritter (1998), and various issues of the *Going Public: The IPO Reporter* and the *Venture Capital Journal.*
Notes: This table compares the distribution of IPOs in this sample versus all IPOs recorded over this period of time. All dollar figures are in millions of 1992 U.S. dollars.

firms they take public (on average, the lead venture capitalist holds a 19 percent stake immediately prior to the IPO, and all venture investors hold 34 percent), and hold about one-third of the board seats. They continue to hold their equity positions in the year after the IPO. Finally, venture-backed IPOs have less of a positive return on their first trading day. The authors suggest that this implies that investors need less of a discount in order to purchase these shares (i.e., the offerings are less "under-priced"), because the venture capitalist has monitored the quality of the offering.

Megginson and Weiss (1991) argue that because venture capitalists repeatedly bring

firms to the public market, they can credibly stake their reputation. Put another way, they can certify to investors that the firms they bring to market are not overvalued. Certification requires that venture capitalists possess reputational capital, that the acquisition of such a reputation is costly, and that the present value of lost reputational capital by cheating is greater than the one-time gain from behaving in a duplicitous manner.

The certification model yields several empirical implications. First, because venture capitalists repeatedly take firms public, they build relationships with underwriters and auditors. These relationships may lead to the average venture-backed IPO having higher-quality underwriters and auditors than nonventure IPOs. Megginson and Weiss (1991) also argue that these relationships and the existence of reputation should lead to greater institutional holdings of the venture-backed firm after IPO. Megginson and Weiss (1991) also argue that the retention of large stakes of equity both before and after the IPO is a "bonding mechanism" that increases the effectiveness of the venture capitalist's certification. Any benefit to issuing overpriced shares would be minimized because the venture capitalist sells few or no shares at IPO. Megginson and Weiss (1991) test these ideas using a matched set of 640 venture-backed and nonventure IPOs between 1983 and 1987, and find results generally consistent with their hypotheses.

More recent research has examined the timing of the decision to take firms public and to liquidate the venture capitalists' holdings (which frequently occurs well after the IPO). Several potential factors affect when venture capitalists choose to bring firms public. One of these is the relative valuation level of publicly traded securities. Lerner (1994b) examines when venture capitalists choose to finance a sample of biotechnology companies in another private round versus taking the firm public. Using a sample of 350 privately held venture-backed firms, he shows that firms are taken public at market peaks, relying on private financings when valuations are lower. Seasoned venture capitalists appear more proficient at timing IPOs. The results are robust to the use of alternative criteria to separate firms and controls for firms' quality. The results are not caused by differences in the speed of executing the IPOs, or in the willingness to withdraw the proposed IPOs.

Another consideration may be the reputation of the venture capital firm. Gompers (1996) argues that young venture capital firms have incentives to "grandstand": that is, they take actions that signal their ability to potential investors. Specifically, young venture capital firms bring companies public earlier than older venture capital firms in an effort to establish a reputation and successfully raise capital for new funds. He examines a sample of 433 venture-backed IPOs between 1978 and 1987, as well

as a second sample consisting of the first IPOs brought to market by 62 venture capital funds. The results support predictions of the grandstanding hypothesis.

The typical venture capital firm, however, does not sell their equity at the time of the IPO. The negative signal that would be sent to the market by an insider "cashing out" would prevent a successful offering. In addition, most investment banks require that all insiders, including the venture capitalists, do not sell any of their equity after the offering for a prespecified period (usually six months). Once that lock-up period is over, however, venture capitalists can return money to investors in one of two ways. They can sell the shares and return cash to investors or distribute the shares themselves. Many institutional investors have received a flood of these distributions during the past several years and have grown increasingly concerned about the incentives of the venture capitalists when they declare these transfers.

Gompers and Lerner (1998) examine how investors might be affected by distributions. These distributions have several features that make them an interesting testing ground for an examination of the impact of transactions by informed insiders on securities prices. Because they are not considered to be "sales", the distributions are exempt from the anti-fraud and anti-manipulation provisions of the securities laws. The legality of distributions provides an important advantage. Comprehensive records of these transactions are compiled by the institutional investors and the intermediaries who invest in venture funds, addressing concerns about sample selection bias.

Like trades by corporate insiders, transactions are not revealed at the time of the transaction. Rather, the occurrence of such distributions can only be discovered from corporate filings with a lag, and even then the distribution date cannot be precisely identified. To identify the time of these transactions, one needs to rely on the records of the partners in the fund. The authors characterize the features of the venture funds making the distributions, the firms whose shares are being distributed, and the changes associated with the transactions in a way that

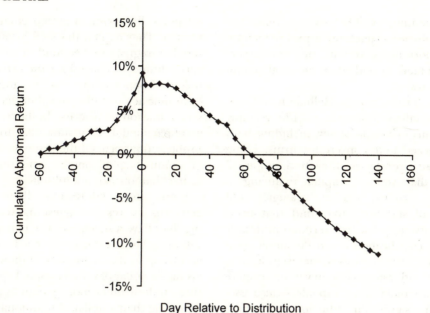

Figure 13.4 Stock price around distribution of equity by venture capitalists. The graph plots the cumulative abnormal return from sixty days prior to distribution to 140 days after distribution. *Source:* Gompers and Lerner (1998a).

allows them to distinguish between various alternative explanations for these patterns.

From the records of four institutions, Gompers and Lerner (1998a) construct a representative set of over 700 transactions by 135 funds over a decade-long period. The results are consistent with venture capitalists possessing inside information and of the (partial) adjustment of the market to that information. As depicted in Figure 13.4, after significant increases in stock prices prior to distribution, abnormal returns around the distribution are a negative and significant −2.0 percent, comparable to the market reaction to publicly announced secondary stock sales. The sign and significance of the cumulative excess returns for the twelve months following the distribution appear to be negative in most specifications, but are sensitive to the benchmark used.

13.4. Venture Capital and Technological Innovation

The research discussed so far in this chapter has focused on how venture capital organizations work. While this research is clearly related to the central issue of this volume—without the unique structural features of the venture capital industry, it is unlikely that this chapter would have been solicited at all!—it does not answer the central question of whether venture capital "matters." Is venture capital particularly effective in stimulating innovation?

This question is very important. A key motivation for policymakers seeking to emulate the U.S. model is the perception that venture capital organizations have had much to do with the rising leadership of U.S. firms in high-technology industries, whether measured through patent counts or more qualitative measures. But demonstrating a casual relationship between innovation and job growth on the one hand and the presence of venture capital investment on the other is a challenging empirical problem.

It might be thought that it would be not difficult to address this question. For instance, one could look in regressions across industries and time whether, controlling for R&D spending, venture capital funding has an impact on the number of patents or other measures of innovation. But even a simple model of the relationship between venture capital, R&D, and innovation suggests that this approach is likely to give misleading estimates. Both venture funding and patenting could be positively related to a third unobserved factor, the arrival of technological opportunities. To date, only two papers have attempted to address these challenging estimation issues.

The first of these papers, Hellmann and Puri (1998), examines a sample of 170 recently formed firms in Silicon Valley, including both venture-backed and nonventure firms. Using questionnaire responses, they find empirical evidence that venture capital financing is related to product market strategies and outcomes of start-ups. They find that firms that are pursuing what they term an innovator strategy (a classification based on the content analysis of survey responses) are significantly more likely and faster to obtain venture capital. The presence of a venture capitalist is also associated with a significant reduction in the time taken to bring a product to market, especially for innovators. Furthermore, firms are more likely to list obtaining venture capital as a significant milestone in the life cycle of the company as compared to other financing events.

The results suggest significant interrelations between investor type and product market dimensions, and a role of venture capital in encouraging innovative companies. Given the small size of the sample and the limited data, they can only modestly address concerns about causality. Unfortunately, the possibility remains that more innovative firms select venture capital for financing, rather than venture capital causing firms to be more innovative.

Kortum and Lerner (2000), by way of contrast, examine whether these patterns can be discerned on an aggregate industry level, rather than on the firm level. They address concerns about causality in two ways. First, they exploit the major discontinuity in the recent history of the venture capital industry: as discussed above, in the late 1970s, the U.S. Department of Labor clarified the Employee Retirement Income Security Act, a policy shift that freed pensions to invest in venture capital. This shift led to a sharp increase in the funds committed to venture capital. This type of exogenous change should identify the role of venture capital, because it is unlikely to be

related to the arrival of entrepreneurial opportunities. They exploit this shift in instrumental variable regressions. Second, they use R&D expenditures to control for the arrival of technological opportunities that are anticipated by economic actors at the time, but that are unobserved to econometricians. In the framework of a simple model, they show that the causality problem disappears if they estimate the impact of venture capital on the patent/R&D ratio, rather than on patenting itself.

Even after addressing these causality concerns, the results suggest that venture funding does have a strong positive impact on innovation. The estimated coefficients vary according to the techniques employed, but on average a dollar of venture capital appears to be three to four times more potent in stimulating patenting than a dollar of traditional corporate R&D. The estimates therefore suggest that venture capital, even though it averaged less than three percent of corporate R&D from 1983 to 1992, is responsible for a much greater share—perhaps ten percent—of U.S. industrial innovations in this decade.

In their concluding remarks, Kortum and Lerner (2000) suggest that the growth of the venture capital industry is one of these key changes in the management of innovative activities that has led to the recent surge in patenting in the United States. Other innovations in organizing research did occur contemporaneously. For example, central R&D facilities of large corporations have been redirected toward more applied problems. They identify the parallel rise of venture capital and other R&D management innovations as an important issue, which, while challenging to explore empirically, is worthy of further investigation.

13.5. Future Research

While financial economists know much more about venture capital than they did a decade ago, there are many unresolved issues that would reward future research. While a number of these are indicted in the course of the discussion, this section highlights the area where research is most needed: the internationalization of venture capital.

The rapid growth in the U.S. venture capital market have led institutional investors to look increasingly at private equity alternatives abroad. Until very recently, outside of the United Kingdom (where performance of funds has been quite poor) and Israel there has been little venture capital activity abroad.[7] (Table 13.6 provides an international comparison of venture capital activity.) Black and Gilson (1998) argue that the key source of the U.S. competitive advantage in venture capital is the existence of a robust IPO market. Venture capitalists can commit to transfer control back to the entrepreneur when a public equity market for new issues exists. This commitment device is unavailable in economies dominated by banks, such as Germany and Japan.

These arguments, however, have less credibility in light of the events of the past two years. There has been a surge in venture capital investment, particularly relating to the Internet, in a wide variety of nations across Asia, Europe, and Latin America. While some of these investments have been made by local groups (many recently established), much of the activities have been driven by U.S.-based organizations.

The changes in Europe are illustrative. On the venture capital side, the same changes have happened on a much more accelerated time frame. As the European private equity industry emerged in the early 1980s, there was a significant representation of venture capital investments. Over time, however, the venture capital portion dwindled dramatically. The shrinking representation of venture capital investments reflected their poor performance. Between 1980 and 1994, for instance, while the average mature large buyout fund in the United

---

[7] One potential source of confusion is that the term venture capital is used differently different in Europe and Asia. Abroad, venture capital often refers to all private equity, including buyout, late stage, and mezzanine financing (which represent the vast majority of the private equity pool in most overseas markets). In the United States, these are separate classes. We confine our discussion of international trends—as the rest of the chapter—to venture capital using the restrictive, U.S. definition.

TABLE 13.6

The Size of the Venture Capital Pool in Twenty-One Nations in 1995 (millions of current U.S.$)

Country	Total venture capital under management
Australia	54
Austria	0.4
Belgium	8
Canada	182
Denmark	4
Finland	1
France	35
Germany	116
Ireland	1
Israel	550
Italy	60
Japan	11
Netherlands	100
New Zealand	1
Norway	7
Portugal	9
Spain	24
Sweden	9
Switzerland	1
United Kingdom	36
United States	3651

Source: Compiled from Jeng and Wells (1999), slightly amended by the author.

Notes: Jeng and Wells' (1999) figures are used for early-stage funds in each country outside the United States because they are most comparable to venture capital funds as defined in the United States. Figures for Australia and New Zealand are 1994 estimated levels; figures for Israel are a 1995 estimate; and figures for Portugal are the actual level in 1994.

Kingdom boasted a net return of 23.1 percent and the average mid-sized buyout fund had a return of 14.7 percent. Meanwhile, the typical venture fund had a net return of 4.0 percent over the same period (*European Venture Capital Journal*, 1996). As a result, most venture capital specialists were unable to new funds, and generalist investors (such as Apax and 3i) shifted to an emphasis on buyouts.

This situation began reversing itself around 1997. The shifting attitudes were in part triggered by U.S. venture groups, particularly East Coast-based organizations such as General

Atlantic and Warburg Pincus. Attracted by the modest valuations of European technology and biotechnology start-ups relative to their U.S. counterparts, general partners began increasingly traveling to Europe to invest in portfolio companies. This trend accelerated at the end of the decade, as U.S. groups such as Benchmark and Draper Fisher Jurvetson began targeting large amounts of capital (sometimes in dedicated funds) for European venture investments. The trend was also helped by the superior performance of venture investments in the last years of the decade. In fact, by the end of 1999, the ten year performance of venture capital funds (17.2 percent) was almost indistinguishable from that of buyout ones (17.5 percent) (Venture Economics, 2000a) (Generalist funds performed significantly more poorly, with 9.5 percent rate of return over this period.)

Meanwhile, European-based funds also became more active. The increase in activity was manifested in three ways. First, groups that had been active for a number of years, such as Atlas Ventures, were able to raise significantly larger amounts of funds. Second, new entrants—in many cases modeled after U.S. groups—became increasingly active. (Examples include Amadeus in the United Kingdom and Early Bird in Germany). Finally, generalist funds increased their allocation to venture capital again: for instance, over the late 1990s, 3i moved from a 15 percent allocation to technology funds to a 40 percent share.

In a pioneering study, Jeng and Wells (1999) examine the factors that influence venture capital fund-raising in twenty-one countries. They find that the strength of the IPO market is an important factor in the determinant of venture capital commitments, echoing the conclusions of Black and Gilson. Jeng and Wells find, however, that the IPO market does not seem to influence commitments to early-stage funds as much as later-stage ones. While this work represents an important initial step, much more remains to be explored regarding the internationalization of venture capital.

One provocative finding from the Jeng and Wells analysis is that government policy can have a dramatic impact on the current and long-term viability of the venture capital sector. In many countries, especially those in Continental Europe, policymakers face a dilemma. The relatively few entrepreneurs active in these markets face numerous daunting regulatory restrictions, a paucity of venture funds focusing on investing in high-growth firms, and illiquid markets where investors do not welcome IPOs by young firms without long histories of positive earnings. It is often unclear where to begin the process of duplicating the success of the United States. Only very recently have researchers begun to examine the ways in which policymakers can catalyze the growth of venture capital and the companies in which they invest. (Three recent exceptions are Irwin and Klenow (1996), Lerner (1999), and Wallsten (1996)). Given the size of recent initiatives undertaken both in the United States and abroad (summarized in Lerner, 1999; Gompers and Lerner, 1999a), much more needs to be done in this arena.

Pharmaceutical Biotechnology

Gary P. Pisano

14.1. Introduction

The last twenty-five years have seen a revolution in the biological sciences. This revolution includes, but is not limited to, the dramatic advances in a constellation of technologies that underpin the discovery of new drugs. Members of this constellation includes genetic engineering, genomics, combinatorial chemistry, high throughput screening, rational drug design, gene therapy, cell therapy, and many others. There has also been very considerable progress in our knowledge of the genetic and molecular processes underpinning a range of diseases. For the purposes of this chapter, these advances are defined collectively as the "Molecular Biology Revolution" (MBR). This revolution has had several dramatic effects on the pharmaceutical industry and, in particular, the system of innovation characterizing drug discovery and development. This chapter explores the impact the molecular biology revolution has had on the structure and organization of pharmaceutical industry.

Many previous studies of innovation have focused on the "disruptive" aspect of technological change on industry structure, and in particular, the performance of established

companies (e.g., Tushman and Anderson, 1985; Henderson and Clark, 1990; Christensen, 1997). The general conclusion from past research is that when technologies are either competence destroying from a technological point of view (Tushman and Anderson, 1985) or disrupt the links between a firm and its market (Christensen, 1997), new entrants have the upper hand and often successfully overturn previously dominant incumbents. However, past studies have generally focused on the impact of specific individual technologies. For example, Christensen examines the impact of successive generations of new disk drive technology. The molecular biology revolution, however, cannot be understood as a single technology, although it is often discussed in such a manner. Rather, as pointed out above, it is a constellation of several distinct, but related, trajectories of scientific advance. As such, it is best understood as a technological system. Moreover, it is a system that is neither completely new nor completely old, but instead is a hybrid of new science (e.g., genomics) and traditional fields (chemistry). Thus, the molecular biology revolution is not a simple story of one broad technological paradigm replacing another, but rather the overlaying of successive waves of scientific knowledge building upon one another in a complex technological landscape. Such a landscape is highly unstable. There is a high degree of uncertainty around which paths of advance will be most promising. The productivity of R&D in one field may be influenced by what occurs elsewhere (e.g., high throughput screening enhances the promise of combinatorial chemistry and genomics). This instability and uncertainty places a premium on institutional and organizational flexibility.

This chapter draws heavily from an earlier published paper entitled, "The Pharmaceutical Industry and the Revolution in Molecular Biology: Interactions Among Scientific, Institutional, and Organizational Change," by Rebecca Henderson, Luigi Orsenigo, and Gary Pisano and published as a chapter in *Source of Industrial Leadership*, ed. David Mowery and Richard Nelson, 1999, Oxford University Press. I am indebted to Richard Nelson, Benn Steil, and David Victor for comments on an earlier draft and to Clarissa Ceruti for research assistance.

In addition, the concept of "technological advance" in pharmaceuticals differs from that of other industries. Unlike other contexts, where technical change involves changes in product technology or manufacturing process technology, technical advance in pharmaceuticals since the last century fundamentally involves changes in the *methods of R&D*. The story of technical advance in pharmaceuticals is one of finding new ways to search for and select therapeutic compounds. In pharmaceuticals, more than in other industries, it is the "technology of R&D" itself which changes. This characteristic reinforces the link between technical advance and organizational flexibility in pharmaceuticals.

This chapter focuses on two questions. The first concerns the role of start-up companies and established pharmaceutical companies in commercializing new technologies. A striking characteristic of the MBR is the extent to which it has proceeded through collaborations between new firms and established firms. The MBR is more than just a scientific revolution; it has also revolutionized the institutional and organizational arrangements through which drug discovery and development take place. A second issue we explore is the dominance of the United States as a locus of commercial R&D in these new technologies. Measured in various ways—formation of new enterprises, origination of new drugs based on these new technologies, R&D investments, and patenting—the United States has been an extremely fertile ground for commercial development of the MBR. Throughout this chapter, we argue that the impact of new science on the pharmaceutical industry has been and continues to be mitigated by two sets of factors. One is the set of institutional conditions (e.g., government funding of basic research, university systems, intellectual property regimes, and regulations) that influence patterns of activity and firm behaviors at the national or at least regional level. Equally important, however, has been a second factor: management. One simply cannot tell the story of the MRB without reference to how the new technologies have changed the way the drug R&D process is managed. Different pharmaceutical firms have developed different capabilities

for drug R&D (Henderson and Cockburn, 1996). And different firms have pursued different strategies with respect to adopting and utilizing the new technologies. The fact that there is significant variation within countries in the performance of pharmaceutical firms suggest that management at the individual firm level matters a great deal.

14.2. Historical Background

The history of the pharmaceutical industry can be divided into approximately three major epochs. Each epoch can be characterized by the dominant approach used by scientists to search for and screen therapeutic compounds. The first, corresponding roughly to the period 1850–1945, can be thought of as the pre–R&D period in which little new drug development occurred, and that which did was based on relatively primitive research methods. The large-scale development of penicillin during World War II marked the emergence of a second period of industry evolution that was characterized by the institution of formalized in-house R&D programs and relatively rapid rates of new drug introduction. As discussed below, this period also witnessed the creation of a particular approach to drug discovery based on random screening of natural and chemically synthesized compounds. The third epoch of the industry, and the one constituting the main focus of this chapter, began during the past decade with the growing application of molecular biology and related bodies of scientific knowledge to the discovery, development, and manufacture of new therapeutics.

In this section, we briefly review the first two of these periods. Section 14.3 turns to the industry during the MBR. Understanding the evolution of the industry during these earlier periods is important for the discussion that comes later, as they played a critical role in building and molding the basic industrial and institutional structure of the industry, as well as the organizational capabilities of individual firms, which still influence the industry today.

14.2.1 Early History

By almost any measure (including R&D intensity, innovative output, and the use of new scientific concepts), pharmaceuticals are a classic "high technology" or "science-based" industry. Yet drugs are as old as antiquity. For example, the Ebers Papyrus lists 811 prescriptions used in Egypt in 550 B.C. Eighteenth century France and Germany had pharmacies where pharmacists working in well-equipped laboratories produced therapeutic ingredients of known identity and purity on a small scale. Mass production of drugs dates back to 1813, when J.B. Trommsdof opened the first specialized pharmaceutical plant in Germany. However, during the first half of the nineteenth century, there were virtually no standardized medicines for treating specific conditions. A patient instead would be given a customized prescription that would be formulated at the local pharmacy by hand.

The birth of the modern pharmaceutical industry can be traced to the mid-nineteenth century with the emergence of the synthetic dye industry in German and Switzerland. At that time, Switzerland and Germany were the leading centers of the synthetic dye industry (this was due in part to the strength of German universities in organic chemistry, and in part to the fact that Basel was close to the leading silk and textile regions of Germany and France). During the 1880s, the medicinal effects (such as antiseptic properties) of dyestuffs and other organic chemicals were discovered. It was thus initially Swiss and German chemical companies such as Ciba, Sandoz, Bayer, and Hoechst, leveraging their technical competencies in organic chemistry and dyestuffs, who began to manufacture drugs (usually based on synthetic dyes) later in the nineteenth century. Aspirin, for example, was first produced in 1899 by the German company Bayer.

In the United States and the United Kingdom, mass production of pharmaceuticals also commenced in the later part of the nineteenth century. However, the pattern of development there was quite different from that of Germany and Switzerland. Whereas Swiss and German pharmaceutical activities tended to emerge within larger chemical producing enterprises, the United States and the United Kingdom witnessed the birth of specialized pharmaceutical producers such as Wyeth (later American Home Products) Eli Lilly, Merck, Pfizer, Warner-Lambert, and Burroughs-Wellcome. However, up until World War I, German companies dominated the industry, producing approximately 80 percent of the world's pharmaceutical output.

While pharmaceuticals might be considered a science-based industry today, it certainly did not begin as such. Until the 1930s, when sulfonamide was discovered, drug companies undertook little formal research on new drugs. Most new drugs were based on existing organic chemicals or derived from natural sources (e.g., herbs) and little formal testing was done to ensure either safety or efficacy.

World War II and wartime needs for antibiotics marked the drug industry's transition to an R&D intensive business. Penicillin and its antibiotic properties were discovered by Alexander Fleming in 1928; however, throughout the 1930s, it was produced only in laboratory-scale quantities and used almost exclusively for experimental purposes. With the outbreak of World War II, the U.S. government organized a massive research and production effort that focused on commercial production techniques and chemical structure analysis. More than twenty companies, several universities, and the Department of Agriculture took part. Pfizer, which had production experience in fermentation, developed a deep-tank fermentation process for producing large quantities of penicillin. This system led to major gains in productivity and, more important, laid out an architecture for the process and created a framework in which future improvements could take place.

The commercialization of penicillin marked a watershed in the industry's development.

Due partially to the technical experience and organizational capabilities accumulated through the intense wartime effort to develop penicillin as well as to the recognition that drug development could be highly profitable, pharmaceutical companies embarked on a period of massive investment in R&D and built large-scale internal R&D capabilities.

14.2.2 Patterns of Competition and Industrial Organization: 1950–90

The period from 1950 to 1990 could be classified as a golden age for the pharmaceutical industry. The industry and particularly the main U.S. players such as Merck, Eli Lilly, Bristol-Myers, and Pfizer grew rapidly and profitably. R&D spending on new drugs literally exploded and with this came a steady flow of new drugs. Drug innovation was a highly profitable activity during most of this period. Statman (1983), for example, estimated that accounting rates of return on new drugs introduced between 1954 and 1978 averaged 20.9 percent (compared to a cost of capital of 10.7 percent). Between 1982 and 1992, firms in the industry grew at an average annual rate of 18 percent. During the early 1980s, double-digit rates of growth in earnings and return-on-equity were the norm for most pharmaceutical companies and the industry as a whole ranked among the most profitable in the United States.

A number of structural factors supported the industry's high average level of innovation and economic performance. One was the sheer magnitude of R&D opportunities and unmet needs. In the early post-war years, there were many physical ailments and diseases for which no drugs existed. In every major therapeutic category from pain killers and anti-inflammatories to cardiovascular and central nervous system products pharmaceutical companies faced a completely open field (it must be kept in mind that before the discovery of penicillin, there were precious few drugs that effectively cured diseases). Faced with such a "target rich" environment but very little detailed knowledge of the biological underpinnings of specific diseases, pharmaceutical companies invented an approach to R&D now referred to as "random screening."

Under this approach, natural and chemically derived compounds were randomly screened in test tube experiments and laboratory animals for potential therapeutic activity. Pharmaceutical companies maintained enormous "libraries" of chemical compounds, and added to their collections by searching for new compounds in swamps, streams, and soil samples. Thousands, if not tens of thousands, of compounds might be subjected to multiple screens before researchers honed in on a promising substance. Serendipity played a key role. In fact, it was not uncommon for companies to discover a drug to treat one disease while searching for a treatment for another. Although random screening may appear ineffective, it worked extremely well for many years. Several hundred chemical entities were introduced in the 1950s and 1960s and, as several important classes of drug were discovered in this way, including a number of important diuretics, all of the early vasodilators, and a number of centrally acting agents including reserpine and guanethidine (Henderson, 1994: 613). Even many drugs hitting the market today still reflect the highly random nature of drug discovery. For instance, Pfizer initially attempted to develop Viagra, the enormously successful drug for erectile dysfunction introduced to the market in 1998, as a treatment for hypertension.

It was also during this period that the industry began to benefit more directly from the explosion in public funding for health-related research. From the mid-1970s onward, substantial advances in physiology, pharmacology, enzymology, and cell biology–the vast majority stemming from publicly funded research–led to enormous progress in the ability to understand the mechanisms of action of existing drugs. This new knowledge made it possible to develop more sophisticated and more sensitive screens for drugs. These more sensitive screens made it possible to search for a wider range of compounds.

As is well known to both practitioners and scholars of innovation, new products do not ensure profits. Thus, the question remains: why was the pharmaceutical industry so profitable during the period 1950–90? Rents from innovation can be competed away unless "isolating mechanisms" (Lippman and Rumelt, 1982) are in place to inhibit imitators and new entrants. For most of the post-war period, pharmaceutical companies (particularly in the United States) had a number of isolating mechanisms working in their favor. One of these was the process of random screening itself. As an organizational process, random screening was anything but random. Over time, early entrants into the pharmaceutical industry developed highly disciplined processes for carrying out mass screening programs. Because random screening capabilities were based on internal organizational processes and tacit skills, they were difficult for potential entrants to imitate and thus became a source of first-mover advantage. In addition, with random screening, spillovers of knowledge between firms were relatively small (Henderson, 1994). When firms essentially rely on the law of large numbers, there is little to be learned from the competition; it is hard to copy luck.

A second isolating mechanism was patent protection. Pharmaceutical compounds have generally enjoyed very strong patent protection (Kleverick et al., 1995). It was historically very difficult for an imitator to come up with a therapeutically equivalent compound that did not infringe on the patent. A third isolating mechanism related to the regulatory approval process. Until the passage of the Waxman-Hatch Act (1982), generic competition was weak. After the initial patent expired, would-be competitors still had to take their compound through extensive clinical trials to demonstrate clinical equivalency. Thus, companies could enjoy monopoly profits long after patent protection on a molecule had lapsed. Finally, successful drugs historically enjoyed fairly long life cycles. It might be a decade or more before a new class of compounds that offered dramatically improved therapeutic performance entered the market and made the original compound obsolete. In sum, pharmaceutical companies enjoyed a combination of factors that contributed to high levels of profitability; imitation was difficult for legal, regulatory, and technological reasons and successful products could earn monopoly rents for a decade or more.

These advantages, combined with the presence of scale economies in pharmaceutical research, may help to explain the dearth of new entry. Until the mid-1970s, only one company, Syntex, the developer of the oral contraceptive, succeeded in entering the industry. Indeed, many of the leading firms during this period globally, companies like Roche, Ciba, Hoechst,

Merck, Pfizer, and Lilly, had gotten their start in the pre–R&D era of the industry.

Vertical integration was also used by pharmaceutical companies as a way to protect rents from new drug discovery. Between 1950 and 1990, vertical integration–from discovery research through manufacturing and global marketing–evolved as the dominant organizational form of the pharmaceutical industry. Although there was some licensing of compounds, the vast majority of major firms established capabilities in research, development, regulatory affairs, manufacturing, and marketing. One exception to this trend could be found in Japan where local Japanese firms undertook little of their own discovery research, but instead licensed compounds from American and European firms. Institutional factors seem to explain this pattern. In Japan, prior to 1967, any drug approved for use in another country could be sold without going through additional clinical trials. As soon as the drug was listed in an accepted official pharmacopoeia, it could be sold in Japan (Reich, 1990). At the same time, Japanese firms were protected from foreign competition and given strong incentives to license products that had been approved overseas. Under this regulatory regime, the primary technology strategy for Japanese pharmaceutical companies became the identification of promising foreign approved drugs to license (Reich, 1990).

14.2.3. International Differences and Institutional Environments

Significant differences in the competitive and innovative performance at the country level suggest that institutional factors have also played a critical role. Although global in nature, the post-war pharmaceutical industry has been dominated by companies from the United States, Switzerland, Germany, and the United Kingdom. Although Japan is the second largest pharmaceutical market in the world, and is dominated by local firms (largely for regulatory reasons), Japanese firms have been consciously absent from the global industry. Only Takeda, for instance, ranks among the top twenty pharmaceutical firms in the world. Only relatively recently, the innovative performance of Japanese pharmaceutical firms has been weak relative to the U.S. and European competitors.

To understand these international differences in performance, we need to probe the differences in institutional forces that have shaped opportunities to both create and exploit intellectual property in drugs in different countries.

From its inception, the evolution of the pharmaceutical industry has been tightly linked to institutions supporting the creation and appropriation of intellectual property. The pharmaceutical industry emerged in Switzerland and Germany, in part, because of strong university research and training in the relevant scientific areas. Organic chemistry was literally invented in Germany by Professor Justus Liebig and German universities in the nineteenth century were leaders in organic chemistry. Basel, Switzerland was the home of the country's oldest university which was a center for medicinal and chemical study. Later, it was the U.S. government's massive wartime investment in the development of penicillin which, as discussed earlier, profoundly altered the evolution of the industry in the United States. In the post-war era, institutional arrangements affecting intellectual property protection, procedures for product testing and approval, and pricing and reimbursement policies have strongly influenced both the process of innovation directly and the economic returns (and thus incentives) for undertaking such innovation. A brief review of these is provided below.

14.2.3.1. Intellectual Property Protection

In many industries, successful new products quickly attract imitators. But rapid imitation of new drugs is difficult in pharmaceuticals for a number of institutional reasons. One of these has to do with patents. Pharmaceuticals have historically been one of the few industries where patents provide solid protection against imitation (Klevorick et al., 1995) because small variants in a molecule's structure can drastically alter its pharmacological properties, potential imitators find it hard to work around the patent. Thus, although other firms might undertake R&D in the same therapeutic class as an inno-

vator, their probability of finding another compound with the same therapeutic properties that did not infringe on the original patent was quite small. However, the scope and efficacy of patent protection has varied significantly across countries. The United States and most European countries have provided relatively strong patent protection in pharmaceuticals. In contrast, in Japan and in Italy, until 1976 and 1978, respectively, patent law did not offer protection for pharmaceutical products; instead, only process technologies could be patented. As a result, Japanese pharmaceutical companies tended to avoid product R&D and concentrated on finding novel processes for making existing foreign or domestically originated molecules.

14.2.3.2. Procedures for Product Approval

Pharmaceuticals are regulated products. Procedures for approval have a profound impact on both the cost of innovating, and the ability of firms to sustain positions once their products have been approved. As in the case of patents, there are substantial differences in product approval processes across countries.

Since the early 1960s, most countries have tended to increase the stringency of controls. However, it was the United States, with the Kefauver-Harris Amendment Act in 1962, and the United Kingdom, with the Medicine Act in 1971, who take by far the most stringent stance among industrialized countries, followed by the Netherlands, Switzerland and the Scandinavian countries. Germany, France, Japan, and Italy were much less demanding.

In the United States, the 1962 Amendments were passed after the thalidomide disaster. They introduced a proof-of-efficacy requirement for approval of new drugs and establishment of FDA regulatory controls over the clinical (human) testing of new drug candidates. Specifically, the amendments required firms to provide substantial evidence of a new drug's efficacy based on "adequate and well controlled trials." As a result, the FDA shifted after 1962 from essentially an evaluator of evidence and research findings at the end of the R&D process to an active participant in the process itself (Grabowski and Vernon, 1983).

The effects of the Amendments on innovative activities and market structure have been the subjects of considerable debate (see, e.g., Chien, 1979). Certainly, they led to large increases in the resources necessary to obtain approval of a new drug application (NDA), mainly through higher development costs and longer time for R&D. In turn, these effects are deemed to have caused sharp increases in R&D costs and gestation times for new chemical entities (NCEs), large declines in the annual rate of NCE introduction for the industry and a lag in the introduction of significant new drugs therapies in the United States when compared to Germany and the United Kingdom. However, the creation of a stringent drug approval process in the United States may have also helped create an isolating mechanism for innovative rents. Although the process of development and approval increased costs, it significantly increased barriers to imitation, even after patents expired. Until the Waxman-Hatch Act was passed in the United States in 1984, generic versions of drugs that had gone off patent still had to undergo extensive human clinical trials before they could be sold in the U.S. market. Even once patents expired, it might be years before a generic version appeared. In 1980, generics held only 2 percent of the U.S. drug market.

The institutional environment concerning drug approval in the United Kingdom was quite similar to that in the United States. In the United Kingdom, regulation of product safety began in 1964 and from the very beginning it turned to formal academic medicine, in particular to well-controlled clinical trials to demonstrate safety and efficacy of new drugs. Extensive documentation and high academic standards were required of all submissions. The Committee on Safety of Drugs (CSD) (since 1971 the Committee on Safety of Medicines (CSM)) comprised independent academic experts, voluntarily organized and supported by the industry. The whole system was based on a strong cooperative attitude between the CSD/CSM, industry and academe, which effectively imposed very high standards on industry (Thomas, 1994; Davies, 1967; Wardell, 1978; Hancher, 1990). Like in the United States after 1962, the introduction of a tougher regulatory environment in the United Kingdom was followed by a sharp fall in the number of new drugs launched into the United Kingdom and a shakeout of innovative firms. Actually, a number of smaller, weaker firms exited the market. Similarly, the proportion of minor local products launched into the U.K. market shrunk significantly and the strongest U.K. firms gradually reoriented their R&D activities towards the development of more ambitious, global products (Thomas, 1994).

Japan represented a very different case from either the United States or the United Kingdom. In Japan, prior to 1967, any drug approved for use in another country could be sold without going through additional clinical trials or regulatory approval. As soon as the drug was listed in an accepted official Pharmacopoeia, it could be sold in Japan (Reich, 1990). At the same time, however, non–Japanese firms were prohibited from applying for drug approval. Thus, Japanese firms were protected from foreign competition and simultaneously had strong incentives to license products that had been approved overseas. Under this regime the primary technology strategy for Japanese pharmaceutical companies became the identification of promising foreign products to license (Reich, 1990).

14.2.3.3. The Structure of the Health Care System and Systems of Reimbursement

Perhaps the biggest difference in institutional environments across countries is in the structure of the health care system. In the U.S., pharmaceutical companies' rents from product innovation were further protected by the fragmented structure of health care markets and the low bargaining power of buyers. Unlike most European countries (with the exception of Germany and the Netherlands) and Japan, drug prices in the United States are unregulated by government intervention. Until the mid-1980s, the overwhelming majority of drugs were sold through retail pharmacies or administered in hospitals to patients, but marketed directly to physicians (who essentially made purchasing decisions by deciding which drug to prescribe).

Buyers, the patients, had little bargaining power, even in those instances where multiple drugs were available for the same condition. Because insurance companies generally did not cover prescription drugs (in 1960, only 4 percent of prescription drug expenditures were funded by third-party payers), they did not provide a major source of pricing leverage. Pharmaceutical companies were afforded a relatively high degree of pricing flexibility. This pricing flexibility, in turn, contributed to the profitability of investments in drug R&D.

Drug prices were also relatively high in other countries that did not have strong government intervention in prices such as Germany and the Netherlands. In the United Kingdom, price regulation was conceived as a voluntary cooperation between the pharmaceutical industry and the Ministry of Health. This scheme left companies to set their own prices, but a global profit margin with each firm was negotiated which was designed to assure each of them an appropriate return on capital investment including research, in the United Kingdom. The allowed rate of rate return was negotiated directly and was set higher for export-oriented firms. In general, this scheme tended to favor both U.K. and foreign R&D intensive companies which operated directly in the United Kingdom. Conversely, it tended to penalize weak, imitative firms as well as those foreign competitors (primarily the Germans) trying to enter the U.K. market without direct innovative effort in loco (Burstall, 1985; Thomas, 1994).

In Japan, the Ministry of Health and Welfare set the prices of all drugs, using suggestions from the manufacturer based on the drug's efficacy and the prices of comparable products. Importantly, moreover, in Japan the price has historically not been allowed to change over the life of the drug (Mitchell et al., 1995). Thus, whereas in many competitive contexts, prices begin to fall as a product matures, this was not the case in Japan. Given that manufacturing costs often fall with cumulative experience, old drugs thus probably offered the highest profit margins to many companies, further curtailing the incentive to introduce new drugs. Moreover, generally high prices in the domestic market provided Japanese pharmaceutical companies with ample profits and little incentive to expand overseas.

14.3. Molecular Biology as a New Technology of Pharmaceutical R&D

In most industries, technological change can be measured as changes in the performance of product or process technology. In pharmaceuticals, technological advance has centered on improvements in the techniques used to synthesize, search for, screen, and select therapeutically promising molecules. Over the past decade, there has been a veritable revolution in the methods by which pharmaceutical scientists discover new drugs. The term "biotechnology" is commonly used to connote this new approach. Unfortunately, this terminology creates the impression that the revolution in pharmaceutical R&D is the story of *one* major new technology. In fact, this is not the case. There is a constellation of technologies which are fundamentally altering the ways in which new drugs are discovered. As a result, there are many different paths or strategies organizations can follow in drug discovery. Technological variety is creating a more complex, multidimensional industrial landscape.

Today, the discovery of new drugs involves three, interrelated processes: the *search* for therapeutic "targets," the *synthesis* of potentially therapeutic compounds, and the *screening* of those compounds for desired therapeutic activity. As noted earlier, the traditional technology of drug R&D—random screening—involved largely the second and third of these processes (in that order). Below is a brief description of the major search, synthesis, and screening technologies that are fundamentally altering the drug discovery process.

14.3.1. Search

As noted earlier, historically, drug compounds were found, not designed. Increasingly, the search for a new drug begins with an attempt to understand the underlying biology of the disease or condition for which a therapy is being sought. *Rational drug design* is an approach that emerged during the 1980s that sought to "design" drugs based on detailed knowledge of the biochemical pathways of diseases. If, to use one common analogy, the action of a drug on a receptor in the body is similar to that of a key fitting into a lock, advances in scientific knowledge in the 1970s and 1980s greatly increased knowledge of which "locks" might be important, thus making the screening process much more precise. More recently, an improved understanding of molecular kinetics, of the physical structure of molecular receptors, and of the relationship between chemical structure and a particular compound's mechanism of action has greatly increased knowledge of what suitable "keys" might look like. This knowledge can be used to guide the search for potential therapeutic molecules or even to "design" compounds that might have particular therapeutic effects. Structure-based molecular design applies principles not only of chemistry, medicinal chemistry, biochemistry and molecular biology to the design and development of drugs, but also of mathematics and computer science. The result is a comprehensive, full molecular level approach that can be of great practical importance in disciplines such as biopharmaceutics, enzymology, toxicology, biotechnology, and molecular medicine. The attention that rational drug design receives from the chemical and pharmaceutical industry comes from the perception that conventional approaches (e.g., screening of natural products) have reached the point of diminishing returns in developing new pharmaceutical agents. Interestingly, all drugs in use as of 1996 addressed only 500 molecular targets; by one estimate, the total number of *potential* drug targets may be in the range of 5,000–10,000 (Drews, 2000).

The potential to understand disease processes at a molecular (genetic) level that will determine the optimal molecular target(s) for drugs is the main promise of molecular biology for drug discovery. *Genomics* itself refers to several technologies focused on characterizing the genetic basis of diseases and using that information to identify promising drug targets. The benefits of genome knowledge, of humans and other species, can potentially transform medicine by introducing safer and more effective drugs, expanding the range of diseases that are treatable, and improving diagnosis. To date, a major focus of genomics research has been to identify the 100,000 human genes and determine the sequence of three billion DNA bases of the human body. This effort was undertaken by both government—through the U.S.$3 billion multiyear Human Genome Project—and by a competitive private company (Celera). The government-sponsored project officially started in 1990 and was, at that time, estimated to be completed in about 15 years. On June 26, 2000 scientists from both the government-sponsored project and Celera jointly announced the creation of a complete map of the human genome. The project was completed earlier than expected (and at lower cost) because of advances in approaches to sequencing. Now that the map has been created, researchers will begin the task of identifying the function of genes, the proteins they code for, and the ways in which these genes cause or contribute to specific diseases at a more molecular level.

14.3.2. Synthesis

Until recently, the arsenal of potential therapeutic compounds at the drug researchers disposal was fairly limited. Essentially, they were limited to substances which could be identified and isolated from natural sources (e.g., mold) or compounds which could be chemically synthesized. Over the past twenty years, a number of techniques have been developed which vastly expand the array of therapeutic substances which can be created. A few of the most critical are described below.

Recombinant DNA (rDNA) is a genetic technique discovered by Herbert Boyer and Stanley Cohen in 1973. The discovery and dissemination of this technique essentially marked the beginning of the "biotechnology" industry. Before the introduction of the rDNA, researchers were severely limited in the size and shape of the compounds that they could hope to synthesize as potential new drugs. In particular, there was no generally available method for the large-scale manufacture of proteins since these are much larger and more complicated than traditional small molecule drugs. With the notable exception of some of the antibiotics, the vast majority of drugs were small molecules that could be manufactured through a series of small, relatively straightforward steps. It was simply infeasible to synthesize a protein through traditional methods of organic chemistry. Those proteins that were used as therapeutic agents—notably insulin—were produced through extraction from natural sources.[1] rDNA is a very powerful technique that enables scientists to transfer genes of one organism into the cell of another. The basic step consists of taking the human gene and inserting it into a plasmid DNA named vector. The resulting construct is then pushed into the DNA of nonhuman cells that can be grown rapidly (usually those of a bacterium named *Escherichia coli,* or from the ovaries of the Chinese hamster). In these cells, the human gene is translated into a protein in the same way as the cell's native genes. The protein can then be extracted and purified. Therapeutic proteins made by rDNA have proved to be extremely successful. For instance, Cohen and Boyer were able to produce 100 percent recombinant human insulin, developed by Genentech but currently sold by Eli Lilly. Over the past 25 years, rDNA has been used as the basis for producing several therapeutic proteins, which have been approved for sale. The best known among these are: recombinant insulin, human growth hormone, Factor VIII, erythropoetin, tissue plasminogen active (tPA), beta interferon, and interleukin-2 (IL-2). In 1998, the combined annual sales of recombinant drugs were about U.S.$13 billion. Companies which were founded to exploit the commercial opportunities offered by rDNA technology include Genentech (co-founded by Boyer), Amgen, Biogen, Chiron, Genzyme, and many other "first generation" biotechnology entrants.

Cohen and Boyer's key contribution was the invention of a method for manipulating the genetics of a cell so that it could be induced to produce a specific protein. This invention

made it possible for the first time to produce proteins synthetically and in so doing opened up an entirely new domain of search for new drugs—the vast store of proteins that the body uses to carry out a wide range of biological functions.

Monoclonal antibody (MAb) technology was invented in 1975 by Kohler and Millstein in the United Kingdom as a way of producing highly pure antibodies by creating an immortal cell line which can produce a single antibody of defined specificity. The success of this technique depends on the development of cultured myeloma cell lines that grow in normal culture medium but do not grow in a defined selection medium because they are genetically modified. Fusing normal cells to these defective myeloma partners provides the necessary biological system of the normal cells and the immortality of the modified ones. The result is the production of virtually unlimited quantities of a single antibody specific for a particular protein. Like rDNA, MAb technology is essentially a *synthesis*-technology. Many early entrants into the biotech industry focused on MAbs or on rDNA. Initially, MAbs were viewed by both scientists and entrepreneurs as having great promise to cure a range of diseases, and in particular cancer. The basic assumption is that diseased cells (e.g., a cancer cell) express specific proteins (markers) on their membrane surface. A MAb developed against the marker, would only trigger that particular marker, and could deliver a specific agent, such as a toxic dose of chemotherapeutic agent, to that specific cell. MAbs were sometimes referred to as "magic bullets" because of the perceived potential to be highly selective in targeting only diseased cells. Unfortunately, MAb technology has proven far more difficult to develop than initially estimated. Many early clinical trials of MAb-based drugs were failures. Problems with the body's response to nonhumanized monoclonals, as well as manufacturing challenges, caused firms to go back to the drawing board on numerous occasions. Recently, after nearly 25 years of frustrated efforts and failure, MAbs are once again beginning to show promise in clinical trials, and the numbers of approved MAbs are increasing. In 1998, biotech products,

---

[1] How were antibiotics manufactured? Is "fermentation" biotech?

most of them recombinant proteins and Mabs, accounted for 26 percent (15 out of 57) of drugs introduced worldwide.

Gene therapy (search and synthesis) is a powerful, and relatively new technique. One major goal of this therapy is to identify a defective gene(s) causing a particular disease, and then fixing it by supplying cells with healthy copies of the missing or flawed gene(s). This approach is revolutionary because it attempts to correct the basic problem from inside the cells, by altering the genetic information of some of the patient's cells instead of giving a drug to treat or control the symptoms of the disorder. Another important use is as a drug delivery system. Gene therapy has been used in several disease treatments. Clinical trials have been in progress for the treatment of melanoma, brain tumors and HIV. Unfortunately, until very recently, the results have been disappointing, mostly because in a particular disease, several different genes can be involved or there is no efficient way to deliver the corrected gene to a patient. As medicine treatments at a molecular level increase, using gene therapy for drug delivery could save much effort and expense. It could be a powerful tool for treating many of the more than 4,000 known genetic disorders, as well as heart disease, cancer, arthritis, and other illnesses.

The idea behind *combinatorial chemistry* is deceptively simple: all the organic molecules can be thought of as made up of modules that may be put together in different ways. By going through all the possible combinations, an incredible number of molecules can be created from a relatively small number of starting modules. Historically, new chemical compounds were synthesized by highly skilled chemists but they were generally limited to searching within libraries of existing compounds. Combinatorial chemistry has unleashed the search across an enormous range of newly synthesized compounds at lower costs. Using traditional organic chemistry, it takes a chemist one month to produce four leads (a leads is a compound that shows promising activity and is potentially capable of being developed into drugs), at an estimated cost of about U.S.$7,500 per compound. In

that same period of time, an organic chemist employing combinatorial approaches would have produced about 3,300 compounds at a cost of about U.S.$12 per compound. Given the potential cost savings of combinatorial chemistry, it is not surprising that right now about one-tenth of 1,800 to 1,900 biotech companies in the world have a formal program in combinatorial chemistry. Combinatorial chemistry started as a tool for the development of pharmaceuticals and agrochemicals, but is presently also used for foods, metals, and catalyst discovery.

14.3.3. Screening

The need to speed up the process of screening drug compounds found by combinatorial chemistry is the base of the *high throughput screening* (HTS) technique. Like chemical synthesis, traditional processes of screening were fairly labor intensive since assays needed to be prepared by hand. HTS is an automated, robotics-based technology for testing vast numbers of new compounds against a large number of assays. HTS is essentially a random screening technology that is much faster and cheaper than traditional labor-intensive drug screening. As knowledge grows about how and why molecules react together, the processes of combinatorial chemistry and HTS can often be mimicked on a computer with impressive cost-saving results. The virtual chemists can view computer representations of the target protein and of the candidate drug molecule on the screen. The candidate can then be altered atom by atom to achieve a better result, and only at that point will the drug be synthesized on a small scale. HTS, along with combinatorial chemistry, is in many ways a return to the principle of random screening, albeit in a vastly quicker and more productive mode.

Several other important components of the drug discovery process technologies are pervading pharmaceutical R&D today. Among the emerging technologies are: tissue engineering, stem cell therapy, chiral chemistry, and proteomics. However, a complete discussion is well beyond the scope of this chapter.

14.4. Patterns of Industry Evolution Since 1980

The growing complexity of the technological landscape in pharmaceuticals is reflected in the growing complexity of the industry landscape and structure. Until the mid-1970s, the pharmaceutical industry was dominated by large, multinational corporations (largely based in the United States, the United Kingdom, Germany, and Switzerland). "The pharmaceutical industry" meant major multinational players like Merck, Hoffman LaRoche, Pfizer, Eli Lilly, and others.

The late 1970s and 1980s witnessed the "first wave" of biotechnology entrants (such as Genentech, Biogen, Amgen, etc.) who focused on rDNA and MAb technology. The first biotechnology product, human insulin, was approved in 1982. As of 2000, there were approximately 59 such biotechnology drugs on the markets (Drews, 2000). In 1998, biotechnology-based rDNA and Mab drugs accounted for 26 percent of the total number of new drugs introduced worldwide (Drews, 2000).

While many new biotechnology companies had visions of becoming fully integrated pharmaceutical companies, the high costs of drug development forced virtually all new entrants to pursue a strategy of collaboration with larger, more established pharmaceutical companies. Only a handful of the new entrants (e.g., Amgen, Biogen, Chiron, Genentech, Genzyme, Immunex, and Genetics Institute) were able to establish themselves as fully integrated pharmaceutical companies. Several of the larger players (Genentech, Chiron, Immunex, and Genetics Institute) sold majority stakes to established pharmaceutical companies. While most of the biotechnology products that have been approved or that are under development have their origins in research conducted at one of the start-ups, most were developed through collaboration with established pharmaceutical companies. Although there is considerable variation between different sources, it appears that since the late 1980s entry into the industry has started to decline. At the same time, exit rates have been increasing rapidly—although in 55 percent of the reported cases, exit was due to mergers and acquisitions and another

30 percent of the cases involved changes in the name of the company (Ryan et al., 1995).

Despite years of predictions of consolidation and shake-out, entry by start-up companies in the United States has continued steadily throughout with new firms specializing in particular emerging technologies: gene therapy, combinatorial chemistry, high throughput screening, and, most recently, genomics. It is thus increasingly difficult to talk about "the pharmaceutical industry" or even "the biotechnology industry." Millenium Pharmaceuticals, for example, was a company that was founded to find attractive drug targets based on genetic information. Broadly speaking, it is considered a "biotechnology" firm; yet its focus is vastly different than that of, say, its Cambridge neighbors like Biogen or other first generation biotechnology companies that sought to develop novel therapeutic proteins from rDNA technology.

There are two striking features of the pattern of development of new drug R&D technologies over the past decade. The first is the dominant role played by start-ups as the instigators of commercial research. The second is the dominance of the United States as a location for this research. Each of these traits is discussed below.

14.4.1. The Dominance of New Entrants in Commercial Research

Almost without exception, new entrants have been on the leading edge of research in each major wave of technology associated with the molecular biology revolution. This was true for rDNA and Mabs in the 1980s (e.g., Amgen, Biogen, Genentech, Genzyme, Immunex, ImmunoGen, and Genetics Institute); it was true for combinatorial chemistry, high throughput screening, and genomics in the 1990s (e.g., Millenium, Incyte, Human Genome Sciences, and literally hundreds of other start-ups). In emerging areas like gene chips and proteomics, the trend also appears to be repeating itself. A notable exception is Celera, a genomics company which competed with the government-sponsored Human Genome Project to sequence the human genome. Celera is a division of PE Corporation.

The dominance of start-up companies in research, however, does not mean that established pharmaceutical companies ignored the new technologies or "missed the wave." This is largely true (with some exceptions) if one views internal investment as the only way in which participation in these technologies is possible. While some established companies have been slow to recognize the potential impact of new discovery technologies, most of the major players have been aggressive, indirect participants in the research through equity investments, collaborative arrangements and licensing deals. Companies such as Roche, Eli Lilly, and American Home Products went on to make acquisitions (or majority investments) in "first generation" biotechnology companies. More recently, the multinational pharmaceutical companies have been major investors in genomics through licensing agreements and technology development deals with new entrants into that space. Consider Millenium Pharmaceuticals, a company founded in Cambridge, MA in 1993, and widely perceived to be a leader in the genomics field. Eli Lilly, Bayer, Bristol-Myers Squibb, Aventis, Monsanto, Pfizer, Warner Lambert, and Hoffman LaRoche have all entered fairly large scale agreements to access Millenium's genomics data and its drug discovery capabilities (the total value of these investments is estimated to be in excess of U.S.$1 billion). The Aventis deal alone is estimated to be worth U.S.$450 million in funding over years. SmithKline Beecham has made major investment in genomics through a multi-year licensing and development agreement with Human Genome Sciences. While some major pharmaceutical companies may have started later than others, virtually major pharmaceutical companies have invested in new approaches to drug discovery through some combination of internal investments and licensing agreements with external partners.

It may be asked why established pharmaceutical companies have chosen to "outsource" such a significant fraction of their investments in new life science technologies. First, it must be clear that while major pharmaceutical companies use more external sources of R&D than in the past, the overwhelming bulk of their budgets (probably around 75–80 percent) is devoted to internal activities. However, two factors appear to be at work in explaining the growing use of external sources of R&D. One is the shear breadth of skills and knowledge represented by the new technologies. Historically, discovery research in pharmaceuticals meant having deep skills in one discipline: medicinal chemistry. As stressed earlier, the molecular biology revolution is a rapidly evolving constellation of many technologies and bodies of scientific knowledge. Even for the largest firms in the industry, whose R&D budgets amount to several billion dollars per year, it is simply infeasible to build deep expertise across the full range of technologies. Second, knowledge bases of the new technologies are by and large quite different from those of traditional medicinal chemistry. Building internal capabilities meant more than simply funding the effort. Completely new organizational routines and philosophies were required. There is a long literature highlighting the difficulties faced by established firms in building capabilities in technologies which fundamentally depart from existing knowledge bases (e.g., Tushman and Anderson, 1985; Henderson and Clark, 1990).

Incorporating new discovery technologies into research has thus been trivial for established pharmaceutical companies, even with the ability to "outsource" components of the process to new entrants. Nor has the transition occurred at the same rate across all firms. The MBR has tightened the connection between drug discovery and basic science. For those firms that were less well connected to basic science, the transition appears to have been more difficult (Gambardella, 1995). It was often hard to recruit scientists of adequate caliber if the firm had no history of publication or of investment in basic science, and once recruited it proved to be difficult to create the communication patterns that the new techniques required. The new techniques also significantly increased returns to scope and scale in the industry (Henderson and Cockburn, 1996). As drug discovery came to rely increasingly on the insights of modern biology, discoveries in one field often had implications for work in other areas, and firms that had the size and scope to capitalize on these opportunities for cross fertilization—and the organizational mechanisms in place to take advantage of these opportunities—reaped significant rewards. Thus, one of the major impacts of the revolution in molecular biology has been to drive a wedge between those firms that have been able to absorb the new science into their research efforts and those that are still struggling to make the transition.

14.4.2. The Dominance of the United States as a Locus for R&D Activities

The United States has been the dominant locus of R&D in virtually all the new technologies associated with the MBR. This is *not* to say that only U.S. firms participated in the technology. Established pharmaceutical companies from the United States, Europe and Japan have been active *users* of the new technology through the collaborative arrangements discussed above. But with the partial exception of the U.K., the rest of the world saw no real parallel to the phenomenon of the specialized start-ups that was such a pronounced feature of the American industry in the early 1980s and 1990s.

This difference is particularly striking given that in most European countries, and in Japan, governments (at various levels: the European Union, national and local governments) have devised a variety of measures to foster industry–university collaboration and the development of venture capital to favor the birth of new biotechnology ventures. To date the results of these policies have not been particularly impressive, although the increase in the rate of formation of new biotechnology-based firms in the 1990s may reflect the fact that these policies are now beginning to have an impact. Ernst and Young (1994) suggest that there are now approximately 380 biotechnology companies in Europe. The United Kingdom has the largest number of new biotechnology firms in Europe, followed by France, Germany and the Netherlands (Escourrou, 1992; SERD, 1996). Recent data, moreover, suggest a dramatic increase in the number of new entrants in Germany, with different sources

estimating their number in the 400–500 range or even more than 600 (Coombs, 1996). However, these numbers need to be kept in perspective. In the area of San Diego, CA, alone there are estimated to be approximately more than 400 firms involved in life sciences research and development.

However, very few of these companies resemble the American prototype. Many of the new European firms are not involved in drug discovery or development but are instead either intermediaries commercializing products developed elsewhere, active in diagnostics, in the agricultural sector (especially in the Netherlands), or in the provision of instrumentation and/or reagents (Merit, 1996; SERD, 1996). Moreover, some of these companies (especially the most important ones, like Celltech and Transgene) have been founded through the direct support and involvement of both governments and large pharmaceutical companies rather than through the venture capital market.

In the absence of extensive founding of new firms, most of the innovation in biotechnology in mainland Europe has occurred within established firms. In France, there has been significant entry, largely from firms diversifying into biotechnology and from other research institutions, while in Germany there has been almost no entry at all. Thus, in mainland Europe a few firms account for a large proportion of biotechnology patents, and innovation in biotechnology rests essentially on the activities of a relatively small and stable group of well-established companies. However, while the majority of the established American pharmaceutical firms adopted the new techniques of drug discovery through acquisition and collaboration with the small American start-ups, the European firms showed considerable variation in the methods through which they acquired the technology.

The U.K. (Glaxo, Wellcome and to a lesser extent ICI) and the Swiss companies (particularly Hoffman La Roche, Ciba Geigy, and Sandoz) moved earlier and above all more decisively in the direction pioneered by the large U.S. firms in collaborating or acquiring American startups. Firms in the rest of Europe tended to focus primarily on the establishment of a network of alliances with local research institutes although it is worth emphasizing that German companies lagged somewhat behind. Hoechst signed a 10-year agreement with Massachusetts General Hospital as early as 1981, but Bayer did not enter seriously until 1985. In general, Germany made little progress in the field and they are not now considered to be among the leaders in European biotechnology. In some countries (e.g., Italy), the scientific community actually took the lead in attempts to promote the commercial development of genetic engineering, through the establishment of linkages and collaboration with the pharmaceutical industry. Besides these companies, the biggest European innovators are a research institution, Institut Pasteur, and two companies that have not been traditional players in the pharmaceutical industry, Gist-Brocades and Novo Nordisk. In Japan, entry in biotechnology was pioneered by the large food and chemical companies with strong capabilities in process technologies (e.g., fermentation), like Takeda, Kyowa Hakko, Ajinomoto, Kirin, and Suntory. However, like their European counterparts, Japanese firms appear to be undertaking most of their life sciences R&D through collaborative arrangements with U.S. start-ups, or by establishing research facilities in the United States, rather than by setting up capabilities in their home country.

This pattern can be observed in statistics on genetic engineering patenting in Europe. As shown in Table 14.1, in the United States, new entrants hold the largest share of European genetic engineering patenting; whereas in

TABLE 14.1
Percentage of Genetic Engineering Patents, by Type of Institution 1987–93

	New firms	Established corporations	Universities
United States	40	38	22
Japan	3	87	10
Germany	3	80	17
United Kingdom	24	45	31
France	17	35	48

Source: Henderson et al. (1999).

Japan and Europe, it is the established firms which dominate. Only the United Kingdom has a pattern that is even remotely similar to the United States.

14.5. Why the Molecular Biology Revolution is Largely a U.S. Commercial Phenomenon

It is clear that the molecular biology revolution will re-shape drug discovery and development on a worldwide basis. Drug companies from around the world—the United States, Europe, and Japan—will utilize the tools of genomics, combinatorial chemistry and HTS, and other tools emerging today. However, the locus of commercial R&D in these new technologies is largely confined to the United States. Why is this?

To some extent, the two features of the MBR discussed above are difficult to separate: most of the initial commercial research has been dominated by *start-up* companies and has been located in the United States. However, the United States tends to be a much more fertile environment for entrepreneurial firms. Thus, it is hard to say which is cause and which is effect. Is the MBR being dominated by start-ups because it is originating from U.S. academic laboratories? Or, is commercial research undertaken largely in the United States because it is a more start-up friendly environment? Both forces are critical, and each has reinforced the other. There are some institutional factors—namely the massive public spending on basic biomedical research, that accounts for the U.S. dominance in the basic science. However, there is another set of institutional factors which have supported the *commercial* development of these technologies by U.S.-based start-up companies.

14.5.1. The U.S. Dominance in Basic Biomedical Research

It is not hard to understand why the molecular biology revolution had its origins in the United States. For several decades, the U.S. government—through the National Institute of Health (NIH) and initiatives like "the war on cancer"—provided massive support to basic biomedical research. This funding supported many of the most critical discoveries in molecular biology research. The NIH, the largest funding agency for biomedical research, spent U.S.\$15.6 billion on basic scientific and clinical research.[2] As noted earlier, the NIH was the chief financial supporter of the 15-year, U.S.\$3 billion initiative to map the human genome. Although difficult to compare because of differences in categorization, the funding of the NIH appears to dwarf public research expenditures in other countries. For example, public expenditures on biotechnology research in all European countries combined totaled only U.S.\$9.1 billion during the entire period 1994–8. The big spenders, Germany (32 percent), the United Kingdom (27 percent), and France (22 percent), were responsible for over 80 percent of all expenditure (Senker et al., 2000). Public expenditure and involvement of industry in biotechnology by European country are summarized in Table 14.2. These data indicate that while countries like the United Kingdom and Germany have funded public research in the life sciences, and in particular molecular biology, they have not come anywhere near the sheer scale of the efforts in the United States.

It might be argued that "science" is public good and diffuses rapidly, particularly in today's global scientific community. Just because the locus of basic research is concentrated in the United States, does not necessarily mean the locus of commercial activity should also be in the United States. After all, the Japanese electronics industry flourished in the 1970s and 1980s despite the fact that much of the basic research in electronics was conducted in the United States. Why is the case of molecular biology different? Indeed, the United Kingdom has a tradition and track record of outstanding scientific research in molecular biology. Monoclonal antibody technology was invented in the United Kingdom, but has been largely developed commercially by U.S. firms.

There are several related institutional factors that may help to explain why the United States has dominated the commercial exploitation of the molecular biology revolution. In the United

TABLE 14.2
Public Expenditures on Biotechnology: 1999 in millions of U.S.\$ (current exchange rate of U.S.\$1 = 0.88 ECU)

Germany	531.7
United Kingdom	453.4
France	372.2
Belgium	97.0
The Netherlands	55.2
Sweden	47.7
Finland	38.7
Italy	36.4
Norway	32.6
Denmark	24.3
Portugal	12.8
Switzerland	8.8
Austria	8.6
Spain	8.3
Ireland	8.1
Greece	3.7
Iceland	0.5

States a combination of factors made it possible for small, newly founded firms to take advantage of the opportunity this created. These factors included a favorable financial climate, strong intellectual property protection, a scientific and medical establishment that could supplement the necessarily limited competencies of small newly founded firms, a regulatory climate that did not restrict genetic experimentation and, perhaps most importantly, a combination of a very strong local scientific base and academic norms that permitted the rapid translation of academic results into competitive enterprises. In Europe (although to a lesser extent in the United Kingdom) and in Japan many of these factors were not in place, and it was left to larger firms to exploit the new technology. In Europe this meant that entry into biotechnology was "late" and in Japan that it was pioneered by firms whose interest in the new techniques was not primarily therapeutic.

14.5.1.1. A Strong Local Scientific Base and Academic Norms that Permitted the Rapid Translation of Academic Results into Competitive Enterprises

The majority of the American biotechnology start-ups were tightly linked to university depart-

[2] http://www4.0d.nih.gov.

ments, and the very strong state of American academic molecular biology clearly played an important role in facilitating the wave of start-ups that characterized the 1980s (Zucker et al., 1997). The strength of the local science base may also be responsible, within Europe, for the relative U.K. advantage and the relative German and French delay. Similarly the weakness of Japanese industry may partially reflect the weakness of Japanese biomedical science. There seems to be little question as to the superiority of the U.S. and U.K. scientific systems in the field of molecular biology, and it is tempting to suggest that the strength of the local science base provides an easy explanation for regional differences in the speed with which molecular biology was exploited as a tool for drug discovery.

Although this explanation might seem unsatisfying to the degree that academic science is rapidly published and thus, in principle, rapidly available across the world, the U.S. lead appears to have been particularly important because in the early years of the industry the exploitation of the new technologies required the mastery of a considerable body of tacit knowledge that could not be easily acquired from the literature (Pisano, 1996; Zucker et al., 1998).

The transmission of this kind of tacit knowledge was probably facilitated by geographic proximity (Jaffe et al., 1993). In the case of biotechnology, however, several authors have suggested that the U.S. start-ups were not simply the result of geographic proximity (Zucker et al., 1998). These authors have suggested that the flexibility of the U.S. academic system, the high mobility characteristic of the scientific labor market, and, in general, the social, institutional, and legal context that made it relatively straightforward for leading academic scientists to become deeply involved with commercial firms were also major factors in the health of the new industry.

The willingness to exploit the results of academic research commercially also distinguishes the U.S. environment from that of either Europe or Japan. In 1980 Congress passed the Patent and Trademark Amendments of 1980 (Public Law 96-517), also known as the Bayh-Dole Act, which gave universities (and other nonprofit institutions, as well as small businesses) the right to retain the property rights to inventions deriving from federally funded research and has encouraged universities to seek commercial licenses for such technology. This law has strengthened the willingness of the universities to seek commercial outlets for research. Indeed, most top research universities in the life sciences (Harvard, MIT, Columbia, University of California, Stanford, etc.) have established fairly aggressive and highly professional licensing operations. At many universities, promising research areas are actively sought out and identified by the university licensing office. There can be little doubt that the Bayh-Dole Act has played a critical role in the commercialization of life sciences research in the United States.

In contrast, links between academe and industry—particularly the ability to freely exchange personnel—appear to have been much weaker in Europe and Japan. Indeed, the efforts of several European governments were targeted precisely toward the strengthening of industry–university collaboration, and it has been argued that the rigidities of the research system of continental Europe and the large role played in France and Germany by the public, nonacademic institutions have significantly hindered the development of biotechnology in those countries. This can be partially seen in the case of the United Kingdom. Despite the strength of U.K. academic science in molecular biology, the United Kingdom has not witnessed the same degree of commercial research activity as the United States.

Gittelman's (2000) research comparing the development of biotechnology in France and the United States highlights the importance of institutional factors affecting linkages between academic science and industry. Gittelman notes that in the careers of academic scientists there are a number of entrepreneurial features. For instance, they must compete for resources and raise funding, and are generally granted a high degree of autonomy in setting their research agenda and managing their laboratories. Academic scientists in the United States can and often do change jobs. Most importantly, U.S. academic scientists often leave academe to join start-up companies, or become involved in such ventures through consulting relationships, advisory boards, or other arrangements. The picture is very different in France, where academic scientists are civil servants and operate in a highly rigid, hierarchical system where moves are rare and where there is little autonomy. And, until July 1999 when the legislation was adopted, academic scientists were forbidden from taking part in the managing board of a private enterprise. Now that the legislation has been relaxed, start-up participating scientists can retain their academic status for as long as six years.

The importance of these kinds of factors, as distinct from the strength of the science base per se, as being absolutely critical to the wave of new entry in biotechnology that occurred in United States in the early 1980s is given further credibility by the rate at which the use of molecular biology diffused across the world.

14.5.1.2. Access to Capital

It is commonly believed that lack of venture capital restricted the start-up activity of biotechnology firms outside the United States. Clearly, venture capital—which is to some extent a largely American institution—played an enormous role in fueling the growth of the new biotechnology-based firms. However, at least in Europe, there appear to have been many other sources of funds (usually through government programs) available to prospective start-ups. In addition, the results of several surveys suggest that financial constraints did not constitute a significant obstacle to the founding of new biotechnology firms in Europe (Ernst and Young, 1994; Merit, 1996). Although venture capital played a critical role in the founding of U.S. biotechnology firms, collaborations between the new firms and the larger, more established firms provided a potentially even more important source of capital. This raises the question, why could prospective European or Japanese biotechnology start-ups not turn to established pharmaceutical firms as a source of capital? Although we can only speculate, a plausible answer revolves around the evolution of the market for know-how. The way the market for know-how in biotechnology evolved created many opportunities for

European and Japanese companies to collaborate with U.S. biotechnology firms. Although some U.S.-based NBFs, such as Amgen, Biogen, Chiron, Genentech, and Genzyme, pursued a strategy of vertical integration from research through marketing in the U.S. market, most firms' strategies emphasized licensing product rights outside the United States to foreign partners. Thus, to an even greater extent than many established U.S. pharmaceutical firms, European and Japanese firms were well positioned as partners for U.S. NBFS. Given the plethora of U.S. NBFs in search of capital, European and Japanese firms interested in commercializing biotechnology had little incentive to invest in local biotechnology firms. Even in the absence of other institutional barriers to entrepreneurial ventures, start-ups in Europe or Japan might have been crowded out by the large number of U.S.-based firms eager to trade non–U.S. marketing rights for capital.

14.5.1.3. Intellectual Property Rights

In section 14.2 we discussed the degree to which strong patent protection (or the lack of it, in the case of Italy and Japan) has shaped the industry's history. The establishment of clearly defined property rights also played a major role in making possible the explosion of new firms founded in the United States, since the new firms, by definition, had few complementary assets that would have enabled them to appropriate returns from the new science in the absence of strong patent rights (Teece, 1986).

In the early years of "biotechnology" considerable confusion surrounded the conditions under which patents could be obtained. In the first place, research in genetic engineering was on the borderline between basic and applied science. Much of it was conducted in universities or was otherwise publicly funded, and the degree to which it was appropriate to patent the results of such research became almost immediately the subject of bitter debate. Millstein and Kohler's groundbreaking discovery—hybridoma technology—was never patented, whereas Stanford University filed a patent for Boyer and Cohen's process in 1974. Boyer and Cohen renounced their own rights to the patent but nevertheless were strongly criticized for having been instrumental in patenting what was considered to be a basic technology. Similarly a growing tension emerged between publishing research results versus patenting them. Whereas the norms of the scientific community and the search for professional recognition had long stressed rapid publication, patent laws prohibited the granting of a patent to an already published discovery (Merton, 1973; Kenney, 1986; Etzkowitz, 1996). In the second place, the law surrounding the possibility of patenting life formats and procedures relating to the modification of life-forms were not defined. This issue involved a variety of problems, but it essentially boiled down first to the question of whether living things could be patented at all and second to the scope of the claims that could be granted to such a patent (Merges and Nelson, 1994).

It is often stressed (see, e.g., Ernst and Young, 1994) that the lack of adequate patent protection was a major obstacle to the development of the biotechnology industry in Europe. First, the grace period introduced in the United States is not available in Europe; any discovery that has been published cannot be patented in Europe. This has made it difficult for European companies to offer attractive positions to scientists who still have a strong interest in publishing. Second, in Europe, the interpretation has prevailed that naturally occurring entities, whether cloned or uncloned, cannot be patented. As a consequence, the scope for broad claims on patents is much less than in the United States. In 1994 the European Parliament *rejected* a draft directive that attempted to strengthen the protection offered to biotechnology. However, in 1998, the European Parliament approved a directive expanding the legal protection of biotechnological invention. Although it is clear that stronger intellectual property protection is not unambiguously advantageous, as the controversy surrounding the NIH's decision to seek patents for human gene sequences clearly illustrated. It can be argued that, at least in the early days of the industry, the United States reaped an advantage from its relatively stronger regime. (For more on this difficult and complex subject, see Merges and Nelson, 1994.)

14.6. Conclusion

The molecular biology revolution can best be understood as the emergence of a constellation of technologies that fundamentally change the processes by which drug researchers search for, select, and screen drugs. Although the technologies are indeed quite distinct, there have been some common patterns in their evolution. Two of these were noted in this chapter. First, the locus of commercial R&D has largely been the domain of specialized new entrants. Second, the locus of commercial R&D has been largely within the United States. These two features are obviously related. The U.S. environment in a range of industries has been far more receptive and encouraging of entrepreneurial firms. What is interesting about the impact of molecular biology on the pharmaceutical industry is that it has not had a classic Schumpeterian effect of driving out the established players. The major pharmaceutical companies continue to be major players in the industry, and, for the most part, have been active participants in the revolution through their use of collaborative arrangements, licensing agreement, and equity investments in the new entrants.

An interesting issue going forward is the future of the large incumbent multinational pharmaceutical firms. To date, they have utilized the tools of the molecular biology revolution to enhance their existing R&D capabilities. Although the tools of the molecular biology revolution are indeed quite different than the traditional tools of drug discovery, the market impacts of these technologies have not been great. Drug companies have aggressively adopted and bought the tools of the molecular biology revolution because they see these as a way of sustaining their existing competitive advantage. As long as the tools of the molecular biology revolution fit within the existing business models of established pharmaceutical companies, they will see these as attractive.

There are, however, some indications that the new tools offered by the molecular biology revolution will create vastly different market opportunities in pharmaceuticals. For instance, better understanding of the genetic basis of diseases is often discussed as creating opportunities for "personalized" medicine, whereby drug treatments would be customized based on an individual's genetics. At the very least, there are expectations that genetics will be used to identify sub-populations where particular types of compounds are more likely to be effective than others. This is already starting to happen. For instance, Genentech's Herceptin is targeted specifically at breast cancer patients who over-express a particular protein (HER-2). As drug development becomes more targeted, it clearly creates wonderful opportunities for therapeutic advances. However, it also means that therapeutic markets will begin to fragment. Rather than there being one compound that serves a U.S.$2 billion market, there could well be twenty different compounds each targeting a U.S.$100 million sub-market. Such fragmented markets, however, represent a major challenge for existing pharmaceutical companies' business models. Over the past fifty years, pharmaceutical company growth has been driven by so-called "blockbuster" products (generally viewed today as products with sales greater than U.S.$1 billion). Large pharmaceutical companies meet their growth goals by launching blockbuster products. Their internal resource allocation processes and their overhead structures all evolved around the blockbuster model. The challenge for most pharmaceutical companies is that U.S.$100 million products do not solve their growth problems. Nor are they very profitable given the high fixed cost structures of the firms.

A related challenge to pharmaceutical company business models has to due with the blurring distinction between "product" and "service." Historically, pharmaceutical companies set up large sales forces and standardized distribution channels to sell high volumes of pills. However, genetic-based medicine, cell therapy, and other more customized treatment regimes do not fit with this "mass distribution" model.

The possibility exists, and we can only speculate at this point, that there will be opportunities for specialists to vertically integrate into these more niche-oriented, customized markets. There are examples of this happening.

For instance, Millenium Pharmaceuticals, a pioneer in the use of genetic data to find drug targets, initially focused on selling their technological services to large pharmaceutical companies. More recently, Millenium has also acquired and built its capabilities to develop drugs on its own.

The evidence to date suggests that incumbent pharmaceutical firms have been quite nimble at adopting or using the new tools of drug discovery that have emerged over the past two decades. This fact is a challenge to those who view established companies as being unable or unwilling to master or at least utilize new technologies. It will be interesting to see whether the incumbents are as aggressive at changing their business models and their strategies to utilize the fruits of the molecular biology revolution in a profitable manner. If they do not, then the industrial landscape of pharmaceuticals is likely to look very different in twenty years.

This chapter has also highlighted the role that government policy and national institutions play in shaping commercial development of new science. The U.S. strength in the basic science underpinning the MBR can be explained largely by the level of sustained public investment (and particularly NIH) investment in basic research over a period of more than forty years. However, such public investment is not enough to explain the ensuing commercial development that occurred. The rapid translation of basic scientific opportunities into commercial development in the United States was greatly facilitated by the permeable boundaries between academe and industry that existed to a much greater degree in the United States than elsewhere in the world. These permeable boundaries were partly rooted in the culture and history of U.S. academic institutions, but interactions between academe and private firms were further stimulated by the passage of the Bayh-Dole Act (Mowery et al., 2001). The U.S. experience in biotechnology suggests that public policies which both strengthen the academic research base *and* facilitate collaboration between academic institutions and private enterprises are critical components of an effective science policy.

15

Agricultural Biotechnology

Robert E. Evenson

15.1. Introduction

Innovations in the agricultural biotechnology (ag biotech, hereafter) industries are of relatively recent origin. The scientific discoveries that have enabled ag biotech invention (i.e., the invention of genetically engineered plants, plant components, animals and techniques) are also of recent origin. Most plant and animal invention (and innovation) prior to the ag biotech era was produced in public sector agricultural experiment station research programs. This was the consequence of weak Intellectual Property Rights (IPRs) for private sector invention in plant and animal improvement.[1] As ag biotech inventions became increasingly enabled by both basic and applied scientific research programs, parallel developments in IPRs occurred. The scope of patent coverage, in particular, was broadened to cover "genes" and plants and animals themselves. The combination of science-driven changes in the methods enabling ag biotech invention (the invention of methods of invention; Griliches, 1957) and the expansion of IPRs is transforming ag biotech invention from a predominantly public sector system to a private sector system (Acharya, 1999; Jones, 1998).

Changes in regulatory systems have also been factors in ag biotech innovation and industrial organization. At present, large "Life Sciences" industrial firms are emerging as dominant firms in the ag biotech industries. These Life Sciences firms have traditionally been suppliers of agricultural chemicals (fertilizers insecticides, herbicides, fungicides, etc.) to the farm production sector. In recent years they have acquired firms in the seed industry to exploit perceived complementarities between ag biotech products in the form of transformed or genetically engineered seeds and agricultural chemicals. Several ag biotech products, notably herbicide-tolerant seeds (enabling better weed control with herbicides) and insect toxic seeds (enabling natural insect damage control) have been rapidly adopted in several countries in the past three to four years.

As new ag biotech products have appeared in food markets, an unexpected degree of consumer resistance to genetically modified organisms (GMOs) has emerged. This resistance (fueled to some degree by political movements) has raised a number of questions regarding the regulatory structure for GM foods and for the nature of food markets that are as yet unresolved. In particular, the prospects for the development of GM-free food markets (other than organic food markets) remain unclear at this time. The uncertainty associated with consumer response has had an adverse effect on investor confidence in the ag biotech industries.

This chapter addresses two major questions. The first is an assessment of factors driving invention and innovation in the sector. The second is an assessment of factors influencing the conversion of invention/innovation into economic performance. This chapter documents a high rate of invention/innovation and attributes this high rate to "enabling science." It also documents a high rate of ag biotech product adoption in the early stages of industrial development with significant associated productivity gains. The industry has not

[1] Until 1930, inventions in plants and animals were not provided with IPRs. The 1930 Plant Patent Act in the United States provided limited protection for asexually reproduced plants. It was not until the 1960s that IPRs in the form of "Breeders Rights" were available for sexually reproduced plants.

yet fully addressed the consumer resistance issues. This raises some questions as to the sustainability of early economic performance.

Invention, innovation, and economic performance in the ag biotech sector are discussed in the following format: section 15.2 provides an overview of the public and private organization in the crop and animal genetic invention/innovation fields in the 1970s, prior to the development of methods enabling modern ag biotech invention. Section 15.3 addresses the factors driving inventions and innovation in the modern ag biotech industry. Two key factors driving invention and innovation in the industry are stressed. The first is the science-enablement of invention. The second is the nature of changes in IPRs and associated incentives for industrial firm investment in R&D (Evenson, 2000). The chapter also discusses the regulatory framework impinging on industrial development and the emerging Life Sciences industrial structure.

Section 15.4 describes industrial structure and performance in the sectors.

Section 15.5 discusses the acceptance of ag biotech products by the farm production sector under conditions where GMO discounts and premiums have not been implemented. This acceptance has been quite impressive. Section 15.6 discusses the consumer response to GMOs and the inherent conflict between the interests and policies of the ag biotech firms, food industry firms, and consumers. Prospects for GM-free food markets are discussed. Section 15.7. concludes with policy implications.

15.2. Ag Biotech Invention/Innovation Pre–1980s

Prior to the 1980s, when the first genetically engineered "transformation" of plants was achieved, the structure of the sector was a mixed public/private structure. Agricultural chemicals (herbicides, insecticides, fungicides) were generally produced in specialized divisions of industrial chemical firms. Many of these firms were multi-national firms and included Monsanto, DuPont, Union Carbide, and others.

The fertilizer sector was also a well-estab-lished industrial sector with some overlap with the agricultural chemical sector. Many small firms, particularly in fertilizer distribution, were active in the fertilizer sector. Animal health products were produced by private firms also. A number of firms in the pharmaceutical industry had (have) animal health divisions producing animal health products that in many cases were closely related to human health products.

The animal breeding sector in the 1970s was primarily a farmer-breeder or rancher-breeder sector with numerous small-scale units in the breeding of horses, cattle, sheep, and pigs. Some breeding was undertaken in public sector experiment station programs, particularly in developing countries (see below). For poultry and dairy cattle breeding, specialized firms had emerged by the 1970s. Poultry breeding firms produced breeding lines for specialized grandparent and parent breeders, and a few breeding firms already were dominating the breeding of broilers and layers. For dairy cattle, the development of artificial insemination markets supported by breeders associations was standard. These systems relied on progeny testing of superior animals and the technology of artificial insemination to expand superior genetic traits rapidly in dairy herds.

The crop seed production sector was very much influenced by IPRs. Until the mid-nineteenth century, plant and animal improvement was achieved through the breeding selection strategies of farmers and animal breeders. By contrast, mechanical and chemical inventions were being made by industrial firms and most of these inventions were given patent protection. The late nineteenth century was actually a period of high rates of agricultural invention in the mechanical and chemical fields (Huffman and Evenson, 1993). Public sector Agricultural Experiment Station systems were developed in the late nineteenth century to provide farmers with agronomic advice (often associated with mechanical and chemical inventions) and with biological inventions through plant and animal breeding programs. These breeding programs produced large numbers of improved plant varieties in the first half of the twentieth century in developed

LAYER/ACTIVITY	THE R & D SYSTEM				
	Mathematical Sciences	Physical Sciences	Biological Sciences		Social Sciences
I. GENERAL SCIENCES (University and public agency research primarily)	Mathematics Probability & Statistics	Atmospherical & Meterological Sciences Chemistry Geological Sciences Physics	Bacteriology Biochemistry Botany Ecology	Genetics Microbiology Molecular Biology Zoology	Economics Psychology
II. PRE-TECHNOLOGY SCIENCES (University and public agency research primarily)	Applied Math Applied Physics Engineering Computer Sciences	Climatology Soil Physics & Chemistry Hydrology & Water Resources	Plant Physiology Plant Genetics Phytopathology	Animal & Human Physiology Animal & Human Genetics Animal Pathology Nutrition	Applied Economics Statistics & Econometrics Political Science Sociology
III. TECHNOLOGY INVENTION (Public and private research)	Agricultural Egineering & Design Mechanics Computer Design	Agricultural Chemistry Soils & Soil Science Irrigation & Water Methods	Agronomy Horticulture Plant Breeding Applied Plant Pathology	Animal & Poultry Science Animal Breeding Animal & Human Nutrition Veterinary Medicine	Farm Management Marketing Resource Economics Rural Sociology Public Policy Studies Human Ecology
IV. PRODUCTS FROM INNOVATION (Agro-Industrial Development)	Farm Machinery & Equipment Farm Buildings Computer Equipment/Software	Commercial Fertilizers Agricultural Chemicals Irrigation Systems Pest Control Systems	Crop Plant Varieties Horticultural/Nursery Species Livestock Feed	Animal Breeds Animal Health Products Food Products	Management Systems Marketing Systems Institutional Innovations Health Care Child Care
V. EXTENSION (Public and private)	Resources & Environment	Commodity Oriented	Management & Marketing	Public Policy	Family & Human Resources
VI. FINAL USERS/SOURCES (Clientele problems)	PRODUCERS		GOVERNMENTS		CONSUMERS

Figure 15.1 The Agriculture Innovation System. *Source:* Huffman and Evenson (1993).

countries. These programs have now been replicated in most countries of the world (Evenson, 2000).

For most improved crop varieties, seed production is coordinated through a system of registered and certified seed growers who multiply seed of released varieties and sell seed to farmers. Most crop seed can be replicated by farmers; thus the traditional seed industry in most crops is diversified among many seed growers and suppliers, and most farmers save much of their own seed.

Beginning with the development of "hybrid" seeds in maize in the 1920s (and later in sorghum and millet, and to a lesser extent in rice and wheat), a more formal seed industry with its own R&D capacity has developed. The hybridization process is such that the hybrid vigor or "heterosis" of the seed cannot be replicated in farmer-saved seed. Thus, farmers must buy new seed each year and hybrid seed companies produce this seed through a multi-year process of inbreeding and crossing to produce hybrid seeds for farmers. The seed industry in the United States in the 1970s had a number of major companies (DeKalb, Pioneer, Holdens, etc.) and most produced seed for a number of other crops. (The proportion of farmer-saved seed has declined for most crops in recent years in developed countries, but remains very high in developing countries.)

In the 1960s, plant breeders rights (PBRs) were introduced to stimulate private sector breeding by providing patent-like protection to new crop varieties. The PBR provides a "right to exclude" (for a period of years) others from using a crop variety subject to a "farmers exemption" allowing farmers to save their own seed and to a "research exemption" allowing a plant breeder to use a protected variety as parent material in a breeding program. PBRs are now used in a number of countries and are subject to an international convention (UPOV). They have stimulated expanded plant breeding by private firms. They are generally regarded to be the favored "sui generis" IPR for plants required under the World Trade Organization (WTO) system (Lesser, 2000).[2]

The conceptual model applied to agricultural invention generally is summarized in Figure 15.1 (Huffman and Evenson, 1993). Here a distinction is made between sciences (Level I), where the derived demand (i.e., derived from inventors) carries little weight in

[2] Developing countries are generally hostile to IPRs and often view them as post-colonial type institutions designed mainly to protect the interests of foreign firms.

project selection and design, and the applied or pre-invention sciences (Level II), where the derived demand mechanism operates in a significant way. The agricultural sciences (Level II) in academic institutions (as well as the health sciences and many fields of engineering) were developed to produce pre-invention services for both public and private sector inventors (Level III). This model has proven to be successful in the pre-biotech era for agriculture. It has been expanded to the point where most regions of the world have National Agricultural Research (experiment stations) Systems (NARS) dedicated to producing inventions for farmers. In developed countries the pre-invention sciences have been incorporated into university systems. In the less developed countries, a system of International Agricultural Research Centers (IARCs) has been built to provide an alternative form of pre-invention science services to NARS. The IARCs undertake relatively little applied science, but do engage in other important activities – notably in the provision of genetic germplasm (plant breeding materials) to NARS (Evenson, 2000).

15.3. The Ag Biotech "Revolution": Factors Driving Invention/Innovation

15.3.1. Science Enablement

Ag biotech products are based on inventions made feasible by developments in applied science in recent years. These advances in applied biological science take the form of genetic engineering techniques enabling "transformation" of plants and animals. Transformation entails the insertion of "foreign" (i.e., from another species) genetic material (DNA) into plant or animal cells.[3] Actually, plant and animal breeders have been achieving transformation between closely related species

using pre-biotech methods for many years.[4] This was achieved in sugarcane, rice, wheat and other crop species many years ago (these pre-biotech transformations produced GMOs but this point is largely lost in the current debate over modern GMOs). The first crop transformation using modern gene transfer methods were reported in 1983 (for tobacco and petunia plants). Today, however, plant and animal transformation using several methods is routine.

The role of biological science as a foundation for biological invention has differed somewhat from the role of the physical sciences. Until the 1930s, biological invention was not closely related to biological sciences. Plant breeders did rely on the biological classification system to characterize potential breeding materials. The rediscovery in 1900 of Mendel's classic (1865) work on heredity did guide plant breeding in subsequent years. The role of mutations was better understood after intensive studies of linked genes in fruit flies. Heterosis was well understood in the early part of the century and the development of "hybrid" varieties of corn, sorghum and millets was achieved by 1920.

Late in the 1950s, however, the gene itself remained an "invisible, formal and abstract unit" (Stout, 1969: 16, cited in Ruttan, 2001). Ruttan (2001) identifies four major advances in molecular biology that enabled modern biotechnology invention.

The first was the identification of DNA as the physical carrier of genetic information by Max Delbruck of the California Institute of Technology in 1938.

The second was the discovery by Watson and Crick of the double helix structure of DNA in 1953. This led to institutional change in the form of the recognition of molecular genetics as a new field of science.

The third was the demonstration of a method for inserting genes from a foreign organism into a host genome by Stanley Cohen and

---

[3] Species are typically defined as having a "breeding barrier." Thus, one cannot achieve a viable natural reproductive cross between distinct species. It is possible to achieve natural reproductive crosses in some cases as with the mule (a cross between two animal species, the horse and the donkey) but the progeny of the cross is typically sterile.

[4] Embryo rescue methods have been used to achieve reproductive crosses between many cultivated crop species (e.g., wheat and rice) and the related noncultivated or "wild" species in the same genus.

Herbert Boyer of Stanford University in 1973. This opened the field of genetic engineering (gene splicing).

The fourth was the invention of hybridoma (fusion) technology by Cesar Millstein and George F. Kohler in 1975. This invention enabled the combination of nuclei and cytoplasm from different cells to form a hybrid cell with desirable characteristics from the donor cells.

As these developments were made and published, potential inventors in the field began to develop invention strategies. Prior to the late 1970s, research in molecular biology was the province of universities. As invention opportunities emerged, a new group of science entrepreneurs responded to these opportunities. In most cases these entrepreneurs were scientists, many with major university appointments. Genetic engineering start-up companies were formed, often with university participation and compliance. This led to university–industrial linkages in the early stage of biotech development. As traditional pharmaceutical and chemical firms recognized the potential for inventions and the value of university scientists in this potential, they reinforced the university–industrial complex by providing research grants to universities.

One of the more interesting university–industry programs in the ag biotech field is a research contract between Novartis (Aventis Crop Science) and the College of Natural Resources at the University of California-Berkeley developed in 1996 (Rausser et al., 2000). In return for a substantial research fund contribution, Novartis receives certain first claim rights to inventions or potential inventions produced in University programs. This contract represents a departure from the university patent model that emerged during the 1980s in U.S. universities. In the university patent model, inventions made in universities are patented in the name of the university (and its inventors), and then these rights are licensed to commercial firms (or in some cases to public enterprises). These patent rights are now generating significant revenues for universities. The Novartis–Berkeley model represents a licensing or sale of potential invention rights.

The development of biotechnology methods and subsequent invention in the first generation of ag biotech products, thus, does not fit the model implicit in Figure 15.1 (previous section) very well. (It is argued below that the second and third generations of agricultural biotech products will conform more closely.)[5] Figure 15.1 implies that fundamental science discoveries were made in Level I science programs (this is basically correct) and that, with a lag, Level II applied science programs would work out the methods enabling inventions in Level III public and private organizations, again with a lag. What actually happened for first generation biotechnology inventions was that both the science and methods emerged to a large extent from leading biological science (Level I) programs and that private firms recognized the potential for invention without extensive pre-invention research (or where the pre-invention work was carried out in the private firms' R&D programs).[6]

The departure from the older model was facilitated by the nature of the technology itself and by two major forms of institutional change. The first institutional change was the expansion of IPRs described below. The second was the change in research incentives for universities embodied in the Bayh-Dole Act of 1980. The Bayh-Dole Act allowed universities to have full IPRs for inventions where the research was funded by federal government programs. This change in incentives has had profound effects on universities and university–industry relationships. This is particularly true in the biotechnology fields.[7]

---

[5] The basis for this argument is that over the long run ag biotech methods will be utilized to produce "platform" crop varieties.

[6] To some extent, this reflects a significant time delay in the development of institutions. Level II sciences emerge largely because of demand from Level III programs, not because of supply developments in Level I sciences.

[7] The implications of the Bayh-Dole Act for the conduct of science, especially applied science, are quite important. The extension of IPRs to plants has also had implications for the conduct of agricultural research in the public sector (see Santaniello et al., 2000).

While several methods of transformation have been developed (for agriculture, *Agrobacterium tumefaciens* (bacterial transfer), biolistic (gene-gun), protoplast and electroporation methods have been most widely used), none allow multi-gene transformation.[8] However, "gene stacking," where several single gene transformations are performed on the same plant are now routine. Effective transformation requires that the genetic expression in the transformed plant be passed on to the sexually reproduced progeny. In many programs, "gene-silencing," that is, reproductive failure, has been a problem. (Actually, genetic engineering refers to the DNA insertion techniques and this can be done with genetic material from the same species.[9])

For animals, similar transformations are possible. The inducement of the production of bovine somatotrophin hormone (Bst) was one of the earliest of the ag biotech products). The problem of sexual reproduction of transformed animals can now be bypassed using cloning techniques.

The potential economic value of single gene trait products was recognized quite readily in the past because traditional plant and animal breeding methods had evolved to incorporate a distinction between *quantitative* traits (governed by multiple genes) and *qualitative* traits (governed by a single gene or few genes). Genetic resources used in plant breeding, that is, "landraces" or distinct farmer-selected varieties collected in seed or germplasm banks, have both quantitative and qualitative trait value. The conventional plant breeder makes a parental cross to produce an F_1 generation of plants and then goes through a multi-generation "backcross" process to eliminate as much of the undesired genetic material from the cross as possible, incorporating the desired traits in the resultant variety. This process works for both quantitative and qualitative traits.

Commercial firms recognized that single gene traits could include changes in product quality such as shelf life in tomatoes, protein content in vegetables, etc. They also recognized that one could incorporate insect resistance and disease resistance in plants as extensions of conventional breeding successes; but with the advantage that they could cross species boundaries with genetic engineering techniques. The opportunities to introduce herbicide tolerance traits in plants to enable greater use of herbicides was also recognized.[10] These traits constitute the first generation of ag biotech products. Many have been produced, tested and commercialized. Many more are in the pipeline.

Second generation ag biotech products are now being developed. These products essentially use plants and animals to produce health and pharmaceutical products ("pharming"). Plants and animals have long been used for this purpose but biotechnology methods have expanded the scope for this activity.

Third generation products are expected to be utilizing genome mapping and genetic markers. The development of a full map for rice was recently reported (*Science*). Complete maps will soon be available for most important crops. Plant breeders already use marker-aided breeding techniques to more effectively identify genetic sources and to target (using markers) DNA insertion to achieve more effective expression of traits.

Fourth generation products will be more sophisticated and will be based on "genomics" and "proteonomics," new fields of applied science. Genomics will allow scientists to identify phenotypic traits associated with specific genes and combinations of genes.[11]

Because of the nature of the location specificity of most plant varieties, the platform (quantitative trait) varieties must be produced with a

---

[8] The Agrobacterium tumefaciens method was the first method used. It was based on the only known natural example of gene transfer in the plant kingdom (Bennett, 1995).

[9] The XA21 gene for host plant resistance to bacterial leaf blight in rice is an example (Khush, 1995).

[10] Most crops are damaged by herbicides designed to control weed species. When herbicide tolerance is incorporated into the seed, herbicides can be used more effectively to control weeds.

[11] Genomics is a new field of applied science where phenotypic function is systematically related to specific genes and DNA sequences.

high degree of tailoring to specific locations. The complex system of NARS and IARCs has produced genetic platform varieties throughout most of the developed and developing world using conventional plant breeding methods. Private firms have invested in platform variety development in developed countries, but not in developing countries. First generation (and probably second generation) ag biotech products can be installed onto these platforms with limited capability on the part of host platform recipient. This transfer will be modified by IPRs and their implementation. Third and fourth generation biotech products will call for platform development itself.

Animal biotech products include products such as the bovine somatotrophin hormone (bST) inducing increased milk production in cows. A number of pharmaceuticals are now being produced by animals using similar technologies. However, a major development in the animal biotech field is the development of cloning techniques. These techniques have implications for human health (e.g., the production of organs for transplantation). They also break the natural breeding barrier limiting the rapid reproduction of superior animals.

The reproduction barrier was partially overcome when artificial insemination methods were utilized in animal breeding. This enabled a single male parent to produce numerous offspring, although this was not the case for the female parent. In recent years, the development of embryo splitting techniques (a type of biotechnology) and the harvesting of multiple embryos from superior female animals further reduced the replication barrier. With cloning technology, the replication barrier no longer exists.

15.3.2. IPR Developments

Since 1970 important developments in patent law and its application to plants, plant parts, biotech processes, and to animals has taken place in the United States. Interestingly, these changes have taken place, not because of a change in U.S. patent law, but because of a change in "case law," that is, in court interpretations of existing laws. While similar changes in patent law have occurred in European coun-

tries, the chief expansion of patent "scope" to cover biotech inventions has occurred in the United States. Some features of this expansion of scope were incorporated into the Trade Related Intellectual Property Rights (TRIPS) component of the Uruguay Round of GATT and members of the WTO have accepted obligations to develop increased patent and breeders' rights protection.

The "opening wedge" in patent expansion was the Chakrabarty decision in 1980 (*Diamond vs. Chakrabarty*, 447 US 303, 206 USPQ 193) where living multi-cellular plants and animals were ruled to be "not excluded" from patent protection. Specific court decisions for crops (*ex parte* Hibbard) and animals (*ex parte* Allen) followed. These court decisions were at least partly responding to the early ag biotech inventions. The U.S. Patent and Trademark Office (USPTO) and other patent offices respond to new "fields" of invention and there is thus a natural IPR expansion associated with invention expansion itself. As with other responses to new fields (e.g., in computers), the early decisions and rules regarding patentability are subject to court interpretations. It has been argued that the USPTO has been too expansive in approving ag biotech patents and granting approval to patents that are too "broad" in scope (Bolton, 1998).

The expansion of IPRs to ag biotech products is stated to be critical to firms assisting in the invention of and commercialization of new products. The parallel development of expanded IPRs for biological invention (bringing biological invention on a par with mechanical, chemical, and electrical inventions) has had a profound effect on the industrial structure of the ag biotech industries. The related changes in patenting policy associated with U.S. universities (the Bayh-Dole Act) has also had a profound effect on Government and university science and applied science programs.

15.3.3. The Invention Record in Ag Biotech

Two recent studies of ag biotech inventions have been completed (Zohrabian and Evenson, 2000; Johnson and Santaniello, 2000). These studies report:

TABLE 15.1
IOM-SOU Matrix of US Biotechnology Patents (as a percentage) for 1976–98

Industry of manufacture	Sector of use						
	Agriculture	Chemicals	Drugs	Food	Health	Other	Total
Agriculture	0.5	0.0	0.0	0.0	0.0	0.1	0.6
Chemicals	1.0	3.8	10.9	1.2	1.5	1.8	20.2
Drugs	1.4	1.6	22.7	2.1	35.7	1.2	64.7
Food	0.1	0.0	0.0	1.1	0.0	0.0	1.2
Other	0.3	1.1	0.7	0.3	5.2	7.7	13.3
Total	3.3	6.5	34.3	4.7	40.4	10.8	100

- rapid increases in ag biotech inventions in the United States;
- high shares of university inventions in the United States;
- high proportions of reference to U.S. university inventions in "front page" references in U.S. patents; and
- strong technological leadership by U.S. enterprises internationally.

The relevant data from the two studies are summarized in Tables 15.1 and 15.2. Table 15.1 reports an Industry of Manufacture (IOM)-Sector of Use (SOU) matrix for all U.S. biotechnology patents over the 1976–98 period. The matrix is based on patent assignments by the Canadian Patent Office (The Yale Technology Concordance, Evenson and Johnson, 1997).

These data indicate that the agricultural sector is the SOU of 3.3 percent of all biotech inventions and the food sector is the SOU of 4.7 percent of all biotech inventions. The chemical and drug industries are the IOMs for 85 percent of all biotech inventions and the SOUs for 41 percent. Many of the inventions used in the chemical and drug industries are process inventions. For the product inventions used outside these industries, roughly 14 percent are used in the agricultural and food sectors and 68 percent in the health sector.

Table 15.2 documents the growth in biotech invention and the significant role of universities. It also reports the high degree of references to academic science papers.

Table 15.3 summarizes the international dimension of ag biotechnology invention in the early 1990s. Eastern European economies granted 3 percent of global biotechnology inventions but less than 1 percent of origin inventions. Developing countries granted 6 percent of ag biotech inventions and originated 3–4 percent. Of the developed countries, the United States is clearly the dominant country. The United States grants 12 percent of all ag biotech patents, but U.S. inventors hold more than 45 percent of all origin patent rights.

TABLE 15.2
Biotech Patents Granted in the United States 1990–8

	1990	1995	1998
Number by sector of use			
Crop production	11	30	79
Animal production	11	21	125
Food industries	38	88	309
Health sector	317	688	2720
Percent granted to industries from:			
University research institutes	18	29	29
Private U.S. firms	55	53	51
Private foreign firms	28	18	20
Percent of "front page" references to:			
Academic papers	32	30	NA
U.S. patents	50	52	NA
Foreign patents	18	13	NA

TABLE 15.3

Biotech Patents Granted Internationally (1995)

Granting country	Number granted by sector of use			Percent by country of origin of invention			
	Agriculture	Food	Health	–	United States	Japan	Other
United States	51	88	688	82	–	8	10
Japan	60	96	780	32	28	–	40
United Kingdom	20	25	245	11	39	19	31
France	23	30	307	24	32	16	28
Germany	19	25	247	15	38	19	28
Other developed	116	141	1512	8	45	15	32
Transition	9	10	115	30	35	15	25
Developing countries	25	25	250	50	30	10	10

15.4. Industrial Structure and Economic Performance

15.4.1. The "Life Science" Model of Industrial Structure

The term, "Life Science," has been used to describe the industrial strategy where traditional agricultural chemical companies have acquired leading seed companies with the objective of designing genetic (ag biotech) products that complement their ag chemicals products. The Life Science industrial strategy is evident in Table 15.4 where the top fifteen ag biotech seed companies are listed. Most of these companies were ag chemical companies in the 1970s (or ag chemical divisions in industrial chemical firms). Almost all have acquired leading seed companies. Often they have made considerable investment in the development of ag biotech products. (As noted above, some have university relationships.)

Most of these companies have large R&D programs, ranging from 8 to 15 percent of sales. This R&D to sales ratio is higher than for traditional ag chemical firms and approaches that of the pharmaceutical industry. It should be noted, however, that the fifteen firms account for 26.1 percent of seed sales in 1998, indicating a concentration ratio about half that observed in pharmaceutical industries (Artuso, 1999) Nonetheless, this degree of concentration is higher than in the traditional

seed industry and is seen as threatening to farmers. (This is often seen as particularly threatening in developing countries where most seed is farmer-saved.)[12] The R&D expenditures of these fifteen companies is roughly equivalent to all expenditures on agricultural research in public sector NARS and IARCs in developing countries. Very little of this R&D is targeted to producing "platform" crop varieties in developing countries, however.

The marketing strategy of the Life Science firms differs from the strategy of traditional seed companies. Traditional seed companies sought to price their seed to include a premium for specific genetic advantages embodied in their product. They thus earned innovation rents through higher product prices. Life Science firms are adopting a different strategy. Increasingly they are licensing the IPRs to a biotech trait on a per hectare basis directly to farmers. This licensing fee is thus independent of seed use. It also allows the selling firm to sell a biotech trait without tying it to a specific platform variety. This means that a supplying firm can arrange to insert its product in the platform varieties of other seed companies and of public sector experiment stations. Success in this marketing strategy depends on the institutional support for contracts binding the purchasers to

---

[12] Countries with little experience with IPRs are subject to considerable potential uncertainty regarding these rights.

TABLE 15.4
Sales and Market Shares of Top 15 Ag Biotech Companies

Company	1998 sales	
	U.S.$ millions	Share (percent)
DuPont/Pioneer	1625	5.4
Novartis Seeds	1056	3.5
Limagraine	1027	3.4
Seminis/DNAP	498	1.7
Monsanto/DeKalb/DPL	1020	3.4
Advanta	445	1.5
Takii	360	1.2
Sakata	349	1.2
Cargill	330	1.1
KWS	329	1.1
Agribiotech	205	0.7
Berenburg	168	0.6
Mycogen/Dow	162	0.5
AgrEvo/Aventis	131	0.4
DLF Trifolium	120	0.4
Total	7824	26.1

Source: Artuso (1999).

conditions protecting the IPRs of the seller. (This has implications for developing countries where IPR protection is weak or nonexistent.)

As shown in Table 15.4, the top fifteen companies are estimated to account for approximately 26 percent of total seed industry sales. However, recent and pending mergers and acquisitions within the industry have resulted in much higher levels of concentration within certain segments of the North American and European seed markets. Two companies, DuPont/Pioneer and Monsanto/DeKalb, account for over 50 percent of North American sales of corn seed and nearly 40 percent of North American soybean seed sales. Monsanto will also control over 60 percent of the North American market for cotton if its acquisition of Delta & Pine Land is approved by the U.S. Justice Department. The vegetable seed market has also become increasingly concentrated due to acquisitions by Empresas la Moderna (ELM) subsidiary Seminis, and the French company, Limagraine. Based upon data contained in their most recent annual reports, these two

companies now account for more than 40 percent of global commercial sales of fruit and vegetable seed.

Leading firms in the market for seed varieties and agricultural biotechnology products also are confronted with significant amounts of both actual and potential competition. In addition to market leaders such as Monsanto and DuPont/Pioneer, several other large, diversified, life science companies are aggressively seeking to increase their shares of the corn, soybean, oilseed, and vegetable seed markets. Novartis has expanded its maize and soybean seed sales in the North American market and has realized strong sales growth for vegetable and horticultural seeds. Aventis Crop Science is actively marketing herbicide-tolerant corn and canola seed and has recently established itself as a strong competitor in the vegetable seed market with the acquisitions of Nunza and Sunseeds. Advanta, which is a joint venture of the life science company Zeneca (soon to be AstraZeneca) and Cooperatie Cosun of the Netherlands, is also competing in the maize, cotton, and oilseed markets. The recent acquisition of Mycogen by Dow Agro Sciences creates another well-financed competitor in the maize and soybean seed markets.

15.4.2. The Regulatory Environment

Regulations have been concerned with two major production issues. For herbicide tolerant (HT) crops, the concern is that herbicide tolerance will be transformed to "weedy relatives" of the crops, thus defeating the economic objective of the product. To date, with numerous field trials, little or no evidence that this is occurring has been produced. More than 25,000 such trials have now been conducted.

The second concern which is influencing deployment of new biotech crops, is the potential of insects resistant to *Bacillus thuringiensis* (Bt) affecting other crops where sprayable Bt is used. Both for farmers not adopting the crop Bt and for users of the sprayable Bt the claim is made that they will lose one of their best and safest pest management tools because of the potential development of insects resistant to crop Bt.

The Environmental Protection Agency (EPA) is requiring as a condition for obtaining registration and the right to sell the crops seeds that all companies must have a resistance management plan. The crops containing Bt are regulated as "plant pesticides" under the standard pesticide law (FIFRA) as are the herbicides that can be used on the HT crop cultivars. In the case of the BHT crops, the force of these property rights restrictions (for health concerns) is illustrated by a recent cancellation of an HT crop herbicide after many years of research and three years of commercial sales.

The EPA is the regulatory agency in the United States. In Canada, the regulation of seed testing and approval of varieties falls on the Plant Biotechnology Office (Agriculture Canada web site). These agencies are responsible for pesticide safety and efficacy. EPA policies and not court rulings, patents or private contracts are the institutional changes that are critical to the deployment of seeds effective against crop pests.

Table 15.5 summarizes some recent events critical to crop biotechnology related to pest control. The U.S. Development Agency (USDA) entries refer to the approval process for conducting field tests. This step in the development process has become more streamlined, and it also provides information on likely new products by crop, company and technology type (Carlson and Marra, 2000).

The federal pesticide law in the United States is FIFRA with amendments. The insecticides expressed in insect-resistant crops developed by biotechnology are being regulated as "plant pesticides." The FIFRA (1947) law required that all pesticides must be registered with USDA before they began market sales. This responsibility was turned over to the EPA in 1970, but the Federal Drug Agency (FDA) retains responsibility for setting the acceptable pesticide residue tolerances. The tolerance setting process has been revised by the 1996 Food Quality Protection Act.

New pesticides usually receive conditional registrations until all safety, efficacy, and other conditions are met. Given the urgency to get approval to begin commercial marketing, manufacturers are willing to respond to agency

TABLE 15.5
Recent History of Crop Protection Biotechnology in North America

1987	First successful insertion of Bt toxin gene into plant
1990	First introduction of Bt into corn plant
1992	First field trials of Bt corn under USDA permit; Flavor Saver tomato approved
1993	USDA simplifies field test approval
1994	BXN (bromoxynil) cotton approved, first HT crop
1994	First trials with plant pharmaceutical objectives begin in Canada
1995	Agriculture Canada approves HT canola and soybeans
3/95	Ceiba Seeds receives limited registration for planting Bt corn
8/95	First full registration of Bt corn by EPA
10/95	First Bt cotton and potatoes approved for planting in United States
1/96	Roundup tolerant soybeans first marketed in United States
1/97	First "stacked" gene product (Bt and RR cotton) approved
7/97	Roundup tolerant corn seed approved for 1998 crop year
9/97	Petition charges EPA with "gross negligence" in regulating genetically engineered plants
11/97	First cancellation of HT crop herbicide
4/98	USEPA reverses cancellation of herbicide for HT cotton

demands for monitoring, label restrictions, and other requests. The primary objective of EPA actions under FIFRA is to avoid "unacceptable adverse effects on the environment."

Since 1972, the registration of new pesticides requires that the manufacturers provide test data on safety and efficacy. Later amendments clarify that re-registration and evaluation are required for all active ingredients. Also, if there are any changes in information on either safety or efficacy of the pesticide, it is the responsibility of the manufacturer to make this information available to the agency. EPA has required "Resistance Management Plans" of manufacturers.

Label restrictions are another way EPA limits the property rights of patent holders and users of pesticides. Label restrictions can specify where a chemical can be used (crops, counties), maximum amounts per application and per season, method of application, applicator equipment and exposure, and when the application can be made (crop stage, pre-harvest intervals). Registrants are usually willing to accept label limitations to obtain registration and early market entry.

FIFRA also provides for cancellation and suspension of registrations. Usually this process involves a consideration of benefits and costs, but the provisions of the 1996 Food Quality Protection Act limit when benefits of pesticides can be considered in the cancellation and registration decisions to times when there might be a "significant disruption" of the food supply.

The resistance management restrictions have taken the form of no planting zones or refugia on which Bt corn or cotton will not be planted on each farm. These conventional corn and cotton fields are intended to provide a place where insects susceptible to Bt can be produced and thus, limit resistance build up over time.

Refugia were required in the first year, 1997, of marketing Bt cotton by Monsanto. Generally, the refugia limits have been set as at least 5 percent of all corn or cotton acreage on each farm if no insecticides are used in the refuge, and 20 percent if insecticides are applied. Scientists supporting the Union of Concerned Scientists are calling for an expansion of minimum refugia size to 50 percent of crop acreage. The main objective of refugia is to prevent future resistance development of target insect species (European cornborer for corn; bollworm, budworm, and pink bollworm for cotton).

15.4.3. Economic Performance: Industry

The economic performance of the ag biotech industry is difficulty to assess at this stage. In the United States, at least twelve ag biotech products have been given regulatory approval. Of these, three are the bST hormone product for dairy producers, the HT seed products and the Bt insect resistance products. The HT and insect resistance products have been intro-

duced in several crops and have been widely adopted by farmers (see below). There is considerable promise that recently approved disease resistant products will succeed as well. Several products, notably the Calgene Flavor Saver Tomato (with longer shelf life) have not had market success.

One of the successful product types is the HT products. These products incorporate genetic tolerance to specific types of herbicides, enabling farmers to use these herbicides for weed control on crops where they would otherwise not be used. The most important products of this type are the "Roundup Ready" products contributing tolerance to Monsanto's Roundup herbicides. The chief Roundup patent expires in 2000 and it is alleged that this product extends the effective patent life for the herbicide. Roundup is the most widely used herbicide in the world. It has a limited market in low wage economies because weed control can be achieved by labor-intensive methods. It has a large market in the United States where wages are high and where minimum tillage methods are practiced. Liberty/Link, a second product with tolerance to the herbicide Liberty is also being sold.

A second successful type is the Bt products. *Bacillus thuringienesis* is a natural insecticide occurring in the soil. This bacteria is toxic to certain classes of insect pests, but not to all insects. It is also presumably not toxic to animals and humans. Plants have been engineered to produce this toxin in plant tissue. This enables more effective control of insects such as the cotton boll weevil, where traditional chemical insecticide control has had limited effectiveness. It also allows effective control for insects where chemical insecticides have been used, enabling reduced use of insecticides.

Both of these products face resistance from consumer groups and from environmental groups (see below). To the degree that GMO discounts emerge in these markets, the acceptance by farmers will be discouraged.

Estimates of the potential market for ag biotech products embodied in seed vary. The International Seed Industry Federation estimates global seed sales to be nearly U.S.$30 billion, with somewhat more than U.S.$20 billion occurring in sixteen countries. The North American market, including Mexico, is estimated to account for approximately 20 percent of commercial seed sales; the European Union for approximately 15 percent; Russia, Ukraine, and eastern Europe for 9 percent; China and Japan for approximately 8 percent each; and Latin America for 7 percent. Global seed exports exceeded U.S.$3.5 billion in 1997 with U.S. exports accounting for approximately 25 percent of that total, followed by 17 percent for the Netherlands and 15 percent for France.

The growth potential of the agricultural biotechnology sector is likely to become increasingly dependent on improvements in output traits, such as taste texture and nutritional characteristics. Products currently available with improved output traits include sunflower, canola, and soybeans with modified oil content (Dow/Mycogen, Optimum Quality Grains), and vegetable varieties with improved taste and texture (Zeneca, Seminis/DNAP). In addition, an increasing number of products currently in development or in field trials are designed to improve output traits such as enhanced shelf life in tomatoes, peppers, strawberries and other fruits, increased nutritional quality, antioxidant and vitamin content in vegetables (carrots (PetoSeed) and tomato (Zeneca)), improved taste (peppers (DNAP)), modified carbohydrates and starch content (potato (Monsanto) and pea (DNAP)), increased protein (corn (DeKalb)), and production of industrial enzymes and pharmaceutical proteins (Monsanto, Nobel Foundation, University of Wisconsin).

Increasingly, both pharmaceuticals and new crop development are also employing similar technologies for new product development. Advances in gene sequencing and analysis, collectively known as genomics, and more recently, analysis of the proteins coded by genes, known as proteomics, have been employed by pharmaceutical companies to develop new gene therapies, identify new drug targets, and understand the biochemical pathways responsible for disease and healing. These technologies are now being employed by agricultural biotechnology companies to map the genomes of the major crop species. Over time,

genomics and proteomics may reduce the marginal cost of developing both new drugs and new crop varieties, but in the short to medium term, substantial initial investments must be made in both human resources and capital equipment. Even the larger life science companies, such as Monsanto, DuPont/Pioneer, and AstraZeneca have created alliances with biotechnology companies specializing in gene sequencing and protein analysis. Each of these companies and the start-up biotechnology companies with which they are collaborating are employing genomics and proteomics for both pharmaceutical and crop development.

From the perspective of investors, the economic success of the ag biotech industry has been disappointing. The significant sales of ag biotech products have not been sufficient to justify high rates of return on the large R&D investments made. Many of the merger combinations in Life Science companies turned out to be difficult to manage because of different cultures in the chemical and seed companies.

15.5. Farmer Acceptance of Ag Biotech Products and Impacts on Production

Three classes of ag biotech products have been adopted by farmers in the United States and in several other countries under conditions where GMO discounts have not been important They are:

- bST or bovine somatotrophin, a genetically engineered synthetic analogue of the naturally produced hormone in cow's milk, was introduced in 1994 to stimulate increased milk production;
- Herbicide-resistant crops. This product enables the use of herbicides to control weeds on these crops. Without the resistance genes, the herbicides cannot be used. These products have been incorporated into corn, soybeans, and canola varieties.
- Bt crops producing bacterial (*Bacillus thuringiensis*) toxicity in plant tissues to specific types of insects. Bt toxicity has been incorporated into corn, cotton, tobacco, and potatoes.

One study of bST adoption in New York showed that farmers adopting the product have produced more milk per cow but not necessarily more profits per cow (Tauer, 2000). A California study (Henriques and Butler, 2000) showed that bST is profitable when complementary feed management practices are adopted. Jarvis (1999) reviews a number of economic studies and concludes that under proper management, profit increases per cow are relatively low (less than U.S.$1,000), but for large herds (2,000 cows) total profits can be quite substantial. Adoption of bST has generally been highest for larger enterprises.

Adoption of herbicide-resistant crops, especially of "Roundup-Ready" soybeans and corn has been very rapid. (Roundup is the most widely used herbicide in the world. It is produced by Monsanto as is the biotech product.) The general consensus is that these products do not necessarily increase yield, but that they do reduce herbicide costs. Actually many farmers adopt this product as an "insurance" device because if weather conditions prevent mechanical weed control measures, herbicide-resistant crops can be treated with herbicides even during adverse weather.

The Bt crops, especially cotton, clearly show cost and profit advantages, because they provide insect control that chemicals cannot provide. Thus, they not only enable reduced insecticide use but enhanced yields as well. Farms in the United States and in China report 4–8 percent yield gains for corn and 6–12 percent yield gains for cotton (James, 1999; Marra et al., 1999; Gianessi and Carpenter, 1999).

Farm studies of adoption of ag biotech products thus show quite rapid diffusion of these products among farmers. Except for the Bt products, however, they also show quite modest cost advantages. Thus, if consumer reaction were sufficient to create a 10 percent discount in the farm price of GM products, it appears that adoption of these products would be low. (Note, as discussed below, products embedded in cotton and in corn for livestock feed will probably have lower consumer resistance than farm products consumed directly as food (some cottonseed oil is consumed directly).)

Data for U.S. acreage planted to GM crops indicate that the proportion of corn area planted to GM seeds declined from 33 percent in 1999 to 25 percent in 2000. This decline reflected a concern that discounts for GM products would begin to emerge. However, GM soybeans in 2000 accounted for 54 percent of area and GM cotton (primarily Bt) was planted on 61 percent of cotton area.

When converted to productivity change terms, the early gains, however, are impressive. The crop products in question have been used by farmers for only five or six years. Even with modest gains of 5–10 percent cost reductions in the field (and they are probably higher than this), this translated into significant additions to total factor production gains in agriculture. (Note, the hybrid corn advantage calculated by Griliches was 28 percent.)

15.6. Consumer Reaction and Implications for GMO Discounts

Each year large numbers of new products meet regulatory standards and are approved for marketing. The ag biotech industry adopted a policy of supporting existing regulatory practices but opposing labeling of food products that are made from GMOs.

In U.S. markets, the first ag biotech products were generally accepted as safe foods. In Europe, however, where several "food scare" episodes had occurred (notably Mad Cow Disease), consumer groups expressed concern over GMOs and demanded labeling as a "consumer right to know." Industry responses, at least in the United States, were to continue to oppose mandatory labeling. They argued that it was costly to segregate GMO products from non–GMO products and to establish separate markets for GMO and non–GMO products. This strategy has essentially "backfired" for several reasons.

First, several major grocery chains in Europe (Sainsbury and others) announced that they would not sell GMO products (to the extent possible at least). Several food manufacturers followed suit. These moves made good marketing sense, as long as consumers expressed some preference for non–GM foods and as long as premiums for non–GMO segregated foods at the farm level were small (or zero). This response has since been translated into import bans on GMO products in many countries.

Second, the Organic Food Industry, which had already developed market segregation for organically grown products adopted a policy excluding GMOs from the organic market (even though some of the GMOs actually enabled more efficient organic (i.e., nonchemical) production). The organic food industry enjoyed an increase in demand because it provided consumers with assurance that the products were non–GMO products.

Third, the GMO issue became part of a larger collection of issues included in the opposition to "globalization" and related policies reflected in political oppositions to the WTO (Seattle) and the World Bank-IMF (Washington). This "movement" may have a considerable element of irrationality and misunderstanding of economics as is probably the case for most movements, but it does have appeal to a large number of groups.

Fourth, stockholders in ag biotech firms have expressed concern that the ag biotech units in larger companies are not generating incomes commensurate with other units in the companies. These factors are probably going to result in industry acceptance of labeling for GMO content in foods. This in turn will require market segregation of GMO crops, for certain products with resultant premiums and discounts. For crops used directly in foods, this may not be too serious, except for vegetable oils. Most fruits and vegetables are segregated for product quality reasons. Soybean oil, however, is based on a major GMO crop and a major vegetable oil. Canola oil is in a similar position. Methods for testing and certifying non–GMO status will have to be developed further.

Recent studies of the costs of segregation and certification have been undertaken. Lin (2000) notes that in 1999 the market for non–GM corn was small (about 1 percent of the crop). Similarly, the market for non–GM soybeans was also only 2 percent of the crop. This market was created by Japan and European Union buyers

as well as a few specialized U.S. firms. Small premiums (5–10 cents per bushel for corn, 10–15 cents for soybeans) were offered for non–GM crops.

This market is likely to grow, however. The cost of segregating non–GM crops from GM crops and the costs of testing and certifying non–GM status become relevant for the emergence of larger non–GM crop markets. Many countries are now implementing labeling requirements.

Lin (2000) notes that there are costs to segregating non–GM crops from GM crops, as well as costs of identity preservation. Estimates of additional costs of handling specialized high oil corn in the United States were 6 cents per bushel. For food grade soybeans these costs were 18 cents per bushel. This represents only 3–5 percent of the farm value of the crop. Estimates of segregation costs for non–GM corn and soybeans, including added marketing costs were 22 cents for corn and 54 cents for soybeans. Costs of testing for GM content were relatively small (3–6 cents per bushel).

The USDA study indicated, however, that with large volume and specialized handling facilities, these costs could be lowered, but that they would probably be between 6 and 10 percent of farm value. This is roughly the order of magnitude of the cost advantage to farmers for corn and soybeans, so if a large market for non–GM foods were to develop it would curtail the use of the current generation of ag biotech products.

Few studies of consumers "willingness to pay" premiums have been made. One recent study (Mendenhall, 2000) made in the United States suggests that few consumers would pay a 20 percent premium for non–GM foods, but that many would pay a 10 percent premium. This is probably less than the premiums paid in the organic food markets. However, for some food products, the farm value component is small (e.g., margarine produced from soybean oil), so a small premium at the retail level can support a substantial premium at the farm level.

The food industry will engage in a number of economic experiments over the next few years to determine whether significant non–GM markets can be developed. One issue will be whether such markets will be developed independently of the organic food markets which now offer non–GM foods.

It is quite likely that many specialized food products such as breakfast food, canned products, etc., will end up being labeled and certified as non–GM products. Consumer resistance sufficient to justify animal products certified to have been produced with non–GM feed grains is less likely.

The food industry is discovering that the "consumer is always right" and that there is a limit to the acceptance of food additives, etc. The consumer is also becoming more concerned with food origins and other special qualities. The industry will change as competition induces it to do so. However, the regulatory agencies supporting the food industry will also have to change.

15.7. Policy Lessons

Two central questions are asked of the experience with ag biotech products from a policy perspective. The first is, what factors were important in guiding and driving innovation in the sector? The second is, what factors were important in guiding the translation of innovation into economic performance?

15.7.1. Factors Driving Innovation

It is useful to distinguish between invention and innovation—the bringing of inventions into commercialization and marketed form in this discussion. This is partly because inventors need not be commercializers or innovators. In fact, inventors need not be integrated into commercial enterprises because they can sell rights to inventions to commercializers (the university patent model).

The key factor driving invention in ag biotech in a most basic sense was the advances made in science and applied science. The key scientific advances discussed earlier were made in university science programs. They were guided by a quest for understanding of plant genetics and biochemistry. As these advances unfolded,

invention (and ultimately commercialization) potentials were recognized.

The next key factor driving invention was the development of university–industry alliances. These were institutional innovations driven by the recognition by industrial entrepreneurs that university (and related science programs) scientists held knowledge and insights vital to invention. These alliances were of three types:

- the university faculty start-up company type;
- the industry-funded university research type; and
- the university patent type.

All three institutional forms were utilized to produce first generation ag biotech inventions. They created "demand expression" to scientists and induced them to move in the direction of invention. The Bayh-Dole Act and related changes in the university culture supported these institutional changes.

To some extent, the line between science and applied science has become blurred as a consequence. Two concerns have emerged regarding the conduct of science and applied science. The first is that the mix of effort has been "tilted" away from science toward more applied science as scientists seek to obtain IPRs for methods (process) inventions. The inference is that the exchange of scientific communication has been damaged in the process.

These are legitimate concerns, of course. It might be argued that a high degree of responsiveness to demands derived from inventions (i.e., demand for methods and for the science associated with method development) makes both science and applied science more productive. It probably does, but the concern that this starves the "unfettered" quest for knowledge has some validity. At least for the present, however, one has to conclude that the productivity of both science and applied science in this field is high.

The concern with the exchange of information and in the sharing of genetic resources is more serious. Private firms do rely on trade secrecy and give up secrecy reluctantly. This does impede discovery (one of the advantages of patent and breeder rights is that they call for removal from secrecy). The institutional traditions of open and free exchange of information in the science and applied science organization also offers at least a partial antidote to the secrecy problem.

This is also a case where IPRs have been important in driving invention as well as innovation. The IPR expansion achieved through case law provided assurances to universities, or to ag biotech start-ups and to the Life Science firms, of protection of key inventions. IPR expansion, however, has been subject to many of the problems associated with new fields of invention. Some patents have been granted that are too "broad" to use in the public interest (Barton, 1999).

The venture capital, risk-taking culture characterizing the United States in recent decades has provided a favorable climate for ag biotech product commercialization. It is important to note that IPRs, chiefly the patent rights, are perceived to be crucial to the product commercialization stage. IPRs are probably more important for this stage than for the invention stage. Trade secrecy is part of product development but does not appear to hamper this stage.

The regulatory environment, calling for extensive field tests for environmental and food safety concerns, appears not to have been a serious barrier to product development. Numerous products have been tested and many more are in the pipeline.

15.7.2. Factors Driving the Translation of Innovation into Economic Performance

At this point (late 2000), it is possible to argue that what has been an impressive innovation performance has also been translated into an impressive economic performance. It cannot be argued, however, that the economic performance is associated with high returns to investors. The adoption of several ag biotech products (Bst, the Bt insect resistance products, and the herbicide tolerance products) has actually been impressive. But the ag biotech industry has not handled the consumer response issue well, and there are prospects for significant regulation and prohibition of sales of GM products. It is also not clear at this point whether existing ag biotech

products will have significant markets in developing countries.

It does appear that the traditional regulatory system has not been an important barrier to economic performance. The processes of testing and approval by several agencies have seemingly worked well and might have been expected to allay consumer fears. Had the ag biotech industry been more sensitive to the concerns of the food industries and not taken a strong stance against labeling and segregation of GM foods, the consumer movement might have taken a different form. The ag biotech industry is now faced with at least some market development that will result in some GM market discounts. These will limit the economic impact of some ag biotech products.

15.7.3. Implications for International Technology Transfer

The United States is the leading generator of ag biotech products and of associated inventions and methods. A number of other OECD countries, however, are also producing these products. There are two channels by which products produced in one country benefit another country. The first is through the direct sale of the products in the second country at prices (licensing fees) that constitute a "bargain" in the purchasing country. The second is the indirect contribution through "adaptive invention" in the second country, that is, where the inventions of the product in the first country enables inventions in the second, with adaptive tailoring of the invention to the soil, climate and economic condition of the second. Both channels are important for ag biotech products.

The direct channel is mediated by IPR systems and related contract and legal systems. It is also affected by regulations and trade policy. The first generation ag biotech products of the single gene trait type can be sold or licensed over a broad range of production environments even though the actual crop varieties in which they are inserted are actually location specific. The Roundup Ready trait, for example, has been incorporated into many soybean varieties. It has been sold in a number of countries, including some developing countries. It has also been regulated and banned in some European countries.

The indirect channel requires both a supportive institutional (IPR) environment and a capacity for adaptive invention. The private sector capacity for adaptive invention (i.e., R&D capacity in private firms) is substantial in OECD countries, but limited to only twenty or so of the most advanced developed countries (Evenson and Johnson, 2000). Public sector capacity for agricultural research is well developed in all developed and most developing countries (80 of the 100 major developing countries have well developed public NARS). However, the biotech research capacity in these NARS is quite limited.

The IARC system developed in partial response to limited applied (pre-invention) science capacity in NARS has been effective in providing various kinds of applied science support to NARS (especially plant breeding germplasm) but it has been very slow to provide biotech method services. This is partly due to the age distribution of scientists in the system and to limited scope for hiring new scientists trained at the biotech method frontiers.

The consumer resistance movement has also made it difficult for international agencies supporting the IARC system to aggressively move to provide essential biotech capacity building services. Ironically, the "movement" which would generally claim to be supportive of the interests of the "poorest of the poor" may be a major impediment to the provision of access to technology already implemented in developed countries; it may also impede indirect transfer to some European countries as well (see Evenson, 2000 for evidence that this can have serious consequences for the poorest developing countries).

Electric Power

David G. Victor

16.1. Introduction

To celebrate the arrival of the new century, the U.S. National Academy of Engineering listed the twenty greatest engineering achievements of the last. Electrification came first. By some measures, the age of electricity began in 1882 when Thomas Edison switched on his first commercial generating station on Pearl Street in lower Manhattan, supplying electricity and incandescent illumination to seven dozen customers, including one of his key financial backers, J.P. Morgan. But the spread of electric technologies, like most other large technological changes, took off slowly. In America, Edison and his competitors dotted cities and towns with generators and distribution networks. But in 1900, sun and kerosene still lit the indoors of nearly all American houses; steam and water power still supplied 95 percent of all mechanical energy, tying factories to messy furnaces and remote rivers. By the 1930s, two-thirds of American households were wired; candles and kerosene were retreating to niche markets—on tables for romantic dinners and stored in closets, ready for those rarer and briefer moments when the electrons stopped. Only by the 1950s was the electrification of American households complete—spread not only through urban areas but also to nearly every distant farm. Europe and Japan also electrified over the century—first in dense urban areas and then across the countryside. Electricity transformed the quantity, flexibility and safety of home lighting; compact AC motors and elec-tric appliances such as vacuum cleaners and washing machines (both invented in 1907) eventually liberated the household—and women in particular—from backbreaking work.[1] Today electrification is spreading its benefits across the developing world as well.

Electrification caused a revolution in industrial productivity. Although Edison is most famously identified with electric lights, he was skeptical that illumination would be electricity's winning punch; gas lighting was a strong competitor. Mechanical drives, Edison thought, were electricity's strong suit and would make electricity the mover of choice in industry (Millard, 1990: chapter 5). Edison was right, but like most engineers he overestimated what was possible in the short run and could not dream of the revolution that would unfold over the much longer term. As Paul David (1990) has shown, it took time for the full benefits of electrification to be felt because they required changing both the paradigm of industrial production as well as the capital stock. Initially, the effects were marginal as factory managers simply replaced steam or water line drives with electric motors and replaced gas lights with incandescent. More profound changes occurred over decades—from 1900 to the 1920s—as the ability to carry power by wire liberated machines from drive shafts and made it possible to redesign factories. In 1900, only one-third of the electricity used by industry went to mechanical force, with the rest mainly for lighting; by 1920, the proportions had

I thank Richard Foster, Richard Nelson and Benn Steil for comments, Nadejda Victor for assistance with the figures, Rebecca Weiner for research assistance, and the Council's programs on Science & Technology and the Project on Innovation and Economic Performance for support.

---

[1] On efforts to measure the improvement and consequences of electric light, see Nordhaus (1997); on lighting technologies and their social impacts, such as on street and family life and in the theater, see Hughes (1983) and Blühm and Lippincott (2000); for a history of electric technologies see Hyman (1995).

reversed as plant managers figured out how to optimize the use of electric motors on the factory floor. Quality and productivity—both difficult to measure—rose sharply; but the complete transformation took about four decades.[2]

Nearly every industry has been affected, although often the impacts have taken even longer to be realized. Modern aluminum smelting depends on electricity to heat smelter pots as well as to electrolyze alumina in bauxite mined from Earth into pure aluminum. That industry did not flourish until demand for high quality aluminum soared with the aircraft industry after the second world war. Electricity also transformed steel production, making possible small batch processing of scrap steel in electric arc furnaces, which excel at tailoring steel production to customer needs and are more efficient than the lumbering giant integrated mills that they replaced. Today, electricity is also the backbone of the computer-intensive "new economy," which in turn is forcing changes in the electric power business by creating demand for new industries that supply backup power sources and devices to "clean" grid power for use in sensitive electronics (Feder, 2000). Transportation is the only major element of modern industrial society, accounting for one-quarter to one-fifth of the total consumption of primary energy, where electricity still remains at the margin. Although a contender in the late nineteenth century, the electric car could not compete with more flexible and longer range internal combustion engines (Kirsch, 2000). Yet even in this area,

electrons may yet transform the industry—in the dirtiest cities with the wealthiest drivers and strongest regulators, pure and "hybrid" electric cars are making inroads by supplying mobility that is cleaner and more efficient than the pure internal combustion engine. Electricity is a "general purpose technology" that has been contributing to the growth of industrial economies for a century.[3] No wonder the engineers listed omnipresent electrification first.

This study puts the spotlight on the generation of electric power itself. Broadly, the development of the industry can be divided into three periods during which three very different forces for innovation were at work. In the earliest period, electric power generation was driven by the competition between the newcomer (electricity) and incumbent energy sources such as town gas and kerosene for illumination and water and steam power for mechanical energy. This was a period of great technological diversity and intense competition between immature business models and technologies. For this first phase, the chapter focuses on the experience in the United States, where competition was particularly intense and technological change was especially rapid. By the 1920s in the United States and in Western Europe, electricity emerged victorious from this great competition and the firms that controlled electric networks were solidifying their position as natural monopolies. By the 1930s, governments controlled the industry in all the major advanced industrialized countries—either directly as owners or indirectly as regulators of privately owned utilities. The United States saw both patterns: regulation, which began in 1907 and was complete by 1935; and also direct government control in the form of large power projects such as the Tennessee Valley Authority. Everywhere, governments justified their intervention not only to avert price gouging by natural monopolists but also as part of a broader, illiberal pattern in government that favored state ownership of firms that provided public goods. The state-controlled system, which marks a second era, helped to stabilize competition and probably aided the diffusion of new

[2] For more on the slow pace at which electrification made its mark on the economy, see Devine (1983) and Schurr et al. (1990).

[3] For early overviews of the impact of electricity on the economy, see National Research Council (1986). For general overviews, see Mowery and Rosenberg (1998: chapter 5) and Rosenberg (1998a). For a compact evaluation of the evolution of electric power technology, see, especially, Marchetti and Ausubel (1996); for a look to the future, see Electric Power Research Institute (1999). On general purpose technologies, such as electricity, see Bresnahan and Trajtenberg (1995); for some similar ideas with different concepts about why electricity is a "different" kind of technology, see Schmidt (1984).

technology. Through the 1960s, the technological frontier for existing generation equipment based on steam turbines remained steps in front of actual industry practice, and it was relatively easy for utilities and regulators to agree on investments in marginal technological changes that raised efficiency and reduced operating costs. Although regulators had limited information, the supply of generation equipment remained a competitive business, and suppliers had a strong incentive to alert utilities and regulators alike to efficiency-enhancing innovations. But as the frontier for steam generation slowed in the late 1960s, performance of traditional coal-fired steam generators stagnated (Joskow and Jones, 1983; Nelson and Wohar, 1983; Joskow and Rose, 1985; Joskow, 1987; Hirsh, 1989).

Finally, the industry appears to be entering a third era of "restructuring" as governments in many markets retreat from direct ownership and control, allowing greater competition in power generation and retailing while continuing to own or regulate as a natural monopoly the wires that transmit power from generators to consumers. That era began in the 1970s with a partial deregulation of a very limited segment of electric power supply in the United States. That change eased the entry of new power supplies, including renewable electric power sources—such as wind and solar—that were also aided by subsidies and favorable accounting rules. Although Chile was the first to restructure its market completely, the first major industrialized nation to fully restructure its electric power system was the United Kingdom. This chapter reviews the U.K. policies, which are the most widely emulated and watched in other jurisdictions that are considering restructuring.

Throughout, the goal is not to recount the full twelve decades of electrification but, rather, to examine the main forces for innovation, the factors that have governed the diffusion (uptake) of innovations, and the ultimate impact of technological changes on performance of entities that generate electric power. Conceptually, the last link is the hardest. From the perspective of consumers, the long term "performance" of the industry has been specta-

cular—electric power has become cheaper and more reliable, mainly because of technological change that has allowed more efficient production at larger scales with denser and more reliable power grids and (during most of the period) state control that restrained monopolists. From the perspective of the generating companies, the link between technological change and performance—such as private or public value-added, or stock valuations—is harder to evaluate, especially during the period of intense state control. The real performance of state-owned firms during this era is particularly shrouded in mystery and hard to probe. Where generators were privately owned, as in most of the United States, "performance" as measured by returns to investors was first and foremost a function of regulatory procedure, not innovation, and attempts to link innovation and performance create the misleading impression that firm managers were free to exploit technological potentials to enhance firm performance. The performance of utility stocks was generally poor and lagged behind other equity investments, especially starting in the 1970s when innovation became more complex because the traditional approach—the installation of ever-larger power plants—ran out of steam. In principle, restructuring is breaking the link between regulation and performance and will allow the most competitive firms to flourish. In practice, however, restructuring is being implemented in ways that do not yield fully open competition, and the era of restructuring is still comparatively short.

While the industry has seen many technological changes over the century, this chapter puts the spotlight on three major changes in technology:

- The basic structure of the industry organized around large steam turbines, mainly fed with coal. That structure dominated the U.S. industry by the 1910s and still dominates in most countries today.
- The arrival and rapid diffusion of nuclear power, which was the most important technological change from the early 1960s through the 1980s. This chapter gives particular attention to nuclear power in three

countries: the United States (the largest single market, accounting for one-third of the world's nuclear power generation), France (the nation with the highest share of nuclear power in its electricity system today, 77 percent), and the United Kingdom (the country where the impacts of restructuring on the nuclear power industry are most transparent).[4]

- The rapid shift to natural gas technologies in the 1990s, often dubbed the "dash to gas," which is especially evident after market restructuring in the United Kingdom and the United States. and was facilitated by the availability of low-cost, flexible and efficient gas turbines.

The explanations for these three clusters of technological changes are woven throughout the main story. The long history of the industry is replete with numerous technological changes and a full history would address them all, but these three are most important; "renewable" power sources such as solar and wind power get only passing attention as they account for much smaller shares of electric power generation, although they may play more important roles in the future. These three fuels—coal, nuclear and natural gas—account for most of the electricity generated in all five of the largest industrialized countries considered in this book (see Figure 16.1). And the experience with these three technological changes illustrates the large diversity in sources of technological change and impacts on performance. Major shifts in technology often arrive unplanned— as in key innovations such as the alternating current motor, commercial nuclear power, and gas turbines. In each case, patient investment was required before the technologies were commercially viable; as the industry matured, the time and cost of key investments has grown. In the case of nuclear power, especially, the experience underscores that rapid technological change is not always a boon for economic performance.

[4] French nuclear share is for 2000 as reported in International Energy Agency (2001: Table 7).

16.2. The Industry: An Overview

Not long after Edison turned on the power for his first customers, the economics that would dominate the industry for the next century became clear. Power plants and distribution systems were costly to build but relatively cheap to operate; innovations solidified that pattern by achieving economies of scale that raised efficiency and reliability, yielding a technology with high fixed costs and low operating expenses. Much like the ".com" firms of the late 1990s, the major electric companies consumed vast quantities of cash as they built out networks and operated on the brink of bankruptcy while signing up customer bases. The central obsession of utilities was raising capital, setting standards and expectations that vanquished competitors, and survival. In the 1880s, Edison competed with four other companies to supply electric power in New York City (Clark, 1977: 140). By 1900, the great electric shakeout was over in major markets. Once a utility was established in an area it was economically prohibitive for others to enter the market.

The economies of scale are most evident in the size and efficiency of turbines, both the result of numerous improvements on the same basic concept: a boiler (usually) fired with coal yielding steam that turns a generator. As shown in Figure 16.2, the maximum capacity for steam turbines has grown in two major pulses: the first associated with perfecting and scaling up the basic concept of a steam turbine; and the second from the introduction, in 1957, of highly efficient "supercritical" boilers and turbines that operated at extremely high pressure and temperature.

Originally, electric generators (dynamos) were belted or bolted to steam engines; since neither the dynamo nor the source of mechanical energy to turn it was optimized for this use, the result was an extremely inefficient system. Edison's Pearl Street station may have converted only about two or three percent of the thermal energy into usable electricity. Introduction of the steam turbine—in which steam directly turned blades on a spindle—enabled a leap in efficiency, both because the turbine itself offered room for improvement and also

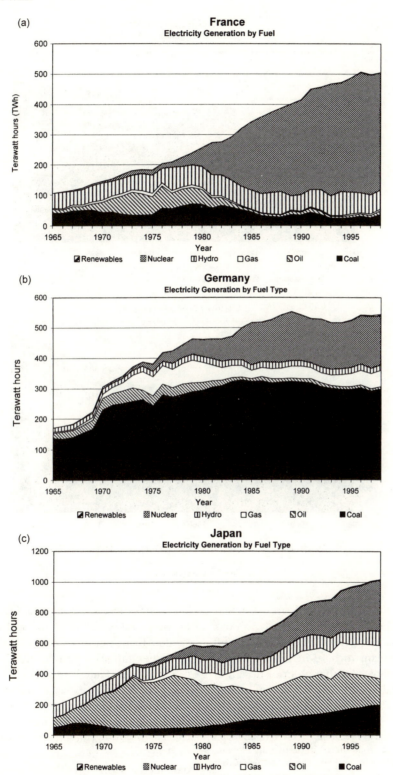

Figure 16.1 Primary energy sources for electric power generation in the five largest advanced industrialized nations: (a) France, (b) Germany, (c) Japan, (d) United Kingdom, and (e) United States. *Source:* IEA (2001).

(d)

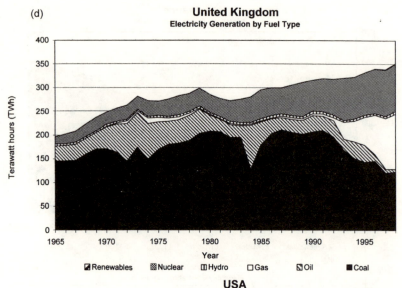

United Kingdom
Electricity Generation by Fuel Type

(e)

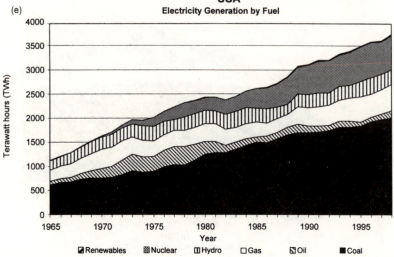

USA
Electricity Generation by Fuel

Figure 16.1 (*continued*)

because complementary technologies—such as boilers—could be designed specifically to work with steam turbines. Westinghouse marketed the first small steam turbine in 1898; General Electric (GE) followed with a superior design in 1903 and quickly captured 80 percent of the market.[5] By the 1920s, GE's share had stabilized

at about 65 percent of the total market, Westinghouse supplied 25 percent, and a handful of smaller firms delivered the rest (Hirsh, 1989)

Three changes in design—all discovered separately and perfected through trial and error—made it possible to scale up steam turbines thereby achieving dramatically higher efficiencies. First, steam turbines were reoriented from vertical design—which made expansion impractical as components could not be reliably balanced one on top of the other—to horizontal. The first horizontal turbine was introduced in 1910; by 1914, no utility would purchase a new

[5] GE had been formed in 1892 from the merger of Edison's firm and a rival firm, orchestrated in part by J.P. Morgan. The new company fought, and lost, the battle for DC but remained the key innovator in electric technologies and operated the two largest electric technology research laboratories.

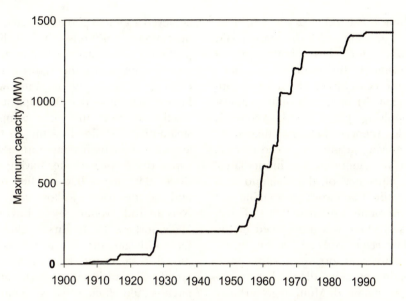

Figure 16.2 Maximum capacity of steam turbine generators. *Source:* U.S. Department of Energy Generating Unit Reference files, redrawn from Schurr et al. (1990) and updated with EIA Inventory of Electric Utility Power Plants (1999).

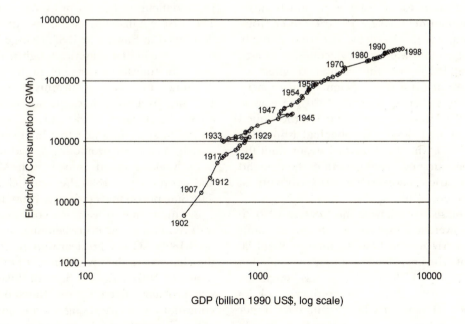

GDP (billion 1990 US$, log scale)

Figure 16.3 National Income and Consumption of Electricity. *Source:* U.S. Department of Commerce (1975) and energy databases of the International Institute for Applied Systems Analysis.

vertical turbine. Second, larger turbines required better dynamos. Edison himself laid the groundwork for these improvements through experiments he launched to make successors to the Pearl Street station more efficient. The original dynamos were built on guesswork, but applying James Clerk Maxwell's magnetic field theory—the first theory to explain how moving magnets induced electric fields—Edison's laboratories immediately doubled the efficiency of the dynamo and created a scientific framework for making still further improvements (Millard, 1990). Third, the multi-stage turbine was introduced in the 1920s. The first stages operated at extremely high temperature and pressure; subsequent stages were optimized to handle the lower pressure steam that remained. Multi-stage turbines made possible a large leap in capacity, and they also required larger custom-designed boiler units. From 1914 to 1929 the average unit capacity increased from 12.5 MW to 24 MW, and the capital cost per MW of new capacity declined 70 percent. In 1929, GE's three-stage turbine achieved a 208 MW capacity. Whereas electric power generation was a boutique industry in the 1880s and open to many entrants as late as 1910, economies of scale grew much more rapidly than demand for electric power. Total consumption of electricity increased dramatically—far more rapidly than economic growth (Figure 16.3)—but the combined effect of increases in plant size, efficiency and capacity factors was even greater. In 1920 there were nearly 2500 steam-driven turbines in the United States; by the 1940s that number had dropped to about 1000, where it remained steady until the late 1960s despite steady growth in the demand for electric power (U.S. Department of Commerce, 1975).

It took sixty years, from the 1880s to 1940, to lift the average efficiency of U.S. power plants from nearly zero in Edison's time to about 20 percent. The next 20 percent took only half that time, after which efficiency has stagnated (Figure 16.4). New "supercritical" plants achieved 41 percent efficiency in 1961 under ideal conditions, and there has been no significant progress in the steam paradigm since. By the middle 1970s the best new steam turbines

achieved about 36 percent efficiency under real operating conditions—the decline due to problems with sustaining the integrity of materials at such high temperatures and pressures, causing more frequent shutdowns. Indeed, Figure 16.5 shows that the capacity factor—the fraction of time the plant is operating—for steam plants declined starting in 1957 with the arrival of new high temperature and pressure supercritical plants, after having risen steadily since 1932. Steam had reached the economic end of the road (Joskow and Jones, 1983; Nelson and Wohar, 1983; Joskow and Rose 1985; Joskow, 1987; Hirsh, 1989: chapter 5). Only with gas turbines as well as gas turbines linked to steam turbines (so-called "combined cycle" gas turbines)—which are discussed later—could efficiencies rise again.

As with generating capacity, transmission systems also increased in size. Edison's Pearl Street plant ran on direct current (DC)—much easier to work with and control, and perhaps more practical in 1882 when reliable alternating current (AC) motors and meters were unavailable. But large quantities of power are costly to transport at low voltages because they require large copper wires, and DC is difficult to transform to higher voltages. The first commercial AC transformers were developed in Europe in 1882; George Westinghouse bought the American rights, built the first U.S. transformer system in 1886, setting the lines for the "war of currents" with Edison's DC. Just as Edison had spread scare stories about the dangers of gaslight, he waged war on AC by spreading fear that high voltage was unsafe, such as by promoting a road show that publicly electrocuted animals with AC power and converting in 1890 the death chamber at Sing Sing prison to electricity to prove his point.

But the benefit of easy, low-cost transmission with AC power was overwhelming, and by the early 1890s AC was the clear winner. The key to the change was the invention of a practical AC motor by Nikola Tesla, a Serbian tinkerer who was probably aided by his (limited) formal education in electrical engineering and theory at the University of Graz in Austria and worked on AC motors mainly because it was one of the great engineering problems of the day. He

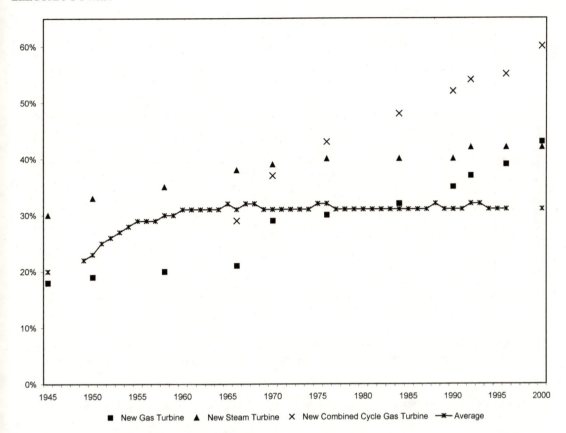

Figure 16.4 Efficiencies of U.S. electric turbines. Note that average efficiencies include both fossil and nuclear plants; because the latter operate at lower temperatures and pressures they are slightly less efficient. *Source:* Gorte and Kaarsberg (2001).

moved to the United States, briefly worked for (and then fell out with) Thomas Edison, and established his own company with private equity investors and focused on invention of electric power equipment. Tesla's firm patented a refined AC motor in 1891, which it licensed exclusively to Westinghouse. When Westinghouse ran into financial trouble in the late 1890s—having over-stretched itself to build AC networks and defeat General Electric's rival DC power—Westinghouse himself convinced Tesla to sell his AC patents outright rather than lease them to Westinghouse. Tesla abandoned any further claim to the rents from his innovation, already worth millions of dollars in the currency of the late 1890s—a financial error that surely ranks as one of the worst in history.[6] Although

DC was first, rapid investment in AC systems and the sheer technical superiority of AC for efficient long-distance transmission meant that AC won the battle. Edison himself did not appreciate that fact until a decade after the battle was lost, but even franchisees in Edison's network of power service areas understood which was best and adopted the AC system. Ever since, the challenge has been to raise line voltages and make long-distance transmission more efficient. Knowing that, Edison's effort to hobble AC in the 1890s included a failed attempt to get New York State to pass a law banning power transmission above 800 volts. In 1900 the maximum line voltage was 60,000 volts; in 1912 that had climbed to 150,000 volts; in 1930 the 240,000 volts mark was reached. Higher voltages have required some complementary innovations. For example, the arcs caused when opening or closing

---

[6] Generally on Tesla, his genius and lack of sophistication in money matters, see Cheney (1981).

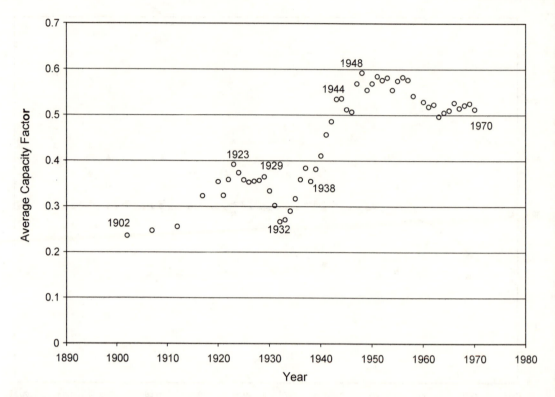

Figure 16.5 Capacity factor for steam turbine plants. *Source:* Department of Commerce, *Historical Statistics of the United States, Colonial Times to the Present.*

extremely high voltage circuits would weld circuit breakers shut; quenching fluids and gases, and gizmos that would inject the quencher when the breaker moved, solved the problem.

The long-term pattern of development—toward greater size and higher voltages, which meant high barriers to entry and exit—were already clear at the turn of the century and meant that the electric power system had characteristics of a natural monopoly. The incentives for monopoly and regulation co-evolved such that by the 1920s basic patterns in the ownership of electric power services had emerged. Vertically integrated electric utilities—which controlled not only generation but also transmission and the distribution of electric power—appeared in the early 1900s, and they carved the market into exclusive franchise areas. In 1907, New York and Wisconsin first created state regulatory commissions, and during the 1910s, when America was already attuned to the dangers of monopolistic corpo-

rate behavior, most other states followed. On the belief that electric power companies were natural monopolies, states sought to regulate the behavior of vertically integrated utilities rather than attempt to promote competition by breaking up the monopolies.

State regulators had only limited control over multi-state holding companies that raised capital for costly investments such as new generating capacity and power lines. Those holding companies also speculated in sundry other unrelated businesses and were highly leveraged when the stock market crashed after 1929. The dysfunctional and anti-competitive nature of the inter-state holding companies partially explains why the reliability of plants decreased sharply in the late 1920s (Figure 16.5). The Federal government sought to set this straight with the 1935 Public Utility Holding Company Act (PUHCA), which empowered regulators to recraft the corporate structure of utility companies and led, after a decade of experimentation, to the tightly regulated and vertically integrated firms that generate, transmit and distribute electric power that persists in much of the United States today. (That basic model of regulated, vertically integrated firms persists today, although a few states are in the process of restructuring their power companies and freeing parts of the business for unregulated competition.) The Federal Power Act (FPA) passed at the same time empowered the federal government to regulate interstate wholesale trade in electrons; recrafting and updating of that Act in the 1970s led to the Federal Energy Regulatory Commission (FERC), which exists today and has power to regulate not only electricity but also inter-state gas markets. At the federal and state levels, regulators assured a rate of return approximately equal to the cost of capital.[7] Divided authority between the federal and state levels is a hallmark of the American constitution and accounts for a strange attribute of the American electric grid. There are three grids: East, West and Texas. But for a brief moment, the Texas grid has been disconnected from the rest, making it possible for Texas to escape federal regulation of its electricity market.

In addition to comprehensive regulation, the 1930s "New Deal" era left two other legacies. One was a more rapid pace of rural electrification—closing what, then, was the equivalent of today's "digital divide." By the middle 1930s over 80 percent of urban households had electric service, but rural areas lagged far behind. Massive government investment in rural electrification as a public works project helped to lower the cost of low voltage transmission lines from about U.S.$2000 per line mile in 1935 to U.S.$600 only four years later. As costs fell and the government strung wires, gradually all of America got connected. Finally, by the middle 1950s, the spread of power to rural households had converged on urban rates.

Depression-era public works projects also bequeathed large generating stations, such as the Tennessee Valley Authority—initiated in

1933 as a public works development agency and a federal power producer—and large dam projects such as the Hoover dam on the Colorado river (1935) and the Columbia river dams managed by the Bonneville Power Administration (1937). Near the end of the spurt of federal dam-building federal power accounted for about one-quarter of U.S. electric supply, but that fraction has declined ever since as most new supply since the 1950s has come from investor-owned utilities.

Starting in 1978, with the passage of the Public Utilities Regulatory Policies Act (PURPA), the United States began a limited process of deregulation by requiring utilities to purchase power from "qualifying facilities" (QFs) at the utility's "avoided cost" of generation. The QF rule was intended to spur development of a partially deregulated market and also to encourage the refinement of new energy technologies; indeed, the definition of "QF" was written to foster three cutting edge technologies in particular: renewable sources, such as solar or wind electric power; "cogeneration" of electricity at industrial sites, with waste heat recycled to industrial processes such as the manufacture of chemicals; and ultra-efficient production of electricity using "combined cycle" generators that link a gas turbine with traditional steam turbines. States set the rules for "avoided cost," and in some cases they were set at close to high peak period rates, which provided a strong incentive to invest in qualifying facilities. The impact of the QFs on gas turbines is addressed later, but briefly it is worth examining the impact of these rules on the development of renewable power sources. At the same time as PURPA, the federal government and some states (notably California) offered large subsidies to builders of renewable power supply. Together, the QF rules and subsidization launched a strong pulse of investment in renewable power, and experts have debated the consequences ever since. On the one hand, this spending spree yielded many investments that made little or no contribution to improving the technology—boondoggles such as wind turbines that never turned and blades that spun off and decapitated onlookers. On the other hand, public investment programs in

[7] For an excellent and brief history of U.S. power regulation and the seeds of deregulation, see Brennan et al. (1996: chapter 2).

TABLE 16.1
Comparative Cost of Renewable and Conventional Fossil Fuel Electric Power Generating Technologies for Selected OECD Countries (U.S. cents/kWh) in 1997–8. *Data source:* IEA (1997)

Country	Projected costs of new baseload plants[a]				
	Coal	Gas	Nuclear	Wind	Biomass
Denmark	3.6	4.3–5.5	–	5.5	11.9
France	5.7	3.2	4.8	6.5[c]	
Germany	n.a.	3.3	n.a.	5.8–11	11–14.4
Japan	7.4	7.8	7.6	13.3[b]	
United Kingdom	3.9[b]		5.5[c]	5.1[d]	
United States	3.3–3.5	2.3–2.6	4.5	4.1	

[a] Ten percent discount rate.
[c] Average bid prices for successful projects, 1997.
[b] 1997 cost estimates from national administrations.
[d] New Zealand Energy Outlook, Ministry of Commerce, February 1997.

the United States and overseas (notably Denmark, Germany and Japan) did bring down the cost of renewable power; today, at good sites with steady winds, wind power is economically competitive with fossil fuels, such as shown in Table 16.1 for the five large industrialized countries plus Denmark, a world leader in wind power. In the United States, wind accounts for only about 0.2 percent of electricity consumption, but its share is rising and wind is the most rapidly increasing source of electric power in the United States today. In Europe, larger and continuous subsidization along with favorable investment rules for wind power have led to even higher shares—in Germany wind accounts for nearly 1 percent of electric supply, and in Denmark the share is more than 5 percent. Most of the advanced industrialized countries have adopted explicit benchmark targets for increasing the share of wind and other renewable power sources in their electric supply systems.[8]

PURPA also made it possible for generators whose facilities did not meet QF standards to enter the wholesale market—known as independent power producers (IPPs). The United States further opened access to supply in 1992 by creating exempt wholesale generators

[8] For wind power market shares, see International Energy Agency (2000, 2001); for a history of the wind power industry in the United States, see especially Asmus (2001).

(EWGs) that were freed from some regulatory rules (Brennan et al., 1996: chapter 2). Together, these three categories—QFs, IPPs and EWGs—are known as nonutility generators, and a 1996 rule by FERC assured them access to the U.S. transmission system. The story of the U.S. market since the early 1980s has been an accelerating shift from utility to nonutility generators. In the middle 1980s about one-fifth of new power has come from nonutility generators; by the middle 1990s that fraction was more than half (Brennan et al., 1996). There is now largely open competition in wholesale markets and a fragmented array of state markets—some unbundled and open to full competition (e.g., California), many in the process of restructuring (e.g., Texas), and some still regulated using the model that goes back to the 1930s with no visible attraction to market forces (e.g., Idaho). The debacle in California has emboldened those who want to keep the status quo or even roll back plans for restructuring and deregulation.

16.3. Measuring Performance?

Broadly, two statistics indicate the performance of the industry as a whole. First, Figure 16.6 shows the performance of a composite of electric utilities against the Standard & Poor's broad index of stocks (S&P 500). Second, Figure 16.7

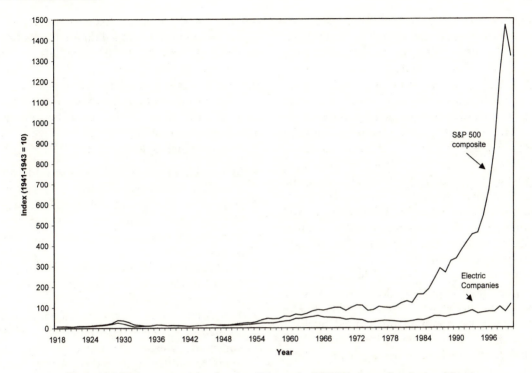

Figure 16.6 Performance of the electric utilities vs. the S&P 500. *Source:* Standard and Poor's.

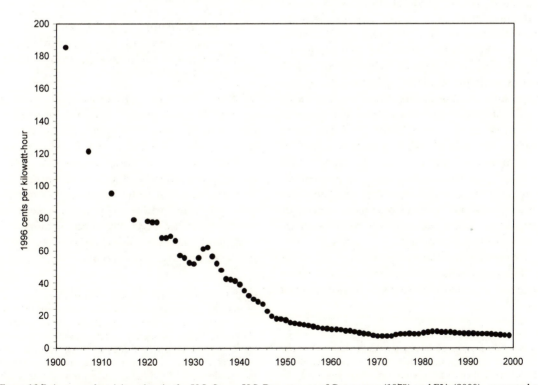

Figure 16.7 Average electricity prices in the U.S. *Source:* U.S. Department of Commerce (1975) and EIA (2000), converted to constant prices using deflators from BEA (2001).

shows the average real price of delivered electricity in the United States. As the U.S. market is in flux in recent years, we focus here on the longer period when regulation was the norm.

It is difficult to draw strong conclusions from these broad indicators, but two trends stand out. First, considerable reductions in electricity prices have occurred during the period of stringent regulation. It is difficult to construct a plausible counterfactual over such a long time period when so much else changed in the economy, but electricity prices (Figure 16.7) and capacity factors (Figure 16.5) during the period of utility consolidation without full regulation (1920–35) suggest that regulation has brought considerable benefits.

The average prices shown in Figure 16.7 obscure many important differences. One is that prices vary widely across the nation. The least expensive power in the United States is found in Wyoming (4.5 ¢/kwh) and Idaho (4.6 ¢/kwh) and neighboring states where cheap hydropower is harnessed from the Columbia river by federally funded dams and managed by the federal Bonneville Power Administration. The most expensive is in New Hampshire (11.7 ¢/kwh) and Vermont (11.5 ¢/kwh), the two states that draw the largest fraction of their electricity from nuclear plants built by regulated private utilities who have suffered handily for their nuclear exposure.[9] Electricity prices also vary widely across countries, as shown in Figure 16.8, but these are extremely hard to assess; data reported by governments suggest that electricity taxes account for only a small share of the price differential (International Energy Agency, 2000), but built-in subsidies and distortions in electricity contracts (which are not reported systematically) probably have a large impact on final prices yet are hard to compare.

The other striking trend is that the market value of electric utilities closely tracked that of

the S&P 500 throughout the period when regulation was imposed and solidified (and when much of the rest of the economy also came under stronger governmental influence). But the two diverge in the late 1950s, just as the most rapid pulse in electrification occurs and when the capital requirements of the industry also grew most rapidly. This divergence may be the consequence of three factors:

- Exhaustion of possibilities for improved technological performance with the existing generation of power plants (coal-fired steam turbines) along with continued pressure from regulators on prices squeezed performance.
- The big pulse in supply starting in the 1960s—nuclear power—turned out to be an economic millstone.
- The combination of traditional monopoly regulation as well as environmental regulation made it especially difficult for utilities to improve their performance. Worse, environmental rules locked in uneconomic coal-burning practices and delayed the shift towards natural gas, which in the early 1980s was technically and economically the most cost-effective source of new supply, but utilities did not embrace gas fully until the middle 1990s.

Whether the gap will continue to grow is unclear. The industry is diffuse and fragmented, consisting of about 3300 entities. A mere three dozen of those utilities supply half the power, and further concentration is under way as the industry restructures to achieve economies of scale that will be needed to succeed in competitive retail and wholesale power markets.[10] A restructured industry may become more efficient and may also deliver returns to shareholders that are more comparable with (or

---

[9] Electricity prices for 2000, average of all sectors, from Energy Information Administration (2001: Table 53). Actually Hawaii has the costliest power (15.1 ¢/kwh) because of the special and costly factors associated with generating on small remote islands, but those factors do not apply to the rest of the U.S. market.

[10] Of these entities, the prospects for integration are greatest for the 342 investor-owned utilities that account for three-quarters of generated power. Of the remaining supply, about 10 percent supplied by federal government entities and 15 percent is supplied by 2000 utilities that are owned by state and municipal authorities. In addition, about 900 rural cooperatives also distribute power as nonprofit organizations but account for a very small share of total power supply.

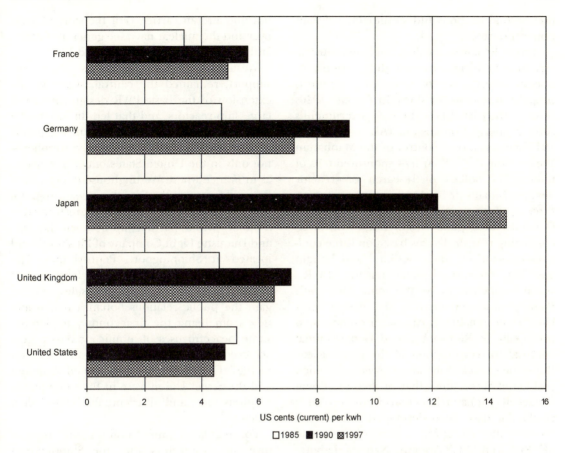

US cents (current) per kwh

□1985 ■1990 ▨1997

Figure 16.8 International comparison of electricity prices, current prices for industry. *Source:* IEA (2000).

even exceed) those in other sectors of the economy.

16.4. Technological Change in a Regulated System: The Nuclear Experience

So far, we have set the scene by focusing on the United States. Some of the key inventions came from Europe but were applied on the largest scale in the United States. The basic structure of vertically integrated utilities emerged quickly and in all the major industrialized countries—with regulation of privately owned utilities (and some state-owned power generators) in the United States and state ownership in most other countries. In such a system, what are the sources of technological innovation? Here we focus on the answer to that question for nuclear power, which, starting in the 1960s, caused a

dramatic shift in the source of energy converted to electricity and a corresponding change in the technologies deployed (see Figure 16.1); later we examine natural gas, which is associated with the other large technological change in electric power generation in recent decades—the introduction of gas turbines.

The foundations for a civilian nuclear power industry lay, first, in the new atomic physics of the early twentieth century. The basic ideas emerged largely autonomously from the scientific community, but the bomb-making program animated by the race to beat Germany to nuclear weapons provided crucial support for vital but costly engineering programs such as the initial experiments to sustain a nuclear chain reaction and the facilities needed to separate and purify fissile material (Rhodes, 1986; Bundy, 1988). With the basic knowledge in hand it became much easier to create nuclear uses beyond weapons and, eventually, a civilian power industry.

Hyman Rickover, a skilled engineer, bureaucrat and politician, carried the concepts of nuclear power from the weapons program to propulsion systems for ships. In the late 1940s through the early 1950s, the U.S. government's Atomic Energy Commission (AEC)—which in 1947 had taken over control of the Manhattan Project from the U.S. Army—sponsored tens of millions of dollars of research on reactor designs. Initially, it funded joint research with three private companies (Allis Chalmers, General Electric, and Westinghouse) on three competing reactor designs based on three coolants—pressurized water, sodium, and helium gas. The pressurized water reactor (PWR), which happened to be the joint effort with Westinghouse, emerged as the design most likely to be reliable. A campaign orchestrated principally by Rickover gained Congressional approval for construction of the first nuclear ship—the attack submarine *Nautilus*, which cost about three times that of a conventional (diesel-electric) attack submarine and probably would not have been developed without the bureaucratic entrepreneurship of someone like Rickover. AEC's Argonne National Laboratory and Westinghouse designed and built the test reactor and the nearly identical reactor that was actually used in *Nautilus*; water at high temperature and pressure circulated between the reactor core and a heat exchanger that generated nonradioactive steam that ultimately turned the propeller—a so-called pressurized water reactor (PWR) design. (A General Electric laboratory also built a sodium-cooled submarine reactor—as an [unused] prototype for *Nautilus* and installed in *Seawolf*, the second nuclear submarine; but sodium proved to be too corrosive and unmanageable as a coolant, and *Seawolf*'s reactor was changed to the PWR design after two years of hazardous operation.) The success of the *Nautilus*, which could operate submerged at high speeds for long periods of time, and Rickover's bureaucratic skill lathered money for reactors on larger, surface ships. The first nuclear powered aircraft carrier, *Enterprise*, was launched in 1961 with eight reactors on board at a cost nearly double that of an oil-burning aircraft carrier. (For the story of Rickover and the nuclear navy, see generally Polmar and Allen, 1982: chapters 6, 7, and 12).

Westinghouse, with Rickover's continuous support, remained the central player in the extension of the basic PWR design for use in large ship reactors, and that led directly to the U.S. civilian nuclear power program, eventually making Westinghouse the anointed supplier—not only in the United States but also overseas, as in France where Westinghouse designs were licensed for use in the French nuclear program. The first commercial reactor was constructed as a public–private partnership between the AEC and Duqusne Light Company of Pittsburgh and located at Shippingport, Pennsylvania. The facility was built quickly and with firm support of the U.S. government, which was desperate to gain the public relations bonanza that would flow from being the first country to demonstrate peaceful uses of atomic power—a goal achieved when Shippingport began operation in 1957. Canada, France, the United Kingdom and the Soviet Union were in the same public relations race, and all eventually built civilian reactors.[11]

For regulated public utilities, the logic of investing in reactors after the Shippingport demonstration was clear. Utilities and regulators alike faced the problem that the rising demand for electricity seemed to be unstoppable, as shown in Figure 16.9, with similar patterns of exponential growth in most other advanced industrialized countries. Even when the first energy crisis tempered the demand for nonelectric energy, total demand for energy continued to rise and electricity accounted for an ever-larger share of the gap. In principle, nuclear power could yield some of the supply.

[11] The French, U.K. and Soviet programs are addressed briefly below. The Canadian program was also a legacy of the wartime Allied bomb-building effort, which included construction of a small pilot heavy water reactor that went critical just after the war ended—the first critical reactor outside the United States. That effort, in turn, laid the framework for Canada's commercial reactor based on heavy water—the Canadian-Deuterium-Uranium (CANDU) reactor, some of which were sold overseas but the design did not define the frontier for reactor building and is not addressed in more detail here. For more on heavy water reactors and the Canadian effort, see Dahl (1999: chapter 15 and 284–9).

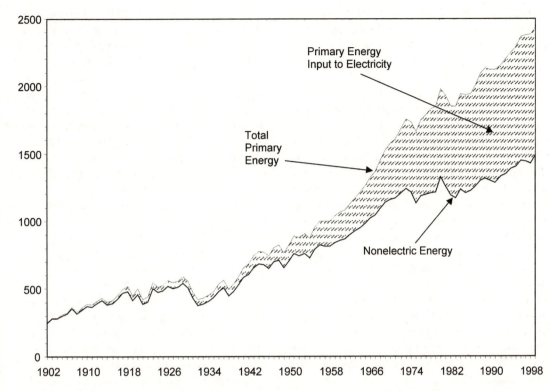

Figure 16.9 U.S. primary energy consumption and its conversion to electricity (units: million metric tons of oil equivalent.) *Sources:* Mitchell (1993) and U.S. Department of Commerce (1975), updated with EIA (2000); estimates for primary energy consumption from databases compiled at the International Institute for Applied Systems Analysis.

The cases of France and the United States reveal different strategies in the commercialization of nuclear power but equally difficult tasks of evaluation. France's approach, in hindsight, is often cited as a most likely case for the success of this technology—the French program is large (accounting for three-quarters of French electric power), makes use of a somewhat standardized design, and is managed mainly as a centralized system that, in principle, could ensure that experience gained in building and operating plants is applied to subsequent plants. The U.S. program has the longest history and is the world's largest, but it has built out with a different model—individual utilities investing in small numbers of plants without standardized design.

In France, as in Japan, the government has been centrally involved in advocating nuclear power, citing national security and the principal reason—a factor that is very hard to include in economic analysis since it can justify a large range of seemingly uneconomic behavior. The popular French riposte explains the nuclear decision: 'no oil, no gas, no coal, no choice.'[12] State-directed application of a single technology also fit with the industrial policy models in these and many other countries. In France, as Messerlin has shown (chapter 6), a process of careful bureaucratic cultivation leads to bold state-backed technology developments—he illustrates with Minitel and Concorde, but nuclear power follows a similar model. In both countries, the suite of technologies developed

---

[12] Today, in fact, France could easily link to the European gas grid and allow its electric power market to move in the same direction—towards gas—as the rest of the European market. But even gas entails some exposure to supply risks, not least because Europe is becoming highly dependent upon Russian sources of gas. Similarly, Japan is now importing gas in liquefied form, but only at great expense and with some exposure to the risk that gas supplies could be interrupted, although the emergence of a spot market in liquefied natural gas can, to some degree, offset that risk.

probably required extensive control from the center as no single firm would be willing to take the risk nor be able to coordinate such far-flung operations that led to complete closure of the nuclear fuel cycle. (The United Kingdom, also, applied commercial nuclear power through central control, which also made it possible to plan an elaborate closed fuel cycle.) France acquired the Westinghouse PWR reactor design—itself the result of the U.S. military nuclear program—and built fifty-six nearly uniform copies. The French government does not publish data to allow proper independent assessment of the economic performance of its investment in nuclear power—the capital and operating costs of the plants are unclear, and the counter-factual (fossil fuel power) is very difficult to assess since the vast majority of the French electric power system is nonfossil. A captive market, subsidies and lack of competition explain much of nuclear's continued success in France (for more detail, see Palfreman, 1998; Bataille and Galley, 1999).

In the United States, the government also affected investment decisions but more indirectly. Although investors were mainly under private ownership, with hindsight it is now clear that they did not give adequate attention to the risks of investing in this new technology—rate of return regulation gave utilities the impression that they would be shielded from many financial risks for approved capital projects. Thus, the innovation probably diffused much more rapidly than if the investors had been more fully exposed, and too rapid diffusion caused an ever-growing drain on firm performance. In the program to nuclearize the navy and even at Shippingport, projects occurred at the frontiers of the technology and were pursued in the engineering style of the Manhattan project rather than the cost-sensitive, risk-averse, financial mode of competitive firms. Yet the full costs of this exposure did not appear until after many utilities had already committed to building reactors. No utility went bankrupt from investing in nuclear power until Public Service of New Hampshire suffered the costs of its Seabrook plant and went bankrupt in the 1980s—but that was long after the Three

Mile Island accident of 1979 and growing costs of nuclear reactors had already dissuaded utilities from ordering new plants. The last firm order for a plant in the United States was in 1973. Shielded by regulatory rules, investors found themselves massively exposed when they learned, often in the middle of construction, that the technology was not as cheap or upwardly scalable as originally hoped. The United States government also shielded investors by limiting the liability that utilities would face in case of a nuclear accident.

One way to measure the performance of the U.S. nuclear industry is to look at marginal costs. Capital costs were sunk long ago; what matters today for the large existing stock is the cost of operation and maintenance (O&M) and whether those costs are competitive with other sources of supply at the margin. Although the marginal cost of nuclear power varies considerably, the mean (2¢/kwh) is competitive with the average cost of coal-fired electricity, and a large fraction of plants generate at even lower cost. About one-fifth of the plants are much more costly (Energy Information Administration, 1998). Differences in management explain much of the variation.

Operators have few options for reducing O&M. About 70 percent of O&M is labor costs, but most labor expenses are the result of the size of the labor force, which is largely dictated by safety regulators. Fuel accounts for most of the balance of the O&M costs, but fuel costs are difficult to control and are, in any case, declining with the growing glut of available fuels, in part because of the large supply of potential fuel from dismantled warheads in the United States and Russia and in part because it is now clear that uranium is abundant and can be mined and refined at relatively low cost from various sources, including seawater. The spot price for uranium fell 80 percent from the middle 1970s through the early 1990s and has remained at historically low levels since.

Because O&M costs are largely invariant with time and are mainly beyond the control of managers, the main avenue for lowering the cost per nuclear kilowatt hour is to increase the capacity factor—the time the reactor is

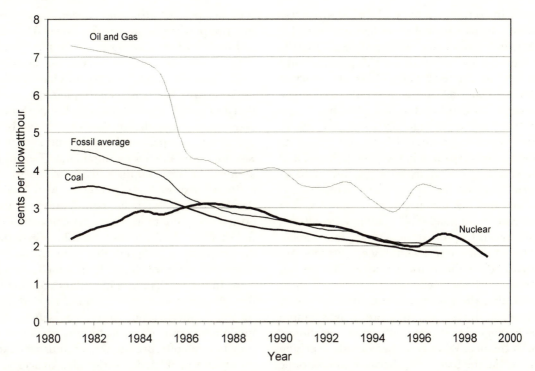

Figure 16.10 Marginal cost of nuclear power compared with coal-fired electricity, oil- and gas-fired electricity and the average of all fossil supply ("fossil"). *Source:* EIA, Report: EIA/DOE-0607(99) *http://www.eia.doe.gov/oiaf/issues/power_plant.html#oct*

online, delivering power. From 1990 to 1995, the *average* capacity of U.S. nuclear plants has risen from 66 percent to 77.4 percent,[13] mainly through improved management. Significant potential remains for further increases in average capacity factors through technological change. For example, a major cause of down time is refueling; Pacific Gas and Electric, for example, is working with fuel suppliers to deliver a higher quality (and more expensive) fuel that will make it possible to extend the refueling cycle from 18 to 24 months by the year 2001 (EIA, 1998). Overall, the capacity factor explains almost all of the shape of the cost curve for nuclear power shown in Figure 16.10—the decline in nuclear generating costs from the peak in the middle 1980s coincides exactly with the start of a long-term rise in capacity factors. The consolidation of the industry, along with more competitive electricity

markets, has encouraged the wider application of best management practices; further consolidation may aid even better performance. The newly consolidated operators of nuclear power plants not only generally manage their plants better than the operators they have supplanted, but they are also investing in new designs that could lead to a new generation of safer and more economically viable nuclear power plants.

Regarding the performance of individual firms that supply nuclear plants, it is instructive to examine Westinghouse—a firm that was consistently at the frontier of U.S. electric technology. Westinghouse placed the first big bet (with private financial backing) on AC power and, with Tesla's patents, set the standard for multi-phase 60 cycle AC power that still exists today. The firm also bet (with the U.S. government's money) on the PWR design, and the firm was at the frontier in other areas such as the development of special circuit breakers essential for very high voltage transmission lines. Today, the firm no longer exists—broken up, with its assets divided among former compe-

[13] Energy Information Administration, Monthy Energy Review (October 1997) update.

titors. In contrast, General Electric—which was formed in part to make the bad bet (with J.P. Morgan's money and Edison's ideas) for DC power and also bet (with the U.S. government's money) on the technology of breeder reactors still exists and delivers stellar returns to stockholders—in part because of a good bet on gas turbines (derived originally from research in the United Kingdom and bolstered by private and public investment in the United States) and in part because of extremely good management. The contrasting experiences of Westinghouse and GE are particular examples of a general point made by Schumpeter (1942), and recently probed by Foster and Kaplan (2001), that even technological leaders are destroyed in the marketplace if they do not sustain performance.

In sum, the experience with nuclear power shows an investment that went awry—rapid technological change with poor economic performance. What is perhaps most surprising is not that the technology became an economic millstone—many technological bets do not pay off—but that the technology entered the marketplace so rapidly when the economic risks were so great. In part the rapid penetration of this new technology is the result of its diffusion into an existing complementary network—the electric power grid. Similarly, catalytic converters diffused into use in the United States over only a decade because they were bolted on to an existing system (the automobile), whereas the automobile itself diffused much more slowly when it first entered the market to supply mobility (Grübler, 1996). Still, the speed of diffusion is remarkable given its large number of complex, risky and innovative elements, uncertainty about safety regulation, exposure to delays, and uncertainty about whether small tested designs could be scaled up to twice or four times their original size. It is doubtful if a competitive market would have made such a singular bet.

In parallel with the Western program, the Soviet Union also supported a large nuclear weapons program from which also emerged technologies for production of electric power from nuclear energy. That effort also emerged from military investments and, in part, a naval

nuclear power program—indeed, the first nuclear powered ship was the Soviet Union's icebreaker *Lenin*. The Soviet reactor program defined the frontier within the Soviet bloc, which had no choice but to purchase Soviet designs, and for some developing countries that also acquired Soviet reactors. But the Soviet program did not define the frontier for best practice in the part of the world industry that was not under the Soviet thumb; the Chernobyl accident in 1986 and the collapse of the Soviet economy exposed the problems with Soviet design. Today, the main contribution of the Soviet program to the world nuclear power industry are indirect and twofold. First, the entire industry suffered the political fallout from the Chernobyl accident, which (along with the 1979 Three Mile Island accident) forced operators of nuclear plants worldwide to share information on reactor safety and implement joint programs to improve safety—they have a collective interest to improve reactor safety and efficiency worldwide. An accident anywhere harms the viability of the nuclear power industry almost everywhere. Second, effective controls on nuclear weapons have liberated large quantities of fissile material from decommissioned warheads, which is glutting the world market for reactor fuel and also generating pressure in the West to purchase and sequester the fuel before it is sold or stolen (Allison et al., 1996). Neither constitutes a profound innovation and neither was a planned development of the industry, but both could have important implications for the industry and its long-term performance. Attention to operations can make plants more efficient and profitable, although it is likely that private ownership would generate that same pressure for efficiency on its own—as is already evident in the United Kingdom and United States, where privately owned nuclear plants are being operated much more efficiently than before. The glut of nuclear fuel, in principle, will further erode the viability of technological innovations in breeder reactors and nuclear fuel reprocessing facilities that have proved to be costly, raise the risk of proliferation, and justifiable only in a world where nuclear fuel is scarce and costly.

16.5. The American Dash to Gas—Delayed by Regulation?

Until the 1990s, the history of electricity production was mainly a history of coal and nuclear power. By the middle 1990s, coal accounted for 52 percent of U.S. electricity, and nuclear power was responsible for one-fifth. Other countries, such as Germany and the United Kingdom, are big coal consumers, getting 55 percent and 43 percent of their electricity from coal, respectively. France and Japan are much less reliant upon coal and other fossil fuels, having pursued nuclear power for reasons of energy security.

Yet today, nearly all of the planned new electric generating capacity in most industrialized countries is slated to use natural gas. Why has this shift occurred, and why now? What are the sources of this innovation, and what are its impacts on the economic performance of the industry? The key to answering these questions is the gas turbine—a technology that uses hot expanding gas from the combustion of fuel to turn a turbine. In this section, we focus on the answers for the United States and generally introduce the technology, which is globally available and not unique to any particular market. The leading world suppliers of gas turbines are, in order of market share for large turbines, GE (United States), Siemens (Germany), Alstom (France–United Kingdom) and Mitsubishi (Japan). In a later section, the answers for the U.K. market are examined when exploring the impact of the restructuring of electricity markets on natural gas technologies.

The earliest development of the gas turbine, as with many technologies, long predates its commercial application; the first patent for a gas turbine was awarded in 1872 in Germany, and the first successful test of a gas turbine was in France in 1903—just at the time that steam turbines were already diffusing into use, and being scaled up to more economic sizes, for the generation of electric power. The gas turbine languished until Whittle published his theory on the use of gas turbines for aircraft propulsion in 1928 in the United Kingdom and patented the first jet engine in 1930. Patenting did not secure control over the idea, and the German air force invested heavily in jet aircraft and claimed the first flight in 1939. The Whittle engine first flew two years later; the race to perfect jet engines was on, but the war ended before the German edge in jet aircraft made much difference. At the end of the war, the United Kingdom was the leading remaining center of research on jet engines, but cooperative agreements with the United States eased diffusion of information about jet engines to U.S. firms and helped foster a U.S.-based industry. Continuing strong investment in jet technology by militaries along with the prospect of sales to a commercial jet aircraft industry spurred additional investment in the 1950s and 1960s, which further refined the technology. Improvements came not only from engine design but also from other fields of research, such as metallurgy that supplied the stronger and less brittle alloys that made higher operating temperatures and efficiencies possible. The result was a classic case of an improving technology—jet aircraft quickly came to dominate long-distance air transport where propeller competitors were too slow and had limited range; with growing engine sales, the generic knowledge about turbines improved and a virtuous cycle of investment, learning and investment led to ever-better performance; spillovers from other fields reinforced progress. The technology was then perfected for niche markets in electric power generation and, again, the path down the learning curve saw cumulative improvement in performance (Argote and Epple, 1990; Grübler et al., 1999). Figure 16.11 shows a "learning curve" for gas turbines and, for comparison, also shows learning curves for wind and solar photovoltaic electric power sources.

Just when gas turbine technology for electric power generation was maturing, the U.S. Congress passed the 1978 Fuel Use Act, which erected barriers to the new technology by banning nearly all uses of natural gas in electric power generation. Guided by the myth that natural gas was extremely scarce, Congress sought to conserve it for applications with higher value-added than electric power genera-

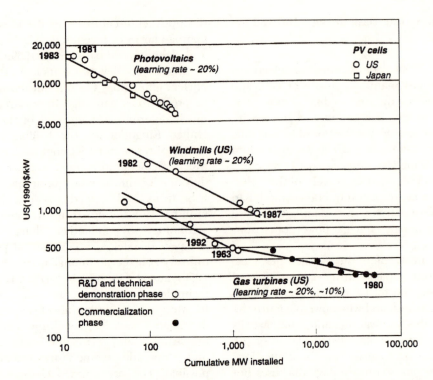

Figure 16.11 Learning curve for gas turbines and other new electric generation technologies. Vertical axis is the capital cost for installing capacity; horizontal axis is the cumulative capacity. Often, the learning curve is steep at the early, pre-commercial stage of the technology and then flattens (i.e., slower learning) as the technology matures and enters into widespread commercial use. Photovoltaic data show estimates for the United States and Japan; wind power estimates from the United States; gas turbine learning is based on data from General Electric in the United States. *Source:* Grübler et al. (1999).

tion. Existing utilities and regulators, who saw the world through coal-tinted lenses, were happy to leave the myth unchallenged.[14] Although the Fuel Use Act barred utilities from burning gas, PURPA's rules on QFs gave gas two openings: in cogeneration and in combined cycle plants.

Even with the benefit of hindsight it is difficult to estimate the impact of the Fuel Use Act and PURPA on the penetration of gas. Combined cycle technology was not mature in the late 1970s, so PURPA initially had minimal effect on the penetration of combined cycle technologies. Gas turbines did have a competitive niche market in some cogeneration applications, although cogeneration was attractive only where firms could make economic use of the combination of heat and electricity (Joskow and Jones, 1983). Plants built under the QF rule helped to demonstrate the potential for gas; in 1987 the government repealed the Fuel Use Act and began to deregulate gas markets, allowing price rather than mandate to determine who could burn gas. In 1992 the Federal Energy Regulatory Commission (FERC) required pipeline companies to publish information on prices and available capacity and ordered a restructuring of the gas market that separated suppliers of gas from the pipeline and distribution companies. The result was a more competitive gas market, which further encouraged investment in gas-fired facilities. The practical implications of

[14] It is now known that gas is abundant; in the late 1970s gas appeared scarce to conventional petroleum economists because drillers rarely sought gas—rather, known gas reserves were mainly the byproduct of looking for oil. In the late 1980s—in part spurred by the repeal of the Fuel Ase Act in 1987—drillers sought gas and were amply rewarded. For more on gas reserves and resources, see Rogner (1997).

these two trends—the arrival of competitive gas turbine technology and deregulation of gas supply—for electric power generation is that gas is now the fuel of choice for supplying peak power. New gas plants are smaller and cleaner than coal-fired facilities, and thus easier to locate close to where peak power will be needed—such as in cities. Gas plants can be constructed more rapidly, and the capital cost per kilowatt of capacity can be as low as one-quarter that of a modern coal-fired plant. The operating costs are higher and probably more volatile; thus, for base loads, the existing coal and nuclear plants remain the most cost effective sources while gas plants have been used to supply additional base load capacity and especially attractive for new generating capacity that is needed for peak periods, such as mid-afternoon on hot summer days when air conditioners are set full blast.

In sum, the main factor affecting the penetration of natural gas had been the maturity of efficient low-cost gas turbines. It is plausible that the technology was sufficiently mature in the late 1970s that, if not for the Fuel Use Act of 1978, the penetration of this technology would have been rapid by the early 1980s—a decade earlier than the technology actually took off.

16.6. Restructuring of Electric Power Markets: The U.K. Experience

So far, regulation has been a lead actor in this story. Electric power generation, transmission, and distribution were typically bundled together as a single vertically integrated enterprise, and the large fixed capital investment required for transmission and distribution meant that the industry was a natural monopoly. The original innovations in the generation and transmission of electric power—central power stations, AC transmission networks, ever-larger turbines, and integrated utilities—emerged in the late nineteenth century in a largely unregulated environment. Since the early twentieth century, however, regulators have controlled every major electric power market, and regulatory decisions have shaped technological

choices and the impacts of those choices on the economy.

Despite the inefficiencies of regulation, a combination of special interests and the fear of unregulated monopolies kept this system locked into place everywhere. Diffuse and poorly organized consumers of electricity—especially households—paid the cost in the form of rates that were higher than they would be otherwise. Over a decade, that cosy arrangement started to change. Chile made the first move, in 1988, by privatizing electric power generators and deregulating some of its electric power system. The Nordic countries and New Zealand followed. Here we focus on the United Kingdom, which began "restructuring"[15] in 1990, concentrating on England and Wales, the United Kingdom's largest coherent power market. The United Kingdom was, by far, the largest of the first wave of countries to restructure their electric power systems, and the U.K. experience has been a model for others, including the restructuring of electric power in the United States led by California and New York. The U.K. and Nordic experience helped to chart the way for competition across Europe—a E.U. directive requires that all E.U. countries open at least one-third of their internal electricity markets to competition by 2003, but many countries already exceed that target (Taylor, 2000a,b)—Finland, Germany, Sweden and the United Kingdom already have full internal competition for electricity supply.

---

[15] The general term "restructuring" is adopted here to describe this process, since it consists of three closely related activities: demerging, privatization, and (partial) deregulation. Demerging has separated generation (which can be competitive) from transmission and local distribution (which has characteristics of natural monopoly) from final marketing and management of customer accounts (which can be competitive). Some countries (e.g., the United Kingdom) have done all three—demerging, privatization and deregulation. Others have engaged in only some of the three activities—in the United States, most generation, local distribution and marketing capacity has long been in private hands and thus the U.S. program has consisted mainly of deregulating the competitive parts of the business while preserving regulatory oversight of natural monopolies in the system. One term, "restructrucuring," is used for the general process of shifting from natural monopoly government ownership or regulation towards a system that is governed much more by market forces.

16.6.1. Key Events

In all the countries that have led this wave, restructuring was the product of an *idea*—that government should intervene less in the economy—rather than a particular crisis or opportunity knocking on the door. Electric power systems were generally reliable; costs of delivered power had generally declined (although in many markets electric power costs had risen since the first oil shock raised fuel prices and high interest rates multiplied capital costs). The power of the idea of restructuring explains why Chile and New Zealand were in the vanguard—these same countries, at the same time they restructured their electric power sectors, also shifted their entire economies from among the most state controlled to among the least. The importance of the idea, rather than a particular event, also explains why the restructuring of electric power was merely one element in a cluster of deregulations and privatizaitons—in telecommunications, air travel, railroads, hospitals, fishing rights, labor markets, and others. In the United Kingdom, the key decisions for restructuring were taken by the ardently pro-market Thatcher government—the most aggressive of the major advanced industrialized countries in shifting from state to markets. Animosity towards pro-Labor striking coal miners—who became the big losers from U.K. restructuring—sweetened the game, but the idea of using markets to allocate resources, rather than government command, was the great attractor for Thatcher. The idea was remarkably powerful—Thatcher's government began to prepare the restructuring of the electric power sector in 1987, after winning a fresh electoral mandate; yet the 1984 privatization of British Telecom (BT) was seen by many, at that time, as a failure—reliability of service was declining and BT was widely seen as exploiting its monopoly position (Green, 1998: 179–80).

Prior to restructuring, the U.K. electric power system was a government-owned entity that controlled generation, transmission, final distribution and "supply" (retailing) of electric power. That entity consisted of the Central Electricity Generating Board (CEGB), which controlled generation and transmission, and twelve Area Electricity Boards, which controlled regional distribution and retailing. The national Electricity Council controlled the entire enterprise as a single entity. The first plans for restructuring were published in 1988, and the first phase began in 1990. The basic principle, followed in essentially all electric power restructurings since, was to separate generation and retailing from control over the wires that actually linked generators with final consumers. Generation, especially, could be a competitive business while the high cost and physical immobility of installed wires made them natural monopolies. The Central Electricity Generating Board was divided into a transmission company (National Grid) and two power generating companies (National Power and Powergen) that were then privatized. The Area Electricity boards were renamed Regional Electric Companies (RECs) and allowed to enter the generation business while also maintaining regulated monopolies over regional and local distribution and marketing.

The original plan was to give National Power 70 percent of the generating capacity, including most of the nation's nuclear power plants. The hope was that the larger market share would allow National Power's investors to subsidize the completion and operation of the nuclear facilities. The government had already paid most of the high construction cost, and operating expenses were anticipated to be low. But real data on operating costs were elusive; some data suggested that costs might be high, and the potential danger of commercial accidents and unknown decommissioning costs added to the commercial risk. These risks scared investors, and the government was forced to retain the nuclear plants. Unable to hide the cost of nuclear power in the fossil generating companies, the government imposed a new "fossil fuel levy" and channeled the revenue back to nuclear power generators. (That levy accounted for about half the revenue of the state-owned company that operated the nuclear power plants; it was finally phased out when that company was privatized.) A smaller fraction of the levy also went to support renewable power and energy efficiency programs. Majority shares in National Power and Power-

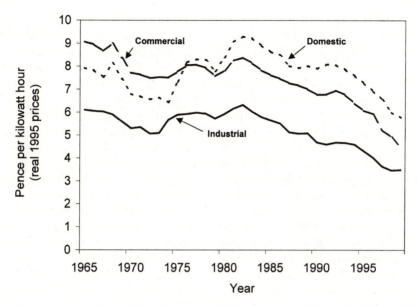

Figure 16.12. U.K. energy prices for domestic (small), commercial and industrial (large) consumers. *Source:* United Kingdom, *Digest of Energy Statistics* (various years).

gen were sold in 1991; a few years later, the fear that these duopolists were abusing their dominant position lead the government to force (by threatening to refer the companies to the Monopolies and Mergers Commission) especially National Power to sell some of its capacity to independent power producers.

Starting in 1990, large electric power users could purchase directly from any generator, including new independent power producers (IPPs) that were also allowed to enter the generation business. In 1994 medium-sized users were also allowed direct access to generators, and four years later the market was to be opened to all consumers. The staged process allowed the kinks to be worked out along the way, with competition beginning in the segment of the market (large industrial power consumers) where consumers are most sensitive to price and most accustomed to shopping for inputs. Another benefit of the staged process was that price discovery in the most competitive market helped regulators set the rules that would affect rates in the rest of the market. Regulators often have incomplete information, and the information base is particularly poor during the transition to a novel market structure.

The best measure, perhaps, of the restructuring is its impact on real electricity prices, shown in Figure 16.12. For the largest consumers (bottom line) electricity prices dropped sharply with the onset of open access. Green (1998) has argued that the very largest of these industrial users actually experience an increase in prices because they had previously enjoyed special arrangements with the CEGB through which they obtained very low cost power. It is not surprising, then, that one of the United Kingdom's very largest consumers of electricity (ICI Chemicals) soon contracted with U.S.-based Enron to build a gas-fired power plant at an ICI facility, supplying low-cost heat and electricity to ICI and selling the excess electricity to the grid. The special pre-competition arrangements that delivered cut-rate power are probably evidence of the large transaction costs in the pre-competitive U.K. electricity market. Typically, purchasers of power had agreed to work with CEGB to manage load in exchange for their cheap power; given the complexity of that task in a nonmarket environment, it is not surprising that only the largest consumers could secure such arrangements.

Two new institutions are key to how the U.K. market has functioned. One is the pool—the formally established wholesale market that links sellers of electricity with the RECs and other buyers. Generators bid supply and price for half-hour slots a day in advance, and a computer generates a dispatch plan that brings the least costly units into service first. Until recently, the price for the final kilowatt-hour of supply selected in the auction determined the price for the whole pool. Thus, plants with very low operating costs (notably nuclear power) have had no effect on the pool price because they bid at very low prices and therefore were called to deliver essentially every kilowatt-hour of supply they could muster. Rather, the price was set by medium-sized coal-fired plants that are the least efficient and thus the last to be dispatched. By far, the largest factor in their costs is the price of coal. Thus, to first approximation, the price of coal has dictated the pool price for electricity.

In addition to this basic wholesale pool pricing arrangement, generation fees are adjusted according to the distance between suppliers and consumers since distant plants must use scarce capacity on the national high voltage grid to transmit their power to final consumers and the stability of the grid is affected by the location of major suppliers and users. Generators are also paid for time when their units are requested in standby mode—with turbines spinning synchronously with the grid's alternating current but not actually generating electricity. Standby power is needed because on-line units might fail and because demand cannot be estimated perfectly. If demand were estimated and controlled through a similar pool as supply then some of this excess standby capacity might not be needed and the system might be more efficient overall; the government's original plan envisioned such a double pool, but the demand portion proved too complicated to implement. Among the difficulties is the lack of real-time metering and control for much of the demand, including essentially all households.

The other key institution is the regulatory oversight of the monopoly portion of the business—National Grid's high voltage transmission system as well as the regional distribution and marketing monopolies. The allowable charges

for both of these transmission types are regulated by an independent authority (the Director General for Electricity Supply, DGES) who is advised by the Office of Electricity Regulation (OFFER). The method of regulation for transmission, distribution and retailing of power involved setting targets for three to five year periods based on the retail price index (RPI) minus a factor "X" that accounts for the potential to innovate, improve management and engage in other activities that lower costs. The choice of X factor became a national obsession not only because it affected what consumers paid for electricity but also because it was the mechanism by which the rents from electric power restructuring were divided between investors (who got to keep the benefits of any efficiencies that went beyond the allowable "RPI-X" change in rates) and consumers.

The United Kingdom never solved what may be an unsolvable regulatory problem: how to impose efficient regulation when regulators have highly incomplete information. The regulator can obtain information from the same market that he regulates, but doing so creates strong incentives for firms not to signal their true potential for innovation. If the regulator simply sets the allowable price (or "X") and then allows the firm to capture any benefits beyond that value then the firm has the strongest incentive to innovate because it can capture all of the extra benefits of innovation. But that strategy may not be politically sustainable, especially during a politically sensitive transition towards free markets. Thus, even in that case, where the regulator professes a credible commitment to let the firm reap the profits of innovation, the firm may be wise to hold back. The U.K. experience reveals these problems. Even as electricity prices have declined, profits have risen sharply. Some of that profit has been the result of cost-cutting innovations, but most was the byproduct of sharply lower coal prices from a more competitive coal industry and was a windfall for electricity vendors. (For more on the impact of restructuring on the economic efficiency of the U.K. electric power system, and the distribution of benefits, see Newbery and Pollitt (1997).) Seeing this, the regulator increased the X factor at the first review in 1994 and also imposed a "one time" reduction in electricity prices for some consumers. The result was a steep rise in stock prices for the RECs and immediate speculation about a generous takeover of one of the RECs, which suggested that private investors thought these companies could still handily beat the new RPI-X targets while also accommodating the "one-time" cut in power prices. In the wake of this new "information," the regulator found a way to impose another "one-time" cut in power prices. Thus, regulation has become endogenous to the market itself. As Brower et al. (1996) suggest, de facto the system has moved towards the same type of regulation as in the United States where regulators set prices to deliver an acceptable rate of return on legitimate investments (see also Burns and Weyman-Jones, 1998). Privatization and "deregulation" have increased the incentive to innovate as compared with state monopolies, but this process may be implemented in ways that make a restructuring much less of a watershed for the electric power industry and for consumers than originally thought.

16.6.2. Impact on Innovation and Performance

The U.K. experience with deregulation is only a decade old, and for many U.K. consumers it is barely under way. Nonetheless, it is possible to explore some impacts on innovation and performance. First, we examine the observed changes in technology and, next, we speculate on possible technological changes in the future.

First, some substantial technological changes are immediately evident in the mix of fuels that has supplied U.K. electric power since the late 1980s (see Figure 16.1). Most important is the emergence of natural gas, which rose from nearly zero in 1990 to supply nearly one-third of all electric power by the late 1990s; the share of nuclear power also increased during the period of restructuring and deregulation. Both these expansions occurred at the expense of oil and, especially, coal. As total consumption of electricity rose, the quantity of electricity produced by burning coal declined one-third from its peak in 1987—the very year that Thatcher received her fresh mandate and

began the process that would lead to the restructuring of the U.K. electric power system. Were the continued shift to nuclear and the dash to gas in the United Kingdom a consequence of restructuring?

For nuclear power, the impacts of restructuring pulled in two directions. In one direction, market forces made nuclear power generation more efficient. During the late 1990s, British Energy—the privatized operator of recent vintage nuclear power plants—increased the fraction of time that plants were on-station and extended the useful life of a few plants. By this method, British Energy lowered the cost per kilowatt-hour of nuclear supply by 15 percent in just three years. (As discussed above, similar effects are evident in the U.S. market as well—when individual utilities were freed to sell their white elephants, often at near zero prices, new owners that specialized in operating nuclear power plants were able to squeeze additional power from the plants at very low marginal cost. Among the new operators in the U.S. market are the North American arm of British Energy, AmerEnergy, which carried its expertise in running plants across the Atlantic.)[16]

In the other direction, market forces revealed that the current generation of nuclear technologies is unsustainable. It survives only because the capital costs from building these plants are already sunk, and the government provided subsidies to keep the enterprise afloat, kept the worst plants for itself, and shielded operators from some risks. The Thatcher government's original plan for restructuring was to include nuclear power plants with National Power—giving National Power a much larger share of the total generating market than PowerGen with the hope that the extra fossil fuel capacity would be used to subsidize nuclear power. When that plan fell apart, the government was able to privatize nuclear power only after it separated nuclear power plants into two distinct companies—British Energy, which

---

[16] Not all of the increased share nuclear power is due to improved operation of existing plants. Some is the result of new plants that had been ordered and largely built by the government but actually came online after privatization.

would own the newer nuclear power plants in England and Scotland, and Magnox electric, which would own the older, riskier and probably costlier nuclear plants. (The newer plants are gas cooled and pressurized water reactors; the older Magnox plants are based on an experimental fuel cycle—what reporter Andy Beckett (2000) termed "an experiment with magnesium oxide, uranium, and optimistic accounting.") British Energy was eventually privatized once the government could supply better information on operating costs and shield owners from some of the commercial risks of nuclear power. Magnox remains in state hands.[17] As in the United States, nuclear power has thrived in the deregulated U.K. market only because the money has already been spent; the task for the operator is to extend and improve the efficiency of the already built plants' lifetime, rather than investing in new plants. With existing technologies, nowhere in the industrial world is it profitable to contemplate building new nuclear power plants. Where such plants already exist, most are slated to run (at very low operating cost) until the end of their useful life. Even in Germany and Sweden—two countries that have made public decisions, strongly supported by anti-nuclear political parties, to close down their nuclear power plants—the process of closure has been slowed by simple economics. What can be built in nuclear's stead that has lower operating costs? Nearly one quarter of Europe's electric power is nuclear; even with a rapid diffusion of gas (as seen in the United Kingdom), such a large source is not easy to replace. Increasingly, power generators are also looking to extend the useful lifetime of existing plants—in the United States, the first license extension (at the Calvert Cliffs plant in 2000) is likely to lead to more. With total demand for nuclear power rising, a "revival" of nuclear power is under way—at present,

that revival is based on better management and longer lifetimes for existing plants, but a new pulse of reactor building with simpler, less costly and financially less risky designs is also possible.

Restructuring of the U.K. power market was a principal cause of the dash to gas. The key innovation, already mentioned in this chapter, is the gas turbine—in particular, the combined cycle gas turbine (CCGT), which can deliver power with efficiencies approaching 60 percent. (Applied in a setting where waste heat can be recovered for useful purposes the effective efficiency is even higher.) CCGT technology did not appear in 1990; nor did gas from the North Sea to power these new plants. What did change was that deregulation of the electric power generation system made the economic advantages of CCGT immediately apparent; indeed, nearly all of the generating capacity added by independent power producers (IPPs) who entered the market to compete with national power companies and the RECs selected CCGT plants; PowerGen, National Power and the RECs that built their own new generating capacity also selected CCGTs. The competitive market gave strong favor to the high efficiency, rapid construction and low capital costs of CCGT; nonetheless, the technology did not immediately enter the market entirely on its own merit. Another key innovation was for equipment operators to link long-term (15 year) gas and electric contracts with performance guarantees by turbine manufacturers, which greatly lowered the risk of investing in these new plants (on the U.K. "dash to gas", see generally Brower et al. (1964)). The large number of competing suppliers in the U.K. market may have also contributed by assuring low gas prices—about 50 firms produce gas from the North Sea and help explain why the U.K. gas market is one of the world's most competitive (Taylor, 2000a,b).

The shift to gas and nuclear power are particularly impressive since Thatcher era reforms also freed coal, the main contender, to fight back against these swaggering competitors. With the onset of restructuring in the electric power sector in 1990, British Coal (itself privatized) shed much of its workforce, closed

[17] On May 23, 2000, the government announced that it would phase out the Magnox reactors, which currently supply about 8 percent of U.K. electricity. The closure includes the 37-year-old Bradwell plant—the "Monster of the Marshes"—which is the world's oldest still running commercial nuclear plant and, at one time, held the world record for greatest production of nuclear power in a year (Beckett, 2000).

mines, raised productivity, and cut the price of long-term coal contracts by half. In 1990, per unit of energy, British coal cost more than twice that of coal in the United States or Canada; of the OECD nations, only Austria, Ireland, Germany and Japan—all with even more dysfunctional coal markets—had costlier coal. Only seven years later, the gap between British coal and lower cost coal producers had narrowed considerably.[18] Since coal still accounts for the single largest share of electric power generated in the United Kingdom, and fuel prices largely determine the marginal cost of coal-fired electricity, these reforms in the U.K. coal industry are the main reason that electric power prices declined. Indeed, the one unequivocal effect of restructuring the U.K. electric power market was in the coal sector; almost overnight, coal mining was transformed from a lumbering giant employment scheme and a darling of the Old Labor party to a more efficient shadow of its former self (and still cutting its way into extinction). The result was much better economic performance—through labor-cutting management, mainly, not technological innovation. Environmental pressure helped to accelerate this trend, but the threat from gas, especially, is the main explanation. Arguably this same effect might have been achieved by intervening in only the coal production system, rather than restructuring the whole power sector. But that would have gone against the Thatcher government's key idea of letting market forces allocate resources, which required restructuring coal's key market (electricity generation) as well as the U.K. coal industry itself.

16.7. Conclusion and the Future

From the 1880s through the first years of the twentieth century, the infant electric power generation industry was unregulated and highly innovative. During this period, essentially all the pieces of the modern power networks were put into place—steam turbines, scientifically designed dynamos, high voltage AC transmis-sion, and systems controls that included tight measurement of plant performance and cost accounting. The industry was highly competitive as it expanded to serve new areas—mainly in dense urban settings and near potentially large industrial consumers. Innovation during this period was intense in part because of competition between systems—notably, electricity versus gas for illumination, AC versus DC, and electricity versus water and steam for mechanical energy—and in part because of competition between equipment suppliers, notably steam turbines. The frontier for improvement in the technology was far beyond contemporary practice, and technological change was rapid as the new industry built out.

With high capital costs and fixed assets, firms rapidly became monopolies and regulation (or state ownership) rapidly followed. Through the 1960s, regulation probably aided the process of diffusing innovations—the technological frontier for steam generators stayed ahead of actual practice, new plants kept getting larger, efficiencies kept rising, reliability continued to improve, and the cost of electricity fell. From the 1960s to the 1980s, industrial performance stagnated. Innovation and technological change continued, and this chapter has examined the two most important changes during the period: the rapid investment in nuclear power and the "dash to gas" made possible with the technology of gas turbines. For nuclear, regulation greatly enhanced the technological investment but only because governments absorbed the risk from investing in nuclear power. Technological change was rapid, but the impact on performance—while hard to assess—appears to have been particularly negative. Measured as technological change, nuclear power had a huge impact on the electricity system; measured as the creation of wealth, it was a disaster. There is a revival of nuclear power under way today—made possible by the fact that better management can squeeze more power from existing (paid for) reactors. That competitive, private owners of nuclear plants are often able to deliver one-third more power from the same plants that had been owned or tightly regulated by the state is one measure of the severe inefficiencies caused by the regula-

---

[18] International Energy Agency (1999: Table 41).

tory apparatus. For gas, regulation appears to have slowed the introduction of combined cycle and single cycle gas turbines—the key technologies for making economic use of the gas fuel—because regulations favored the existing suite of mainly coal-based technologies. As markets in the United States and the United Kingdom deregulated, the shift to gas accelerated because gas-fired technologies were more cost effective than the alternatives and power generators were more responsive to market-like forces. Market forces caused technological change, and that in turn caused better economic performance.

Briefly speculating on the future of innovation in the electric power industry, first, it is important to be humble when projecting futures. The two largest shifts in technology over the last half century—nuclear power and gas turbines—arrived unexpectedly from research programs in other fields backed by governments and private investors for purposes other than generating electricity. The next wave of electric power generation technologies may, similarly, come from outside the industry rather than an extension of existing technologies—it may take the form of fuel cells, for example, which originated in the space program and are now the subject of intense investment for use in electricity-based automobile propulsion systems and also possible use in distributed generation of electric power in homes and businesses—as backup power sources or even as an alternative to a system based on centralized generation and delivery by grid. The inability to predict which technologies will be successful should give policy makers pause before designing rules that favor or discourage particular choices, as U.S. regulators did when they sidelined gas from most electric power generation in the late 1970s just when gas was poised to enter.

Second, the industry is in the midst of a broad restructuring and exposure to market forces. Yet it is difficult to assess the impact of restructuring on the long-term incentives for innovation. On the one hand, it is undeniable

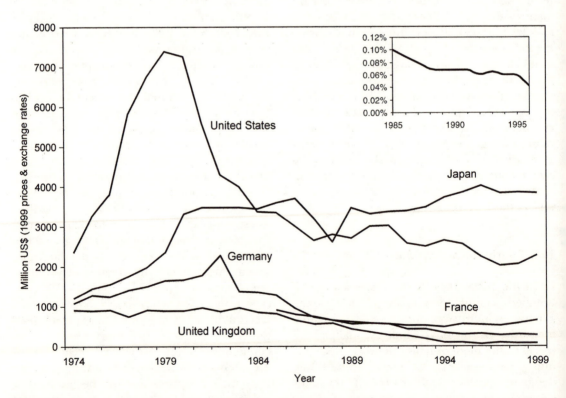

Figure 16.13 Government spending on energy R&D in five countries, million U.S.$, 1974–99. Inset: spending as a fraction of GDP for all industrialized countries that are members of the International Energy Agency, 1986–96. *Source:* IEA (2001).

that the shift towards market forces has put the focus on short-term profitability and survival rather than investment in the next generation of technology. This is evident not only in shrinking private R&D budgets but also in public spending on energy R&D, which has also declined in the major industrialized countries that account for nearly all of the world's spending on energy R&D (Figure 16.13). On the other hand, the incentives to uptake superior technologies are stronger than before, and those forces will presumably lead to swifter and more efficient selection of superior technologies—as they did in the dash to gas in the United States and the United Kingdom—and that, in turn, has put pressure on equipment manufacturers to develop superior generation equipment. That set of forces may lead to the conclusion that during this period of extreme uncertainty there will be rapid but marginal changes in technology but the seeds will not be sown for the more important, future radical changes in technology. Yet even that conclusion is hard to support because the sources of the next generation of technology are hard to pinpoint. While the long-term decline in public and private investment in R&D is extremely worrying (Dooley, 1997; Morgan and Tierney, 1998), much of the decline in government investment has been in the support of old generations of nuclear technology that were unlikely to become economic winners. Meanwhile, a next generation of nuclear technology is taking shape—funded partially by governments and also by private companies that are attuned to market conditions that will determine the success of nuclear technologies. A model for securing socially optimal long-term investment in fickle technology has not emerged.

17

Automobiles

Charles H. Fine and Daniel M.G. Raff

17.1. Introduction

The automobile industry is a classic among the prominent mature sectors of the industrialized economies. The industry has existed in most of those economies for roughly a century. Economies of scale in manufacturing mean that the total number of firms making final product is relatively small. That final product is complex, and so inevitably are the coordination burdens of assembling it in volume. These coordination problems are the more extreme because the industry's supply chains and the channels of distribution are deep as well as broad. The scale of all these operations is generally very large in absolute terms and typically accounts for a significant fraction of both gross domestic product (GDP) and national employment.

The adjective "mature" may suggest stagnancy. But the historical development of the industry exhibits dramatic change. This point is most simply defended with examples from the industry's earlier years, although we argue below that innovations of first-order importance have taken place relatively recently and may still be emerging. The product was initially so expensive that only the wealthy could afford it; but its real price fell dramatically and a mass market emerged. The industry's history of product and process innovation is long and relatively intricate. So too is the industry's organizational history. Furthermore, the industry represents an enabling technology that spurred

We thank Susan Helper, Michael Jacobides, John Paul MacDuffie, the Innovation and Economic Performance authors and study group, and, particularly, the editors for helpful comments and for patience when it was needed. We thank the International Motor Vehicle Program and the Reginald Jones Center at Wharton for financial support. The usual disclaimer applies.

change among its consumers. It is difficult to believe that the spatial distribution of work and residence in the United States, for example, would have evolved as it did in the absence of the automobile.

There have been notable bursts of productivity improvement in the industry's history as well as long periods of modest but relatively steady growth. Productivity was clearly affected by law and policy as well as the course of technology and managerial innovation. Other aspects of economic performance also changed in noteworthy ways. This industry, thus, provides an interesting context in which to examine the themes of innovation and economic performance, both historically and in the context of recent technological developments.

The chapter is organized around a distinction. We consider three types of innovation: product innovation, process innovation, and organization innovation. We begin with the categories and a discussion of how performance might be measured in each. We then describe the most significant innovations in each of the categories, also discussing the drivers of these innovations, the reasons the innovations occurred where they did, and the performance consequences. We conclude with forward-looking discussion. Our range of reference is global though the text generally focuses on developments in America. The reason behind this focus is simple. America is the largest home market. The earliest major innovations happened here because of this. America remains by far the most competitive market. Europe (as a region as well as nation-by-nation) and Japan are quite protected by comparison, American measures in the past thirty years notwithstanding. America is thus where the development of innovations counts most heavily and where firms with inefficient techniques face the most severe consequences. It is, ultimately, the market from which the analyst has the most to learn.

17.2. Innovation Categorized and the Question of Quantity

The most obvious form innovation might take is product innovation, that is, the development of new and more desired or sophisticated (or both) features for the basic product. The automotive industry has seen tremendous innovation of this type, particularly in its early years. The most casual comparisons of product photographs of models from the beginning and end of the first forty years of the industry's commercial existence suffice to document radical changes in, for example, power sources, body shapes and functions, steering control mechanisms, wheels, and even tires.

It is certainly possible to chronicle these immensely heterogeneous changes systematically.[1] Measuring them quantitatively requires a common standard and is harder. Raff and Trajtenberg (1996) have made a start at this on data from the (well-documented) American marketplace from 1906 to 1940. Their calculations suggest quite notable progress over the period (Table 17.1 reproduces the key results). The limitations of the underlying hedonic estimation methods are well known and the fine quantitative detail should therefore be interpreted with caution.[2] But the basic pattern is plain. The value placed upon new features in the market rose over these years by an average of 2 percent per annum in real terms. This is substantial by any reasonable standard.

What happened to prices themselves? There are no long-term calculations for the industry for anywhere other than America. There, the estimates of Raff and Trajtenberg (1996) can be linked up with previous computations by Griliches (1961) and Gordon (1990) to create a much longer time series running from 1906 to 1982 (see Table 17.2). These estimates give

[1] See, for example, Newcomb and Spurr (1989).

[2] See the comment by Triplett (1996).

TABLE 17.1

Price and Quality Indices for American Automobiles (prices in constant 1993 U.S. dollars)

Year	Mean price	Mean QA price	Percentage change quality
1906	52640	52640	
1908	46640	36848	0.19
1910	39860	27583	0.10
1912	41400	24214	0.16
1914	44242	20424	0.23
1916	29483	14423	−0.03
1918	24875	12160	0.00
1920	24566	12528	−0.04
1922	27146	13634	0.02
1924	22732	11528	0.00
1926	22082	10002	0.10
1928	21241	8791	0.08
1930	20702	7896	0.07
1932	25803	7843	0.25
1934	23236	7370	−0.04
1936	17842	7264	−0.21
1938	19036	8422	−0.09
1940	16565	8107	−0.09
Annual			0.02

Source: Raff and Trajtenberg (1996: 87).
Notes: Mean price is the mean price in the paper's database for the given year, stated in constant 1993 U.S. dollars. Mean quality-adjusted (QA) price is the mean hedonic price for the year as calculated in the paper. Percentage change quality is calculated as the residual percentage change in mean price less the percentage change in mean quality-adjusted price.

equal weight to each model for sale (rather than weighting the significance of each model by its sales) and therefore underestimate the effects of scale economies in production. They are also corrected for changes in the general price level. The series shows real prices dropping very sharply, just as volumes were exploding, in the first several decades of the twentieth century. By the time of the Great Depression, even the Dustbowl farmers forced off their land could load their meager possessions into a car when giving up and leaving for California. The performance of the American industry in getting the product before an increasingly larger population of potential consumers was remarkable.

TABLE 17.2

Nominal and Real Hedonic Prices for American Automobiles 1906–83

Year	Index (nominal)	Index (real)
1906	100.0	100.0
1908	70.0	70.0
1910	54.0	52.1
1912	49.3	45.9
1914	43.3	38.8
1916	33.1	27.2
1918	38.4	22.8
1920	53.4	23.9
1922	47.9	25.6
1924	41.2	21.6
1926	37.3	18.9
1928	34.8	18.3
1930	33.4	17.9
1932	27.4	17.9
1934	25.3	16.9
1936	25.5	16.6
1938	30.2	19.2
1940	28.8	18.4
1948	39.9	14.8
1950	45.0	16.7
1952	49.7	16.8
1954	48.3	16.1
1956	49.7	16.4
1958	49.7	15.4
1960	50.3	15.2
1962	52.8	15.7
1964	51.3	14.8
1966	50.8	14.1
1968	53.4	13.8
1970	53.9	12.5
1972	55.6	11.9
1974	58.4	10.6
1976	72.0	11.3
1978	85.4	11.7
1980	99.2	10.8
1982	135.3	12.6

Source: Raff and Trajtenberg (1996: 90); U.S. Bureau of the Census (1997, Series E-135, "Avg." column).

Process change is another important form of innovation. We see three basic domains for process change in the industry's history: design,

manufacturing, and quality assurance. Hard data on design performance are relatively recent and not extensive. The regional differences they highlight are nonetheless very striking. We discuss the data in context in section 17.3. The second arena concerns the manufacturing process itself. Here one might measure productivity, either crudely with some measure of output per capita (or per employee hour) or with more sophistication by also capturing the utilization of inputs other than labor. This is an industry that has been transformed by capital investment from very early on—this is the message of the famous passage in the film *Modern Times*—so leaving capital out seems a distortion. But aggregation problems in nonlabor data series such as capital make leaving it in problematic in industry-level calculations, as do problems with series continuity over time and with including firms carrying out widely differing sets of activities.[3] The third aspect of process innovation is even more elusive, since none of the standard measurements of productivity in this industry for which long-term comparisons can be made incorporates any consideration of product quality or post-production longevity. Two rounds of international plant-level surveys designed in part to overcome all these problems were carried out in the mid-1980s and 1990s, however. These take the progress that the initial development of mass production methods represents as a given and ask "And then what?" The answers are discussed in section 17.4. Overall, again the basic facts are clear. Recent developments represent a substantial improvement over classic American mass production methods. Those were in themselves a radical transformation.[4] This is an industry that once produced on a very small scale essentially by hand and sold to fairly well-to-do clien-

[3] The aggregation problems were the reason the Census Bureau stopped collecting capital data with the 1919 Census of Manufactures. Collection did not resume until well after World War II.

[4] Raff (1996) gives preliminary total factor productivity growth figures for Ford. The underlying data are not problematic in the way industry data are and they home in on the firm (indeed, the plant) in which the innovation was actually happening.

tele, the only potential customers who could afford them. It grew into an industry with tremendous scale economies and a mass market. Subsequent developments enabled far more productive manufacturing. This is innovation on a grand scale.

Organization innovations are even less easily measured quantitatively over a long period of time than are product and process innovation. Nevertheless, we view these as the key to understanding the evolution of the automotive sector over the past century. We attempt to put the important developments in context in section 17.5.

17.3. Product and Design Innovation

The basic elements of an automobile are an engine, a mechanical system to translate the actions of the engine into motive power, a steering system to guide the vehicle, and a system to carry the users and their belongings.[5] The engine is complex in itself, and the basic set of systems, none of which are simple mechanically, needs augmentation to make the experience of riding tolerable. All of these must, as a matter of design, work well and work well together. Each system works better when its own physical parts and components have tighter tolerances relative to specifications. Since the parts and components are very numerous even in the simplest and least sophisticated designs (a round figure of 10,000 basic parts is a reasonable baseline figure over the period discussed here), manufacturing and assembly in a timely, efficient, and reliable way inevitably represents a difficult coordination task.

None of this is simplified by the fact that designs inevitably change over time with advances in materials and in engineering knowledge. In the early years, as described above, the pace of this change was rapid. The American industry, during a period in which it was unambiguously the world's most vibrant, also intentionally adopted elements of rapid

change by using frequent and superficial design changes as a marketing tool.[6] High-frequency changes (and the inventory problems associated with relatively long-lived products) have thus been part of this industry for a long time.

A long view of the industry's history suggests a striking observation about the evolution of the product.[7] Profound uncertainties attended the character of many mechanical systems in the earliest years, even concerning elements as fundamental as whether the source of power should be steam, electricity, or internal combustion.[8] But dominant designs generally emerged relatively quickly. With the development of deep draw presses in the early 1920s, the technology for making bodies with recognizably modern materials and contours was also available.

From about 1910 to the 1960s at least, the American firms Ford and, from the late 1920s, General Motors (GM) were the dominant automotive firms in the world. The bulk of this dominance owed to massive scale economies and widespread local assembly plants rather than to product innovation (Ford manufactured the Model T from 1908 through 1927!), although GM developed and maintained a formidable R&D capability that was responsible for a number of genuine if not radical innovations.[9] One consequence of the decimation of Japanese and German industrial plant during World War II was that large-scale foreign competition in autos did not develop immediately after the war. Ford and GM subsidiaries in Japan and Europe did continue to function.

---

[5] For finer detail on automotive engineering systems, see Society of Automotive Engineers Historical Committee (1997).

[6] Sloan (1964: 152, 165–8, 240) gives the traditional account of how the annual model change began. Perusal of the trade journals during the teens suggests that Sloan may have given himself excessive credit.

[7] Abernathy (1978) is an early and important source of this line of thought.

[8] See, for example, Flink (1970: chapter 8). These uncertainties soon resolved, although steam cars remained in production for many years thereafter.

[9] The most notable of these was probably the automatic transmission of the late 1930s.

TABLE 17.3
Selected Data on Product Development Performance 1980–7

	Japanese volume producer	United States volume producer	European volume producer	European high-end specialist	Overall
Number of organizations	8	5	5	4	22
Number of projects	12	6	7	4	29
Years of introduction	1981–5	1984–7	1980–7	1982–6	1980–7
Average engineering hours (millions)	1.2	3.5	3.4	3.4	2.5
Lead time (months)	42.6	61.9	57.6	71.5	54.2
Total product quality index	58	41	41	84	55

Source: Clark and Fujimoto (1991: 73).
Notes: Year of introduction is the calendar year when the first version of the model was introduced to the market. Engineering hours are hours spent directly on the project excluding process engineering. Lead time is the time elapsed between the start of the project (concept study) and the start of sales. The total product quality index is constructed from quality and market share data; details are given in Clark and Fujimoto (1991: Appendix).

European industry contributed important product innovations in the postwar period, however, including electronic fuel injection and anti-lock braking systems. These innovations reflect the European bias toward high-performance automobiles (designed to take full advantage of the unregulated speeds on Germany's autobahns, for example) in contrast to the American orientation to the mass market.

Both Japanese and European firms devoted far more resources to small car design in the postwar period than did American firms. Space in urban areas was more constrained in both regions and income levels for the bulk of the population were lower. Fuel costs also had an effect on product innovation. Originally plentiful domestic sources accustomed Americans to cheap fuel, and the voters have ever since encouraged their political leaders to keep it that way. With fuel costs of secondary importance, the most profitable path to producing upscale vehicles in the United States was to make them large and heavy.[10] This required little innovative input. In Europe, by contrast, fuel was heavily taxed. For upscale cars to deliver superior performance and comfort with fuel expenses the customers would regard as toler-

able, innovation in powertrain and the overall driving experience was an absolute requirement.

Regulation can also have a more direct effect on product innovation. Regulation of safety, exhaust emissions, and fuel economy in the United States has had a significant effect on the features of cars offered for sale.

Even in the absence of fundamental product innovation, the design of an entirely new model (i.e., one not made from off-the-shelf components) always involved substantial fixed costs in terms of time and other resources. Given the level of complexity that today's products have attained, these now routinely come to billions of dollars. A careful survey conducted in the 1980s yielded the comparative data given in Table 17.3.

One striking feature of the data in this table is the large differences between Japanese product development efficiency and that of the Americans and Europeans. While the Japanese have not placed any sustained emphasis to date on product innovation, they have become strikingly good at developing relatively standard offerings with great efficiency. In the context of other aspects of their capabilities discussed below, this is of particularly great value to them.

Very recently, however, the Japanese firms of Toyota and Honda have taken the worldwide

[10] The famous unattributed slogan is "We make 'em by the piece and we sell 'em by the pound."

lead in offering a distinctively new form of powertrain known as hybrid gasoline-electric. Such vehicles have two power plants and use the gasoline engine both to propel the vehicle as well as to generate electricity for use by a second, all-electric, drive train. The electric drive train can serve as the principle source of propulsion at low speeds and can augment power at high speeds when surges are needed. This allows the internal combustion engine to spend more of its time operating under the conditions that are optimal for its economy and cleanliness. Overall improvements to fuel economy relative to the standard technology are in the 50–100 percent range. The motivation for investing in these innovations seems to be getting the jump on a technology that will deliver fuel economy at a level that may ultimately be mandated by many governments around the world. Whether this investment represents investment in a new capability, as opposed to no more than a new set of features, remains to be seen.

17.4. Innovation in Production Systems

One cannot always draw a bright line distinguishing innovations in production systems from those in overall organization. But because the automotive industry has been the source of two fundamentally paradigm-altering innovations in the domain of production systems, mass production at Ford and lean production at Toyota, we believe it useful to distinguish these, and others born on the factory floor, from other types of organizational innovations.

Industry production itself began in a fragmented fashion. Once adequately efficient internal combustion engines became reasonably widely available, the mechanically skilled and inventive began to dream and to tinker. The spirit of enterprise was widespread and companies formed in profusion. Their products were made in small numbers. Skilled mechanics—artisans—worked in a skill-intensive fashion. Unit costs were high. But entry barriers were low and those with the wherewithal to be customers in those early days were willing to buy what firms, especially local firms, were offering.

Henry Ford soon became the leading figure among the tinkerers. Ford tinkered with product but also with process. His vision of the relationship between the two was quite concrete, namely that

> [t]he way to make automobiles is to make one automobile like another, to make them all alike, to make them come through the factory just alike, like one pin is like another when it comes from the pin factory and one match is like another when it comes from the match factory.[11]

He sought a simple product, undifferentiated and cheap, sturdy, and easy to repair. It was to be a car for the multitudes, a theretofore essentially unaddressed market segment. This so-called mass market rapidly became the most important one economically.

The implications of Ford's approach were systemic and powerful. Implementation required, as a practical matter, interchangeable parts and thus the whole expensive panoply of American System measurement and (machine) manufacturing methods for parts and components.[12] Economies of scale became very important as a consequence. But the economies of scale were there to be seized. Prices were lowered. Volumes shot up. Unit costs sank. And from 1911, profit as a percentage of sales price rose virtually monotonically for half a decade, from 17 percent to 31 percent.[13]

The shift to truly interchangeable parts facilitated the wholesale departure from the factory floor of highly skilled mechanics in favor of semi-skilled machine-minders working with standalone machines or on the side of a moving assembly line. With this departure went the last traces of the artisanal coincidence of task definition and task execution.[14] With all the routinization came the challenges of coordination,

[11] Ford (1922: 59).

[12] On the American System, see Hounshell (1984).

[13] Williams et al. (1994: 98, Table 7.1).

[14] Meyer (1981).

which were very demanding at the output volumes in question even with what was essentially just a single model in production at any one time.[15] For the Ford company soon became by a very wide margin the largest producer in the industry. Its new mother plant became in its time the largest single manufacturing establishment in the Western world. Ford's interchangeable factory workers (with their fabulous pay levels of five dollars a day) became for a time the best-paid essentially unskilled laborers in the world.[16]

Ford's factory in the 1910s and 1920s was the cynosure of the world of manufacturing. It was a triumph of scale, of coordination, and of management more broadly. Industrialists—as well as dignitaries, newspaper reporters, and even Charlie Chaplin—came from far and wide to observe and to marvel.[17] Many went home planning on imitation (although even with the benefit of trade barriers and the partiality of local consumers to domestic producers, few of the European mass producers were in the end great financial successes).

The post-World War II era witnessed the development of automatic transfer machines.[18] These are machines which perform a sequence of operations on a given piece, mechanically moving the piece from one machine element to the next and automatically orienting the piece at each stage. They were first created specifically for engine plants in the interwar years but saw their most widespread implemen-

tation after World War II. As an innovation, they represent a sort of nth degree development of the moving assembly line. The machines were expensive enough that they naturally were developed in the largest market. The machines that emerged were, however, highly dedicated to specific designs. This product inflexibility, as much as downtime, became a major problem that was not adequately addressed until the development of numerically controlled (i.e., programmable) machine tools and so-called robots in recent years.[19]

Apart from the reference to Ford's (transitory) wage policy, the account given thus far of the industry's development during the middle third of the century is in one important respect seriously incomplete. It all but leaves out labor; and labor was increasingly not the infinitely malleable factor of production of neoclassical economic theory.

The roots of labor's complex role begin in America in the interwar years. The diffusion of mass production methods drove the skill requirements of typical industry jobs sharply downwards. Efforts by unions in the 1910s and 1920s to organize in the industry were by turns quixotic and ambivalent. They were certainly never successful. By the 1930s, management was generally mobilized and ready to resist. But the New Deal labor legislation made organizing easier and resistance more difficult. When (in the eyes of GM) the judicial response to the bitter sit-down strike at its Flint plants in 1937 was to decline to enforce GM's rights to control its property, the companies could see that organization had become inevitable.[20] All the principal manufacturers soon signed contracts with the United Auto Workers. By the end of the war, the unions were clearly there to stay.

The first postwar contracts in America set a pattern that was reminiscent of military hierar-

---

[15] The single model represents the famous philosophy that "the customer can have any color he wants so long as it is black." The facts that the basic mechanical elements could be fitted at the end with a (small) variety of basic body types and that there were, over the years, minor changes in some of the mechanical systems are of the most minor significance to the point being made in the text.

[16] Raff (1987).

[17] On the industrialists, see Fridenson (1978) and Laux (1992: 54). For some specific examples with important consequences, see Schweitzer (1992: 36), on Citröen (see also Cohen, 1991) and Lewchuk (1987: 171) on Austin. For the influence on Fiat, see Bigazzi (1987: 81).

[18] See Hounshell (2000).

[19] See Noble (1984). Jaikumar (1986) exposes the fact that the most sophisticated and flexible of these more recent machines were at that time actually deployed more flexibly in Japan than elsewhere. This observation is compatible with the argument about Japanese production methods developed below.

[20] On the strike, see Fine (1963).

chy but was perhaps less valuable in manufacturing. The union members were responsible for effort input, management for everything else.[21] Ford, and even the theorist Frederick Taylor, could hardly have wished for more.[22] This simplified the position of union officials and may have been helpful in maintaining solidarity among the rank-and-file; but it had its own longer-run costs. The people who carried out the tasks often had the opportunity to observe and invent in ways that would have considerably enhanced productivity. But drawing such a radical distinction between what management did and what the workers did in effect threw away these possibilities. It also made for more routine, and ultimately more stultifying, jobs. It gave any management looking for ways to enhance productivity an incentive to find it simply by making the work more demanding. It gave any management looking for ways to enhance profits an incentive, at least at the margin, to find it through marketing or keeping a lid on product market competition rather than by inevitably disruptive and costly innovation in its operations.

The job characteristics and incentives identified above proved to be the dragon's teeth of worker discontent. By the early 1970s, on the eve of the oil price shock, the U.S. auto industry was vulnerable. The blue-collar employees were alienated.[23] Production quality was low. Management itself had gone slack as well. An increasingly tight oligopoly had enjoyed long decades of a vast and steadily growing domestic market essentially free from foreign competition. The oligopolists competed among themselves more on the basis of advertising than of importantly different technology.

All these features were basically common to the principal European firms as well. Their product markets were largely national, with only a little intra-European trade and for the most part relatively little extra-European

exporting. The European unions were organized primarily on a national basis, and they saw their interests as more closely aligned with management and the fate of the firm than the Americans did. But—perhaps because of the political culture, perhaps because of the social background of the labor force, perhaps because the production technology had for the most part changed jobs in the same way jobs had changed in the United States—an oppositional attitude was still common.[24]

There were alternatives to be contemplated. Most strikingly on the labor side, a small number of European firms, most notably Volvo, had begun to experiment with meliorative models of productive organization.[25] These initiatives could be interpreted as job design oriented towards engaging and satisfying employees. German workers had by statutory right from the postwar years a place on a so-called supervisory board involved in the overall governance of the enterprise.[26] The American firms were aware of these experiments but initially thought them responses to European firms' different competitive strategies, organizations, and legal environments. They felt no need to change themselves. Nor did the initiatives diffuse much within Europe. In fact, the Europeans seemed to focus primarily on product innovation throughout this period.

The relative neglect of process innovation by the American and European firms became a decisive challenge in the mid-1970s. The source of the challenge was less internal strains than consumers and international competition. The pressure began soon after oil prices went up and was, at first, most conspicuous in America. The flexibility that the old-style system could not deliver became particularly important when consumers discovered that Japanese automobile manufacturers were able to offer oil-

---

[21] See Lichtenstein (1995: 277–8), for management's perspective.

[22] The locus classicus is Taylor (1911).

[23] See especially Bardou et al. (1982: 263–4).

[24] Bardou et al. (1982: 258ff), and Laux (1992: chapters 9–11 passim).

[25] See inter alia Davis et al. (1975). Some of these experiments were joint company/union initiatives.

[26] On the German "co-determination" statutes and their consequences, see, for example, Hunnius et al. (1973: 194–210).

shocked American car buyers attractively small and fuel-efficient cars. Worse, it rapidly became clear that the Japanese had levels of manufacturing quality far higher than Detroit could offer. The previously reliable consumers began to desert the Detroit firms in droves. Defensive trade policy did not thwart this as much as it might have since Japanese firms built plants (and eventually whole supply chains) in the United States and Europe in response to protectionist trade agreements. This was good for local labor but bad news for the local car manufacturers. These established producers had a new set of competitors who were doing something unanticipated and important right.

The most widely appreciated consequence of this was the intense attention devoted to the production system developed by Toyota, sometimes called the Toyota Production System (TPS) and sometimes more simply lean production.[27] The central focus of that system was not on specific models or features but rather flexibility, efficiency, and quality in the production process. (That is, it was a lucky coincidence that the models and features, initially just well adapted to the small spaces of Japanese cities and the small budgets of Japanese consumers, became attractive in the vast American market. The appeal of the system's performance characteristics was not coincidental at all.) The system represented a radical change from the Ford-style approach to mass production. Whereas it had previously seemed that efficiency and quality had to be traded off against each other, for example, TPS showed that quality improvement could actually drive improved efficiency.[28]

The system and its virtues evolved from Toyota's postwar drive to rebuild an auto industry in an environment of low capital availability and very small market size. Before the war, the Toyota company's automotive operations were

sustained by government assistance.[29] Taiichi Ohno, the engineer who eventually transformed the Toyota automotive operations, had studied Ford and GM factories in the interwar period. He was awed by the scale and capital intensity of the American production technology. He realized that Toyota could not set out by trying to replicate the American mass production system and certainly could not make a success of it in the relatively modest Japanese market. He also saw vulnerabilities in the American approach. He therefore set about finding ways to carry out efficient small-batch production with consistent high-quality output. Toyota's lean production system was born from necessity and scarcity.[30]

This so-called lean system had at its center a taut supply chain ("just-in-time manufacturing"), which minimized working capital tied up in stocks, facilitated mistake-catching, and nurtured an ability, grounded in both human and institutional capital, to learn from mistakes and continuously improve operations.[31] The performance contrasts to classic mass production were in important respects quite noteworthy. The first clear measurement in the literature (see Table 17.4) dates from the mid-1980s but compares two plants that close observation confirmed to be good representatives of their system archetypes. The differences are large.

These figures incorporate a careful, even if not completely robust, attempt to adjust measures so as to compare apples with apples. Even on such a basis, the Toyota plant requires only about half the production hours. It requires less than five-eighths the assembly space per car. Its defect rate is less than one-third that of its American counterpart. And its parts inventories are a tiny fraction of those of the American plant. These are gaps to be reckoned with.

Both the supply chain organization and the within-the-plant activities represented complex

---

[27] See Cusumano (1985: chapter 5), for an example of description and analysis and Womack et al. (1990) for an example of proslytization.

[28] See, for example, Fine (1986, 1988), and Fine and Porteus (1989) for models.

[29] Cusumano (1985: 17).

[30] Cusumano (1985: chapter 5) describes this process in detail.

[31] This was supported by the organization of labor into company, rather than industrial, unions.

TABLE 17.4
Classic Mass Production Compared to the Lean System: A 1986 Snapshot

	Classic mass production: GM Framingham assembly plant	Lean production: Toyota Takaoka assembly plant
Adjusted assembly hours per car	31	16
Assembly defects per 100 cars	130	45
Assembly space per car	8.1	4.8
Inventories of parts (average)	2 weeks	2 hours

Source: Womack et al. (1990: 81).
Notes: Adjusted assembly hours per car is gross assembly hours adjusted to make the measurement comparable across the two plants and then divided by the total number of cars produced. The adjustments are described in Womack et al. (1990: 80–1). The assembly defects data were estimated from the J.D. Power Initial Quality Survey for 1987. Assembly space per car is square feet per vehicle per year, adjusted for vehicle size. The inventories figure is a rough average for major parts.

and difficult-to-transfer sets of routines. The process of their diffusion to Detroit has at best been slow and incomplete. Some of this was already under way by the mid-1980s and bearing measurable fruit. Table 17.5 reports the results of a broad survey. Yet the basic pattern remained. The hours input measure of productivity for the American-owned plants remains half the level of the Japanese. The quality gap is much smaller, but the American level is still more than one-third higher than the Japanese. This survey gives more details of work organization, and the contrasts there are very great. The same is true, on a smaller scale, of automation. The role of the union in this state of affairs is certainly substantial. (One can also see from the table that these differences were not primarily due to the use of the American workforce, since the Japanese plants sited in America did better than the American-owned ones.)

A second round of the survey, giving data from a 1994 follow-up survey, shows continued progress but a continued gap as well,[32] (see Table 17.6). Productivity levels were slowly converging, but the American labor requirements were still in excess of one-third higher than those of the Japanese home plants. Absolute defect levels were down but the relative performance remained about the same. A new

measure of the complexity of model mix within each factory—that is, a measure of how much model mix each factory can cope with—has the Japanese at twice the level of the Americans.

All these consequences for efficiency and quality represented deep changes. An equally profound consequence of the collision, however, concerned manufacturing flexibility itself. In the (immediate) absence of the system and infrastructure of the Japanese and in the face of the Japanese cost advantages, the question of how else the Detroit manufacturers might economically make heterogeneous offerings available to American customers had to be confronted. The historic method had been oriented towards batchwork with a view towards very large markets and squeezing the maximum value available out of set-up costs. If an individual customer wanted something specific and out of sequence, and no inventory was available somewhere in the distribution channels, then he or she simply waited. The wait would certainly be weeks and could well be significantly longer. Shifts in market preferences across models were even harder to meet. Some of the roots of this lay in the planning and coordination functions and in supply chain organization (and ultimately in information technology), but part lay in plant and equipment design. American automobile plants have not historically been particularly flexible. Throughout the postwar period to the late 1970s and early 1980s, plants were generally

[32] A third round is under way but still incomplete as of this writing.

TABLE 17.5
Assembly Plant Characteristics for Volume Producers: 1989
IMVP Survey

	Japanese in Japan	Japanese in North America	American in North America
Performance			
Productivity	16.8	21.2	25.1
Quality	60.0	65.0	82.3
Layout			
Space	5.7	9.1	7.8
Size of repair area	4.1	4.9	12.9
Inventories	.2	1.6	2.9
Workforce			
Percent in teams	69.3	71.3	17.3
Degree of job rotation	3.0	2.7	0.9
Suggestions/employee	61.6	1.4	0.4
Number of job classes	11.9	8.7	67.1
Training of new production employee	380.3	370.0	46.4
Absenteeism	5.0	4.8	11.7
Automation (percent direct steps)			
Welding	86.2	85.0	76.2
Painting	54.6	40.7	33.6
Assembly	1.7	1.1	1.2

Source: Womack et al. (1990: 92).
Notes: Productivity is hours per vehicle. Quality is defects per one hundred vehicles. Space is square feet per vehicle per year. Size of repair area is given as a percentage of assembly space. Inventories for eight sample parts and is measured in days. Degree of job rotation is measured on a scale running from 0 (none) to 4 (frequent). Training of new production employees is measured in hours.

TABLE 17.6
Assembly Plant Characteristics for Volume Producers: 1994
IMVP Survey

	Japanese in Japan	Japanese in North America	American in North America
Productivity	16.2	17.3	21.9
Quality	52	48	71
Model mix complexity index	39.5	24	20

Source: MacDuffie and Pil (1999: 385).
Notes: Productivity is labor hours per vehicle. Quality is defects per one hundred vehicles. The Model Mix Complexity Index is scaled from 0 (simplest model mix) to 100 (most complex).

17.5. Organization Innovation: Internal Operations and the Extended Enterprise

In the earliest years of a recognizable industry in America, firms were predominantly assemblers of bought-in parts and components. The entrepreneurs were often engineers as much as businessmen.[33] Even as the early firms grew relatively large, most remained assemblers. (Some high-end firms such as Packard backward integrated—and, indeed, claimed this as a virtue in their advertising—but the practice was not common.) Through 1908 there were a few firms that produced their cars by any means other than batch production using relatively low tolerance parts, highly skilled mechanics fitting the parts together, and relatively modest production runs. Relatively customized orders were widely entertained and a quite a number of firms included among their priced offerings bodiless chassis to be completed by custom coachbuilders.[34]

There were a number of noteworthy consolidations of firms in the period through World War I, but these appear to have been motivated

designed and outfitted to be dedicated to a single model. In the course of the 1980s, there began to be plants dedicated to platforms but able to put together any of the models sharing that platform. It has only been since the late 1980s and early 1990s that American plants have been capable of manufacturing multiple platforms from a single facility. The Japanese were consistently a step ahead at each stage of this progression (as the bottom row of Table 17.6 clearly suggests).

[33] See Kimes and Clark (1996) for American examples.

[34] This is most easily reviewed through the price-and-specification tables in the annual statistical issues of, for example, The Automobile (the predecessor publication to Automotive Industries). For European parallels, see Laux (1992: chapters 2–3).

more by financial distress than by any detailed vision of economies of scale or scope.[35] The early years saw tremendous rates of entry and exit, and the fact that there was not more consolidation than actually happened suggests that both strategies and managerial capabilities generally were really not ready for the demands of large-scale enterprise.[36]

Automotive industry supply initially came from firms in the business of supplying previously established downstream industries with commodities like metal stampings and castings. Downstream industries with relevant needs were plentiful in the upper Midwest, which encouraged the early automobile industry to congregate in that region.

The early auto firms bought from these firms either off-the-rack or on a job basis. As industry demands grew, supply firms began to see profit in specializing in auto parts (and relationships). But initially there was a problem. The large firm, Ford, seemed a dangerous partner. Ford found some suppliers willing to dedicate equipment and time to its growing needs but seems to have had real difficulties sustaining the old supply system. The most obvious explanation is the fear of ex post expropriation.[37] Ford's degree of backward integration grew to very substantial proportions quite apart from the famous iron mines and rubber plantation.[38] Many of the other producers of the day had idiosyncratic specifications for basic parts, and there were few really common specifications. This put all the small firms at a considerable cost disadvantage regarding intermediate inputs. The incentives to develop common standards were powerful but apparently less powerful than other, countervailing, forces: the standards movement was for some time not particularly successful.[39]

The tremendous expansion of the market in the decade after World War I was a great boon to the supply firms. The largest manufacturers were still integrating backward; but as a mass market and second-hand market developed, a lucrative market for replacement parts that the manufacturers did not really want to address developed in tandem. The loss of business on the one front was more than offset by the gain on the other. To compete in this replacement parts market, the suppliers had to offer (to a discerning trade) a combination of quality, durability, and price superior to those of the manufacturers. This the suppliers learned to do.[40] They were then well placed, over time and as conditions evolved, to share in the activities and costs of actual innovation in the manufacturers' annual model changes.[41] Relationships appear to have been long-term and cooperative, even between supply firms linked primarily to one final manufacturer but supplying others.[42]

Ford was at this point the paradigm case of the large firm, but it was not horizontally diversified. GM pushed largeness farther. In the early 1920s, GM was a holding company of a number of distinct automobile brands and a variety of parts suppliers and more or less related firms. Coordinated operating management began with the appointment, in chaotic circumstances, of Alfred Sloan as chief executive.[43] One of his first, and most famous, initiatives was to create an orderly product line in a way that minimized the degree of competition between divisions producing final goods. Sloan intended to offer a car "for every purse and purpose". He also imported financial control concepts from Dupont (a major GM shareholder), and refined these tools for managerial control of his large and growing industrial empire. A less widely appreciated but quite important (and highly complemen-

---

[35] See, for example, Kennedy (1941: 48–58).

[36] On entry and exit, see Epstein (1928).

[37] See Helper (1991).

[38] See Nevins and Hill (1957).

[40] Schwartz (2000: 67).

[41] See Heldt (1933).

[42] See Heldt (1933).

[43] See Chandler and Salsbury (1971: chapter 18, especially 482–91).

tary) innovation involved getting the separate divisions to use common parts.[44] This exploited, to one extent or another, the collective scale of the divisions without depressing divisional profits. It should probably be understood as making the provision of variety economically attractive, since it seems to have been both quantitatively important and easily imitated given sufficient overall scale.[45]

This organization innovation history demonstrates the successful development of American industry's ability to mobilize resources to address a mass market—in particular, its own vast domestic market—and the slower and still incomplete development of its ability to respond comparably to address profitably the latent demands for quality and variety, both at any moment in time and as the tastes of that market develop over time.

The situation after the war was very different. The great bursts of product innovation were largely at an end. So was the long industry shakeout; most of the smaller firms were gone and the mid-sized firms were dying.[46] Only Ford, GM, American Motors, and Chrysler were left in remotely robust health. The focus of competition among them shifted to marketing. Concurrently, the focus of the procurement officials shifted to minimizing unit costs of supply.

This led to a very different sort of relationship between the suppliers and their immediate customers. Parts design returned from the suppliers to the big manufacturers. The manufacturers kept their suppliers on short-term contracts. There were multiple sources for each part, and all suppliers knew the manufacturers kept other possible sources in the wings. Differences were sorted out by changing contractors rather than by discussion and mutual accommodation. This is a reasonable approach if the production model, and indeed business model, is essentially Ford-like: the

supply strategy was complementary to the idea of manufacturing organized around long production runs of a fixed and small number of basic designs in order to minimize unit costs.

This may indeed have kept costs low, but it did not encourage suppliers to invest in quality or indeed in anything beyond what was specified in the contract. Little information flowed. When Detroit sought, in the 1980s, to replicate Toyota's relations with its suppliers, there was little infrastructure and less trust upon which to build.

Chrysler initially developed its so-called Extended Enterprise system in crisis. Its financial condition was weak and weakening, and perennially standing third in the suppliers' queues behind the larger of the Big Three firms was not helping the situation. It needed somehow to offer a better deal. The deal it offered, based to a significant degree upon the model of Japan's Honda Motor Corporation, involved stepping back from this regime of pitting the suppliers against one another. Chrysler proposed committing to long-term relationships, devolving more responsibility to its suppliers, and sharing the rents and any incremental cost-savings. It also stepped up outsourcing. In essence, Chrysler increased the modularity of its product design while simultaneously modularizing its supply chain practices relative to most other companies in the industry.[47] This was appealing enough from the perspective of the suppliers—there was more business, it was more reliable, the margins were better, and it built up the capabilities of the firms—but it was even more appealing at the time from the perspective of Chrysler. Corporate overheads went down and Chrysler devoted its own attentions more to the stages of the value chain where it had distinctive expertise or really needed to operate and less to those where it did not. Its advantage in minivans and jeeps gave Chrysler just enough breathing room to refine its new business model and race ahead (in unit profit, return on assets, and product launch speed) of its larger American rivals, an outcome which was not widely anticipated as late as 1990, but was quite in evidence

---

[44] Sloan (1964: 155–8).

[45] See Raff (1991) on the quantitative importance.

[46] On the shakeout, see Bresnahan and Raff (1991, 2001) and Vatter (1952).

[47] See Fine (1999) for a more extended discussion.

TABLE 17.7

Chrysler Profit and Market Share Performance Relative to Ford and GM (1988–98)

Performance measure	1988	1989	1990	1991	1992	1993	1994	1995	1996	1997	1998
Return on assets (percent)											
Chrysler	3.5	1.1	0.3	−1.9	2.3	8.8	11.8	9.8	15.0	9.5	11.1
Ford	5.8	3.7	0.8	−0.1	−1.4	2.0	8.5	4.5	3.2	8.2	7.5
GM	5.4	5.1	−1.3	−1.8	−3.1	1.3	6.9	6.7	4.3	0.0	2.8
Profit per unit (U.S.$)											
Chrysler	649	249	209	(427)	445	1709	2110	1290	2059	1468	2055
Ford	1014	663	53	(700)	(307)	240	775	479	378	1000	1019
GM	684	645	(462)	(883)	(541)	208	270	594	542	683	312
Market share (percent)											
Chrysler	13.9	13.7	13.2	12.2	12.2	14.7	14.6	14.7	16.2	15.1	16.1
Ford	23.7	24.6	23.8	22.8	24.6	25.6	25.3	25.8	25.8	25.2	24.6
GM	34.9	35.0	35.5	35.1	33.9	33.4	33.1	32.6	30.9	31.0	28.9

Source: Dyer (2000).

Notes: Return on assets is pretax automotive operating income divided by total automotive assets as given in the companies' annual reports. Profit per unit is pretax profit per unit sold, with the data drawn from Chilton's Automotive Industries, Report Card Issues. Market Share is the percentage of the U.S. market by units, with the data drawn from Chilton's Automotive Industries, Report Card Issues.

by 1995, as is illustrated by the data in Table 17.7.

While Chrysler was building much more cooperative relationships with a stronger, more technologically capable supply base than the industry had previously known, GM moved in the opposite direction. In the early 1990s, GM's procurement function, under the leadership of the forceful and colorful Ignacio Lopez, pared its supply costs by attempting to squeeze every last penny from supplier profit margins and every last ounce of goodwill from supplier dispositions. GM reported over U.S.$4 billion in annual savings from this effort, but the data in Table 17.7 suggest that the Chrysler approach was far more fruitful.

More recently, GM has shown some appreciation of the merits of the Chrysler approach to supplier relations, in word and at least to some extent in deed. Ford began between the two and remains there. Daimler Benz allegedly acquired Chrysler in part to master its Extended Enterprise model, but has, ironically, largely dismantled the model as well as the team that built it, with little but red ink to show for its trouble.

Marketing and distribution in Europe and Japan largely resemble their counterparts in the United States but with less competition and stronger legal rights of the manufacturers over the dealers.[48] (Local differences persist, however. One seemingly quaint example is the tradition of door-to-door sales of cars in Japan, still widely practiced well into the 1990s.) The American market has seen have seen more radical change and generally seen it sooner.

The three most important innovations in marketing have been brand management, the institutionalization of the annual model change and the growth of the latter into a design strategy of planned obsolescence. Brand management has its roots in Sloan's reorganization of GM in the early 1920s: once divisional managers were held accountable for and evaluated on the basis of brand results, they developed an interest in brand identity far beyond keeping out of the way of other GM divisions. This certainly diffused into the culture of GM upper management, entry into which was typically from below

[48] Womack et al. (1990: 175ff). See also Altshuler et al. (1984: 168).

rather than from outside. At GM, annual model changes were originally principally a coordination device; but they eventually became a key marketing tool, appealing to fashion impulses in the American buyer. Once the tapering off of product innovation was well under way and the model changes had relatively little real technical advance to offer, planned obsolescence was next, particularly given that the new car market began to be saturated in the 1920s (in the sense of the end of the discovery of previously unserved automobile customers and also of the development of a secondhand market). To further stimulate sales, the manufacturers established consumer finance units to help potential customers purchase their (increasingly expensive) products in the 1920s. These rapidly became big businesses in themselves.

The sales system has been oriented to legally independent (but generally exclusive) dealers from the start. The early manufacturers were not flush with capital and the prospect of finding others to invest in facilities and inventory for sale was attractive. The agency problems were less extreme as well. The financial risk-spreading was also welcome.

The contractual relations between the manufacturers and the dealers came to be complex and have a long and somewhat tangled history.[49] This history has important political as well as economic elements.[50] The most striking development in it from our perspective is the passage in 1956, at the end of a long campaign, of a federal statute known as the Dealer's Day In Court Act which essentially gave the dealers legally enforceable rights in their territorial franchises and their ability to sell the manufacturer's cars in these. The Act in effect entrenched the dealers and made management of the distribution channel as a whole fairly difficult for the automakers.

This system has been changing in a way that gives even more power to the dealers in recent years. There have been increasing numbers of multiple-site and even multiple-nameplate dealers. Attempts by the manufacturers to establish sales channels owned by themselves have been resisted fiercely. It is unclear how the development of the Internet will ultimately affect this balance of power.

Yet it appears that the main significance of the Internet for automobile marketing will not ultimately concern this balance at all but rather relations between customer and dealer and their effect on operations. Historically, the manufacturers have made to stock rather than to order. A selection of alternative purchase options are available in dealer inventory and regionally; but, as remarked above, options outside of this set can only be supplied with a delay, potentially a substantial one. As the Internet makes information about alternatives and desires easily available to both buyer and seller, and Internet firms such as Amazon and Dell begin to accustom potential purchasers of increasingly diverse products to very wide selections and to rapid, sometimes even make-to-order, fulfillment, the question arises of how long the traditional (and costly) make-to-stock regime can survive.[51] The number of possible combinations of features on offer to automobile customers is extraordinarily large The coordination challenges of a rapid make-to-order system under such circumstances would be intimidating even with a technically stable product, the difficulties of transition entirely aside. But this is the challenge currently facing the manufacturers. Again, the complementarities all along the value chain are powerful; and the commercial appeal of being able to offer customers exactly what they want is potentially quite large.[52]

---

[49] See, for example, White (1971: chapter 9). In Japan, in particular, relations between manufacturers and dealers have historically been somewhat closer. See Shimokawa (1994: 82ff).

[50] The foundations of the economic elements lie in what economists call the problem of double monopoly: the manufacturers would be better off if the dealers would sell more cars than the dealers, in their capacity as local monopolists, would otherwise wish to sell. The manufacturers naturally sought for ways to force cars on the dealers. The instigation of the massive Federal Trade Commission investigation of the industry in the late 1930s was only the first vivid example of the political clout of the dealers in fighting back.

[51] See Lapidus (2000).

[52] See Lapidus (2000).

17.6. Conclusions

The automotive industry has a long and rich history from which to observe the processes and outcomes of innovation. Innovations sometimes come as radical shocks that trigger dramatic restructuring and sometimes as a long series of incremental changes. We find both types in abundance in automobiles. We discussed above a collection of innovations, some radical and abrupt, others incremental and gradual, that have occurred in the automotive industry over the last century. We believe these innovations are usefully classified as product innovations, production system process innovations, and organizational innovations.

In the domain of production system processes, we find that radical innovations sometimes come from the entrepreneurial drive to exploit a market opportunity (Ford's mass production system) and sometimes from the desire to overcome scarcity and adverse conditions (Toyota's lean production system). However, the incremental process innovations that occurred in the half-century between these shifts in process paradigms, as well as the process innovations that have occurred since the initial implementations of lean production, have been collectively enormously important as well.[53] These incremental improvements generally arise from ongoing competitive pressures to reduce costs while improving quality and customer service. Thus the openness of markets to competition is of great importance in both cases.

The two radical process innovations discussed ultimately proved to be of the first order of importance for the whole of the industrialized economy. No manufacturing industry in the developed world has been left untouched by the examples of Ford's mass production system and Toyota's lean production system. The Ford system itself benefited greatly from the earlier development of manufacturing methods utilizing interchangeable parts in industries such as firearms and bicycles. The Toyota system emerged in part as a reaction to the Ford approach. One can only conclude from this that inter- as well as intra-industry diffusion of process innovation can play a key role in industrial evolution.

Aside from the basic initial idea of connecting an inanimate power source to the wagons once pulled by horses, product innovations in the industry have in our opinion been primarily incremental. That is, the basic form of the automobile has not changed abruptly at any point in the past hundred years and the system forms have not changed abruptly since the dominant designs emerged. The changes that have occurred since then are significant in the aggregate but have appeared quite gradually. These incremental product innovations have emerged from technical innovations in areas such as drive trains, suspensions, chassis, bodies, interiors, and, more recently, electronics as well as from responses to customer desires for greater speed, comfort, safety, and so on. Some of the product innovations were stimulated by regional needs. Japan perfected small cars because the spaces available for cars were small. Germany developed high-performance cars and engines that could exploit fully the high-speed autobahns that were built for relatively rapid automotive transit.

Complementary innovations in infrastructure (e.g., paved roads and limited access highways) have also played an important role in the development of incremental product innovations to satisfy automobile buyers' demands and uses. Here social investment supported consumer desires to exploit fully the personal transportation opportunities afforded by owning a car. Government regulation drove product innovation as well. American regulation of noxious emissions, fuel economy, and safety, for example, enabled automobile usage to grow enormously without (yet) having its public health side effects and other negative environmental and congestion externalities overwhelm the collective transportation benefits.

Organizational innovations can have significant consequences for economic performance

---

[53] This is not unusual. Hollander (1965), in a famous and detailed study of radical and incremental innovations in Dupont factories over several decades, found that the cumulative impact of incremental innovations was roughly equal to that of the radical innovations.

as well. But such innovations appear to be much more difficult to import from one company to another than product innovations. Ford and GM have labored long and hard to accomplish organizational change to replicate Toyota's performance with the lean production system. The resulting progress has been most definitely gradual and incremental, when evident at all. Such organizations' ability to change their ways of working depend deeply upon their histories, their persistent institutional characteristics, and upon the complex interactions among their many actors.

Nevertheless, organizational innovations can be significant and can be copied by others (at least in part). A variety of forces can catalyze such change. Sloan's creation of the multidivisional GM was stimulated primarily by a desire to exploit the enormous opportunities for market segmentation in the still-young industry. Roughly a half-century later, Toyota, Honda, and Nissan each launched their first premium brand divisions to compete more directly with the luxury brands of other automakers. In contrast to Sloan's expansion motivations, Chrysler's Extended Enterprise system was an innovation dictated by stark challenges to the company's survival. That system, was, in turn, conceived in part by an attempt to replicate some of the institutional characteristics observed in Honda's supply chain relationships.

What lies ahead? The automobile plays a central role in the lives of citizens of the industrialized world. Our landscape and our daily lives are organized around the availability and ubiquity of personal motorized transportation and the huge infrastructure we have developed to support our driving needs and desires. Our competitive system will continue to reward the efficient exploitation of resources for consumer satisfaction and will ultimately punish firms that stray too far from the frontier. In the automo-bile industry, however, market share adjustments have sometimes been surprisingly slow due to governmental protection of domestic automakers (on all continents), high entry barriers resulting from the industry's huge economies of scale, and significant market clout within a tight oligopoly. We note, for example, that GM has been demonstrably quite far from the efficient frontier in the core activities of design, product development, and manufacturing for a quarter of a century, yet remains the world's largest automaker.

In each of the major industrialized regions, governments have on occasion found ways to blunt the effects of global competition on domestic producers. Reductions in trade barriers have begun to force adjustments, however. In the past five years, we have seen the acquisition of the weaker firms in Japan, Korea, Europe, and North America by a few of the remaining giants—Ford, GM, Daimler, Chrysler, Renault, and Volkswagen. (Toyota alone among the giants has resisted any urges to merge with or acquire weakened companies.) Such consolidation may slow further the weeding out of inefficiencies among the remaining giants due to internal sources of resistance and the large firms' scale and marketing powers. But market shares do show clear evidence of shifting, however slowly, towards the more efficient producers.

In addition to competitive pressures, the undesirable externalities of foul air, global warming, and congestion will also drive innovation even as other product innovations make the automobile an ever more desirable product. Since humans seem unlikely ever to abandon their cars, innovation in aid of livable compromises will surely continue. Because of the industry's enormous economic and social impact, we expect that these issues will continue to be addressed through public policy as well as private investment and competition.

Abernathy, William J. 1978. *The Productivity Dilemma: Road-blocks to Innovation in the Automobile Industry.* Baltimore, MD: Johns Hopkins University Press.

Abernathy, William J., and James Utterback. 1978. "Patterns of Industrial Innovation," *Technology Review* June/July: 40–7.

Abernathy, William J., and James Utterback. 1978. "Patterns of Industrial Innovation," *Technology Review* June/July: 41.

Abernathy, William J., Kim B. Clark, and Alan M. Kantrow. 1983. *Industrial Renaissance: Producing a Competitive Future in America.* Boston, MA: Basic Books.

Abramowitz, Moses. 1956. "Resource and Output Trends in the United States Since 1970," *American Economic Review* 46 (29 May): 5–23.

Accardo, Jérôme, Laurent Bouscharain, and Mahmoud Jlassi. 1999. "Le Progrès Technique a-t-il été Ralenti Depuis 1990?" *Economie et Statistiques* 323: 53–72.

Acharya, R. 1999. *The Emergence and Growth of Biotechnology.* Northampton, MA: Edward Elgar.

Ackerman, Bruce A., and William T. Hassler. 1981. *Clean Coal/Dirty Air, or How the Clean Air Act Became a Multibillion-Dollar Bail-Out for High-Sulfur Coal Producers and What Should be Done About It.* New Haven, CT: Yale University Press.

Adams, William J. 1989. *Restructuring the French Economy.* Washington, DC: Brookings Institution.

Admati, Anat, and Paul Pfleiderer. 1994. "Robust Financial Contracting and the Role for Venture Capitalists," *Journal of Finance* 49: 371–402.

Afuah, Allan. 1999. "Strategies to Turn Adversity into Profits," *Sloan Management Review* 40 (Winter): 99–109.

Agrawal, Raj, Stephen Findley, Sean Greene, Kathryn Huang, Aly Jeddy, William W. Lewis, and Markus Petry. 1996. "Capital Productivity: Why the U.S. Leads and Why It Matters," *The McKinsey Quarterly* 3: 38–55.

Akerlof, George. 1970. "The Market for 'Lemons': Qualitative Uncertainty and the Market Mechanism," *Quarterly Journal of Economics* 84: 488–500.

Alder, Kenneth. 1997. *Engineering the Revolution: Arms, Enlightenment, and the Making of Modern France.* Princeton, NJ: Princeton University Press.

Alexander, C., C. Fernandez and R. Goodhue. 2000. "Determinants of GMO Use: A Survey of Iowa Corn Soybean Farmers' Acreage Allocation," *Economics of Agricultural Biotechnologies, IACBR.* Ravello, Italy, August, 635.

Alexander, W.O. 1978. "The Utilization of Metals," In Trevor I. Williams, ed. *A History of Technology, Vol. VI, The Twentieth Century.* Oxford: Oxford University Press, 427–61.

Ali-Yrkkö, Laura Paijan, Catherine Reilly, and Pekka Ylä-Anttila. 1999. *Nokia: A Big Company in a Small Country.* ETLA B 162.

Allison, Graham T., Owen R. Coté, Jr., Richard A. Falkenrath, and Steven E. Miller. 1996. *Avoiding Nuclear Anarchy: Containing the Threat of Loose Russian Nuclear Weapons and Fissile Material.* Cambridge, MA: MIT Press.

Altshuler, Alan, Martin Anderson, Daniel Jones, Daniel Roos, and James Womack. 1984. *The Future of the Automobile: The Report of MIT's International Automobile Project.* Cambridge, MA: MIT Press.

Amihud, Yakov, and Haim Mendelson. 2000. "The Liquidity Route to a Lower Cost of Capital," *Journal of Applied Corporate Finance* 12: 8–25.

Amit, Raphael, Lawrence Glosten, and Eitan Muller. 1990a. "Does Venture Capital Foster the Most Promising Entrepreneurial Firms?" *California Management Review* 32: 102–11.

Amit, Raphael, Lawrence Glosten, and Eitan Muller. 1990b. "Entrepreneurial Ability, Venture Investments, and risk sharing," *Management Science* 36: 1232–45.

Analyseinstitut for Forskning. 2000. *Nordic R&D Statistics for 1997.* Åarhus: analyseinstitut for Forskning.

Angel, David P. 1994. *Restructuring for Innovation: the Remaking of the U.S. Semiconductor Industry.* New York: Guilford Press.

Aoki, Masahiko, and Hugh Patrick, eds. 1994. *The Japanese Main Bank System: Its Relevance for Developing and Transforming Economies.* New York: Oxford University Press.

Argote, L., and D. Epple 1990. "Learning Curves in Manufacturing," *Science* 247: 920–4.

Arnold, Tom, Philip Hersch, J. Harold Mulherin, and Jeffrey Netter. 1999. "Merging Markets," *Journal of Finance* 54: 1083–107.

Arora, Ashish, and Alfonso Gambardella. 1990. "Complementary and External Linkage: The Strategies of the Large Firms in Biotechnology," *Journal of Industrial Economics* 37 (4): 361–79.

Arora, Ashish, and Alfonso Gambardella. 1994. "The Changing Technology of Technological Change: General and Abstract Knowledge and the Division of Innovative Labor," *Research Policy* 23 (5): 523–32.

Arora, Ashish, Ralph Landau, and Rosenberg, Nathan, eds. 1998. *Chemicals and Long-Term Economic Growth.* New York: Wiley.

Artuso, A. 2000. "Endogenous Demand and Optimal Product Regulation: the Case of Agricultural Biotechnology," *Economics of Agricultural Biotechnologies, IACBR.* Ravello, Italy, August, 232.

Asmus, Peter. 2001. *Reaping the Wind: How Mechanical Wizards, Visionaries, and Profiteers Helped Shape Our Energy Future*. Washington, DC: Island Press.

Ausubel, Jesse H., and Arnulf Grübler. 1995. "Working Less and Living Longer: Long-Term Trends in Working Time and Time Budgets," *Technological Forecasting and Social Change* 50: 113–31.

Babbage, Charles. 1835. *On the Economy of Machinery and Manufactures*. Fairfield, NJ: Kelley.

Baer, Walter S. 1997. "Will the Global Information Infrastructure Need Transnational (or Any) Governance?" In Brian Kahin, and Ernest J. Wilson, III, eds. *National Information Infrastructure Initiatives: Vision and Policy Design*. Cambridge, MA: MIT Press.

Bailey, Joseph P., and Lee W. McKnight. 1997a. *Internet Economics*. Cambridge, MA: MIT Press.

Bailey, Joseph P., and Lee W. McKnight. 1997b. "Scalable Internet Interconnection Agreements and Integrated Services," In Brian Kahin, and James H. Keller, eds. *Coordinating the Internet*. Cambridge, MA: MIT Press.

Balassa, Bela. 1965. "Trade Liberalization and 'Revealed' Comparative Advantage," *The Manchester School of Economic and Social Studies* 23 (2): 99–123.

Baldwin, Carliss Y., and Kim B. Clark. 1997. "Sun Wars— Competition within a Modular Cluster," In David B. Yoffie, ed. *Competing in the Age of Digital Convergence*. Boston, MA: Harvard Business School Press.

Bank for International Settlements (various years). *Annual Report*.

Barbanti, R., A. Gambardella, and L. Orsenigo. 1998. "The Evolution of the Forms of Organization of Innovative Activities in Biotechnology," *Biotechnology International Journal of Technology Management*.

Bardou, J.P., J.J. Chanaron, P. Fridenson, and J.M. Laux. 1982. *The Automobile Revolution: The Impact of an Industry*. Chapel Hill, NC: University of North Carolina Press.

Barro, Robert. 1997. *Determinants of Economic Growth: A Cross-Country Empirical Study*. Cambridge, MA: MIT Press.

Barro, Robert J. 2001. "Human Capital and Growth," *AEA Papers and Proceedings* 91: 12–17.

Barry, Christopher B., Chris J. Muscarella, John W. Peavy III, and Michael R. Vetsuypens. 1990. "The Role of Venture Capital in the Creation of Public Companies: Evidence from the Going Public Process," *Journal of Financial Economics* 27: 447–71.

Bartlett, Joseph W. 1995. *Equity Finance: Venture Capital, Buyouts, Restructurings, and Reorganizations*. New York: Wiley.

Bashe, Charles J., Lyle R. Johnson, John H. Palmer, and Emerson W. Pugh. 1986. *IBM's Early Computers*. Cambridge, MA: MIT Press.

Bataille, Christian, and Robert Galley. 1999. "L'Aval du Cycle Nucléaire Tome II: les Coûts de Production de l' Electricité," *Report of the Office Parlementaire d'Évaluation des Choix Scientifiques et Technologiques* No. 1359. Paris: Assemblée Nationale, February 2.

Bean, Charles, and Crafts, Nicholas. 1996. "British Economic Growth Since 1945: Relative Economic Decline and Renaissance?" In Nicholas Crafts, and Gianni Toniolo, eds. *Economic Growth in Europe Since 1945*. Cambridge: Cambridge University Press (for the Centre for Economic Policy Research).

Beck, Thorsten, Asli Demirguc-Kunt, and Ross Levine. 1999. "A New Database on Financial Development and Structure," *Policy Research Working Paper No. 2146*. World Bank, July.

Becker, Gary S., and Kevin M. Murphy. 1992. "The Division of Labor, Coordination Costs, and Knowledge," *Quarterly Journal of Economics* 107: 1137–61.

Beckett, Andy. 2000. "Power Failure," *The Guardian* 28 June.

Beim, David O., and Charles W. Calomiris. 2000. *Emerging Financial Markets*. New York: McGraw Hill-Irwin.

Bello, Francis. 1953. "The Year of the Transistor," *Fortune* March.

Ben-David, J. 1977. *Centers of Learning: Britain, France, Germany and the United States*. New York: McGraw-Hill.

Bergemann, Dirk, and Ulirich Hege. 1998. "Dynamic Venture Capital Financing, Learning, and Moral Hazard," *Journal of Banking and Finance* 22: 703–35.

Berger, Allen, Gerald A. Hanweck, and David B. Humphrey. 1987. "Competitive Viability in Banking: Scale, Scope and Product Mix Economies," *Journal of Monetary Economics* 20: 501–20.

Berglöf, Erik. 1994. "A Control Theory of Venture Capital Finance," *Journal of Law, Economics, and Organizations* 10: 247–67.

Besson, James, and Eric Maskin. 1999. *Intellectual Property Rights*. Mimeo.

Bienz-Tadmore, Brigitta, Patricia A. Decerbo, Gilead Tadmore, and Louis Lasagna. 1992. "Biopharmaceuticals and Conventional Drugs: Clinical Success Rates," *Bio/Technology* 10: 521–5.

Bigazzi, D. 1987. "Management and Labor in Italy 1906– 1945." In S. Tolliday, and J. Zeitlin, eds., *The Automobile Industry and its Workers: Between Fordism and Flexibility*. New York: St. Martin's.

Bank for International Settlements (BIS) 1998. *Statistics on Payment Systems in the Group of the Countries*. Basle: Bank for International Settlements.

Blacconiere, Walter G., Marilyn F. Johnson, and Mark S. Johnson. 2000. "Market Valuation and Deregulation of Electric Utilities," *Journal of Accounting and Economics* 29: 231–60.

Black, Bernard, and Ronald Gilson. 1998. "Venture Capital and the Structure of Capital Markets: Banks versus Stock Markets," *Journal of Financial Economics* 47: 243–77.

Bloom, Nick, and John Van Reenen. 1998. "Pharmaceutical Regulation in the UK: Where do We Go from Here?" *Fiscal Studies* 19 (4): 347–74.

Bloom, Nick, Rachel Griffith, and John Van Reenen. 1999. *Do R&D Tax Credits Work? Evidence from a Panel of Countries 1979–97*. Working Paper 99/8 (revised), Institute for Fiscal Studies.

Blühm, Andreas, and Louise Lippincott. 2000. *Light: The Industrial Age 1750–1900, Art & Science, Technology and Society*. Amsterdam: Van Gogh Museum.

Boltho, Andrew, and Jenny Corbett. 2000. "The Assessment: Japan's Stagnation – Can Policy Revive the Economy?" *Oxford Review of Economic Policy* 16 (2): 1–17.

Bond, Stephen, and Timothy Jenkinson. 1996. "The Assessment: Investment Performance and Policy," *Oxford Review of Economic Policy* 12 (2): 1–29.

Bond, Stephen, Bruno Crepon, Jacques Mairesse, and Benoir Mulkey. 1997. "Financial Factors and Investment in Belgium, France, Germany and the UK," *NBER Working Paper No. 5900.*

Bond, Stephen, Dietmar Harhoff, and John Van Reenen. 1999. "Investment, R&D and Financial Constraints in Britain and Germany," *IFS Working Paper 99/5.*

Bond, Stephen, Costas Meghir, and Frank Windmeijer. 1998. *Productivity, Investment and the Threat of Takeover.* Mimeo, Institute for Fiscal Studies, London.

Borrus, Michael, James E. Millstein, and John Zysman. 1983. "Trade and Development in the Semiconductor Industry: Japanese Challenge and American Response," In John Zysman, and Laura Tyson, eds. *American Industry in International Competition: Government Policies and Corporate Strategies.* Ithaca, NY: Cornell University Press, 142–248.

Boswell, Stewart M. 2000. "Buying and Selling Companies in the New Millenium," *Journal of Applied Corporate Finance* 12 (Winter): 70–80.

Botosan, Christine A. 2000. "Evidence That Greater Disclosure Lowers the Cost of Equity Capital," *Journal of Applied Corporate Finance* 12: 60–9.

Boyer, Robert, and Michel Didier. 1998. *Innovation et Croissance.* Conseil d'Analyse Economique.

Bradburg, Katherine L. 1999. "Job Creation and Destruction in Massachusetts: Gross Flows Among Industries," *New England Economic Review* September/October.

Braun, D. 1994. *Structure and Dynamics of Health Research and Public Funding: an International Institutional Comparison.* Amsterdam: Kluwer Academic Publishers.

Braun, Ernest, and Stuart Macdonald. 1978. *Revolution in Miniature,* (2nd edition, 1982). Cambridge: Cambridge University Press.

Brennan, Michael J., and Claudia Tamarowski. 2000. "Investor Relations, Liquidity, and Stock Prices," *Journal of Applied Corporate Finance* 12: 26–37.

Brennan, Timothy J., Karen L. Palmer, Raymond L. Kopp, Alan J. Krupnick, Vito Stagliano, and Dallas Burtraw. 1996. *A Shock to the System: Restructuring America's Electricity Industry.* Washington, DC: Resources for the Future.

Bresnahan, Timothy F. 1999. "New Modes of Competition: Implications for the Future Structure of the Computer Industry," In Jeffrey A. Eisenach, and Thomas M. Lenard, eds. *Competition, Innovation, and the Microsoft Monopoly: antitrust in the Digital Marketplace.* Boston, MA: Kluwer Academic Publishers, 155–208.

Bresnahan, Timothy F., and Alfonso Gambardella. 1998. "The Division of Inventive Labor and the Extent of the Market," In Elhanan Helpman, ed. *General Purpose Technologies and Economic Growth.* Cambridge, MA: MIT Press, 253–81.

Bresnahan, Timothy F., and Robert J. Gordon. 1997. "Introduction," In *The Economics of New Goods.* Chicago, IL: University of Chicago Press (for NBER), 1–26.

Bresnahan, Timothy F., and Shane Greenstein. 1996. "The Competitive Crash in Large-Scale Commercial Computing," In Ralph Landau, Timothy Taylor, and Gavin Wright, eds. *The Mosaic of Economic Growth.* Stanford, CA: Stanford University Press, 357–97.

Bresnahan, Timothy F., and Shane Greenstein. 1997. "Technical Progress and Co-invention in Computing and the Use of Computers," In Martin Neil Bailey, Peter C. Reiss, and Clifford Winston, eds. *Brookings Papers on Economic Activity: Microeconomics 1996.* Washington, DC: Brookings Institution, 1–77.

Bresnahan, Timothy F., and Shane Greenstein. 1998. *The Economic Contribution of Information Technology: Value Indicators in International Perspective.* Paris: OECD.

Bresnahan, Timothy F., and F. Malerba. 1999. "Industrial Dynamics and the Evaluation of Firms' and Nations' Dynamic Capabilities," In David C. Mowery, and Richard R. Nelson, eds. *The Sources of Industrial Leadership.* Cambridge: Cambridge University Press, 79–132.

Bresnahan, Timothy F., and Daniel M.G. Raff. 1991. "Intra-Industry Heterogeneity and the Great Depression: The American Motor Vehicle Industry 1929–1935," *Journal of Economic History* 51(2): 317–31.

Bresnahan, Timothy F., and Daniel M.G. Raff. 2001. "Plant Shutdown Behavior during the Great Depression and the Structure of the American Automobile Industry," *Journal of Economic History.*

Bresnahan, Timothy F., and Manuel Trajtenberg. 1995. "General Purpose Technologies: Engines of Growth?" *Journal of Econometrics* 65 (January): 83–108.

Bresnahan, Timothy, Erik Brynjolfsson, and Lorin Hitt. 1998. "Information Technology, Workplace Organization and the Demand for Skilled Labor: Firm-Level Evidence," *NBER Working Paper No. 7136.*

Brewer, Elijah, III, Bernadette A. Minton, and James T. Moser. 2000. "Interest-Rate Derivatives and Bank Lending," *Journal of Banking and Finance* 24 (March): 353–80.

Brock, William H. 1992. *The Norton History of Chemistry.* New York: W.W. Norton.

Bromley, Alan. 2001. *The New York Times* 9 March.

Brower, Michael C., Stephen D. Thomas, and Catherine Mitchell. 1996. *The British Electric Utility Experience: History and Lessons for the United States.* Montpelier, VT: National Council on Competition and the Electric Industry, http://www.ncouncil.org/pubs/restdeba.html.

Bryant, Lynwood. 1967. "The Beginnings of the Internal Combustion Engine," In Melvin Kranzberg, and Carroll W. Pursell, Jr., eds. *Technology in Western Civilization*, Vol. 1. New York: Oxford University Press, 648–63.

Brynjolfsson, Erik, and Lorin M. Hitt. 2000. "Beyond Computation: Information Technology, Organizational Transformation and Business Performance," *Journal of Economic Perspectives* 14: 23–48.

Brynjolfsson, Erik. 1996. "The Contribution of Information Technology to Consumer Welfare," *Information Systems Research* 7: (3, September): 281–300.

Bundesministerium für Bildung und Forschung (BMBF). 1996. *Bundesbericht Forschung 1996.* Bonn.

Bundesministerium für Bildung und Forschung (BMBF). 1998. *Faktenbericht 1998 zum Bundesbericht Forschung.* Bonn.

Bundesministerium für Bildung und Forschung (BMBF).

2000. *Zur technologischen Leistungsfähigkeit Deutschlands.* Zusammenfassender Endberich 1999. Bonn.

Bundy, McGeorge. 1988. *Danger and Survival.* New York: Random House.

Bureau of Economic Analysis. 2001. *National Income and Product Accounts* http://www.bea.doc.gov/bea/dn/gdplev.htm

Burns, Philip, and Thomas Weyman-Jones. 1998. "Periodic Regulatory Review in UK Electricity Markets: Developments Within a Deregulated System," In Georges Zaccour, ed. *Deregulation of Electric Utilities.* Boston, MA: Kluwer Academic Publishers, 75–99.

Burstall, M.L. 1985. *The Community's Pharmaceutical Industry.* Brussels: Commission of the European Communities.

Business Software Alliance and Software Publishers Association. 1997. "Global Software Piracy Report," Washington, DC: Business Software Alliance and Software Publishers Association.

Bylinsky, Gene. 1980. "Here Comes the Second Computer Revolution," In Tom Forester, ed. *The Microelectronics Revolution.* Oxford: Basil Blackwell, 9–15.

Caballero, Ricardo, and Mohamed Hammour. 2000. "Creative Destruction and Development: Institution, Crisis, and Restructuring," *NBER Working Paper No. 7849.*

Callon, Scott. 1995. *Divided Sun: MITI and the Breakdown of Japanese High-Tech Industrial Policy, 1975–1993.* Stanford, CA: Stanford University Press.

Calomiris, Charles W. 2000. *U.S. Bank Deregulation in Historical Perspective.* Cambridge: Cambridge University Press.

Calomiris, Charles W., and Berry Wilson. 1998. "Bank Capital and Portfolio Management: the 1930s 'Capital Crunch' and Scramble to Shed Risk," *NBER Working Paper No. 6649,* July.

Calomiris, Charles W., and Charles P. Himmelberg. 2000. "Equity Underpricing, Underwriting, and the Cost of External Capital," *Working Paper,* Columbia Business School.

Calomiris, Charles W., and Daniel M.G. Raff. 1995. "The Evolution of Market Structure, Information, and Spreads in American Investment Banking," In Michael D. Bordo, and Richard Sylla, eds. *Anglo-American Financial Systems: Institutions and Markets in the Twentieth Century.* New York: Irwin, 103–60.

Campbell-Kelly, Martin, and William Aspray. 1996. *Computer: A History of the Information Machine.* New York: Basic Books.

Cardwell, Donald S.L. 1971. *From Watt to Clausius: The Rise of Thermodynamics in the Early Industrial Age.* Ithaca, NY: Cornell University Press.

Cardwell, Donald S.L. 1994. *The Fontana History of Technology.* London: Fontana Press.

Carlson, Gerald A., and Michelle Marra 2000, "Property Rights and Regulations for Transgenic Crops in North America," In V. Santaniello, R.E. Evenson, D. Zilberman, and G.A. Carlson, eds. *Agriculture and Intellectual Property Rights: Economic, Institutional and Implementation Issues in Biotechnology,* Chapter 13. Wallingford, UK: CABI Publishing.

Carlton, Dennis, and Jeffrey Perloff. 1990. *Modern Industrial Organization.* Boston, MA: Little Brown.

Carnot, Sadi. 1824/1986. *Reflections on the Motive Power of Fire.* Translated and edited by Robert Fox. Manchester: Manchester University Press.

Carr, J.C., and W. Taplin. 1962. *A History of the British Steel Industry.* Oxford: Basil Blackwell.

Casper, Steven. 1997. "Automobile Supplier Network Organisation in East Germany: A Challenge to the German Model of Industrial Organisation," *Industry and Innovation* 4 (1): 97–113.

Casper, Steven, Marc Lehrer, and David Soskice. 1999. "Can High-technology Industries Prosper in Germany? Institutional Frameworks and the Evolution of the Germany Software and Biotechnology Industries," *Industry and Innovation* 6 (1): 5–20.

Cawley, Richard A. 1997. "Interconnection, Pricing, Settlements: Some Healthy Jostling in the Growth of the Internet," In Brian Kahin, and James H. Keller, eds. *Coordinating the Internet.* Cambridge, MA: MIT Press.

CBI. 1996. *Investment in the UK.* London: Confederation of British Industry.

Cerf, Vinton G., Barry M. Leiner, David D. Clark, Robert E. Kahn, Leonard Kleinrock, Daniel C. Lynch, Jon Postel, Larry G. Roberts, and Stephen Wolff. 2000. *A Brief History of the Internet,* www.isoc.org/internet/history/.

Ceruzzi, Paul E. 1998. *A History of Modern Computing.* Cambridge, MA: MIT Press.

Chan, Yuk-Shee. 1983. "On the Positive Role of Financial Intermediation in Allocation of Venture Capital in a Market with Imperfect Information," *Journal of Finance* 38: 1543–68.

Chandler, Alfred D. 1990. *Scale and Scope: The Dynamics of Industrial Capitalism.* Cambridge, MA: Harvard University Press.

Chandler, Alfred D. Jr., and S. Salsbury. 1971. *Pierre S. Dupont and the Making of the Modern Corporation.* New York: Harper and Row.

Chapman, Stanley D. 1974. "The Textile Factory Before Arkwright: a Typology of Factory Development," *Business History Review* 48 (4): 451–78.

Charlesworth, Brian, and Alan R. Templeton. 1982. "Hopeful Monsters Cannot Fly," *Paleobiology* 8(4): 469–74.

Cheney, Margaret. 1981. *Tesla: Man Out of Time.* Englewood Cliffs, NJ: Prentice Hall.

Chesnais, François. 1993. "The French National System of Innovation", In Richard Nelson, ed. *National Innovation Systems: A Comparative Analysis.* New York: Oxford University Press, 192–229.

Chien, R.I. 1979. *Issues in Pharmaceutical Economics.* Lexington, MA: Lexington Books.

Chinoy, Bilal, and Timothy J. Salo. 1997. "Internet Exchanges: Policy-Driven Evolution," In Brian Kahin, and James H. Keller, eds. *Coordinating the Internet.* Cambridge, MA: MIT Press.

Christensen, Clayton M. 1997. *The Innovator's Dilemma: When New Technologies Cause Great Firms to Fail.* Cambridge, MA: Harvard Business School Press.

Christensen, Jesper Lindgaard. 1992. "The Role of Finance in National Systems of Innovation," In B. Lundval, ed. *National Systems of Innovation: Towards a Theory of Innovation and Interactive Learning.* London: Pinter.

Claessens, Stijn, Thomas Glaessner, and Daniela Klingebiel. 2000. "Electronic Finance: Reshaping the Financial Landscape Around the World," *Financial Sector Discussion Paper No. 4*. World Bank, September.

Clark, Kim B., and Takahiro Fujimoto. 1991. *Product Development Performance: Strategy, Organization, and Management in the World Automobile Industry.* Boston, MA: Harvard Business School Press.

Clark, Ronald W. 1977. *Edison: The Man Who Made the Future.* New York: G.P. Putnam & Sons.

Clymer, H.A. 1975. "The Economic and Regulatory Climate: US. and Overseas Trends," In R.B. Helms, ed. *Drug Development and Marketing.* Washington, DC: American Enterprise Institute.

Cockburn, Iain M., and Rebecca Henderson. 1996. "Public-Private Interaction in Pharmaceutical Research," In *Proceedings of the National Academy of Sciences*, Vols. 93/23 (November 12): 12725–30.

Cockburn, Iain M., and Rebecca Henderson. 1998. "Absorptive Capacity, Coauthoring behavior and the Organization of Research in Drug Discovery," *The Journal of Industrial Economics* 46: 157–82.

Cockburn, Iain M., Rebecca Henderson, and Scott Stem. 1997. *Fixed Effects and the Diffusion of Organizational Practice in Pharmaceutical Research.* Mimeo, Cambridge, MA: MIT Press.

Cockburn, Iain M., Rebecca Henderson, and Scott Stem. 1998. *Balancing Research and Production: Internal Capital Markets and Promotion Policies as Incentive Instruments.* Mimeo, Cambridge, MA: MIT Press.

Cohen, Elie, and Michel Bauer. 1985. *Les Grandes Manoeuvres Industrielles.* Paris: Belfond.

Cohen, Jack, and Ian Stewart. 1994. *The Collapse of Chaos.* New York: Penguin.

Cohen, Jessica, William Dickens, and Adam Posen. 2001. "Changing Human Resource Management Practices in U.S. Manufacturing and the Decline in the NAIRU," In Alan Krueger, and Robert Solow, eds. *Sustainable Employment.* Russell Sage Foundation.

Cohen, Linda R., and Roger G. Noll. 1991. *The Technology Pork Barrel.* Washington, DC: Brookings Institution.

Cohen, W., and R. Levin. 1989. "Empirical Studies of Innovation and Market Structure," In Richard Schmalensee, and Robert D. Willig, eds. *Handbook of Industrial Organization*, Vol. 2. New York: North-Holland, 1059–107.

Cohen, Wesley M., and Daniel A. Levinthal. 1989. "Innovation and Learning: The Two Faces of R&D," *The Economic Journal* 99 (397): 569–96.

Cohen, Wesley M., Richard Nelson, and John Walsh. 2000. "Protecting Their Intellectual Assets: Appropriability Conditions and Why U.S. Manufacturing Firms Patent (and Don't)," In *NBER Working Paper No. 7552.* Cambridge, MA: National Bureau of Economic Research.

Cohen, Y. 1991. "The Modernization of Production in the French Automobile Industry between the Wars: A Photographic Essay," *Business History Review* 65(4): 754–80.

Commissariat Général du Plan (CGP). 1999. *Recherche et Innovation: la France dans la Compétition Mondiale.*

Committee for Strategic Economic Policies. 1999. *Nihan Keisai Saisei Eno Seneyaku (The Strategy for Reviving the Japanese Economy)* Prime Minister's Office, Tokyo.

Constant, Edward W. 1980. *The Origins of the Turbojet Revolution.* Baltimore, MD: Johns Hopkins Press.

Coombs, Aston. 1996. *The European Biotechnology Yearbook.* EBUS, Netherlands.

Cooper, Carolyn. 1984. "The Portsmouth System of Manufacture," *Technology and Culture* 25 (April): 182–225.

Coopers and Lybrand. 1993. *Final Report for Study of International Differences in the Cost of Capital for the European Commission*, April. Brussels: European Commission.

Coppejans, Mark, and Ian Domowitz. 2000. "The Impact of Foreign Ownership on Emerging Market Share Volatility," *International Finance* 3: 95–122.

Coppejans, Mark, Ian Domowitz, and Ananth Madhavan. 2000. "Liquidity in an Automated Auction," *Working Paper.* Pennsylvania State University.

Cornelli, Francesca, and Oved Yosha. 1997. "Stage Financing and the Role of Convertible Debt," *Working Paper.* London Business School and Tel Aviv University.

Council of Economic Advisers. 2000. *The Economic Report of the President.* Washington, DC: US Government Printing Office.

Council of Economic Advisers. 2001. *The Economic Report of the President.* Washington, DC: US Government Printing Office.

Cour des Comptes. 1989. *Rapport au Président de la République* 36–44.

Cowan, Robin, and Dominique Foray. 1999. "The Economics of Codification and the Diffusion of Knowledge," *Industrial and Corporate Change* 6 (3, September): 595–622.

Cox, W. Michael, and Richard Alm. 1998. *The Right Stuff: America's Move to Mass-customization.* Federal Reserve Bank of Dallas, 1998 Annual Report.

Crafts, Nicholas, and Mary O'Mahony. 2000. *A Perspective on UK Productivity Performance.* Mimeo, London School of Economics.

Crafts, Nicholas, and Gianni Toniolo. 1996. "Postwar Growth: an Overview," In Nicholas Crafts, and Gianni Toniolo, eds. *Economic Growth in Europe since 1945.* Cambridge: Cambridge University Press (for the Centre for Economic Policy Research).

Craggs, Anthony, and Peter Jones. 1998. "UK Results from the Community Innovation Survey," *Economic Trends* 539 (October): 51–7.

Credit Suisse First Boston Global Bank Team. 1999. *Special Internet Banking Review.* New York: Credit Suisse First Boston Global Bank.

Crouch, Tom. 1989. *The Bishop's Boys: A Life of Wilbur and Orville Wright.* New York: Norton.

Cullen, M.J. 1975. *The Statistical Movement in Early Victorian Britain.* New York: Barnes and Noble.

Cusumano, Michael 1985. *The Japanese Automobile Industry: Technology and Management at Nissan and Toyota.* Cambridge, MA: Harvard University Press.

Cusumano, Michael, and David B. Yoffie. 1998. *Competing on Internet Time: Lessons From Netscape and its Battle with Microsoft.* New York: Free Press.

Cyert, Richard M., and David C. Mowery, eds. 1987. *Technology and Employment: Innovation and Growth in the U.S. Economy.* Washington, DC: National Academy Press.

Dahl, Per H. 1999. *Heavy Water and the Wartime Race for Nuclear Energy.* Bristol, UK: Institute of Physics Publishing.

Danthine, Jean-Pierre, Francesco Giavazzi, and Ernst-Ludwig von Thadden. 2000. "European Financial Markets After EMU: A First Assessment," *Working Paper.* Universite de Lausanne.

David, Paul A. 1975. *Technical Choice, Innovation and Economic Growth.* Cambridge, UK: Cambridge University Press.

David, Paul A. 1990. "The Dynamo and the Computer: an Historical Perspective on the Modern Productivity Paradox," *American Economic Review* 80 (May): 355–61.

David, Paul A. 2000. "Understanding Digital Technology's Evolution and the Path of Measured Productivity Growth: Present and Future in the Mirror of the Past," In E. Brynjolffson, and B. Kahin, eds. *Understanding the Digital Economy.* Cambridge, MA: MIT Press.

David, Paul A., and Dominique Foray. 1995. "Accessing and Expanding the Science and Technology Knowledge Base," *STI Review:* 13–68.

David, Paul A., and Shane Greenstein. 1990. "The Economics of Compatibility Standards: an Introduction to Recent Research," *Economics of Innovation and New Technology* 1: 3.

David, Paul A., David C. Mowery, and Edward Steinmueller. 1994. "Analyzing the Economic Payoffs from Basic Research," In D.C. Mowery, ed. *Science and Technology Policy in Interdependent Economies.* Boston, MA: Kluwer.

Davies, W. 1967. *The Pharmaceutical Industry: A Personal Study.* Oxford: Pergamon Press.

Davis, E. Philip, and Benn Steil. 2001. *Institutional Investors.* Cambridge, MA: MIT Press.

Davis, Louis E., and Albert B. Cherns, eds. 1975. *The Quality of Working Life,* 2 vols. New York: Free Press.

Davis, Steven J., and Kevin M. Murphy. 2000. "A Competitive Perspective on Internet Explorer," *American Economic Review* May: 184–7.

De Long, B. 1999. "Liquidation Cycles: Old Fashioned Real Business Cycle Theory and the Great Depression," *NBER Working Paper No. 3546.*

Décennie, *Une Analyse en Comparaison Internationale,* 8 Juillet, Mimeo, Paris: INSEE.

DeLong, J. Bradford. 2000. "Cornucopia: The Pace of Economic Growth in the Twentieth century," *NBER Working Paper No. 7602.*

Dempsey, Bert J., Debra Weiss, Paul Jones, and Jane Greenberg. 1999. *A Quantitative Profile of a Community of Open Source Linux Developers.* UNC Open Source Research Team. Chapel Hill, NC: School of Information and Library Science, University of North Carolina. Internet: http://www.ibiblio.org/osrt/develpro.html.

Denison, Edward. 1962. *The Sources of Economic Growth in the United States and the Alternatives Before Us.* New York: Committee for Economic Development.

Deutsches Aktieninstitut. 1998. *DAI-Factbook.* Frankfurt: DAI.

Devine, Warren. 1983. "From Shafts to Wires: Historical Perspective on Electrification," *Journal of Economic History* 43: 347–72.

Dixit, Avinash K., and Robert S. Pindyck. 1994. *Investment under Uncertainty.* Princeton, NJ: Princeton University Press.

Domowitz, Ian, and Benn Steil. 1999. "Automation, Trading Cost, and the Structure of the Securities Trading Industry," *Brookings-Wharton Papers on Financial Services* 2: 33–92.

Domowitz, Ian, and Benn Steil. 2001. "Automation, Trading Cost, and the Equity Cost of Capital," *Working Paper.* Pennsylvania State University.

Domowitz, Ian, Jack Glen, and Ananth Madhavan. 2001. "Liquidity, Volatility, and Equity Trading Costs Across Countries and Over Time," *International Finance* 4 (2, Summer).

Domowitz, Ian. 1993. "A Taxonomy of Automated Trade Execution Systems," *Journal of International Money and Finance* 12: 607–31.

Dooley, James J. 1997. "Unintended Consequences: Energy R&D in a Deregulated Energy Market," *Energy Policy* 26: 547–55.

Dorfman, Nancy S. 1987. *Innovation and Market Structure: Lessons from the Computer and Semiconductor Industries.* Cambridge: Ballinger.

Dosi, Giovanni, 1981. *Technical Change and Survival: Europe's Semiconductor Industry.* Sussex: Sussex European Research Center.

Dosi, Giovanni. 1982. "Technological Paradigms and Technological Trajectories," *Research Policy* 11: 147–62.

Dosi, Giovanni. 1984. *Technical Change and Industrial Transformation.* New York: St. Martin's Press.

Dosi, Giovanni, and Richard R. Nelson. 1994. "An Introduction to Evolution Theories in Economics," *Journal of Evolutionary Economics* 4 (3, September): 153–172.

Drews, Jurgen. 2000. "Drug Discovery: A Historical Perspective," *Science* 287: 1960–4.

DuBoff, Richard B. 1983. "The Telegraph and the Structure of Markets in the United States, 1845–1890," *Research in Economic History* 8: 253.

Dummer, G.W.A. 1978. *Electronic Inventions and Discoveries.* New York: Pergamon Press.

Dyer, Jeff. 2000. *Collaborative Advantage.* Oxford: Oxford University Press.

Dyson, Freeman. 1997. *Imagined Worlds.* Cambridge, MA: Harvard University Press.

Eaton, Jonathan, Eva Gutierrez, and Samuel Kortum. 1998. "European Technology Policy," *Economic Policy* 27: 403–38.

Economides Nicholas. 1996. "The Economics of Networks" *International Journal of Industrial Organization* 17: 673.

Edqvist, C., and Bengt-Ake Lundvall. 1993. "Comparing the Danish and Swedish Systems of Innovations," In Richard Nelson (ed.), *National Innovation Systems: A Comparative Analysis.* New York: Oxford University Press, 265–98.

Electric Power Research Institute. 1999. *Electricity Technology Roadmap.* Palo Alto, CA: EPRI.

Electronic Publication. North Carolina State University (available online at http://www.ag-econ.ncsu.edu/faculty/marra/FirstCrops/sld001.htm).

Eller, Jonathan. May 2000. "U. S. Inflation and Unemployment in the Late 1990s: A Re-examination of the Time-

Varying NAIRU," *Senior Honors Thesis* Northwestern University.

Energy Information Administration. 1998. *Challenges of Electric Power Industry Restructuring for Fuel Suppliers.* DOE/EIA-0623. Washington, DC: Department of Energy.

Energy Information Administration. 2000. *Annual Energy Review 1999.* Washington, DC: Department of Energy. http://tonto.eia.doe.gov/aer/index99.htm.

Energy Information Administration. 2001. *Electric Power Monthly* March http://www.eia.doe.gov/cneaf/electricity/epm/epm_sum.html.

Epstein, R.C. 1928. *The Automobile Industry: Its Economic and Commercial Development.* Chicago, IL: A.W. Shaw.

Ernst and Young. 1994. "Biotechnology in Europe," *Ernst & Young Annual Report.* London: Ernst and Young.

Ernst and Young. 1995. "European Biotech 95: Gathering Momentum," *Ernst & Young Annual Report.* London: Ernst and Young.

Ernst and Young. 2000. *Zweiter Biotechnologiereport Deutschland.* Mimeo, Stuttgart: Ernst and Young.

Escourrou, N. 1992. "Les Sociétés de Biotechnologie Européennes: Un Reseau Trts Imbriqué," *Biofutur* July/August, 40–2.

Etzkowitz, Henry. 1996. "Conflict of Interest and Commitment in Academic Science in the United States," *Minerva* 34 (3): 326–60.

European Central Bank. 1999. *The Effects of Technology on the EU Banking Systems.* Frankfurt: European Central Bank.

European Central Bank. 2000. *EU Banks' Income Structure.* Frankfurt: European Central Bank.

European Commission. 2000. *8th Review of Government Subsidies in the European Union.* Com (2000) 205. Brussels: European Commission.

European Venture Capital Journal. 1996. "European Performance Surveyed – A Tentative First Step," *European Venture Capital Journal.* 3–6.

Evenett, Simon J., Alexander Lehman, and Benn Steil. 2000. *Antitrust Goes Global: What Future for Transatlantic Cooperation?* London: Royal Institute for International Affairs.

Evenson, Robert E., and Daniel K. Johnson. 1999. "R&D Spillovers to Agriculture: Measurement and Application," *Contemporary Economic Policy* 17(4): 432–456.

Evenson, Robert E., and Daniel K.N. Johnson. 1997. "Introduction: Invention Input-Output Analysis," *Economic Systems Research* 9(2): 149–60.

Fama, Eugene F., and Michael C. Jensen. 1983. "Separation of Ownership and Control," *Journal of Law and Economics* 26: 301–25.

FED. 2000. "Productivity Developments Abroad," *Federal Reserve Bulletin* October: 665–81.

Feder, Barnaby J. 2000. "Digital Economy's Demand for Steady Power Strains Utilities," *New York Times*, 3 July, C1 & C4.

Federal Communications Commission: www.fcc.gov.

Federal Reserve Board. 2000. *Report to Congress on Markets for Small Business- and Commercial-Mortgage-Related Securities.* September. (Jointly authored with Securities and Exchange Commission.)

Ferguson, Charles H. 1985. *American Microelectronics in Decline: Evidence, Analysis, and Alternatives.* VLSI Memo No. 85-284, Cambridge, MA: Microsystems Research Center, Massachusetts Institute of Technology.

Ferguson, Charles H., and Charles R. Morris. 1993. *Computer Wars: How the West Can Win in a Post-IBM World.* New York: Times Books.

Fine, Charles H. 1986. "Quality Improvement and Learning in Productive Systems," *Management Science* 32 (10): 1301–15.

Fine, Charles H. 1988. "A Quality Control Model with Learning Effects," *Operations Research* 36 (3): 437–444.

Fine, Charles H. 1999. *Clockspeed: Winning Industry Control in the Age of Temporary Advantage.* Reading, MA: Perseus Books.

Fine, Charles H., and E. van Porteus. 1989. "Dynamic Process Improvement," *Operations Research* 37 (4): 580–91.

Fine, Charles H., and Richard St. Clair. 1996. *Meeting the Challenge: U.S. Industry Faces the 21st Century: The U.S. Automobile Manufacturing Industry.* Washington, DC: U.S. Department of Commerce Office of Technology Policy.

Fine, S. 1963. *The Automobile under the Blue Eagle: Labor, Management, and the Automobile Manufacturing Code.* Ann Arbor, MI: University of Michigan Press.

Fine, S. 1969. *Sit-Down: The General Motors Strike of 1936–1937.* Ann Arbor, MI: University of Michigan Press.

Fisher, Franklin. 2000. "The IBM and Microsoft Cases: What's the Difference," *American Economic Review* 90 (May): 180–3.

Fisher, Franklin M., James W. McKie, and Richard B. Mancke. 1983. *IBM and The U.S. Data Processing Industry.* New York: Praeger.

Flamm, Kenneth. 1988. *Creating the Computer.* Washington, DC: Brookings Institution.

Flamm, Kenneth. 1996. *Mismanaged Trade? Strategic Policy and the Semiconductor Industry.* Washington, DC: Brookings Institution Press.

Flanagan, Chris, Ralph DiSerio, and Ryan Asato. 1998. "More Growth Ahead," *Mortgage Banking* January: 46–56.

Flink, J.J. 1970. *America Adopts the Automobile, 1895–1970.* Cambridge, MA: MIT Press.

Ford, H. 1922. *My Life and Work.* Garden City, NY: Doubleday.

Forester, Tom. 1993. "Japan's Move up the Technology 'Food Chain'," *Prometheus* 11 (June): 73–94.

Foster, Richard N. 1986. *Innovation: The Attacker's Advantage.* New York: Summit Books.

Foster, Richard, and Sarah Kaplan. 2001. *Creative Destruction: Why Companies that are Built to Last Underperform the Market—and How to Successfully Transform Them.* New York: Doubleday.

Franks, Julian, and Mayer, Colin. 1992. *Hostile Takeovers and the Correction of Managerial Failure.* Mimeo, London Business School.

Fransman, Martin. 1990. *The Market and Beyond: Information Technology in Japan.* Cambridge: Cambridge University Press.

Fransman, Martin. 1995. *Japan's Computer and Communications Industry: the Evolution of Industrial Giants and Global Competitiveness.* Oxford: Oxford University Press.

Fransman, Martin. 1999. *Visions of Innovation: The Firm and Japan*. New York: Oxford University Press.

Freeman, Christopher, and Francisco Louca. 2001. *As Time Goes By*. Oxford: Oxford University Press.

Freeman, Christopher, and Luc Soete. 1997. *The Economics of Industrial Innovation*, 3rd edition. Cambridge, MA: MIT Press.

Fridenson, P. 1978. "The Coming of the Assembly Line to Europe," In W. Krohn et. al., eds., *The Dynamics of Science and Technology: Social Values, Technical Norms, and Scientific Criteria in the Development of Knowledge*. Dordrecht: Reidel.

Friend, Irwin, Marshall Blume, and Jean Crockett. 1970. *Mutual Funds and Other Institutional Investors*. New York: McGraw Hill.

Froot, Kenneth A., and Jeremy C. Stein. 1998. "Risk Management, Capital Budgeting, and Capital Structure Policy for Financial Institutions: an Integrated Approach," *Working Paper*. Cambridge, MA: MIT Sloan School.

Fujitsu Research Institute. 1997. "The Economic Impact of Information Technology in Japan: A Growth Accounting Analysis of the Contribution of Information Technology Capital to Economic Growth," *Report No. 8*.

Fukuyama, Francis. 1992. *The End of History and the Last Man*. New York: Maxwell Macmillan.

Furst, Karen, William W. Lang, and Daniel E. Nolle. 2000. "Internet Banking: Developments and Prospects," *Economic and Policy Analysis Working Paper 2000–9* September, Comptroller of the Currency.

Gall, Lothar, Gerald D. Feldman, Harold James, Carl-Ludwig Holtfrerich, and Hans Egon Büschgen. 1995. *Die Deutsche Bank 1870–1995*. Munich: C.H. Beck.

Gambardella, A. 1995. *Science and Innovation in the US Pharmaceutical Industry*. Cambridge: Cambridge University Press.

Garud, Raghu, and Arun Kumaraswamy. 1993. "Changing Competitive Dynamics in Network Industries: an Exploration of Sun Microsystems' Open Systems Strategy," *Strategic Management Journal* 14: 351–69.

Geczy, Christopher, Bernadette A. Minton, and Catherine Schrand. 1997. "Why Firms Use Currency Derivatives," *Journal of Finance* 52 (September): 1323–54.

Genda, Yuji, and Marcus Rebick. 2000. "Japanese Labour in the 1990s: Stability and Stagnation," *Oxford Review of Economic Policy* 16 (2): 85–107.

Geroski, Paul A. 1990. "Innovation, Technological Opportunity and Market Structure," *Oxford Economic Papers* 42: 586–602.

Gianessi, Leonard P., and Janet E. Carpenter. 1999. *Agricultural Biotechnology: Insect Control Benefits*. Washington, DC: National Center for Food and Agricultural Policy, July.

Gilder, George. 1989. *Microcosm: the Quantum Revolution in Economics and Technology*. New York: Simon and Schuster.

Gilpin, Robert. 1981. *War and Change in World Politics*. Cambridge: Cambridge University Press.

Gittleman, L. 2000. "Mapping National Knowledge Networks: Scientists, Firms, and Institutions in Biotechnology in the United States and France," *Working Paper*. New York University.

Goldin, Claudia. 1998. "America's Graduation from High School: The Evolution and Spread of Secondary Schooling in the Twentieth Century," *Journal of Economic History* 58 (June): 345–74.

Gompers, Paul. 1995. "Optimal Investment, Monitoring, and the Staging of Venture Capital," *Journal of Finance* 5: 1461–89.

Gompers, Paul. 1996. "Grandstanding in the Venture Capital Industry," *Journal of Financial Economics* 42: 133–56.

Gompers, Paul, and Josh Lerner. 1998. "Venture capital distributions: short- and long-run reactions," *Journal of Finance* 53: 2161–83.

Gompers, Paul, and Josh Lerner. 1999a. *Capital Market Imperfections in Venture Markets: A Report to the Advanced Technology Program*. Washington, DC: Advanced Technology Program, U.S. Department of Commerce.

Gompers, Paul, and Josh Lerner. 1999b. *The Venture Capital Cycle*. Cambridge, MA: MIT Press.

Gompers, Paul, and Josh Lerner. 2000. "Money Chasing Deals? The Impact of Fund Inflows on Private Equity Valuations," *Journal of Financial Economics* 55: 239–79.

Gompers, Paul, and Josh Lerner. 2001. *The Venture Capital Revolutions*. Boston, MA: Harvard Business School Press.

Gordon, Robert J. 1977. "Can the Inflation of the 1970s Be Explained?" *BPEA* 1: 253–77.

Gordon, Robert J. 1982. "Inflation, Flexible Exchange Rates, and the Natural Rate of Unemployment," In Martin N. Baily, ed. *Workers, Jobs, and Inflation*. Washington, DC: Brookings, 88–152.

Gordon, Robert. 1990. *The Measurement of Durable Goods Prices*. Chicago, IL: University of Chicago Press (for NBER).

Gordon, Robert. 1997. "The Time-Varying NAIRU and its Implications for Economic Policy," *Journal of Economic Perspectives* 11(1): 11–32.

Gordon, Robert. 1998. "Foundations of the Goldilocks Economy: Supply Shocks and the Time-Varying NAIRU," *Brookings Papers on Economic Activity* 29 (2): 297–333.

Gordon, Robert G. 2000a. "Does the 'New Economy' Measure up to the Great Inventions of the Past?" *Journal of Economic Perspectives* 14 (Fall): 49–74.

Gordon, Robert. 2000b. "Interpreting the 'One Big Wave' in U.S. Long-term Productivity Growth," In Bart van Ark, Simon Kuipers, and Gerard Kuper, eds. *Productivity, Technology, and Economic Growth*. Dordrecht: Kluwer Publishers, 19–65.

Gorman, Michael, and William A. Sahlman. 1989. "What do Venture Capitalists do?" *Journal of Business Venturing* 4: 231–48.

Gorte, Julie Fox, and Tina Kaarsberg, 2001. *Electricity Restructuring, Innovation and Efficiency*. Washington, DC: Northeast-Midwest Institute at http://www.nemw.org/ER_ERIE.htm

Goto, Akira, and Hiroyuki Odagiri. 1993. "The Japanese System of Innovation: Past, Present, and Future," In Richard Nelson, ed. *National Innovation System: A Comparative Analysis*. New York: Oxford University Press.

Goto, Akira, and Hiroyuki Odagiri, eds. 1997. *Innovation in Japan*. New York: Oxford University Press.

Goux, Dominique. 1996. *Les Transformations de la Demande de Travail par Qualifications: le Cas de la France, 1970–93*, STI, No. 18. Paris: OECD.

Grabowski, H. and J. Vernon. 1983. *The Regulation of Pharmaceuticals*. Washington, DC and London: American Enterprise Institute for Public Policy Research.

Grabowski, H. and J. Vernon. 1994. "Innovation and Structural Change in Pharmaceuticals and Biotechnology," *Industrial and Corporate Change* 3(2): 435–50.

Graham, Stuart, and David C. Mowery. 2000. "Intellectual Property Protection in the Software Industry," *Paper Presented at the National Research Council Conference on Intellectual Property and Policy*. Washington, DC, February 2–3.

Green, Richard. 1998. "Electricity Deregulation in England and Wales," In Georges Zaccour, ed. *Deregulation of Electric Utilities*. Boston, MA: Kluwer Academic Publishers, 179–202.

Greenstein, Shane. 2000a. "Commercialization of the Internet: The Interaction of Public Policy and Private Choices or Why Introducing the Market Worked So Well," *Paper written for the NBER program on Innovation, Policy and the Economy*. Washington DC, April 11.

Greenstein, Shane. 2000b. "Framing Empirical Work on the Evolving Structure of Commercial Internet Markets," In E. Brynjolffson, and B. Kahin, eds. *Understanding the Digital Economy*. Cambridge, MA: MIT Press.

Greenwald, Bruce C., Joseph E. Stiglitz, and Andrew Weiss. 1984. "Information Imperfections in the Capital Market and Macroeconomic Fluctuations," *American Economic Review Papers and Proceedings* 74: 194–9.

Griffith, Rachel, Stephen Redding, and John Van Reenen. 1999. *Mapping the Two Faces of R&D: Productivity Growth in a Panel of OECD Manufacturing Industries*. Mimeo, Institute for Fiscal Studies, London.

Griliches, Z. 1957. "Hybrid Corn: an Exploration in the Economics of Technological Change," *Econometrics* 25 (October): 501–22.

Griliches, Z. 1961. *Hedonic Price Indices for Automobiles: an Econometric Analysis of Quality Change. In Price Statistics of the Federal Government*. Hearings before the Joint Economic Committee of the U.S. Congress, 173–76. Pt. 1, 87th Cong., 1st sess. Reprinted in Z. Griliches, ed. 1971. *Price Indices and Quality Change: Studies in New Methods of Measurement*. Cambridge, MA: Harvard University Press.

Grindley, Peter, David C. Mowery, and Brian Silverman. 1994. "Sematech and Collaborative Research Lessons in the Design of High-Technology Consortia," *Journal of Policy Analysis and Management* 13 (Fall): 723–58.

Grossman, Sanford, and Oliver Hart. 1986. "The Costs and Benefits of Ownership: a Theory of Vertical and Lateral Integration," *Journal of Political Economy* 94: 691–719.

Grubel, Herbert G., and Rolf Weder. 1993. "The New Growth Theory and Coasean Economics: Institutions to Capture Externalities," *Weltwirtschaftliches Archiv* 129 (3): 488–513.

Grübler, Arnulf, Neboja Nakiænoviæ, and David G. Victor. 1999. "Dynamics of Energy Technologies and Global Change," *Energy Policy* 27: 247–80.

Grübler, Arnulf. 1996. "Time for a Change: on the Patterns of Diffusion of Innovation," *Daedalus* 125: 19-42.

Guillaume, Henri. 1998. *La Technologie et l'Innovation*. Rapport pour le Premier Ministre.

Gust and Marquez. 2000. "Productivity Developments Abroad," *Federal Reserve Bulletin* 86 (October): 665–81.

Hall, A. Rupert. 1974. "What Did the Industrial Revolution in Britain Owe to Science?" In Neil McKendrick, ed., *Historical Perspectives: Studies in English Thought and Society*. London: Europa Publications.

Hall, Bronwyn H., and Rosemarie Ham Ziedonis. 2001. "The Patent Paradox Revisited: an Empirical Study of Patenting in the U.S Semiconductor Industry, 1979–1995," *Rand Journal of Economics* 32 (1): 101–28.

Hall, Chris, and Robert H. Hall. 2000. "Towards a Quantification of the Effects of Microsoft's Conduct," *American Economic Review* (90): 188–91.

Halloran, Michael J., ed. 1996. *Venture Capital and Public Offering Negotiation*. Englewood Cliffs, NJ: Aspen Law and Business.

Hancher, L. 1990. *Regulating for Competition: Government, Law and the Pharmaceutical Industry in the United Kingdom and France*. Oxford: Oxford University Press.

Hansen, Robert, and P. Torregrossa. 1992. "Underwriter Compensation and Corporate Monitoring," *Journal of Finance* 47 (September): 1537–55.

Hartnett, Michael, and Matthew Higgins. 2000. *Global Ranking System: Ranking the World's Fast-Track Economies*. New York: Merrill Lynch.

Harris, Ron. 2000. *Industrializing English Law: Entrepreneurship and Business Organization, 1720–1844*. Cambridge: Cambridge University Press.

Hart, Oliver, and John Moore. 1990. "Property Rights and the Nature of the Firm," *Journal of Political Economy* 98: 1119–58.

Hart, Oliver, and John Moore. 1998. "Default and Renegotiation: A Dynamic Model of Debt," *Quarterly Journal of Economics* 113: 1–41.

Hayami, Yujiro, and Vernon W. Ruttan. 1971. *Agricultural Development: an International Perspective*. Baltimore, MD: John Hopkins Press.

Headrick, Daniel R. 1989. *The Invisible Weapon: Telecommunications and International Politics, 1851–1945*. New York: Oxford University Press.

Headrick, Daniel. 2000. *When Information Came of Age: Technologies of Knowledge in the Age of Reason and Revolution, 1700–1850*. New York: Oxford University Press.

Heldt, P. 1933. "Parts Makers' Role Gets Bigger as Automotive History Unfolds," *Automotive Industries* (6, May): 546–8, 554.

Hellmann, Thomas, and Manju Puri. 1998. "The Interaction Between Product Market and Financing Strategy: the Role of Venture Capital," *Review of Financial Studies* 13: 959–84.

Hellmann, Thomas. 1998. "The Allocation of Control Rights in Venture Capital Contracts," *Rand Journal of Economics* 29: 57–76.

Helm, Leslie. 1995. "In the Chips," *The Los Angeles Times* (March 5): D1.

Helper, Susan R. 1991. "Strategy and Irreversibility in Supplier Relations: The Case of the U.S. Auto Industry," *Business History Review* 65(4): 781–824.

Helper, Susan R. and J.P. MacDuffie. 2000. *E-volving the Auto Industry: E-commerce Effects on Consumer and Supplier Relationships.* Typescript.

Helpman, Elhanan, and Trajtenberg, Manuel. 1998. "Diffusion of General Purpose Technologies," In Elhanan Helpman, ed. *General Purpose Technologies.* Cambridge, MA: MIT Press, 85–120.

Elhanan Helpman, ed. 1998. *General Purpose Technologies.* Cambridge, MA: MIT Press.

Henderson, Rebecca. 1994. "The Evolution of Integrative Competence: Innovation in Cardiovascular Drug Discovery," *Industrial and Corporate Change* 3(3): 607–30.

Henderson, Rebecca, and Iain Cockburn. 1994. "Measuring Competence? Exploring Firm Effects in Pharmaceutical Research," *Strategic Management Journal* 15 (Winter Special Issue): 63–84.

Henderson, Rebecca, and Iain Cockburn. 1996. "Scale, Scope and Spillovers: The Determinants of Research Productivity in Drug Discovery," *Rand Journal of Economics* 27(1): 32–59.

Henderson, Rebecca M., and Kim B. Clark. 1990. "Architectural Innovation: the Reconfiguration of Existing Product Technologies and the Failure of Established Firms," *Administrative Science Quarterly* 35: 9–30.

Henderson, Rebecca, Luigi Orsenigo, and Gary. P. Pisano. 1999. "The Pharmaceutical Industry and the Revolution in Molecular Biology: Interactions Among Scientific, Institutional, and Organizational Change," In David C. Mowery, and Richard R. Nelson, eds. *Sources of Industrial Leadership.* Cambridge: Cambridge University Press, 267–311.

Henriques, Irene, and Lee J. Butler. 2000. "The Importance of Feed Management Technologies in the Decision to Adopt Bovine Somatotropin (bST): an Application to California Dairy Producers," *Economics of Agricultural Biotechnologies,* IACBR Ravello, Italy, August, 165.

Hermalin, Benjamin E., and Michael S. Weisbach. 1988. "The Determinants of Board Composition," *Rand Journal of Economics* 19: 589–606.

Hirsh, Richard F. 1989. *Technology and Transformation in the American Electric Utility Industry.* New York: Cambridge University Press.

Hobday, Michael. 1991. "Semiconductor Technology and the Newly Industrializing Countries: The Diffusion of ASICs (Application Specific Integrated Circuits)," *World Development* 19 (April): 375–97.

Holbrook, Daniel. 1999. "Technical Diversity and Technological Change in the American Semiconductor Industry, 1952–1965," Ph.D. dissertation, Carnegie Mellon University.

Hollander, S. 1965. *The Sources of Increased Efficiency: A Study of DuPont Rayon Plants.* Cambridge, MA: MIT Press.

Hoshi, Takeo, and Anil Kashyap 2001. *Keiretsu Financing.* Cambridge, MA: MIT Press.

Hoshi, Takeo, Anil Kashyap, and David Scharfstein. 1990. "Bank Monitoring and Investment: Evidence from the Changing Nature of Japanese Corporate Banking Relationships," In R. Glenn Hubbard, ed. *Asymmetric Information, Corporate Finance, and Investment.* Chicago, IL: University of Chicago Press.

Hoshi, Takeo, Anil Kashyap, and David Scharfstein. 1990. "The Role of Banks in Reducing the Costs of Financial Distress in Japan," *Journal of Financial Economics* 45: 33–60.

Hounshell, D.A. 1984. *From the American System to Mass Production: The Development of Manufacturing Technology in the United States.* Baltimore, MD: Johns Hopkins University Press.

Hounshell, D.A. 2000. "Automation, Transfer Machinery, and Mass Production in the U.S. Automobile Industry in the Post-World War II Era," *Economy and Society* 1(1): 100–38.

Howell, Thomas R., Brent Bartlett, and Warren Davis. 1992. *Creating Advantage: Semiconductors and Government Industrial Policy in the 1990s.* Cupertino, CA and Washington, DC: Semiconductor Industry Association and Dewey Ballintine. http://www.isoc.org/guest/zakon/Internet/History/HIT.html.

Huffman, Wallace E., and Robert E. Evenson. 1993. *Science for Agriculture: A Long Term Perspective.* Aimes, IA: Iowa State University Press.

Hughes, Thomas P. 1983. *Networks of Power: Electrification in Western Society, 1880–1930.* Baltimore, MD: Johns Hopkins University Press.

Hunnius, Gerry, G. David Garson, and John Case, eds. 1975. *Workers' Control: A Reader on Labor and Social Change.* New York: Vintage.

Hyman, Leonard S., ed. 1995. *America's Electric Utilities: Past, Present and Future,* 5th edition. Vienna, VA: Public Utilities Reports.

Industrial Policy Bureau. 1998. *Action Plan for Economic Structural Reform.* Tokyo: MITI.

Innovation Systems: A Comparative Study. Cambridge, UK: Oxford University Press.

Integrated Circuit Engineering Corporation (ICE). (Various years). *Status of the Integrated Circuit Industry.* Scottsdale, AZ: ICE.

International Energy Agency (IEA). 1997. *Renewable Energy Policy in IEA Countries, Vol. 2: Country Reports.* Paris: IEA. http//www.iea.org/pubs/studies/files/renenp2/table4.pdf.

International Energy Agency (IEA). 1998. *Projected Costs of Generating Electricity.* Paris: OECD.

International Energy Agency (IEA). 2000. *Energy Policies of IEA Countries: 1999 Review.* Paris: OECD.

International Energy Agency (IEA). 2001. *Monthly Electricity Survey* January, http://www.iea.org.

IMD. 2000. *International Management Development Institute World Competitiveness Yearbook 2000.* Lausanne: IMD.

Ip, Greg. 2000. "Market on a High Wire," *Wall Street Journal* January 18, C1.

Irvine, J., B. Martin, and P. Isard. 1990. *Investing in the Future: an International Comparison of Government Funding of Academic and Related Research.* Cheltenham: Edward Elgar, 219.

Irwin, Douglas A., and Peter J. Klenow. 1996. "High Tech

R&D Subsidies: Estimating the Effects of Sematech," *Journal of International Economics* 40: 323–44.

Iung, Nicolas, and Phillippe Lagarde. 1998. "L'evolution des Industries Francaise de Haute Technologies: Elements Descriptifs," In Robert Boyer ,and Michel Didier. *Innovation et Croissance.* Conseil d'Analyse Economique.

Jaffe, Adam B., Manuel Trajtenberg, and Rebecca Henderson. 1993. "Geographic Localization of Knowledge Spillovers as Evidenced by Patent Citations," *Quarterly Journal of Economics* August: 578–98.

Jaffe, Adam, Manuel Trajtenberg, and Michael S. Fogarty. 2000. "The Meaning of Patent Citations," Canadian Institute for Advanced Research, *Working Paper No. 137* April.

Jaikumar, R. 1986. "Post-Industrial Manufacturing," *Harvard Business Review* Nov/Dec: 69–76.

James, Christopher. 1987. "Some Evidence on the Uniqueness of Bank Loans," *Journal of Financial Economics* 19: 217–35.

James, Clive. 1999. *Global Review of Commercialized Transgenic Crops: 1999.* Ithaca, NY: ISAAA.

Japan Development Bank. 1996. "Recent Research and Development Trends in Japanese Enterprises: Technological Fusion," *Research Report No. 91.* Tokyo: Japan Development Bank.

Japan Development Bank. 1998. "Structural Changes in Unemployment of Japan: an Approach from Labor Flow," *Research Report No. 86.* Tokyo: Japan Development Bank.

Jarvis, Lovell S. 1999. "The Potential Effect of Recombinant Bovine Somatotropin (rbSt) on World Dairying," presented at The Shape of the Coming Agricultural Biotechnology Transformation, International Consortium on Agricultural Biotechnology Research, Rome, Italy, June 17–18.

Jeng, Leslie, and Philippe Wells. 1999. "The Determinants of Venture Capital Funding: an Empirical Analysis," *Unpublished Working Paper.* Harvard University.

Jensen, Michael C., and William H. Meckling. 1976. "Theory of the Firm: Managerial Behavior, Agency Costs and Ownership Structure," *Journal of Financial Economics* 3: 305–60.

Jewkes, John, David Sawers, and Richard Stillerman. 1969. *The Sources of Invention,* 2nd edition. New York: Norton.

Johnson, Daniel K.N., and Vittorio Santaniello. 2000, "Biotechnology Inventions: What Can We Learn from Patents?" In V. Santaniello, R.E. Evenson, D. Zilberman, and G.A. Carlson, eds. *Agriculture and Intellectual Property Rights: Economic, Institutional and Implementation Issues in Biotechnology,* Chapter 11. Wallingford, UK: CABI Publishing.

Johnstone, Bob. 1999. *We Were Burning: Japanese Entrepreneurs and the Forging of the Electronic Age.* New York: Basic Books.

Jorgenson, Dale W., and Kevin J. Stiroh. 2000. "Raising the Speed Limit: U.S. Economic Growth in the Information Age," *Brookings Papers on Economic Activity* 31(1): 125–211.

Joskow, Paul L. 1987. "Productivity Growth and Technical Change in the Generation of Electricity," *The Energy Journal* 8: 17–38.

Joskow, Paul L., and Donald R. Jones. 1983. "The Simple Economics of Industrial Cogeneration," *The Energy Journal* 4: 1–22.

Joskow, Paul L., and Nancy L. Rose. 1985. "The Effects of Technological Change, Experience and Environmental Regulation on the Construction Cost of Coal-Burning Generating Units," *Rand Journal of Economics* 16: 1–27.

Kahin, Brian. 1997. "The U.S. National Information Infrastructure Initiative: The Market, the Net, and the Virtual Project," In B. Kahin, and E.J. Wilson, III, eds. *National Information Infrastructure Initiatives: Vision and Policy Design.* Cambridge, MA: MIT Press.

Kaplan, S., and P. Stromberg. 1999. "Financial Contracting Theory Meets the Real World: Evidence from Venture Capital Contracts," *Unpublished Working Paper.* Chicago, IL: University of Chicago.

Kaserman, David L., and John W. Mayo. 1995. *Government and Business: The Economics of Antitrust and Regulation.* Fort Worth, TX: Harcourt Brace College Publishers.

Katz, Barbara, and Almarin Phillips. 1982. "The Computer Industry," In Richard R. Nelson, ed. *Government and Technical Progress: A Cross-Industry Analysis.* New York: Pergamon Press, 162–232.

Katz, Lawrence F., and Alan B. Krueger. 1999. "The High-Pressure U.S. Labor Market of the 1990s," *Brookings Papers on Economic Activity* 301: 1–65.

Kauffman, Stuart A. 1995. *At Home in the Universe: The Search for the Laws of Self-Organization and Complexity.* New York: Oxford University Press.

Keim, Donald B., and Ananth Madhavan. 1998. "The Cost of Institutional Equity Trades," *Financial Analysts Journal:* 50–69.

Kennedy, E.D. 1941. *The Automobile Industry: The Coming of Age of Capitalism's Favorite Child.* New York: Reynal and Hitchcock.

Kennedy, Paul M. 1987. *The Rise and Fall of the Great Powers: Economic Change and Military Conflict from 1500 to 2000.* New York: Random House.

Kenney, M. 1986. *Biotechnology: The Industry-University Complex.* Ithaca, NY: Cornell University Press.

Kimes, B.R. and H.A. Clark, Jr. 1996. *Standard Catalogue of American Cars 1805–1942,* 3rd edition. Osceola, WI: Krause.

Kingston, William. 2000. "Antibiotics, Invention, and Innovation," *Research Policy* 29, 679–710.

Kirsch, David A. 2000. *The Electric Vehicle and the Burden of History.* Rutgers, NJ: Rutgers University Press.

Klette, Jacob, and Jarle Moen. 1999. "From Growth Theory to Technology Policy Coordination Problems in Theory and Practice," *Nordic Journal of Political Economy* 35: 53–74.

Klevorick, A., R. Levin, R. Nelson, and S. Winter. 1995. "On the Sources and Significance of Interindustry Differences in Technological Opportunities," *Research Policy* 24 (2, March): 185.

Klodt, Henning. 1998. "German Technology Policy: Institutions, Objectives and Economic Efficiency," *Zeitschrift für Wirtschaftspolitik* 47 (2): 142–63.

Kortum, Samuel, and Josh Lerner. 2000. "Assessing the

Contribution of Venture Capital to Innovation," *Rand Journal of Economics* 31 (Winter): 674–92.

Kortum, Steven, and Josh Lerner. 1998. "Stronger Protection or Technological Revolution: What is Behind the Recent Surge in Patenting?" *Carnegie-Rochester Conference Series on Public Policy* 48: 247–304.

Kraus, Jerome. 1971. "An Economic Study of the U.S. Semiconductor Industry," Ph.D. Dissertation. New School for Social Research.

Kregel, Jan. 1992. "Some Considerations on the Causes of Structural Change in Financial Markets," *Journal of Economic Issues* September XXVI: 3.

Kruger, Alan, and Mikael Lindahl. 2000. "Education for Growth: Why and for Whom?" *NBER Working Paper No. 7591.*

Kuan, Jennifer. 2000. "Open-Source Software as Consumer Integration into Production," *Unpublished Manuscript.* Berkeley, CA: Haas School of Business, U.C. Berkeley.

Kurzweil, Raymond. 1999. *The Age of Spiritual Machines.* New York: Viking.

Kuznets, Simon. 1965. *Economic Growth and Structure.* New York: W.W. Norton.

Lamoreaux, Naomi R., and Kenneth L. Sokoloff. 2000. "Intermediaries in the U.S. Market for Technology, 1870–2000," *Unpublished Working Paper.* University of California at Los Angeles.

Landau, Ralph, Basil Achilladelis, and Alexander Scriabine. 1999. *Pharmaceutical Innovation: Revolutionizing Human Health.* Philadelphia, PA: Chemical Heritage Foundation.

Landes, David S. 1998. *The Wealth and Poverty of Nations: Why Some are so Rich and Some so Poor.* New York: W.W. Norton.

Langlois, Richard N. 1992. "External Economies and Economic Progress: The Case of the Microcomputer Industry," *Business History Review* 66 (Spring): 1–50.

Langlois, Richard N., and David C. Mowery. 1996. "The Federal Government Role in the Development of the U.S. Software Industry," In D.C. Mowery ed. *The International Computer Software Industry: A Comparative Study of Industry Evolution and Structure.* New York: Oxford University Press.

Langlois, Richard N., and Paul L. Robertson. 1992. "Networks and Innovation in a Modular System: Lessons from the Microcomputer and Stereo Component Industries," *Research Policy* 21: 297–313.

Langlois, Richard N., and Paul L. Robertson. 1995. *Firms, Markets, and Economic Change: A Dynamic Theory of Business Institutions.* London: Routledge.

Langlois, Richard N., and W. Edward Steinmueller. 1999. "The Evolution of Competitive Advantage in the Worldwide Semiconductor Industry, 1947–1996," In David C. Mowery, and Richard R. Nelson, eds. *The Sources of Industrial Leadership.* New York: Cambridge University Press, 19–78.

Langlois, Richard N., Thomas A. Pugel, Carmela S. Haklisch, Richard R. Nelson, and William G. Egelhoff. 1988. *Microelectronics: an Industry in Transition.* London: Unwin Hyman.

Lapidus, Gary. 2000. *Gentlemen Start Your Search Engines.* New York: Goldman Sachs.

Laragh, J.H. et al. 1972. "Renin, Angiotensin and Aldosterone System in Pathogenesis and Management of Hypertensive Vascular Disease," *American Journal of Medicine* 52: 644–52.

Lavoie, Brian F., and Ian M. Sheldon. 2000. "Market Structure in Biotechnology: Implications for Long Run Comparative Advantage," *Economics of Agricultural Biotechnologies IACBR.* Ravello, Italy, August, 335.

Lawrence, Robert, and David Weinstein. 1999. "Trade and Growth: Import-Led or Export-Led? Evidence from Japan and Korea," *NBER Working Paper No. 7264.*

Layard, Richard, and Stephen J. Nickell. 1989. "The Thatcher Miracle?" *American Economic Review, Papers and Proceedings* 215–9.

Laux, James M. 1992. *The European Automobile Industry.* New York: Twayne.

Lee, Gwendolyn K., and Robert E. Cole. 2000. "The Linux Kernel Development as a Model of Open Source Knowledge Creation," *Unpublished Manuscript.* Berkeley, CA: Haas School of Business, U.C. Berkeley.

Lee, Kong-Rae, and John Kantwell, eds. 1998. *The Sources of Capital Goods Innovation: The Rule of User Firms in Japan and Korea.* London: Gordon & Brach.

Lerner, Josh. 1994a. "The Syndication of Venture Capital Investments," *Financial Management* 23: 16–27.

Lerner, Josh. 1994b. "Venture Capitalists and the Decision to Go Public," *Journal of Financial Economics* 35: 293–316.

Lerner, Josh. 1995. "Venture Capitalists and the Oversight of Private Firms," *Journal of Finance* 50: 301–18.

Lerner, Josh. 1997. "An Empirical Exploration of a Technology Race," *Rand Journal of Economics* 28: 228–47.

Lerner, Josh. 1998. "Angel Financing and Public Policy: an Overview," *Journal of Banking and Finance* 22: 773–83.

Lerner, Josh. 1999. "The Government as Venture Capitalist: the Long-Run Effects of the SBIR Program," *Journal of Business* 72: 285–318.

Lesser, William H. 2000. "Intellectual Property Rights Under the Convention on Biological Diversity," In V. Santaniello, R.E. Evenson, D. Zilberman, and G.A. Carlson, eds. *Agriculture and Intellectual Property Rights: Economic, Institutional and Implementation Issues in Biotechnology,* Chapter 3. Wallingford, UK: CABI Publishing.

Lessig, Lawrence. 1999. *CODE: and Other Laws of Cyberspace.* New York: Basic Books.

Levin, Jack S. 1995. *Structuring Venture Capital, Private Equity, and Entrepreneurial Transactions.* Boston, MA: Little, Brown & Co.

Levin, Richard C. 1982. "The Semiconductor Industry," In Richard R. Nelson, ed. *Government and Technical Progress: A Cross-Industry Analysis.* New York: Pergamon Press, 9–100.

Levin, Richard C., Alvin K. Klevorick, Richard R. Nelson, Sidney G. Winter, Richard Gilbert, and Zvi Griliches. 1987. "Appropriating the Returns to Industrial Research and Development," In *Brookings Papers on Economic Activity.* Washington, DC: Brookings, 783–832.

Lewchuk, W. 1987. *American Technology and the British Vehicle Industry.* New York: Cambridge University Press.

Lichtenstein, Nelson. 1995. *The Most Dangerous Man in*

Detroit: Walter Reuther and the Fate of American Labor. New York: Basic Books.

Liles, Patrick. 1977. *Sustaining the Venture Capital Firm.* Cambridge: Management Analysis Center.

Lincoln, Edward. 1998. *Japan: Facing Economic Maturity.* Washington, DC: Brookings Institution.

Lin, William. 2000. "Estimating the Cost of Segregation for Nonbiotech Corn and Soya," *Economics of Agricultural Biotechnologies IACBR* Ravello, Italy, August, 499.

Lindgren, Nilo. 1969. "The Splintering of the Solid State Electronics Industry," *Innovation* 8: 2–16.

Lippman, Steven A., and Richard P. Rumelt. 1982. "Uncertain Imitability: an Analysis of Interfirm Differences in Efficiency Under Competition," *The Bell Journal of Economics* 13(2): 418–38.

Lipsey, Richard G., Cliff Bekar, and Kenneth Carlaw. 2000. "What Requires Explanation?" In Elhanan Helpman, ed. *General Purpose Technologies and Economic Growth.* Cambridge, MA: MIT Press.

List, Friedrich. 1841. *The National System of Political Economy.* English edition in 1904. London.

Litan, Robert E., and Alice M. Rivlin. 2001. *Beyond the Dot.coms: The Economic Promise of the Internet.* Washington, DC: Brookings Institution.

Lucas, Robert E. 1988. "On the Mechanics of Economic Development," *Journal of Monetary Economics* 22: 3–42.

Lum, Sherlene K.S., and Brian C. Moyer. 2000. "Gross Domestic Product by Industry for 1997–99," *Survey of Current Business* 80 (12, December): 24–35.

Lutterbeck, Bernd, Robert Gehring, and Axel H. Horns 2000. *Sicherheit in der Informationstechnologie und Patentschutz für Software-Produkte — Ein Widerspruch?* Kurzgutachten im Auftrag des Bundesministeriums für Wirtschaft und Technologie. Berlin: Technische Universität.

Lydon, James, and Richard Bambrick. 1987. "Fairchild Semiconductor, the Lily of the Valley, 1957–1987," *Electronic News* 33 (September 28).

MacDuffie, John Paul, and Frits Pil. 1999. "What Makes Transplants Thrive? Managing the Transfer of 'Best Practices' at Japanese Auto Plants in North America," *Journal of World Business* 34(4): 372–91.

Macher, Jeffrey, David C. Mowery, and David Hodges. 1998. "Performance and Innovation in the U.S. Semiconductor Industry, 1980–1996," In Ralph Landau, and David C. Mowery, eds. *Explaining America's Industrial Resurgence.* Washington, DC: National Academy Press.

MacLeod, Christine. 1992. "Strategies for Innovation: The Diffusion of New Technology in Nineteenth-Century British Industry," *Economic History Review* 45: 285–307.

Malerba, Franco. 1985. *The Semiconductor Business: The Economics of Rapid Growth and Decline.* Madison, WI: University of Wisconsin Press.

Malkiel, Burton G. 1992. "The Cost of Capital, Institutional Arrangements, and Business Fixed Investment: an International Comparison," *Paper Presented to the Osaka-Wharton Conference on Corporate Financial Policy and International Competition.*

Malone, Michael S. 1985. *The Big Score.* New York: Doubleday.

March, James G. 1991. "Exploration and Exploitation in Organizational Learning," *Organizational Science* 2: 71–87.

Marchetti, Cesare, and Jesse H. Ausubel. 1996. "Elektron: Electrical Systems in Retrospect and Prospect," *Daedalus* 125: 139–169.

Marra, Michelle, Brian Hubbell, and Gerald Carlson. 2000. "Information Quality, Technology Depreciation and Bt Cotton Adoption in the Southeastern US," *Economics of Agricultural Biotechnologies IACBR.* Ravello, Italy, August, 77.

Marra, Michelle, Gerald Carlson, and Brian Hubbell. 1999. *Economic Impacts of the First Crop Biotechnologies.*

Marron, Donald, and David G. Steel. 2000. "Which Countries Protect Intellectual Property? The Case of Software Piracy," *Economic Inquiry* 38: 159–74.

Marx, Leslie. 1994. "Negotiation and Renegotiation of Venture Capital Contracts," *Working Paper.* University of Rochester.

Mason, Geoff, and Karin Wagner. 1999. "Knowledge Transfer and Innovation in Germany and Britain: 'Intermediate Institution' Models of Knowledge Transfer under Strain?" *Industry and Innovation* 6 (1): 85–109.

Matsuoku, Mikihiro, and Chris Calderwood. 1999. *Corporate Restructuring: Waiting for More Progress?* Mimeo, Tokyo: Jardine Fleming Securities (Asia).

Maxwell, Robert A., and Shohreh B. Eckhardt. 1990. *Drug Discovery: A Case Book and Analysis.* Clifton, NJ: Humana Press.

McCauley, Robert N., and Steven A. Zimmer. 1989. "Explaining International Differences in the Cost of Capital," *Federal Research Bank of New York Quarterly Review* Summer: 7–28.

McConnell, John J., and Chris J. Muscarella. 1985. "Corporate Capital Expenditures and the Market Value of the Firm," *Journal of Financial Economics* 14: 399–422.

McHugh, K.S. 1949. "Bell System Patents and Patent Licensing," *Bell Telephone Magazine* January: 1–4.

McKinsey Global Institute. 1998. *Driving Productivity and Growth in the UK Economy.* Washington, DC: McKinsey Global Institute.

McKinsey Global Institute. 2000. *Why the Japanese Economy is Not Growing: Micro Barriers to Productivity Growth.* Mimeo, July. Washington, DC: McKinsey Global Institute.

Megginson, William C., and Kathleen A. Weiss. 1991. "Venture Capital Certification in Initial Public Offerings," *Journal of Finance* 46: 879–93.

Meissner, Gerd. 1997. *SAP — Die heimliche Softwaremacht: Wie ein mittelständisches Unternehmen den Weltmarkt eroberte.* Hamburg: Hoffmann & Kampe.

Mendelson, Morris. 1967. "Underwriter Compensation," In I. Friend, J.R. Longstreet, M. Mendelson, E. Miller, and A.P. Hess, Jr., eds. *Investment Banking and the New Issues Market.* New York: World Publishing Co., 394–479.

Mendenhall, Catherine. 2000. "Willingness to Pay a Premium for Non-Genetically Modified Foods," *Economics of Agricultural Biotechnologies, IACBR.* Ravello, Italy, August, 923.

Merges, R., and R.R. Nelson. 1994. "On Limiting or Encouraging Rivalry in Technical Progress: The Effect of Patent Scope Decisions," *Journal of Economic Behavior and Organization* 25: 1–24.

Merit. 1996. "The Organization of Innovative Activities in the European Biotechnology Industry and Its Implications for Future Competitiveness," *Report for the European Commission*. Maastricht: European Commission.

Merton, D. 1973. In N.W. Starer, ed. *The Sociology of Science: Theoretical and Empirical Investigation*. Chicago, IL: University of Chicago Press.

Merton, Robert K. 1961. "Singletons and Multiples in Scientific Discovery," *Proceedings of the American Philosophical Society* 105.

Messerlin, Patrick A. 2001. *Measuring the Costs of Protection in the European Community*. Washington, DC.

Methé, David T. 1991. *Technological Competition in Global Industries: Marketing and Planning Strategies for American Industry*. Westport: Quorum Books.

Meyer, S. 1981. *The Five-Dollar Day: Labor Management and Social Control in the Ford Motor Company, 1908–1921*. Albany, NY: State University of New York Press.

Mikitani, Ryoichi, and Adam Posen, eds. 2000. *Japan's Financial Crisis and Its Parallels with U.S. Experience*. Washington, DC: Institute for International Economics.

Miles, David. 1993. "Testing for Short Termism in the UK Stock Market," *Economic Journal* 103: 1379–96.

Miles, Ian, Birgitte Andersen, Mark Boden, and Jeremy Howells. 1999. "Service Production and Intellectual Property," *International Journal of Technology Management*.

Millard, Andre. 1990. *Edison and the Business of Invention* Baltimore, MD: Johns Hopkins Press.

Ministere de l'Industrie. 1995. Quoted in *Commissariat General du Plan*, 1999.

Mishel, Lawrence, Jared Bernstein, and John Schmitt. 1999. *The State of Working America 1998–99*. Ithaca, NY: Cornell University Press.

Mitchell, B.R. 1993. *International Historical Statistics. The Americas, 1750–1988*. New York: Stockton Press.

Mitchell, W., T. Roehl, and R.J. Slattery. 1995. "Influences on R&D Growth Among Japanese Pharmaceutical Firms, 1975–1990," *Journal of High Technology Management Research* 6(1): 17–31.

MITI. 1997. *White Paper on International Trade 1997*. Tokyo: MITI.

MITI. 1998. *White Paper on International Trade 1998*. Tokyo: MITI.

MITI. 1999. *White Paper on International Trade 1999*. Tokyo: MITI.

MITI. 2000. *White Paper on International Trade 2000*. Tokyo: MITI.

Mokyr, Joel. 1990a. "Punctuated Equilibria and Technological Progress," *American Economic Review* 80 (May): 350–4.

Mokyr, Joel. 1990b. *The Lever of Riches: Technological Creativity and Economic Progress*. New York: Oxford University Press.

Mokyr, Joel. 1996. "La Tecnologia, l'informazione e le famiglie," In Renato Ginanetti, ed. *Nel Mitu di Prometeo*. Firinze: Ponte alle Grazie, 147–84.

Mokyr, Joel. 1998a. "Editor's Introduction: The New Economic history and the Industrial Revolution," In Joel Mokyr, ed. *The British Industrial Revolution: an Economic Perspective*. Boulder, CO: Westview Press, 1–127.

Mokyr, Joel. 1998b. "Science, Technology, and Knowledge: What Historians Can Learn from an Evolutionary Approach," *Working Paper No. 9803*. Max Planck Institute on Evolutionary Economics.

Mokyr, Joel. 1999. "The Second Industrial Revolution," In Valerio Castronovo, ed. *Storia dell'economica Mondiale*. Rome: Laterza Publishing.

Mokyr, Joel. 2000a. "Knowledge, Technology, and Economic Growth During the Industrial Revolution," In Bart Van Ark, Simon K. Kuipers, and Gerard Kuper, eds. *Productivity, Technology and Economic Growth*. The Hague: Kluwer Academic Press, 253–92.

Mokyr, Joel. 2000b. "The Rise and Fall of the Factory System: Technology, Firms, and Households since the Industrial Revolution," *Unpublished Paper*. Northwestern University.

Mokyr, Joel. 2000c. "Innovation and Selection in Evolutionary Models of Technology: Some Definitional Issues," In John Ziman, ed., *Technological Innovation as an Evolutionary Process*. Cambridge: Cambridge University Press, 52–65.

Moore, Gordon. 1965. "Cramming More Components onto Integrated Circuits," *Electronics* 38 (April 19): 114–7.

Moore, Gordon. 1997. "An Update on Moore's Law," *Keynote Address to the Intel Developer Forum*, September 30, San Francisco, CA.

Morgan, M. Granger, and Susan F. Tierney. 1998. "Research Support for the Power Industry," *Issues in Science & Technology* 15: 81–7.

Morris, Peter R. 1990. *A History of the World Semiconductor Industry*. London: Peter Peregrinus (on behalf of the Institution of Electrical Engineers).

Motonishi, Tarzo, and Hiroshi Yoshikawa. 1999. "Causes of the Lag Stagnation of Japan During the 1990s: Financial or Real?" *Journal of the Japanese and the International Economies* 13: 181–200.

Mowery, David C. 1995. "The Boundaries of the US Firm in R & D," In Naomi Lamoureaux, and Daniel Raff, eds. *Coordination and Information: Historical Perspectives on the Organization of Enterprise*. Chicago, IL: Chicago University Press and NBER, 147–76.

Mowery, David C. 1996. *The International Computer Software Industry: A Comparative Study of Industry Evolution and Structure*. Oxford, UK: Oxford University Press.

Mowery, David C. 1999. "The Computer Software Industry," In David C. Mowery, and Richard R. Nelson, eds. *Sources of Industrial Leadership*. New York: Cambridge University Press.

Mowery, David C. 2001. "The Resurgence of Growth in the Late 1990s: Is Information Technology the Story?" *Updated Presentation at the Meetings of the American Economic Association* January 7.

Mowery, David C., and Richard R. Nelson, eds. 1999. *Sources of Industrial Leadership: Studies of Seven Industries*. Cambridge, UK: Cambridge University Press.

Mowery, David C., and Nathan Rosenberg. 1989. "New Developments in US Technology Policy: Implications for Competitiveness and International Trade Policy," *California Management Review* 32 (Fall): 107–24.

Mowery, David C., and Nathan Rosenberg. 1993. "The U.S. National Innovation System," In Richard R. Nelson, ed.

National Innovation Systems: A Comparative Analysis. New York: Oxford University Press.

Mowery, David C., and Nathan Rosenberg. 1998. *Paths of Innovation: Technological Change in 20th Century America.* New York: Cambridge University Press.

Mowery, David C., and W. Edward Steinmueller. 1994. "Prospects for Entry by Developing Countries into the Global Integrated Circuit Industry: Lessons from the United States, Japan, and the NIEs, 1955–1990," In David C. Mowery, ed. *Science and Technology Policy in Interdependent Economies,* Boston, MA: Kluwer.

Mowery, David, Richard Nelson, Bhaven Sampat, and Arvids Ziedonis. 2001. "The Growth of Patenting and Licensing by U.S. Universities: an Assessment of the Bayh-Dole act of 1980," *Research Policy* 30: 99–119.

Murmann, Johann Peter. 1998. "Knowledge and Competitive Advantage in the Synthetic Dye Industry, 1850–1914," Unpublished Doctoral Dissertation. Columbia University.

Myers, Stewart. 1977. "Determinants of Corporate Borrowing," *Journal of Financial Economics* 5: 147–75.

Myers, Stewart, and Christopher Howe. 1997. "A Life Cycle Financial Model of Pharmaceutical R&D," *Working Paper No. 41-97.* MIT Program on the Pharmaceutical Industry.

Myers, Stewart, and Nicholas Majluf. 1984. "Corporate Financing and Investment Decisions When Firms Have Information That Investors Do Not Have," *Journal of Financial Economics* 13: 187–221.

Nakayama, Wataru; William Boulton; and Michael Pecht. 1999. *The Japanese Electronics Industry.* Boca Raton, FL: Chapman & Hall/CRC.

National Industrial Technology Strategy Development Committee. 1999. *National Industrial Technology Strategies in Japan.* Mimeo, Tokyo.

National Research Council and the Japan Society for the Promotion of Science. 1999. *New Strategies for New Challenges: Corporate Innovation in the U.S. and Japan.* Washington, DC: National Academy of Sciences.

National Research Council. 1986. *Electricity in Economic Growth.* Washington, DC: National Academy Press.

National Research Council. 1999a. *Funding a Revolution: Government Support for Computing Research.* Washington, DC: National Academy Press.

National Research Council. 1999b. *Securing America's Industrial Strength.* Washington, DC: National Academy Press.

National Science Foundation. 1998. *Science and Engineering Indicators.*

National Telecommunications and Information Administration. *Falling Through the Net,* www.ntia.doc.gov/ntiahome/digitaldivide/.

Nelson, Randy A., and Mark E. Wohar. 1983. "Regulation, Scale Economies and Productivity in Steam-Electric Generation," *International Economic Review* 24: 57–79.

Nelson, Richard R. 1962. "The Link between Science and Invention: the Case of the Transistor," In Richard R. Nelson, ed. *The Rate and Direction of Inventive Activity.* Princeton, NJ: Princeton University Press, 549–83.

Nelson, Richard R. 1984. *High-Technology Policies: A Five-Nation Comparison.* Washington, DC: American Enterprise Institute.

Nelson, Richard. 1990. "Capitalism as an Engine of Progress," *Research Policy* 19 (3, June): 193–214.

Nelson, Richard R., ed. 1992. *National Systems of Innovation,* Oxford, UK: Oxford University Press.

Nelson, Richard R., ed. 1993. *National Innovation Systems: A Comparative Analysis.* New York: Oxford University Press.

Nelson, Richard R. 1994. "Economic growth through the Co-evolution of Technology and Institutions," In Loet Leydesdorff, and Peter Van Den Besselaar, eds., *Evolutionary Economics and Chaos Theory: New Directions in Technology Studies.* New York: St Martin's.

Nelson, Richard R. 1995a. "Co-evolution of Industry, Structure, Technology and Supporting Institutions, and the Making of Comparative Advantages," *International Journal of the Economics of Business* 2(2): 171–84.

Nelson, Richard R. 1995b. "Recent Evolutionary Theorizing About Economic Change," *Journal of Economic Literature,* Vol. XXXIII (March): 48–90.

Nelson, Richard. 1996. *The Sources of Economic Growth.* Cambridge, MA: Harvard University Press.

Nelson, Richard. 1998. "The Agenda for Growth Theory: A Different Point of View," *Cambridge Journal of Economics* 22: 497–520.

Nelson, Richard R. 2000. "Selection Criteria and Selection Processes in Cultural Evolution Theories," In John Ziman, ed. *Technological Innovation as an Evolutionary Process.* Cambridge: Cambridge University Press, 66–74.

Nelson, Richard R., and Sidney G. Winter. 1977. "In Search of More Useful Theory of Innovation," *Research Policy* 5: 36–76.

Network Wizard. 1999. *Internet Domain Survey.* http://www.nw.com.

Nevins, A., and F.E. Hill. 1957. *Ford: Expansion and Challenge, 1915–1933.* New York: Scribner.

New Business Promotion Department. 2000. *Current Status of Business Start-Up and Venture Businesses.* Mimeo, Tokyo: MITI.

Newbery, David M., and Michael G. Pollitt. 1997. "The Restructuring and Privatisation of the CEGB Was it Worth It?" *Journal of Industrial Economics* 45: 269–303.

Newcomb, T.P., and R.T. Spurr. 1989. *A Technical History of the Motor Car.* Bristol, UK: Hilger.

Nickell, Stephen J. 1996. "Competition and Corporate Performance," *Journal of Political Economy* 104: 724–46.

Nickell, Stephen J., Sushil Wadhwani, and Martin Wall. 1992. "Productivity Growth in UK Companies, 1975–1986," *European Economic Review* 36: 1055–91.

Nishiyama, Hidebiko. 2000. "Japan's Regulatory Reform: Part I," *Inside/Outside Japan* 9: 9.

Niskanen, William A. 1971. *Bureaucracy and Representative Government.* Chicago, IL: Aldine-Atherton.

Noble, David 1984. *Forces of Production: A Social History of Industrial Automation.* New York: Knopf.

Nonaka, Ikujiro, and Horitaku Takeuchi. 1995. *The Knowledge-Creating Company: How Japanese Companies Foster Creativity and Innovation.* New York: Oxford University Press.

Norberg, Arthur L. 1993. "New Engineering Companies and the Evolution of the United States Computer Industry," *Business and Economic History* 22 (Fall): 181–193.

Nordhaus, William D. 1997. "Do Real-Output and Real-

Wage Measures Capture Reality? The History of Lighting Suggests Not," In Timothy F. Bresnahan, and Robert Gordon, eds. *The Economics of New Goods*. Chicago, IL: University of Chicago Press.

Nordic Council of Ministers. 1998. *The Information and Communication Technology Sectors in the Nordic Countries*. TemaNord 587, Copenhagen.

Noyce, Robert N., and Marcian E. Hoff, Jr. 1981. "A History of Microprocessor Development at Intel," *IEEE Micro* 1 (February): 8–21.

Nuttall, Robin. 1998. *An Empirical Study of the Effect of the Threat of Takeover on UK Company Performance*. Mimeo, Oxford: Nuffield College.

Observatoire des Sciences et Techniques. 1998. *Science et Technologie. Indicateurs 1998*. Paris: Economica.

O'Mahony, Mary. 1999. *Britain's Productivity Performance 1959–1996: an International Perspective*. London: National Institute of Economic and Social Research.

Ockenden, Giles. 2000. *NASDAQ Japan: Let Battle Commence* Mimeo, Tokyo: Jardine Fleming Securities (Asia).

OECD. 1985. *A New Economy? The Changing Role of Innovation and Information Technology in Growth*. Paris: OECD.

OECD. 1987. *Reviews of National Science and Technology Policy: Sweden*. Paris: OECD.

OECD. 1988. *Reviews of National Science and Technology Policy: Denmark*. Paris: OECD.

OECD. 1994. *Jobs Study: Evidence and Explanations, Part II*. Paris: OECD.

OECD. 1995. *National Systems for Financing Innovation*. Paris: OECD.

OECD. 1996. *Globalization of Industry: Overview and Sector Reports*. Paris: OECD.

OECD. 1997. *Historical Statistics*. Paris: OECD.

OECD. 1998a. *Main Science and Technology Indicators*, Vols. 1 & 2. Paris: OECD.

OECD. 1998b. *OECD Economic Survey: Japan 1997–1998*. Paris: OECD.

OECD. 1998c. *France's Experience with the Minitel: Lessons for Electronic Commerce over the Internet*. Paris: OECD.

OECD. 1998d. *OECD Economic Surveys 1997–1998: Germany*. Paris: OECD.

OECD. 1998e. *Fostering Entrepreneurship*. Paris: OECD.

OECD. 1998f. *The STAN Database for Industrial Analysis 1978–1997*. Paris: OECD.

OECD. 1999a. *OECD Science, Technology and Industry Scoreboard: Benchmarking Knowledge Based Economics*. Paris: OECD.

OECD. 1999b. *OECD Science, Technology and Industry Scoreboard: Benchmarking Knowledge Based Economics*. Paris: OECD.

OECD. 1999c. *OECD Communications Outlook 1999*. Paris: OECD.

OECD. 1999d. *The Economic and Social Impact of Electronic Commerce*. Paris: OECD.

OECD. 1999e. "New Enterprise Work Practices and their Labour market implications," *Employment Outlook*, Chapter 4. Paris: OECD.

OECD. 1999f. *Building Infrastructure Capacity for Electronic Commerce: Leased Line Developments and Pricing*. Paris: OECD.

OECD. 1999g. *Communications Outlook 1999*. Paris: OECD.

OECD. 1999h. *Employment Outlook*. Paris: OECD.

OECD. 2000a. *A New Economy? The Changing Role of Innovation and Information Technology in Growth*. Paris: OECD.

OECD. 2000b. *Education at a Glance. OECD Indicators*. Paris: OECD.

Okimoto, Daniel I., Takuo Sugano, and Franklin B. Weinstein. 1984. *Competitive Edge: The Semiconductor Industry in the U.S. and Japan*. Stanford, CA: Stanford University Press.

Oliner, Stephen D., and Daniel E. Sichel. 2000. "The Resurgence of Growth in the Late 1990's: Is Information Technology the Story?" *Journal of Economic Perspectives* 14 (4, Fall): 3–22.

Olmstead, Alan L., and Paul W. Rhode. 2000. *Biological Innovation and American Agricultural Development*. Davis, CA: Institute of Government Affairs, University of California.

Oppel, Richard A. 2000. "Deregulation has Given Power to the Power People," *New York Times* 30 April.

Orsenigo, Luigi. 1995. *The Emergence of Biotechnology*. London, UK: Pinter Publishers.

Ostry, Sylvia, and Richard Nelson. 1995. *Techno-Nationalism and Techno-Globalism: Conflict and Cooperation*. Washington, DC: Brooking Institution Press.

Owen, Geoffrey. 1999. *From Empire to Europe*. London: Harper-Collins.

Pajarinen, Mika, Petri Rouvinen, and Pekka Ylä-Anttila. 1998. *Small Country Strategies in Global Competition: Benchmarking the Finnish Case*. Helsinki: ETLA, B144.

Palfreman, Jon. 1998. "Why the French Like Nuclear Energy," *Frontline*, PBS Online.

Parker, Robert, and Bruce Grimm. 2000. *Software Prices and Real Output: Recent Developments at the Bureau of Economic Analysis*. Paper Presented at NBER Productivity Workshop, March 17.

Parsons, Charles. 1911. *The Steam Turbine: The Rede Lecture*. Cambridge: Cambridge University Press. (http://www.history.rochester.edu/steam/parsons/).

Pavitt, Keith, and W. Edward Steinmueller. 1999. "Technology in Corporate Strategy: Change, Continuity and the Information Revolution," In A. Pettigrew, H. Thomas, and R. Whittington, eds. *Handbook of Strategy and Management*. London: Sage Publications.

Peltzman, Sam. 1974. *Regulation of Pharmaceutical Innovation: The 1962 Amendments*. Washington DC: American Enterprise Institute for Public Policy.

Perold, Andre, and Erik Sirri. 1993. "The Cost of International Equity Trading," *Working Paper*. Boston, MA: Harvard University.

Petersen, Mitchell A., and Raghuram G. Rajan. 1994. "The Benefits of Lending Relationships: Evidence from Small Business Data," *Journal of Finance* 49: 3–37.

Petersen, Mitchell A., and Raghuram G. Rajan. 1995. "The Effect of Credit Market Competition on Lending Relationships," *Quarterly Journal of Economics* 110: 407–43.

Petersen, Mitchell, and Raghuram G. Rajan. 2000. "Does Distance Still Matter? The Information Revolution in Small Business Lending," *NBER Working Paper No. 7685*, May.

Pisano, Gary. 1991. "The Governance of Innovation: Vertical Integration and Collaborative Arrangements in the Biotechnology Industry," *Research Policy* 20: 237–49.

Pisano, Gary. 1996. *The Development Factory: Unlocking the Potential of Process Innovation.* Boston, MA: Harvard Business School Press.

Pisano, Gary, and Paul Y. Mang. 1993. "Collaborative Product Development and the Market for Know-How: Strategies and Structures in the Biotechnology Industry," In R. Rosenbloom, and R. Burgelmon, eds. *Research on Technological Innovation, Management and Policy*, Vol. 5. Greenwich, CT: JAI Press.

Plotkin, Henry. 1993. *Darwin, Machines, and the Nature of Knowledge.* Cambridge, MA: Harvard University Press.

Polanyi, Michael. 1962. *Personal Knowledge: Towards a Post-Critical Philosophy.* Chicago, IL: Chicago University Press.

Policy Planning and Research Office. 2000. *Trend of Industrial Property Right Applications and Registration.* Japanese Patent Office, http://www.jpo-miti.go.jp/tousie/218.html.

Pollard, Sidney. 1965/1968. *The Genesis of Modern Management.* London: Penguin.

Polmar, Norman, and Thomas B. Allen. 1982. *Rickover: Controversy and Genius.* New York: Simon and Schuster.

Porter, Michael. 1990. *The Competitive Advantage of Nations.* New York: The Free Press.

Porter, Roy. 1997. *The Greatest Benefit to Mankind: A Medical History of Humanity.* New York: Norton.

Porter, Theodore. 1986. *The Rise of Statistical Thinking, 1820–1900.* Princeton, NJ: Princeton University Press.

Portes, Richard, and Helene Rey. 2000. "The Determinants of Cross-Border Equity Flows: The Geography of Information," *Working Paper.* London Business School.

Posen, Adam. 1998. *Restoring Japan's Economic Growth.* Washington, DC: Institute for International Economics.

Posen, Adam. 2001. "Economic Viewpoint: Recognizing Japan's Rising Potential Growth," *NIRA Review* Winter.

Posner, Richard A. 1999. *Natural Monopoly and its Regulation.* Washington, DC: Cato Institute.

Proudman, Jonathan, and Stephen Redding, eds. 1998. *Openness and Growth.* London: Bank of England.

Pugh, Emerson W. 1984. *Memories that Shaped an Industry.* Cambridge, MA: MIT Press.

Pugh, Emerson W., Lyle R. Johnson, and John H. Palmer. 1991. *IBM's 360 and Early 370 Systems.* Cambridge, MA: MIT Press.

Rae, J.B. 1959. *American Automobile Manufacturers: The First Forty Years.* Philadelphia, PA: Chilton.

Raff, Daniel M.G. 1987. Wage Determination Theory and the Five-Dollar Day at Ford: A Detailed Examination, Ph.D. Dissertation. Cambridge, MA: MIT Press.

Raff, Daniel M.G. 1991. "Making Cars and Making Money in the Interwar Automobile Industry Economies of Scale, Economies of Scope, and the Manufacturing Behind the Marketing," *Business History Review* 65(4): 521–753.

Raff, Daniel M.G. 1996. "Productivity Growth at Ford in the Coming of Mass Production: A Preliminary Analysis," *Business and Economic History* 25(1): 176–85.

Raff, Daniel M.G., and M. Trajtenberg. 1996. "Quality-Adjusted Price Indices for the American Automobile Industry, 1906–1940," In T.F. Bresnahan, and R.J. Gordon, eds. *The Economics of New Goods.* Chicago, IL: University of Chicago Press, 71–101.

Raff, Daniel M.G., and M. Trajtenberg. 1997. *Innovation, Prices, and the Structure of Competition in the American Automobile Industry 1901–1918: Data, Methods, and Some Preliminary Findings.* Typescript.

Rausser, G., L.K. Simm, and H.A. Amedin, *Biotechnology R&D in Developing Countries: Negotiating Public-Private Research Partnerships.* Presented at the 4th International Conference on Agricultural Biotechnology, Ravello, Italy.

Redmond, Kent C., and Thomas M. Smith. 1980. *Project Whirlwind: History of a Pioneer Computer.* Bedford, MA: Digital Press.

Reich, Michael. 1990. "Why Japanese Don't Export More Pharmaceuticals: Health Policy as Industrial Policy," *California Management Review* Winter: 124–50.

Reid, T.R. 1984. *The Chip: How Two Americans Invented the Microchip and Launched a Revolution.* New York: Simon and Schuster.

Request for Comments (various), Jon Postel, ed. www.faqs.org/rfcs/.

Rexecode. 1998. "Les performances comparées de l'Europe et des Etats-Unis," *Revue de Rexecode* 58: 39–69.

Rhodes, Richard. 1986. *The Making of the Atomic Bomb.* New York: Simon and Schuster.

Rifkin, Glenn, and George Harrar. 1988. *The Ultimate Entrepreneur: The Story of Ken Olsen and Digital Equipment Corporation.* Chicago, IL: Contemporary Books.

Ritter, Jay R. 1998. "Initial Public Offerings," In D. Logue, and J. Seward, eds. *Warren, Gorham, and Lamont Handbook of Modern Finance.* New York: WGL/RIA.

Rogner, Hans Holger. 1997. "An Assessment of World Hydrocarbon Resources," *Annual Review of Energy and the Environment* 22: 217–62.

Romer, Paul M. 1990. "Endogenous Technological Change," *Journal of Political Economy* 98: 71–102.

Rosenberg, Nathan. 1963. "Technological Change in the Machine Tool Industry, 1840–1910," *Journal of Economic History* 23 (December): 414–43.

Rosenberg, Nathan. 1983. *Inside the Black Box: Technology and Economics.* Cambridge: Cambridge University Press.

Rosenberg, Nathan. 1986. "The Impact of Technological Innovation: A Historical View," In Ralph Landau, and Nathan Rosenberg, eds. *The Positive Sum Strategy: Harnessing Technology for Economic Growth.* Washington DC: National Academy Press, 17–32.

Rosenberg, Nathan. 1992. "Scientific Instrumentation and University Research," *Research Policy* 21: 381–90.

Rosenberg, Nathan. 1994. *Exploring the Black Box.* Cambridge: Cambridge University Press.

Rosenberg, Nathan. 1996. "Uncertainty and Technological Change," In R. Landau, G. Wright, and T. Taylor, eds. *The Mosaic of Economic Growth.* Stanford, CA: Stanford University Press.

Rosenberg, Nathan. 1998a. "The Role of Electricity in Industrial Development," *The Energy Journal* 19: 7–24.

Rosenberg, Nathan. 1998b. "Chemical Engineering as a General Purpose Technology," In Elhanan Helpman, ed. *General Purpose Technologies and Economic Growth.* Cambridge, MA: MIT Press, 167–92.

Rosenberg, Nathan. 1998c. "Technological Change in Chemicals: The Role of University-Industry Relations," In A. Arora, R. Landau, and N. Rosenberg, eds. *Chemicals and Long-Term Economic Growth.* New York: Wiley, 193–230.

Rosenberg, Nathan, and Richard R. Nelson. 1994. "American Universities and Technical Advance in Industry," *Research Policy* 23: 323–48.

Ruigrok, Winfred, Andrew M. Pettigrew, Simon Peck, and Richard Whittington. 1999. "Corporate Restructuring and New Forms of Organising: Evidence from Europe," *Management International Review* 41–64.

Ruttan, Vernon W. 2001. *Technology, Growth and Development: an Induced Innovation Perspective.* Oxford: Oxford University Press.

Ryan, A., J. Freenan, and R. Hybels. 1994. "Biotechnology Firms," In G. Carroll, and M. Hannan, eds. *Organizations in Industry Strategy, Structure, and Selection.* New York: Oxford University Press.

Ryle, Gilbert. 1949. *The Concept of Mind.* Chicago, IL: University of Chicago Press.

Sachverständigenrat zur Begutachtung der gesamtwirtschaftlichen Entwicklung. *Jahresbericht.* Various issues.

Sahlman, William A. 1990. "The Structure and Governance of Venture Capital Organizations," *Journal of Financial Economics* 27: 473–524.

Sahlman, William A., and Howard Stevenson. 1987. "Capital Market Myopia," *Journal of Business Venturing* 1: 7–30.

Santaniello, Vittorio 2000, "Intellectual Property Rights of Plant Varieties and of Biotechnology in the European Union," In V. Santaniello, R.E. Evenson, D. Zilberman, and G.A. Carlson, eds. *Agriculture and Intellectual Property Rights: Economic, Institutional and Implementation Issues in Biotechnology,* Chapter 2. Wallingford, UK: CABI Publishing.

Saviotti, Pier Paolo. 1996. *Technological Evolution, Variety, and the Economy.* Cheltenham: Edward Elgar.

Scarpetta, Stefan, Andreas Bassanini, Dirk Pilat, and Paul Schreyer. 2000. "Economic Growth in the OECD Area: Recent Trends at the Aggregate and Sectoral Level," *ECO/WKP 2000 21.* Paris: Economics Department, OECD.

Schienstock, Gerd, and Osmo Kuusi, eds. 1999. *Transformation Towards a Learning Society.* Helsinki: SITRA.

Schmalensee, Richard, and Paul L. Joskow, 1986. "Estimated Parameters as Independent Variables: an Application to the Costs of Electric Generating Units," *Journal of Econometrics* 31: 275–305.

Schmidt, Philip S. 1984. *Electricity and Industrial Productivity.* Palo Alto, CA: EPRI.

Schmookler, Jacob. 1966. *Invention and Economic Growth.* Cambridge, MA: Harvard University Press.

Schor, Juliet B. 1993. *The Overworked American: The Unexpected Decline of Leisure.* New York: Basic Books.

Schumpeter, Joseph A. 1934. *The Theory of Economic Development: an Inquiry into Profits, Capital, Credit, Interest, and the Business Cycle.* Originally Published in German, 1912. Cambridge, MA: Cambridge University Press.

Schumpeter, Joseph A. 1942. *Capitalism, Socialism and Democracy.* New York: Harper & Brothers.

Schurr, Sam H., Calvin C. Burwell, Warren Devine, and Sidney Sonenblum. 1990. *Electricity in the American Economy: Agent of Technological Progress.* New York: Greenwood Press.

Schwartz, M. 2000. "Markets, Networks, and the Rise of Chrysler in Old Detroit, 1920–1940," *Enterprise and Society* 1(1): 63–99.

Schweitzer, S. 1992. *André Citröen. 1878–1935: Le Risque et le Défi.* Paris: Fayard.

Securities and Exchange Commission (SEC). 1971.

Semiconductor Industry Association. 1999. *International Technology Roadmap for Semiconductors: 1999 edition.* Austin, TX: International SEMATECH.

Senker, J., C. Enzing, P. Joly, and T. Reiss. 2000. "European Exploitation of Biotechnology—Do Government Policies Help?" *Nature Biotechnology* 18: 605–8.

SERD. 1996. "The Role of SMEs in Technology Creation and Diffusion: Implications for European Competitiveness in Biotechnology," *Report for the European Commission.* Maastricht: European Commission.

Shimizu, Yoshinori. 2000. "Convoy Regulation, Bank Management, and the Financial Crisis in Japan," In Ryoichi Mikitani, and Adam Posen, eds. *Japan's Financial Crisis and Its Parallels with U.S. Experience.* Washington, DC: Institute for International Economics, 57–100.

Shimokawa, Koichi. 1994. *The Japanese Automobile Industry: A Business History.* London and Atlantic Highlands, NJ: Athlone.

Shockley, William. 1976. "The Path to the Conception of the Junction Transistor," *IEEE Transactions on Electron Devices* ED-23: 567–620 (July)

Shy, Oz. 2001. *The Economics of Network Industries.* Cambridge: Cambridge University Press.

Sichel, Daniel E. 1997. *The Computer Revolution: an Economic Perspective.* Washington, DC: Brookings.

Sicsic, Pierre, and Charles Wyplosz. 1996. "France 1945–92," In Nicholas Crafts, and Gianni Toniolo, eds. *Economic Growth in Europe Since 1945.* Cambridge: Cambridge University Press (for the Centre for Economic Policy Research).

Siebert, Horst. 1992. "Why has Potential Growth Declined? The Case of Germany," In Federal Reserve Bank of Kansas City, ed. *Policies for Long-run Economic Growth.* Jackson Hole, WY: Federal Reserve Bank of Kansas City.

Siebert, Horst. 1994. *Geht den Deutschen die Arbeit aus? Wege zu mehr Beschaeftigung.* Guetersloh: Bertelsmann.

Siebert, Horst. 1997. "Labor Market Rigidities: at the Root of Unemployment in Europe," *Journal of Economic Perspectives* 11 (3): 37–54.

Siegmann, Ken. 1993. "An American Tale of Semi-Success: How American Chip Companies Regained Lead," *The San Francisco Chronicle,* December 20.

Single Market Review. 1997. *Capital Market Liberalisation.* Subseries III, Vol. 5. London: Kogan.

Sinn, Hans-Werner. 1997. *Der Staat im Bankwesen. Zur Rolle der Landesbanken in Deutschland.* Munich: Verlag C.H. Beck.

Sloan, Alfred P. 1964. *My Years with General Motors.* Garden City, NY: Doubleday.

Smith, Adam. 1776/1937. *The Wealth of Nations.* New York: Random House Modern Library.

Smith, Merritt Roe. 1994. "Technological Determinism in American Culture," In Merritt Roe Smith, and Leo Marx, eds. *Does Technology Drive History?* Cambridge, MA: MIT Press, 2–35.

Smith, Michael D., Joseph Bailey, and Erik Brynjolfsson. 2000. "Understanding Digital Markets: Review and Assessment," In E. Brynjolfsson, and B. Kahin, eds. *Understanding the Digital Economy.* Cambridge, MA: MIT Press.

Society of Automotive Engineers Historical Committee. 1997. *The Automobile: A Century of Progress.* Warrendale, PA: Society of Automotive Engineers.

Solow, Robert M. 1957. "Technological Change and the Aggregate Production Function," *Review of Economics and Statistics* 39 (3, August): 312–20.

Solow, Robert M. 1987. "We'd Better Watch Out," *New York Times Book Review* July 12, 36.

Soskice, David. 1997. "German Technology Policy, Innovation, and National Institutional Frameworks," *Industry and Innovation* 4 (1): 75–96.

Sparkes, J.J. 1973. "The First Decade of Transistor Development," *Radio and Electronic Engineering* 43: 8–9.

Standard and Poor's. 2000a. *Global Financial Data system.* http://ww.globalfindata.com.

Standard and Poor's. 2000b. *S&P 500 Composite Prices.* http://www.census.gov/statab/freq/00s0831.txt.

Stanley, Steven M. 1981. *The New Evolutionary Timetable.* New York: Basic Books.

Statistics Denmark. 1999. *Production Statistics.* Copenhagen: Statistics Denmark.

Statistics Finland. 1999a. *R&D Activity in Finland.* Annual reports since 1969, Helsinki: Statistics Finland.

Statistics Finland. 1999b. *Towards to an Information Society* (In Finnish: the Finnish title: Tiedolla Tietoyhteiskuntaan). Helsinki: Statistics Finland.

Statistics Finland. 1999c. *Production Statistics* (in Finnish). Helsinki: Statistics Finland.

Statistics Norway. 1999. *Production Statistics.* Oslo: Statistics Norway.

Statistics Sweden. 1999. *Production Statistics* (in Swedish). Stokholm: Statistics Sweden.

Statman, Meir. 1983. *Competition in the Pharmaceutical Industry: The Declining Profitability of Drug Innovation.* Washington, DC: American Enterprise Institute.

Stedman, Edmund C., ed. 1905. *The New York Stock Exchange.*

Steedman, Hilary, and Karen Wagner. 1987. "A Second Look at Productivity, Machinery and Skills in Britain and Germany," *National Institute Economic Review* 122 (November).

Steedman, Hilary. 1999. "Looking into the Qualifications 'Black Box': What can International Surveys Tell us about Basic Competence?" *Centre for Economic Performance*

Doiscussion Paper No. 431. London: London School of Economics.

Stern, Nancy. 1981. *From ENIAC to Univac.* Bedford, MA: Digital Press.

Stifterverband für die Deutsche Wissenschaft. 1995. *Forschung und Entwicklung in der deutschen Wirtschaft 1993. Mit ersten Ergebnissen für 1995.* Mimeo, Essen.

Stiglitz, Joseph, and Andrew Weiss. 1981. "Credit Rationing in Markets with Incomplete Information," *American Economic Review* 71: 393–409.

Stiroh, Kevin J. 2000. "How Did Bank Holding Companies Prosper in the 1990s?" *Journal of Banking and Finance* 24 (November): 1703–45.

Stolpe, Michael. 1995. *Technology and the Dynamics of Specialization in Open Economies.* Kieler Studien 271. Tübingen: Mohr.

Stolpe, Michael. 2000. "Protection Against Software Piracy: A Study of Technology Adoption for the Enforcement of Intellectual Property Rights," *Economics of Innovation and New Technology* 7 (1): 25–52.

Tanaka, Nobuo. 2000. *A New Economy for Japan?* Mimeo, Tokyo: MITI.

Tauer, Loren. 2000. "The Impact of Bovine Somatotropine on Farm Profits," *Economics of Agricultural Biotechnologies, IACBR.* Ravello, Italy, August, 17.

Taylor, Andrew. 2000a. "Consumers Get Early Chance to Choose," *Financial Times Energy & Utilities Review* 6 June, 2: II.

Taylor, Andrew. 2000b. "Obstacles Remain to Unfettered Market," *Financial Times Energy & Utilities Review* 6 June, 2: III.

Taylor, Frederick W. 1911. *Principles of Shop Management.* New York: Harper and Row.

Teece, David J. 1986. "Profiting from Technological Innovation: Implications for Integration, Collaboration,Licensing and Public Policy," *Research Policy* 15(6): 185–219.

Telecommunication Statistics. 1999. Compiled by *Edita and the Ministry of Transport and Communications Finland.* Helsinki: Edita.

Thomas, L.G. 1994. "Implicit Industrial Policy: The Triumph of Britain and the Failure of France in Global Pharmaceuticals," *Industrial and Corporate Change* 3(2): 451–89.

Thompson, G. 1954. "Intercompany Technical Standardization in the Early American Automobile Industry," *Journal of Economic History* 14(1): 1–20.

Tilton, John E. 1971. *International Diffusion of Technology: the Case of Semiconductors.* Washington, DC: Brookings Institution.

Triplett, Jack E. 1996. "Comment," In T.F. Bresnahan, and R.J. Gordon, eds., *The Economics of New Goods.* Chicago, IL: University of Chicago Press, 102–7.

Triplett, Jack E. 1999. "The Solow Computer Paradox: What do Computers do to Productivity?" *Canadian Journal of Economics* 32 (2, April): 309–34.

Trischler, Helmuth, and Rüdiger vom Bruch. 1999. *Forschung für den Markt: Geschichte der Fraunhofer-Gesellschaft.* Munich: C.H. Beck.

Tushman, M.L., and R. Anderson. 1986. "Technological

Discontinuities and Organizational Environments," *Administrative Science Quarterly* 31: 439–465.

Tylecote, Andrew, and Emmanuelle Conesa. 1999. "Corporate Governance, Innovation Systems and Industrial Performance," *Industry and Innovation* 6 (1): 25–50.

Tyson, Laura D'Andrea. 1992. *Who's Bashing Whom? Trade Conflict in High Technology Industries.* Washington, DC: Institute for International Economics.

Tyson, Laura D'Andrea, and David B. Yoffie. 1993. "Semiconductors: From Manipulated to Managed Trade," In David B. Yoffie, ed. *Beyond Free Trade: Firms, Governments, and Global Competition.* Boston, MA: Harvard Business School Press.

US Bureau of the Census. 1997. *Historical Statistics of the United States: Colonial Times to 1970.* (Compact disc version edited by Susan B. Carter et al.) New York: Cambridge University Press.

US Department of Commerce. 1975. *Historical Statistics Colonial Times to the Present.* Washington, DC: US Government Printing Office.

US Federal Trade Commission. 1938. *Report on the Automobile Industry.* Washington, DC: US Government Printing Office.

Uchitelle, Louis. 2000a. "Economic View: Productivity Finally Shows the Impact of Computers," *New York Times* March 12, section 3, 4.

Uchitelle, Louis. 2000b. "In a Productivity Surge, no Proof of a 'New Economy'," *New York Times* October 8.

UNICE. 1999. *Fostering Entrepreneurship in Europe: The Unice Benchmarking Report 1999.* Brussels: UNICE.

Urata, Masutaro. 2000. "Japan Expands Investment Opportunities," *Inside/Outside Japan* 9: 9.

Usselman, Steven W. 1993. "IBM and Its Imitators: Organizational Capabilities and the Emergence of the International Computer Industry," *Business and Economic History* 22 (Winter): 1–35.

Utterback, James M. 1979. "The Dynamics of Product and Process Innovation in Industry," In C.T. Hill, and J.M. Utterback, eds. *Technological Innovation for a Dynamic Economy.* New York: Pergamon Press, 40–65.

Utterback, James M., and F. Suarez. 1993. "Innovation, Competition and Industry Structure," *Research Policy* 22 (1, February): 1–22.

Van Reenen, John. 1997. "Why Has Britain Had Slow R&D Growth," *Research Policy* 26: 493–507.

Vatter, H. 1952. "The Closure of Entry in the American Automobile Industry," *Oxford Economic Papers* 4 (3): 213–34.

Venture Economics. 2000a. *Investment Benchmark Reports: International Private Equity.* Newark, NJ: Venture Economics.

Venture Economics. 2000b. *Investment Benchmark Reports: Venture Capital.* Newark, NJ: Venture Economics.

Verband der Chemischen Industrie (VCI). 2000. *Biotechnologie-Statistik September.* Frankfurt: Deutsche Industrievereinigung Biotechnologie.

Vermeij, Geerat J. 1994. "The Evolutionary Interaction Among Species: Selection, Escalation, and Coevolution," *Annual Review of Ecological Systems,* 25: 219–236.

Vickery, William, and Northcott, John. 1995. "Diffusion of Micro-electronics and Advanced Manufacturing Technology: a Review of National Surveys," *Economics of Innovation and New Technology* 3: 253–76.

Villa, Pierre. 1993. *Productivité et Accumulation du Capital en France Depuis 1896.*

Vincenti, Walter G. 1990. *What Engineers Know and How They Know It.* Baltimore, MD: Johns Hopkins Press.

Vincenti, Walter G. 2000. "Real-world Variation-selection in the Evolution of Technological Form: Historical Examples," In John Ziman, ed. *Technological Innovation as an Evolutionary Process.* Cambridge: Cambridge University Press, 174–89.

Von Neumann, John. 1945. "First Draft of a Report on the EDVAC," In William Aspray, and Arthur Burks, eds. *Papers of John von Neumann on Computing and Computer Theory* 1987. Cambridge, MA: MIT Press.

Von Tunzelmann, G.N. 1995. *Technology and Industrial Progress.* Aldershot, UK: Edward Elgar.

Wagner, Wayne, and Mark Edwards. 1993. "Best execution," *Financial Analysts Journal* 49: 65–71.

Wallsten, Scott J. 1996. "The Small Business Innovation Research Program: Encouraging Technological Innovation and Commercialization in Small Firms?" *Unpublished Working Paper.* Stanford University.

Ward, Michael, and David Dranove. 1995. "The Vertical Chain of R&D in the Pharmaceutical Industry," *Economic Inquiry* 33: 1–18.

Wardell, W. 1978. *Controlling the Use of Therapeutic Drugs: an International Comparison.* Washington, DC: American Enterprise Institute.

Weinhaus, Carol L., and Anthony G. Oettinger. 1988. *Behind the Telephone Debates.* Ablex Publishing.

Weinstein, David, and Yishay Yafeh. 1998. "On the Costs of a Bank Centered Financial Sector: Evidence from the Changing Main Bank Relationships in Japan," *Journal of Finance.* 635–72.

Weitzman, Eric. 1999. *Note on the New Venture Business in Japan.* Mimeo, Palo Alto, CA: Stanford Graduate School of Business.

Whelan, Karl. 2000. "Computers, Obsolescence, and Productivity," *Finance and Economics Discussion Series.* Washington, DC: The Federal Reserve Board.

White, Lawrence J. 1971. *The American Automobile Industry since 1945.* Cambridge, MA: Harvard University Press.

Wildes, Karl L., and Nilo A. Lindgren. 1985. *A Century of Electrical Engineering and Computer Science at MIT, 1882–1982.* Cambridge, MA: MIT Press.

Williams, K., C. Haslam, S. Johal, and J. Williams. 1994. *Cars: Analysis, History, Cases.* Providence, RI: Berghahn.

Williamson, Oliver E. 1983. "Organization Form, Residual Claimants, and Corporate Control," *Journal of Law and Economics* 26: 351–66.

Wilson, Robert W., Peter K. Ashton, and Thomas P. Egan. 1980. *Innovation, Competition, and Government Policy in the Semiconductor Industry.* Lexington, MA: D.C. Heath.

WIPO (World Intellectual Property Organisation). 2000. *Patent Statistics.* Geneva: WIPO.

Wolff, Edward. 1999. "Has Japan Specialized in the Wrong Industries?" *Working Paper.* New York: New York University Economics Department .

Womack, J.P., D.T. Jones, and D. Roos. 1990. *The Machine that Changed the World*. New York: Rawson.

World Bank. 1998. *World Development Indicators* (CD-ROM). Washington, DC: World Bank.

World Bank. 2000a. *World Development Indicators* (CD-ROM). Washington, DC: World Bank.

World Bank. 2000b. *Global Development Finance*. Washington, DC: World Bank.

World Bank. 2000c. *World Development Indicators*. Washington, DC: World Bank.

World Bank. 2001. *World Development Indicators*. (CD-ROM). Washington, DC: World Bank.

Wright, Gavin. 1990. "The Origins of American Industrial Success: 1879–1940," *American Economic Review* 80 (September): 651–68.

Wuketits, Franz. 1990. *Evolutionary Epistemology and Its Implications for Humankind*. Albany, NY: SUNY Press.

Yoshikawa, Hiroshi. 2000. "Technical Progress and the Growth of the Japanese Economy—Past and Future," *Oxford Review of Economic Policy* 16 (2): 34–45.

Young, Allyn A. 1928. "Increasing Returns and Economic Progress," *Economic Journal* 38: 523–42.

Zakon, Robert H. 2000. *Hobbe's Internet Timeline v5.1*.

Zimmerman, Michael R., and Lisa Dicarlo. 1999. "Who Would've Known Where the PC Would Go? Nearly 20 Years after the IBM PC Was Born, It Still Rules — Thanks to Its Ability to Evolve," *ZDNet News*, December 23.

Zohrabyan, Ariak and Robert E. Evenson 2000, "Biotechnology Inventions: Patent Data Evidence," In V. Santaniello, R.E. Evenson, D. Zilberman, and G.A. Carlson, eds. *Agriculture and Intellectual Property Rights: Economic, Institutional and Implementation Issues in Biotechnology*, Chapter 12. Wallingford, UK: CABI Publishing.

Zucker, G. Lynne, and Michael R. Darby. 1996. "Costly Information in Firm Transformation, Exit, or Persistent Failure," *American Behavioral Scientist* 39: 959–74.

Zucker, G. Lynne, and Michael R. Darby. 1997. "Present at the Revolution: Transformation of Technical Identity for a Large Incumbent Pharmaceutical Firm After the Biotechnological Breakthrough," *Research Policy* 26 (4/5): 429–47.

Zucker, Lynne G., Michael L. Darby, and Jeff Armstrong. 1994. "Intellectual Capital and the Firm: The Technology of Geographically Localized Knowledge Spillovers," *NBER Working Paper 4946*. Cambridge, MA: National Bureau of Economic Research.

Zucker, Lynne, Michael Darby, and Marilynn Brewer. 1997. "Intellectual Human Capital and the Birth of U.S. Biotechnology Enterprises," *American Economic Review* 87 (3, June).

Subject Index

acceleration 39
adaptive invention 383, 384
Advanta 376
adverse selection 286, 287, 299, 308
AEC see Atomic Energy Commission
AEG 127, 129
Africa
    capital flows 311
    Internet 249, 250
agency costs 336n, 337
agriculture 11, 16
    biotechnology 37, 367–84
    Denmark 221n
    mass production 39
    United Kingdom 184, 194
Airbus 118, 154
Ajinomoto 361
Alcatel 174
allocative efficiency 19–20
ALP see average labor productivity
Alstom 405
Altair 276–7
Amadeus 346
Amazon.com 258, 430
AMD 280
America Online (AOL) 237, 257
American Home Products 349, 359
American Motors 428
American Research and Development (ARD) 328
Amgen 356, 358, 364
animal breeding 368, 370, 372, 373
antibiotics 36–7, 41
antitrust policy
    anti-competitive practices 19, 20
    Internet 230, 240, 243, 245, 246, 257
    software 69
AOL see America Online
Apple Computer 277, 329
appropriability 11–13
ARD see American Research and Development
Argentina 296
ARPANET 233, 234, 235, 241, 242, 246, 248
Asia
    capital flows 311
    Internet 249, 250, 296
    securitization 309
    trading costs 320n
assets
    banking/corporate finance 290, 291, 292, 296, 297
    liquidity 286, 288

    pension funds 303
    securitization 286, 298, 308–9
    venture capital 337
AstraZeneca 195, 376, 379
AT&T 234n, 238, 243, 267–8, 269, 274n
Atlas Ventures 346
ATMs 212, 215, 285
Atomic Energy Commission (AEC) 400
Australia
    banking/corporate finance 296, 309
    Internet 247, 248, 252, 253, 296
    labor productivity 254
    venture capital 345
Austria
    banking/corporate finance 296, 303
    biotechnology 362
    coal 413
    Internet 253, 296
    productivity 122
    venture capital 345
automatic transfer machines 422
automation of securities trading 314, 315, 316–18, 323–5
automobile industry 13, 404, 416–32
    France 150, 157
    Germany 112, 113, 118, 119, 120, 124, 127, 128–9
    Japan 87, 90, 197
    United Kingdom 194, 197–8
    United States 68, 72
Aventis 127, 134, 359, 376
average labor productivity (ALP) 62–3, 67

bandwidth 251, 264
banking 285–313
    France 165
    Germany 117, 129, 136, 137–8
    Japan 77, 80, 93, 94–5, 104
    Nordic Countries 200, 211–12, 213, 215, 224
    venture capital 337
bankruptcies
    Japan 76, 82, 95–6
    Nordic Countries 218–20
BASF 127, 128
basic research 15–16, 17–18
Bay Networks 236
Bayer 118, 127, 349, 359, 361
Bayh-Dole Act (1980) 16, 17, 363, 366, 371, 382
Bayh-Dole Amendment (1983) 91, 110
BBN see Bolt, Beranek and Newman Inc.
Belgium
    banking/corporate finance 303